In Praise of *Digital Design and Computer Architecture*

Harris and Harris have taken the popular pedagogy from Computer Organization and Design *to the next level of refinement, showing in detail how to build a MIPS microprocessor in both Verilog and VHDL. Given the exciting opportunity that students have to run large digital designs on modern FGPAs, the approach the authors take in this book is both informative and enlightening.*

David A. Patterson University of California, Berkeley

Digital Design and Computer Architecture *brings a fresh perspective to an old discipline. Many textbooks tend to resemble overgrown shrubs, but Harris and Harris have managed to prune away the deadwood while preserving the fundamentals and presenting them in a contemporary context. In doing so, they offer a text that will benefit students interested in designing solutions for tomorrow's challenges.*

Jim Frenzel University of Idaho

Harris and Harris have a pleasant and informative writing style. Their treatment of the material is at a good level for introducing students to computer engineering with plenty of helpful diagrams. Combinational circuits, microarchitecture, and memory systems are handled particularly well.

James Pinter-Lucke Claremont McKenna College

Harris and Harris have written a book that is very clear and easy to understand. The exercises are well-designed and the real-world examples are a nice touch. The lengthy and confusing explanations often found in similar textbooks are not seen here. It's obvious that the authors have devoted a great deal of time and effort to create an accessible text. I strongly recommend Digital Design and Computer Architecture.

Peiyi Zhao Chapman University

Harris and Harris have created the first book that successfully combines digital system design with computer architecture. Digital Design and Computer Architecture *is a much-welcomed text that extensively explores digital systems designs and explains the MIPS architecture in fantastic detail. I highly recommend this book.*

James E. Stine, Jr., Oklahoma State University

Digital Design and Computer Architecture *is a brilliant book. Harris and Harris seamlessly tie together all the important elements in microprocessor design—transistors, circuits, logic gates, finite state machines, memories, arithmetic units—and conclude with computer architecture. This text is an excellent guide for understanding how complex systems can be flawlessly designed.*

Jaeha Kim Rambus, Inc.

Digital Design and Computer Architecture *is a very well-written book that will appeal to both young engineers who are learning these subjects for the first time and also to the experienced engineers who want to use this book as a reference. I highly recommend it.*

A. Utku Diril Nvidia Corporation

Digital Design and
Computer Architecture

About the Authors

David Money Harris is an associate professor of engineering at Harvey Mudd College. He received his Ph.D. in electrical engineering from Stanford University and his M.Eng. in electrical engineering and computer science from MIT. Before attending Stanford, he worked at Intel as a logic and circuit designer on the Itanium and Pentium II processors. Since then, he has consulted at Sun Microsystems, Hewlett-Packard, Evans & Sutherland, and other design companies.

David's passions include teaching, building chips, and exploring the outdoors. When he is not at work, he can usually be found hiking, mountaineering, or rock climbing. He particularly enjoys hiking with his son, Abraham, who was born at the start of this book project. David holds about a dozen patents and is the author of three other textbooks on chip design, as well as two guidebooks to the Southern California mountains.

Sarah L. Harris is an assistant professor of engineering at Harvey Mudd College. She received her Ph.D. and M.S. in electrical engineering from Stanford University. Before attending Stanford, she received a B.S. in electrical and computer engineering from Brigham Young University. Sarah has also worked with Hewlett-Packard, the San Diego Supercomputer Center, Nvidia, and Microsoft Research in Beijing.

Sarah loves teaching, exploring and developing new technologies, traveling, wind surfing, rock climbing, and playing the guitar. Her recent exploits include researching sketching interfaces for digital circuit design, acting as a science correspondent for a National Public Radio affiliate, and learning how to kite surf. She speaks four languages and looks forward to adding a few more to the list in the near future.

Digital Design and Computer Architecture

David Money Harris
Sarah L. Harris

AMSTERDAM • BOSTON • HEIDELBERG • LONDON
NEW YORK • OXFORD • PARIS • SAN DIEGO
SAN FRANCISCO • SINGAPORE • SYDNEY • TOKYO

Morgan Kaufmann Publishers is an imprint of Elsevier

ELSEVIER

Publisher: Denise E. M. Penrose
Senior Developmental Editor: Nate McFadden
Publishing Services Manager: George Morrison
Project Manager: Marilyn E Rash
Assistant Editor: Mary E. James
Editorial Assistant: Kimberlee Honjo
Cover and Editorial Illustrations: Duane Bibby
Interior Design: Frances Baca Design
Composition: Integra
Technical Illustrations: Harris and Harris/Integra
Production Services: Graphic World Inc.
Interior Printer: Courier-Westford
Cover Printer: Phoenix Color Corp.

Morgan Kaufmann Publishers is an imprint of Elsevier.
500 Sansome Street, Suite 400, San Francisco, CA 94111

This book is printed on acid-free paper.

Permissions may be sought directly from Elsevier's Science & Technology Rights Department
in Oxford, UK: phone: (+44) 1865 843830, fax: (+44) 1865 853333, e-mail: permissions
@elsevier.co.uk. You may also complete your request on-line via the Elsevier homepage
(*http://elsevier.com*) by selecting "Customer Support" and then "Obtaining Permissions."

Library of Congress Cataloging-in-Publication Data

Harris, David Money.
Digital design and computer architecture / David Money Harris and
   Sarah L. Harris.—1st ed.
     p. cm.
   Includes bibliographical references and index.
   ISBN 13: 978-0-12-370497-9 (alk. paper)
   ISBN 10: 0-12-370497-9
   1. Digital electronics. 2. Logic design. 3. Computer architecture. I. Harris, Sarah L. II. Title.
   TK7868.D5H298 2007
   621.381—dc22

                                  2006030554

For information on all Morgan Kaufmann publications,
visit our Web site at *www.mkp.com*

Printed in the United States of America
   09   10   11   5   4   3

To my family, Jennifer and Abraham
– DMH

To my sisters, Lara and Jenny
– SLH

Contents

Preface

Why publish yet another book on digital design and computer architecture? There are dozens of good books in print on digital design. There are also several good books about computer architecture, especially the classic texts of Patterson and Hennessy. This book is unique in its treatment in that it presents digital logic design from the perspective of computer architecture, starting at the beginning with 1's and 0's, and leading students through the design of a MIPS microprocessor.

We have used several editions of Patterson and Hennessy's *Computer Organization and Design* (COD) for many years at Harvey Mudd College. We particularly like their coverage of the MIPS architecture and microarchitecture because MIPS is a commercially successful microprocessor architecture, yet it is simple enough to clearly explain and build in an introductory class. Because our class has no prerequisites, the first half of the semester is dedicated to digital design, which is not covered by *COD*. Other universities have indicated a need for a book that combines digital design and computer architecture. We have undertaken to prepare such a book.

We believe that building a microprocessor is a special rite of passage for engineering and computer science students. The inner workings of a processor seem almost magical to the uninitiated, yet prove to be straightforward when carefully explained. Digital design in itself is a powerful and exciting subject. Assembly language programming unveils the inner language spoken by the processor. Microarchitecture is the link that brings it all together.

This book is suitable for a rapid-paced, single-semester introduction to digital design and computer architecture or for a two-quarter or two-semester sequence giving more time to digest the material and experiment in the lab. The only prerequisite is basic familiarity with a high-level programming language such as C, C++, or Java. The material is usually taught at the sophomore- or junior-year level, but may also be accessible to bright freshmen who have some programming experience.

FEATURES

This book offers a number of special features.

Side-by-Side Coverage of Verilog and VHDL

Hardware description languages (HDLs) are at the center of modern digital design practices. Unfortunately, designers are evenly split between the two dominant languages, Verilog and VHDL. This book introduces HDLs in Chapter 4 as soon as combinational and sequential logic design has been covered. HDLs are then used in Chapters 5 and 7 to design larger building blocks and entire processors. Nevertheless, Chapter 4 can be skipped and the later chapters are still accessible for courses that choose not to cover HDLs.

This book is unique in its side-by-side presentation of Verilog and VHDL, enabling the reader to quickly compare and contrast the two languages. Chapter 4 describes principles applying to both HDLs, then provides language-specific syntax and examples in adjacent columns. This side-by-side treatment makes it easy for an instructor to choose either HDL, and for the reader to transition from one to the other, either in a class or in professional practice.

Classic MIPS Architecture and Microarchitecture

Chapters 6 and 7 focus on the MIPS architecture adapted from the treatment of Patterson and Hennessy. MIPS is an ideal architecture because it is a real architecture shipped in millions of products yearly, yet it is streamlined and easy to learn. Moreover, hundreds of universities around the world have developed pedagogy, labs, and tools around the MIPS architecture.

Real-World Perspectives

Chapters 6, 7, and 8 illustrate the architecture, microarchitecture, and memory hierarchy of Intel IA-32 processors. These real-world perspective chapters show how the concepts in the chapter relate to the chips found in most PCs.

Accessible Overview of Advanced Microarchitecture

Chapter 7 includes an overview of modern high-performance microarchitectural features including branch prediction, superscalar and out-of-order operation, multithreading, and multicore processors. The treatment is accessible to a student in a first course and shows how the microarchitectures in the book can be extended to modern processors.

End-of-Chapter Exercises and Interview Questions

The best way to learn digital design is to do it. Each chapter ends with numerous exercises to practice the material. The exercises are followed by a set of interview questions that our industrial colleagues have asked students applying for work in the field. These questions provide a helpful glimpse into the types of problems job applicants will typically encounter during the interview process. (Exercise solutions are available via the book's companion and instructor Web pages. For more details, see the next section, Online Supplements.)

ONLINE SUPPLEMENTS

Supplementary materials are available online at *textbooks.elsevier.com/ 9780123704979*. This companion site (accessible to all readers) includes:

▶ Solutions to odd-numbered exercises

▶ Links to professional-strength computer-aided design (CAD) tools from Xilinx® and Synplicity®

▶ Link to PCSPIM, a Windows-based MIPS simulator

▶ Hardware description language (HDL) code for the MIPS processor

▶ Xilinx Project Navigator helpful hints

▶ Lecture slides in PowerPoint (PPT) format

▶ Sample course and lab materials

▶ List of errata

The instructor site (linked to the companion site and accessible to adopters who register at *textbooks.elsevier.com*) includes:

▶ Solutions to even-numbered exercises

▶ Links to professional-strength computer-aided design (CAD) tools from Xilinx® and Synplicity®. (Instructors from qualified universities can access *free* Synplicity tools for use in their classroom and laboratories. More details are available at the instructor site.)

▶ Figures from the text in JPG and PPT formats

Additional details on using the Xilinx, Synplicity, and PCSPIM tools in your course are provided in the next section. Details on the sample lab materials are also provided here.

HOW TO USE THE SOFTWARE TOOLS IN A COURSE

Xilinx ISE WebPACK

Xilinx ISE WebPACK is a free version of the professional-strength Xilinx ISE Foundation FPGA design tools. It allows students to enter their digital designs in schematic or using either the Verilog or VHDL hardware description language (HDL). After entering the design, students can simulate their circuits using ModelSim MXE III Starter, which is included in the Xilinx WebPACK. Xilinx WebPACK also includes XST, a logic synthesis tool supporting both Verilog and VHDL.

The difference between WebPACK and Foundation is that WebPACK supports a subset of the most common Xilinx FPGAs. The difference between ModelSim MXE III Starter and ModelSim commercial versions is that Starter degrades performance for simulations with more than 10,000 lines of HDL.

Synplify Pro

Synplify Pro® is a high-performance, sophisticated logic synthesis engine for FPGA and CPLD designs. Synplify Pro also contains HDL Analyst, a graphical interface tool that generates schematic views of the HDL source code. We have found that this is immensely useful in the learning and debugging process.

Synplicity has generously agreed to donate Synplify Pro to qualified universities and will provide as many licenses as needed to fill university labs. Instructors should visit the instructor Web page for this text for more information on how to request Synplify Pro licenses. For additional information on Synplicity and its other software, visit *www.synplicity.com/university*.

PCSPIM

PCSPIM, also called simply SPIM, is a Windows-based MIPS simulator that runs MIPS assembly code. Students enter their MIPS assembly code into a text file and run it using PCSPIM. PCSPIM displays the instructions, memory, and register values. Links to the user's manual and an example file are available at the companion site (textbooks.elsevier.com/9780123704979).

LABS

The companion site includes links to a series of labs that cover topics from digital design through computer architecture. The labs teach students how to use the Xilinx WebPACK or Foundation tools to enter, simulate, synthesize, and implement their designs. The labs also include topics on assembly language programming using the PCSPIM simulator.

After synthesis, students can implement their designs using the Digilent Spartan 3 Starter Board or the XUP-Virtex 2 Pro (V2Pro) Board. Both of these powerful and competitively priced boards are available from *www.digilentinc.com*. The boards contain FPGAs that can be programmed to implement student designs. We provide labs that describe how to implement a selection of designs using Digilent's Spartan 3 Board using

WebPACK. Unfortunately, Xilinx WebPACK does not support the huge FPGA on the V2Pro board. Qualified universities may contact the Xilinx University Program to request a donation of the full Foundation tools.

To run the labs, students will need to download and install the Xilinx WebPACK, PCSPIM, and possibly Synplify Pro. Instructors may also choose to install the tools on lab machines. The labs include instructions on how to implement the projects on the Digilent's Spartan 3 Starter Board. The implementation step may be skipped, but we have found it of great value. The labs will also work with the XST synthesis tool, but we recommend using Synplify Pro because the schematics it produces give students invaluable feedback.

We have tested the labs on Windows, but the tools are also available for Linux.

BUGS

As all experienced programmers know, any program of significant complexity undoubtedly contains bugs. So too do books. We have taken great care to find and squash the bugs in this book. However, some errors undoubtedly do remain. We will maintain a list of errata on the book's Web page.

Please send your bug reports to *ddcabugs@onehotlogic.com*. The first person to report a substantive bug with a fix that we use in a future printing will be rewarded with a $1 bounty! (Be sure to include your mailing address.)

ACKNOWLEDGMENTS

First and foremost, we thank David Patterson and John Hennessy for their pioneering MIPS microarchitectures described in their *Computer Organization and Design* textbook. We have taught from various editions of their book for many years. We appreciate their gracious support of this book and their permission to build on their microarchitectures.

Duane Bibby, our favorite cartoonist, labored long and hard to illustrate the fun and adventure of digital design. We also appreciate the enthusiasm of Denise Penrose, Nate McFadden, and the rest of the team at Morgan Kaufmann who made this book happen. Jeff Somers at Graphic World Publishing Services has ably guided the book through production.

Numerous reviewers have substantially improved the book. They include John Barr (Ithaca College), Jack V. Briner (Charleston Southern University), Andrew C. Brown (SK Communications), Carl Baumgaertner (Harvey Mudd College), A. Utku Diril (Nvidia Corporation), Jim Frenzel (University of Idaho), Jaeha Kim (Rambus, Inc.), Phillip King

(ShotSpotter, Inc.), James Pinter-Lucke (Claremont McKenna College), Amir Roth, Z. Jerry Shi (University of Connecticut), James E. Stine (Oklahoma State University), Luke Teyssier, Peiyi Zhao (Chapman University), and an anonymous reviewer. Simon Moore was a wonderful host during David's sabbatical visit to Cambridge University, where major sections of this book were written.

We also appreciate the students in our course at Harvey Mudd College who have given us helpful feedback on drafts of this textbook. Of special note are Casey Schilling, Alice Clifton, Chris Acon, and Stephen Brawner.

I, David, particularly thank my wife, Jennifer, who gave birth to our son Abraham at the beginning of the project. I appreciate her patience and loving support through yet another project at a busy time in our lives.

From Zero to One

1.1 THE GAME PLAN

Microprocessors have revolutionized our world during the past three decades. A laptop computer today has far more capability than a room-sized mainframe of yesteryear. A luxury automobile contains about 50 microprocessors. Advances in microprocessors have made cell phones and the Internet possible, have vastly improved medicine, and have transformed how war is waged. Worldwide semiconductor industry sales have grown from US $21 billion in 1985 to $227 billion in 2005, and microprocessors are a major segment of these sales. We believe that microprocessors are not only technically, economically, and socially important, but are also an intrinsically fascinating human invention. By the time you finish reading this book, you will know how to design and build your own microprocessor. The skills you learn along the way will prepare you to design many other digital systems.

We assume that you have a basic familiarity with electricity, some prior programming experience, and a genuine interest in understanding what goes on under the hood of a computer. This book focuses on the design of digital systems, which operate on 1's and 0's. We begin with digital logic gates that accept 1's and 0's as inputs and produce 1's and 0's as outputs. We then explore how to combine logic gates into more complicated modules such as adders and memories. Then we shift gears to programming in assembly language, the native tongue of the microprocessor. Finally, we put gates together to build a microprocessor that runs these assembly language programs.

A great advantage of digital systems is that the building blocks are quite simple: just 1's and 0's. They do not require grungy mathematics or a profound knowledge of physics. Instead, the designer's challenge is to combine these simple blocks into complicated systems. A microprocessor may be the first system that you build that is too complex to fit in your

3

head all at once. One of the major themes weaved through this book is how to manage complexity.

1.2 THE ART OF MANAGING COMPLEXITY

One of the characteristics that separates an engineer or computer scientist from a layperson is a systematic approach to managing complexity. Modern digital systems are built from millions or billions of transistors. No human being could understand these systems by writing equations describing the movement of electrons in each transistor and solving all of the equations simultaneously. You will need to learn to manage complexity to understand how to build a microprocessor without getting mired in a morass of detail.

1.2.1 Abstraction

The critical technique for managing complexity is *abstraction*: hiding details when they are not important. A system can be viewed from many different levels of abstraction. For example, American politicians abstract the world into cities, counties, states, and countries. A county contains multiple cities and a state contains many counties. When a politician is running for president, the politician is mostly interested in how the state as a whole will vote, rather than how each county votes, so the state is the most useful level of abstraction. On the other hand, the Census Bureau measures the population of every city, so the agency must consider the details of a lower level of abstraction.

Figure 1.1 illustrates levels of abstraction for an electronic computer system along with typical building blocks at each level. At the lowest level of abstraction is the physics, the motion of electrons. The behavior of electrons is described by quantum mechanics and Maxwell's equations. Our system is constructed from electronic *devices* such as transistors (or vacuum tubes, once upon a time). These devices have well-defined connection points called *terminals* and can be modeled by the relationship between voltage and current as measured at each terminal. By abstracting to this device level, we can ignore the individual electrons. The next level of abstraction is *analog circuits*, in which devices are assembled to create components such as amplifiers. Analog circuits input and output a continuous range of voltages. *Digital circuits* such as logic gates restrict the voltages to discrete ranges, which we will use to indicate 0 and 1. In logic design, we build more complex structures, such as adders or memories, from digital circuits.

Microarchitecture links the logic and architecture levels of abstraction. The *architecture* level of abstraction describes a computer from the programmer's perspective. For example, the Intel IA-32 architecture used by microprocessors in most *personal computers* (PCs) is defined by a set of

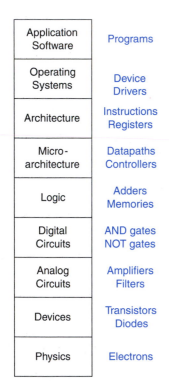

Application Software	Programs
Operating Systems	Device Drivers
Architecture	Instructions Registers
Micro-architecture	Datapaths Controllers
Logic	Adders Memories
Digital Circuits	AND gates NOT gates
Analog Circuits	Amplifiers Filters
Devices	Transistors Diodes
Physics	Electrons

Figure 1.1 Levels of abstraction for electronic computing system

instructions and registers (memory for temporarily storing variables) that the programmer is allowed to use. Microarchitecture involves combining logic elements to execute the instructions defined by the architecture. A particular architecture can be implemented by one of many different microarchitectures with different price/performance/power trade-offs. For example, the Intel Core 2 Duo, the Intel 80486, and the AMD Athlon all implement the IA-32 architecture with different microarchitectures.

Moving into the software realm, the operating system handles low-level details such as accessing a hard drive or managing memory. Finally, the application software uses these facilities provided by the operating system to solve a problem for the user. Thanks to the power of abstraction, your grandmother can surf the Web without any regard for the quantum vibrations of electrons or the organization of the memory in her computer.

This book focuses on the levels of abstraction from digital circuits through computer architecture. When you are working at one level of abstraction, it is good to know something about the levels of abstraction immediately above and below where you are working. For example, a computer scientist cannot fully optimize code without understanding the architecture for which the program is being written. A device engineer cannot make wise trade-offs in transistor design without understanding the circuits in which the transistors will be used. We hope that by the time you finish reading this book, you can pick the level of abstraction appropriate to solving your problem and evaluate the impact of your design choices on other levels of abstraction.

1.2.2 Discipline

Discipline is the act of intentionally restricting your design choices so that you can work more productively at a higher level of abstraction. Using interchangeable parts is a familiar application of discipline. One of the first examples of interchangeable parts was in flintlock rifle manufacturing. Until the early 19th century, rifles were individually crafted by hand. Components purchased from many different craftsmen were carefully filed and fit together by a highly skilled gunmaker. The discipline of interchangeable parts revolutionized the industry. By limiting the components to a standardized set with well-defined tolerances, rifles could be assembled and repaired much faster and with less skill. The gunmaker no longer concerned himself with lower levels of abstraction such as the specific shape of an individual barrel or gunstock.

In the context of this book, the digital discipline will be very important. Digital circuits use discrete voltages, whereas analog circuits use continuous voltages. Therefore, digital circuits are a subset of analog circuits and in some sense must be capable of less than the broader class of analog circuits. However, digital circuits are much simpler to design. By limiting ourselves to digital circuits, we can easily combine components into sophisticated systems that ultimately outperform those built from analog components in many applications. For example, digital televisions, compact disks (CDs), and cell phones are replacing their analog predecessors.

1.2.3 The Three -Y's

In addition to abstraction and discipline, designers use the three "-y's" to manage complexity: hierarchy, modularity, and regularity. These principles apply to both software and hardware systems.

▶ *Hierarchy* involves dividing a system into modules, then further subdividing each of these modules until the pieces are easy to understand.

▶ *Modularity* states that the modules have well-defined functions and interfaces, so that they connect together easily without unanticipated side effects.

▶ *Regularity* seeks uniformity among the modules. Common modules are reused many times, reducing the number of distinct modules that must be designed.

To illustrate these "-y's" we return to the example of rifle manufacturing. A flintlock rifle was one of the most intricate objects in common use in the early 19th century. Using the principle of hierarchy, we can break it into components shown in Figure 1.2: the lock, stock, and barrel.

The barrel is the long metal tube through which the bullet is fired. The lock is the firing mechanism. And the stock is the wooden body that holds the parts together and provides a secure grip for the user. In turn, the lock contains the trigger, hammer, flint, frizzen, and pan. Each of these components could be hierarchically described in further detail.

Modularity teaches that each component should have a well-defined function and interface. A function of the stock is to mount the barrel and lock. Its interface consists of its length and the location of its mounting pins. In a modular rifle design, stocks from many different manufacturers can be used with a particular barrel as long as the stock and barrel are of the correct length and have the proper mounting mechanism. A function of the barrel is to impart spin to the bullet so that it travels more accurately. Modularity dictates that there should be no side effects: the design of the stock should not impede the function of the barrel.

Regularity teaches that interchangeable parts are a good idea. With regularity, a damaged barrel can be replaced by an identical part. The barrels can be efficiently built on an assembly line, instead of being painstakingly hand-crafted.

We will return to these principles of hierarchy, modularity, and regularity throughout the book.

Captain Meriwether Lewis of the Lewis and Clark Expedition was one of the early advocates of interchangeable parts for rifles. In 1806, he explained:

The guns of Drewyer and Sergt. Pryor were both out of order. The first was repared with a new lock, the old one having become unfit for use; the second had the cock screw broken which was replaced by a duplicate which had been prepared for the lock at Harpers Ferry where she was manufactured. But for the precaution taken in bringing on those extra locks, and parts of locks, in addition to the ingenuity of John Shields, most of our guns would at this moment been entirely unfit for use; but fortunately for us I have it in my power here to record that they are all in good order.

See Elliott Coues, ed., *The History of the Lewis and Clark Expedition...* (4 vols), New York: Harper, 1893; reprint, 3 vols, New York: Dover, 3:817.

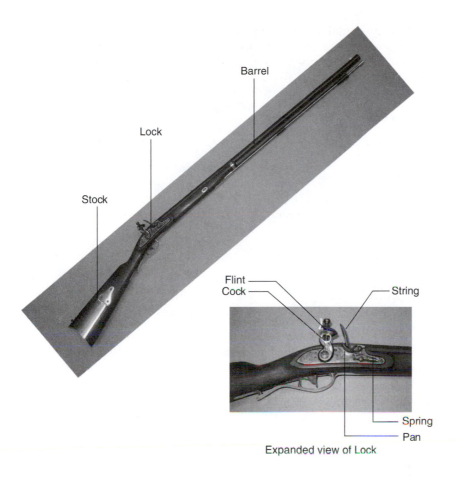

Barrel

Lock

Stock

Flint
Cock

String

Spring
Pan

Expanded view of Lock

Figure 1.2 Flintlock rifle with a close-up view of the lock (Image by Euroams Italia. www.euroarms.net © 2006).

Charles Babbage, 1791–1871. Attended Cambridge University and married Georgiana Whitmore in 1814. Invented the Analytical Engine, the world's first mechanical computer. Also invented the cowcatcher and the universal postage rate. Interested in lock-picking, but abhorred street musicians (image courtesy of Fourmilab Switzerland, www. fourmilab.ch).

1.3 THE DIGITAL ABSTRACTION

Most physical variables are continuous. For example, the voltage on a wire, the frequency of an oscillation, or the position of a mass are all continuous quantities. Digital systems, on the other hand, represent information with *discrete-valued variables*—that is, variables with a finite number of distinct values.

An early digital system using variables with ten discrete values was Charles Babbage's Analytical Engine. Babbage labored from 1834 to 1871,[1] designing and attempting to build this mechanical computer. The Analytical Engine used gears with ten positions labeled 0 through 9, much like a mechanical odometer in a car. Figure 1.3 shows a prototype

---

[1] And we thought graduate school was long!

Figure 1.3 Babbage's Analytical Engine, under construction at the time of his death in 1871 (image courtesy of Science Museum/Science and Society Picture Library).

George Boole, 1815–1864. Born to working-class parents and unable to afford a formal education, Boole taught himself mathematics and joined the faculty of Queen's College in Ireland. He wrote *An Investigation of the Laws of Thought* (1854), which introduced binary variables and the three fundamental logic operations: AND, OR, and NOT (image courtesy of xxx).

of the Analytical Engine, in which each row processes one digit. Babbage chose 25 rows of gears, so the machine has 25-digit precision.

Unlike Babbage's machine, most electronic computers use a binary (two-valued) representation in which a high voltage indicates a '1' and a low voltage indicates a '0,' because it is easier to distinguish between two voltages than ten.

The *amount of information D* in a discrete valued variable with *N* distinct states is measured in units of *bits* as

$$D = \log_2 N \text{ bits} \qquad (1.1)$$

A binary variable conveys $\log_2 2 = 1$ bit of information. Indeed, the word bit is short for *binary digit*. Each of Babbage's gears carried $\log_2 10 = 3.322$ bits of information because it could be in one of $2^{3.322} = 10$ unique positions. A continuous signal theoretically contains an infinite amount of information because it can take on an infinite number of values. In practice, noise and measurement error limit the information to only 10 to 16 bits for most continuous signals. If the measurement must be made rapidly, the information content is lower (e.g., 8 bits).

This book focuses on digital circuits using binary variables: 1's and 0's. George Boole developed a system of logic operating on binary variables that is now known as *Boolean logic*. Each of Boole's variables could be TRUE or FALSE. Electronic computers commonly use a positive voltage to represent '1' and zero volts to represent '0'. In this book, we will use the terms '1,' TRUE, and HIGH synonymously. Similarly, we will use '0,' FALSE, and LOW interchangeably.

The beauty of the *digital abstraction* is that digital designers can focus on 1's and 0's, ignoring whether the Boolean variables are physically represented with specific voltages, rotating gears, or even hydraulic fluid levels. A computer programmer can work without needing to know the intimate details of the computer hardware. On the other hand, understanding the details of the hardware allows the programmer to optimize the software better for that specific computer.

An individual bit doesn't carry much information. In the next section, we examine how groups of bits can be used to represent numbers. In later chapters, we will also use groups of bits to represent letters and programs.

1.4 NUMBER SYSTEMS

You are accustomed to working with decimal numbers. In digital systems consisting of 1's and 0's, binary or hexadecimal numbers are often more convenient. This section introduces the various number systems that will be used throughout the rest of the book.

1.4.1 Decimal Numbers

In elementary school, you learned to count and do arithmetic in *decimal*. Just as you (probably) have ten fingers, there are ten decimal digits, 0, 1, 2, ..., 9. Decimal digits are joined together to form longer decimal numbers. Each column of a decimal number has ten times the weight of the previous column. From right to left, the column weights are 1, 10, 100, 1000, and so on. Decimal numbers are referred to as *base 10*. The base is indicated by a subscript after the number to prevent confusion when working in more than one base. For example, Figure 1.4 shows how the decimal number 9742_{10} is written as the sum of each of its digits multiplied by the weight of the corresponding column.

An N-digit decimal number represents one of 10^N possibilities: 0, 1, 2, 3, ..., 10^{N-1}. This is called the *range* of the number. For example, a three-digit decimal number represents one of 1000 possibilities in the range of 0 to 999.

1.4.2 Binary Numbers

Bits represent one of two values, 0 or 1, and are joined together to form *binary numbers*. Each column of a binary number has twice the weight

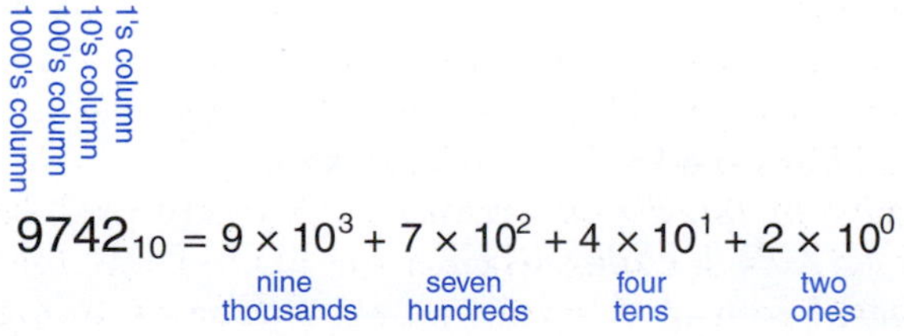

1's column
10's column
100's column
1000's column

$$9742_{10} = 9 \times 10^3 + 7 \times 10^2 + 4 \times 10^1 + 2 \times 10^0$$

nine thousands   seven hundreds   four tens   two ones

Figure 1.4 Representation of a decimal number

of the previous column, so binary numbers are *base 2*. In binary, the column weights (again from right to left) are 1, 2, 4, 8, 16, 32, 64, 128, 256, 512, 1024, 2048, 4096, 8192, 16384, 32768, 65536, and so on. If you work with binary numbers often, you'll save time if you remember these powers of two up to 2^{16}.

An N-bit binary number represents one of 2^N possibilities: 0, 1, 2, 3, ..., 2^{N-1}. Table 1.1 shows 1, 2, 3, and 4-bit binary numbers and their decimal equivalents.

Example 1.1 BINARY TO DECIMAL CONVERSION

Convert the binary number 10110_2 to decimal.

Solution: Figure 1.5 shows the conversion.

Table 1.1 Binary numbers and their decimal equivalent

1-Bit Binary Numbers	2-Bit Binnary Numbers	3-Bit Binary Numbers	4-Bit Binary Numbers	Decimal Equivalents
0	00	000	0000	0
1	01	001	0001	1
	10	010	0010	2
	11	011	0011	3
		100	0100	4
		101	0101	5
		110	0110	6
		111	0111	7
			1000	8
			1001	9
			1010	10
			1011	11
			1100	12
			1101	13
			1110	14
			1111	15

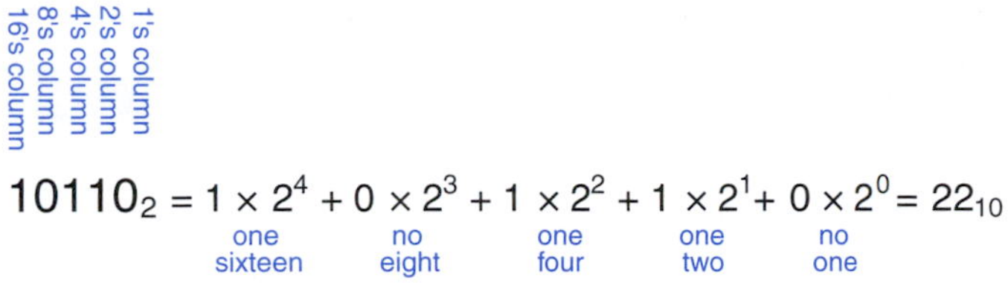

$$10110_2 = 1 \times 2^4 + 0 \times 2^3 + 1 \times 2^2 + 1 \times 2^1 + 0 \times 2^0 = 22_{10}$$

one sixteen · no eight · one four · one two · no one

Figure 1.5 **Conversion of a binary number to decimal**

Example 1.2 DECIMAL TO BINARY CONVERSION

Convert the decimal number 84_{10} to binary.

Solution: Determine whether each column of the binary result has a 1 or a 0. We can do this starting at either the left or the right column.

Working from the left, start with the largest power of 2 less than the number (in this case, 64). $84 \geq 64$, so there is a 1 in the 64's column, leaving $84 - 64 = 20$. $20 < 32$, so there is a 0 in the 32's column. $20 \geq 16$, so there is a 1 in the 16's column, leaving $20 - 16 = 4$. $4 < 8$, so there is a 0 in the 8's column. $4 \geq 4$, so there is a 1 in the 4's column, leaving $4 - 4 = 0$. Thus there must be 0's in the 2's and 1's column. Putting this all together, $84_{10} = 1010100_2$.

Working from the right, repeatedly divide the number by 2. The remainder goes in each column. $84/2 = 42$, so 0 goes in the 1's column. $42/2 = 21$, so 0 goes in the 2's column. $21/2 = 10$ with a remainder of 1 going in the 4's column. $10/2 = 5$, so 0 goes in the 8's column. $5/2 = 2$ with a remainder of 1 going in the 16's column. $2/2 = 1$, so 0 goes in the 32's column. Finally $1/2 = 0$ with a remainder of 1 going in the 64's column. Again, $84_{10} = 1010100_2$

1.4.3 Hexadecimal Numbers

Writing long binary numbers becomes tedious and prone to error. A group of four bits represents one of $2^4 = 16$ possibilities. Hence, it is sometimes more convenient to work in *base 16*, called *hexadecimal*. Hexadecimal numbers use the digits 0 to 9 along with the letters A to F, as shown in Table 1.2. Columns in base 16 have weights of 1, 16, 16^2 (or 256), 16^3 (or 4096), and so on.

"Hexadecimal," a term coined by IBM in 1963, derives from the Greek *hexi* (six) and Latin *decem* (ten). A more proper term would use the Latin *sexa* (six), but *sexidecimal* sounded too risqué.

Example 1.3 HEXADECIMAL TO BINARY AND DECIMAL CONVERSION

Convert the hexadecimal number $2ED_{16}$ to binary and to decimal.

Solution: Conversion between hexadecimal and binary is easy because each hexadecimal digit directly corresponds to four binary digits. $2_{16} = 0010_2$, $E_{16} = 1110_2$ and $D_{16} = 1101_2$, so $2ED_{16} = 001011101101_2$. Conversion to decimal requires the arithmetic shown in Figure 1.6.

Table 1.2 Hexadecimal number system

Hexadecimal Digit	Decimal Equivalent	Binary Equivalent
0	0	0000
1	1	0001
2	2	0010
3	3	0011
4	4	0100
5	5	0101
6	6	0110
7	7	0111
8	8	1000
9	9	1001
A	10	1010
B	11	1011
C	12	1100
D	13	1101
E	14	1110
F	15	1111

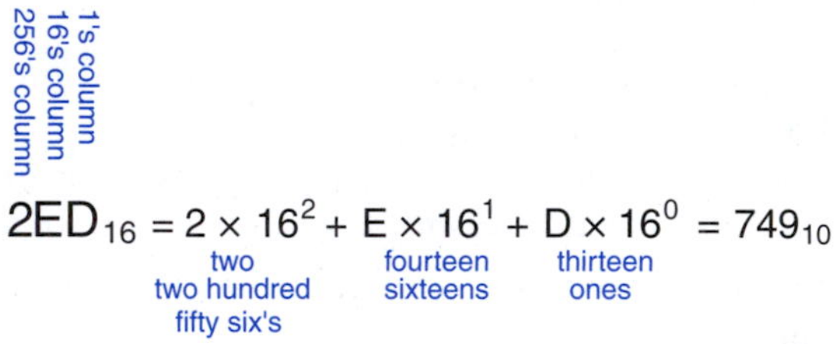

Figure 1.6 Conversion of hexadecimal number to decimal

$$2ED_{16} = 2 \times 16^2 + E \times 16^1 + D \times 16^0 = 749_{10}$$

two hundred fifty six's (256's column) — fourteen sixteens (16's column) — thirteen ones (1's column)

Example 1.4 BINARY TO HEXADECIMAL CONVERSION

Convert the binary number 1111010_2 to hexadecimal.

Solution: Again, conversion is easy. Start reading from the right. The four least significant bits are $1010_2 = A_{16}$. The next bits are $111_2 = 7_{16}$. Hence $1111010_2 = 7A_{16}$.

Example 1.5 DECIMAL TO HEXADECIMAL AND BINARY CONVERSION

Convert the decimal number 333_{10} to hexadecimal and binary.

Solution: Like decimal to binary conversion, decimal to hexadecimal conversion can be done from the left or the right.

Working from the left, start with the largest power of 16 less than the number (in this case, 256). 256 goes into 333 once, so there is a 1 in the 256's column, leaving $333 - 256 = 77$. 16 goes into 77 four times, so there is a 4 in the 16's column, leaving $77 - 16 \times 4 = 13$. $13_{10} = D_{16}$, so there is a D in the 1's column. In summary, $333_{10} = 14D_{16}$. Now it is easy to convert from hexadecimal to binary, as in Example 1.3. $14D_{16} = 101001101_2$.

Working from the right, repeatedly divide the number by 16. The remainder goes in each column. $333/16 = 20$ with a remainder of $13_{10} = D_{16}$ going in the 1's column. $20/16 = 1$ with a remainder of 4 going in the 16's column. $1/16 = 0$ with a remainder of 1 going in the 256's column. Again, the result is $14D_{16}$.

1.4.4 Bytes, Nibbles, and All That Jazz

A group of eight bits is called a *byte*. It represents one of $2^8 = 256$ possibilities. The size of objects stored in computer memories is customarily measured in bytes rather than bits.

A group of four bits, or half a byte, is called a *nibble*. It represents one of $2^4 = 16$ possibilities. One hexadecimal digit stores one nibble and two hexadecimal digits store one full byte. Nibbles are no longer a commonly used unit, but the term is cute.

Microprocessors handle data in chunks called *words*. The size of a word depends on the architecture of the microprocessor. When this chapter was written in 2006, most computers had 32-bit processors, indicating that they operate on 32-bit words. At the time, computers handling 64-bit words were on the verge of becoming widely available. Simpler microprocessors, especially those used in gadgets such as toasters, use 8- or 16-bit words.

Within a group of bits, the bit in the 1's column is called the *least significant bit (lsb)*, and the bit at the other end is called the *most significant bit (msb)*, as shown in Figure 1.7(a) for a 6-bit binary number. Similarly, within a word, the bytes are identified as *least significant byte (LSB)* through *most significant byte (MSB)*, as shown in Figure 1.7(b) for a four-byte number written with eight hexadecimal digits.

A *microprocessor* is a processor built on a single chip. Until the 1970's, processors were too complicated to fit on one chip, so mainframe processors were built from boards containing many chips. Intel introduced the first 4-bit microprocessor, called the 4004, in 1971. Now, even the most sophisticated supercomputers are built using microprocessors. We will use the terms microprocessor and processor interchangeably throughout this book.

Figure 1.7 Least and most significant bits and bytes

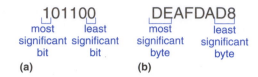

$$101100$$

most significant bit — least significant bit

(a)

$$DEAFDAD8$$

most significant byte — least significant byte

(b)

By handy coincidence, $2^{10} = 1024 \approx 10^3$. Hence, the term *kilo* (Greek for thousand) indicates 2^{10}. For example, 2^{10} bytes is one kilobyte (1 KB). Similarly, *mega* (million) indicates $2^{20} \approx 10^6$, and *giga* (billion) indicates $2^{30} \approx 10^9$. If you know $2^{10} \approx 1$ thousand, $2^{20} \approx 1$ million, $2^{30} \approx 1$ billion, and remember the powers of two up to 2^9, it is easy to estimate any power of two in your head.

Example 1.6 ESTIMATING POWERS OF TWO

Find the approximate value of 2^{24} without using a calculator.

Solution: Split the exponent into a multiple of ten and the remainder. $2^{24} = 2^{20} \times 2^4$. $2^{20} \approx 1$ million. $2^4 = 16$. So $2^{24} \approx 16$ million. Technically, $2^{24} = 16,777,216$, but 16 million is close enough for marketing purposes.

1024 bytes is called a *kilobyte* (KB). 1024 bits is called a *kilobit* (Kb or Kbit). Similarly, MB, Mb, GB, and Gb are used for millions and billions of bytes and bits. Memory capacity is usually measured in bytes. Communication speed is usually measured in bits/sec. For example, the maximum speed of a dial-up modem is usually 56 Kbits/sec.

1.4.5 Binary Addition

Binary addition is much like decimal addition, but easier, as shown in Figure 1.8. As in decimal addition, if the sum of two numbers is greater than what fits in a single digit, we *carry* a 1 into the next column. Figure 1.8 compares addition of decimal and binary numbers. In the right-most column of Figure 1.8(a), $7 + 9 = 16$, which cannot fit in a single digit because it is greater than 9. So we record the 1's digit, 6, and carry the 10's digit, 1, over to the next column. Likewise, in binary, if the sum of two numbers is greater than 1, we carry the 2's digit over to the next column. For example, in the right-most column of Figure 1.8(b), the sum

Figure 1.8 Addition examples showing carries: (a) decimal (b) binary

```
       11    ← carries →      11
     4277                   1011
  +  5499                +  0011
     9776                   1110
      (a)                    (b)
```

$1 + 1 = 2_{10} = 10_2$ cannot fit in a single binary digit. So we record the 1's digit (0) and carry the 2's digit (1) of the result to the next column. In the second column, the sum is $1 + 1 + 1 = 3_{10} = 11_2$. Again, we record the 1's digit (1) and carry the 2's digit (1) to the next column. For obvious reasons, the bit that is carried over to the neighboring column is called the *carry bit*.

Example 1.7 BINARY ADDITION

Compute $0111_2 + 0101_2$.

Solution: Figure 1.9 shows that the sum is 1100_2. The carries are indicated in blue. We can check our work by repeating the computation in decimal. $0111_2 = 7_{10}$. $0101_2 = 5_{10}$. The sum is $12_{10} = 1100_2$.

```
  111
  0111
+ 0101
  1100
```

Figure 1.9 Binary addition example

Digital systems usually operate on a fixed number of digits. Addition is said to *overflow* if the result is too big to fit in the available digits. A 4-bit number, for example, has the range [0, 15]. 4-bit binary addition overflows if the result exceeds 15. The fifth bit is discarded, producing an incorrect result in the remaining four bits. Overflow can be detected by checking for a carry out of the most significant column.

Example 1.8 ADDITION WITH OVERFLOW

Compute $1101_2 + 0101_2$. Does overflow occur?

Solution: Figure 1.10 shows the sum is 10010_2. This result overflows the range of a 4-bit binary number. If it must be stored as four bits, the most significant bit is discarded, leaving the incorrect result of 0010_2. If the computation had been done using numbers with five or more bits, the result 10010_2 would have been correct.

```
  11 1
  1101
+ 0101
 10010
```

Figure 1.10 Binary addition example with overflow

1.4.6 Signed Binary Numbers

So far, we have considered only *unsigned* binary numbers that represent positive quantities. We will often want to represent both positive and negative numbers, requiring a different binary number system. Several schemes exist to represent *signed* binary numbers; the two most widely employed are called sign/magnitude and two's complement.

Sign/Magnitude Numbers

Sign/magnitude numbers are intuitively appealing because they match our custom of writing negative numbers with a minus sign followed by the magnitude. An *N*-bit sign/magnitude number uses the most significant bit

The $7 billion Ariane 5 rocket, launched on June 4, 1996, veered off course 40 seconds after launch, broke up, and exploded. The failure was caused when the computer controlling the rocket overflowed its 16-bit range and crashed.

The code had been extensively tested on the Ariane 4 rocket. However, the Ariane 5 had a faster engine that produced larger values for the control computer, leading to the overflow.

(Photograph courtesy ESA/CNES/ ARIANESPACE-Service Optique CS6.)

as the sign and the remaining $N - 1$ bits as the magnitude (absolute value). A sign bit of 0 indicates positive and a sign bit of 1 indicates negative.

Example 1.9 SIGN/MAGNITUDE NUMBERS

Write 5 and -5 as 4-bit sign/magnitude numbers

Solution: Both numbers have a magnitude of $5_{10} = 101_2$. Thus, $5_{10} = 0101_2$ and $-5_{10} = 1101_2$.

Unfortunately, ordinary binary addition does not work for sign/magnitude numbers. For example, using ordinary addition on $-5_{10} + 5_{10}$ gives $1101_2 + 0101_2 = 10010_2$, which is nonsense.

An N-bit sign/magnitude number spans the range $[-2^{N-1} + 1, 2^{N-1} - 1]$. Sign/magnitude numbers are slightly odd in that both $+0$ and -0 exist. Both indicate zero. As you may expect, it can be troublesome to have two different representations for the same number.

Two's Complement Numbers

Two's complement numbers are identical to unsigned binary numbers except that the most significant bit position has a weight of -2^{N-1} instead of 2^{N-1}. They overcome the shortcomings of sign/magnitude numbers: zero has a single representation, and ordinary addition works.

In two's complement representation, zero is written as all zeros: $00...000_2$. The most positive number has a 0 in the most significant position and 1's elsewhere: $01...111_2 = 2^{N-1} - 1$. The most negative number has a 1 in the most significant position and 0's elsewhere: $10...000_2 = -2^{N-1}$. And -1 is written as all ones: $11...111_2$.

Notice that positive numbers have a 0 in the most significant position and negative numbers have a 1 in this position, so the most significant bit can be viewed as the sign bit. However, the remaining bits are interpreted differently for two's complement numbers than for sign/magnitude numbers.

The sign of a two's complement number is reversed in a process called *taking the two's complement*. The process consists of inverting all of the bits in the number, then adding 1 to the least significant bit position. This is useful to find the representation of a negative number or to determine the magnitude of a negative number.

Example 1.10 TWO'S COMPLEMENT REPRESENTATION
                OF A NEGATIVE NUMBER

Find the representation of -2_{10} as a 4-bit two's complement number.

Solution: Start with $+2_{10} = 0010_2$. To get -2_{10}, invert the bits and add 1. Inverting 0010_2 produces 1101_2. $1101_2 + 1 = 1110_2$. So -2_{10} is 1110_2.

Example 1.11 VALUE OF NEGATIVE TWO'S COMPLEMENT NUMBERS

Find the decimal value of the two's complement number 1001_2.

Solution: 1001_2 has a leading 1, so it must be negative. To find its magnitude, invert the bits and add 1. Inverting $1001_2 = 0110_2$. $0110_2 + 1 = 0111_2 = 7_{10}$. Hence, $1001_2 = -7_{10}$.

Two's complement numbers have the compelling advantage that addition works properly for both positive and negative numbers. Recall that when adding N-bit numbers, the carry out of the Nth bit (i.e., the $N + 1^{\text{th}}$ result bit), is discarded.

Example 1.12 ADDING TWO'S COMPLEMENT NUMBERS

Compute (a) $-2_{10} + 1_{10}$ and (b) $-7_{10} + 7_{10}$ using two's complement numbers.

Solution: (a) $-2_{10} + 1_{10} = 1110_2 + 0001_2 = 1111_2 = -1_{10}$.   (b) $-7_{10} + 7_{10} = 1001_2 + 0111_2 = 10000_2$. The fifth bit is discarded, leaving the correct 4-bit result 0000_2.

Subtraction is performed by taking the two's complement of the second number, then adding.

Example 1.13 SUBTRACTING TWO'S COMPLEMENT NUMBERS

Compute (a) $5_{10} - 3_{10}$ and (b) $3_{10} - 5_{10}$ using 4-bit two's complement numbers.

Solution: (a) $3_{10} = 0011_2$. Take its two's complement to obtain $-3_{10} = 1101_2$. Now add $5_{10} + (-3_{10}) = 0101_2 + 1101_2 = 0010_2 = 2_{10}$. Note that the carry out of the most significant position is discarded because the result is stored in four bits.   (b) Take the two's complement of 5_{10} to obtain $-5_{10} = 1011$. Now add $3_{10} + (-5_{10}) = 0011_2 + 1011_2 = 1110_2 = -2_{10}$.

The two's complement of 0 is found by inverting all the bits (producing $11...111_2$) and adding 1, which produces all 0's, disregarding the carry out of the most significant bit position. Hence, zero is always represented with all 0's. Unlike the sign/magnitude system, the two's complement system has no separate -0. Zero is considered positive because its sign bit is 0.

Like unsigned numbers, N-bit two's complement numbers represent one of 2^N possible values. However the values are split between positive and negative numbers. For example, a 4-bit unsigned number represents 16 values: 0 to 15. A 4-bit two's complement number also represents 16 values: -8 to 7. In general, the range of an N-bit two's complement number spans $[-2^{N-1}, 2^{N-1} - 1]$. It should make sense that there is one more negative number than positive number because there is no -0. The most negative number $10...000_2 = -2^{N-1}$ is sometimes called the *weird number*. Its two's complement is found by inverting the bits (producing $01...111_2$ and adding 1, which produces $10...000_2$, the weird number, again). Hence, this negative number has no positive counterpart.

Adding two N-bit positive numbers or negative numbers may cause overflow if the result is greater than $2^{N-1} - 1$ or less than -2^{N-1}. Adding a positive number to a negative number never causes overflow. Unlike unsigned numbers, a carry out of the most significant column does not indicate overflow. Instead, overflow occurs if the two numbers being added have the same sign bit and the result has the opposite sign bit.

Example 1.14 ADDING TWO'S COMPLEMENT NUMBERS
WITH OVERFLOW

Compute (a) $4_{10} + 5_{10}$ using 4-bit two's complement numbers. Does the result overflow?

Solution: (a) $4_{10} + 5_{10} = 0100_2 + 0101_2 = 1001_2 = -7_{10}$. The result overflows the range of 4-bit positive two's complement numbers, producing an incorrect negative result. If the computation had been done using five or more bits, the result $01001_2 = 9_{10}$ would have been correct.

When a two's complement number is extended to more bits, the sign bit must be copied into the most significant bit positions. This process is called *sign extension*. For example, the numbers 3 and -3 are written as 4-bit two's complement numbers 0011 and 1101, respectively. They are sign-extended to seven bits by copying the sign bit into the three new upper bits to form *000*0011 and *111*1101, respectively.

Comparison of Number Systems

The three most commonly used binary number systems are unsigned, two's complement, and sign/magnitude. Table 1.3 compares the range of N-bit numbers in each of these three systems. Two's complement numbers are convenient because they represent both positive and negative integers and because ordinary addition works for all numbers.

Table 1.3 Range of *N*-bit numbers

System	Range
Unsigned	$[0, 2^N - 1]$
Sign/Magnitude	$[-2^{N-1} + 1, 2^{N-1} - 1]$
Two's Complement	$[-2^{N-1}, 2^{N-1} - 1]$

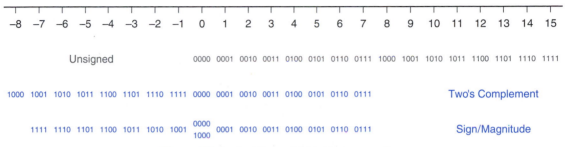

Figure 1.11 Number line and 4-bit binary encodings

Subtraction is performed by negating the second number (i.e., taking the two's complement), and then adding. Unless stated otherwise, assume that all signed binary numbers use two's complement representation.

Figure 1.11 shows a number line indicating the values of 4-bit numbers in each system. Unsigned numbers span the range $[0, 15]$ in regular binary order. Two's complement numbers span the range $[-8, 7]$. The nonnegative numbers $[0, 7]$ share the same encodings as unsigned numbers. The negative numbers $[-8, -1]$ are encoded such that a larger unsigned binary value represents a number closer to 0. Notice that the weird number, 1000, represents -8 and has no positive counterpart. Sign/magnitude numbers span the range $[-7, 7]$. The most significant bit is the sign bit. The positive numbers $[1, 7]$ share the same encodings as unsigned numbers. The negative numbers are symmetric but have the sign bit set. 0 is represented by both 0000 and 1000. Thus, *N*-bit sign/magnitude numbers represent only $2^N - 1$ integers because of the two representations for 0.

1.5 LOGIC GATES

Now that we know how to use binary variables to represent information, we explore digital systems that perform operations on these binary variables. *Logic gates* are simple digital circuits that take one or more binary inputs and produce a binary output. Logic gates are drawn with a symbol showing the input (or inputs) and the output. Inputs are usually drawn on the left (or top) and outputs on the right (or bottom). Digital designers typically use letters near the beginning of the alphabet for gate inputs and the letter Y for the gate output. The relationship between the inputs and the output can be described with a truth table or a Boolean equation. A *truth table* lists inputs on the left and the corresponding output on the right. It has one row for each possible combination of inputs. A *Boolean equation* is a mathematical expression using binary variables.

1.5.1 NOT Gate

A *NOT gate* has one input, A, and one output, Y, as shown in Figure 1.12. The NOT gate's output is the inverse of its input. If A is FALSE, then Y is TRUE. If A is TRUE, then Y is FALSE. This relationship is summarized by the truth table and Boolean equation in the figure. The line over A in the Boolean equation is pronounced *NOT*, so $Y = \overline{A}$ is read "Y equals NOT A." The NOT gate is also called an *inverter*.

Other texts use a variety of notations for NOT, including $Y = A'$, $Y = \neg A$, $Y = !A$ or $Y = \sim A$. We will use $Y = \overline{A}$ exclusively, but don't be puzzled if you encounter another notation elsewhere.

1.5.2 Buffer

The other one-input logic gate is called a *buffer* and is shown in Figure 1.13. It simply copies the input to the output.

From the logical point of view, a buffer is no different from a wire, so it might seem useless. However, from the analog point of view, the buffer might have desirable characteristics such as the ability to deliver large amounts of current to a motor or the ability to quickly send its output to many gates. This is an example of why we need to consider multiple levels of abstraction to fully understand a system; the digital abstraction hides the real purpose of a buffer.

The triangle symbol indicates a buffer. A circle on the output is called a *bubble* and indicates inversion, as was seen in the NOT gate symbol of Figure 1.12.

1.5.3 AND Gate

Two-input logic gates are more interesting. The *AND gate* shown in Figure 1.14 produces a TRUE output, Y, if and only if both A *and* B are TRUE. Otherwise, the output is FALSE. By convention, the inputs are listed in the order 00, 01, 10, 11, as if you were counting in binary. The Boolean equation for an AND gate can be written in several ways: $Y = A \bullet B$, $Y = AB$, or $Y = A \cap B$. The $\cap$ symbol is pronounced "intersection" and is preferred by logicians. We prefer $Y = AB$, read "Y equals A and B," because we are lazy.

NOT

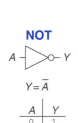

$$Y = \overline{A}$$

A	Y
0	1
1	0

Figure 1.12 NOT gate

BUF

$$Y = A$$

A	Y
0	0
1	1

Figure 1.13 Buffer

AND

$$Y = AB$$

A	B	Y
0	0	0
0	1	0
1	0	0
1	1	1

Figure 1.14 AND gate

According to Larry Wall, inventor of the Perl programming language, "the three principal virtues of a programmer are Laziness, Impatience, and Hubris."

1.5.4 OR Gate

The *OR gate* shown in Figure 1.15 produces a TRUE output, *Y*, if either *A* or *B* (or both) are TRUE. The Boolean equation for an OR gate is written as $Y = A + B$ or $Y = A \cup B$. The $\cup$ symbol is pronounced union and is preferred by logicians. Digital designers normally use the + notation, $Y = A + B$ is pronounced "*Y* equals *A* or *B*".

1.5.5 Other Two-Input Gates

Figure 1.16 shows other common two-input logic gates. *XOR* (exclusive OR, pronounced "ex-OR") is TRUE if *A* or *B*, but not both, are TRUE. Any gate can be followed by a bubble to invert its operation. The *NAND gate* performs NOT AND. Its output is TRUE unless both inputs are TRUE. The *NOR gate* performs NOT OR. Its output is TRUE if neither *A* nor *B* is TRUE.

OR

$$Y = A + B$$

A	B	Y
0	0	0
0	1	1
1	0	1
1	1	1

Figure 1.15 OR gate

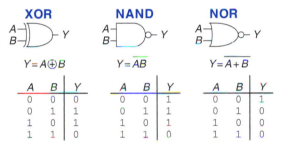

Figure 1.16 More two-input logic gates

XOR

$$Y = A \oplus B$$

A	B	Y
0	0	0
0	1	1
1	0	1
1	1	0

NAND

$$Y = \overline{AB}$$

A	B	Y
0	0	1
0	1	1
1	0	1
1	1	0

NOR

$$Y = \overline{A + B}$$

A	B	Y
0	0	1
0	1	0
1	0	0
1	1	0

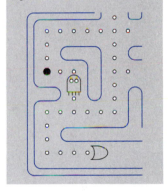

A silly way to remember the OR symbol is that it's input side is curved like Pacman's mouth, so the gate is hungry and willing to eat any TRUE inputs it can find!

Example 1.15 XNOR GATE

Figure 1.17 shows the symbol and Boolean equation for a two-input *XNOR gate* that performs the inverse of an XOR. Complete the truth table.

Solution: Figure 1.18 shows the truth table. The XNOR output is TRUE if both inputs are FALSE or both inputs are TRUE. The two-input XNOR gate is sometimes called an *equality* gate because its output is TRUE when the inputs are equal.

1.5.6 Multiple-Input Gates

Many Boolean functions of three or more inputs exist. The most common are AND, OR, XOR, NAND, NOR, and XNOR. An *N*-input AND gate produces a TRUE output when all *N* inputs are TRUE. An *N*-input OR gate produces a TRUE output when at least one input is TRUE.

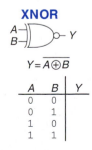

XNOR

$$Y = \overline{A \oplus B}$$

A	B	Y
0	0	
0	1	
1	0	
1	1	

Figure 1.17 XNOR gate

A	B	Y
0	0	1
0	1	0
1	0	0
1	1	1

Figure 1.18 XNOR truth table

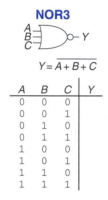

$$Y = \overline{A + B + C}$$

A	B	C	Y
0	0	0	
0	0	1	
0	1	0	
0	1	1	
1	0	0	
1	0	1	
1	1	0	
1	1	1	

Figure 1.19 Three-input NOR gate

A	B	C	Y
0	0	0	1
0	0	1	0
0	1	0	0
0	1	1	0
1	0	0	0
1	0	1	0
1	1	0	0
1	1	1	0

Figure 1.20 Three-input NOR truth table

$$Y = ABCD$$

Figure 1.21 Four-input AND gate

An N-input XOR gate is sometimes called a *parity* gate and produces a TRUE output if an odd number of inputs are TRUE. As with two-input gates, the input combinations in the truth table are listed in counting order.

Example 1.16 THREE-INPUT NOR GATE

Figure 1.19 shows the symbol and Boolean equation for a three-input NOR gate. Complete the truth table.

Solution: Figure 1.20 shows the truth table. The output is TRUE only if none of the inputs are TRUE.

Example 1.17 FOUR-INPUT AND GATE

Figure 1.21 shows the symbol and Boolean equation for a four-input AND gate. Create a truth table.

Solution: Figure 1.22 shows the truth table. The output is TRUE only if all of the inputs are TRUE.

1.6 BENEATH THE DIGITAL ABSTRACTION

A digital system uses discrete-valued variables. However, the variables are represented by continuous physical quantities such as the voltage on a wire, the position of a gear, or the level of fluid in a cylinder. Hence, the designer must choose a way to relate the continuous value to the discrete value.

For example, consider representing a binary signal A with a voltage on a wire. Let 0 volts (V) indicate $A = 0$ and 5 V indicate $A = 1$. Any real system must tolerate some noise, so 4.97 V probably ought to be interpreted as $A = 1$ as well. But what about 4.3 V? Or 2.8 V? Or 2.500000 V?

1.6.1 Supply Voltage

Suppose the lowest voltage in the system is 0 V, also called *ground* or GND. The highest voltage in the system comes from the power supply and is usually called V_{DD}. In 1970's and 1980's technology, V_{DD} was generally 5 V. As chips have progressed to smaller transistors, V_{DD} has dropped to 3.3 V, 2.5 V, 1.8 V, 1.5 V, 1.2 V, or even lower to save power and avoid overloading the transistors.

1.6.2 Logic Levels

The mapping of a continuous variable onto a discrete binary variable is done by defining *logic levels*, as shown in Figure 1.23. The first gate is called the *driver* and the second gate is called the *receiver*. The output of the driver is connected to the input of the receiver. The driver produces a LOW (0) output in the range of 0 to V_{OL} or a HIGH (1) output in the range of V_{OH} to V_{DD}. If the receiver gets an input in the range of 0 to V_{IL}, it will consider the input to be LOW. If the receiver gets an input in the range of V_{IH} to V_{DD}, it will consider the input to be HIGH. If, for some reason such as noise or faulty components, the receiver's input should fall in the *forbidden zone* between V_{IL} and V_{IH}, the behavior of the gate is unpredictable. V_{OH}, V_{OL}, V_{IH}, and V_{IL} are called the output and input high and low logic levels.

1.6.3 Noise Margins

If the output of the driver is to be correctly interpreted at the input of the receiver, we must choose $V_{OL} < V_{IL}$ and $V_{OH} > V_{IH}$. Thus, even if the output of the driver is contaminated by some noise, the input of the receiver will still detect the correct logic level. The *noise margin* is the amount of noise that could be added to a worst-case output such that the signal can still be interpreted as a valid input. As can be seen in Figure 1.23, the low and high noise margins are, respectively

$$NM_L = V_{IL} - V_{OL} \tag{1.2}$$
$$NM_H = V_{OH} - V_{IH} \tag{1.3}$$

A	C	B	D	Y
0	0	0	0	0
0	0	0	1	0
0	0	1	0	0
0	0	1	1	0
0	1	0	0	0
0	1	0	1	0
0	1	1	0	0
0	1	1	1	0
1	0	0	0	0
1	0	0	1	0
1	0	1	0	0
1	0	1	1	0
1	1	0	0	0
1	1	0	1	0
1	1	1	0	0
1	1	1	1	1

Figure 1.22 Four-input AND truth table

Example 1.18

Consider the inverter circuit of Figure 1.24. V_{O1} is the output voltage of inverter I1, and V_{I2} is the input voltage of inverter I2. Both inverters have the following characteristics: $V_{DD} = 5$ V, $V_{IL} = 1.35$ V, $V_{IH} = 3.15$ V, $V_{OL} = 0.33$ V, and $V_{OH} = 3.84$ V. What are the inverter low and high noise margins? Can the circuit tolerate 1 V of noise between V_{O1} and V_{I2}?

Solution: The inverter noise margins are: $NM_L = V_{IL} - V_{OL} = (1.35$ V $- 0.33$ V$)$ $= 1.02$ V, $NM_H = V_{OH} - V_{IH} = (3.84$ V $- 3.15$ V$) = 0.69$ V. The circuit can tolerate 1 V of noise when the output is LOW ($NM_L = 1.02$ V) but not when the output is HIGH ($NM_H = 0.69$ V). For example, suppose the driver, I1, outputs its worst-case HIGH value, $V_{O1} = V_{OH} = 3.84$ V. If noise causes the voltage to droop by 1 V before reaching the input of the receiver, $V_{I2} = (3.84$ V $- 1$ V$) =$ 2.84 V. This is less than the acceptable input HIGH value, $V_{IH} = 3.15$ V, so the receiver may not sense a proper HIGH input.

1.6.4 DC Transfer Characteristics

To understand the limits of the digital abstraction, we must delve into the analog behavior of a gate. The *DC transfer characteristics* of a gate describe the output voltage as a function of the input voltage when the

V_{DD} stands for the voltage on the *drain* of a metal-oxide-semiconductor transistor, used to build most modern chips. The power supply voltage is also sometimes called V_{CC}, standing for the voltage on the *collector* of a bipolar transistor used to build chips in an older technology. Ground is sometimes called V_{SS} because it is the voltage on the *source* of a metal-oxide-semiconductor transistor. See Section 1.7 for more information on transistors.

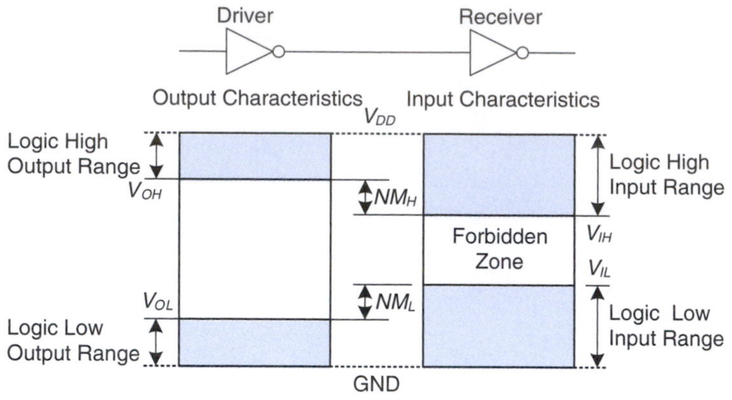

Figure 1.23 Logic levels and noise margins

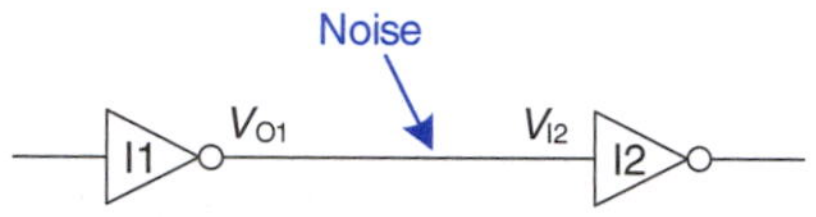

Figure 1.24 Inverter circuit

input is changed slowly enough that the output can keep up. They are called transfer characteristics because they describe the relationship between input and output voltages.

An ideal inverter would have an abrupt switching threshold at $V_{DD}/2$, as shown in Figure 1.25(a). For $V(A) < V_{DD}/2$, $V(Y) = V_{DD}$. For $V(A) > V_{DD}/2$, $V(Y) = 0$. In such a case, $V_{IH} = V_{IL} = V_{DD}/2$. $V_{OH} = V_{DD}$ and $V_{OL} = 0$.

A real inverter changes more gradually between the extremes, as shown in Figure 1.25(b). When the input voltage $V(A)$ is 0, the output voltage $V(Y) = V_{DD}$. When $V(A) = V_{DD}$, $V(Y) = 0$. However, the transition between these endpoints is smooth and may not be centered at exactly $V_{DD}/2$. This raises the question of how to define the logic levels.

A reasonable place to choose the logic levels is where the slope of the transfer characteristic $dV(Y) / dV(A)$ is -1. These two points are called the *unity gain points*. Choosing logic levels at the unity gain points usually maximizes the noise margins. If V_{IL} were reduced, V_{OH} would only increase by a small amount. But if V_{IL} were increased, V_{OH} would drop precipitously.

1.6.5 The Static Discipline

To avoid inputs falling into the forbidden zone, digital logic gates are designed to conform to the *static discipline*. The static discipline requires that, given logically valid inputs, every circuit element will produce logically valid outputs.

By conforming to the static discipline, digital designers sacrifice the freedom of using arbitrary analog circuit elements in return for the

DC indicates behavior when an input voltage is held constant or changes slowly enough for the rest of the system to keep up. The term's historical root comes from direct current, a method of transmitting power across a line with a constant voltage. In contrast, the transient response of a circuit is the behavior when an input voltage changes rapidly. Section 2.9 explores transient response further.

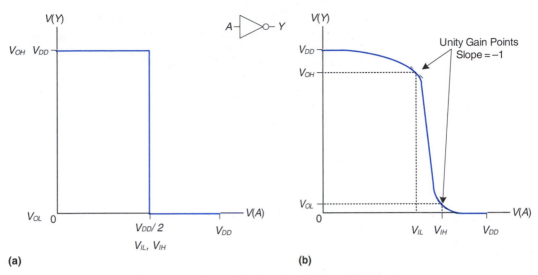

Figure 1.25 DC transfer characteristics and logic levels

simplicity and robustness of digital circuits. They raise the level of abstraction from analog to digital, increasing design productivity by hiding needless detail.

The choice of V_{DD} and logic levels is arbitrary, but all gates that communicate must have compatible logic levels. Therefore, gates are grouped into *logic families* such that all gates in a logic family obey the static discipline when used with other gates in the family. Logic gates in the same logic family snap together like Legos in that they use consistent power supply voltages and logic levels.

Four major logic families that predominated from the 1970's through the 1990's are *Transistor-Transistor Logic* (*TTL*), *Complementary Metal-Oxide-Semiconductor Logic* (*CMOS*, pronounced *sea-moss*), *Low Voltage TTL Logic* (*LVTTL*), and *Low Voltage CMOS Logic* (*LVCMOS*). Their logic levels are compared in Table 1.4. Since then, logic families have balkanized with a proliferation of even lower power supply voltages. Appendix A.6 revisits popular logic families in more detail.

Table 1.4 Logic levels of 5 V and 3.3 V logic families

Logic Family	V_{DD}	V_{IL}	V_{IH}	V_{OL}	V_{OH}
TTL	5 (4.75–5.25)	0.8	2.0	0.4	2.4
CMOS	5 (4.5–6)	1.35	3.15	0.33	3.84
LVTTL	3.3 (3–3.6)	0.8	2.0	0.4	2.4
LVCMOS	3.3 (3–3.6)	0.9	1.8	0.36	2.7

Table 1.5 Compatibility of logic families

		Receiver			
		TTL	CMOS	LVTTL	LVCMOS
Driver	TTL	OK	NO: $V_{OH} < V_{IH}$	MAYBE[a]	MAYBE[a]
	CMOS	OK	OK	MAYBE[a]	MAYBE[a]
	LVTTL	OK	NO: $V_{OH} < V_{IH}$	OK	OK
	LVCMOS	OK	NO: $V_{OH} < V_{IH}$	OK	OK

[a] As long as a 5 V HIGH level does not damage the receiver input

Robert Noyce, 1927–1990. Born in Burlington, Iowa. Received a B.A. in physics from Grinnell College and a Ph.D. in physics from MIT. Nicknamed "Mayor of Silicon Valley" for his profound influence on the industry.

Cofounded Fairchild Semiconductor in 1957 and Intel in 1968. Coinvented the integrated circuit. Many engineers from his teams went on to found other seminal semiconductor companies (© 2006, Intel Corporation. Reproduced by permission).

Example 1.19 LOGIC FAMILY COMPATIBILITY

Which of the logic families in Table 1.4 can communicate with each other reliably?

Solution: Table 1.5 lists which logic families have compatible logic levels. Note that a 5 V logic family such as TTL or CMOS may produce an output voltage as HIGH as 5 V. If this 5 V signal drives the input of a 3.3 V logic family such as LVTTL or LVCMOS, it can damage the receiver, unless the receiver is specially designed to be "5-volt compatible."

1.7 CMOS TRANSISTORS*

This section and other sections marked with a * are optional and are not necessary to understand the main flow of the book.

Babbage's Analytical Engine was built from gears, and early electrical computers used relays or vacuum tubes. Modern computers use transistors because they are cheap, small, and reliable. *Transistors* are electrically controlled switches that turn ON or OFF when a voltage or current is applied to a control terminal. The two main types of transistors are *bipolar transistors* and *metal-oxide-semiconductor field effect transistors* (*MOSFETs* or *MOS transistors,* pronounced "moss-fets" or "M-O-S", respectively).

In 1958, Jack Kilby at Texas Instruments built the first integrated circuit containing two transistors. In 1959, Robert Noyce at Fairchild Semiconductor patented a method of interconnecting multiple transistors on a single silicon chip. At the time, transistors cost about $10 each.

Thanks to more than three decades of unprecedented manufacturing advances, engineers can now pack roughly one billion MOSFETs onto a 1 cm^2 chip of silicon, and these transistors cost less than 10 microcents apiece. The capacity and cost continue to improve by an order of magnitude every 8 years or so. MOSFETs are now the building blocks of almost all digital systems. In this section, we will peer beneath the digital abstraction to see how logic gates are built from MOSFETs.

1.7.1 Semiconductors

MOS transistors are built from silicon, the predominant atom in rock and sand. Silicon (Si) is a group IV atom, so it has four electrons in its valence shell and forms bonds with four adjacent atoms, resulting in a crystalline *lattice*. Figure 1.26(a) shows the lattice in two dimensions for ease of drawing, but remember that the lattice actually forms a cubic crystal. In the figure, a line represents a covalent bond. By itself, silicon is a poor conductor because all the electrons are tied up in covalent bonds. However, it becomes a better conductor when small amounts of impurities, called *dopant* atoms, are carefully added. If a group V dopant such as arsenic (As) is added, the dopant atoms have an extra electron that is not involved in the bonds. The electron can easily move about the lattice, leaving an ionized dopant atom (As^+) behind, as shown in Figure 1.26(b). The electron carries a negative charge, so we call arsenic an *n-type* dopant. On the other hand, if a group III dopant such as boron (B) is added, the dopant atoms are missing an electron, as shown in Figure 1.26(c). This missing electron is called a *hole*. An electron from a neighboring silicon atom may move over to fill the missing bond, forming an ionized dopant atom (B^-) and leaving a hole at the neighboring silicon atom. In a similar fashion, the hole can migrate around the lattice. The hole is a lack of negative charge, so it acts like a positively charged particle. Hence, we call boron a *p-type* dopant. Because the conductivity of silicon changes over many orders of magnitude depending on the concentration of dopants, silicon is called a *semiconductor*.

1.7.2 Diodes

The junction between p-type and n-type silicon is called a *diode*. The p-type region is called the *anode* and the n-type region is called the *cathode*, as illustrated in Figure 1.27. When the voltage on the anode rises above the voltage on the cathode, the diode is *forward biased,* and

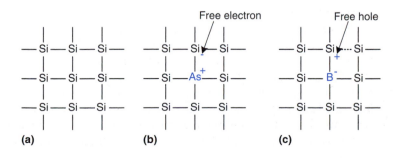

Figure 1.26 Silicon lattice and dopant atoms

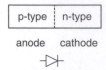

Figure 1.27 The p-n junction diode structure and symbol

Figure 1.28 Capacitor symbol

Technicians in an Intel clean room wear Gore-Tex bunny suits to prevent particulates from their hair, skin, and clothing from contaminating the microscopic transistors on silicon wafers (© 2006, Intel Corporation. Reproduced by permission).

A 40-pin dual-inline package (DIP) contains a small chip (scarcely visible) in the center that is connected to 40 metal pins, 20 on a side, by gold wires thinner than a strand of hair (photograph by Kevin Mapp. © Harvey Mudd College).

current flows through the diode from the anode to the cathode. But when the anode voltage is lower than the voltage on the cathode, the diode is *reverse biased,* and no current flows. The diode symbol intuitively shows that current only flows in one direction.

1.7.3 Capacitors

A *capacitor* consists of two conductors separated by an insulator. When a voltage V is applied to one of the conductors, the conductor accumulates electric *charge* Q and the other conductor accumulates the opposite charge $-Q$. The *capacitance* C of the capacitor is the ratio of charge to voltage: $C = Q/V$. The capacitance is proportional to the size of the conductors and inversely proportional the distance between them. The symbol for a capacitor is shown in Figure 1.28.

Capacitance is important because charging or discharging a conductor takes time and energy. More capacitance means that a circuit will be slower and require more energy to operate. Speed and energy will be discussed throughout this book.

1.7.4 nMOS and pMOS Transistors

A MOSFET is a sandwich of several layers of conducting and insulating materials. MOSFETs are built on thin flat *wafers* of silicon of about 15 to 30 cm in diameter. The manufacturing process begins with a bare wafer. The process involves a sequence of steps in which dopants are implanted into the silicon, thin films of silicon dioxide and silicon are grown, and metal is deposited. Between each step, the wafer is *patterned* so that the materials appear only where they are desired. Because transistors are a fraction of a micron[2] in length and the entire wafer is processed at once, it is inexpensive to manufacture billions of transistors at a time. Once processing is complete, the wafer is cut into rectangles called *chips* or *dice* that contain thousands, millions, or even billions of transistors. The chip is tested, then placed in a plastic or ceramic *package* with metal pins to connect it to a circuit board.

The MOSFET sandwich consists of a conducting layer called the *gate* on top of an insulating layer of *silicon dioxide* (SiO_2) on top of the silicon wafer, called the *substrate.* Historically, the gate was constructed from metal, hence the name metal-oxide-semiconductor. Modern manufacturing processes use polycrystalline silicon for the gate, because it does not melt during subsequent high-temperature processing steps. Silicon dioxide is better known as glass and is often simply called *oxide* in the semiconductor industry. The metal-oxide-semiconductor sandwich forms a capacitor, in which a thin layer of insulating oxide called a *dielectric* separates the metal and semiconductor plates.

---

[2] 1 μm = 1 micron = 10^{-6} m.

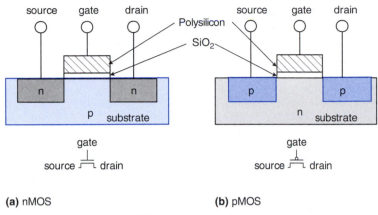

(a) nMOS   **(b)** pMOS

Figure 1.29 nMOS and pMOS transistors

There are two flavors of MOSFETs: nMOS and pMOS (pronounced "n-moss" and "p-moss"). Figure 1.29 shows cross-sections of each type, made by sawing through a wafer and looking at it from the side. The n-type transistors, called *nMOS*, have regions of n-type dopants adjacent to the gate called the *source* and the *drain* and are built on a p-type semiconductor substrate. The *pMOS* transistors are just the opposite, consisting of p-type source and drain regions in an n-type *substrate*.

A MOSFET behaves as a voltage-controlled switch in which the gate voltage creates an electric field that turns ON or OFF a connection between the source and drain. The term *field effect transistor* comes from this principle of operation. Let us start by exploring the operation of an nMOS transistor.

The substrate of an nMOS transistor is normally tied to GND, the lowest voltage in the system. First, consider the situation when the gate is also at 0 V, as shown in Figure 1.30(a). The diodes between the source or drain and the substrate are reverse biased because the source or drain voltage is nonnegative. Hence, there is no path for current to flow between the source and drain, so the transistor is OFF. Now, consider when the gate is raised to V_{DD}, as shown in Figure 1.30(b). When a positive voltage is applied to the top plate of a capacitor, it establishes an electric field that attracts positive charge on the top plate and negative charge to the bottom plate. If the voltage is sufficiently large, so much negative charge is attracted to the underside of the gate that the region *inverts* from p-type to effectively become n-type. This inverted region is called the *channel*. Now the transistor has a continuous path from the n-type source through the n-type channel to the n-type drain, so electrons can flow from source to drain. The transistor is ON. The gate voltage required to turn on a transistor is called the *threshold voltage*, V_t, and is typically 0.3 to 0.7 V.

The source and drain terminals are physically symmetric. However, we say that charge flows from the source to the drain. In an nMOS transistor, the charge is carried by electrons, which flow from negative voltage to positive voltage. In a pMOS transistor, the charge is carried by holes, which flow from positive voltage to negative voltage. If we draw schematics with the most positive voltage at the top and the most negative at the bottom, the source of (negative) charges in an nMOS transistor is the bottom terminal and the source of (positive) charges in a pMOS transistor is the top terminal.

A technician holds a 12-inch wafer containing hundreds of microprocessor chips (© 2006, Intel Corporation. Reproduced by permission).

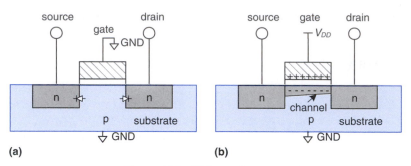

Figure 1.30 nMOS transistor operation

Gordon Moore, 1929–. Born in San Francisco. Received a B.S. in chemistry from UC Berkeley and a Ph.D. in chemistry and physics from Caltech. Cofounded Intel in 1968 with Robert Noyce. Observed in 1965 that the number of transistors on a computer chip doubles every year. This trend has become known as *Moore's Law*. Since 1975, transistor counts have doubled every two years.

A corollary of Moore's Law is that microprocessor performance doubles every 18 to 24 months. Semiconductor sales have also increased exponentially. Unfortunately, power consumption has increased exponentially as well (© 2006, Intel Corporation. Reproduced by permission).

pMOS transistors work in just the opposite fashion, as might be guessed from the bubble on their symbol. The substrate is tied to V_{DD}. When the gate is also at V_{DD}, the pMOS transistor is OFF. When the gate is at GND, the channel inverts to p-type and the pMOS transistor is ON.

Unfortunately, MOSFETs are not perfect switches. In particular, nMOS transistors pass 0's well but pass 1's poorly. Specifically, when the gate of an nMOS transistor is at V_{DD}, the drain will only swing between 0 and $V_{DD} - V_t$. Similarly, pMOS transistors pass 1's well but 0's poorly. However, we will see that it is possible to build logic gates that use transistors only in their good mode.

nMOS transistors need a p-type substrate, and pMOS transistors need an n-type substrate. To build both flavors of transistors on the same chip, manufacturing processes typically start with a p-type wafer, then implant n-type regions called *wells* where the pMOS transistors should go. These processes that provide both flavors of transistors are called Complementary MOS or *CMOS*. CMOS processes are used to build the vast majority of all transistors fabricated today.

In summary, CMOS processes give us two types of electrically controlled switches, as shown in Figure 1.31. The voltage at the gate (g) regulates the flow of current between the source (s) and drain (d). nMOS transistors are OFF when the gate is 0 and ON when the gate is 1.

Figure 1.31 Switch models of MOSFETs

pMOS transistors are just the opposite: ON when the gate is 0 and OFF when the gate is 1.

1.7.5 CMOS NOT Gate

Figure 1.32 shows a schematic of a NOT gate built with CMOS transistors. The triangle indicates GND, and the flat bar indicates V_{DD}; these labels will be omitted from future schematics. The nMOS transistor, *N1*, is connected between GND and the *Y* output. The pMOS transistor, *P1*, is connected between V_{DD} and the *Y* output. Both transistor gates are controlled by the input, *A*.

If $A = 0$, *N1* is OFF and *P1* is ON. Hence, *Y* is connected to V_{DD} but not to GND, and is pulled up to a logic 1. *P1* passes a good 1. If $A = 1$, *N1* is ON and *P1* is OFF, and *Y* is pulled down to a logic 0. *N1* passes a good 0. Checking against the truth table in Figure 1.12, we see that the circuit is indeed a NOT gate.

Figure 1.32 NOT gate schematic

1.7.6 Other CMOS Logic Gates

Figure 1.33 shows a schematic of a two-input NAND gate. In schematic diagrams, wires are always joined at three-way junctions. They are joined at four-way junctions only if a dot is shown. The nMOS transistors *N1* and *N2* are connected in series; both nMOS transistors must be ON to pull the output down to GND. The pMOS transistors *P1* and *P2* are in parallel; only one pMOS transistor must be ON to pull the output up to V_{DD}. Table 1.6 lists the operation of the pull-down and pull-up networks and the state of the output, demonstrating that the gate does function as a NAND. For example, when $A = 1$ and $B = 0$, *N1* is ON, but *N2* is OFF, blocking the path from *Y* to GND. *P1* is OFF, but *P2* is ON, creating a path from V_{DD} to *Y*. Therefore, *Y* is pulled up to 1.

Figure 1.34 shows the general form used to construct any inverting logic gate, such as NOT, NAND, or NOR. nMOS transistors are good at passing 0's, so a pull-down network of nMOS transistors is placed between the output and GND to pull the output down to 0. pMOS transistors are

Figure 1.33 Two-input NAND gate schematic

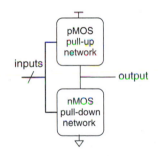

Figure 1.34 General form of an inverting logic gate

Table 1.6 NAND gate operation

A	B	Pull-Down Network	Pull-Up Network	Y
0	0	OFF	ON	1
0	1	OFF	ON	1
1	0	OFF	ON	1
1	1	ON	OFF	0

Experienced designers claim that electronic devices operate because they contain *magic smoke*. They confirm this theory with the observation that if the magic smoke is ever let out of the device, it ceases to work.

good at passing 1's, so a pull-up network of pMOS transistors is placed between the output and V_{DD} to pull the output up to 1. The networks may consist of transistors in series or in parallel. When transistors are in parallel, the network is ON if either transistor is ON. When transistors are in series, the network is ON only if both transistors are ON. The slash across the input wire indicates that the gate may receive multiple inputs.

If both the pull-up and pull-down networks were ON simultaneously, a *short circuit* would exist between V_{DD} and GND. The output of the gate might be in the forbidden zone and the transistors would consume large amounts of power, possibly enough to burn out. On the other hand, if both the pull-up and pull-down networks were OFF simultaneously, the output would be connected to neither V_{DD} nor GND. We say that the output *floats*. Its value is again undefined. Floating outputs are usually undesirable, but in Section 2.6 we will see how they can occasionally be used to the designer's advantage.

In a properly functioning logic gate, one of the networks should be ON and the other OFF at any given time, so that the output is pulled HIGH or LOW but not shorted or floating. We can guarantee this by using the rule of *conduction complements*. When nMOS transistors are in series, the pMOS transistors must be in parallel. When nMOS transistors are in parallel, the pMOS transistors must be in series.

Example 1.20   THREE-INPUT NAND SCHEMATIC

Draw a schematic for a three-input NAND gate using CMOS transistors.

Solution: The NAND gate should produce a 0 output only when all three inputs are 1. Hence, the pull-down network should have three nMOS transistors in series. By the conduction complements rule, the pMOS transistors must be in parallel. Such a gate is shown in Figure 1.35; you can verify the function by checking that it has the correct truth table.

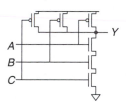

Figure 1.35 Three-input NAND gate schematic

Example 1.21   TWO-INPUT NOR SCHEMATIC

Draw a schematic for a two-input NOR gate using CMOS transistors.

Solution: The NOR gate should produce a 0 output if either input is 1. Hence, the pull-down network should have two nMOS transistors in parallel. By the conduction complements rule, the pMOS transistors must be in series. Such a gate is shown in Figure 1.36.

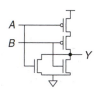

Figure 1.36 Two-input NOR gate schematic

Example 1.22   TWO-INPUT AND SCHEMATIC

Draw a schematic for a two-input AND gate.

Solution: It is impossible to build an AND gate with a single CMOS gate. However, building NAND and NOT gates is easy. Thus, the best way to build an AND gate using CMOS transistors is to use a NAND followed by a NOT, as shown in Figure 1.37.

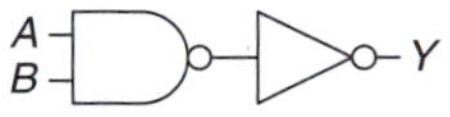

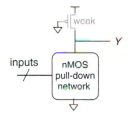

Figure 1.37 Two-input AND gate schematic

1.7.7 Transmission Gates

At times, designers find it convenient to use an ideal switch that can pass both 0 and 1 well. Recall that nMOS transistors are good at passing 0 and pMOS transistors are good at passing 1, so the parallel combination of the two passes both values well. Figure 1.38 shows such a circuit, called a *transmission gate* or *pass gate*. The two sides of the switch are called *A* and *B* because a switch is bidirectional and has no preferred input or output side. The control signals are called *enables*, *EN* and $\overline{EN}$. When *EN* = 0 and $\overline{EN}$ = 1, both transistors are OFF. Hence, the transmission gate is OFF or disabled, so *A* and *B* are not connected. When *EN* = 1 and $\overline{EN}$ = 0, the transmission gate is ON or enabled, and any logic value can flow between *A* and *B*.

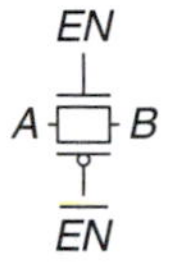

Figure 1.38 Transmission gate

1.7.8 Pseudo-nMOS Logic

An *N*-input CMOS NOR gate uses *N* nMOS transistors in parallel and *N* pMOS transistors in series. Transistors in series are slower than transistors in parallel, just as resistors in series have more resistance than resistors in parallel. Moreover, pMOS transistors are slower than nMOS transistors because holes cannot move around the silicon lattice as fast as electrons. Therefore the parallel nMOS transistors are fast and the series pMOS transistors are slow, especially when many are in series.

Pseudo-nMOS logic replaces the slow stack of pMOS transistors with a single weak pMOS transistor that is always ON, as shown in Figure 1.39. This pMOS transistor is often called a *weak pull-up*. The physical dimensions of the pMOS transistor are selected so that the pMOS transistor will pull the output, *Y*, HIGH weakly—that is, only if none of the nMOS transistors are ON. But if any nMOS transistor is ON, it overpowers the weak pull-up and pulls *Y* down close enough to GND to produce a logic 0.

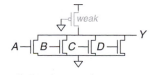

Figure 1.39 Generic pseudo-nMOS gate

The advantage of pseudo-nMOS logic is that it can be used to build fast NOR gates with many inputs. For example, Figure 1.40 shows a pseudo-nMOS four-input NOR. Pseudo-nMOS gates are useful for certain memory and logic arrays discussed in Chapter 5. The disadvantage is that a short circuit exists between V_{DD} and GND when the output is LOW; the weak pMOS and nMOS transistors are both ON. The short circuit draws continuous power, so pseudo-nMOS logic must be used sparingly.

Figure 1.40 Pseudo-nMOS four-input NOR gate

Pseudo-nMOS gates got their name from the 1970's, when manufacturing processes only had nMOS transistors. A weak nMOS transistor was used to pull the output HIGH because pMOS transistors were not available.

1.8 POWER CONSUMPTION*

Power consumption is the amount of energy used per unit time. Power consumption is of great importance in digital systems. The battery life of portable systems such as cell phones and laptop computers is limited by power consumption. Power is also significant for systems that are plugged in, because electricity costs money and because the system will overheat if it draws too much power.

Digital systems draw both *dynamic* and *static* power. Dynamic power is the power used to charge capacitance as signals change between 0 and 1. Static power is the power used even when signals do not change and the system is idle.

Logic gates and the wires that connect them have capacitance. The energy drawn from the power supply to charge a capacitance C to voltage V_{DD} is CV_{DD}^2. If the voltage on the capacitor switches at frequency f (i.e., f times per second), it charges the capacitor $f/2$ times and discharges it $f/2$ times per second. Discharging does not draw energy from the power supply, so the dynamic power consumption is

$$P_{\text{dynamic}} = \frac{1}{2}CV_{DD}^2 f \qquad (1.4)$$

Electrical systems draw some current even when they are idle. When transistors are OFF, they leak a small amount of current. Some circuits, such as the pseudo-nMOS gate discussed in Section 1.7.8, have a path from V_{DD} to GND through which current flows continuously. The total static current, I_{DD}, is also called the *leakage current* or the *quiescent supply current* flowing between V_{DD} and GND. The static power consumption is proportional to this static current:

$$P_{\text{static}} = I_{DD}V_{DD} \qquad (1.5)$$

Example 1.23 POWER CONSUMPTION

A particular cell phone has a 6 watt-hour (W-hr) battery and operates at 1.2 V. Suppose that, when it is in use, the cell phone operates at 300 MHz and the average amount of capacitance in the chip switching at any given time is 10 nF (10^{-8} Farads). When in use, it also broadcasts 3 W of power out of its antenna. When the phone is not in use, the dynamic power drops to almost zero because the signal processing is turned off. But the phone also draws 40 mA of quiescent current whether it is in use or not. Determine the battery life of the phone (a) if it is not being used, and (b) if it is being used continuously.

Solution: The static power is $P_{\text{static}} = (0.040\ \text{A})(1.2\ \text{V}) = 48\ \text{mW}$. If the phone is not being used, this is the only power consumption, so the battery life is (6 W-hr)/(0.048 W) = 125 hours (about 5 days). If the phone is being used, the dynamic power is $P_{\text{dynamic}} = (0.5)(10^{-8}\ \text{F})(1.2\ \text{V})^2(3 \times 10^8\ \text{Hz}) = 2.16\ \text{W}$. Together with the static and broadcast power, the total active power is 2.16 W + 0.048 W + 3 W = 5.2 W, so the battery life is 6 W-hr/5.2 W = 1.15 hours. This example somewhat oversimplifies the actual operation of a cell phone, but it illustrates the key ideas of power consumption.

1.9 SUMMARY AND A LOOK AHEAD

There are 10 kinds of people in this world: those who can count in binary and those who can't.

This chapter has introduced principles for understanding and designing complex systems. Although the real world is analog, digital designers discipline themselves to use a discrete subset of possible signals. In particular, binary variables have just two states: 0 and 1, also called FALSE and TRUE or LOW and HIGH. Logic gates compute a binary output from one or more binary inputs. Some of the common logic gates are:

- ▶ **NOT:** TRUE when input is FALSE

- ▶ **AND:** TRUE when all inputs are TRUE

- ▶ **OR:** TRUE when any inputs are TRUE

- ▶ **XOR:** TRUE when an odd number of inputs are TRUE

Logic gates are commonly built from CMOS transistors, which behave as electrically controlled switches. nMOS transistors turn ON when the gate is 1. pMOS transistors turn ON when the gate is 0.

In Chapters 2 through 5, we continue the study of digital logic. Chapter 2 addresses *combinational logic,* in which the outputs depend only on the current inputs. The logic gates introduced already are examples of combinational logic. You will learn to design circuits involving multiple gates to implement a relationship between inputs and outputs specified by a truth table or Boolean equation. Chapter 3 addresses *sequential logic,* in which the outputs depend on both current and past inputs. *Registers* are common sequential elements that remember their previous input. *Finite state machines,* built from registers and combinational logic, are a powerful way to build complicated systems in a systematic fashion. We also study timing of digital systems to analyze how fast the systems can operate. Chapter 4 describes hardware description languages (HDLs). HDLs are related to conventional programming languages but are used to simulate and build hardware rather than software. Most digital systems today are designed with HDLs. Verilog and VHDL are the two prevalent languages, and they are covered side-by-side in this book. Chapter 5 studies other combinational and sequential building blocks such as adders, multipliers, and memories.

Chapter 6 shifts to computer architecture. It describes the MIPS processor, an industry-standard microprocessor used in consumer electronics, some Silicon Graphics workstations, and many communications systems such as televisions, networking hardware and wireless links. The MIPS architecture is defined by its registers and assembly language instruction set. You will learn to write programs in assembly language for the MIPS processor so that you can communicate with the processor in its native language.

Chapters 7 and 8 bridge the gap between digital logic and computer architecture. Chapter 7 investigates microarchitecture, the arrangement of digital building blocks, such as adders and registers, needed to construct a processor. In that chapter, you learn to build your own MIPS processor. Indeed, you learn three microarchitectures illustrating different trade-offs of performance and cost. Processor performance has increased exponentially, requiring ever more sophisticated memory systems to feed the insatiable demand for data. Chapter 8 delves into memory system architecture and also describes how computers communicate with peripheral devices such as keyboards and printers.

Exercises

Exercise 1.1 Explain in one paragraph at least three levels of abstraction that are used by

a)   biologists studying the operation of cells.

b)   chemists studying the composition of matter.

Exercise 1.2 Explain in one paragraph how the techniques of hierarchy, modularity, and regularity may be used by

a)   automobile designers.

b)   businesses to manage their operations.

Exercise 1.3 Ben Bitdiddle is building a house. Explain how he can use the principles of hierarchy, modularity, and regularity to save time and money during construction.

Exercise 1.4 An analog voltage is in the range of 0–5 V. If it can be measured with an accuracy of $\pm$ 50 mV, at most how many bits of information does it convey?

Exercise 1.5 A classroom has an old clock on the wall whose minute hand broke off.

a)   If you can read the hour hand to the nearest 15 minutes, how many bits of information does the clock convey about the time?

b)   If you know whether it is before or after noon, how many additional bits of information do you know about the time?

Exercise 1.6 The Babylonians developed the *sexagesimal* (base 60) number system about 4000 years ago. How many bits of information is conveyed with one sexagesimal digit? How do you write the number 4000_{10} in sexagesimal?

Exercise 1.7 How many different numbers can be represented with 16 bits?

Exercise 1.8 What is the largest unsigned 32-bit binary number?

Exercise 1.9 What is the largest 16-bit binary number that can be represented with

a)   unsigned numbers?

b)   two's complement numbers?

c)   sign/magnitude numbers?

Exercise 1.10 What is the smallest (most negative) 16-bit binary number that can be represented with

a)   unsigned numbers?

b)   two's complement numbers?

c)   sign/magnitude numbers?

Exercise 1.11 Convert the following unsigned binary numbers to decimal.

a) 1010_2

b) 110110_2

c) 11110000_2

d) 0001100010100111_2

Exercise 1.12 Repeat Exercise 1.11, but convert to hexadecimal.

Exercise 1.13 Convert the following hexadecimal numbers to decimal.

a) $A5_{16}$

b) $3B_{16}$

c) $FFFF_{16}$

d) $D0000000_{16}$

Exercise 1.14 Repeat Exercise 1.13, but convert to unsigned binary.

Exercise 1.15 Convert the following two's complement binary numbers to decimal.

a) 1010_2

b) 110110_2

c) 01110000_2

d) 10011111_2

Exercise 1.16 Repeat Exercise 1.15, assuming the binary numbers are in sign/magnitude form rather than two's complement representation.

Exercise 1.17 Convert the following decimal numbers to unsigned binary numbers.

a) 42_{10}

b) 63_{10}

c) 229_{10}

d) 845_{10}

Exercise 1.18   Repeat Exercise 1.17, but convert to hexadecimal.

Exercise 1.19   Convert the following decimal numbers to 8-bit two's complement numbers or indicate that the decimal number would overflow the range.

a) 42_{10}

b) -63_{10}

c) 124_{10}

d) -128_{10}

e) 133_{10}

Exercise 1.20   Repeat Exercise 1.19, but convert to 8-bit sign/magnitude numbers.

Exercise 1.21   Convert the following 4-bit two's complement numbers to 8-bit two's complement numbers.

a) 0101_2

b) 1010_2

Exercise 1.22   Repeat Exercise 1.21 if the numbers are unsigned rather than two's complement.

Exercise 1.23   Base 8 is referred to as *octal*. Convert each of the numbers from Exercise 1.17 to octal.

Exercise 1.24   Convert each of the following octal numbers to binary, hexadecimal, and decimal.

a) 42_8

b) 63_8

c) 255_8

d) 3047_8

Exercise 1.25   How many 5-bit two's complement numbers are greater than 0? How many are less than 0? How would your answers differ for sign/magnitude numbers?

Exercise 1.26 How many bytes are in a 32-bit word? How many nibbles are in the word?

Exercise 1.27 How many bytes are in a 64-bit word?

Exercise 1.28 A particular DSL modem operates at 768 kbits/sec. How many bytes can it receive in 1 minute?

Exercise 1.29 Hard disk manufacturers use the term "megabyte" to mean 10^6 bytes and "gigabyte" to mean 10^9 bytes. How many real GBs of music can you store on a 50 GB hard disk?

Exercise 1.30 Estimate the value of 2^{31} without using a calculator.

Exercise 1.31 A memory on the Pentium II microprocessor is organized as a rectangular array of bits with 2^8 rows and 2^9 columns. Estimate how many bits it has without using a calculator.

Exercise 1.32 Draw a number line analogous to Figure 1.11 for 3-bit unsigned, two's complement, and sign/magnitude numbers.

Exercise 1.33 Perform the following additions of unsigned binary numbers. Indicate whether or not the sum overflows a 4-bit result.

a) $1001_2 + 0100_2$

b) $1101_2 + 1011_2$

Exercise 1.34 Perform the following additions of unsigned binary numbers. Indicate whether or not the sum overflows an 8-bit result.

a) $10011001_2 + 01000100_2$

b) $11010010_2 + 10110110_2$

Exercise 1.35 Repeat Exercise 1.34, assuming that the binary numbers are in two's complement form.

Exercise 1.36 Convert the following decimal numbers to 6-bit two's complement binary numbers and add them. Indicate whether or not the sum overflows a 6-bit result.

a) $16_{10} + 9_{10}$

b) $27_{10} + 31_{10}$

c) $-4_{10} + 19_{10}$

d) $3_{10} + -32_{10}$

e) $-16_{10} + -9_{10}$

f) $-27_{10} + -31_{10}$

Exercise 1.37 Perform the following additions of unsigned hexadecimal numbers. Indicate whether or not the sum overflows an 8-bit (two hex digit) result.

a) $7_{16} + 9_{16}$

b) $13_{16} + 28_{16}$

c) $AB_{16} + 3E_{16}$

d) $8F_{16} + AD_{16}$

Exercise 1.38 Convert the following decimal numbers to 5-bit two's complement binary numbers and subtract them. Indicate whether or not the difference overflows a 5-bit result.

a) $9_{10} - 7_{10}$

b) $12_{10} - 15_{10}$

c) $-6_{10} - 11_{10}$

d) $4_{10} - -8_{10}$

Exercise 1.39 In a *biased* N-bit binary number system with bias B, positive and negative numbers are represented as their value plus the bias B. For example, for 5-bit numbers with a bias of 15, the number 0 is represented as 01111, 1 as 10000, and so forth. Biased number systems are sometimes used in floating point mathematics, which will be discussed in Chapter 5. Consider a biased 8-bit binary number system with a bias of 127_{10}.

a) What decimal value does the binary number 10000010_2 represent?

b) What binary number represents the value 0?

c) What is the representation and value of the most negative number?

d) What is the representation and value of the most positive number?

Exercise 1.40 Draw a number line analogous to Figure 1.11 for 3-bit biased numbers with a bias of 3 (see Exercise 1.39 for a definition of biased numbers).

Exercise 1.41 In a *binary coded decimal* (BCD) system, 4 bits are used to represent a decimal digit from 0 to 9. For example, 37_{10} is written as 00110111_{BCD}.

a)   Write 289_{10} in BCD.

b)   Convert 100101010001_{BCD} to decimal.

c)   Convert 01101001_{BCD} to binary.

d)   Explain why BCD might be a useful way to represent numbers.

Exercise 1.42 A flying saucer crashes in a Nebraska cornfield. The FBI investigates the wreckage and finds an engineering manual containing an equation in the Martian number system: $325 + 42 = 411$. If this equation is correct, how many fingers would you expect Martians have?

Exercise 1.43 Ben Bitdiddle and Alyssa P. Hacker are having an argument. Ben says, "All integers greater than zero and exactly divisible by six have exactly two 1's in their binary representation." Alyssa disagrees. She says, "No, but all such numbers have an even number of 1's in their representation." Do you agree with Ben or Alyssa or both or neither? Explain.

Exercise 1.44 Ben Bitdiddle and Alyssa P. Hacker are having another argument. Ben says, "I can get the two's complement of a number by subtracting 1, then inverting all the bits of the result." Alyssa says, "No, I can do it by examining each bit of the number, starting with the least significant bit. When the first 1 is found, invert each subsequent bit." Do you agree with Ben or Alyssa or both or neither? Explain.

Exercise 1.45 Write a program in your favorite language (e.g., C, Java, Perl) to convert numbers from binary to decimal. The user should type in an unsigned binary number. The program should print the decimal equivalent.

Exercise 1.46 Repeat Exercise 1.45 but convert from decimal to hexadecimal.

Exercise 1.47 Repeat Exercise 1.45 but convert from an arbitrary base b_1 to another base b_2, as specified by the user. Support bases up to 16, using the letters of the alphabet for digits greater than 9. The user should enter b_1, b_2, and then the number to convert in base b_1. The program should print the equivalent number in base b_2.

Exercise 1.48 Draw the symbol, Boolean equation, and truth table for

a)   a three-input OR gate.

b)   a three-input exclusive OR (XOR) gate.

c)   a four-input XNOR gate

Exercise 1.49 A *majority gate* produces a TRUE output if and only if more than half of its inputs are TRUE. Complete a truth table for the three-input majority gate shown in Figure 1.41.

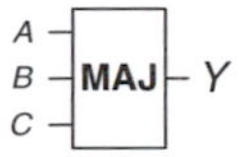

Figure 1.41 Three-input majority gate

Exercise 1.50 A three-input *AND-OR (AO) gate* shown in Figure 1.42 produces a TRUE output if both *A* and *B* are TRUE, or if *C* is TRUE. Complete a truth table for the gate.

Figure 1.42 Three-input AND-OR gate

Exercise 1.51 A three-input *OR-AND-INVERT (OAI) gate* shown in Figure 1.43 produces a FALSE input if *C* is TRUE and *A* or *B* is TRUE. Otherwise it produces a TRUE output. Complete a truth table for the gate.

Figure 1.43 Three-input OR-AND-INVERT gate

Exercise 1.52 There are 16 different truth tables for Boolean functions of two variables. List each truth table. Give each one a short descriptive name (such as OR, NAND, and so on).

Exercise 1.53 How many different truth tables exist for Boolean functions of *N* variables?

Exercise 1.54 Is it possible to assign logic levels so that a device with the transfer characteristics shown in Figure 1.44 would serve as an inverter? If so, what are the input and output low and high levels (V_{IL}, V_{OL}, V_{IH}, and V_{OH}) and noise margins (NM_L and NM_H)? If not, explain why not.

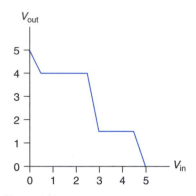

Figure 1.44 DC transfer characteristics

Exercise 1.55 Repeat Exercise 1.54 for the transfer characteristics shown in Figure 1.45.

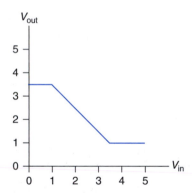

Figure 1.45 DC transfer characteristics

Exercise 1.56 Is it possible to assign logic levels so that a device with the transfer characteristics shown in Figure 1.46 would serve as a buffer? If so, what are the input and output low and high levels (V_{IL}, V_{OL}, V_{IH}, and V_{OH}) and noise margins (NM_L and NM_H)? If not, explain why not.

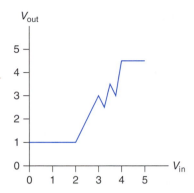

Figure 1.46 DC transfer characteristics

Exercise 1.57 Ben Bitdiddle has invented a circuit with the transfer characteristics shown in Figure 1.47 that he would like to use as a buffer. Will it work? Why or why not? He would like to advertise that it is compatible with LVCMOS and LVTTL logic. Can Ben's buffer correctly receive inputs from those logic families? Can its output properly drive those logic families? Explain.

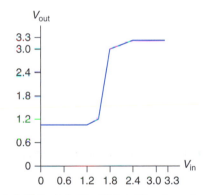

Figure 1.47 Ben's buffer DC transfer characteristics

Exercise 1.58 While walking down a dark alley, Ben Bitdiddle encounters a two-input gate with the transfer function shown in Figure 1.48. The inputs are A and B and the output is Y.

a)   What kind of logic gate did he find?

b)   What are the approximate high and low logic levels?

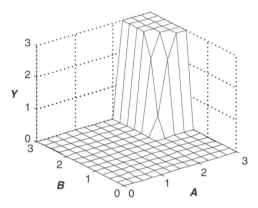

Figure 1.48 Two-input DC transfer characteristics

Exercise 1.59 Repeat Exercise 1.58 for Figure 1.49.

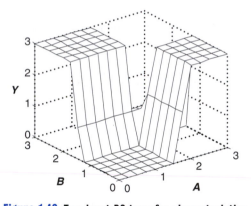

Figure 1.49 Two-input DC transfer characteristics

Exercise 1.60 Sketch a transistor-level circuit for the following CMOS gates. Use a minimum number of transistors.

a)   A four-input NAND gate.

b)   A three-input OR-AND-INVERT gate (see Exercise 1.51).

c)   A three-input AND-OR gate (see Exercise 1.50).

Exercise 1.61 A *minority gate* produces a TRUE output if and only if fewer than half of its inputs are TRUE. Otherwise it produces a FALSE output. Sketch a transistor-level circuit for a CMOS minority gate. Use a minimum number of transistors.

Exercise 1.62 Write a truth table for the function performed by the gate in Figure 1.50. The truth table should have two inputs, *A* and *B*. What is the name of this function?

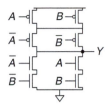

Figure 1.50 Mystery schematic

Exercise 1.63 Write a truth table for the function performed by the gate in Figure 1.51. The truth table should have three inputs, *A*, *B*, and *C*.

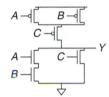

Figure 1.51 Mystery schematic

Exercise 1.64 Implement the following three-input gates using **only** pseudo-nMOS logic gates. Your gates receive three inputs, *A*, *B*, and *C*. Use a minimum number of transistors.

a)   three-input NOR gate

b)   three-input NAND gate

a)   three-input AND gate

Exercise 1.65 *Resistor-Transistor Logic (RTL)* uses nMOS transistors to pull the gate output LOW and a weak resistor to pull the output HIGH when none of the paths to ground are active. A NOT gate built using RTL is shown in Figure 1.52. Sketch a three-input RTL NOR gate. Use a minimum number of transistors.

weak

A —│ ├— *Y*

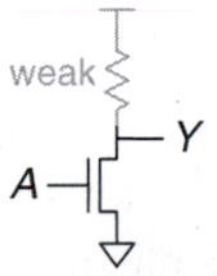

Figure 1.52 RTL NOT gate

Interview Questions

These questions have been asked at interviews for digital design jobs.

Question 1.1 Sketch a transistor-level circuit for a CMOS four-input NOR gate.

Question 1.2 The king receives 64 gold coins in taxes but has reason to believe that one is counterfeit. He summons you to identify the fake coin. You have a balance that can hold coins on each side. How many times do you need to use the balance to find the lighter, fake coin?

Question 1.3 The professor, the teaching assistant, the digital design student, and the freshman track star need to cross a rickety bridge on a dark night. The bridge is so shakey that only two people can cross at a time. They have only one flashlight among them and the span is too long to throw the flashlight, so somebody must carry it back to the other people. The freshman track star can cross the bridge in 1 minute. The digital design student can cross the bridge in 2 minutes. The teaching assistant can cross the bridge in 5 minutes. The professor always gets distracted and takes 10 minutes to cross the bridge. What is the fastest time to get everyone across the bridge?

Combinational Logic Design

2.1 INTRODUCTION

In digital electronics, a *circuit* is a network that processes discrete-valued variables. A circuit can be viewed as a black box, shown in Figure 2.1, with

▶ one or more discrete-valued *input terminals*

▶ one or more discrete-valued *output terminals*

▶ a *functional specification* describing the relationship between inputs and outputs

▶ a *timing specification* describing the delay between inputs changing and outputs responding.

Peering inside the black box, circuits are composed of nodes and elements. An *element* is itself a circuit with inputs, outputs, and a specification. A *node* is a wire, whose voltage conveys a discrete-valued variable. Nodes are classified as *input, output,* or *internal.* Inputs receive values from the external world. Outputs deliver values to the external world. Wires that are not inputs or outputs are called internal nodes. Figure 2.2

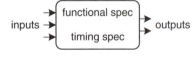

Figure 2.1 Circuit as a black box with inputs, outputs, and specifications

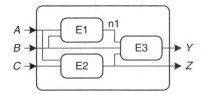

Figure 2.2 Elements and nodes

51

illustrates a circuit with three elements, E1, E2, and E3, and six nodes. Nodes *A*, *B*, and *C* are inputs. *Y* and *Z* are outputs. n1 is an internal node between E1 and E3.

Digital circuits are classified as *combinational* or *sequential*. A combinational circuit's outputs depend only on the current values of the inputs; in other words, it combines the current input values to compute the output. For example, a logic gate is a combinational circuit. A sequential circuit's outputs depend on both current and previous values of the inputs; in other words, it depends on the input sequence. A combinational circuit is *memoryless*, but a sequential circuit has *memory*. This chapter focuses on combinational circuits, and Chapter 3 examines sequential circuits.

The functional specification of a combinational circuit expresses the output values in terms of the current input values. The timing specification of a combinational circuit consists of lower and upper bounds on the delay from input to output. We will initially concentrate on the functional specification, then return to the timing specification later in this chapter.

Figure 2.3 shows a combinational circuit with two inputs and one output. On the left of the figure are the inputs, *A* and *B*, and on the right is the output, *Y*. The symbol ℭ inside the box indicates that it is implemented using only combinational logic. In this example, the function, *F*, is specified to be OR: *Y* = *F*(*A*, *B*) = *A* + *B*. In words, we say the output, *Y*, is a function of the two inputs, *A* and *B*, namely *Y* = *A* OR *B*.

Figure 2.4 shows two possible *implementations* for the combinational logic circuit in Figure 2.3. As we will see repeatedly throughout the book, there are often many implementations for a single function. You choose which to use given the building blocks at your disposal and your design constraints. These constraints often include area, speed, power, and design time.

Figure 2.5 shows a combinational circuit with multiple outputs. This particular combinational circuit is called a *full adder* and we will revisit it in Section 5.2.1. The two equations specify the function of the outputs, *S* and C_{out}, in terms of the inputs, *A*, *B*, and C_{in}.

To simplify drawings, we often use a single line with a slash through it and a number next to it to indicate a *bus*, a bundle of multiple signals. The number specifies how many signals are in the bus. For example, Figure 2.6(a) represents a block of combinational logic with three inputs and two outputs. If the number of bits is unimportant or obvious from the context, the slash may be shown without a number. Figure 2.6(b) indicates two blocks of combinational logic with an arbitrary number of outputs from one block serving as inputs to the second block.

The rules of *combinational composition* tell us how we can build a large combinational circuit from smaller combinational circuit

$$Y = F(A, B) = A + B$$

Figure 2.3 Combinational logic circuit

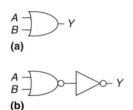

(a)

(b)

Figure 2.4 Two OR implementations

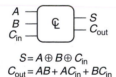

$$S = A \oplus B \oplus C_{in}$$
$$C_{out} = AB + AC_{in} + BC_{in}$$

Figure 2.5 Multiple-output combinational circuit

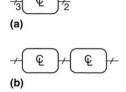

(a)

(b)

Figure 2.6 Slash notation for multiple signals

elements. A circuit is combinational if it consists of interconnected circuit elements such that

▶ Every circuit element is itself combinational.

▶ Every node of the circuit is either designated as an input to the circuit or connects to exactly one output terminal of a circuit element.

▶ The circuit contains no cyclic paths: every path through the circuit visits each circuit node at most once.

The rules of combinational composition are sufficient but not strictly necessary. Certain circuits that disobey these rules are still combinational, so long as the outputs depend only on the current values of the inputs. However, determining whether oddball circuits are combinational is more difficult, so we will usually restrict ourselves to combinational composition as a way to build combinational circuits.

Example 2.1 COMBINATIONAL CIRCUITS

Which of the circuits in Figure 2.7 are combinational circuits according to the rules of combinational composition?

Solution: Circuit (a) is combinational. It is constructed from two combinational circuit elements (inverters I1 and I2). It has three nodes: n1, n2, and n3. n1 is an input to the circuit and to I1; n2 is an internal node, which is the output of I1 and the input to I2; n3 is the output of the circuit and of I2. (b) is not combinational, because there is a cyclic path: the output of the XOR feeds back to one of its inputs. Hence, a cyclic path starting at n4 passes through the XOR to n5, which returns to n4. (c) is combinational. (d) is not combinational, because node n6 connects to the output terminals of both I3 and I4. (e) is combinational, illustrating two combinational circuits connected to form a larger combinational circuit. (f) does not obey the rules of combinational composition because it has a cyclic path through the two elements. Depending on the functions of the elements, it may or may not be a combinational circuit.

Large circuits such as microprocessors can be very complicated, so we use the principles from Chapter 1 to manage the complexity. Viewing a circuit as a black box with a well-defined interface and function is an

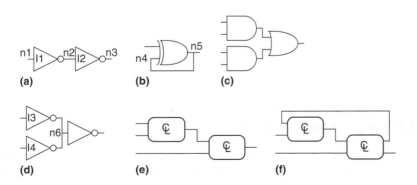

Figure 2.7 Example circuits

application of abstraction and modularity. Building the circuit out of smaller circuit elements is an application of hierarchy. The rules of combinational composition are an application of discipline.

The functional specification of a combinational circuit is usually expressed as a truth table or a Boolean equation. In the next sections, we describe how to derive a Boolean equation from any truth table and how to use Boolean algebra and Karnaugh maps to simplify equations. We show how to implement these equations using logic gates and how to analyze the speed of these circuits.

2.2 BOOLEAN EQUATIONS

Boolean equations deal with variables that are either TRUE or FALSE, so they are perfect for describing digital logic. This section defines some terminology commonly used in Boolean equations, then shows how to write a Boolean equation for any logic function given its truth table.

2.2.1 Terminology

The *complement* of a variable, A, is its inverse, $\overline{A}$. The variable or its complement is called a *literal*. For example, A, $\overline{A}$, B, and $\overline{B}$ are literals. We call A the *true form* of the variable and $\overline{A}$ the *complementary form*; "true form" does not mean that A is TRUE, but merely that A does not have a line over it.

The AND of one or more literals is called a *product* or an *implicant*. $\overline{A}B$, $A\overline{B}\overline{C}$, and B are all implicants for a function of three variables. A *minterm* is a product involving all of the inputs to the function. $A\overline{B}\overline{C}$ is a minterm for a function of the three variables A, B, and C, but $\overline{A}B$ is not, because it does not involve C. Similarly, the OR of one or more literals is called a *sum*. A *maxterm* is a sum involving all of the inputs to the function. $A + \overline{B} + C$ is a maxterm for a function of the three variables A, B, and C.

The *order of operations* is important when interpreting Boolean equations. Does $Y = A + BC$ mean $Y = (A$ OR $B)$ AND C or $Y = A$ OR $(B$ AND $C)$? In Boolean equations, NOT has the highest *precedence*, followed by AND, then OR. Just as in ordinary equations, products are performed before sums. Therefore, the equation is read as $Y = A$ OR $(B$ AND $C)$. Equation 2.1 gives another example of order of operations.

$$\overline{A}B + BC\overline{D} = ((\overline{A})B) + (BC(\overline{D})) \qquad (2.1)$$

2.2.2 Sum-of-Products Form

A truth table of N inputs contains 2^N rows, one for each possible value of the inputs. Each row in a truth table is associated with a minterm that is TRUE for that row. Figure 2.8 shows a truth table of two inputs, *A* and *B*. Each row shows its corresponding minterm. For example, the minterm for the first row is $\overline{A}\overline{B}$ because $\overline{A}\overline{B}$ is TRUE when $A = 0, B = 0$.

We can write a Boolean equation for any truth table by summing each of the minterms for which the output, *Y*, is TRUE. For example, in Figure 2.8, there is only one row (or minterm) for which the output *Y* is TRUE, shown circled in blue. Thus, $Y = \overline{A}B$. Figure 2.9 shows a truth table with more than one row in which the output is TRUE. Taking the sum of each of the circled minterms gives $Y = \overline{A}B + AB$.

This is called the *sum-of-products canonical form* of a function because it is the sum (OR) of products (ANDs forming minterms). Although there are many ways to write the same function, such as $Y = B\overline{A} + BA$, we will sort the minterms in the same order that they appear in the truth table, so that we always write the same Boolean expression for the same truth table.

A	B	Y	minterm
0	0	0	$\overline{A}\,\overline{B}$
0	1	1	$\overline{A}\,B$
1	0	0	$A\,\overline{B}$
1	1	0	$A\,B$

Figure 2.8 Truth table and minterms

Canonical form is just a fancy word for standard form. You can use the term to impress your friends and scare your enemies.

A	B	Y	minterm
0	0	0	$\overline{A}\,\overline{B}$
0	1	1	$\overline{A}\,B$
1	0	0	$A\,\overline{B}$
1	1	1	$A\,B$

Figure 2.9 Truth table with multiple TRUE minterms

Example 2.2 SUM-OF-PRODUCTS FORM

Ben Bitdiddle is having a picnic. He won't enjoy it if it rains or if there are ants. Design a circuit that will output TRUE *only* if Ben enjoys the picnic.

Solution: First define the inputs and outputs. The inputs are *A* and *R*, which indicate if there are ants and if it rains. *A* is TRUE when there are ants and FALSE when there are no ants. Likewise, *R* is TRUE when it rains and FALSE when the sun smiles on Ben. The output is *E*, Ben's enjoyment of the picnic. *E* is TRUE if Ben enjoys the picnic and FALSE if he suffers. Figure 2.10 shows the truth table for Ben's picnic experience.

Using sum-of-products form, we write the equation as: $E = \overline{A}\overline{R}$. We can build the equation using two inverters and a two-input AND gate, shown in Figure 2.11(a). You may recognize this truth table as the NOR function from Section 1.5.5: $E = A$ NOR $R = \overline{A + R}$. Figure 2.11(b) shows the NOR implementation. In Section 2.3, we show that the two equations, $\overline{A}\overline{R}$ and $\overline{A + R}$, are equivalent.

The sum-of-products form provides a Boolean equation for any truth table with any number of variables. Figure 2.12 shows a random three-input truth table. The sum-of-products form of the logic function is

$$Y = \overline{A}\overline{B}\overline{C} + A\overline{B}\overline{C} + A\overline{B}C \qquad (2.2)$$

Unfortunately, sum-of-products form does not necessarily generate the simplest equation. In Section 2.3 we show how to write the same function using fewer terms.

A	R	E
0	0	1
0	1	0
1	0	0
1	1	0

Figure 2.10 Ben's truth table

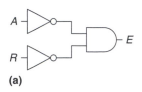

(a)

(b)

Figure 2.11 Ben's circuit

A	B	C	Y
0	0	0	1
0	0	1	0
0	1	0	0
0	1	1	0
1	0	0	1
1	0	1	1
1	1	0	0
1	1	1	0

Figure 2.12 Random three-input truth table

A	B	Y	maxterm
0	0	0	$A + B$
0	1	1	$A + \overline{B}$
1	0	0	$\overline{A} + B$
1	1	1	$\overline{A} + \overline{B}$

Figure 2.13 Truth table with multiple FALSE maxterms

2.2.3 Product-of-Sums Form

An alternative way of expressing Boolean functions is the *product-of-sums canonical form*. Each row of a truth table corresponds to a maxterm that is FALSE for that row. For example, the maxterm for the first row of a two-input truth table is $(A + B)$ because $(A + B)$ is FALSE when $A = 0$, $B = 0$. We can write a Boolean equation for any circuit directly from the truth table as the AND of each of the maxterms for which the output is FALSE.

Example 2.3 PRODUCT-OF-SUMS FORM

Write an equation in product-of-sums form for the truth table in Figure 2.13.

Solution: The truth table has two rows in which the output is FALSE. Hence, the function can be written in product-of-sums form as $Y = (A + B)(\overline{A} + B)$. The first maxterm, $(A + B)$, guarantees that $Y = 0$ for $A = 0$, $B = 0$, because any value AND 0 is 0. Likewise, the second maxterm, $(\overline{A} + B)$, guarantees that $Y = 0$ for $A = 1$, $B = 0$. Figure 2.13 is the same truth table as Figure 2.9, showing that the same function can be written in more than one way.

Similarly, a Boolean equation for Ben's picnic from Figure 2.10 can be written in product-of-sums form by circling the three rows of 0's to obtain $E = (A + \overline{R})(\overline{A} + R)(\overline{A} + \overline{R})$. This is uglier than the sum-of-products equation, $E = \overline{A}\,\overline{R}$, but the two equations are logically equivalent.

Sum-of-products produces the shortest equations when the output is TRUE on only a few rows of a truth table; product-of-sums is simpler when the output is FALSE on only a few rows of a truth table.

2.3 BOOLEAN ALGEBRA

In the previous section, we learned how to write a Boolean expression given a truth table. However, that expression does not necessarily lead to the simplest set of logic gates. Just as you use algebra to simplify mathematical equations, you can use *Boolean algebra* to simplify Boolean equations. The rules of Boolean algebra are much like those of ordinary algebra but are in some cases simpler, because variables have only two possible values: 0 or 1.

Boolean algebra is based on a set of axioms that we assume are correct. Axioms are unprovable in the sense that a definition cannot be proved. From these axioms, we prove all the theorems of Boolean algebra. These theorems have great practical significance, because they teach us how to simplify logic to produce smaller and less costly circuits.

Table 2.1 Axioms of Boolean algebra

	Axiom		Dual	Name
A1	$B = 0$ if $B \neq 1$	A1′	$B = 1$ if $B \neq 0$	Binary field
A2	$\overline{0} = 1$	A2′	$\overline{1} = 0$	NOT
A3	$0 \bullet 0 = 0$	A3′	$1 + 1 = 1$	AND/OR
A4	$1 \bullet 1 = 1$	A4′	$0 + 0 = 0$	AND/OR
A5	$0 \bullet 1 = 1 \bullet 0 = 0$	A5′	$1 + 0 = 0 + 1 = 1$	AND/OR

Axioms and theorems of Boolean algebra obey the principle of *duality*. If the symbols 0 and 1 and the operators • (AND) and + (OR) are interchanged, the statement will still be correct. We use the prime (′) symbol to denote the *dual* of a statement.

2.3.1 Axioms

Table 2.1 states the axioms of Boolean algebra. These five axioms and their duals define Boolean variables and the meanings of NOT, AND, and OR. Axiom A1 states that a Boolean variable B is 0 if it is not 1. The axiom's dual, A1′, states that the variable is 1 if it is not 0. Together, A1 and A1′ tell us that we are working in a Boolean or binary field of 0's and 1's. Axioms A2 and A2′ define the NOT operation. Axioms A3 to A5 define AND; their duals, A3′ to A5′ define OR.

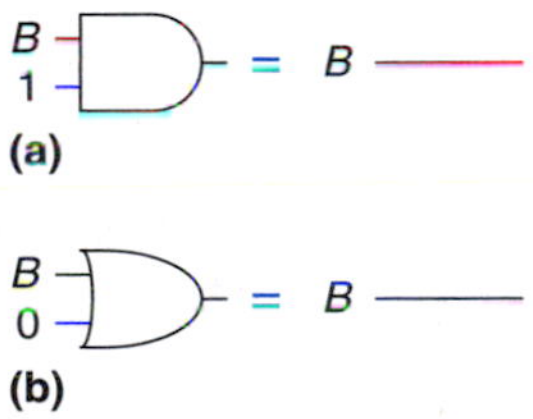

2.3.2 Theorems of One Variable

Theorems T1 to T5 in Table 2.2 describe how to simplify equations involving one variable.

The *identity* theorem, T1, states that for any Boolean variable B, B AND $1 = B$. Its dual states that B OR $0 = B$. In hardware, as shown in Figure 2.14, T1 means that if one input of a two-input AND gate is always 1, we can remove the AND gate and replace it with a wire connected to the variable input (B). Likewise, T1′ means that if one input of a two-input OR gate is always 0, we can replace the OR gate with a wire connected to B. In general, gates cost money, power, and delay, so replacing a gate with a wire is beneficial.

The *null element theorem*, T2, says that B AND 0 is always equal to 0. Therefore, 0 is called the *null* element for the AND operation, because it nullifies the effect of any other input. The dual states that B OR 1 is always equal to 1. Hence, 1 is the null element for the OR operation. In hardware, as shown in Figure 2.15, if one input of an AND gate is 0, we can replace the AND gate with a wire that is tied

Figure 2.14 Identity theorem in hardware: (a) T1, (b) T1′

The null element theorem leads to some outlandish statements that are actually true! It is particularly dangerous when left in the hands of advertisers: YOU WILL GET A MILLION DOLLARS or we'll send you a toothbrush in the mail. (You'll most likely be receiving a toothbrush in the mail.)

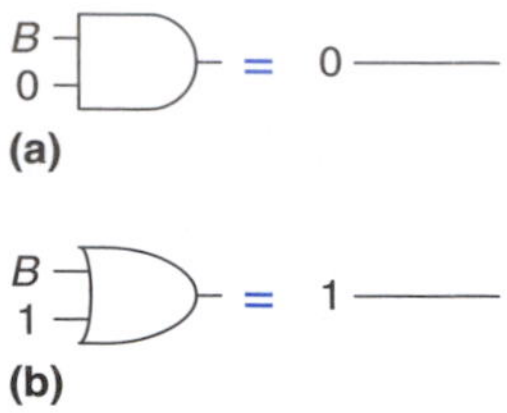

Figure 2.15 Null element theorem in hardware: (a) T2, (b) T2′

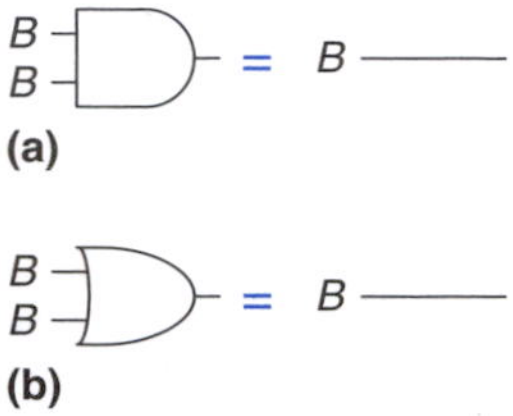

Table 2.2 Boolean theorems of one variable

	Theorem		Dual	Name
T1	$B \bullet 1 = B$	T1′	$B + 0 = B$	Identity
T2	$B \bullet 0 = 0$	T2′	$B + 1 = 1$	Null Element
T3	$B \bullet B = B$	T3′	$B + B = B$	Idempotency
T4			$\overline{\overline{B}} = B$	Involution
T5	$B \bullet \overline{B} = 0$	T5′	$B + \overline{B} = 1$	Complements

Figure 2.16 Idempotency theorem in hardware: (a) T3, (b) T3′

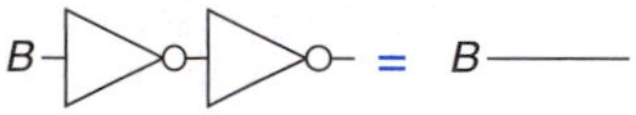

Figure 2.17 Involution theorem in hardware: T4

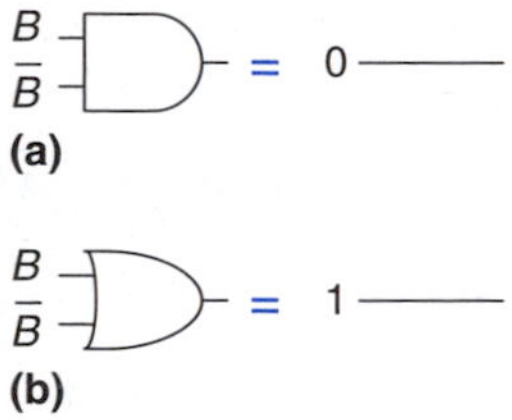

Figure 2.18 Complement theorem in hardware: (a) T5, (b) T5′

LOW (to 0). Likewise, if one input of an OR gate is 1, we can replace the OR gate with a wire that is tied HIGH (to 1).

Idempotency, T3, says that a variable AND itself is equal to just itself. Likewise, a variable OR itself is equal to itself. The theorem gets its name from the Latin roots: *idem* (same) and *potent* (power). The operations return the same thing you put into them. Figure 2.16 shows that idempotency again permits replacing a gate with a wire.

Involution, T4, is a fancy way of saying that complementing a variable twice results in the original variable. In digital electronics, two wrongs make a right. Two inverters in series logically cancel each other out and are logically equivalent to a wire, as shown in Figure 2.17. The dual of T4 is itself.

The *complement theorem*, T5 (Figure 2.18), states that a variable AND its complement is 0 (because one of them has to be 0). And, by duality, a variable OR its complement is 1 (because one of them has to be 1).

2.3.3 Theorems of Several Variables

Theorems T6 to T12 in Table 2.3 describe how to simplify equations involving more than one Boolean variable.

Commutativity and *associativity*, T6 and T7, work the same as in traditional algebra. By commutativity, the *order* of inputs for an AND or OR function does not affect the value of the output. By associativity, the specific groupings of inputs do not affect the value of the output.

The *distributivity theorem*, T8, is the same as in traditional algebra, but its dual, T8′, is not. By T8, AND distributes over OR, and by T8′, OR distributes over AND. In traditional algebra, multiplication distributes over addition but addition does not distribute over multiplication, so that $(B + C) \times (B + D) \neq B + (C \times D)$.

The *covering*, *combining*, and *consensus* theorems, T9 to T11, permit us to eliminate redundant variables. With some thought, you should be able to convince yourself that these theorems are correct.

Table 2.3 Boolean theorems of several variables

	Theorem		Dual	Name
T6	$B \bullet C = C \bullet B$	T6′	$B + C = C + B$	Commutativity
T7	$(B \bullet C) \bullet D = B \bullet (C \bullet D)$	T7′	$(B + C) + D = B + (C + D)$	Associativity
T8	$(B \bullet C) + (B \bullet D) = B \bullet (C + D)$	T8′	$(B + C) \bullet (B + D) = B + (C \bullet D)$	Distributivity
T9	$B \bullet (B + C) = B$	T9′	$B + (B \bullet C) = B$	Covering
T10	$(B \bullet C) + (B \bullet \overline{C}) = B$	T10′	$(B + C) \bullet (B + \overline{C}) = B$	Combining
T11	$(B \bullet C) + (\overline{B} \bullet D) + (C \bullet D)$ $= B \bullet C + \overline{B} \bullet D$	T11′	$(B + C) \bullet (\overline{B} + D) \bullet (C + D)$ $= (B + C) \bullet (\overline{B} + D)$	Consensus
T12	$\overline{B_0 \bullet B_1 \bullet B_2 ...}$ $= (\overline{B_0} + \overline{B_1} + \overline{B_2} ...)$	T12′	$\overline{B_0 + B_1 + B_2 ...}$ $= (\overline{B_0} \bullet \overline{B_1} \bullet \overline{B_2})$	De Morgan's Theorem

De Morgan's Theorem, T12, is a particularly powerful tool in digital design. The theorem explains that the complement of the product of all the terms is equal to the sum of the complement of each term. Likewise, the complement of the sum of all the terms is equal to the product of the complement of each term.

According to De Morgan's theorem, a NAND gate is equivalent to an OR gate with inverted inputs. Similarly, a NOR gate is equivalent to an AND gate with inverted inputs. Figure 2.19 shows these *De Morgan equivalent gates* for NAND and NOR gates. The two symbols shown for each function are called *duals.* They are logically equivalent and can be used interchangeably.

Augustus De Morgan, died 1871.
A British mathematician, born in India. Blind in one eye. His father died when he was 10. Attended Trinity College, Cambridge, at age 16, and was appointed Professor of Mathematics at the newly founded London University at age 22. Wrote widely on many mathematical subjects, including logic, algebra, and paradoxes. De Morgan's crater on the moon is named for him. He proposed a riddle for the year of his birth: "I was x years of age in the year x^2."

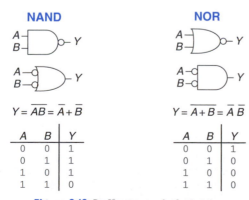

Figure 2.19 De Morgan equivalent gates

The inversion circle is called a *bubble*. Intuitively, you can imagine that "pushing" a bubble through the gate causes it to come out at the other side and flips the body of the gate from AND to OR or vice versa. For example, the NAND gate in Figure 2.19 consists of an AND body with a bubble on the output. Pushing the bubble to the left results in an OR body with bubbles on the inputs. The underlying rules for bubble pushing are

▶ Pushing bubbles backward (from the output) or forward (from the inputs) changes the body of the gate from AND to OR or vice versa.

▶ Pushing a bubble from the output back to the inputs puts bubbles on all gate inputs.

▶ Pushing bubbles on *all* gate inputs forward toward the output puts a bubble on the output.

Section 2.5.2 uses bubble pushing to help analyze circuits.

A	B	Y	$\overline{Y}$
0	0	0	1
0	1	0	1
1	0	1	0
1	1	1	0

FIGURE 2.20 Truth table showing Y and $\overline{Y}$

Example 2.4 DERIVE THE PRODUCT-OF-SUMS FORM

Figure 2.20 shows the truth table for a Boolean function, Y, and its complement, $\overline{Y}$. Using De Morgan's Theorem, derive the product-of-sums canonical form of Y from the sum-of-products form of $\overline{Y}$.

Solution: Figure 2.21 shows the minterms (circled) contained in $\overline{Y}$. The sum-of-products canonical form of $\overline{Y}$ is

$$\overline{Y} = \overline{A}\,\overline{B} + \overline{A}B \tag{2.3}$$

A	B	Y	$\overline{Y}$	minterm
0	0	0	1	$\overline{A}\ \overline{B}$
0	1	0	1	$\overline{A}\ B$
1	0	1	0	$A\ \overline{B}$
1	1	1	0	$A\ B$

Figure 2.21 Truth table showing minterms for $\overline{Y}$

Taking the complement of both sides and applying De Morgan's Theorem twice, we get:

$$\overline{\overline{Y}} = Y = \overline{\overline{A}\,\overline{B} + \overline{A}B} = (\overline{\overline{A}\,\overline{B}})(\overline{\overline{A}B}) = (A + B)(A + \overline{B}) \tag{2.4}$$

2.3.4 The Truth Behind It All

The curious reader might wonder how to prove that a theorem is true. In Boolean algebra, proofs of theorems with a finite number of variables are easy: just show that the theorem holds for all possible values of these variables. This method is called *perfect induction* and can be done with a truth table.

Example 2.5 PROVING THE CONSENSUS THEOREM

Prove the consensus theorem, T11, from Table 2.3.

Solution: Check both sides of the equation for all eight combinations of B, C, and D. The truth table in Figure 2.22 illustrates these combinations. Because $BC + \overline{B}D + CD = BC + \overline{B}D$ for all cases, the theorem is proved.

B	C	D	$BC + \overline{B}D + CD$	$BC + \overline{B}D$
0	0	0	0	0
0	0	1	1	1
0	1	0	0	0
0	1	1	1	1
1	0	0	0	0
1	0	1	0	0
1	1	0	1	1
1	1	1	1	1

Figure 2.22 Truth table proving T11

2.3.5 Simplifying Equations

The theorems of Boolean algebra help us simplify Boolean equations. For example, consider the sum-of-products expression from the truth table of Figure 2.9: $Y = \overline{A}\overline{B} + A\overline{B}$. By Theorem T10, the equation simplifies to $Y = \overline{B}$. This may have been obvious looking at the truth table. In general, multiple steps may be necessary to simplify more complex equations.

The basic principle of simplifying sum-of-products equations is to combine terms using the relationship $PA + P\overline{A} = P$, where P may be any implicant. How far can an equation be simplified? We define an equation in sum-of-products form to be *minimized* if it uses the fewest possible implicants. If there are several equations with the same number of implicants, the minimal one is the one with the fewest literals.

An implicant is called a *prime implicant* if it cannot be combined with any other implicants to form a new implicant with fewer literals. The implicants in a minimal equation must all be prime implicants. Otherwise, they could be combined to reduce the number of literals.

Example 2.6 EQUATION MINIMIZATION

Minimize Equation 2.2: $\overline{A}\overline{B}\overline{C} + A\overline{B}\overline{C} + A\overline{B}C$.

Solution: We start with the original equation and apply Boolean theorems step by step, as shown in Table 2.4.

Have we simplified the equation completely at this point? Let's take a closer look. From the original equation, the minterms $\overline{A}\overline{B}\overline{C}$ and $A\overline{B}\overline{C}$ differ only in the variable A. So we combined the minterms to form $\overline{B}\overline{C}$. However, if we look at the original equation, we note that the last two minterms $A\overline{B}\overline{C}$ and $A\overline{B}C$ also differ by a single literal (C and $\overline{C}$). Thus, using the same method, we could have combined these two minterms to form the minterm $A\overline{B}$. We say that implicants $\overline{B}\overline{C}$ and $A\overline{B}$ *share* the minterm $A\overline{B}\overline{C}$.

So, are we stuck with simplifying only one of the minterm pairs, or can we simplify both? Using the idempotency theorem, we can duplicate terms as many times as we want: $B = B + B + B + B \ldots$. Using this principle, we simplify the equation completely to its two prime implicants, $\overline{B}\overline{C} + A\overline{B}$, as shown in Table 2.5.

Table 2.4 Equation minimization

Step	Equation	Justification
	$\overline{A}\,\overline{B}\,\overline{C} + A\overline{B}\,\overline{C} + A\overline{B}C$	
1	$\overline{B}\,\overline{C}\,(\overline{A} + A) + A\overline{B}C$	T8: Distributivity
2	$\overline{B}\,\overline{C}\,(1) + A\overline{B}C$	T5: Complements
3	$\overline{B}\,\overline{C} + A\overline{B}C$	T1: Identity

Table 2.5 Improved equation minimization

Step	Equation	Justification
	$\overline{A}\,\overline{B}\,\overline{C} + A\overline{B}\,\overline{C} + A\overline{B}C$	
1	$\overline{A}\,\overline{B}\,\overline{C} + A\overline{B}\,\overline{C} + A\overline{B}\,\overline{C} + A\overline{B}C$	T3: Idempotency
2	$\overline{B}\,\overline{C}(\overline{A} + A) + A\overline{B}(\overline{C} + C)$	T8: Distributivity
3	$\overline{B}\,\overline{C}(1) + A\overline{B}(1)$	T5: Complements
4	$\overline{B}\,\overline{C} + A\overline{B}$	T1: Identity

Although it is a bit counterintuitive, *expanding* an implicant (for example, turning AB into $ABC + AB\overline{C}$) is sometimes useful in minimizing equations. By doing this, you can repeat one of the expanded minterms to be combined (shared) with another minterm.

You may have noticed that completely simplifying a Boolean equation with the theorems of Boolean algebra can take some trial and error. Section 2.7 describes a methodical technique called Karnaugh maps that makes the process easier.

Why bother simplifying a Boolean equation if it remains logically equivalent? Simplifying reduces the number of gates used to physically implement the function, thus making it smaller, cheaper, and possibly faster. The next section describes how to implement Boolean equations with logic gates.

2.4 FROM LOGIC TO GATES

A *schematic* is a diagram of a digital circuit showing the elements and the wires that connect them together. For example, the schematic in Figure 2.23 shows a possible hardware implementation of our favorite logic function, Equation 2.2:

$$Y = \overline{A}\,\overline{B}\,\overline{C} + A\overline{B}\,\overline{C} + A\overline{B}C.$$

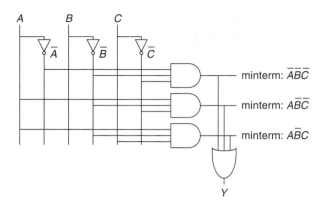

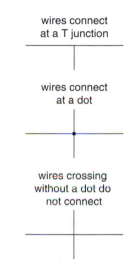

Figure 2.23 Schematic of $Y = \overline{A}\,\overline{B}\,\overline{C} + A\overline{B}\,\overline{C} + A\overline{B}C$

By drawing schematics in a consistent fashion, we make them easier to read and debug. We will generally obey the following guidelines:

▸ Inputs are on the left (or top) side of a schematic.

▸ Outputs are on the right (or bottom) side of a schematic.

▸ Whenever possible, gates should flow from left to right.

▸ Straight wires are better to use than wires with multiple corners (jagged wires waste mental effort following the wire rather than thinking of what the circuit does).

▸ Wires always connect at a T junction.

▸ A dot where wires cross indicates a connection between the wires.

▸ Wires crossing *without* a dot make no connection.

The last three guidelines are illustrated in Figure 2.24.

Any Boolean equation in sum-of-products form can be drawn as a schematic in a systematic way similar to Figure 2.23. First, draw columns for the inputs. Place inverters in adjacent columns to provide the complementary inputs if necessary. Draw rows of AND gates for each of the minterms. Then, for each output, draw an OR gate connected to the minterms related to that output. This style is called a *programmable logic array (PLA)* because the inverters, AND gates, and OR gates are arrayed in a systematic fashion. PLAs will be discussed further in Section 5.6.

Figure 2.25 shows an implementation of the simplified equation we found using Boolean algebra in Example 2.6. Notice that the simplified circuit has significantly less hardware than that of Figure 2.23. It may also be faster, because it uses gates with fewer inputs.

We can reduce the number of gates even further (albeit by a single inverter) by taking advantage of inverting gates. Observe that $\overline{BC}$ is an

wires connect
at a T junction

wires connect
at a dot

wires crossing
without a dot do
not connect

Figure 2.24 Wire connections

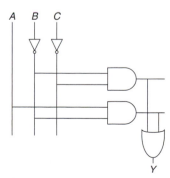

Figure 2.25 Schematic of $Y = \overline{B}\,\overline{C} + A\overline{B}$

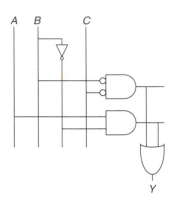

Figure 2.26 Schematic using fewer gates

AND with inverted inputs. Figure 2.26 shows a schematic using this optimization to eliminate the inverter on C. Recall that by De Morgan's theorem the AND with inverted inputs is equivalent to a NOR gate. Depending on the implementation technology, it may be cheaper to use the fewest gates or to use certain types of gates in preference to others. For example, NANDs and NORs are preferred over ANDs and ORs in CMOS implementations.

Many circuits have multiple outputs, each of which computes a separate Boolean function of the inputs. We can write a separate truth table for each output, but it is often convenient to write all of the outputs on a single truth table and sketch one schematic with all of the outputs.

Example 2.7 MULTIPLE-OUTPUT CIRCUITS

The dean, the department chair, the teaching assistant, and the dorm social chair each use the auditorium from time to time. Unfortunately, they occasionally conflict, leading to disasters such as the one that occurred when the dean's fundraising meeting with crusty trustees happened at the same time as the dorm's BTB[1] party. Alyssa P. Hacker has been called in to design a room reservation system.

The system has four inputs, $A_3, \ldots, A_0$, and four outputs, $Y_3, \ldots, Y_0$. These signals can also be written as $A_{3:0}$ and $Y_{3:0}$. Each user asserts her input when she requests the auditorium for the next day. The system asserts at most one output, granting the auditorium to the highest priority user. The dean, who is paying for the system, demands highest priority (3). The department chair, teaching assistant, and dorm social chair have decreasing priority.

Write a truth table and Boolean equations for the system. Sketch a circuit that performs this function.

Solution: This function is called a four-input *priority circuit*. Its symbol and truth table are shown in Figure 2.27.

We could write each output in sum-of-products form and reduce the equations using Boolean algebra. However, the simplified equations are clear by inspection from the functional description (and the truth table): Y_3 is TRUE whenever A_3 is asserted, so $Y_3 = A_3$. Y_2 is TRUE if A_2 is asserted and A_3 is not asserted, so $Y_2 = \overline{A}_3 A_2$. Y_1 is TRUE if A_1 is asserted and neither of the higher priority inputs is asserted: $Y_1 = \overline{A}_3\overline{A}_2 A_1$. And Y_0 is TRUE whenever A_0 and no other input is asserted: $Y_0 = \overline{A}_3\overline{A}_2\overline{A}_1 A_0$. The schematic is shown in Figure 2.28. An experienced designer can often implement a logic circuit by inspection. Given a clear specification, simply turn the words into equations and the equations into gates.

---

[1] Black light, twinkies, and beer.

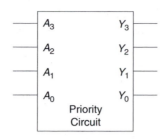

A_3	A_2	A_1	A_0	Y_3	Y_2	Y_1	Y_0
0	0	0	0	0	0	0	0
0	0	0	1	0	0	0	1
0	0	1	0	0	0	1	0
0	0	1	1	0	0	1	0
0	1	0	0	0	1	0	0
0	1	0	1	0	1	0	0
0	1	1	0	0	1	0	0
0	1	1	1	0	1	0	0
1	0	0	0	1	0	0	0
1	0	0	1	1	0	0	0
1	0	1	0	1	0	0	0
1	0	1	1	1	0	0	0
1	1	0	0	1	0	0	0
1	1	0	1	1	0	0	0
1	1	1	0	1	0	0	0
1	1	1	1	1	0	0	0

Figure 2.27 Priority circuit

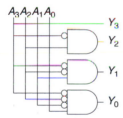

Figure 2.28 Priority circuit
schematic

A_3	A_2	A_1	A_0	Y_3	Y_2	Y_1	Y_0
0	0	0	0	0	0	0	0
0	0	0	1	0	0	0	1
0	0	1	X	0	0	1	0
0	1	X	X	0	1	0	0
1	X	X	X	1	0	0	0

Figure 2.29 Priority circuit truth table
with don't cares (X's)

Notice that if A_3 is asserted in the priority circuit, the outputs *don't care* what the other inputs are. We use the symbol X to describe inputs that the output doesn't care about. Figure 2.29 shows that the four-input priority circuit truth table becomes much smaller with don't cares. From this truth table, we can easily read the Boolean equations in sum-of-products form by ignoring inputs with X's. Don't cares can also appear in truth table outputs, as we will see in Section 2.7.3.

2.5 MULTILEVEL COMBINATIONAL LOGIC

Logic in sum-of-products form is called *two-level logic* because it consists of literals connected to a level of AND gates connected to a level of

X is an overloaded symbol that means "don't care" in truth tables and "contention" in logic simulation (see Section 2.6.1). Think about the context so you don't mix up the meanings. Some authors use D or ? instead for "don't care" to avoid this ambiguity.

OR gates. Designers often build circuits with more than two levels of logic gates. These multilevel combinational circuits may use less hardware than their two-level counterparts. Bubble pushing is especially helpful in analyzing and designing multilevel circuits.

2.5.1 Hardware Reduction

Some logic functions require an enormous amount of hardware when built using two-level logic. A notable example is the XOR function of multiple variables. For example consider building a three-input XOR using the two-level techniques we have studied so far.

Recall that an N-input XOR produces a TRUE output when an odd number of inputs are TRUE. Figure 2.30 shows the truth table for a three-input XOR with the rows circled that produce TRUE outputs. From the truth table, we read off a Boolean equation in sum-of-products form in Equation 2.5. Unfortunately, there is no way to simplify this equation into fewer implicants.

$$Y = \overline{A}\,\overline{B}C + \overline{A}B\overline{C} + A\overline{B}\,\overline{C} + ABC \tag{2.5}$$

On the other hand, $A \oplus B \oplus C = (A \oplus B) \oplus C$ (prove this to yourself by perfect induction if you are in doubt). Therefore, the three-input XOR can be built out of a cascade of two-input XORs, as shown in Figure 2.31.

Similarly, an eight-input XOR would require 128 eight-input AND gates and one 128-input OR gate for a two-level sum-of-products implementation. A much better option is to use a tree of two-input XOR gates, as shown in Figure 2.32.

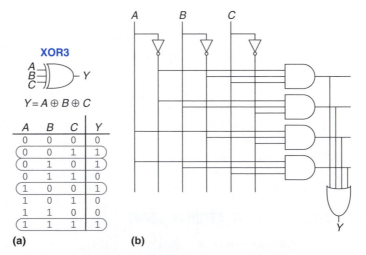

Figure 2.30 Three-input XOR: (a) functional specification and (b) two-level logic implementation

XOR3

$Y = A \oplus B \oplus C$

A	B	C	Y
0	0	0	0
0	0	1	1
0	1	0	1
0	1	1	0
1	0	0	1
1	0	1	0
1	1	0	0
1	1	1	1

(a)   (b)

Selecting the best multilevel implementation of a specific logic function is not a simple process. Moreover, "best" has many meanings: fewest gates, fastest, shortest design time, least cost, least power consumption. In Chapter 5, you will see that the "best" circuit in one technology is not necessarily the best in another. For example, we have been using ANDs and ORs, but in CMOS, NANDs and NORs are more efficient. With some experience, you will find that you can create a good multilevel design by inspection for most circuits. You will develop some of this experience as you study circuit examples through the rest of this book. As you are learning, explore various design options and think about the trade-offs. Computer-aided design (CAD) tools are also available to search a vast space of possible multilevel designs and seek the one that best fits your constraints given the available building blocks.

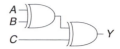

Figure 2.31 Three-input XOR using two two-input XORs

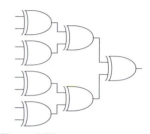

Figure 2.32 Eight-input XOR using seven two-input XORs

2.5.2 Bubble Pushing

You may recall from Section 1.7.6 that CMOS circuits prefer NANDs and NORs over ANDs and ORs. But reading the equation by inspection from a multilevel circuit with NANDs and NORs can get pretty hairy. Figure 2.33 shows a multilevel circuit whose function is not immediately clear by inspection. Bubble pushing is a helpful way to redraw these circuits so that the bubbles cancel out and the function can be more easily determined. Building on the principles from Section 2.3.3, the guidelines for bubble pushing are as follows:

▸ Begin at the output of the circuit and work toward the inputs.

▸ Push any bubbles on the final output back toward the inputs so that you can read an equation in terms of the output (for example, Y) instead of the complement of the output ($\overline{Y}$).

▸ Working backward, draw each gate in a form so that bubbles cancel. If the current gate has an input bubble, draw the preceding gate with an output bubble. If the current gate does not have an input bubble, draw the preceding gate without an output bubble.

Figure 2.34 shows how to redraw Figure 2.33 according to the bubble pushing guidelines. Starting at the output, Y, the NAND gate has a bubble on the output that we wish to eliminate. We push the output bubble back to form an OR with inverted inputs, shown in

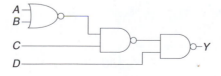

Figure 2.33 Multilevel circuit using NANDs and NORs

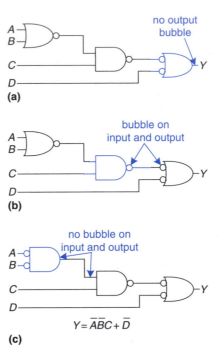

Figure 2.34 Bubble-pushed circuit

Figure 2.34(a). Working to the left, the rightmost gate has an input bubble that cancels with the output bubble of the middle NAND gate, so no change is necessary, as shown in Figure 2.34(b). The middle gate has no input bubble, so we transform the leftmost gate to have no output bubble, as shown in Figure 2.34(c). Now all of the bubbles in the circuit cancel except at the inputs, so the function can be read by inspection in terms of ANDs and ORs of true or complementary inputs: $Y = \overline{A}\overline{B}C + \overline{D}$.

For emphasis of this last point, Figure 2.35 shows a circuit logically equivalent to the one in Figure 2.34. The functions of internal nodes are labeled in blue. Because bubbles in series cancel, we can ignore the bubble on the output of the middle gate and the input of the rightmost gate to produce the logically equivalent circuit of Figure 2.35.

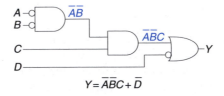

Figure 2.35 Logically equivalent bubble-pushed circuit

Example 2.8 BUBBLE PUSHING FOR CMOS LOGIC

Most designers think in terms of AND and OR gates, but suppose you would like to implement the circuit in Figure 2.36 in CMOS logic, which favors NAND and NOR gates. Use bubble pushing to convert the circuit to NANDs, NORs, and inverters.

Solution: A brute force solution is to just replace each AND gate with a NAND and an inverter, and each OR gate with a NOR and an inverter, as shown in Figure 2.37. This requires eight gates. Notice that the inverter is drawn with the bubble on the front rather than back, to emphasize how the bubble can cancel with the preceding inverting gate.

For a better solution, observe that bubbles can be added to the output of a gate and the input of the next gate without changing the function, as shown in Figure 2.38(a). The final AND is converted to a NAND and an inverter, as shown in Figure 2.38(b). This solution requires only five gates.

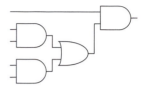

Figure 2.36 Circuit using ANDs and ORs

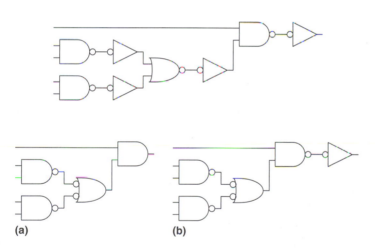

Figure 2.37 Poor circuit using NANDs and NORs

Figure 2.38 Better circuit using NANDs and NORs

(a) (b)

2.6 X'S AND Z'S, OH MY

Boolean algebra is limited to 0's and 1's. However, real circuits can also have illegal and floating values, represented symbolically by X and Z.

2.6.1 Illegal Value: X

The symbol X indicates that the circuit node has an *unknown* or *illegal* value. This commonly happens if it is being driven to both 0 and 1 at the same time. Figure 2.39 shows a case where node Y is driven both HIGH and LOW. This situation, called *contention,* is considered to be an error

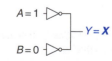

Figure 2.39 Circuit with contention

and must be avoided. The actual voltage on a node with contention may be somewhere between 0 and V_{DD}, depending on the relative strengths of the gates driving HIGH and LOW. It is often, but not always, in the forbidden zone. Contention also can cause large amounts of power to flow between the fighting gates, resulting in the circuit getting hot and possibly damaged.

X values are also sometimes used by circuit simulators to indicate an uninitialized value. For example, if you forget to specify the value of an input, the simulator may assume it is an X to warn you of the problem.

As mentioned in Section 2.4, digital designers also use the symbol X to indicate "don't care" values in truth tables. Be sure not to mix up the two meanings. When X appears in a truth table, it indicates that the value of the variable in the truth table is unimportant. When X appears in a circuit, it means that the circuit node has an unknown or illegal value.

2.6.2 Floating Value: Z

The symbol Z indicates that a node is being driven neither HIGH nor LOW. The node is said to be *floating*, *high impedance*, or *high Z*. A typical misconception is that a floating or undriven node is the same as a logic 0. In reality, a floating node might be 0, might be 1, or might be at some voltage in between, depending on the history of the system. A floating node does not always mean there is an error in the circuit, so long as some other circuit element does drive the node to a valid logic level when the value of the node is relevant to circuit operation.

One common way to produce a floating node is to forget to connect a voltage to a circuit input, or to assume that an unconnected input is the same as an input with the value of 0. This mistake may cause the circuit to behave erratically as the floating input randomly changes from 0 to 1. Indeed, touching the circuit may be enough to trigger the change by means of static electricity from the body. We have seen circuits that operate correctly only as long as the student keeps a finger pressed on a chip.

The *tristate buffer*, shown in Figure 2.40, has three possible output states: HIGH (1), LOW (0), and floating (Z). The tristate buffer has an input, *A*, an output, *Y*, and an *enable*, *E*. When the enable is TRUE, the tristate buffer acts as a simple buffer, transferring the input value to the output. When the enable is FALSE, the output is allowed to float (Z).

The tristate buffer in Figure 2.40 has an *active high* enable. That is, when the enable is HIGH (1), the buffer is enabled. Figure 2.41 shows a tristate buffer with an *active low* enable. When the enable is LOW (0),

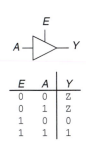

E	A	Y
0	0	Z
0	1	Z
1	0	0
1	1	1

Figure 2.40 Tristate buffer

$\bar{E}$	A	Y
0	0	0
0	1	1
1	0	Z
1	1	Z

Figure 2.41 Tristate buffer with active low enable

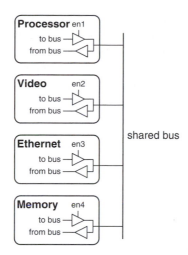

Figure 2.42 Tristate bus connecting multiple chips

the buffer is enabled. We show that the signal is active low by putting a bubble on its input wire. We often indicate an active low input by drawing a bar over its name, $\overline{E}$, or appending the word "bar" after its name, *Ebar*.

Tristate buffers are commonly used on *busses* that connect multiple chips. For example, a microprocessor, a video controller, and an Ethernet controller might all need to communicate with the memory system in a personal computer. Each chip can connect to a shared memory bus using tristate buffers, as shown in Figure 2.42. Only one chip at a time is allowed to assert its enable signal to drive a value onto the bus. The other chips must produce floating outputs so that they do not cause contention with the chip talking to the memory. Any chip can read the information from the shared bus at any time. Such tristate busses were once common. However, in modern computers, higher speeds are possible with *point-to-point links,* in which chips are connected to each other directly rather than over a shared bus.

2.7 KARNAUGH MAPS

After working through several minimizations of Boolean equations using Boolean algebra, you will realize that, if you're not careful, you sometimes end up with a completely *different* equation instead of a simplified equation. *Karnaugh maps (K-maps)* are a graphical method for simplifying Boolean equations. They were invented in 1953 by Maurice Karnaugh, a telecommunications engineer at Bell Labs. K-maps work well for problems with up to four variables. More important, they give insight into manipulating Boolean equations.

Maurice Karnaugh, 1924–. Graduated with a bachelor's degree in physics from the City College of New York in 1948 and earned a Ph.D. in physics from Yale in 1952. Worked at Bell Labs and IBM from 1952 to 1993 and as a computer science professor at the Polytechnic University of New York from 1980 to 1999.

Gray codes were patented (U.S. Patent 2,632,058) by Frank Gray, a Bell Labs researcher, in 1953. They are especially useful in mechanical encoders because a slight misalignment causes an error in only one bit.

Gray codes generalize to any number of bits. For example, a 3-bit Gray code sequence is:

```
000, 001, 011, 010,
110, 111, 101, 100
```

Lewis Carroll posed a related puzzle in *Vanity Fair* in 1879.

"The rules of the Puzzle are simple enough. Two words are proposed, of the same length; and the puzzle consists of linking these together by interposing other words, each of which shall differ from the next word in one letter only. That is to say, one letter may be changed in one of the given words, then one letter in the word so obtained, and so on, till we arrive at the other given word."

For example, SHIP to DOCK:

```
SHIP, SLIP, SLOP,
SLOT, SOOT, LOOT,
LOOK, LOCK, DOCK.
```

Can you find a shorter sequence?

Recall that logic minimization involves combining terms. Two terms containing an implicant, *P*, and the true and complementary forms of some variable, *A*, are combined to eliminate *A*: $PA + P\overline{A} = P$. Karnaugh maps make these combinable terms easy to see by putting them next to each other in a grid.

Figure 2.43 shows the truth table and K-map for a three-input function. The top row of the K-map gives the four possible values for the *A* and *B* inputs. The left column gives the two possible values for the *C* input. Each square in the K-map corresponds to a row in the truth table and contains the value of the output, *Y*, for that row. For example, the top left square corresponds to the first row in the truth table and indicates that the output value $Y = 1$ when $ABC = 000$. Just like each row in a truth table, each square in a K-map represents a single minterm. For the purpose of explanation, Figure 2.43(c) shows the minterm corresponding to each square in the K-map.

Each square, or minterm, differs from an adjacent square by a change in a single variable. This means that adjacent squares share all the same literals except one, which appears in true form in one square and in complementary form in the other. For example, the squares representing the minterms $\overline{A}\,\overline{B}\,\overline{C}$ and $\overline{A}\,\overline{B}C$ are adjacent and differ only in the variable *C*. You may have noticed that the *A* and *B* combinations in the top row are in a peculiar order: 00, 01, 11, 10. This order is called a *Gray code*. It differs from ordinary binary order (00, 01, 10, 11) in that adjacent entries differ only in a single variable. For example, 01 : 11 only changes *A* from 0 to 1, while 01 : 10 would change *A* from 1 to 0 and *B* from 0 to 1. Hence, writing the combinations in binary order would not have produced our desired property of adjacent squares differing only in one variable.

The K-map also "wraps around." The squares on the far right are effectively adjacent to the squares on the far left, in that they differ only in one variable, *A*. In other words, you could take the map and roll it into a cylinder, then join the ends of the cylinder to form a torus (i.e., a donut), and still guarantee that adjacent squares would differ only in one variable.

2.7.1 Circular Thinking

In the K-map in Figure 2.43, only two minterms are present in the equation, $\overline{A}\,\overline{B}\,\overline{C}$ and $\overline{A}\,\overline{B}C$, as indicated by the 1's in the left column. Reading the minterms from the K-map is exactly equivalent to reading equations in sum-of-products form directly from the truth table.

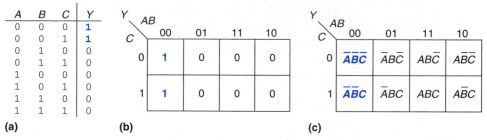

Figure 2.43 Three-input function: (a) truth table, (b) K-map, (c) K-map showing minterms

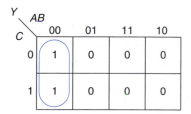

Figure 2.44 K-map minimization

As before, we can use Boolean algebra to minimize equations in sum-of-products form.

$$Y = \overline{A}\,\overline{B}\,\overline{C} + \overline{A}\,\overline{B}C = \overline{A}\,\overline{B}(\overline{C} + C) = \overline{A}\,\overline{B} \qquad (2.6)$$

K-maps help us do this simplification graphically by *circling* 1's in adjacent squares, as shown in Figure 2.44. For each circle, we write the corresponding implicant. Remember from Section 2.2 that an implicant is the product of one or more literals. Variables whose true *and* complementary forms are both in the circle are excluded from the implicant. In this case, the variable C has both its true form (1) and its complementary form (0) in the circle, so we do not include it in the implicant. In other words, Y is TRUE when A = B = 0, independent of C. So the implicant is $\overline{A}\,\overline{B}$. This K-map gives the same answer we reached using Boolean algebra.

2.7.2 Logic Minimization with K-Maps

K-maps provide an easy visual way to minimize logic. Simply circle all the rectangular blocks of 1's in the map, using the fewest possible number of circles. Each circle should be as large as possible. Then read off the implicants that were circled.

More formally, recall that a Boolean equation is minimized when it is written as a sum of the fewest number of prime implicants. Each circle on the K-map represents an implicant. The largest possible circles are prime implicants.

For example, in the K-map of Figure 2.44, $\overline{A}\overline{B}\overline{C}$ and $\overline{A}\overline{B}C$ are implicants, but *not* prime implicants. Only $\overline{A}\overline{B}$ is a prime implicant in that K-map. Rules for finding a minimized equation from a K-map are as follows:

▶   Use the fewest circles necessary to cover all the 1's.

▶   All the squares in each circle must contain 1's.

▶   Each circle must span a rectangular block that is a power of 2 (i.e., 1, 2, or 4) squares in each direction.

▶   Each circle should be as large as possible.

▶   A circle may wrap around the edges of the K-map.

▶   A 1 in a K-map may be circled multiple times if doing so allows fewer circles to be used.

Example 2.9 MINIMIZATION OF A THREE-VARIABLE FUNCTION
                USING A K-MAP

Suppose we have the function $Y = F(A, B, C)$ with the K-map shown in Figure 2.45. Minimize the equation using the K-map.

Solution: Circle the 1's in the K-map using as few circles as possible, as shown in Figure 2.46. Each circle in the K-map represents a prime implicant, and the dimension of each circle is a power of two (2×1 and 2×2). We form the prime implicant for each circle by writing those variables that appear in the circle only in true or only in complementary form.

For example, in the 2×1 circle, the true and complementary forms of B are included in the circle, so we *do not* include B in the prime implicant. However, only the true form of $A(A)$ and complementary form of $C(\overline{C})$ are in this circle, so we include these variables in the prime implicant $A\overline{C}$. Similarly, the 2×2 circle covers all squares where $B = 0$, so the prime implicant is $\overline{B}$.

Notice how the top-right square (minterm) is covered twice to make the prime implicant circles as large as possible. As we saw with Boolean algebra techniques, this is equivalent to sharing a minterm to reduce the size of the

Figure 2.45 K-map for Example 2.9

Y $\diagdown$ AB C	00	01	11	10
0	1	0	1	1
1	1	0	0	1

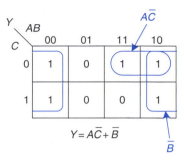

Figure 2.46 Solution for Example 2.9

implicant. Also notice how the circle covering four squares wraps around the sides of the K-map.

Example 2.10 SEVEN-SEGMENT DISPLAY DECODER

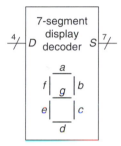

Figure 2.47 Seven-segment display decoder icon

A *seven-segment display decoder* takes a 4-bit data input, $D_{3:0}$, and produces seven outputs to control light-emitting diodes to display a digit from 0 to 9. The seven outputs are often called segments a through g, or S_a–S_g, as defined in Figure 2.47. The digits are shown in Figure 2.48. Write a truth table for the outputs, and use K-maps to find Boolean equations for outputs S_a and S_b. Assume that illegal input values (10–15) produce a blank readout.

Solution: The truth table is given in Table 2.6. For example, an input of 0000 should turn on all segments except S_g.

Each of the seven outputs is an independent function of four variables. The K-maps for outputs S_a and S_b are shown in Figure 2.49. Remember that adjacent squares may differ in only a single variable, so we label the rows and columns in Gray code order: 00, 01, 11, 10. Be careful to also remember this ordering when *entering* the output values into the squares.

Next, circle the prime implicants. Use the fewest number of circles necessary to cover all the 1's. A circle can wrap around the edges (vertical *and* horizontal), and a 1 may be circled more than once. Figure 2.50 shows the prime implicants and the simplified Boolean equations.

Note that the minimal set of prime implicants is not unique. For example, the 0000 entry in the S_a K-map was circled along with the 1000 entry to produce the $\overline{D_2}\,\overline{D_1}\,\overline{D_0}$ minterm. The circle could have included the 0010 entry instead, producing a $\overline{D_3}\,\overline{D_2}\,\overline{D_0}$ minterm, as shown with dashed lines in Figure 2.51.

Figure 2.52 illustrates (see page 78) a common error in which a nonprime implicant was chosen to cover the 1 in the upper left corner. This minterm, $\overline{D_3}\,\overline{D_2}\,\overline{D_1}\,\overline{D_0}$, gives a sum-of-products equation that is *not* minimal. The minterm could have been combined with either of the adjacent ones to form a larger circle, as was done in the previous two figures.

Figure 2.48 Seven-segment display digits

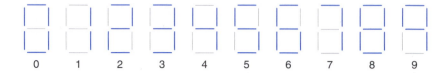

| 0 | 1 | 2 | 3 | 4 | 5 | 6 | 7 | 8 | 9 |

Table 2.6 Seven-segment display decoder truth table

$D_{3:0}$	S_a	S_b	S_c	S_d	S_e	S_f	S_g
0000	1	1	1	1	1	1	0
0001	0	1	1	0	0	0	0
0010	1	1	0	1	1	0	1
0011	1	1	1	1	0	0	1
0100	0	1	1	0	0	1	1
0101	1	0	1	1	0	1	1
0110	1	0	1	1	1	1	1
0111	1	1	1	0	0	0	0
1000	1	1	1	1	1	1	1
1001	1	1	1	0	0	1	1
others	0	0	0	0	0	0	0

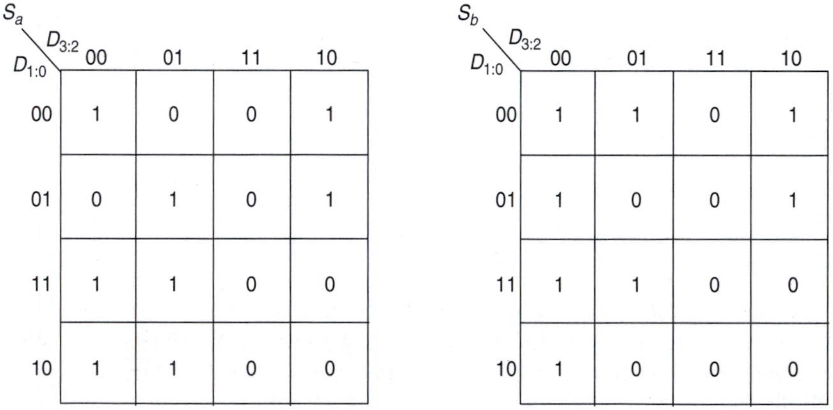

Figure 2.49 Karnaugh maps for S_a and S_b

S_a

$D_{1:0}$ \ $D_{3:2}$	00	01	11	10
00	1	0	0	1
01	0	1	0	1
11	1	1	0	0
10	1	1	0	0

S_b

$D_{1:0}$ \ $D_{3:2}$	00	01	11	10
00	1	1	0	1
01	1	0	0	1
11	1	1	0	0
10	1	0	0	0

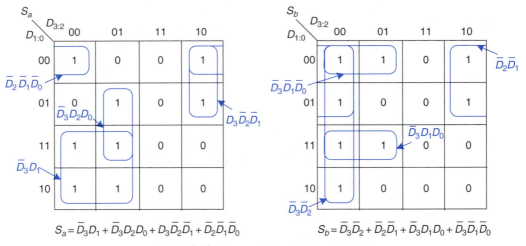

$$S_a = \bar{D}_3 D_1 + \bar{D}_3 D_2 D_0 + D_3 \bar{D}_2 \bar{D}_1 + \bar{D}_2 \bar{D}_1 \bar{D}_0$$

$$S_b = \bar{D}_3 \bar{D}_2 + \bar{D}_2 \bar{D}_1 + \bar{D}_3 D_1 D_0 + \bar{D}_3 \bar{D}_1 \bar{D}_0$$

Figure 2.50 K-map solution for Example 2.10

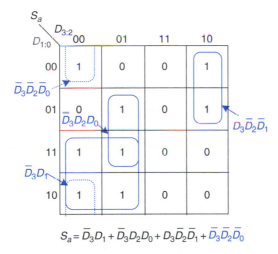

$$S_a = \bar{D}_3 D_1 + \bar{D}_3 D_2 D_0 + D_3 \bar{D}_2 \bar{D}_1 + \bar{D}_3 \bar{D}_2 \bar{D}_0$$

Figure 2.51 Alternative K-map for S_a showing different set of prime implicants

2.7.3 Don't Cares

Recall that "don't care" entries for truth table inputs were introduced in Section 2.4 to reduce the number of rows in the table when some variables do not affect the output. They are indicated by the symbol X, which means that the entry can be either 0 or 1.

Don't cares also appear in truth table outputs where the output value is unimportant or the corresponding input combination can never happen. Such outputs can be treated as either 0's or 1's at the designer's discretion.

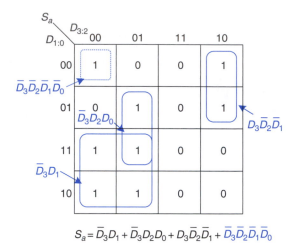

Figure 2.52 Alternative K-map for S_a showing incorrect nonprime implicant

$$S_a = \overline{D}_3 D_1 + \overline{D}_3 D_2 D_0 + D_3 \overline{D}_2 \overline{D}_1 + \overline{D}_3 \overline{D}_2 \overline{D}_1 \overline{D}_0$$

In a K-map, X's allow for even more logic minimization. They can be circled if they help cover the 1's with fewer or larger circles, but they do not have to be circled if they are not helpful.

Example 2.11 SEVEN-SEGMENT DISPLAY DECODER WITH DON'T CARES

Repeat Example 2.10 if we don't care about the output values for illegal input values of 10 to 15.

Solution: The K-map is shown in Figure 2.53 with X entries representing don't care. Because don't cares can be 0 or 1, we circle a don't care if it allows us to cover the 1's with fewer or bigger circles. Circled don't cares are treated as 1's, whereas uncircled don't cares are 0's. Observe how a 2×2 square wrapping around all four corners is circled for segment S_a. Use of don't cares simplifies the logic substantially.

2.7.4 The Big Picture

Boolean algebra and Karnaugh maps are two methods for logic simplification. Ultimately, the goal is to find a low-cost method of implementing a particular logic function.

In modern engineering practice, computer programs called *logic synthesizers* produce simplified circuits from a description of the logic function, as we will see in Chapter 4. For large problems, logic synthesizers are much more efficient than humans. For small problems, a human with a bit of experience can find a good solution by inspection. Neither of the authors has ever used a Karnaugh map in real life to

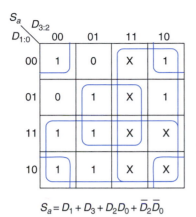

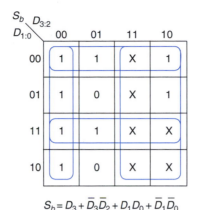

$$S_a = D_1 + D_3 + D_2 D_0 + \overline{D}_2 \overline{D}_0$$

$$S_b = D_3 + \overline{D}_3 \overline{D}_2 + D_1 D_0 + \overline{D}_1 \overline{D}_0$$

Figure 2.53 K-map solution with don't cares

solve a practical problem. But the insight gained from the principles underlying Karnaugh maps is valuable. And Karnaugh maps often appear at job interviews!

2.8 COMBINATIONAL BUILDING BLOCKS

Combinational logic is often grouped into larger building blocks to build more complex systems. This is an application of the principle of abstraction, hiding the unnecessary gate-level details to emphasize the function of the building block. We have already studied three such building blocks: full adders (from Section 2.1), priority circuits (from Section 2.4), and seven-segment display decoders (from Section 2.7). This section introduces two more commonly used building blocks: multiplexers and decoders. Chapter 5 covers other combinational building blocks.

2.8.1 Multiplexers

Multiplexers are among the most commonly used combinational circuits. They choose an output from among several possible inputs based on the value of a *select* signal. A multiplexer is sometimes affectionately called a *mux*.

2:1 Multiplexer

Figure 2.54 shows the schematic and truth table for a 2:1 multiplexer with two data inputs, D_0 and D_1, a select input, S, and one output, Y. The multiplexer chooses between the two data inputs based on the select: if $S = 0$, $Y = D_0$, and if $S = 1$, $Y = D_1$. S is also called a *control* signal because it controls what the multiplexer does.

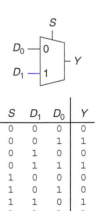

S	D_1	D_0	Y
0	0	0	0
0	0	1	1
0	1	0	0
0	1	1	1
1	0	0	0
1	0	1	0
1	1	0	1
1	1	1	1

Figure 2.54 2:1 multiplexer symbol and truth table

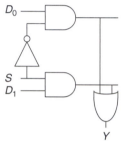

$$Y = D_0\bar{S} + D_1S$$

Figure 2.55 **2:1 multiplexer implementation using two-level logic**

> Shorting together the outputs of multiple gates technically violates the rules for combinational circuits given in Section 2.1. But because exactly one of the outputs is driven at any time, this exception is allowed.

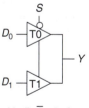

$$Y = D_0\bar{S} + D_1S$$

Figure 2.56 **Multiplexer using tristate buffers**

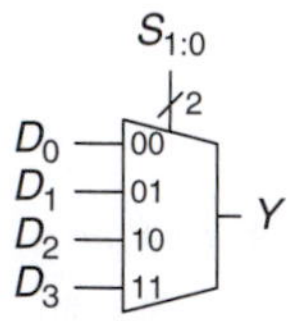

Figure 2.57 **4:1 multiplexer**

A 2:1 multiplexer can be built from sum-of-products logic as shown in Figure 2.55. The Boolean equation for the multiplexer may be derived with a Karnaugh map or read off by inspection (Y is 1 if $S = 0$ AND D_0 is 1 OR if $S = 1$ AND D_1 is 1).

Alternatively, multiplexers can be built from tristate buffers, as shown in Figure 2.56. The tristate enables are arranged such that, at all times, exactly one tristate buffer is active. When $S = 0$, tristate T0 is enabled, allowing D_0 to flow to Y. When $S = 1$, tristate T1 is enabled, allowing D_1 to flow to Y.

Wider Multiplexers

A 4:1 multiplexer has four data inputs and one output, as shown in Figure 2.57. Two select signals are needed to choose among the four data inputs. The 4:1 multiplexer can be built using sum-of-products logic, tristates, or multiple 2:1 multiplexers, as shown in Figure 2.58.

The product terms enabling the tristates can be formed using AND gates and inverters. They can also be formed using a decoder, which we will introduce in Section 2.8.2.

Wider multiplexers, such as 8:1 and 16:1 multiplexers, can be built by expanding the methods shown in Figure 2.58. In general, an N:1 multiplexer needs $\log_2 N$ select lines. Again, the best implementation choice depends on the target technology.

Multiplexer Logic

Multiplexers can be used as *lookup tables* to perform logic functions. Figure 2.59 shows a 4:1 multiplexer used to implement a two-input

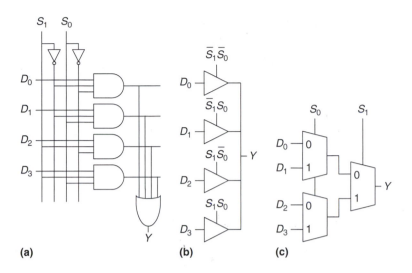

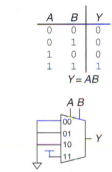

Figure 2.58 4:1 multiplexer implementations: (a) two-level logic, (b) tristates, (c) hierarchical

AND gate. The inputs, *A* and *B*, serve as select lines. The multiplexer data inputs are connected to 0 or 1 according to the corresponding row of the truth table. In general, a 2^N-input multiplexer can be programmed to perform any *N*-input logic function by applying 0's and 1's to the appropriate data inputs. Indeed, by changing the data inputs, the multiplexer can be reprogrammed to perform a different function.

With a little cleverness, we can cut the multiplexer size in half, using only a 2^{N-1}-input multiplexer to perform any *N*-input logic function. The strategy is to provide one of the literals, as well as 0's and 1's, to the multiplexer data inputs.

To illustrate this principle, Figure 2.60 shows two-input AND and XOR functions implemented with 2:1 multiplexers. We start with an ordinary truth table, and then combine pairs of rows to eliminate the rightmost input variable by expressing the output in terms of this variable. For example, in the case of AND, when $A = 0$, $Y = 0$, regardless of *B*. When $A = 1$, $Y = 0$ if $B = 0$ and $Y = 1$ if $B = 1$, so $Y = B$. We then use the multiplexer as a lookup table according to the new, smaller truth table.

A	B	Y
0	0	0
0	1	0
1	0	0
1	1	1

$Y = AB$

Figure 2.59 4:1 multiplexer implementation of two-input AND function

Example 2.12 LOGIC WITH MULTIPLEXERS

Alyssa P. Hacker needs to implement the function $Y = A\overline{B} + \overline{B}\,\overline{C} + \overline{A}BC$ to finish her senior project, but when she looks in her lab kit, the only part she has left is an 8:1 multiplexer. How does she implement the function?

Solution: Figure 2.61 shows Alyssa's implementation using a single 8:1 multiplexer. The multiplexer acts as a lookup table where each row in the truth table corresponds to a multiplexer input.

Figure 2.60 Multiplexer logic using variable inputs

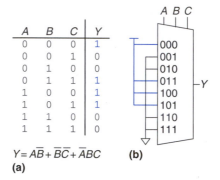

$Y = AB$

A	B	Y
0	0	0
0	1	0
1	0	0
1	1	1

A	Y
0	0
1	B

(a)

$Y = A \oplus B$

A	B	Y
0	0	0
0	1	1
1	0	1
1	1	0

A	Y
0	B
1	$\overline{B}$

(b)

Figure 2.61 Alyssa's circuit: (a) truth table, (b) 8:1 multiplexer implementation

A	B	C	Y
0	0	0	1
0	0	1	0
0	1	0	0
0	1	1	1
1	0	0	1
1	0	1	1
1	1	0	0
1	1	1	0

$Y = A\overline{B} + \overline{B}\,\overline{C} + \overline{A}BC$

(a)

(b)

Example 2.13 LOGIC WITH MULTIPLEXERS, REPRISED

Alyssa turns on her circuit one more time before the final presentation and blows up the 8:1 multiplexer. (She accidently powered it with 20 V instead of 5 V after not sleeping all night.) She begs her friends for spare parts and they give her a 4:1 multiplexer and an inverter. Can she build her circuit with only these parts?

Solution: Alyssa reduces her truth table to four rows by letting the output depend on C. (She could also have chosen to rearrange the columns of the truth table to let the output depend on A or B.) Figure 2.62 shows the new design.

2.8.2 Decoders

A decoder has N inputs and 2^N outputs. It asserts exactly one of its outputs depending on the input combination. Figure 2.63 shows a 2:4 decoder. When $A_{1:0} = 00$, Y_0 is 1. When $A_{1:0} = 01$, Y_1 is 1. And so forth. The outputs are called *one-hot*, because exactly one is "hot" (HIGH) at a given time.

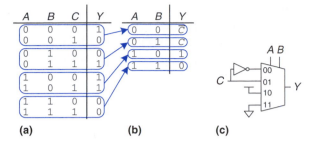

A	B	C	Y
0	0	0	1
0	0	1	0
0	1	0	0
0	1	1	1
1	0	0	1
1	0	1	1
1	1	0	0
1	1	1	0

A	B	Y
0	0	$\overline{C}$
0	1	C
1	0	1
1	1	0

(a)   (b)   (c)

Figure 2.62 Alyssa's new circuit

Example 2.14 DECODER IMPLEMENTATION

Implement a 2:4 decoder with AND, OR, and NOT gates.

Solution: Figure 2.64 shows an implementation for the 2:4 decoder using four AND gates. Each gate depends on either the true or the complementary form of each input. In general, an $N:2^N$ decoder can be constructed from 2^N N-input AND gates that accept the various combinations of true or complementary inputs. Each output in a decoder represents a single minterm. For example, Y_0 represents the minterm $\overline{A}_1\overline{A}_0$. This fact will be handy when using decoders with other digital building blocks.

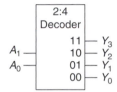

A_1	A_0	Y_3	Y_2	Y_1	Y_0
0	0	0	0	0	1
0	1	0	0	1	0
1	0	0	1	0	0
1	1	1	0	0	0

Figure 2.63 2:4 decoder

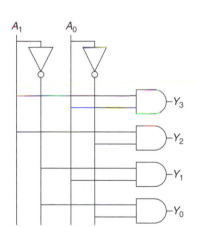

Figure 2.64 2:4 decoder implementation

Decoder Logic

Decoders can be combined with OR gates to build logic functions. Figure 2.65 shows the two-input XNOR function using a 2:4 decoder and a single OR gate. Because each output of a decoder represents a single minterm, the function is built as the OR of all the minterms in the function. In Figure 2.65, $Y = \overline{A}\overline{B} + AB = \overline{A \oplus B}$.

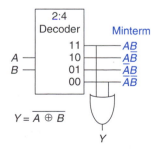

Figure 2.65 Logic function using decoder

When using decoders to build logic, it is easiest to express functions as a truth table or in canonical sum-of-products form. An N-input function with M 1's in the truth table can be built with an $N:2^N$ decoder and an M-input OR gate attached to all of the minterms containing 1's in the truth table. This concept will be applied to the building of Read Only Memories (ROMs) in Section 5.5.6.

2.9 TIMING

In previous sections, we have been concerned primarily with whether the circuit works—ideally, using the fewest gates. However, as any seasoned circuit designer will attest, one of the most challenging issues in circuit design is *timing*: making a circuit run fast.

An output takes time to change in response to an input change. Figure 2.66 shows the *delay* between an input change and the subsequent output change for a buffer. The figure is called a *timing diagram*; it portrays the *transient response* of the buffer circuit when an input changes. The transition from LOW to HIGH is called the *rising edge*. Similarly, the transition from HIGH to LOW (not shown in the figure) is called the *falling edge*. The blue arrow indicates that the rising edge of Y is caused by the rising edge of A. We measure delay from the *50% point* of the input signal, A, to the 50% point of the output signal, Y. The 50% point is the point at which the signal is half-way (50%) between its LOW and HIGH values as it transitions.

2.9.1 Propagation and Contamination Delay

> When designers speak of calculating the *delay* of a circuit, they generally are referring to the worst-case value (the propagation delay), unless it is clear otherwise from the context.

Combinational logic is characterized by its *propagation delay* and *contamination delay*. The propagation delay, t_{pd}, is the maximum time from when an input changes until the output or outputs reach their final value. The contamination delay, t_{cd}, is the minimum time from when an input changes until any output starts to change its value.

Figure 2.66 Circuit delay

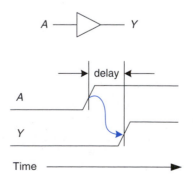

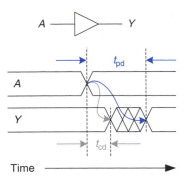

Figure 2.67 **Propagation and contamination delay**

Figure 2.67 illustrates a buffer's propagation delay and contamination delay in blue and gray, respectively. The figure shows that A is initially either HIGH or LOW and changes to the other state at a particular time; we are interested only in the fact that it changes, not what value it has. In response, Y changes some time later. The arcs indicate that Y may start to change t_{cd} after A transitions and that Y definitely settles to its new value within t_{pd}.

The underlying causes of delay in circuits include the time required to charge the capacitance in a circuit and the speed of light. t_{pd} and t_{cd} may be different for many reasons, including

▸ different rising and falling delays

▸ multiple inputs and outputs, some of which are faster than others

▸ circuits slowing down when hot and speeding up when cold

Calculating t_{pd} and t_{cd} requires delving into the lower levels of abstraction beyond the scope of this book. However, manufacturers normally supply data sheets specifying these delays for each gate.

Along with the factors already listed, propagation and contamination delays are also determined by the *path* a signal takes from input to output. Figure 2.68 shows a four-input logic circuit. The *critical path*, shown in blue, is the path from input A or B to output Y. It is the longest, and therefore the slowest, path, because the input travels

Circuit delays are ordinarily on the order of picoseconds (1 ps = 10^{-12} seconds) to nanoseconds (1 ns = 10^{-9} seconds). Trillions of picoseconds have elapsed in the time you spent reading this sidebar.

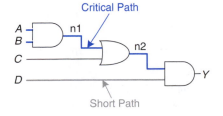

Figure 2.68 **Short path and critical path**

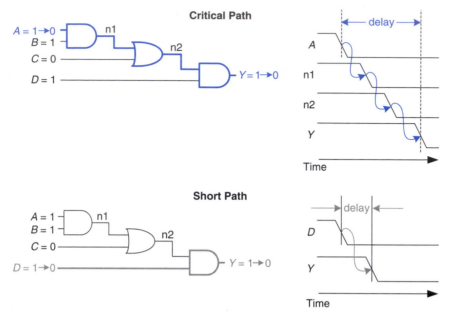

Figure 2.69 Critical and short path waveforms

through three gates to the output. This path is critical because it limits the speed at which the circuit operates. The *short path* through the circuit, shown in gray, is from input D to output Y. This is the shortest, and therefore the fastest, path through the circuit, because the input travels through only a single gate to the output.

The propagation delay of a combinational circuit is the sum of the propagation delays through each element on the critical path. The contamination delay is the sum of the contamination delays through each element on the short path. These delays are illustrated in Figure 2.69 and are described by the following equations:

$$t_{pd} = 2t_{pd\_AND} + t_{pd\_OR} \tag{2.7}$$

$$t_{cd} = t_{cd\_AND} \tag{2.8}$$

Although we are ignoring wire delay in this analysis, digital circuits are now so fast that the delay of long wires can be as important as the delay of the gates. The speed of light delay in wires is covered in Appendix A.

Example 2.15 FINDING DELAYS

Ben Bitdiddle needs to find the propagation delay and contamination delay of the circuit shown in Figure 2.70. According to his data book, each gate has a propagation delay of 100 picoseconds (ps) and a contamination delay of 60 ps.

Solution: Ben begins by finding the critical path and the shortest path through the circuit. The critical path, highlighted in blue in Figure 2.71, is from input A

or *B* through three gates to the output, *Y*. Hence, t_{pd} is three times the propagation delay of a single gate, or 300 ps.

The shortest path, shown in gray in Figure 2.72, is from input *C, D,* or *E* through two gates to the output, *Y*. There are only two gates in the shortest path, so t_{cd} is 120 ps.

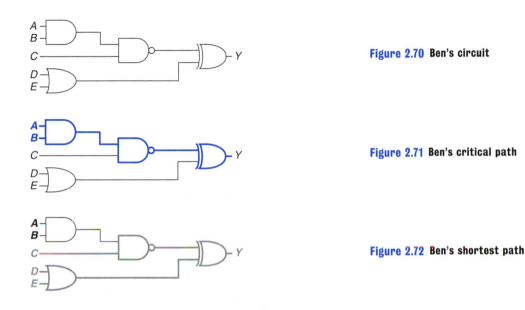

Figure 2.70 Ben's circuit

Figure 2.71 Ben's critical path

Figure 2.72 Ben's shortest path

Example 2.16 MULTIPLEXER TIMING: CONTROL-CRITICAL VS. DATA-CRITICAL

Compare the worst-case timing of the three four-input multiplexer designs shown in Figure 2.58 in Section 2.8.1. Table 2.7 lists the propagation delays for the components. What is the critical path for each design? Given your timing analysis, why might you choose one design over the other?

Solution: One of the critical paths for each of the three design options is highlighted in blue in Figures 2.73 and 2.74. t_{pd_sy} indicates the propagation delay from input *S* to output *Y*; t_{pd_dy} indicates the propagation delay from input *D* to output *Y*; t_{pd} is the worst of the two: $\max(t_{pd\_sy}, t_{pd\_dy})$.

For both the two-level logic and tristate implementations in Figure 2.73, the critical path is from one of the control signals, *S*, to the output, *Y*: $t_{pd} = t_{pd\_sy}$. These circuits are *control critical*, because the critical path is from the control signals to the output. Any additional delay in the control signals will add directly to the worst-case delay. The delay from *D* to *Y* in Figure 2.73(b) is only 50 ps, compared with the delay from *S* to *Y* of 125 ps.

Figure 2.74 shows the hierarchical implementation of the 4:1 multiplexer using two stages of 2:1 multiplexers. The critical path is from any of the D inputs to the output. This circuit is *data critical*, because the critical path is from the data input to the output: ($t_{pd} = t_{pd\_dy}$).

If data inputs arrive well before the control inputs, we would prefer the design with the shortest control-to-output delay (the hierarchical design in Figure 2.74). Similarly, if the control inputs arrive well before the data inputs, we would prefer the design with the shortest data-to-output delay (the tristate design in Figure 2.73(b)).

The best choice depends not only on the critical path through the circuit and the input arrival times, but also on the power, cost, and availability of parts.

Table 2.7 Timing specifications for multiplexer circuit elements

Gate	t_{pd} (ps)
NOT	30
2-input AND	60
3-input AND	80
4-input OR	90
tristate (A to Y)	50
tristate (enable to Y)	35

2.9.2 Glitches

So far we have discussed the case where a single input transition causes a single output transition. However, it is possible that a single input transition can cause *multiple* output transitions. These are called *glitches* or *hazards*. Although glitches usually don't cause problems, it is important to realize that they exist and recognize them when looking at timing diagrams. Figure 2.75 shows a circuit with a glitch and the Karnaugh map of the circuit.

The Boolean equation is correctly minimized, but let's look at what happens when $A = 0$, $C = 1$, and B transitions from 1 to 0. Figure 2.76 (see page 90) illustrates this scenario. The short path (shown in gray) goes through two gates, the AND and OR gates. The critical path (shown in blue) goes through an inverter and two gates, the AND and OR gates.

Hazards have another meaning related to microarchitecture in Chapter 7, so we will stick with the term *glitches* for multiple output transitions to avoid confusion.

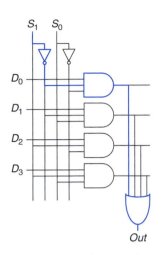

$$t_{pd\_sy} = t_{pd\_INV} + t_{pd\_AND3} + t_{pd\_OR4}$$
$$= 30 \text{ ps} + 80 \text{ ps} + 90 \text{ ps}$$

(a) $= \mathbf{200\ ps}$

$$t_{pd\_dy} = t_{pd\_AND3} + t_{pd\_OR4}$$
$$= \mathbf{170\ ps}$$

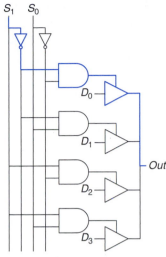

$$t_{pd\_sy} = t_{pd\_INV} + t_{pd\_AND2} + t_{pd\_TRI\_SY}$$
$$= 30 \text{ ps} + 60 \text{ ps} + 35 \text{ ps}$$

(b) $= \mathbf{125\ ps}$

$$t_{pd\_dy} = t_{pd\_TRI\_AY}$$
$$= \mathbf{50\ ps}$$

Figure 2.73 4:1 multiplexer propagation delays: (a) two-level logic, (b) tristate

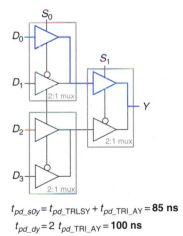

$$t_{pd\_s0y} = t_{pd\_TRLSY} + t_{pd\_TRI\_AY} = \mathbf{85\ ns}$$
$$t_{pd\_dy} = 2\, t_{pd\_TRI\_AY} = \mathbf{100\ ns}$$

Figure 2.74 4:1 multiplexer propagation delays: hierarchical using 2:1 multiplexers

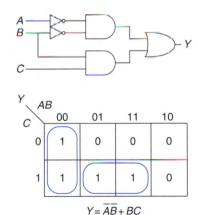

Y \ AB	00	01	11	10
C				
0	1	0	0	0
1	1	1	1	0

$$Y = \overline{A}\,\overline{B} + BC$$

Figure 2.75 Circuit with a glitch

As B transitions from 1 to 0, n2 (on the short path) falls before n1 (on the critical path) can rise. Until n1 rises, the two inputs to the OR gate are 0, and the output Y drops to 0. When n1 eventually rises, Y returns to 1. As shown in the timing diagram of Figure 2.76, Y starts at 1 and ends at 1 but momentarily glitches to 0.

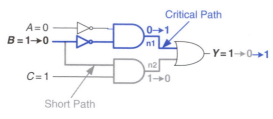

Figure 2.76 Timing of a glitch

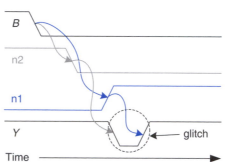

As long as we wait for the propagation delay to elapse before we depend on the output, glitches are not a problem, because the output eventually settles to the right answer.

If we choose to, we can avoid this glitch by adding another gate to the implementation. This is easiest to understand in terms of the K-map. Figure 2.77 shows how an input transition on B from $ABC = 001$ to $ABC = 011$ moves from one prime implicant circle to another. The transition across the boundary of two prime implicants in the K-map indicates a possible glitch.

As we saw from the timing diagram in Figure 2.76, if the circuitry implementing one of the prime implicants turns *off* before the circuitry of the other prime implicant can turn *on,* there is a glitch. To fix this, we add another circle that *covers* that prime implicant boundary, as shown in Figure 2.78. You might recognize this as the consensus theorem, where the added term, $\overline{A}\,\overline{C}$, is the consensus or redundant term.

Figure 2.77 Input change crosses implicant boundary

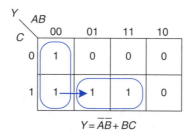

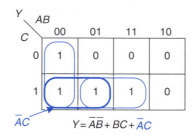

Figure 2.78 **K-map without glitch**

$$Y = \overline{A}\,\overline{B} + BC + \overline{A}C$$

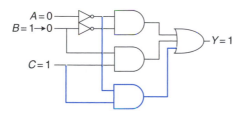

Figure 2.79 **Circuit without glitch**

Figure 2.79 shows the glitch-proof circuit. The added AND gate is highlighted in blue. Now a transition on B when $A = 0$ and $C = 1$ does not cause a glitch on the output, because the blue AND gate outputs 1 throughout the transition.

In general, a glitch can occur when a change in a single variable crosses the boundary between two prime implicants in a K-map. We can eliminate the glitch by adding redundant implicants to the K-map to cover these boundaries. This of course comes at the cost of extra hardware.

However, simultaneous transitions on multiple variables can also cause glitches. These glitches cannot be fixed by adding hardware. Because the vast majority of interesting systems have simultaneous (or near-simultaneous) transitions on multiple variables, glitches are a fact of life in most circuits. Although we have shown how to eliminate one kind of glitch, the point of discussing glitches is not to eliminate them but to be aware that they exist. This is especially important when looking at timing diagrams on a simulator or oscilloscope.

2.10 SUMMARY

A digital circuit is a module with discrete-valued inputs and outputs and a specification describing the function and timing of the module. This chapter has focused on combinational circuits, circuits whose outputs depend only on the current values of the inputs.

The function of a combinational circuit can be given by a truth table or a Boolean equation. The Boolean equation for any truth table can be obtained systematically using sum-of-products or product-of-sums form. In sum-of-products form, the function is written as the sum (OR) of one or more implicants. Implicants are the product (AND) of literals. Literals are the true or complementary forms of the input variables.

Boolean equations can be simplified using the rules of Boolean algebra. In particular, they can be simplified into minimal sum-of-products form by combining implicants that differ only in the true and complementary forms of one of the literals: $PA + P\overline{A} = P$. Karnaugh maps are a visual tool for minimizing functions of up to four variables. With practice, designers can usually simplify functions of a few variables by inspection. Computer-aided design tools are used for more complicated functions; such methods and tools are discussed in Chapter 4.

Logic gates are connected to create combinational circuits that perform the desired function. Any function in sum-of-products form can be built using two-level logic with the literals as inputs: NOT gates form the complementary literals, AND gates form the products, and OR gates form the sum. Depending on the function and the building blocks available, multilevel logic implementations with various types of gates may be more efficient. For example, CMOS circuits favor NAND and NOR gates because these gates can be built directly from CMOS transistors without requiring extra NOT gates. When using NAND and NOR gates, bubble pushing is helpful to keep track of the inversions.

Logic gates are combined to produce larger circuits such as multiplexers, decoders, and priority circuits. A multiplexer chooses one of the data inputs based on the select input. A decoder sets one of the outputs HIGH according to the input. A priority circuit produces an output indicating the highest priority input. These circuits are all examples of combinational building blocks. Chapter 5 will introduce more building blocks, including other arithmetic circuits. These building blocks will be used extensively to build a microprocessor in Chapter 7.

The timing specification of a combinational circuit consists of the propagation and contamination delays through the circuit. These indicate the longest and shortest times between an input change and the consequent output change. Calculating the propagation delay of a circuit involves identifying the critical path through the circuit, then adding up the propagation delays of each element along that path. There are many different ways to implement complicated combinational circuits; these ways offer trade-offs between speed and cost.

The next chapter will move to sequential circuits, whose outputs depend on previous as well as current values of the inputs. In other words, sequential circuits have *memory* of the past.

Exercises

Exercise 2.1 Write a Boolean equation in sum-of-products canonical form for each of the truth tables in Figure 2.80.

(a)

A	B	Y
0	0	1
0	1	0
1	0	1
1	1	1

(b)

A	B	C	Y
0	0	0	1
0	0	1	0
0	1	0	0
0	1	1	0
1	0	0	0
1	0	1	0
1	1	0	0
1	1	1	1

(c)

A	B	C	Y
0	0	0	1
0	0	1	0
0	1	0	1
0	1	1	0
1	0	0	1
1	0	1	1
1	1	0	0
1	1	1	1

(d)

A	B	C	D	Y
0	0	0	0	1
0	0	0	1	1
0	0	1	0	1
0	0	1	1	1
0	1	0	0	0
0	1	0	1	0
0	1	1	0	0
0	1	1	1	0
1	0	0	0	1
1	0	0	1	0
1	0	1	0	1
1	0	1	1	0
1	1	0	0	0
1	1	0	1	0
1	1	1	0	1
1	1	1	1	0

(e)

A	B	C	D	Y
0	0	0	0	1
0	0	0	1	0
0	0	1	0	0
0	0	1	1	1
0	1	0	0	0
0	1	0	1	1
0	1	1	0	1
0	1	1	1	0
1	0	0	0	0
1	0	0	1	1
1	0	1	0	1
1	0	1	1	0
1	1	0	0	1
1	1	0	1	0
1	1	1	0	0
1	1	1	1	1

Figure 2.80 Truth tables

Exercise 2.2 Write a Boolean equation in product-of-sums canonical form for the truth tables in Figure 2.80.

Exercise 2.3 Minimize each of the Boolean equations from Exercise 2.1.

Exercise 2.4 Sketch a reasonably simple combinational circuit implementing each of the functions from Exercise 2.3. Reasonably simple means that you are not wasteful of gates, but you don't waste vast amounts of time checking every possible implementation of the circuit either.

Exercise 2.5 Repeat Exercise 2.4 using only NOT gates and AND and OR gates.

Exercise 2.6 Repeat Exercise 2.4 using only NOT gates and NAND and NOR gates.

Exercise 2.7 Simplify the following Boolean equations using Boolean theorems. Check for correctness using a truth table or K-map.

(a) $Y = AC + \overline{A}\overline{B}C$

(b) $Y = \overline{A}\overline{B} + \overline{A}B\overline{C} + \overline{(A + \overline{C})}$

(c) $Y = \overline{A}\overline{B}\overline{C}D + A\overline{B}C + \overline{A}B\overline{C}D + AB\overline{D} + \overline{A}\overline{B}C\overline{D} + B\overline{C}D + \overline{A}$

Exercise 2.8 Sketch a reasonably simple combinational circuit implementing each of the functions from Exercise 2.7.

Exercise 2.9 Simplify each of the following Boolean equations. Sketch a reasonably simple combinational circuit implementing the simplified equation.

(a) $Y = BC + \overline{A}B\overline{C} + B\overline{C}$

(b) $Y = \overline{A + \overline{A}B + \overline{A}\overline{B}} \ + A + \overline{B}$

(c) $Y = ABC + ABD + ABE + ACD + ACE + (\overline{A + D + E}) + \overline{B}CD$
   $+ \ \overline{B}CE + \overline{B}\,\overline{D}\,\overline{E} + \overline{C}\,\overline{D}\,\overline{E}$

Exercise 2.10 Give an example of a truth table requiring between 3 billion and 5 billion rows that can be constructed using fewer than 40 (but at least 1) two-input gates.

Exercise 2.11 Give an example of a circuit with a cyclic path that is nevertheless combinational.

Exercise 2.12 Alyssa P. Hacker says that any Boolean function can be written in minimal sum-of-products form as the sum of all of the prime implicants of the function. Ben Bitdiddle says that there are some functions whose minimal equation does not involve all of the prime implicants. Explain why Alyssa is right or provide a counterexample demonstrating Ben's point.

Exercise 2.13 Prove that the following theorems are true using perfect induction. You need not prove their duals.

(a)   The idempotency theorem (T3)

(b)   The distributivity theorem (T8)

(c)   The combining theorem (T10)

Exercise 2.14 Prove De Morgan's Theorem (T12) for three variables, B_2, B_1, B_0, using perfect induction.

Exercise 2.15 Write Boolean equations for the circuit in Figure 2.81. You need not minimize the equations.

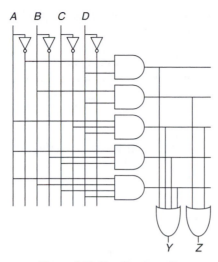

Figure 2.81 Circuit schematic

Exercise 2.16 Minimize the Boolean equations from Exercise 2.15 and sketch an improved circuit with the same function.

Exercise 2.17 Using De Morgan equivalent gates and bubble pushing methods, redraw the circuit in Figure 2.82 so that you can find the Boolean equation by inspection. Write the Boolean equation.

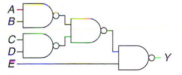

Figure 2.82 Circuit schematic

Exercise 2.18 Repeat Exercise 2.17 for the circuit in Figure 2.83.

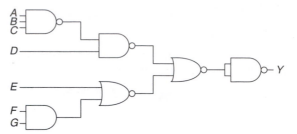

Figure 2.83 Circuit schematic

Exercise 2.19 Find a minimal Boolean equation for the function in Figure 2.84. Remember to take advantage of the don't care entries.

A	B	C	D	Y
0	0	0	0	X
0	0	0	1	X
0	0	1	0	X
0	0	1	1	0
0	1	0	0	0
0	1	0	1	X
0	1	1	0	0
0	1	1	1	X
1	0	0	0	1
1	0	0	1	0
1	0	1	0	X
1	0	1	1	1
1	1	0	0	1
1	1	0	1	1
1	1	1	0	X
1	1	1	1	1

Figure 2.84 Truth table

Exercise 2.20 Sketch a circuit for the function from Exercise 2.19.

Exercise 2.21 Does your circuit from Exercise 2.20 have any potential glitches when one of the inputs changes? If not, explain why not. If so, show how to modify the circuit to eliminate the glitches.

Exercise 2.22 Ben Bitdiddle will enjoy his picnic on sunny days that have no ants. He will also enjoy his picnic any day he sees a hummingbird, as well as on days where there are ants and ladybugs. Write a Boolean equation for his enjoyment (E) in terms of sun (S), ants (A), hummingbirds (H), and ladybugs (L).

Exercise 2.23 Complete the design of the seven-segment decoder segments S_c through S_g (see Example 2.10):

(a) Derive Boolean equations for the outputs S_c through S_g assuming that inputs greater than 9 must produce blank (0) outputs.

(b) Derive Boolean equations for the outputs S_c through S_g assuming that inputs greater than 9 are don't cares.

(c) Sketch a reasonably simple gate-level implementation of part (b). Multiple outputs can share gates where appropriate.

Exercise 2.24 A circuit has four inputs and two outputs. The inputs, $A_{3:0}$, represent a number from 0 to 15. Output P should be TRUE if the number is prime (0 and 1 are not prime, but 2, 3, 5, and so on, are prime). Output D should be TRUE if the number is divisible by 3. Give simplified Boolean equations for each output and sketch a circuit.

Exercise 2.25 A *priority encoder* has 2^N inputs. It produces an N-bit binary output indicating the most significant bit of the input that is TRUE, or 0 if none of the inputs are TRUE. It also produces an output *NONE* that is TRUE if none of the input bits are TRUE. Design an eight-input priority encoder with inputs $A_{7:0}$ and outputs $Y_{2:0}$ and *NONE*. For example, if the input is 00100000, the output Y should be 101 and *NONE* should be 0. Give a simplified Boolean equation for each output, and sketch a schematic.

Exercise 2.26 Design a modified priority encoder (see Exercise 2.25) that receives an 8-bit input, $A_{7:0}$, and produces two 3-bit outputs, $Y_{2:0}$ and $Z_{2:0}$. Y indicates the most significant bit of the input that is TRUE. Z indicates the second most significant bit of the input that is TRUE. Y should be 0 if none of the inputs are TRUE. Z should be 0 if no more than one of the inputs is TRUE. Give a simplified Boolean equation for each output, and sketch a schematic.

Exercise 2.27 An M-bit *thermometer code* for the number k consists of k 1's in the least significant bit positions and $M - k$ 0's in all the more significant bit positions. A *binary-to-thermometer code converter* has N inputs and 2^N-1 outputs. It produces a 2^N-1 bit thermometer code for the number specified by the input. For example, if the input is 110, the output should be 0111111. Design a 3:7 binary-to-thermometer code converter. Give a simplified Boolean equation for each output, and sketch a schematic.

Exercise 2.28 Write a minimized Boolean equation for the function performed by the circuit in Figure 2.85.

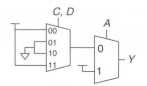

Figure 2.85 Multiplexer circuit

Exercise 2.29 Write a minimized Boolean equation for the function performed by the circuit in Figure 2.86.

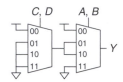

Figure 2.86 Multiplexer circuit

Exercise 2.30 Implement the function from Figure 2.80(b) using

(a) an 8:1 multiplexer

(b) a 4:1 multiplexer and one inverter

(c) a 2:1 multiplexer and two other logic gates

Exercise 2.31 Implement the function from Exercise 2.9(a) using

(a) an 8:1 multiplexer

(b) a 4:1 multiplexer and no other gates

(c) a 2:1 multiplexer, one OR gate, and an inverter

Exercise 2.32 Determine the propagation delay and contamination delay of the circuit in Figure 2.83. Use the gate delays given in Table 2.8.

Table 2.8 Gate delays for Exercises 2.32–2.35

Gate	t_{pd} (ps)	t_{cd} (ps)
NOT	15	10
2-input NAND	20	15
3-input NAND	30	25
2-input NOR	30	25
3-input NOR	45	35
2-input AND	30	25
3-input AND	40	30
2-input OR	40	30
3-input OR	55	45
2-input XOR	60	40

Exercise 2.33 Sketch a schematic for a fast 3:8 decoder. Suppose gate delays are given in Table 2.8 (and only the gates in that table are available). Design your decoder to have the shortest possible critical path, and indicate what that path is. What are its propagation delay and contamination delay?

Exercise 2.34 Redesign the circuit from Exercise 2.24 to be as fast as possible. Use only the gates from Table 2.8. Sketch the new circuit and indicate the critical path. What are its propagation delay and contamination delay?

Exercise 2.35 Redesign the priority encoder from Exercise 2.25 to be as fast as possible. You may use any of the gates from Table 2.8. Sketch the new circuit and indicate the critical path. What are its propagation delay and contamination delay?

Exercise 2.36 Design an 8:1 multiplexer with the shortest possible delay from the data inputs to the output. You may use any of the gates from Table 2.7 on page 88. Sketch a schematic. Using the gate delays from the table, determine this delay.

Interview Questions

The following exercises present questions that have been asked at interviews for digital design jobs.

Question 2.1 Sketch a schematic for the two-input XOR function using only NAND gates. How few can you use?

Question 2.2 Design a circuit that will tell whether a given month has 31 days in it. The month is specified by a 4-bit input, $A_{3:0}$. For example, if the inputs are 0001, the month is January, and if the inputs are 1100, the month is December. The circuit output, Y, should be HIGH only when the month specified by the inputs has 31 days in it. Write the simplified equation, and draw the circuit diagram using a minimum number of gates. (Hint: Remember to take advantage of don't cares.)

Question 2.3 What is a tristate buffer? How and why is it used?

Question 2.4 A gate or set of gates is universal if it can be used to construct any Boolean function. For example, the set {AND, OR, NOT} is universal.

(a) Is an AND gate by itself universal? Why or why not?

(b) Is the set {OR, NOT} universal? Why or why not?

(c) Is a NAND gate by itself universal? Why or why not?

Question 2.5 Explain why a circuit's contamination delay might be less than (instead of equal to) its propagation delay.

Sequential Logic Design

3.1 INTRODUCTION

In the last chapter, we showed how to analyze and design combinational logic. The output of combinational logic depends only on current input values. Given a specification in the form of a truth table or Boolean equation, we can create an optimized circuit to meet the specification.

In this chapter, we will analyze and design *sequential* logic. The outputs of sequential logic depend on both current and prior input values. Hence, sequential logic has memory. Sequential logic might explicitly remember certain previous inputs, or it might distill the prior inputs into a smaller amount of information called the *state* of the system. The state of a digital sequential circuit is a set of bits called *state variables* that contain all the information about the past necessary to explain the future behavior of the circuit.

The chapter begins by studying latches and flip-flops, which are simple sequential circuits that store one bit of state. In general, sequential circuits are complicated to analyze. To simplify design, we discipline ourselves to build only synchronous sequential circuits consisting of combinational logic and banks of flip-flops containing the state of the circuit. The chapter describes finite state machines, which are an easy way to design sequential circuits. Finally, we analyze the speed of sequential circuits and discuss parallelism as a way to increase clock speed.

3.2 LATCHES AND FLIP-FLOPS

The fundamental building block of memory is a *bistable* element, an element with two stable states. Figure 3.1(a) shows a simple bistable element consisting of a pair of inverters connected in a loop. Figure 3.1(b) shows the same circuit redrawn to emphasize the symmetry. The inverters are *cross-coupled,* meaning that the input of I1 is the output of I2 and vice versa. The circuit has no inputs, but it does have two outputs,

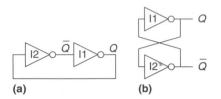

Figure 3.1 Cross-coupled inverter pair

(a)   (b)

Q and $\overline{Q}$. Analyzing this circuit is different from analyzing a combinational circuit because it is cyclic: Q depends on $\overline{Q}$, and $\overline{Q}$ depends on Q.

Consider the two cases, Q is 0 or Q is 1. Working through the consequences of each case, we have:

▶ *Case I:* $Q = 0$
As shown in Figure 3.2(a), I2 receives a FALSE input, Q, so it produces a TRUE output on $\overline{Q}$. I1 receives a TRUE input, $\overline{Q}$, so it produces a FALSE output on Q. This is consistent with the original assumption that $Q = 0$, so the case is said to be *stable*.

▶ *Case II:* $Q = 1$
As shown in Figure 3.2(b), I2 receives a TRUE input and produces a FALSE output on $\overline{Q}$. I1 receives a FALSE input and produces a TRUE output on Q. This is again stable.

Because the cross-coupled inverters have two stable states, $Q = 0$ and $Q = 1$, the circuit is said to be bistable. A subtle point is that the circuit has a third possible state with both outputs approximately halfway between 0 and 1. This is called a *metastable* state and will be discussed in Section 3.5.4.

An element with N stable states conveys $\log_2 N$ bits of information, so a bistable element stores one bit. The state of the cross-coupled inverters is contained in one binary state variable, Q. The value of Q tells us everything about the past that is necessary to explain the future behavior of the circuit. Specifically, if $Q = 0$, it will remain 0 forever, and if $Q = 1$, it will remain 1 forever. The circuit does have another node, $\overline{Q}$, but $\overline{Q}$ does not contain any additional information because if Q is known, $\overline{Q}$ is also known. On the other hand, $\overline{Q}$ is also an acceptable choice for the state variable.

Figure 3.2 Bistable operation of cross-coupled inverters

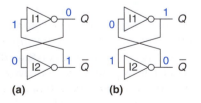

(a)   (b)

When power is first applied to a sequential circuit, the initial state is unknown and usually unpredictable. It may differ each time the circuit is turned on.

Although the cross-coupled inverters can store a bit of information, they are not practical because the user has no inputs to control the state. However, other bistable elements, such as *latches* and *flip-flops,* provide inputs to control the value of the state variable. The remainder of this section considers these circuits.

3.2.1 SR Latch

One of the simplest sequential circuits is the *SR latch,* which is composed of two cross-coupled NOR gates, as shown in Figure 3.3. The latch has two inputs, S and R, and two outputs, Q and $\overline{Q}$. The SR latch is similar to the cross-coupled inverters, but its state can be controlled through the S and R inputs, which *set* and *reset* the output Q.

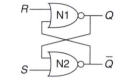

Figure 3.3 SR latch schematic

A good way to understand an unfamiliar circuit is to work out its truth table, so that is where we begin. Recall that a NOR gate produces a FALSE output when either input is TRUE. Consider the four possible combinations of R and S.

- *Case I: R = 1, S = 0*
  N1 sees at least one TRUE input, R, so it produces a FALSE output on Q. N2 sees both Q and S FALSE, so it produces a TRUE output on $\overline{Q}$.

- *Case II: R = 0, S = 1*
  N1 receives inputs of 0 and $\overline{Q}$. Because we don't yet know $\overline{Q}$, we can't determine the output Q. N2 receives at least one TRUE input, S, so it produces a FALSE output on $\overline{Q}$. Now we can revisit N1, knowing that both inputs are FALSE, so the output Q is TRUE.

- *Case III: R = 1, S = 1*
  N1 and N2 both see at least one TRUE input (R or S), so each produces a FALSE output. Hence Q and $\overline{Q}$ are both FALSE.

- *Case IV: R = 0, S = 0*
  N1 receives inputs of 0 and $\overline{Q}$. Because we don't yet know $\overline{Q}$, we can't determine the output. N2 receives inputs of 0 and Q. Because we don't yet know Q, we can't determine the output. Now we are stuck. This is reminiscent of the cross-coupled inverters. But we know that Q must either be 0 or 1. So we can solve the problem by checking what happens in each of these subcases.

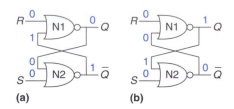

Figure 3.4 Bistable states of SR latch

(a)   (b)

▶ *Case IVa:* $Q = 0$
Because S and Q are FALSE, N2 produces a TRUE output on $\overline{Q}$, as shown in Figure 3.4(a). Now N1 receives one TRUE input, $\overline{Q}$, so its output, Q, is FALSE, just as we had assumed.

▶ *Case IVb:* $Q = 1$
Because Q is TRUE, N2 produces a FALSE output on $\overline{Q}$, as shown in Figure 3.4(b). Now N1 receives two FALSE inputs, R and $\overline{Q}$, so its output, Q, is TRUE, just as we had assumed.

Putting this all together, suppose Q has some known prior value, which we will call Q_{prev}, before we enter Case IV. Q_{prev} is either 0 or 1, and represents the state of the system. When R and S are 0, Q will remember this old value, Q_{prev}, and $\overline{Q}$ will be its complement, $\overline{Q}_{prev}$. This circuit has memory.

The truth table in Figure 3.5 summarizes these four cases. The inputs S and R stand for *Set* and *Reset*. To *set* a bit means to make it TRUE. To *reset* a bit means to make it FALSE. The outputs, Q and $\overline{Q}$, are normally complementary. When R is asserted, Q is reset to 0 and $\overline{Q}$ does the opposite. When S is asserted, Q is set to 1 and $\overline{Q}$ does the opposite. When neither input is asserted, Q remembers its old value, Q_{prev}. Asserting both S and R simultaneously doesn't make much sense because it means the latch should be set and reset at the same time, which is impossible. The poor confused circuit responds by making both outputs 0.

The SR latch is represented by the symbol in Figure 3.6. Using the symbol is an application of abstraction and modularity. There are various ways to build an SR latch, such as using different logic gates or transistors. Nevertheless, any circuit element with the relationship specified by the truth table in Figure 3.5 and the symbol in Figure 3.6 is called an SR latch.

Like the cross-coupled inverters, the SR latch is a bistable element with one bit of state stored in Q. However, the state can be controlled through the S and R inputs. When R is asserted, the state is reset to 0. When S is asserted, the state is set to 1. When neither is asserted, the state retains its old value. Notice that the entire history of inputs can be

Case	S	R	Q	$\overline{Q}$
IV	0	0	Q_{prev}	$\overline{Q}_{prev}$
I	0	1	0	1
II	1	0	1	0
III	1	1	0	0

Figure 3.5 SR latch truth table

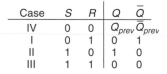

Figure 3.6 SR latch symbol

accounted for by the single state variable Q. No matter what pattern of setting and resetting occurred in the past, all that is needed to predict the future behavior of the SR latch is whether it was most recently set or reset.

3.2.2 D Latch

The SR latch is awkward because it behaves strangely when both S and R are simultaneously asserted. Moreover, the S and R inputs conflate the issues of *what* and *when*. Asserting one of the inputs determines not only *what* the state should be but also *when* it should change. Designing circuits becomes easier when these questions of what and when are separated. The D latch in Figure 3.7(a) solves these problems. It has two inputs. The *data* input, D, controls what the next state should be. The *clock* input, CLK, controls when the state should change.

Again, we analyze the latch by writing the truth table, given in Figure 3.7(b). For convenience, we first consider the internal nodes $\overline{D}$, S, and R. If $CLK = 0$, both S and R are FALSE, regardless of the value of D. If $CLK = 1$, one AND gate will produce TRUE and the other FALSE, depending on the value of D. Given S and R, Q and $\overline{Q}$ are determined using Figure 3.5. Observe that when $CLK = 0$, Q remembers its old value, Q_{prev}. When $CLK = 1$, $Q = D$. In all cases, $\overline{Q}$ is the complement of Q, as would seem logical. The D latch avoids the strange case of simultaneously asserted R and S inputs.

Putting it all together, we see that the clock controls when data flows through the latch. When $CLK = 1$, the latch is *transparent*. The data at D flows through to Q as if the latch were just a buffer. When $CLK = 0$, the latch is *opaque*. It blocks the new data from flowing through to Q, and Q retains the old value. Hence, the D latch is sometimes called a *transparent latch* or a *level-sensitive* latch. The D latch symbol is given in Figure 3.7(c).

The D latch updates its state continuously while $CLK = 1$. We shall see later in this chapter that it is useful to update the state only at a specific instant in time. The D flip-flop described in the next section does just that.

> Some people call a latch open or closed rather than transparent or opaque. However, we think those terms are ambiguous—does *open* mean transparent like an open door, or opaque, like an open circuit?

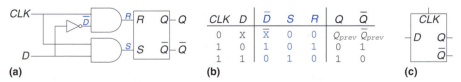

CLK	D	$\overline{D}$	S	R	Q	$\overline{Q}$
0	X	$\overline{X}$	0	0	Q_{prev}	$\overline{Q}_{prev}$
1	0	1	0	1	0	1
1	1	0	1	0	1	0

(a)   (b)   (c)

Figure 3.7 D latch: (a) schematic, (b) truth table, (c) symbol

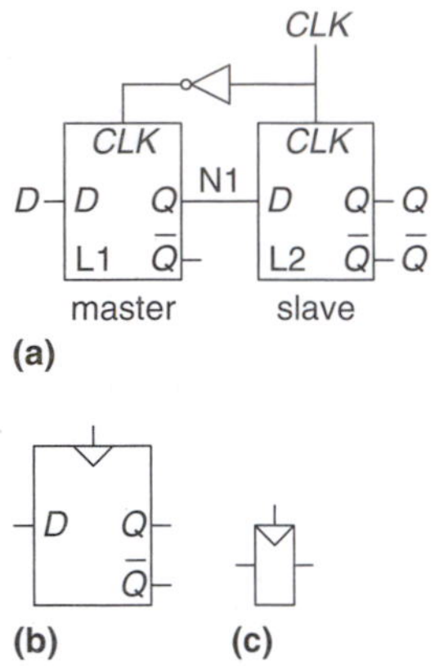

Figure 3.8 D flip-flop:
(a) schematic, (b) symbol,
(c) condensed symbol

The precise distinction between *flip-flops* and *latches* is somewhat muddled and has evolved over time. In common industry usage, a flip-flop is *edge-triggered*. In other words, it is a bistable element with a *clock* input. The state of the flip-flop changes only in response to a clock edge, such as when the clock rises from 0 to 1. Bistable elements without an edge-triggered clock are commonly called latches.

The term flip-flop or latch by itself usually refers to a *D flip-flop* or *D latch*, respectively, because these are the types most commonly used in practice.

3.2.3 D Flip-Flop

A *D flip-flop* can be built from two back-to-back D latches controlled by complementary clocks, as shown in Figure 3.8(a). The first latch, L1, is called the *master*. The second latch, L2, is called the *slave*. The node between them is named N1. A symbol for the D flip-flop is given in Figure 3.8(b). When the $\overline{Q}$ output is not needed, the symbol is often condensed as in Figure 3.8(c).

When $CLK = 0$, the master latch is transparent and the slave is opaque. Therefore, whatever value was at D propagates through to N1. When $CLK = 1$, the master goes opaque and the slave becomes transparent. The value at N1 propagates through to Q, but N1 is cut off from D. Hence, whatever value was at D immediately before the clock rises from 0 to 1 gets copied to Q immediately after the clock rises. At all other times, Q retains its old value, because there is always an opaque latch blocking the path between D and Q.

In other words, *a D flip-flop copies D to Q on the rising edge of the clock, and remembers its state at all other times*. Reread this definition until you have it memorized; one of the most common problems for beginning digital designers is to forget what a flip-flop does. The rising edge of the clock is often just called the *clock edge* for brevity. The D input specifies what the new state will be. The clock edge indicates when the state should be updated.

A D flip-flop is also known as a *master-slave flip-flop*, an *edge-triggered flip-flop*, or a *positive edge-triggered flip-flop*. The triangle in the symbols denotes an edge-triggered clock input. The $\overline{Q}$ output is often omitted when it is not needed.

Example 3.1 FLIP-FLOP TRANSISTOR COUNT

How many transistors are needed to build the D flip-flop described in this section?

Solution: A NAND or NOR gate uses four transistors. A NOT gate uses two transistors. An AND gate is built from a NAND and a NOT, so it uses six transistors. The SR latch uses two NOR gates, or eight transistors. The D latch uses an SR latch, two AND gates, and a NOT gate, or 22 transistors. The D flip-flop uses two D latches and a NOT gate, or 46 transistors. Section 3.2.7 describes a more efficient CMOS implementation using transmission gates.

3.2.4 Register

An *N*-bit register is a bank of *N* flip-flops that share a common *CLK* input, so that all bits of the register are updated at the same time.

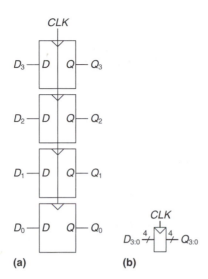

Figure 3.9 A 4-bit register:
(a) schematic and (b) symbol

Registers are the key building block of most sequential circuits. Figure 3.9 shows the schematic and symbol for a four-bit register with inputs $D_{3:0}$ and outputs $Q_{3:0}$. $D_{3:0}$ and $Q_{3:0}$ are both 4-bit busses.

3.2.5 Enabled Flip-Flop

An *enabled flip-flop* adds another input called *EN* or ENABLE to determine whether data is loaded on the clock edge. When *EN* is TRUE, the enabled flip-flop behaves like an ordinary D flip-flop. When *EN* is FALSE, the enabled flip-flop ignores the clock and retains its state. Enabled flip-flops are useful when we wish to load a new value into a flip-flop only some of the time, rather than on every clock edge.

Figure 3.10 shows two ways to construct an enabled flip-flop from a D flip-flop and an extra gate. In Figure 3.10(a), an input multiplexer chooses whether to pass the value at *D*, if *EN* is TRUE, or to recycle the old state from *Q*, if *EN* is FALSE. In Figure 3.10(b), the clock is *gated*.

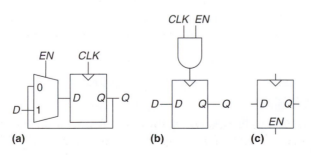

Figure 3.10 Enabled flip-flop:
(a, b) schematics, (c) symbol

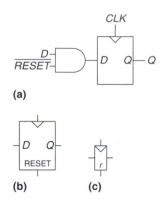

(a)

(b)   **(c)**

Figure 3.11 Synchronously resettable flip-flop: (a) schematic, (b, c) symbols

If *EN* is TRUE, the *CLK* input to the flip-flop toggles normally. If *EN* is FALSE, the *CLK* input is also FALSE and the flip-flop retains its old value. Notice that *EN* must not change while *CLK* = 1, lest the flip-flop see a clock *glitch* (switch at an incorrect time). Generally, performing logic on the clock is a bad idea. Clock gating delays the clock and can cause timing errors, as we will see in Section 3.5.3, so do it only if you are sure you know what you are doing. The symbol for an enabled flip-flop is given in Figure 3.10(c).

3.2.6 Resettable Flip-Flop

A *resettable flip-flop* adds another input called RESET. When RESET is FALSE, the resettable flip-flop behaves like an ordinary D flip-flop. When RESET is TRUE, the resettable flip-flop ignores *D* and resets the output to 0. Resettable flip-flops are useful when we want to force a known state (i.e., 0) into all the flip-flops in a system when we first turn it on.

Such flip-flops may be *synchronously* or *asynchronously resettable*. Synchronously resettable flip-flops reset themselves only on the rising edge of *CLK*. Asynchronously resettable flip-flops reset themselves as soon as RESET becomes TRUE, independent of *CLK*.

Figure 3.11(a) shows how to construct a synchronously resettable flip-flop from an ordinary D flip-flop and an AND gate. When $\overline{\text{RESET}}$ is FALSE, the AND gate forces a 0 into the input of the flip-flop. When $\overline{\text{RESET}}$ is TRUE, the AND gate passes *D* to the flip-flop. In this example, $\overline{\text{RESET}}$ is an *active low* signal, meaning that the reset signal performs its function when it is 0, not 1. By adding an inverter, the circuit could have accepted an active high RESET signal instead. Figures 3.11(b) and 3.11(c) show symbols for the resettable flip-flop with active high RESET.

Asynchronously resettable flip-flops require modifying the internal structure of the flip-flop and are left to you to design in Exercise 3.10; however, they are frequently available to the designer as a standard component.

As you might imagine, settable flip-flops are also occasionally used. They load a 1 into the flip-flop when SET is asserted, and they too come in synchronous and asynchronous flavors. Resettable and settable flip-flops may also have an enable input and may be grouped into *N*-bit registers.

3.2.7 Transistor-Level Latch and Flip-Flop Designs*

Example 3.1 showed that latches and flip-flops require a large number of transistors when built from logic gates. But the fundamental role of a latch is to be transparent or opaque, much like a switch. Recall from Section 1.7.7 that a transmission gate is an efficient way to build a CMOS switch, so we might expect that we could take advantage of transmission gates to reduce the transistor count.

A compact D latch can be constructed from a single transmission gate, as shown in Figure 3.12(a). When $CLK = 1$ and $\overline{CLK} = 0$, the transmission gate is ON, so D flows to Q and the latch is transparent. When $CLK = 0$ and $\overline{CLK} = 1$, the transmission gate is OFF, so Q is isolated from D and the latch is opaque. This latch suffers from two major limitations:

▶ *Floating output node:* When the latch is opaque, Q is not held at its value by any gates. Thus Q is called a *floating* or *dynamic* node. After some time, noise and charge leakage may disturb the value of Q.

▶ *No buffers:* The lack of buffers has caused malfunctions on several commercial chips. A spike of noise that pulls D to a negative voltage can turn on the nMOS transistor, making the latch transparent, even when $CLK = 0$. Likewise, a spike on D above V_{DD} can turn on the pMOS transistor even when $CLK = 0$. And the transmission gate is symmetric, so it could be driven backward with noise on Q affecting the input D. The general rule is that neither the input of a transmission gate nor the state node of a sequential circuit should ever be exposed to the outside world, where noise is likely.

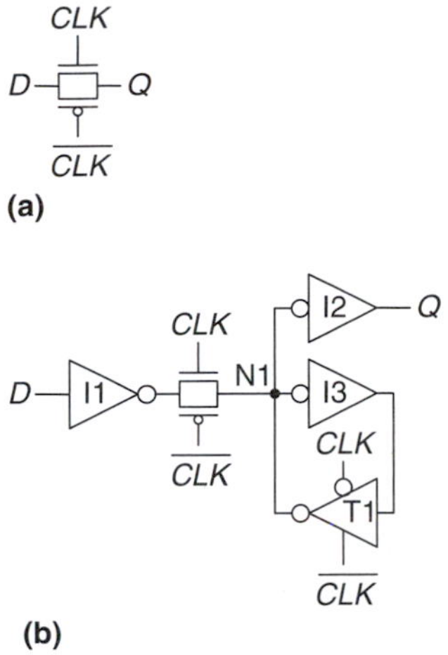

Figure 3.12(b) shows a more robust 12-transistor D latch used on modern commercial chips. It is still built around a clocked transmission gate, but it adds inverters I1 and I2 to buffer the input and output. The state of the latch is held on node N1. Inverter I3 and the tristate buffer, T1, provide feedback to turn N1 into a *static node.* If a small amount of noise occurs on N1 while $CLK = 0$, T1 will drive N1 back to a valid logic value.

Figure 3.13 shows a D flip-flop constructed from two static latches controlled by $\overline{CLK}$ and CLK. Some redundant internal inverters have been removed, so the flip-flop requires only 20 transistors.

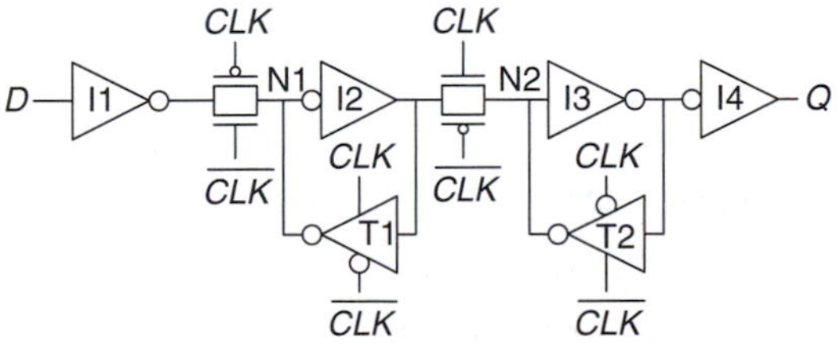

(a)

(b)

Figure 3.12 D latch schematic

This circuit assumes CLK and $\overline{CLK}$ are both available. If not, two more transistors are needed for a CLK inverter.

Figure 3.13 D flip-flop schematic

3.2.8 Putting It All Together

Latches and flip-flops are the fundamental building blocks of sequential circuits. Remember that a D latch is level-sensitive, whereas a D flip-flop is edge-triggered. The D latch is transparent when $CLK = 1$, allowing the input D to flow through to the output Q. The D flip-flop copies D to Q on the rising edge of CLK. At all other times, latches and flip-flops retain their old state. A register is a bank of several D flip-flops that share a common CLK signal.

Example 3.2 FLIP-FLOP AND LATCH COMPARISON

Ben Bitdiddle applies the D and CLK inputs shown in Figure 3.14 to a D latch and a D flip-flop. Help him determine the output, Q, of each device.

Solution: Figure 3.15 shows the output waveforms, assuming a small delay for Q to respond to input changes. The arrows indicate the cause of an output change. The initial value of Q is unknown and could be 0 or 1, as indicated by the pair of horizontal lines. First consider the latch. On the first rising edge of CLK, $D = 0$, so Q definitely becomes 0. Each time D changes while $CLK = 1$, Q also follows. When D changes while $CLK = 0$, it is ignored. Now consider the flip-flop. On each rising edge of CLK, D is copied to Q. At all other times, Q retains its state.

CLK

D

Q (latch)

Q (flop)

Figure 3.14 Example waveforms

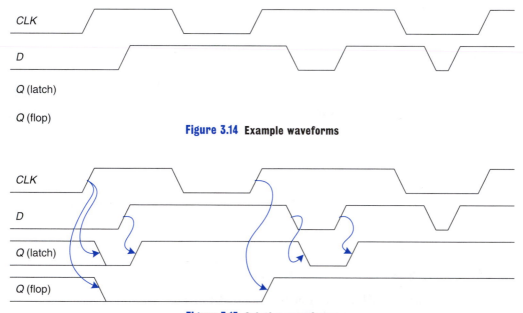

Figure 3.15 Solution waveforms

3.3 SYNCHRONOUS LOGIC DESIGN

In general, sequential circuits include all circuits that are not combinational—that is, those whose output cannot be determined simply by looking at the current inputs. Some sequential circuits are just plain kooky. This section begins by examining some of those curious circuits. It then introduces the notion of synchronous sequential circuits and the dynamic discipline. By disciplining ourselves to synchronous sequential circuits, we can develop easy, systematic ways to analyze and design sequential systems.

3.3.1 Some Problematic Circuits

Example 3.3 ASTABLE CIRCUITS

Alyssa P. Hacker encounters three misbegotten inverters who have tied themselves in a loop, as shown in Figure 3.16. The output of the third inverter is *fed back* to the first inverter. Each inverter has a propagation delay of 1 ns. Determine what the circuit does.

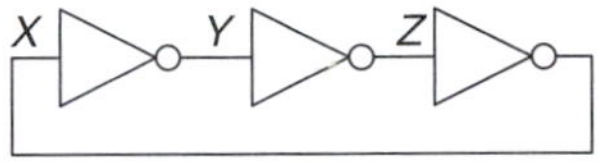

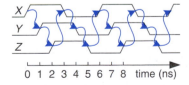

Figure 3.16 Three-inverter loop

Solution: Suppose node X is initially 0. Then $Y = 1$, $Z = 0$, and hence $X = 1$, which is inconsistent with our original assumption. The circuit has no stable states and is said to be *unstable* or *astable*. Figure 3.17 shows the behavior of the circuit. If X rises at time 0, Y will fall at 1 ns, Z will rise at 2 ns, and X will fall again at 3 ns. In turn, Y will rise at 4 ns, Z will fall at 5 ns, and X will rise again at 6 ns, and then the pattern will repeat. Each node oscillates between 0 and 1 with a *period* (repetition time) of 6 ns. This circuit is called a *ring oscillator*.

The period of the ring oscillator depends on the propagation delay of each inverter. This delay depends on how the inverter was manufactured, the power supply voltage, and even the temperature. Therefore, the ring oscillator period is difficult to accurately predict. In short, the ring oscillator is a sequential circuit with zero inputs and one output that changes periodically.

$$\begin{array}{c} X \\ Y \\ Z \end{array}$$

0 1 2 3 4 5 6 7 8   time (ns)

Figure 3.17 Ring oscillator waveforms

Example 3.4 RACE CONDITIONS

Ben Bitdiddle designed a new D latch that he claims is better than the one in Figure 3.17 because it uses fewer gates. He has written the truth table to find

Figure 3.18 An improved (?) D latch

CLK	D	Q_{prev}	Q
0	0	0	0
0	0	1	1
0	1	0	0
0	1	1	1
1	0	0	0
1	0	1	0
1	1	0	1
1	1	1	1

$Q = CLK{\cdot}D + \overline{CLK}{\cdot}Q_{prev}$

$N1 = CLK{\cdot}D$

$N2 = \overline{CLK}{\cdot}Q_{prev}$

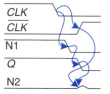

Figure 3.19 Latch waveforms illustrating race condition

the output, Q, given the two inputs, D and CLK, and the old state of the latch, Q_{prev}. Based on this truth table, he has derived Boolean equations. He obtains Q_{prev} by feeding back the output, Q. His design is shown in Figure 3.18. Does his latch work correctly, independent of the delays of each gate?

Solution: Figure 3.19 shows that the circuit has a *race condition* that causes it to fail when certain gates are slower than others. Suppose $CLK = D = 1$. The latch is transparent and passes D through to make $Q = 1$. Now, CLK falls. The latch should remember its old value, keeping $Q = 1$. However, suppose the delay through the inverter from CLK to $\overline{CLK}$ is rather long compared to the delays of the AND and OR gates. Then nodes N1 and Q may both fall before $\overline{CLK}$ rises. In such a case, N2 will never rise, and Q becomes stuck at 0.

This is an example of *asynchronous* circuit design in which outputs are directly fed back to inputs. Asynchronous circuits are infamous for having race conditions where the behavior of the circuit depends on which of two paths through logic gates is fastest. One circuit may work, while a seemingly identical one built from gates with slightly different delays may not work. Or the circuit may work only at certain temperatures or voltages at which the delays are just right. These mistakes are extremely difficult to track down.

3.3.2 Synchronous Sequential Circuits

The previous two examples contain loops called *cyclic paths,* in which outputs are fed directly back to inputs. They are sequential rather than combinational circuits. Combinational logic has no cyclic paths and no races. If inputs are applied to combinational logic, the outputs will always settle to the correct value within a propagation delay. However, sequential circuits with cyclic paths can have undesirable races or unstable behavior. Analyzing such circuits for problems is time-consuming, and many bright people have made mistakes.

To avoid these problems, designers break the cyclic paths by inserting registers somewhere in the path. This transforms the circuit into a collection of combinational logic and registers. The registers contain the state of the system, which changes only at the clock edge, so we say the state is *synchronized* to the clock. If the clock is sufficiently slow, so that the inputs to all registers settle before the next clock edge, all races are eliminated. Adopting this discipline of always using registers in the feedback path leads us to the formal definition of a synchronous sequential circuit.

Recall that a circuit is defined by its input and output terminals and its functional and timing specifications. A sequential circuit has a finite set of discrete *states* $\{S_0, S_1, \ldots, S_{k-1}\}$. A *synchronous sequential circuit* has a clock input, whose rising edges indicate a sequence of times at which state transitions occur. We often use the terms *current state* and *next state* to distinguish the state of the system at the present from the state to which it will enter on the next clock edge. The functional specification details the next state and the value of each output for each possible combination of current state and input values. The timing specification consists of an upper bound, t_{pcq}, and a lower bound, t_{ccq}, on the time from the rising edge of the clock until the *output* changes, as well as *setup* and *hold* times, t_{setup} and t_{hold}, that indicate when the *inputs* must be stable relative to the rising edge of the clock.

The rules of *synchronous sequential circuit composition* teach us that a circuit is a synchronous sequential circuit if it consists of interconnected circuit elements such that

▶ Every circuit element is either a register or a combinational circuit

▶ At least one circuit element is a register

▶ All registers receive the same clock signal

▶ Every cyclic path contains at least one register.

Sequential circuits that are not synchronous are called *asynchronous*.

A flip-flop is the simplest synchronous sequential circuit. It has one input, *D*, one clock, *CLK*, one output, *Q*, and two states, {0, 1}. The functional specification for a flip-flop is that the next state is *D* and that the output, *Q*, is the current state, as shown in Figure 3.20.

We often call the current state variable *S* and the next state variable *S'*. In this case, the prime after *S* indicates next state, not inversion. The timing of sequential circuits will be analyzed in Section 3.5.

Two other common types of synchronous sequential circuits are called finite state machines and pipelines. These will be covered later in this chapter.

t_{pcq} stands for the time of propagation from clock to *Q*, where *Q* indicates the output of a synchronous sequential circuit. t_{ccq} stands for the time of contamination from clock to *Q*. These are analogous to t_{pd} and t_{cd} in combinational logic.

This definition of a synchronous sequential circuit is sufficient, but more restrictive than necessary. For example, in high-performance microprocessors, some registers may receive delayed or gated clocks to squeeze out the last bit of performance or power. Similarly, some microprocessors use latches instead of registers. However, the definition is adequate for all of the synchronous sequential circuits covered in this book and for most commercial digital systems.

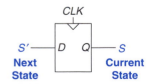

Figure 3.20 Flip-flop current state and next state

Figure 3.21 Example circuits

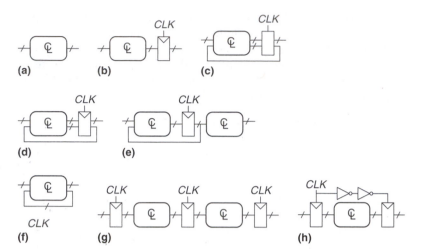

Example 3.5 SYNCHRONOUS SEQUENTIAL CIRCUITS

Which of the circuits in Figure 3.21 are synchronous sequential circuits?

Solution: Circuit (a) is combinational, not sequential, because it has no registers. (b) is a simple sequential circuit with no feedback. (c) is neither a combinational circuit nor a synchronous sequential circuit, because it has a latch that is neither a register nor a combinational circuit. (d) and (e) are synchronous sequential logic; they are two forms of finite state machines, which are discussed in Section 3.4. (f) is neither combinational nor synchronous sequential, because it has a cyclic path from the output of the combinational logic back to the input of the same logic but no register in the path. (g) is synchronous sequential logic in the form of a pipeline, which we will study in Section 3.6. (h) is not, strictly speaking, a synchronous sequential circuit, because the second register receives a different clock signal than the first, delayed by two inverter delays.

3.3.3 Synchronous and Asynchronous Circuits

Asynchronous design in theory is more general than synchronous design, because the timing of the system is not limited by clocked registers. Just as analog circuits are more general than digital circuits because analog circuits can use any voltage, asynchronous circuits are more general than synchronous circuits because they can use any kind of feedback. However, synchronous circuits have proved to be easier to design and use than asynchronous circuits, just as digital are easier than analog circuits. Despite decades of research on asynchronous circuits, virtually all digital systems are essentially synchronous.

Of course, asynchronous circuits are occasionally necessary when communicating between systems with different clocks or when receiving inputs at arbitrary times, just as analog circuits are necessary when communicating with the real world of continuous voltages. Furthermore, research in asynchronous circuits continues to generate interesting insights, some of which can improve synchronous circuits too.

3.4 FINITE STATE MACHINES

Synchronous sequential circuits can be drawn in the forms shown in Figure 3.22. These forms are called *finite state machines* (*FSMs*). They get their name because a circuit with k registers can be in one of a finite number (2^k) of unique states. An FSM has M inputs, N outputs, and k bits of state. It also receives a clock and, optionally, a reset signal. An FSM consists of two blocks of combinational logic, *next state logic* and *output logic*, and a register that stores the state. On each clock edge, the FSM advances to the next state, which was computed based on the current state and inputs. There are two general classes of finite state machines, characterized by their functional specifications. In *Moore machines,* the outputs depend only on the current state of the machine. In *Mealy machines,* the outputs depend on both the current state and the current inputs. Finite state machines provide a systematic way to design synchronous sequential circuits given a functional specification. This method will be explained in the remainder of this section, starting with an example.

3.4.1 FSM Design Example

To illustrate the design of FSMs, consider the problem of inventing a controller for a traffic light at a busy intersection on campus. Engineering students are moseying between their dorms and the labs on Academic Ave. They are busy reading about FSMs in their favorite

Moore and Mealy machines are named after their promoters, researchers who developed *automata theory,* the mathematical underpinnings of state machines, at Bell Labs.

Edward F. Moore (1925–2003), not to be confused with Intel founder Gordon Moore, published his seminal article, *Gedanken-experiments on Sequential Machines* in 1956. He subsequently became a professor of mathematics and computer science at the University of Wisconsin.

George H. Mealy published *A Method of Synthesizing Sequential Circuits* in 1955. He subsequently wrote the first Bell Labs operating system for the IBM 704 computer. He later joined Harvard University.

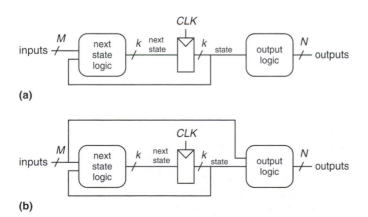

(a)

(b)

Figure 3.22 Finite state machines: (a) Moore machine, (b) Mealy machine

textbook and aren't looking where they are going. Football players are hustling between the athletic fields and the dining hall on Bravado Boulevard. They are tossing the ball back and forth and aren't looking where they are going either. Several serious injuries have already occurred at the intersection of these two roads, and the Dean of Students asks Ben Bitdiddle to install a traffic light before there are fatalities.

Ben decides to solve the problem with an FSM. He installs two traffic sensors, T_A and T_B, on Academic Ave. and Bravado Blvd., respectively. Each sensor indicates TRUE if students are present and FALSE if the street is empty. He also installs two traffic lights, L_A and L_B, to control traffic. Each light receives digital inputs specifying whether it should be green, yellow, or red. Hence, his FSM has two inputs, T_A and T_B, and two outputs, L_A and L_B. The intersection with lights and sensors is shown in Figure 3.23. Ben provides a clock with a 5-second period. On each clock tick (rising edge), the lights may change based on the traffic sensors. He also provides a reset button so that Physical Plant technicians can put the controller in a known initial state when they turn it on. Figure 3.24 shows a black box view of the state machine.

Ben's next step is to sketch the *state transition diagram*, shown in Figure 3.25, to indicate all the possible states of the system and the transitions between these states. When the system is reset, the lights are green on Academic Ave. and red on Bravado Blvd. Every 5 seconds, the controller examines the traffic pattern and decides what to do next. As long

Figure 3.23 Campus map

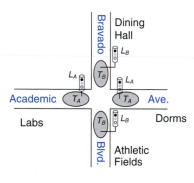

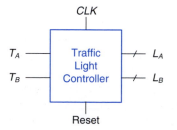

Figure 3.24 Black box view of finite state machine

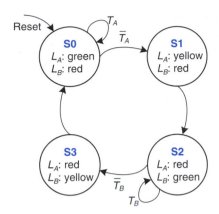

Figure 3.25 State transition diagram

as traffic is present on Academic Ave., the lights do not change. When there is no longer traffic on Academic Ave., the light on Academic Ave. becomes yellow for 5 seconds before it turns red and Bravado Blvd.'s light turns green. Similarly, the Bravado Blvd. light remains green as long as traffic is present on the boulevard, then turns yellow and eventually red.

In a state transition diagram, circles represent states and arcs represent transitions between states. The transitions take place on the rising edge of the clock; we do not bother to show the clock on the diagram, because it is always present in a synchronous sequential circuit. Moreover, the clock simply controls when the transitions should occur, whereas the diagram indicates which transitions occur. The arc labeled Reset pointing from outer space into state S0 indicates that the system should enter that state upon reset, regardless of what previous state it was in. If a state has multiple arcs leaving it, the arcs are labeled to show what input triggers each transition. For example, when in state S0, the system will remain in that state if T_A is TRUE and move to S1 if T_A is FALSE. If a state has a single arc leaving it, that transition always occurs regardless of the inputs. For example, when in state S1, the system will always move to S2. The value that the outputs have while in a particular state are indicated in the state. For example, while in state S2, L_A is red and L_B is green.

Ben rewrites the state transition diagram as a *state transition table* (Table 3.1), which indicates, for each state and input, what the next state, S', should be. Note that the table uses don't care symbols (X) whenever the next state does not depend on a particular input. Also note that Reset is omitted from the table. Instead, we use resettable flip-flops that always go to state S0 on reset, independent of the inputs.

The state transition diagram is abstract in that it uses states labeled {S0, S1, S2, S3} and outputs labeled {red, yellow, green}. To build a real circuit, the states and outputs must be assigned *binary encodings*. Ben chooses the simple encodings given in Tables 3.2 and 3.3. Each state and each output is encoded with two bits: $S_{1:0}$, $L_{A1:0}$, and $L_{B1:0}$.

Table 3.1 State transition table

Current State S	Inputs T_A	T_B	Next State S'
S0	0	X	S1
S0	1	X	S0
S1	X	X	S2
S2	X	0	S3
S2	X	1	S2
S3	X	X	S0

Table 3.2 State encoding

State	Encoding $S_{1:0}$
S0	00
S1	01
S2	10
S3	11

Table 3.3 Output encoding

Output	Encoding $L_{1:0}$
green	00
yellow	01
red	10

Ben updates the state transition table to use these binary encodings, as shown in Table 3.4. The revised state transition table is a truth table specifying the next state logic. It defines next state, S', as a function of the current state, S, and the inputs. The revised output table is a truth table specifying the output logic. It defines the outputs, L_A and L_B, as functions of the current state, S.

From this table, it is straightforward to read off the Boolean equations for the next state in sum-of-products form.

$$S'_1 = \overline{S}_1 S_0 + S_1 \overline{S}_0 \overline{T}_B + S_1 \overline{S}_0 T_B$$
$$S'_0 = \overline{S}_1 \overline{S}_0 \overline{T}_A + S_1 \overline{S}_0 \overline{T}_B \tag{3.1}$$

The equations can be simplified using Karnaugh maps, but often doing it by inspection is easier. For example, the T_B and $\overline{T}_B$ terms in the S'_1 equation are clearly redundant. Thus S'_1 reduces to an XOR operation. Equation 3.2 gives the *next state equations*.

Table 3.4 State transition table with binary encodings

Current State S_1	S_0	Inputs T_A	T_B	Next State S'_1	S'_0
0	0	0	X	0	1
0	0	1	X	0	0
0	1	X	X	1	0
1	0	X	0	1	1
1	0	X	1	1	0
1	1	X	X	0	0

Table 3.5 Output table

Current State S_1	S_0	Outputs L_{A1}	L_{A0}	L_{B1}	L_{B0}
0	0	0	0	1	0
0	1	0	1	1	0
1	0	1	0	0	0
1	1	1	0	0	1

$$S_1' = S_1 \oplus S_0$$
$$S_0' = \overline{S}_1 \overline{S}_0 \overline{T}_A + S_1 \overline{S}_0 \overline{T}_B \qquad (3.2)$$

Similarly, Ben writes an *output table* (Table 3.5) indicating, for each state, what the output should be in that state. Again, it is straightforward to read off and simplify the Boolean equations for the outputs. For example, observe that L_{A1} is TRUE only on the rows where S_1 is TRUE.

$$L_{A1} = S_1$$
$$L_{A0} = \overline{S}_1 S_0$$
$$L_{B1} = \overline{S}_1 \qquad (3.3)$$
$$L_{B0} = S_1 S_0$$

Finally, Ben sketches his Moore FSM in the form of Figure 3.22(a). First, he draws the 2-bit state register, as shown in Figure 3.26(a). On each clock edge, the state register copies the next state, $S'_{1:0}$, to become the state, $S_{1:0}$. The state register receives a synchronous or asynchronous reset to initialize the FSM at startup. Then, he draws the next state logic, based on Equation 3.2, which computes the next state, based on the current state and inputs, as shown in Figure 3.26(b). Finally, he draws the output logic, based on Equation 3.3, which computes the outputs based on the current state, as shown in Figure 3.26(c).

Figure 3.27 shows a timing diagram illustrating the traffic light controller going through a sequence of states. The diagram shows CLK, Reset, the inputs T_A and T_B, next state S', state S, and outputs L_A and L_B. Arrows indicate causality; for example, changing the state causes the outputs to change, and changing the inputs causes the next state to change. Dashed lines indicate the rising edge of CLK when the state changes.

The clock has a 5-second period, so the traffic lights change at most once every 5 seconds. When the finite state machine is first turned on, its state is unknown, as indicated by the question marks. Therefore, the system should be reset to put it into a known state. In this timing diagram,

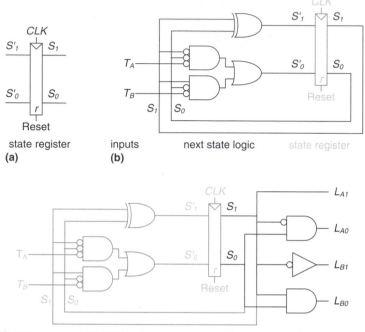

This schematic uses some AND gates with bubbles on the inputs. They might be constructed with AND gates and input inverters, with NOR gates and inverters for the non-bubbled inputs, or with some other combination of gates. The best choice depends on the particular implementation technology.

Figure 3.26 State machine circuit for traffic light controller

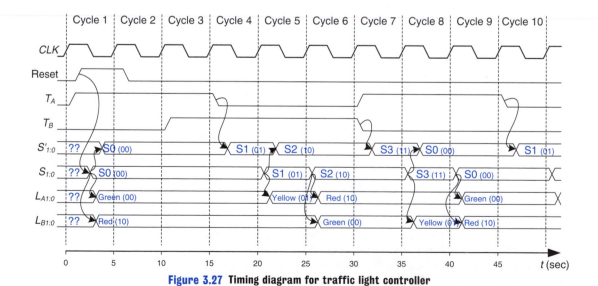

Figure 3.27 Timing diagram for traffic light controller

S immediately resets to S0, indicating that asynchronously resettable flip-flops are being used. In state S0, light L_A is green and light L_B is red.

In this example, traffic arrives immediately on Academic Ave. Therefore, the controller remains in state S0, keeping L_A green even though traffic arrives on Bravado Blvd. and starts waiting. After 15 seconds, the traffic on Academic Ave. has all passed through and T_A falls. At the following clock edge, the controller moves to state S1, turning L_A yellow. In another 5 seconds, the controller proceeds to state S2 in which L_A turns red and L_B turns green. The controller waits in state S2 until all the traffic on Bravado Blvd. has passed through. It then proceeds to state S3, turning L_B yellow. 5 seconds later, the controller enters state S0, turning L_B red and L_A green. The process repeats.

Despite Ben's best efforts, students don't pay attention to traffic lights and collisions continue to occur. The Dean of Students next asks him to design a catapult to throw engineering students directly from their dorm roofs through the open windows of the lab, bypassing the troublesome intersection all together. But that is the subject of another textbook.

3.4.2 State Encodings

In the previous example, the state and output encodings were selected arbitrarily. A different choice would have resulted in a different circuit. A natural question is how to determine the encoding that produces the circuit with the fewest logic gates or the shortest propagation delay. Unfortunately, there is no simple way to find the best encoding except to try all possibilities, which is infeasible when the number of states is large. However, it is often possible to choose a good encoding by inspection, so that related states or outputs share bits. Computer-aided design (CAD) tools are also good at searching the set of possible encodings and selecting a reasonable one.

One important decision in state encoding is the choice between binary encoding and one-hot encoding. With *binary encoding*, as was used in the traffic light controller example, each state is represented as a binary number. Because K binary numbers can be represented by $\log_2 K$ bits, a system with K states only needs $\log_2 K$ bits of state.

In *one-hot encoding*, a separate bit of state is used for each state. It is called one-hot because only one bit is "hot" or TRUE at any time. For example, a one-hot encoded FSM with three states would have state encodings of 001, 010, and 100. Each bit of state is stored in a flip-flop, so one-hot encoding requires more flip-flops than binary encoding. However, with one-hot encoding, the next-state and output logic is often simpler, so fewer gates are required. The best encoding choice depends on the specific FSM.

Example 3.6 FSM STATE ENCODING

A *divide-by-N counter* has one output and no inputs. The output Y is HIGH for one clock cycle out of every N. In other words, the output divides the frequency of the clock by N. The waveform and state transition diagram for a divide-by-3 counter is shown in Figure 3.28. Sketch circuit designs for such a counter using binary and one-hot state encodings.

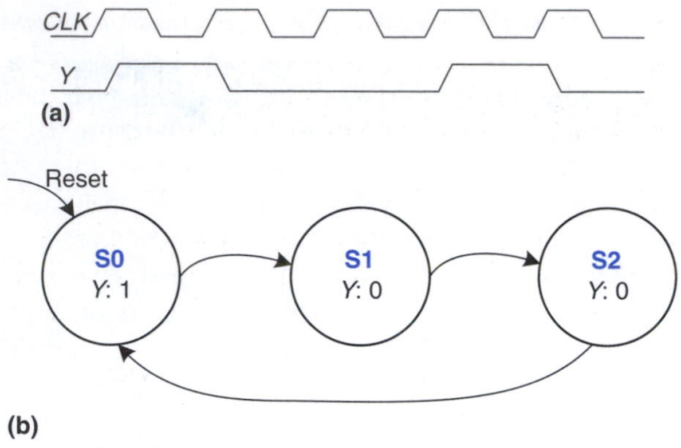

Figure 3.28 Divide-by-3 counter (a) waveform and (b) state transition diagram

Table 3.6 Divide-by-3 counter state transition table

Current State	Next State
S0	S1
S1	S2
S2	S0

Table 3.7 Divide-by-3 counter output table

Current State	Output
S0	1
S1	0
S2	0

Solution: Tables 3.6 and 3.7 show the abstract state transition and output tables before encoding.

Table 3.8 compares binary and one-hot encodings for the three states.

The binary encoding uses two bits of state. Using this encoding, the state transition table is shown in Table 3.9. Note that there are no inputs; the next state depends only on the current state. The output table is left as an exercise to the reader. The next-state and output equations are:

$$S_1' = \overline{S}_1 S_0$$
$$S_0' = \overline{S}_1 \overline{S}_0 \tag{3.4}$$

$$Y = \overline{S}_1 \overline{S}_0 \tag{3.5}$$

The one-hot encoding uses three bits of state. The state transition table for this encoding is shown in Table 3.10 and the output table is again left as an exercise to the reader. The next-state and output equations are as follows:

$$S_2' = S_1$$
$$S_1' = S_0 \tag{3.6}$$
$$S_0' = S_2$$

$$Y = S_0 \tag{3.7}$$

Figure 3.29 shows schematics for each of these designs. Note that the hardware for the binary encoded design could be optimized to share the same gate for Y and S'_0. Also observe that the one-hot encoding requires both settable (s) and resettable (r) flip-flops to initialize the machine to S0 on reset. The best implementation choice depends on the relative cost of gates and flip-flops, but the one-hot design is usually preferable for this specific example.

A related encoding is the *one-cold* encoding, in which K states are represented with K bits, exactly one of which is FALSE.

Table 3.8 Binary and one-hot encodings for divide-by-3 counter

State	Binary Encoding			One-Hot Encoding	
	S_2	S_1	S_0	S_1	S_0
S0	0	0	1	0	1
S1	0	1	0	1	0
S2	1	0	0	0	0

Table 3.9 State transition table with binary encoding

Current State		Next State	
S_1	S_0	S'_1	S'_0
0	0	0	1
0	1	1	0
1	0	0	0

Table 3.10 State transition table with one-hot encoding

Current State			Next State		
S_2	S_1	S_0	S'_2	S'_1	S'_0
0	0	1	0	1	0
0	1	0	1	0	0
1	0	0	0	0	1

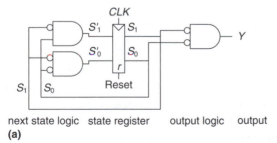

next state logic   state register   output logic   output
(a)

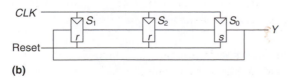

(b)

Figure 3.29 Divide-by-3 circuits for (a) binary and (b) one-hot encodings

3.4.3 Moore and Mealy Machines

So far, we have shown examples of Moore machines, in which the output depends only on the state of the system. Hence, in state transition diagrams for Moore machines, the outputs are labeled in the circles. Recall that Mealy machines are much like Moore machines, but the outputs can depend on inputs as well as the current state. Hence, in state transition diagrams for Mealy machines, the outputs are labeled on the arcs instead of in the circles. The block of combinational logic that computes the outputs uses the current state and inputs, as was shown in Figure 3.22(b).

An easy way to remember the difference between the two types of finite state machines is that a Moore machine typically has *more* states than a Mealy machine for a given problem.

Example 3.7 MOORE VERSUS MEALY MACHINES

Alyssa P. Hacker owns a pet robotic snail with an FSM brain. The snail crawls from left to right along a paper tape containing a sequence of 1's and 0's. On each clock cycle, the snail crawls to the next bit. The snail smiles when the last four bits that it has crawled over are, from left to right, 1101. Design the FSM to compute when the snail should smile. The input A is the bit underneath the snail's antennae. The output Y is TRUE when the snail smiles. Compare Moore and Mealy state machine designs. Sketch a timing diagram for each machine showing the input, states, and output as your snail crawls along the sequence 111011010.

Solution: The Moore machine requires five states, as shown in Figure 3.30(a). Convince yourself that the state transition diagram is correct. In particular, why is there an arc from S4 to S2 when the input is 1?

In comparison, the Mealy machine requires only four states, as shown in Figure 3.30(b). Each arc is labeled as A/Y. A is the value of the input that causes that transition, and Y is the corresponding output.

Tables 3.11 and 3.12 show the state transition and output tables for the Moore machine. The Moore machine requires at least three bits of state. Consider using a binary state encoding: S0 = 000, S1 = 001, S2 = 010, S3 = 011, and S4 = 100. Tables 3.13 and 3.14 rewrite the state transition and output tables with these encodings (These four tables follow on page 128).

From these tables, we find the next state and output equations by inspection. Note that these equations are simplified using the fact that states 101, 110, and 111 do not exist. Thus, the corresponding next state and output for the non-existent states are don't cares (not shown in the tables). We use the don't cares to minimize our equations.

$$S_2' = S_1 S_0 A$$
$$S_1' = \overline{S}_1 S_0 A + S_1 \overline{S}_0 + S_2 A \qquad (3.8)$$
$$S_0' = \overline{S}_2 \overline{S}_1 \overline{S}_0\, A + S_1 \overline{S}_0 \overline{A}$$

$$Y = S_2 \tag{3.9}$$

Table 3.15 shows the combined state transition and output table for the Mealy machine. The Mealy machine requires at least two bits of state. Consider using a binary state encoding: $S0 = 00$, $S1 = 01$, $S2 = 10$, and $S3 = 11$. Table 3.16 rewrites the state transition and output table with these encodings.

From these tables, we find the next state and output equations by inspection.

$$S_1' = S_1\overline{S}_0 + \overline{S}_1 S_0 A$$
$$S_0' = \overline{S}_1 \overline{S}_0 A + S_1 \overline{S}_0 \overline{A} + S_1 S_0 A \tag{3.10}$$

$$Y = S_1 S_0 A \tag{3.11}$$

The Moore and Mealy machine schematics are shown in Figure 3.31(a) and 3.31(b), respectively.

The timing diagrams for the Moore and Mealy machines are shown in Figure 3.32 (see page 131). The two machines follow a different sequence of states. Moreover, the Mealy machine's output rises a cycle sooner because it responds to the input rather than waiting for the state change. If the Mealy output were delayed through a flip-flop, it would match the Moore output. When choosing your FSM design style, consider when you want your outputs to respond.

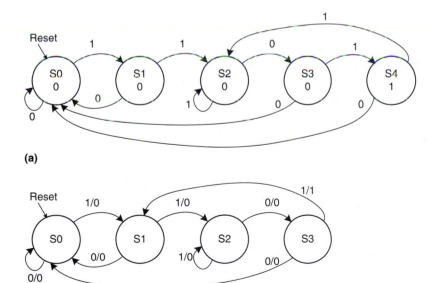

(a)

(b)

Figure 3.30 FSM state transition diagrams: (a) Moore machine, (b) Mealy machine

Table 3.11 Moore state transition table

Current State S	Input A	Next State S'
S0	0	S0
S0	1	S1
S1	0	S0
S1	1	S2
S2	0	S3
S2	1	S2
S3	0	S0
S3	1	S4
S4	0	S0
S4	1	S2

Table 3.12 Moore output table

Current State S	Output Y
S0	0
S1	0
S2	0
S3	0
S4	1

Table 3.13 Moore state transition table with state encodings

S_2	S_1	S_0	Input A	S'_2	S'_1	S'_0
0	0	0	0	0	0	0
0	0	0	1	0	0	1
0	0	1	0	0	0	0
0	0	1	1	0	1	0
0	1	0	0	0	1	1
0	1	0	1	0	1	0
0	1	1	0	0	0	0
0	1	1	1	1	0	0
1	0	0	0	0	0	0
1	0	0	1	0	1	0

Table 3.14 Moore output table with state encodings

S_2	S_1	S_0	Output Y
0	0	0	0
0	0	1	0
0	1	0	0
0	1	1	0
1	0	0	1

Table 3.15 Mealy state transition and output table

Current State S	Input A	Next State S'	Output Y
S0	0	S0	0
S0	1	S1	0
S1	0	S0	0
S1	1	S2	0
S2	0	S3	0
S2	1	S2	0
S3	0	S0	0
S3	1	S1	1

Table 3.16 Mealy state transition and output table with state encodings

Current State		Input	Next State		Output
S_1	S_0	A	S'_1	S'_0	Y
0	0	0	0	0	0
0	0	1	0	1	0
0	1	0	0	0	0
0	1	1	1	0	0
1	0	0	1	1	0
1	0	1	1	0	0
1	1	0	0	0	0
1	1	1	0	1	1

3.4.4 Factoring State Machines

Designing complex FSMs is often easier if they can be broken down into multiple interacting simpler state machines such that the output of some machines is the input of others. This application of hierarchy and modularity is called *factoring* of state machines.

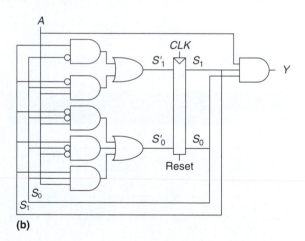

Figure 3.31 FSM schematics for (a) Moore and (b) Mealy machines

Example 3.8 UNFACTORED AND FACTORED STATE MACHINES

Modify the traffic light controller from Section 3.4.1 to have a parade mode, which keeps the Bravado Boulevard light green while spectators and the band march to football games in scattered groups. The controller receives two more inputs: P and R. Asserting P for at least one cycle enters parade mode. Asserting R for at least one cycle leaves parade mode. When in parade mode, the controller proceeds through its usual sequence until L_B turns green, then remains in that state with L_B green until parade mode ends.

First, sketch a state transition diagram for a single FSM, as shown in Figure 3.33(a). Then, sketch the state transition diagrams for two interacting FSMs, as

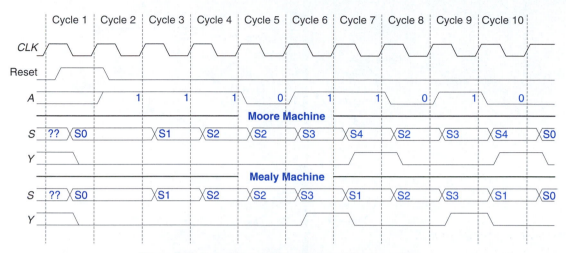

Figure 3.32 Timing diagrams for Moore and Mealy machines

shown in Figure 3.33(b). The Mode FSM asserts the output M when it is in parade mode. The Lights FSM controls the lights based on M and the traffic sensors, T_A and T_B.

Solution: Figure 3.34(a) shows the single FSM design. States S0 to S3 handle normal mode. States S4 to S7 handle parade mode. The two halves of the diagram are almost identical, but in parade mode, the FSM remains in S6 with a green light on Bravado Blvd. The P and R inputs control movement between these two halves. The FSM is messy and tedious to design. Figure 3.34(b) shows the factored FSM design. The mode FSM has two states to track whether the lights are in normal or parade mode. The Lights FSM is modified to remain in S2 while M is TRUE.

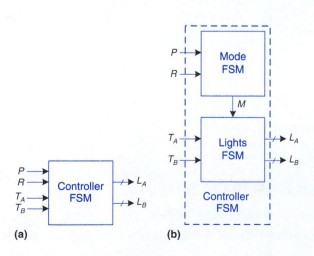

Figure 3.33 (a) single and (b) factored designs for modified traffic light controller FSM

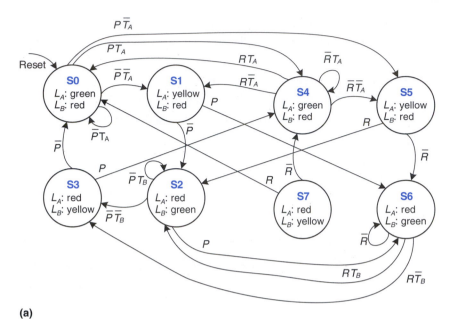

Figure 3.34 State transition diagrams: (a) unfactored, (b) factored

(a)

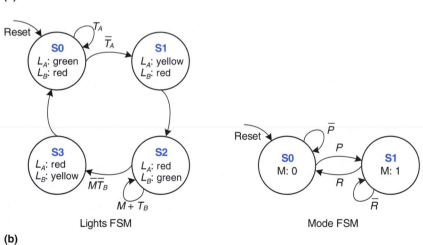

(b)

3.4.5 FSM Review

Finite state machines are a powerful way to systematically design sequential circuits from a written specification. Use the following procedure to design an FSM:

▶ Identify the inputs and outputs.

▶ Sketch a state transition diagram.

- For a Moore machine:
  - Write a state transition table.
  - Write an output table.

- For a Mealy machine:
  - Write a combined state transition and output table.

- Select state encodings—your selection affects the hardware design.

- Write Boolean equations for the next state and output logic.

- Sketch the circuit schematic.

We will repeatedly use FSMs to design complex digital systems throughout this book.

3.5 TIMING OF SEQUENTIAL LOGIC

Recall that a flip-flop copies the input D to the output Q on the rising edge of the clock. This process is called *sampling* D on the clock edge. If D is *stable* at either 0 or 1 when the clock rises, this behavior is clearly defined. But what happens if D is changing at the same time the clock rises?

This problem is similar to that faced by a camera when snapping a picture. Imagine photographing a frog jumping from a lily pad into the lake. If you take the picture before the jump, you will see a frog on a lily pad. If you take the picture after the jump, you will see ripples in the water. But if you take it just as the frog jumps, you may see a blurred image of the frog stretching from the lily pad into the water. A camera is characterized by its *aperture time*, during which the object must remain still for a sharp image to be captured. Similarly, a sequential element has an aperture time around the clock edge, during which the input must be stable for the flip-flop to produce a well-defined output.

The aperture of a sequential element is defined by a *setup* time and a *hold* time, before and after the clock edge, respectively. Just as the static discipline limited us to using logic levels outside the forbidden zone, the *dynamic discipline* limits us to using signals that change outside the aperture time. By taking advantage of the dynamic discipline, we can think of time in discrete units called clock cycles, just as we think of signal levels as discrete 1's and 0's. A signal may glitch and oscillate wildly for some bounded amount of time. Under the dynamic discipline, we are concerned only about its final value at the end of the clock cycle, after it has settled to a stable value. Hence, we can simply write $A[n]$, the value of signal A at the end of the nth clock cycle, where n is an integer, rather than $A(t)$, the value of A at some instant t, where t is any real number.

The clock period has to be long enough for all signals to settle. This sets a limit on the speed of the system. In real systems, the clock does not reach all flip-flops at precisely the same time. This variation in time, called clock skew, further increases the necessary clock period.

Sometimes it is impossible to satisfy the dynamic discipline, especially when interfacing with the real world. For example, consider a circuit with an input coming from a button. A monkey might press the button just as the clock rises. This can result in a phenomenon called metastability, where the flip-flop captures a value partway between 0 and 1 that can take an unlimited amount of time to resolve into a good logic value. The solution to such asynchronous inputs is to use a synchronizer, which has a very small (but nonzero) probability of producing an illegal logic value.

We expand on all of these ideas in the rest of this section.

3.5.1 The Dynamic Discipline

So far, we have focused on the functional specification of sequential circuits. Recall that a synchronous sequential circuit, such as a flip-flop or FSM, also has a timing specification, as illustrated in Figure 3.35. When the clock rises, the output (or outputs) may start to change after the clock-to-Q *contamination delay, t_{ccq},* and must definitely settle to the final value within the clock-to-Q *propagation delay, t_{pcq}.* These represent the fastest and slowest delays through the circuit, respectively. For the circuit to sample its input correctly, the input (or inputs) must have stabilized at least some *setup time, t_{setup},* before the rising edge of the clock and must remain stable for at least some *hold time, t_{hold},* after the rising edge of the clock. The sum of the setup and hold times is called the *aperture time* of the circuit, because it is the total time for which the input must remain stable.

The *dynamic discipline* states that the inputs of a synchronous sequential circuit must be stable during the setup and hold aperture time around the clock edge. By imposing this requirement, we guarantee that the flip-flops sample signals while they are not changing. Because we are concerned only about the final values of the inputs at the time they are sampled, we can treat signals as discrete in time as well as in logic levels.

Figure 3.35 Timing specification for synchronous sequential circuit

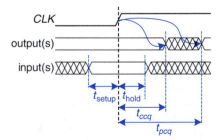

3.5.2 System Timing

The *clock period* or *cycle time*, T_c, is the time between rising edges of a repetitive clock signal. Its reciprocal, $f_c = 1/T_c$, is the *clock frequency*. All else being the same, increasing the clock frequency increases the work that a digital system can accomplish per unit time. Frequency is measured in units of Hertz (Hz), or cycles per second: 1 megahertz (MHz) = 10^6 Hz, and 1 gigahertz (GHz) = 10^9 Hz.

Figure 3.36(a) illustrates a generic path in a synchronous sequential circuit whose clock period we wish to calculate. On the rising edge of the clock, register R1 produces output (or outputs) Q1. These signals enter a block of combinational logic, producing D2, the input (or inputs) to register R2. The timing diagram in Figure 3.36(b) shows that each output signal may start to change a contamination delay after its input change and settles to the final value within a propagation delay after its input settles. The gray arrows represent the contamination delay through R1 and the combinational logic, and the blue arrows represent the propagation delay through R1 and the combinational logic. We analyze the timing constraints with respect to the setup and hold time of the second register, R2.

In the three decades from when one of the authors' families bought an Apple II+ computer to the present time of writing, microprocessor clock frequencies have increased from 1 MHz to several GHz, a factor of more than 1000. This speedup partially explains the revolutionary changes computers have made in society.

Setup Time Constraint

Figure 3.37 is the timing diagram showing only the maximum delay through the path, indicated by the blue arrows. To satisfy the setup time of R2, D2 must settle no later than the setup time before the next clock edge.

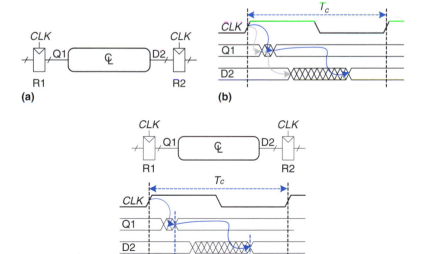

Figure 3.36 Path between registers and timing diagram

Figure 3.37 Maximum delay for setup time constraint

Hence, we find an equation for the minimum clock period:

$$T_c \geq t_{\overline{pcq}} + t_{pd} + t_{\text{setup}} \quad\quad (3.12)$$

In commercial designs, the clock period is often dictated by the Director of Engineering or by the marketing department (to ensure a competitive product). Moreover, the flip-flop clock-to-Q propagation delay and setup time, t_{pcq} and t_{setup}, are specified by the manufacturer. Hence, we rearrange Equation 3.12 to solve for the maximum propagation delay through the combinational logic, which is usually the only variable under the control of the individual designer.

$$t_{pd} \leq T_c - (t_{pcq} + t_{\text{setup}}) \quad\quad (3.13)$$

The term in parentheses, $t_{pcq} + t_{\text{setup}}$, is called the *sequencing overhead*. Ideally, the entire cycle time, T_c, would be available for useful computation in the combinational logic, t_{pd}. However, the sequencing overhead of the flip-flop cuts into this time. Equation 3.13 is called the *setup time constraint* or *max-delay constraint*, because it depends on the setup time and limits the maximum delay through combinational logic.

If the propagation delay through the combinational logic is too great, D2 may not have settled to its final value by the time R2 needs it to be stable and samples it. Hence, R2 may sample an incorrect result or even an illegal logic level, a level in the forbidden region. In such a case, the circuit will malfunction. The problem can be solved by increasing the clock period or by redesigning the combinational logic to have a shorter propagation delay.

Hold Time Constraint

The register R2 in Figure 3.36(a) also has a *hold time constraint*. Its input, D2, must not change until some time, t_{hold}, after the rising edge of the clock. According to Figure 3.38, D2 might change as soon as $t_{ccq} + t_{cd}$ after the rising edge of the clock.

Figure 3.38 Minimum delay for hold time constraint

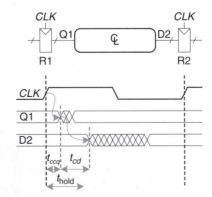

Hence, we find

$$t_{ccq} + t_{cd} \geq t_{hold} \qquad (3.14)$$

Again, t_{ccq} and t_{hold} are characteristics of the flip-flop that are usually outside the designer's control. Rearranging, we can solve for the minimum contamination delay through the combinational logic:

$$t_{cd} \geq t_{hold} - t_{ccq} \qquad (3.15)$$

Equation 3.15 is also called the *min-delay constraint* because it limits the minimum delay through combinational logic.

We have assumed that any logic elements can be connected to each other without introducing timing problems. In particular, we would expect that two flip-flops may be directly cascaded as in Figure 3.39 without causing hold time problems.

In such a case, $t_{cd} = 0$ because there is no combinational logic between flip-flops. Substituting into Equation 3.15 yields the requirement that

$$t_{hold} \leq t_{ccq} \qquad (3.16)$$

Figure 3.39 Back-to-back flip-flops

In other words, a reliable flip-flop must have a hold time shorter than its contamination delay. Often, flip-flops are designed with $t_{hold} = 0$, so that Equation 3.16 is always satisfied. Unless noted otherwise, we will usually make that assumption and ignore the hold time constraint in this book.

Nevertheless, hold time constraints are critically important. If they are violated, the only solution is to increase the contamination delay through the logic, which requires redesigning the circuit. Unlike setup time constraints, they cannot be fixed by adjusting the clock period. Redesigning an integrated circuit and manufacturing the corrected design takes months and millions of dollars in today's advanced technologies, so *hold time violations* must be taken extremely seriously.

Putting It All Together

Sequential circuits have setup and hold time constraints that dictate the maximum and minimum delays of the combinational logic between flip-flops. Modern flip-flops are usually designed so that the minimum delay through the combinational logic is 0—that is, flip-flops can be placed back-to-back. The maximum delay constraint limits the number of consecutive gates on the critical path of a high-speed circuit, because a high clock frequency means a short clock period.

Example 3.9 TIMING ANALYSIS

Ben Bitdiddle designed the circuit in Figure 3.40. According to the data sheets for the components he is using, flip-flops have a clock-to-Q contamination delay

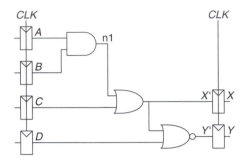

Figure 3.40 Sample circuit for timing analysis

of 30 ps and a propagation delay of 80 ps. They have a setup time of 50 ps and a hold time of 60 ps. Each logic gate has a propagation delay of 40 ps and a contamination delay of 25 ps. Help Ben determine the maximum clock frequency and whether any hold time violations could occur. This process is called *timing analysis.*

Solution: Figure 3.41(a) shows waveforms illustrating when the signals might change. The inputs, *A* to *D,* are registered, so they change shortly after *CLK* rises only.

The critical path occurs when $B = 1$, $C = 0$, $D = 0$, and *A* rises from 0 to 1, triggering n1 to rise, X' to rise and Y' to fall, as shown in Figure 3.41(b). This path involves three gate delays. For the critical path, we assume that each gate requires its full propagation delay. Y' must setup before the next rising edge of the *CLK*. Hence, the minimum cycle time is

$$T_c \ge t_{pcq} + 3\, t_{pd} + t_{\text{setup}} = 80 + 3 \times 40 + 50 = 250 \text{ ps} \qquad (3.17)$$

The maximum clock frequency is $f_c = 1/T_c = 4$ GHz.

A short path occurs when $A = 0$ and *C* rises, causing X' to rise, as shown in Figure 3.41(c). For the short path, we assume that each gate switches after only a contamination delay. This path involves only one gate delay, so it may occur after $t_{ccq} + t_{cd} = 30 + 25 = 55$ ps. But recall that the flip-flop has a hold time of 60 ps, meaning that X' must remain stable for 60 ps after the rising edge of *CLK* for the flip-flop to reliably sample its value. In this case, $X' = 0$ at the first rising edge of *CLK*, so we want the flip-flop to capture $X = 0$. Because X' did not hold stable long enough, the actual value of *X* is unpredictable. The circuit has a hold time violation and may behave erratically at any clock frequency.

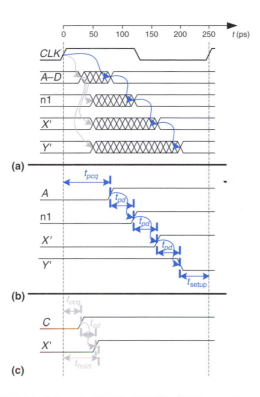

Figure 3.41 Timing diagram: (a) general case, (b) critical path, (c) short path

---

Example 3.10 FIXING HOLD TIME VIOLATIONS

Alyssa P. Hacker proposes to fix Ben's circuit by adding buffers to slow down the short paths, as shown in Figure 3.42. The buffers have the same delays as other gates. Determine the maximum clock frequency and whether any hold time problems could occur.

Solution: Figure 3.43 shows waveforms illustrating when the signals might change. The critical path from A to Y is unaffected, because it does not pass through any buffers. Therefore, the maximum clock frequency is still 4 GHz. However, the short paths are slowed by the contamination delay of the buffer. Now X' will not change until $t_{ccq} + 2t_{cd} = 30 + 2 \times 25 = 80$ ps. This is after the 60 ps hold time has elapsed, so the circuit now operates correctly.

This example had an unusually long hold time to illustrate the point of hold time problems. Most flip-flops are designed with $t_{hold} < t_{ccq}$ to avoid such problems. However, several high-performance microprocessors, including the Pentium 4, use an element called a *pulsed latch* in place of a flip-flop. The pulsed latch behaves like a flip-flop but has a short clock-to Q delay and a long hold time. In general, adding buffers can usually, but not always, solve hold time problems without slowing the critical path.

Figure 3.42 Corrected circuit to fix hold time problem

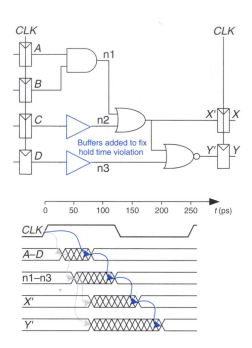

Figure 3.43 Timing diagram with buffers to fix hold time problem

3.5.3 Clock Skew*

In the previous analysis, we assumed that the clock reaches all registers at exactly the same time. In reality, there is some variation in this time. This variation in clock edges is called *clock skew*. For example, the wires from the clock source to different registers may be of different lengths, resulting in slightly different delays, as shown in Figure 3.44. Noise also results in different delays. Clock gating, described in Section 3.2.5, further delays the clock. If some clocks are gated and others are not, there will be substantial skew between the gated and ungated clocks. In

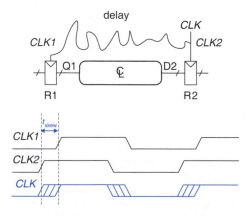

Figure 3.44 Clock skew caused by wire delay

Figure 3.44, *CLK2* is *early* with respect to *CLK1*, because the clock wire between the two registers follows a scenic route. If the clock had been routed differently, *CLK1* might have been early instead. When doing timing analysis, we consider the worst-case scenario, so that we can guarantee that the circuit will work under all circumstances.

Figure 3.45 adds skew to the timing diagram from Figure 3.36. The heavy clock line indicates the latest time at which the clock signal might reach any register; the hashed lines show that the clock might arrive up to t_{skew} earlier.

First, consider the setup time constraint shown in Figure 3.46. In the worst case, R1 receives the latest skewed clock and R2 receives the earliest skewed clock, leaving as little time as possible for data to propagate between the registers.

The data propagates through the register and combinational logic and must setup before R2 samples it. Hence, we conclude that

$$T_c \geq t_{pcq} + t_{pd} + t_{\text{setup}} + t_{\text{skew}} \tag{3.18}$$

$$t_{pd} \leq T_c - (t_{pcq} + t_{\text{setup}} + t_{\text{skew}}) \tag{3.19}$$

Next, consider the hold time constraint shown in Figure 3.47. In the worst case, R1 receives an early skewed clock, *CLK1*, and R2 receives a late skewed clock, *CLK2*. The data zips through the register

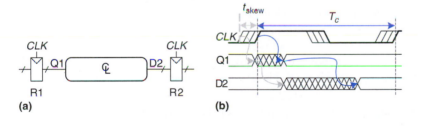

Figure 3.45 Timing diagram with clock skew

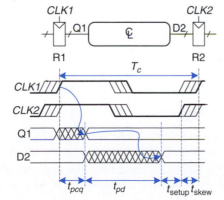

Figure 3.46 Setup time constraint with clock skew

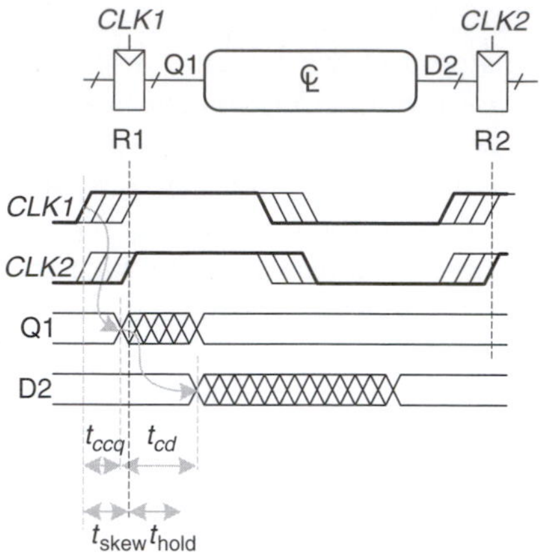

Figure 3.47 Hold time constraint with clock skew

and combinational logic but must not arrive until a hold time after the late clock. Thus, we find that

$$t_{ccq} + t_{cd} \geq t_{hold} + t_{skew} \tag{3.20}$$

$$t_{cd} \geq t_{hold} + t_{skew} - t_{ccq} \tag{3.21}$$

In summary, clock skew effectively increases both the setup time and the hold time. It adds to the sequencing overhead, reducing the time available for useful work in the combinational logic. It also increases the required minimum delay through the combinational logic. Even if $t_{hold} = 0$, a pair of back-to-back flip-flops will violate Equation 3.21 if $t_{skew} > t_{ccq}$. To prevent serious hold time failures, designers must not permit too much clock skew. Sometimes flip-flops are intentionally designed to be particularly slow (i.e., large t_{ccq}), to prevent hold time problems even when the clock skew is substantial.

Example 3.11 TIMING ANALYSIS WITH CLOCK SKEW

Revisit Example 3.9 and assume that the system has 50 ps of clock skew.

Solution: The critical path remains the same, but the setup time is effectively increased by the skew. Hence, the minimum cycle time is

$$\begin{aligned} T_c &\geq t_{pcq} + 3t_{pd} + t_{setup} + t_{skew} \\ &= 80 + 3 \times 40 + 50 + 50 = 300 \text{ ps} \end{aligned} \tag{3.22}$$

The maximum clock frequency is $f_c = 1/T_c = 3.33$ GHz.

The short path also remains the same at 55 ps. The hold time is effectively increased by the skew to $60 + 50 = 110$ ps, which is much greater than 55 ps. Hence, the circuit will violate the hold time and malfunction at any frequency. The circuit violated the hold time constraint even without skew. Skew in the system just makes the violation worse.

Example 3.12 FIXING HOLD TIME VIOLATIONS

Revisit Example 3.10 and assume that the system has 50 ps of clock skew.

Solution: The critical path is unaffected, so the maximum clock frequency remains 3.33 GHz.

The short path increases to 80 ps. This is still less than $t_{hold} + t_{skew} = 110$ ps, so the circuit still violates its hold time constraint.

To fix the problem, even more buffers could be inserted. Buffers would need to be added on the critical path as well, reducing the clock frequency. Alternatively, a better flip-flop with a shorter hold time might be used.

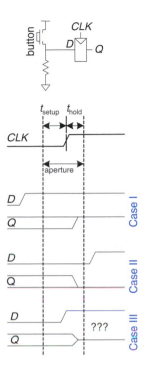

Figure 3.48 Input changing before, after, or during aperture

3.5.4 Metastability

As noted earlier, it is not always possible to guarantee that the input to a sequential circuit is stable during the aperture time, especially when the input arrives from the external world. Consider a button connected to the input of a flip-flop, as shown in Figure 3.48. When the button is not pressed, $D = 0$. When the button is pressed, $D = 1$. A monkey presses the button at some random time relative to the rising edge of CLK. We want to know the output Q after the rising edge of CLK. In Case I, when the button is pressed much before CLK, $Q = 1$.

In Case II, when the button is not pressed until long after CLK, $Q = 0$. But in Case III, when the button is pressed sometime between t_{setup} before CLK and t_{hold} after CLK, the input violates the dynamic discipline and the output is undefined.

Metastable State

In reality, when a flip-flop samples an input that is changing during its aperture, the output Q may momentarily take on a voltage between 0 and V_{DD} that is in the forbidden zone. This is called a *metastable* state. Eventually, the flip-flop will resolve the output to a *stable state* of either 0 or 1. However, the *resolution time* required to reach the stable state is unbounded.

The metastable state of a flip-flop is analogous to a ball on the summit of a hill between two valleys, as shown in Figure 3.49. The two valleys are stable states, because a ball in the valley will remain there as long as it is not disturbed. The top of the hill is called metastable because the ball would remain there if it were perfectly balanced. But because nothing is perfect, the ball will eventually roll to one side or the other. The time required for this change to occur depends on how nearly well balanced the ball originally was. Every bistable device has a metastable state between the two stable states.

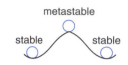

Figure 3.49 Stable and metastable states

Resolution Time

If a flip-flop input changes at a random time during the clock cycle, the resolution time, t_{res}, required to resolve to a stable state is also a random variable. If the input changes outside the aperture, then $t_{res} = t_{pcq}$. But if the input happens to change within the aperture, t_{res} can be substantially longer. Theoretical and experimental analyses (see Section 3.5.6) have shown that the probability that the resolution time, t_{res}, exceeds some arbitrary time, t, decreases exponentially with t:

$$ P(t_{res} > t) = \frac{T_0}{T_c} e^{-\frac{t}{\tau}} \tag{3.23} $$

where T_c is the clock period, and T_0 and τ are characteristic of the flip-flop. The equation is valid only for t substantially longer than t_{pcq}.

Intuitively, T_0/T_c describes the probability that the input changes at a bad time (i.e., during the aperture time); this probability decreases with the cycle time, T_c. τ is a time constant indicating how fast the flip-flop moves away from the metastable state; it is related to the delay through the cross-coupled gates in the flip-flop.

In summary, if the input to a bistable device such as a flip-flop changes during the aperture time, the output may take on a metastable value for some time before resolving to a stable 0 or 1. The amount of time required to resolve is unbounded, because for any finite time, t, the probability that the flip-flop is still metastable is nonzero. However, this probability drops off exponentially as t increases. Therefore, if we wait long enough, much longer than t_{pcq}, we can expect with exceedingly high probability that the flip-flop will reach a valid logic level.

3.5.5 Synchronizers

Asynchronous inputs to digital systems from the real world are inevitable. Human input is asynchronous, for example. If handled carelessly, these asynchronous inputs can lead to metastable voltages within the system, causing erratic system failures that are extremely difficult to track down and correct. The goal of a digital system designer should be to ensure that, given asynchronous inputs, the probability of encountering a metastable voltage is sufficiently small. "Sufficiently" depends on the context. For a digital cell phone, perhaps one failure in 10 years is acceptable, because the user can always turn the phone off and back on if it locks up. For a medical device, one failure in the expected life of the universe (10^{10} years) is a better target. To guarantee good logic levels, all asynchronous inputs should be passed through *synchronizers*.

A synchronizer, shown in Figure 3.50, is a device that receives an asynchronous input, *D*, and a clock, *CLK*. It produces an output, *Q*, within a bounded amount of time; the output has a valid logic level with extremely high probability. If *D* is stable during the aperture, *Q* should take on the same value as *D*. If *D* changes during the aperture, *Q* may take on either a HIGH or LOW value but must not be metastable.

Figure 3.51 shows a simple way to build a synchronizer out of two flip-flops. F1 samples *D* on the rising edge of *CLK*. If *D* is changing at that time, the output D2 may be momentarily metastable. If the clock period is long enough, D2 will, with high probability, resolve to a valid logic level before the end of the period. F2 then samples D2, which is now stable, producing a good output *Q*.

We say that a synchronizer *fails* if *Q*, the output of the synchronizer, becomes metastable. This may happen if D2 has not resolved to a valid level by the time it must setup at F2—that is, if $t_{res} > T_c - t_{setup}$. According to Equation 3.23, the probability of failure for a single input change at a random time is

$$P(\text{failure}) = \frac{T_0}{T_c} e^{-\frac{T_c - t_{setup}}{\tau}} \tag{3.24}$$

The probability of failure, *P*(failure), is the probability that the output, *Q*, will be metastable upon a single change in *D*. If *D* changes once per second, the probability of failure per second is just *P*(failure). However, if *D* changes *N* times per second, the probability of failure per second is *N* times as great:

$$P(\text{failure})/\text{sec} = N \frac{T_0}{T_c} e^{-\frac{T_c - t_{setup}}{\tau}} \tag{3.25}$$

Figure 3.50 Synchronizer symbol

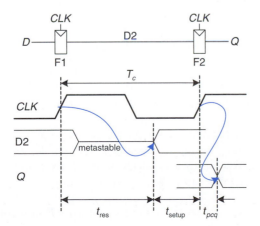

Figure 3.51 Simple synchronizer

System reliability is usually measured in *mean time between failures* (*MTBF*). As the name might suggest, MTBF is the average amount of time between failures of the system. It is the reciprocal of the probability that the system will fail in any given second

$$MTBF = \frac{1}{P(\text{failure})/\text{sec}} = \frac{T_c\, e^{\frac{T_c - t_{\text{setup}}}{\tau}}}{NT_0} \quad (3.26)$$

Equation 3.26 shows that the MTBF improves exponentially as the synchronizer waits for a longer time, T_c. For most systems, a synchronizer that waits for one clock cycle provides a safe MTBF. In exceptionally high-speed systems, waiting for more cycles may be necessary.

Example 3.13 SYNCHRONIZER FOR FSM INPUT

The traffic light controller FSM from Section 3.4.1 receives asynchronous inputs from the traffic sensors. Suppose that a synchronizer is used to guarantee stable inputs to the controller. Traffic arrives on average 0.2 times per second. The flip-flops in the synchronizer have the following characteristics: $\tau = 200$ ps, $T_0 = 150$ ps, and $t_{\text{setup}} = 500$ ps. How long must the synchronizer clock period be for the MTBF to exceed 1 year?

Solution: 1 year $\approx \pi \times 10^7$ seconds. Solve Equation 3.26.

$$\pi \times 10^7 = \frac{T_c e^{\frac{T_c - 500 \times 10^{-12}}{200 \times 10^{-12}}}}{(0.2)(150 \times 10^{-12})} \quad (3.27)$$

This equation has no closed form solution. However, it is easy enough to solve by guess and check. In a spreadsheet, try a few values of T_c and calculate the MTBF until discovering the value of T_c that gives an MTBF of 1 year: $T_c = 3.036$ ns.

3.5.6 Derivation of Resolution Time*

Equation 3.23 can be derived using a basic knowledge of circuit theory, differential equations, and probability. This section can be skipped if you are not interested in the derivation or if you are unfamiliar with the mathematics.

A flip-flop output will be metastable after some time, *t,* if the flip-flop samples a changing input (causing a metastable condition) and the output does not resolve to a valid level within that time after the clock edge. Symbolically, this can be expressed as

$$P(t_{res} > t) = P(\text{samples changing input}) \times P(\text{unresolved}) \quad (3.28)$$

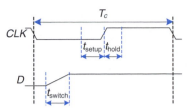

Figure 3.52 **Input timing**

We consider each probability term individually. The asynchronous input signal switches between 0 and 1 in some time, t_{switch}, as shown in Figure 3.52. The probability that the input changes during the aperture around the clock edge is

$$P(\text{samples changing input}) = \frac{t_{switch} + t_{setup} + t_{hold}}{T_c} \qquad (3.29)$$

If the flip-flop does enter metastability—that is, with probability P(samples changing input)—the time to resolve from metastability depends on the inner workings of the circuit. This resolution time determines P(unresolved), the probability that the flip-flop has not yet resolved to a valid logic level after a time t. The remainder of this section analyzes a simple model of a bistable device to estimate this probability.

A bistable device uses storage with positive feedback. Figure 3.53(a) shows this feedback implemented with a pair of inverters; this circuit's behavior is representative of most bistable elements. A pair of inverters behaves like a buffer. Let us model it as having the symmetric DC transfer characteristics shown in Figure 3.53(b), with a slope of G. The buffer can deliver only a finite amount of output current; we can model this as an output resistance, R. All real circuits also have some capacitance, C, that must be charged up. Charging the capacitor through the resistor causes an RC delay, preventing the buffer from switching instantaneously. Hence, the complete circuit model is shown in Figure 3.53(c), where $v_{out}(t)$ is the voltage of interest conveying the state of the bistable device.

The metastable point for this circuit is $v_{out}(t) = v_{in}(t) = V_{DD}/2$; if the circuit began at exactly that point, it would remain there indefinitely in the

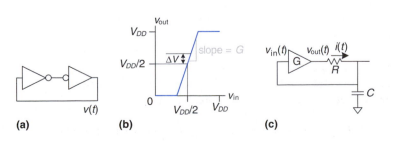

Figure 3.53 **Circuit model of bistable device**

absence of noise. Because voltages are continuous variables, the chance that the circuit will begin at exactly the metastable point is vanishingly small. However, the circuit might begin at time 0 near metastability at $v_{out}(0) = V_{DD}/2 + \Delta V$ for some small offset ΔV. In such a case, the positive feedback will eventually drive $v_{out}(t)$ to V_{DD} if $\Delta V > 0$ and to 0 if $\Delta V < 0$. The time required to reach V_{DD} or 0 is the resolution time of the bistable device.

The DC transfer characteristic is nonlinear, but it appears linear near the metastable point, which is the region of interest to us. Specifically, if $v_{in}(t) = V_{DD}/2 + \Delta V/G$, then $v_{out}(t) = V_{DD}/2 + \Delta V$ for small ΔV. The current through the resistor is $i(t) = (v_{out}(t) - v_{in}(t))/R$. The capacitor charges at a rate $dv_{in}(t)/dt = i(t)/C$. Putting these facts together, we find the governing equation for the output voltage.

$$\frac{dv_{out}(t)}{dt} = \frac{(G-1)}{RC}\left[v_{out}(t) - \frac{V_{DD}}{2}\right] \qquad (3.30)$$

This is a linear first-order differential equation. Solving it with the initial condition $v_{out}(0) = V_{DD}/2 + \Delta V$ gives

$$v_{out}(t) = \frac{V_{DD}}{2} + \Delta V e^{\frac{(G-1)t}{RC}} \qquad (3.31)$$

Figure 3.54 plots trajectories for $v_{out}(t)$ given various starting points. $v_{out}(t)$ moves exponentially away from the metastable point $V_{DD}/2$ until it saturates at V_{DD} or 0. The output voltage eventually resolves to 1 or 0. The amount of time this takes depends on the initial voltage offset (ΔV) from the metastable point $(V_{DD}/2)$.

Solving Equation 3.31 for the resolution time t_{res}, such that $v_{out}(t_{res}) = V_{DD}$ or 0, gives

$$|\Delta V| e^{\frac{(G-1)t_{res}}{RC}} = \frac{V_{DD}}{2} \qquad (3.32)$$

$$t_{res} = \frac{RC}{G-1} \ln\frac{V_{DD}}{2|\Delta V|} \qquad (3.33)$$

Figure 3.54 Resolution trajectories

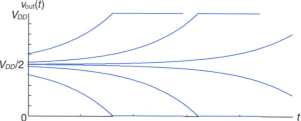

In summary, the resolution time increases if the bistable device has high resistance or capacitance that causes the output to change slowly. It decreases if the bistable device has high *gain*, G. The resolution time also increases logarithmically as the circuit starts closer to the metastable point ($\Delta V \rightarrow 0$).

Define τ as $\frac{RC}{G-1}$. Solving Equation 3.33 for ΔV finds the initial offset, ΔV_{res}, that gives a particular resolution time, t_{res}:

$$\Delta V_{res} = \frac{V_{DD}}{2} e^{-t_{res}/\tau} \qquad (3.34)$$

Suppose that the bistable device samples the input while it is changing. It measures a voltage, $v_{in}(0)$, which we will assume is uniformly distributed between 0 and V_{DD}. The probability that the output has not resolved to a legal value after time t_{res} depends on the probability that the initial offset is sufficiently small. Specifically, the initial offset on v_{out} must be less than ΔV_{res}, so the initial offset on v_{in} must be less than $\Delta V_{res}/G$. Then the probability that the bistable device samples the input at a time to obtain a sufficiently small initial offset is

$$P(\text{unresolved}) = P\left(\left|v_{in}(0) - \frac{V_{DD}}{2}\right| < \frac{\Delta V_{res}}{G}\right) = \frac{2\Delta V_{res}}{GV_{DD}} \qquad (3.35)$$

Putting this all together, the probability that the resolution time exceeds some time, t, is given by the following equation:

$$P\left(t_{res} > t\right) = \frac{t_{switch} + t_{setup} + t_{hold}}{GT_c} e^{-\frac{t}{\tau}} \qquad (3.36)$$

Observe that Equation 3.36 is in the form of Equation 3.23, where $T_0 = (t_{switch} + t_{setup} + t_{hold})/G$ and $\tau = RC/(G-1)$. In summary, we have derived Equation 3.23 and shown how T_0 and τ depend on physical properties of the bistable device.

3.6 PARALLELISM

The speed of a system is measured in latency and throughput of tokens moving through a system. We define a *token* to be a group of inputs that are processed to produce a group of outputs. The term conjures up the notion of placing subway tokens on a circuit diagram and moving them around to visualize data moving through the circuit. The *latency* of a system is the time required for one token to pass through the system from start to end. The *throughput* is the number of tokens that can be produced per unit time.

Example 3.14 COOKIE THROUGHPUT AND LATENCY

Ben Bitdiddle is throwing a milk and cookies party to celebrate the installation of his traffic light controller. It takes him 5 minutes to roll cookies and place them on his tray. It then takes 15 minutes for the cookies to bake in the oven. Once the cookies are baked, he starts another tray. What is Ben's throughput and latency for a tray of cookies?

Solution: In this example, a tray of cookies is a token. The latency is 1/3 hour per tray. The throughput is 3 trays/hour.

As you might imagine, the throughput can be improved by processing several tokens at the same time. This is called *parallelism,* and it comes in two forms: spatial and temporal. With *spatial parallelism,* multiple copies of the hardware are provided so that multiple tasks can be done at the same time. With *temporal parallelism,* a task is broken into stages, like an assembly line. Multiple tasks can be spread across the stages. Although each task must pass through all stages, a *different* task will be in each stage at any given time so multiple tasks can overlap. Temporal parallelism is commonly called *pipelining.* Spatial parallelism is sometimes just called parallelism, but we will avoid that naming convention because it is ambiguous.

Example 3.15 COOKIE PARALLELISM

Ben Bitdiddle has hundreds of friends coming to his party and needs to bake cookies faster. He is considering using spatial and/or temporal parallelism.

Spatial Parallelism: Ben asks Alyssa P. Hacker to help out. She has her own cookie tray and oven.

Temporal Parallelism: Ben gets a second cookie tray. Once he puts one cookie tray in the oven, he starts rolling cookies on the other tray rather than waiting for the first tray to bake.

What is the throughput and latency using spatial parallelism? Using temporal parallelism? Using both?

Solution: The latency is the time required to complete one task from start to finish. In all cases, the latency is 1/3 hour. If Ben starts with no cookies, the latency is the time needed for him to produce the first cookie tray.

The throughput is the number of cookie trays per hour. With spatial parallelism, Ben and Alyssa each complete one tray every 20 minutes. Hence, the throughput doubles, to 6 trays/hour. With temporal parallelism, Ben puts a new tray in the oven every 15 minutes, for a throughput of 4 trays/hour. These are illustrated in Figure 3.55.

If Ben and Alyssa use both techniques, they can bake 8 trays/hour.

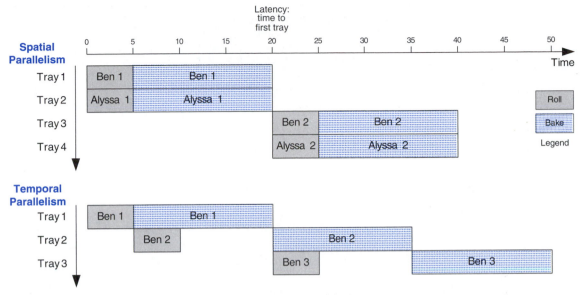

Figure 3.55 Spatial and temporal parallelism in the cookie kitchen

Consider a task with latency L. In a system with no parallelism, the throughput is $1/L$. In a spatially parallel system with N copies of the hardware, the throughput is N/L. In a temporally parallel system, the task is ideally broken into N steps, or stages, of equal length. In such a case, the throughput is also N/L, and only one copy of the hardware is required. However, as the cookie example showed, finding N steps of equal length is often impractical. If the longest step has a latency L_1, the pipelined throughput is $1/L_1$.

Pipelining (temporal parallelism) is particularly attractive because it speeds up a circuit without duplicating the hardware. Instead, registers are placed between blocks of combinational logic to divide the logic into shorter stages that can run with a faster clock. The registers prevent a token in one pipeline stage from catching up with and corrupting the token in the next stage.

Figure 3.56 shows an example of a circuit with no pipelining. It contains four blocks of logic between the registers. The critical path passes through blocks 2, 3, and 4. Assume that the register has a clock-to-Q propagation delay of 0.3 ns and a setup time of 0.2 ns. Then the cycle time is $T_c = 0.3 + 3 + 2 + 4 + 0.2 = 9.5$ ns. The circuit has a latency of 9.5 ns and a throughput of 1/9.5 ns = 105 MHz.

Figure 3.57 shows the same circuit partitioned into a two-stage pipeline by adding a register between blocks 3 and 4. The first stage has a minimum clock period of $0.3 + 3 + 2 + 0.2 = 5.5$ ns. The second

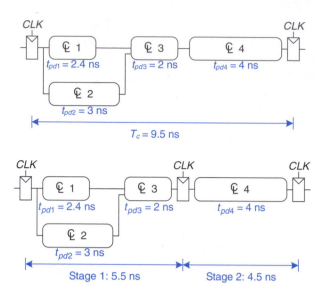

Figure 3.56 Circuit with no pipelining

Figure 3.57 Circuit with two-stage pipeline

stage has a minimum clock period of $0.3 + 4 + 0.2 = 4.5$ ns. The clock must be slow enough for all stages to work. Hence, $T_c = 5.5$ ns. The latency is two clock cycles, or 11 ns. The throughput is $1/5.5$ ns $= 182$ MHz. This example shows that, in a real circuit, pipelining with two stages almost doubles the throughput and slightly increases the latency. In comparison, ideal pipelining would exactly double the throughput at no penalty in latency. The discrepancy comes about because the circuit cannot be divided into two exactly equal halves and because the registers introduce more sequencing overhead.

Figure 3.58 shows the same circuit partitioned into a three-stage pipeline. Note that two more registers are needed to store the results of blocks 1 and 2 at the end of the first pipeline stage. The cycle time is now limited by the third stage to 4.5 ns. The latency is three cycles, or 13.5 ns. The throughput is $1/4.5$ ns $= 222$ MHz. Again, adding a pipeline stage improves throughput at the expense of some latency.

Although these techniques are powerful, they do not apply to all situations. The bane of parallelism is *dependencies*. If a current task is

Figure 3.58 Circuit with three-stage pipeline

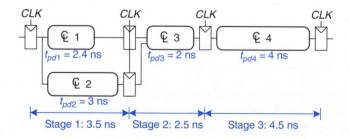

dependent on the result of a prior task, rather than just prior steps in the current task, the task cannot start until the prior task has completed. For example, if Ben wants to check that the first tray of cookies tastes good before he starts preparing the second, he has a dependency that prevents pipelining or parallel operation. Parallelism is one of the most important techniques for designing high-performance microprocessors. Chapter 7 discusses pipelining further and shows examples of handling dependencies.

3.7 SUMMARY

This chapter has described the analysis and design of sequential logic. In contrast to combinational logic, whose outputs depend only on the current inputs, sequential logic outputs depend on both current and prior inputs. In other words, sequential logic remembers information about prior inputs. This memory is called the state of the logic.

Sequential circuits can be difficult to analyze and are easy to design incorrectly, so we limit ourselves to a small set of carefully designed building blocks. The most important element for our purposes is the flip-flop, which receives a clock and an input, D, and produces an output, Q. The flip-flop copies D to Q on the rising edge of the clock and otherwise remembers the old state of Q. A group of flip-flops sharing a common clock is called a register. Flip-flops may also receive reset or enable control signals.

Although many forms of sequential logic exist, we discipline ourselves to use synchronous sequential circuits because they are easy to design. Synchronous sequential circuits consist of blocks of combinational logic separated by clocked registers. The state of the circuit is stored in the registers and updated only on clock edges.

Finite state machines are a powerful technique for designing sequential circuits. To design an FSM, first identify the inputs and outputs of the machine and sketch a state transition diagram, indicating the states and the transitions between them. Select an encoding for the states, and rewrite the diagram as a state transition table and output table, indicating the next state and output given the current state and input. From these tables, design the combinational logic to compute the next state and output, and sketch the circuit.

Synchronous sequential circuits have a timing specification including the clock-to-Q propagation and contamination delays, t_{pcq} and t_{ccq}, and the setup and hold times, t_{setup} and t_{hold}. For correct operation, their inputs must be stable during an aperture time that starts a setup time before the rising edge of the clock and ends a hold time after the rising edge of the clock. The minimum cycle time, T_c, of the system is equal to the propagation delay, t_{pd}, through the combinational logic plus

> Anyone who could invent logic whose outputs depend on future inputs would be fabulously wealthy!

$t_{pcq} + t_{\text{setup}}$ of the register. For correct operation, the contamination delay through the register and combinational logic must be greater than t_{hold}. Despite the common misconception to the contrary, hold time does not affect the cycle time.

Overall system performance is measured in latency and throughput. The latency is the time required for a token to pass from start to end. The throughput is the number of tokens that the system can process per unit time. Parallelism improves the system throughput.

Exercises

Exercise 3.1 Given the input waveforms shown in Figure 3.59, sketch the output, Q, of an SR latch.

Figure 3.59 Input waveform of SR latch

Exercise 3.2 Given the input waveforms shown in Figure 3.60, sketch the output, Q, of a D latch.

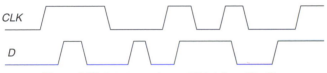

Figure 3.60 Input waveform of D latch or flip-flop

Exercise 3.3 Given the input waveforms shown in Figure 3.60, sketch the output, Q, of a D flip-flop.

Exercise 3.4 Is the circuit in Figure 3.61 combinational logic or sequential logic? Explain in a simple fashion what the relationship is between the inputs and outputs. What would you call this circuit?

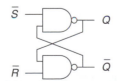

Figure 3.61 Mystery circuit

Exercise 3.5 Is the circuit in Figure 3.62 combinational logic or sequential logic? Explain in a simple fashion what the relationship is between the inputs and outputs. What would you call this circuit?

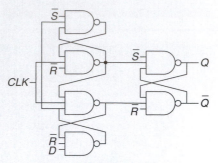

Figure 3.62 Mystery circuit

Exercise 3.6 The *toggle (T) flip-flop* has one input, *CLK*, and one output, *Q*. On each rising edge of *CLK*, *Q* toggles to the complement of its previous value. Draw a schematic for a T flip-flop using a D flip-flop and an inverter.

Exercise 3.7 A *JK flip-flop* receives a clock and two inputs, *J* and *K*. On the rising edge of the clock, it updates the output, *Q*. If *J* and *K* are both 0, *Q* retains its old value. If only *J* is 1, *Q* becomes 1. If only *K* is 1, *Q* becomes 0. If both *J* and *K* are 1, *Q* becomes the opposite of its present state.

(a)   Construct a JK flip-flop using a D flip-flop and some combinational logic.

(b)   Construct a D flip-flop using a JK flip-flop and some combinational logic.

(c)   Construct a T flip-flop (see Exercise 3.6) using a JK flip-flop.

Exercise 3.8 The circuit in Figure 3.63 is called a *Muller C-element*. Explain in a simple fashion what the relationship is between the inputs and output.

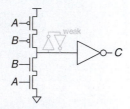

Figure 3.63 Muller C-element

Exercise 3.9 Design an asynchronously resettable D latch using logic gates.

Exercise 3.10 Design an asynchronously resettable D flip-flop using logic gates.

Exercise 3.11 Design a synchronously settable D flip-flop using logic gates.

Exercise 3.12 Design an asynchronously settable D flip-flop using logic gates.

Exercise 3.13 Suppose a ring oscillator is built from N inverters connected in a loop. Each inverter has a minimum delay of t_{cd} and a maximum delay of t_{pd}. If N is odd, determine the range of frequencies at which the oscillator might operate.

Exercise 3.14 Why must N be odd in Exercise 3.13?

Exercise 3.15 Which of the circuits in Figure 3.64 are synchronous sequential circuits? Explain.

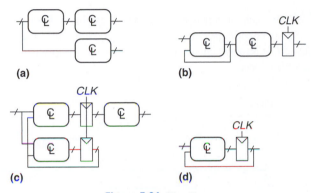

Figure 3.64 Circuits

Exercise 3.16 You are designing an elevator controller for a building with 25 floors. The controller has two inputs: *UP* and *DOWN*. It produces an output indicating the floor that the elevator is on. There is no floor 13. What is the minimum number of bits of state in the controller?

Exercise 3.17 You are designing an FSM to keep track of the mood of four students working in the digital design lab. Each student's mood is either HAPPY (the circuit works), SAD (the circuit blew up), BUSY (working on the circuit), CLUELESS (confused about the circuit), or ASLEEP (face down on the circuit board). How many states does the FSM have? What is the minimum number of bits necessary to represent these states?

Exercise 3.18 How would you factor the FSM from Exercise 3.17 into multiple simpler machines? How many states does each simpler machine have? What is the minimum total number of bits necessary in this factored design?

Exercise 3.19 Describe in words what the state machine in Figure 3.65 does. Using binary state encodings, complete a state transition table and output table for the FSM. Write Boolean equations for the next state and output and sketch a schematic of the FSM.

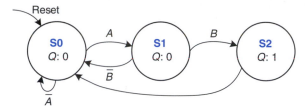

Figure 3.65 State transition diagram

Exercise 3.20 Describe in words what the state machine in Figure 3.66 does. Using binary state encodings, complete a state transition table and output table for the FSM. Write Boolean equations for the next state and output and sketch a schematic of the FSM.

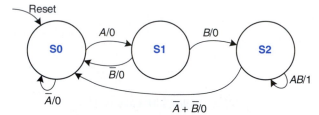

Figure 3.66 State transition diagram

Exercise 3.21 Accidents are still occurring at the intersection of Academic Avenue and Bravado Boulevard. The football team is rushing into the intersection the moment light B turns green. They are colliding with sleep-deprived CS majors who stagger into the intersection just before light A turns red. Extend the traffic light controller from Section 3.4.1 so that both lights are red for 5 seconds before either light turns green again. Sketch your improved Moore machine state transition diagram, state encodings, state transition table, output table, next state and output equations, and your FSM schematic.

Exercise 3.22 Alyssa P. Hacker's snail from Section 3.4.3 has a daughter with a Mealy machine FSM brain. The daughter snail smiles whenever she slides over the pattern 1101 or the pattern 1110. Sketch the state transition diagram for this happy snail using as few states as possible. Choose state encodings and write a

combined state transition and output table using your encodings. Write the next
state and output equations and sketch your FSM schematic.

Exercise 3.23 You have been enlisted to design a soda machine dispenser for
your department lounge. Sodas are partially subsidized by the student chapter of
the IEEE, so they cost only 25 cents. The machine accepts nickels, dimes, and
quarters. When enough coins have been inserted, it dispenses the soda and
returns any necessary change. Design an FSM controller for the soda machine.
The FSM inputs are *Nickel*, *Dime*, and *Quarter*, indicating which coin was
inserted. Assume that exactly one coin is inserted on each cycle. The outputs are
Dispense, *ReturnNickel*, *ReturnDime*, and *ReturnTwoDimes*. When the FSM
reaches 25 cents, it asserts *Dispense* and the necessary *Return* outputs required
to deliver the appropriate change. Then it should be ready to start accepting
coins for another soda.

Exercise 3.24 Gray codes have a useful property in that consecutive numbers
differ in only a single bit position. Table 3.17 lists a 3-bit Gray code representing
the numbers 0 to 7. Design a 3-bit modulo 8 Gray code counter FSM with no
inputs and three outputs. (A modulo N counter counts from 0 to $N-1$, then
repeats. For example, a watch uses a modulo 60 counter for the minutes and seconds that counts from 0 to 59.) When reset, the output should be 000. On each
clock edge, the output should advance to the next Gray code. After reaching
100, it should repeat with 000.

Table 3.17 3-bit Gray code

Number	Gray code		
0	0	0	0
1	0	0	1
2	0	1	1
3	0	1	0
4	1	1	0
5	1	1	1
6	1	0	1
7	1	0	0

Exercise 3.25 Extend your modulo 8 Gray code counter from Exercise 3.24 to be
an UP/DOWN counter by adding an *UP* input. If *UP* = 1, the counter advances
to the next number. If *UP* = 0, the counter retreats to the previous number.

Exercise 3.26 Your company, Detect-o-rama, would like to design an FSM that takes two inputs, A and B, and generates one output, Z. The output in cycle n, Z_n, is either the Boolean AND or OR of the corresponding input A_n and the previous input A_{n-1}, depending on the other input, B_n:

$$Z_n = A_n A_{n-1} \quad \text{if } B_n = 0$$
$$Z_n = A_n + A_{n-1} \text{ if } B_n = 1$$

(a) Sketch the waveform for Z given the inputs shown in Figure 3.67.

(b) Is this FSM a Moore or a Mealy machine?

(c) Design the FSM. Show your state transition diagram, encoded state transition table, next state and output equations, and schematic.

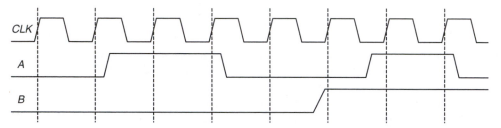

Figure 3.67 FSM input waveforms

Exercise 3.27 Design an FSM with one input, A, and two outputs, X and Y. X should be 1 if A has been 1 for at least three cycles altogether (not necessarily consecutively). Y should be 1 if A has been 1 for at least two consecutive cycles. Show your state transition diagram, encoded state transition table, next state and output equations, and schematic.

Exercise 3.28 Analyze the FSM shown in Figure 3.68. Write the state transition and output tables and sketch the state transition diagram. Describe in words what the FSM does.

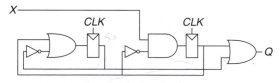

Figure 3.68 FSM schematic

Exercise 3.29 Repeat Exercise 3.28 for the FSM shown in Figure 3.69. Recall that the r and s register inputs indicate set and reset, respectively.

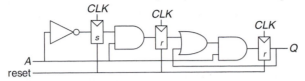

Figure 3.69 FSM schematic

Exercise 3.30 Ben Bitdiddle has designed the circuit in Figure 3.70 to compute a registered four-input XOR function. Each two-input XOR gate has a propagation delay of 100 ps and a contamination delay of 55 ps. Each flip-flop has a setup time of 60 ps, a hold time of 20 ps, a clock-to-Q maximum delay of 70 ps, and a clock-to-Q minimum delay of 50 ps.

(a) If there is no clock skew, what is the maximum operating frequency of the circuit?

(b) How much clock skew can the circuit tolerate if it must operate at 2 GHz?

(c) How much clock skew can the circuit tolerate before it might experience a hold time violation?

(d) Alyssa P. Hacker points out that she can redesign the combinational logic between the registers to be faster *and* tolerate more clock skew. Her improved circuit also uses three two-input XORs, but they are arranged differently. What is her circuit? What is its maximum frequency if there is no clock skew? How much clock skew can the circuit tolerate before it might experience a hold time violation?

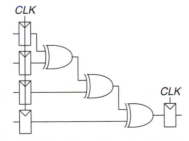

Figure 3.70 Registered four-input XOR circuit

Exercise 3.31 You are designing an adder for the blindingly fast 2-bit RePentium Processor. The adder is built from two full adders such that the carry out of the first adder is the carry in to the second adder, as shown in Figure 3.71. Your adder has input and output registers and must complete the

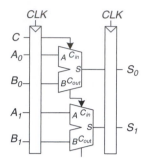

Figure 3.71 2-bit adder schematic

addition in one clock cycle. Each full adder has the following propagation delays: 20 ps from C_{in} to C_{out} or to *Sum* (S), 25 ps from A or B to C_{out}, and 30 ps from A or B to S. The adder has a contamination delay of 15 ps from C_{in} to either output and 22 ps from A or B to either output. Each flip-flop has a setup time of 30 ps, a hold time of 10 ps, a clock-to-Q propagation delay of 35 ps, and a clock-to-Q contamination delay of 21 ps.

(a) If there is no clock skew, what is the maximum operating frequency of the circuit?

(b) How much clock skew can the circuit tolerate if it must operate at 8 GHz?

(c) How much clock skew can the circuit tolerate before it might experience a hold time violation?

Exercise 3.32 A *field programmable gate array* (FPGA) uses *configurable logic blocks* (CLBs) rather than logic gates to implement combinational logic. The Xilinx Spartan 3 FPGA has propagation and contamination delays of 0.61 and 0.30 ns, respectively for each CLB. It also contains flip-flops with propagation and contamination delays of 0.72 and 0.50 ns, and setup and hold times of 0.53 and 0 ns, respectively.

(a) If you are building a system that needs to run at 40 MHz, how many consecutive CLBs can you use between two flip-flops? Assume there is no clock skew and no delay through wires between CLBs.

(b) Suppose that all paths between flip-flops pass through at least one CLB. How much clock skew can the FPGA have without violating the hold time?

Exercise 3.33 A synchronizer is built from a pair of flip-flops with $t_{setup} = 50$ ps, $T_0 = 20$ ps, and $\tau = 30$ ps. It samples an asynchronous input that changes 10^8 times per second. What is the minimum clock period of the synchronizer to achieve a mean time between failures (MTBF) of 100 years?

Exercise 3.34 You would like to build a synchronizer that can receive asynchronous inputs with an MTBF of 50 years. Your system is running at 1 GHz, and you use sampling flip-flops with $\tau = 100$ ps, $T_0 = 110$ ps, and $t_{setup} = 70$ ps. The synchronizer receives a new asynchronous input on average 0.5 times per second (i.e., once every 2 seconds). What is the required probability of failure to satisfy this MTBF? How many clock cycles would you have to wait before reading the sampled input signal to give that probability of error?

Exercise 3.35 You are walking down the hallway when you run into your lab partner walking in the other direction. The two of you first step one way and are still in each other's way. Then you both step the other way and are still in each other's way. Then you both wait a bit, hoping the other person will step aside. You can model this situation as a metastable point and apply the same theory that has been applied to synchronizers and flip-flops. Suppose you create a mathematical model for yourself and your lab partner. You start the unfortunate encounter in the metastable state. The probability that you remain in this state after t seconds is $e^{-\frac{t}{\tau}}$. τ indicates your response rate; today, your brain has been blurred by lack of sleep and has $\tau = 20$ seconds.

(a) How long will it be until you have 99% certainty that you will have resolved from metastability (i.e., figured out how to pass one another)?

(b) You are not only sleepy, but also ravenously hungry. In fact, you will starve to death if you don't get going to the cafeteria within 3 minutes. What is the probability that your lab partner will have to drag you to the morgue?

Exercise 3.36 You have built a synchronizer using flip-flops with $T_0 = 20$ ps and $\tau = 30$ ps. Your boss tells you that you need to increase the MTBF by a factor of 10. By how much do you need to increase the clock period?

Exercise 3.37 Ben Bitdiddle invents a new and improved synchronizer in Figure 3.72 that he claims eliminates metastability in a single cycle. He explains that the circuit in box M is an analog "metastability detector" that produces a HIGH output if the input voltage is in the forbidden zone between V_{IL} and V_{IH}. The metastability detector checks to determine

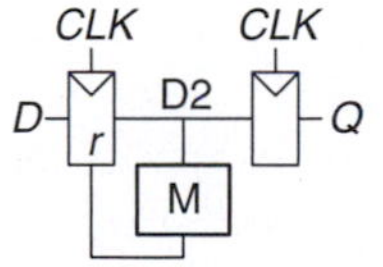

Figure 3.72 "New and improved" synchronizer

whether the first flip-flop has produced a metastable output on $D2$. If so, it asynchronously resets the flip-flop to produce a good 0 at $D2$. The second flip-flop then samples $D2$, always producing a valid logic level on Q. Alyssa P. Hacker tells Ben that there must be a bug in the circuit, because eliminating metastability is just as impossible as building a perpetual motion machine. Who is right? Explain, showing Ben's error or showing why Alyssa is wrong.

Interview Questions

The following exercises present questions that have been asked at interviews for digital design jobs.

Question 3.1 Draw a state machine that can detect when it has received the serial input sequence 01010.

Question 3.2 Design a serial (one bit at a time) two's complementer FSM with two inputs, *Start* and *A*, and one output, *Q*. A binary number of arbitrary length is provided to input *A*, starting with the least significant bit. The corresponding bit of the output appears at *Q* on the same cycle. *Start* is asserted for one cycle to initialize the FSM before the least significant bit is provided.

Question 3.3 What is the difference between a latch and a flip-flop? Under what circumstances is each one preferable?

Question 3.4 Design a 5-bit counter finite state machine.

Question 3.5 Design an edge detector circuit. The output should go HIGH for one cycle after the input makes a 0 › 1 transition.

Question 3.6 Describe the concept of pipelining and why it is used.

Question 3.7 Describe what it means for a flip-flop to have a negative hold time.

Question 3.8 Given signal *A*, shown in Figure 3.73, design a circuit that produces signal *B*.

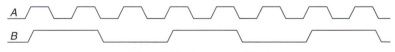

Figure 3.73 Signal waveforms

Question 3.9 Consider a block of logic between two registers. Explain the timing constraints. If you add a buffer on the clock input of the receiver (the second flip-flop), does the setup time constraint get better or worse?

Hardware Description Languages

4.1 INTRODUCTION

Thus far, we have focused on designing combinational and sequential digital circuits at the schematic level. The process of finding an efficient set of logic gates to perform a given function is labor intensive and error prone, requiring manual simplification of truth tables or Boolean equations and manual translation of finite state machines (FSMs) into gates. In the 1990's, designers discovered that they were far more productive if they worked at a higher level of abstraction, specifying just the logical function and allowing a *computer-aided design* (*CAD*) tool to produce the optimized gates. The specifications are generally given in a *hardware description language* (*HDL*). The two leading hardware description languages are *Verilog* and *VHDL*.

Verilog and VHDL are built on similar principles but have different syntax. Discussion of these languages in this chapter is divided into two columns for literal side-by-side comparison, with Verilog on the left and VHDL on the right. When you read the chapter for the first time, focus on one language or the other. Once you know one, you'll quickly master the other if you need it.

Subsequent chapters show hardware in both schematic and HDL form. If you choose to skip this chapter and not learn one of the HDLs, you will still be able to master the principles of computer organization from the schematics. However, the vast majority of commercial systems are now built using HDLs rather than schematics. If you expect to do digital design at any point in your professional life, we urge you to learn one of the HDLs.

4.1.1 Modules

A block of hardware with inputs and outputs is called a *module*. An AND gate, a multiplexer, and a priority circuit are all examples of hardware modules. The two general styles for describing module functionality are *behavioral* and *structural*. Behavioral models describe what a module does. Structural models describe how a module is built from simpler pieces; it is an application of hierarchy. The Verilog and VHDL code in HDL Example 4.1 illustrate behavioral descriptions of a module that computes the Boolean function from Example 2.6, $y = \overline{a}\,\overline{b}\,\overline{c} + a\overline{b}\,\overline{c} + a\overline{b}c$. In both languages, the module is named `sillyfunction` and has three inputs, a, b, and c, and one output, y.

HDL Example 4.1 COMBINATIONAL LOGIC

Verilog

```
module sillyfunction (input a, b, c,
                      output y);

  assign y = ~a & ~b & ~c |
             a & ~b & ~c |
             a & ~b &  c;

endmodule
```

A Verilog module begins with the module name and a listing of the inputs and outputs. The `assign` statement describes combinational logic. ~ indicates NOT, & indicates AND, and | indicates OR.

   Verilog signals such as the inputs and outputs are Boolean variables (0 or 1). They may also have floating and undefined values, as discussed in Section 4.2.8.

VHDL

```
library IEEE; use IEEE.STD_LOGIC_1164.all;

entity sillyfunction is
  port(a, b, c: in  STD_LOGIC;
       y:       out STD_LOGIC);
end;

architecture synth of sillyfunction is
begin
  y <= ((not a) and (not b) and (not c)) or
       (a and (not b) and (not c)) or
       (a and (not b) and c);
end;
```

VHDL code has three parts: the `library` use clause, the `entity` declaration, and the `architecture` body. The `library` use clause is required and will be discussed in Section 4.2.11. The `entity` declaration lists the module name and its inputs and outputs. The `architecture` body defines what the module does.

   VHDL signals, such as inputs and outputs, must have a *type declaration*. Digital signals should be declared to be `STD_LOGIC` type. `STD_LOGIC` signals can have a value of '0' or '1', as well as floating and undefined values that will be described in Section 4.2.8. The `STD_LOGIC` type is defined in the `IEEE.STD_LOGIC_1164` library, which is why the library must be used.

   VHDL lacks a good default order of operations, so Boolean equations should be parenthesized.

A module, as you might expect, is a good application of modularity. It has a well defined interface, consisting of its inputs and outputs, and it performs a specific function. The particular way in which it is coded is unimportant to others that might use the module, as long as it performs its function.

4.1.2 Language Origins

Universities are almost evenly split on which of these languages is taught in a first course, and industry is similarly split on which language is preferred. Compared to Verilog, VHDL is more verbose and cumbersome,

Verilog	**VHDL**
Verilog was developed by Gateway Design Automation as a proprietary language for logic simulation in 1984. Gateway was acquired by Cadence in 1989 and Verilog was made an open standard in 1990 under the control of Open Verilog International. The language became an IEEE standard[1] in 1995 (IEEE STD 1364) and was updated in 2001.	VHDL is an acronym for the *VHSIC Hardware Description Language*. VHSIC is in turn an acronym for the *Very High Speed Integrated Circuits* program of the US Department of Defense. VHDL was originally developed in 1981 by the Department of Defense to describe the structure and function of hardware. Its roots draw from the Ada programming language. The IEEE standardized it in 1987 (IEEE STD 1076) and has updated the standard several times since. The language was first envisioned for documentation but was quickly adopted for simulation and synthesis.

as you might expect of a language developed by committee. U.S. military contractors, the European Space Agency, and telecommunications companies use VHDL extensively.

Both languages are fully capable of describing any hardware system, and both have their quirks. The best language to use is the one that is already being used at your site or the one that your customers demand. Most CAD tools today allow the two languages to be mixed, so that different modules can be described in different languages.

4.1.3 Simulation and Synthesis

The two major purposes of HDLs are logic *simulation* and *synthesis*. During simulation, inputs are applied to a module, and the outputs are checked to verify that the module operates correctly. During synthesis, the textual description of a module is transformed into logic gates.

Simulation

Humans routinely make mistakes. Such errors in hardware designs are called *bugs*. Eliminating the bugs from a digital system is obviously important, especially when customers are paying money and lives depend on the correct operation. Testing a system in the laboratory is time-consuming. Discovering the cause of errors in the lab can be extremely difficult, because only signals routed to the chip pins can be observed. There is no way to directly observe what is happening inside a chip. Correcting errors after the system is built can be devastatingly expensive. For example, correcting a mistake in a cutting-edge integrated circuit costs more than a million dollars and takes several months. Intel's infamous FDIV (floating point division) bug in the Pentium processor forced the company to recall chips after they had shipped, at a total cost of $475 million. Logic simulation is essential to test a system before it is built.

The term "bug" predates the invention of the computer. Thomas Edison called the "little faults and difficulties" with his inventions "bugs" in 1878.

The first real computer bug was a moth, which got caught between the relays of the Harvard Mark II electromechanical computer in 1947. It was found by Grace Hopper, who logged the incident, along with the moth itself and the comment "first actual case of bug being found."

Source: Notebook entry courtesy Naval Historical Center, US Navy; photo No. NII 96566-KN

---

[1] The Institute of Electrical and Electronics Engineers (IEEE) is a professional society responsible for many computing standards including WiFi (802.11), Ethernet (802.3), and floating-point numbers (754) (see Chapter 5).

Figure 4.1 Simulation waveforms

Now: 800 ns		0 ns 160 320 ns 480 640 ns 800
a	0	
b	0	
c	0	
y	0	

Figure 4.1 shows waveforms from a simulation[2] of the previous `sillyfunction` module demonstrating that the module works correctly. y is TRUE when a, b, and c are 000, 100, or 101, as specified by the Boolean equation.

Synthesis

Logic synthesis transforms HDL code into a *netlist* describing the hardware (e.g., the logic gates and the wires connecting them). The logic synthesizer might perform optimizations to reduce the amount of hardware required. The netlist may be a text file, or it may be drawn as a schematic to help visualize the circuit. Figure 4.2 shows the results of synthesizing the `sillyfunction` module.[3] Notice how the three three-input AND gates are simplified into two two-input AND gates, as we discovered in Example 2.6 using Boolean algebra.

Circuit descriptions in HDL resemble code in a programming language. However, you must remember that the code is intended to represent hardware. Verilog and VHDL are rich languages with many commands. Not all of these commands can be synthesized into hardware. For example, a command to print results on the screen during simulation does not translate into hardware. Because our primary interest is

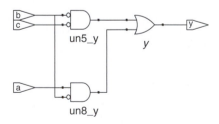

Figure 4.2 Synthesized circuit

---

[2] The simulation was performed with the Xilinx ISE Simulator, which is part of the Xilinx ISE 8.2 software. The simulator was selected because it is used commercially, yet is freely available to universities.

[3] Synthesis was performed with Synplify Pro from Synplicity. The tool was selected because it is the leading commercial tool for synthesizing HDL to field-programmable gate arrays (see Section 5.6.2) and because it is available inexpensively for universities.

to build hardware, we will emphasize a *synthesizable subset* of the languages. Specifically, we will divide HDL code into *synthesizable* modules and a *testbench*. The synthesizable modules describe the hardware. The testbench contains code to apply inputs to a module, check whether the output results are correct, and print discrepancies between expected and actual outputs. Testbench code is intended only for simulation and cannot be synthesized.

One of the most common mistakes for beginners is to think of HDL as a computer program rather than as a shorthand for describing digital hardware. If you don't know approximately what hardware your HDL should synthesize into, you probably won't like what you get. You might create far more hardware than is necessary, or you might write code that simulates correctly but cannot be implemented in hardware. Instead, think of your system in terms of blocks of combinational logic, registers, and finite state machines. Sketch these blocks on paper and show how they are connected before you start writing code.

In our experience, the best way to learn an HDL is by example. HDLs have specific ways of describing various classes of logic; these ways are called *idioms*. This chapter will teach you how to write the proper HDL idioms for each type of block and then how to put the blocks together to produce a working system. When you need to describe a particular kind of hardware, look for a similar example and adapt it to your purpose. We do not attempt to rigorously define all the syntax of the HDLs, because that is deathly boring and because it tends to encourage thinking of HDLs as programming languages, not shorthand for hardware. The IEEE Verilog and VHDL specifications, and numerous dry but exhaustive textbooks, contain all of the details, should you find yourself needing more information on a particular topic. (See Further Readings section at back of the book.)

4.2 COMBINATIONAL LOGIC

Recall that we are disciplining ourselves to design synchronous sequential circuits, which consist of combinational logic and registers. The outputs of combinational logic depend only on the current inputs. This section describes how to write behavioral models of combinational logic with HDLs.

4.2.1 Bitwise Operators

Bitwise operators act on single-bit signals or on multi-bit busses. For example, the inv module in HDL Example 4.2 describes four inverters connected to 4-bit busses.

HDL Example 4.2 INVERTERS

Verilog

```
module inv(input  [3:0] a,
           output [3:0] y);

  assign y = ~a;
endmodule
```

a[3:0] represents a 4-bit bus. The bits, from most significant to least significant, are a[3], a[2], a[1], and a[0]. This is called *little-endian* order, because the least significant bit has the smallest bit number. We could have named the bus a[4:1], in which case a[4] would have been the most significant. Or we could have used a[0:3], in which case the bits, from most significant to least significant, would be a[0], a[1], a[2], and a[3]. This is called *big-endian* order.

VHDL

```
library IEEE; use IEEE.STD_LOGIC_1164.all;
entity inv is
  port(a: in  STD_LOGIC_VECTOR(3 downto 0);
       y: out STD_LOGIC_VECTOR(3 downto 0));
end;

architecture synth of inv is
begin
  y <= not a;
end;
```

VHDL uses STD_LOGIC_VECTOR, to indicate busses of STD_LOGIC. STD_LOGIC_VECTOR (3 downto 0) represents a 4-bit bus. The bits, from most significant to least significant, are 3, 2, 1, and 0. This is called *little-endian* order, because the least significant bit has the smallest bit number. We could have declared the bus to be STD_LOGIC_VECTOR (4 downto 1), in which case bit 4 would have been the most significant. Or we could have written STD_LOGIC_VECTOR (0 to 3), in which case the bits, from most significant to least significant, would be 0, 1, 2, and 3. This is called *big-endian* order.

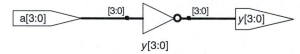

Figure 4.3 inv **synthesized circuit**

The endianness of a bus is purely arbitrary. (See the sidebar in Section 6.2.2 for the origin of the term.) Indeed, endianness is also irrelevant to this example, because a bank of inverters doesn't care what the order of the bits are. Endianness matters only for operators, such as addition, where the sum of one column carries over into the next. Either ordering is acceptable, as long as it is used consistently. We will consistently use the little-endian order, [$N-1$:0] in Verilog and ($N-1$ downto 0) in VHDL, for an N-bit bus.

After each code example in this chapter is a schematic produced from the Verilog code by the Synplify Pro synthesis tool. Figure 4.3 shows that the inv module synthesizes to a bank of four inverters, indicated by the inverter symbol labeled y[3:0]. The bank of inverters connects to 4-bit input and output busses. Similar hardware is produced from the synthesized VHDL code.

The gates module in HDL Example 4.3 demonstrates bitwise operations acting on 4-bit busses for other basic logic functions.

HDL Example 4.3 LOGIC GATES

Verilog

```
module gates(input  [3:0] a, b,
             output [3:0] y1, y2,
                          y3, y4, y5);

  /* Five different two-input logic
     gates acting on 4 bit busses */
  assign y1 = a & b;    // AND
  assign y2 = a | b;    // OR
  assign y3 = a ^ b;    // XOR
  assign y4 = ~(a & b); // NAND
  assign y5 = ~(a | b); // NOR
endmodule
```

~, ^, and | are examples of Verilog *operators*, whereas a, b, and y1 are *operands*. A combination of operators and operands, such as a & b, or ~(a | b), is called an *expression*. A complete command such as assign y4 = ~(a & b); is called a *statement*.

   assign out = in1 op in2; is called a *continuous assignment statement*. Continuous assignment statements end with a semicolon. Anytime the inputs on the right side of the = in a continuous assignment statement change, the output on the left side is recomputed. Thus, continuous assignment statements describe combinational logic.

VHDL

```
library IEEE; use IEEE.STD_LOGIC_1164.all;

entity gates is
  port(a, b: in  STD_LOGIC_VECTOR(3 downto 0);
       y1, y2, y3, y4,
       y5:   out STD_LOGIC_VECTOR(3 downto 0));
end;

architecture synth of gates is
begin
  -- Five different two-input logic gates
  --acting on 4 bit busses
  y1 <= a and b;
  y2 <= a or b;
  y3 <= a xor b;
  y4 <= a nand b;
  y5 <= a nor b;
end;
```

not, xor, and or are examples of VHDL *operators*, whereas a, b, and y1 are *operands*. A combination of operators and operands, such as a and b, or a nor b, is called an *expression*. A complete command such as y4 <= a nand b; is called a *statement*.

   out <= in1 op in2; is called a *concurrent signal assignment statement*. VHDL assignment statements end with a semicolon. Anytime the inputs on the right side of the <= in a concurrent signal assignment statement change, the output on the left side is recomputed. Thus, concurrent signal assignment statements describe combinational logic.

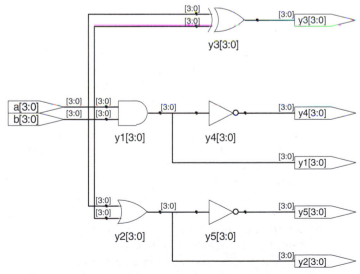

Figure 4.4 gates **synthesized circuit**

4.2.2 Comments and White Space

The `gates` example showed how to format comments. Verilog and VHDL are not picky about the use of white space (i.e., spaces, tabs, and line breaks). Nevertheless, proper indenting and use of blank lines is helpful to make nontrivial designs readable. Be consistent in your use of capitalization and underscores in signal and module names. Module and signal names must not begin with a digit.

Verilog	VHDL
Verilog comments are just like those in C or Java. Comments beginning with /* continue, possibly across multiple lines, to the next */. Comments beginning with // continue to the end of the line. Verilog is case-sensitive. y1 and Y1 are different signals in Verilog.	VHDL comments begin with −− and continue to the end of the line. Comments spanning multiple lines must use −− at the beginning of each line. VHDL is not case-sensitive. y1 and Y1 are the same signal in VHDL. However, other tools that may read your file might be case sensitive, leading to nasty bugs if you blithely mix upper and lower case.

4.2.3 Reduction Operators

Reduction operators imply a multiple-input gate acting on a single bus. HDL Example 4.4 describes an eight-input AND gate with inputs a_7, $a_6, \ldots, a_0$.

HDL Example 4.4 EIGHT-INPUT AND

Verilog	VHDL
| ```verilog
module and8(input [7:0] a,
            output      y);

  assign y = &a;

  // &a is much easier to write than
  // assign y = a[7] & a[6] & a[5] & a[4] &
  //            a[3] & a[2] & a[1] & a[0];
endmodule
``` | VHDL does not have reduction operators. Instead, it provides the `generate` command (see Section 4.7). Alternatively, the operation can be written explicitly, as shown below. |
| As one would expect, \|, ^, ~&, and ~\| reduction operators are available for OR, XOR, NAND, and NOR as well. Recall that a multi-input XOR performs parity, returning TRUE if an odd number of inputs are TRUE. | ```vhdl
library IEEE; use IEEE.STD_LOGIC_1164.all;

entity and8 is
  port(a: in  STD_LOGIC_VECTOR (7 downto 0);
       y: out STD_LOGIC);
end;

architecture synth of and8 is
begin
  y <= a(7) and a(6) and a(5) and a(4) and
       a(3) and a(2) and a(1) and a(0);
end;
``` |

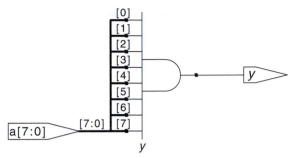

Figure 4.5 and8 **synthesized circuit**

4.2.4 Conditional Assignment

Conditional assignments select the output from among alternatives based on an input called the *condition*. HDL Example 4.5 illustrates a 2:1 multiplexer using conditional assignment.

HDL Example 4.5 2:1 MULTIPLEXER

Verilog

The *conditional operator* ?: chooses, based on a first expression, between a second and third expression. The first expression is called the *condition*. If the condition is 1, the operator chooses the second expression. If the condition is 0, the operator chooses the third expression.

?: is especially useful for describing a multiplexer because, based on the first input, it selects between two others. The following code demonstrates the idiom for a 2:1 multiplexer with 4-bit inputs and outputs using the conditional operator.

```
module mux2(input  [3:0] d0, d1,
            input        s,
            output [3:0] y);

   assign y = s ? d1 : d0;
endmodule
```

If s is 1, then y = d1. If s is 0, then y = d0.

?: is also called a *ternary operator,* because it takes three inputs. It is used for the same purpose in the C and Java programming languages.

VHDL

Conditional signal assignments perform different operations depending on some condition. They are especially useful for describing a multiplexer. For example, a 2:1 multiplexer can use conditional signal assignment to select one of two 4-bit inputs.

```
library IEEE; use IEEE.STD_LOGIC_1164.all;

entity mux2 is
  port(d0, d1: in  STD_LOGIC_VECTOR(3 downto 0);
       s:      in  STD_LOGIC;
       y:      out STD_LOGIC_VECTOR(3 downto 0));
end;

architecture synth of mux2 is
begin
  y <= d0 when s = '0' else d1;
end;
```

The conditional signal assignment sets y to d0 if s is 0. Otherwise it sets y to d1.

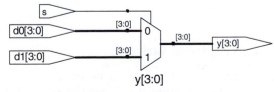

Figure 4.6 mux2 **synthesized circuit**

HDL Example 4.6 shows a 4:1 multiplexer based on the same principle as the 2:1 multiplexer in HDL Example 4.5.

Figure 4.7 shows the schematic for the 4:1 multiplexer produced by Synplify Pro. The software uses a different multiplexer symbol than this text has shown so far. The multiplexer has multiple data (d) and one-hot enable (e) inputs. When one of the enables is asserted, the associated data is passed to the output. For example, when s[1] = s[0] = 0, the bottom AND gate, un1_s_5, produces a 1, enabling the bottom input of the multiplexer and causing it to select d0[3:0].

HDL Example 4.6 4:1 MULTIPLEXER

Verilog

A 4:1 multiplexer can select one of four inputs using nested conditional operators.

```
module mux4(input  [3:0] d0, d1, d2, d3,
            input  [1:0] s,
            output [3:0] y);

  assign y = s[1] ? (s[0] ? d3 : d2)
                  : (s[0] ? d1 : d0);
endmodule
```

If s[1] is 1, then the multiplexer chooses the first expression, (s[0] ? d3 : d2). This expression in turn chooses either d3 or d2 based on s[0] (y = d3 if s[0] is 1 and d2 if s[0] is 0). If s[1] is 0, then the multiplexer similarly chooses the second expression, which gives either d1 or d0 based on s[0].

VHDL

A 4:1 multiplexer can select one of four inputs using multiple else clauses in the conditional signal assignment.

```
library IEEE; use IEEE.STD_LOGIC_1164.all;
entity mux4 is
  port (d0, d1,
        d2, d3: in  STD_LOGIC_VECTOR (3 downto 0);
        s:      in  STD_LOGIC_VECTOR (1 downto 0);
        y:      out STD_LOGIC_VECTOR (3 downto 0));
end;

architecture synth1 of mux4 is
begin
  y <= d0 when s = "00" else
       d1 when s = "01" else
       d2 when s = "10" else
       d3;
end;
```

VHDL also supports *selected signal assignment statements* to provide a shorthand when selecting from one of several possibilities. This is analogous to using a case statement in place of multiple if/else statements in some programming languages. The 4:1 multiplexer can be rewritten with selected signal assignment as follows:

```
architecture synth2 of mux4 is
begin
  with a select y <=
    d0 when "00",
    d1 when "01",
    d2 when "10",
    d3 when others;
end;
```

4.2.5 Internal Variables

Often it is convenient to break a complex function into intermediate steps. For example, a full adder, which will be described in Section 5.2.1,

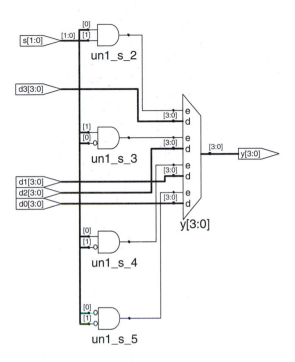

Figure 4.7 mux4 **synthesized circuit**

is a circuit with three inputs and two outputs defined by the following equations:

$$S = A \oplus B \oplus C_{in}$$
$$C_{out} = AB + AC_{in} + BC_{in}$$

(4.1)

If we define intermediate signals, P and G,

$$P = A \oplus B$$
$$G = AB$$

(4.2)

we can rewrite the full adder as follows:

$$S = P \oplus C_{in}$$
$$C_{out} = G + PC_{in}$$

(4.3)

P and G are called *internal variables*, because they are neither inputs nor outputs but are used only internal to the module. They are similar to local variables in programming languages. HDL Example 4.7 shows how they are used in HDLs.

HDL assignment statements (`assign` in Verilog and <= in VHDL) take place concurrently. This is different from conventional programming languages such as C or Java, in which statements are evaluated in the order in which they are written. In a conventional language, it is

Check this by filling out the truth table to convince yourself it is correct.

HDL Example 4.7 FULL ADDER

Verilog	VHDL
In Verilog, *wires* are used to represent internal variables whose values are defined by `assign` statements such as `assign p = a ^ b;` Wires technically have to be declared only for multibit busses, but it is good practice to include them for all internal variables; their declaration could have been omitted in this example.	In VHDL, *signals* are used to represent internal variables whose values are defined by *concurrent signal assignment statements* such as `p <= a xor b;`

```
module fulladder(input  a, b, cin,
                 output s, cout);

  wire p, g;

  assign p = a ^ b;
  assign g = a & b;

  assign s = p ^ cin;
  assign cout = g | (p & cin);
endmodule
```

```
library IEEE; use IEEE.STD_LOGIC_1164.all;

entity fulladder is
  port(a, b, cin: in  STD_LOGIC;
       s, cout:   out STD_LOGIC);
end;

architecture synth of fulladder is
  signal p, g: STD_LOGIC;
begin
  p <= a xor b;
  g <= a and b;

  s <= p xor cin;
  cout <= g or (p and cin);
end;
```

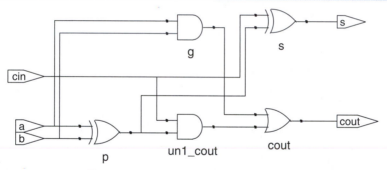

Figure 4.8 `fulladder` **synthesized circuit**

important that $S = P \oplus C_{in}$ comes after $P = A \oplus B$, because statements are executed sequentially. In an HDL, the order does not matter. Like hardware, HDL assignment statements are evaluated any time the inputs, signals on the right hand side, change their value, regardless of the order in which the assignment statements appear in a module.

4.2.6 Precedence

Notice that we parenthesized the `cout` computation in HDL Example 4.7 to define the order of operations as $C_{out} = G + (P \cdot C_{in})$, rather than $C_{out} = (G + P) \cdot C_{in}$. If we had not used parentheses, the default operation order is defined by the language. HDL Example 4.8 specifies operator precedence from highest to lowest for each language. The tables include arithmetic, shift, and comparison operators that will be defined in Chapter 5.

HDL Example 4.8 OPERATOR PRECEDENCE

Verilog

Table 4.1 Verilog operator precedence

	Op	Meaning
H **i** **g** **h** **e** **s** **t**	~	NOT
	*, /, %	MUL, DIV, MOD
	+, −	PLUS, MINUS
	<<, >>	Logical Left/Right Shift
	<<<, >>>	Arithmetic Left/Right Shift
	<, <=, >, >=	Relative Comparison
	==, !=	Equality Comparison
L **o** **w** **e** **s** **t**	&, ~&	AND, NAND
	^, ~^	XOR, XNOR
	|, ~|	OR, NOR
	?:	Conditional

The operator precedence for Verilog is much like you would expect in other programming languages. In particular, AND has precedence over OR. We could take advantage of this precedence to eliminate the parentheses.

```
assign cout = g | p & cin;
```

VHDL

Table 4.2 VHDL operator precedence

	Op	Meaning
H **i** **g** **h** **e** **s** **t**	not	NOT
	*, /, mod, rem	MUL, DIV, MOD, REM
	+, −, &	PLUS, MINUS, CONCATENATE
L **o** **w** **e** **s** **t**	rol, ror, srl, sll, sra, sla	Rotate, Shift logical, Shift arithmetic
	=, /=, <, <=, >, >=	Comparison
	and, or, nand, nor, xor	Logical Operations

Multiplication has precedence over addition in VHDL, as you would expect. However, unlike Verilog, all of the logical operations (and, or, etc.) have equal precedence, unlike what one might expect in Boolean algebra. Thus, parentheses are necessary; otherwise cout <= g or p and cin would be interpreted from left to right as cout <= (g or p) and cin.

4.2.7 Numbers

Numbers can be specified in a variety of bases. Underscores in numbers are ignored and can be helpful in breaking long numbers into more readable chunks. HDL Example 4.9 explains how numbers are written in each language.

4.2.8 Z's and X's

HDLs use z to indicate a floating value. z is particularly useful for describing a tristate buffer, whose output floats when the enable is 0. Recall from Section 2.6 that a bus can be driven by several tristate buffers, exactly one of which should be enabled. HDL Example 4.10 shows the idiom for a tristate buffer. If the buffer is enabled, the output is the same as the input. If the buffer is disabled, the output is assigned a floating value (z).

HDL Example 4.9 NUMBERS

Verilog

Verilog numbers can specify their base and size (the number of bits used to represent them). The format for declaring constants is N'Bvalue, where N is the size in bits, B is the base, and value gives the value. For example 9'h25 indicates a 9-bit number with a value of $25_{16} = 37_{10} = 000100101_2$. Verilog supports 'b for binary (base 2), 'o for octal (base 8), 'd for decimal (base 10), and 'h for hexadecimal (base 16). If the base is omitted, the base defaults to decimal.

If the size is not given, the number is assumed to have as many bits as the expression in which it is being used. Zeros are automatically padded on the front of the number to bring it up to full size. For example, if w is a 6-bit bus, assign w = 'b11 gives w the value 000011. It is better practice to explicitly give the size.

VHDL

In VHDL, STD_LOGIC numbers are written in binary and enclosed in single quotes: '0' and '1' indicate logic 0 and 1.

STD_LOGIC_VECTOR numbers are written in binary or hexadecimal and enclosed in double quotation marks. The base is binary by default and can be explicitly defined with the prefix X for hexadecimal or B for binary.

Table 4.4 VHDL numbers

Numbers	Bits	Base	Val	Stored
"101"	3	2	5	101
B"101"	3	2	5	101
X"AB"	8	16	161	10101011

Table 4.3 Verilog numbers

Numbers	Bits	Base	Val	Stored
3'b101	3	2	5	101
'b11	?	2	3	000 ... 0011
8'b11	8	2	3	00000011
8'b1010_1011	8	2	171	10101011
3'd6	3	10	6	110
6'o42	6	8	34	100010
8'hAB	8	16	171	10101011
42	?	10	42	00 ... 0101010

HDL Example 4.10 TRISTATE BUFFER

Verilog

```
module tristate(input  [3:0] a,
                input        en,
                output [3:0] y);

  assign y = en ? a : 4'bz;
endmodule
```

VHDL

```
library IEEE; use IEEE.STD_LOGIC_1164.all;

entity tristate is
  port(a:  in  STD_LOGIC_VECTOR(3 downto 0);
       en: in  STD_LOGIC;
       y:  out STD_LOGIC_VECTOR(3 downto 0));
end;

architecture synth of tristate is
begin
  y <= "ZZZZ" when en = '0' else a;
end;
```

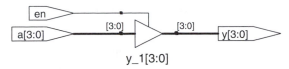

Figure 4.9 `tristate` **synthesized circuit**

Similarly, HDLs use x to indicate an invalid logic level. If a bus is simultaneously driven to 0 and 1 by two enabled tristate buffers (or other gates), the result is x, indicating contention. If all the tristate buffers driving a bus are simultaneously OFF, the bus will float, indicated by z.

At the start of simulation, state nodes such as flip-flop outputs are initialized to an unknown state (x in Verilog and u in VHDL). This is helpful to track errors caused by forgetting to reset a flip-flop before its output is used.

If a gate receives a floating input, it may produce an x output when it can't determine the correct output value. Similarly, if it receives an illegal or uninitialized input, it may produce an x output. HDL Example 4.11 shows how Verilog and VHDL combine these different signal values in logic gates.

HDL Example 4.11 TRUTH TABLES WITH UNDEFINED AND FLOATING INPUTS

Verilog

Verilog signal values are 0, 1, z, and x. Verilog constants starting with z or x are padded with leading z's or x's (instead of 0's) to reach their full length when necessary.

Table 4.5 shows a truth table for an AND gate using all four possible signal values. Note that the gate can sometimes determine the output despite some inputs being unknown. For example 0 & z returns 0 because the output of an AND gate is always 0 if either input is 0. Otherwise, floating or invalid inputs cause invalid outputs, displayed as x in Verilog.

VHDL

VHDL `STD_LOGIC` signals are '0', '1', 'z', 'x', and 'u'.

Table 4.6 shows a truth table for an AND gate using all five possible signal values. Notice that the gate can sometimes determine the output despite some inputs being unknown. For example, '0' and 'z' returns '0' because the output of an AND gate is always '0' if either input is '0.' Otherwise, floating or invalid inputs cause invalid outputs, displayed as 'x' in VHDL. Uninitialized inputs cause uninitialized outputs, displayed as 'u' in VHDL.

Table 4.5 Verilog AND gate truth table with z and x

&		A			
		0	1	z	x
B	0	0	0	0	0
	1	0	1	x	x
	z	0	x	x	x
	x	0	x	x	x

Table 4.6 VHDL AND gate truth table with z, x, and u

AND		A				
		0	1	z	x	u
B	0	0	0	0	0	0
	1	0	1	x	x	u
	z	0	x	x	x	u
	x	0	x	x	x	u
	u	0	u	u	u	u

HDL Example 4.12 BIT SWIZZLING

Verilog	VHDL

`assign y = {c[2:1], {3{d[0]}}, c[0], 3'b101};`
 	
The `{}` operator is used to concatenate busses. `{3{d[0]}}` indicates three copies of `d[0]`.
 	
   Don't confuse the 3-bit binary constant `3'b101` with a bus named b. Note that it was critical to specify the length of 3 bits in the constant; otherwise, it would have had an unknown number of leading zeros that might appear in the middle of `y`.
 	
   If `y` were wider than 9 bits, zeros would be placed in the most significant bits.
	`y <= c(2 downto 1) & d(0) & d(0) & d(0) &`
	    `c(0) & "101";`
	
	The `&` operator is used to concatenate busses. `y` must be a 9-bit `STD_LOGIC_VECTOR`. Do not confuse `&` with the `and` operator in VHDL.

Seeing x or u values in simulation is almost always an indication of a bug or bad coding practice. In the synthesized circuit, this corresponds to a floating gate input, uninitialized state, or contention. The x or u may be interpreted randomly by the circuit as 0 or 1, leading to unpredictable behavior.

4.2.9 Bit Swizzling

Often it is necessary to operate on a subset of a bus or to concatenate (join together) signals to form busses. These operations are collectively known as *bit swizzling*. In HDL Example 4.12, y is given the 9-bit value $c_2c_1d_0d_0d_0c_0101$ using bit swizzling operations.

4.2.10 Delays

HDL statements may be associated with delays specified in arbitrary units. They are helpful during simulation to predict how fast a circuit will work (if you specify meaningful delays) and also for debugging purposes to understand cause and effect (deducing the source of a bad output is tricky if all signals change simultaneously in the simulation results). These delays are ignored during synthesis; the delay of a gate produced by the synthesizer depends on its t_{pd} and t_{cd} specifications, not on numbers in HDL code.

   HDL Example 4.13 adds delays to the original function from HDL Example 4.1, $y = \overline{a}\,\overline{b}\,\overline{c} + a\overline{b}\,\overline{c} + a\overline{b}c$. It assumes that inverters have a delay of 1 ns, three-input AND gates have a delay of 2 ns, and three-input OR gates have a delay of 4 ns. Figure 4.10 shows the simulation waveforms, with y lagging 7 ns after the inputs. Note that y is initially unknown at the beginning of the simulation.

HDL Example 4.13 LOGIC GATES WITH DELAYS

Verilog

```
`timescale 1ns/1ps

module example(input  a, b, c,
               output y);
  wire ab, bb, cb, n1, n2, n3;

  assign #1 {ab, bb, cb} = ~ {a, b, c};
  assign #2 n1 = ab & bb & cb;
  assign #2 n2 = a & bb & cb;
  assign #2 n3 = a & bb & c;
  assign #4 y = n1 | n2 | n3;
endmodule
```

Verilog files can include a timescale directive that indicates the value of each time unit. The statement is of the form `timescale unit/precision. In this file, each unit is 1 ns, and the simulation has 1 ps precision. If no timescale directive is given in the file, a default unit and precision (usually 1 ns for both) is used. In Verilog, a # symbol is used to indicate the number of units of delay. It can be placed in assign statements, as well as non-blocking (<=) and blocking (=) assignments, which will be discussed in Section 4.5.4.

VHDL

```
library IEEE; use IEEE.STD_LOGIC_1164.all;

entity example is
  port(a, b, c: in  STD_LOGIC;
       y:       out STD_LOGIC);
end;

architecture synth of example is
signal ab, bb, cb, n1, n2, n3: STD_LOGIC;
begin
  ab <= not a after 1 ns;
  bb <= not b after 1 ns;
  cb <= not c after 1 ns;
  n1 <= ab and bb and cb after 2 ns;
  n2 <= a and bb and cb after 2 ns;
  n3 <= a and bb and c after 2 ns;
  y <= n1 or n2 or n3 after 4 ns;
end;
```

In VHDL, the after clause is used to indicate delay. The units, in this case, are specified as nanoseconds.

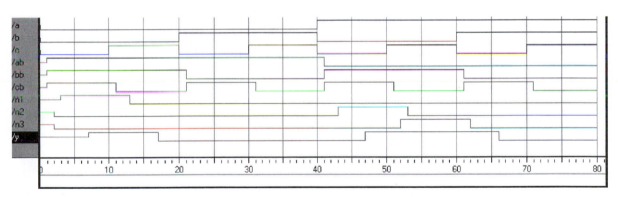

Figure 4.10 Example simulation waveforms with delays (from the ModelSim simulator)

4.2.11 VHDL Libraries and Types*

(This section may be skipped by Verilog users.) Unlike Verilog, VHDL enforces a strict data typing system that can protect the user from some errors but that is also clumsy at times.

Despite its fundamental importance, the STD_LOGIC type is not built into VHDL. Instead, it is part of the IEEE.STD_LOGIC_1164 library. Thus, every file must contain the library statements shown in the previous examples.

Moreover, IEEE.STD_LOGIC_1164 lacks basic operations such as addition, comparison, shifts, and conversion to integers for the STD_LOGIC_VECTOR data. Most CAD vendors have adopted yet more libraries containing these functions: IEEE.STD_LOGIC_UNSIGNED and IEEE.STD_LOGIC_SIGNED. See Section 1.4 for a discussion of unsigned and signed numbers and examples of these operations.

VHDL also has a BOOLEAN type with two values: true and false. BOOLEAN values are returned by comparisons (such as the equality comparison, s = '0') and are used in conditional statements such as when. Despite the temptation to believe a BOOLEAN true value should be equivalent to a STD_LOGIC '1' and BOOLEAN false should mean STD_LOGIC '0', these types are not interchangeable. Thus, the following code is illegal:

```
y <= d1 when s else d0;
q <= (state = S2);
```

Instead, we must write

```
y <= d1 when (s = '1') else d0;
q <= '1' when (state = S2) else '0';
```

Although we do not declare any signals to be BOOLEAN, they are automatically implied by comparisons and used by conditional statements.

Similarly, VHDL has an INTEGER type that represents both positive and negative integers. Signals of type INTEGER span at least the values -2^{31} to $2^{31} - 1$. Integer values are used as indices of busses. For example, in the statement

```
y <= a(3) and a(2) and a(1) and a(0);
```

0, 1, 2, and 3 are integers serving as an index to choose bits of the a signal. We cannot directly index a bus with a STD_LOGIC or STD_LOGIC_VECTOR signal. Instead, we must convert the signal to an INTEGER. This is demonstrated in HDL Example 4.14 for an 8:1 multiplexer that selects one bit from a vector using a 3-bit index. The CONV_INTEGER function is defined in the IEEE.STD_LOGIC_UNSIGNED library and performs the conversion from STD_LOGIC_VECTOR to INTEGER for positive (unsigned) values.

VHDL is also strict about out ports being exclusively for output. For example, the following code for two and three-input AND gates is illegal VHDL because v is an output and is also used to compute w.

```
library IEEE; use IEEE.STD_LOGIC_1164.all;

entity and23 is
  port(a, b, c: in  STD_LOGIC;
       v, w:    out STD_LOGIC);
end;
```

HDL Example 4.14 8:1 MULTIPLEXER WITH TYPE CONVERSION

```
library IEEE;
use IEEE.STD_LOGIC_1164.all;
use IEEE.STD_LOGIC_UNSIGNED.all;

entity mux8 is
  port(d: in  STD_LOGIC_VECTOR(7 downto 0);
       s: in  STD_LOGIC_VECTOR(2 downto 0);
       y: out STD_LOGIC);
end;

architecture synth of mux8 is
begin
  y <= d(CONV_INTEGER(s));
end;
```

Figure follows on next page.

```
architecture synth of and23 is
begin
  v <= a and b;
  w <= v and c;
end;
```

VHDL defines a special port type, `buffer`, to solve this problem. A signal connected to a `buffer` port behaves as an output but may also be used within the module. The corrected entity definition follows. Verilog does not have this limitation and does not require buffer ports.

```
entity and23 is
  port(a, b, c: in      STD_LOGIC;
       v:       buffer STD_LOGIC;
       w:       out    STD_LOGIC);
end;
```

VHDL supports *enumeration* types as an abstract way of representing information without assigning specific binary encodings. For example, the divide-by-3 FSM described in Section 3.4.2 uses three states. We can give the states names using the enumeration type rather than referring to them by binary values. This is powerful because it allows VHDL to search for the best state encoding during synthesis, rather than depending on an arbitrary encoding specified by the user.

```
type statetype is (S0, S1, S2);
signal state, nextstate: statetype;
```

4.3 STRUCTURAL MODELING

The previous section discussed *behavioral* modeling, describing a module in terms of the relationships between inputs and outputs. This section

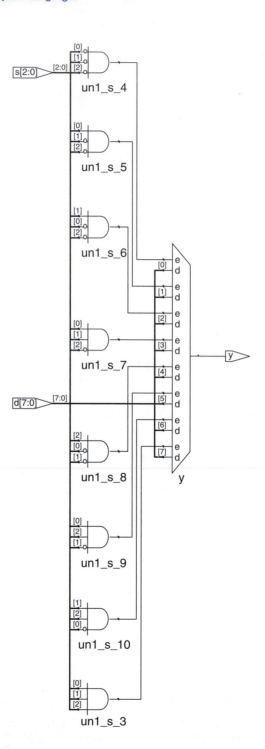

Figure 4.11 mux8 **synthesized circuit**

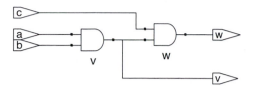

Figure 4.12 and23 **synthesized circuit**

examines *structural* modeling, describing a module in terms of how it is composed of simpler modules.

For example, HDL Example 4.15 shows how to assemble a 4:1 multiplexer from three 2:1 multiplexers. Each copy of the 2:1 multiplexer

---

HDL Example 4.15 STRUCTURAL MODEL OF 4:1 MULTIPLEXER

Verilog

```
module mux4 (input   [3:0] d0, d1, d2, d3,
             input   [1:0] s,
             output  [3:0] y);

  wire [3:0] low, high;

  mux2 lowmux (d0, d1, s[0], low);
  mux2 highmux (d2, d3, s[0], high);
  mux2 finalmux (low, high, s[1], y);
endmodule
```

The three `mux2` instances are called `lowmux`, `highmux`, and `finalmux`. The `mux2` module must be defined elsewhere in the Verilog code.

VHDL

```
library IEEE; use IEEE.STD_LOGIC_1164.all;

entity mux4 is
  port (d0, d1,
        d2, d3: in  STD_LOGIC_VECTOR (3 downto 0);
        s:      in  STD_LOGIC_VECTOR (1 downto 0);
        y:      out STD_LOGIC_VECTOR (3 downto 0));
end;

architecture struct of mux4 is
  component mux2
    port (d0,
          d1: in  STD_LOGIC_VECTOR (3 downto 0);
          s:  in  STD_LOGIC;
          y:  out STD_LOGIC_VECTOR (3 downto 0));
  end component;
  signal low, high: STD_LOGIC_VECTOR (3 downto 0);
begin
  lowmux:   mux2 port map (d0, d1, s(0), low);
  highmux:  mux2 port map (d2, d3, s(0), high);
  finalmux: mux2 port map (low, high, s(1), y);
end;
```

The architecture must first declare the `mux2` ports using the `component` declaration statement. This allows VHDL tools to check that the component you wish to use has the same ports as the entity that was declared somewhere else in another entity statement, preventing errors caused by changing the entity but not the instance. However, component declaration makes VHDL code rather cumbersome.

Note that this architecture of `mux4` was named `struct`, whereas architectures of modules with behavioral descriptions from Section 4.2 were named `synth`. VHDL allows multiple architectures (implementations) for the same entity; the architectures are distinguished by name. The names themselves have no significance to the CAD tools, but `struct` and `synth` are common. Synthesizable VHDL code generally contains only one architecture for each entity, so we will not discuss the VHDL syntax to configure which architecture is used when multiple architectures are defined.

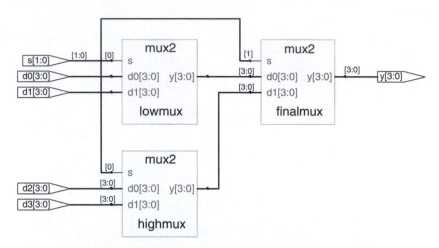

Figure 4.13 mux4 **synthesized circuit**

is called an *instance*. Multiple instances of the same module are distinguished by distinct names, in this case lowmux, highmux, and finalmux. This is an example of regularity, in which the 2:1 multiplexer is reused many times.

HDL Example 4.16 uses structural modeling to construct a 2:1 multiplexer from a pair of tristate buffers.

HDL Example 4.16 STRUCTURAL MODEL OF 2:1 MULTIPLEXER

Verilog

```
module mux2 (input   [3:0] d0, d1,
             input        s,
             output [3:0] y);

  tristate t0 (d0, ~s, y);
  tristate t1 (d1, s, y);
endmodule
```

In Verilog, expressions such as ~s are permitted in the port list for an instance. Arbitrarily complicated expressions are legal but discouraged because they make the code difficult to read.

VHDL

```
library IEEE; use IEEE.STD_LOGIC_1164.all;

entity mux2 is
  port (d0, d1: in  STD_LOGIC_VECTOR (3 downto 0);
        s:      in  STD_LOGIC;
        y:      out STD_LOGIC_VECTOR (3 downto 0));
end;

architecture struct of mux2 is
  component tristate
    port (a:  in  STD_LOGIC_VECTOR (3 downto 0);
          en: in  STD_LOGIC;
          y:  out STD_LOGIC_VECTOR (3 downto 0));
  end component;
  signal sbar: STD_LOGIC;
begin
  sbar <= not s;
  t0: tristate port map (d0, sbar, y);
  t1: tristate port map (d1, s, y);
end;
```

In VHDL, expressions such as not s are not permitted in the port map for an instance. Thus, sbar must be defined as a separate signal.

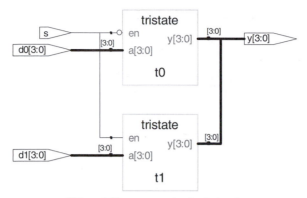

Figure 4.14 mux2 **synthesized circuit**

HDL Example 4.17 shows how modules can access part of a bus. An 8-bit wide 2:1 multiplexer is built using two of the 4-bit 2:1 multiplexers already defined, operating on the low and high nibbles of the byte.

In general, complex systems are designed *hierarchically*. The overall system is described structurally by instantiating its major components. Each of these components is described structurally from its building blocks, and so forth recursively until the pieces are simple enough to describe behaviorally. It is good style to avoid (or at least to minimize) mixing structural and behavioral descriptions within a single module.

HDL Example 4.17 ACCESSING PARTS OF BUSSES

Verilog

```
module mux2_8 (input  [7:0] d0, d1,
               input       s,
               output [7:0] y);

  mux2 lsbmux (d0[3:0], d1[3:0], s, y[3:0]);
  mux2 msbmux (d0[7:4], d1[7:4], s, y[7:4]);
endmodule
```

VHDL

```
library IEEE; use IEEE.STD_LOGIC_1164.all;

entity mux2_8 is
  port(d0, d1: in  STD_LOGIC_VECTOR(7 downto 0);
       s:      in  STD_LOGIC;
       y:      out STD_LOGIC_VECTOR(7 downto 0));
end;

architecture struct of mux2_8 is
  component mux2
    port(d0, d1: in  STD_LOGIC_VECTOR(3
                                      downto 0);
         s:      in  STD_LOGIC;
         y:      out STD_LOGIC_VECTOR(3 downto 0));
  end component;
begin

  lsbmux: mux2
    port map(d0(3 downto 0), d1(3 downto 0),
             s, y(3 downto 0));
  msbhmux: mux2
    port map(d0(7 downto 4), d1(7 downto 4),
             s, y(7 downto 4));
end;
```

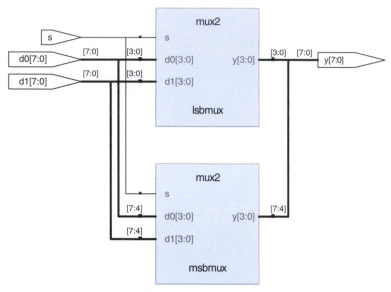

Figure 4.15 mux2_8 **synthesized circuit**

4.4 SEQUENTIAL LOGIC

HDL synthesizers recognize certain idioms and turn them into specific sequential circuits. Other coding styles may simulate correctly but synthesize into circuits with blatant or subtle errors. This section presents the proper idioms to describe registers and latches.

4.4.1 Registers

The vast majority of modern commercial systems are built with registers using positive edge-triggered D flip-flops. HDL Example 4.18 shows the idiom for such flip-flops.

In Verilog `always` statements and VHDL `process` statements, signals keep their old value until an event in the sensitivity list takes place that explicitly causes them to change. Hence, such code, with appropriate sensitivity lists, can be used to describe sequential circuits with memory. For example, the flip-flop includes only `clk` in the sensitive list. It remembers its old value of q until the next rising edge of the `clk`, even if d changes in the interim.

In contrast, Verilog continuous assignment statements (`assign`) and VHDL concurrent assignment statements (`<=`) are reevaluated anytime any of the inputs on the right hand side changes. Therefore, such code necessarily describes combinational logic.

HDL Example 4.18 REGISTER

Verilog

```
module flop(input          clk,
            input    [3:0] d,
            output reg [3:0] q);

  always @ (posedge clk)
    q <= d;
endmodule
```

A Verilog always **statement is written in the form**

```
always @ (sensitivity list)
  statement;
```

The statement is executed only when the event specified in the sensitivity list occurs. In this example, the statement is q <= d (pronounced "q gets d"). Hence, the flip-flop copies d to q on the positive edge of the clock and otherwise remembers the old state of q.

<= is called a *nonblocking assignment*. Think of it as a regular = sign for now; we'll return to the more subtle points in Section 4.5.4. Note that <= is used instead of assign inside an always statement.

All signals on the left hand side of <= or = in an always statement must be declared as reg. In this example, q is both an output and a reg, so it is declared as output reg [3:0] q. Declaring a signal as reg does not mean the signal is actually the output of a register! All it means is that the signal appears on the left hand side of an assignment in an always statement. We will see later examples of always statements describing combinational logic in which the output is declared reg but does not come from a flip-flop.

VHDL

```
library IEEE; use IEEE.STD_LOGIC_1164.all;

entity flop is
  port(clk: in  STD_LOGIC;
       d:   in  STD_LOGIC_VECTOR(3 downto 0);
       q:   out STD_LOGIC_VECTOR(3 downto 0));
end;

architecture synth of flop is
begin
  process(clk) begin
    if clk'event and clk = '1' then
      q <= d;
    end if;
  end process;
end;
```

A VHDL process **is written in the form**

```
process(sensitivity list) begin
  statement;
end process;
```

The statement is executed when any of the variables in the sensitivity list change. In this example, the if statement is executed when clk changes, indicated by clk'event. If the change is a rising edge (clk = '1' after the event), then q <= d (pronounced "q gets d"). Hence, the flip-flop copies d to q on the positive edge of the clock and otherwise remembers the old state of q.

An alternative VHDL idiom for a flip-flop is

```
process(clk) begin
  if RISING_EDGE(clk) then
    q <= d;
  end if;
end process;
```

RISING_EDGE(clk) is synonymous with clk'event and clk = 1.

Figure 4.16 flop **synthesized circuit**

4.4.2 Resettable Registers

When simulation begins or power is first applied to a circuit, the output of a flop or register is unknown. This is indicated with x in Verilog and 'u' in VHDL. Generally, it is good practice to use resettable registers so that on powerup you can put your system in a known state. The reset may be either asynchronous or synchronous. Recall that asynchronous reset occurs immediately, whereas synchronous reset clears the output only on the next rising edge of the clock. HDL Example 4.19 demonstrates the idioms for flip-flops with asynchronous and synchronous resets. Note that distinguishing synchronous and asynchronous reset in a schematic can be difficult. The schematic produced by Synplify Pro places asynchronous reset at the bottom of a flip-flop and synchronous reset on the left side.

HDL Example 4.19 RESETTABLE REGISTER

Verilog

```
module flopr (input             clk,
              input             reset,
              input    [3:0] d,
              output reg [3:0] q);

  // asynchronous reset
  always @ (posedge clk, posedge reset)
    if (reset) q <= 4'b0;
    else       q <= d;
endmodule

module flopr (input             clk,
              input             reset,
              input    [3:0] d,
              output reg [3:0] q);

  // synchronous reset
  always @ (posedge clk)
    if (reset) q <= 4'b0;
    else       q <= d;
endmodule
```

Multiple signals in an `always` statement sensitivity list are separated with a comma or the word `or`. Notice that `posedge reset` is in the sensitivity list on the asynchronously resettable flop, but not on the synchronously resettable flop. Thus, the asynchronously resettable flop immediately responds to a rising edge on `reset`, but the synchronously resettable flop responds to `reset` only on the rising edge of the clock.

Because the modules have the same name, `flopr`, you may include only one or the other in your design.

VHDL

```
library IEEE; use IEEE.STD_LOGIC_1164.all;

entity flopr is
  port (clk,
        reset: in  STD_LOGIC;
        d:     in  STD_LOGIC_VECTOR (3 downto 0);
        q:     out STD_LOGIC_VECTOR (3 downto 0));
end;

architecture asynchronous of flopr is
begin
  process (clk, reset) begin
    if reset = '1' then
      q <= "0000";
    elsif clk' event and clk = '1' then
      q <= d;
    end if;
  end process;
end;

architecture synchronous of flopr is
begin
  process (clk) begin
    if clk'event and clk = '1' then
      if reset = '1' then
        q <= "0000";
      else q <= d;
      end if;
    end if;
  end process;
end;
```

Multiple signals in a `process` sensitivity list are separated with a comma. Notice that `reset` is in the sensitivity list on the asynchronously resettable flop, but not on the synchronously resettable flop. Thus, the asynchronously resettable flop immediately responds to a rising edge on `reset`, but the synchronously resettable flop responds to `reset` only on the rising edge of the clock.

Recall that the state of a flop is initialized to 'u' at startup during VHDL simulation.

As mentioned earlier, the name of the architecture (`asynchronous` or `synchronous`, in this example) is ignored by the VHDL tools but may be helpful to the human reading the code. Because both architectures describe the entity `flopr`, you may include only one or the other in your design.

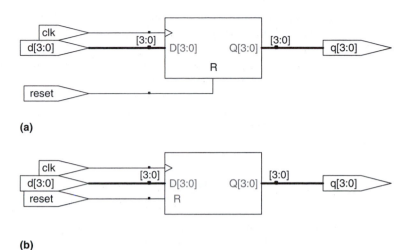

Figure 4.17 flopr **synthesized circuit (a) asynchronous reset, (b) synchronous reset**

4.4.3 Enabled Registers

Enabled registers respond to the clock only when the enable is asserted. HDL Example 4.20 shows an asynchronously resettable enabled register that retains its old value if both reset and en are FALSE.

HDL Example 4.20 RESETTABLE ENABLED REGISTER

Verilog

```
module flopenr (input          clk,
                input          reset,
                input          en,
                input    [3:0] d,
                output reg [3:0] q);

  // asynchronous reset
  always @ (posedge clk, posedge reset)
    if (reset) q <= 4'b0;
    else if (en) q <= d;
endmodule
```

VHDL

```
library IEEE; use IEEE.STD_LOGIC_1164.all;

entity flopenr is
  port (clk,
        reset,
        en: in  STD_LOGIC;
        d:  in  STD_LOGIC_VECTOR (3 downto 0);
        q:  out STD_LOGIC_VECTOR (3 downto 0));
end;

architecture asynchronous of flopenr is
-- asynchronous reset
begin
  process (clk, reset) begin
    if reset = '1' then
      q <= "0000";
    elsif clk'event and clk = '1' then
      if en = '1' then
        q <= d;
      end if;
    end if;
  end process;
end;
```

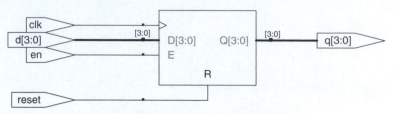

Figure 4.18 `flopenr` **synthesized circuit**

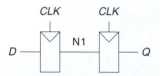

Figure 4.19 Synchronizer circuit

4.4.4 Multiple Registers

A single `always/process` statement can be used to describe multiple pieces of hardware. For example, consider the synchronizer from Section 3.5.5 made of two back-to-back flip-flops, as shown in Figure 4.19. HDL Example 4.21 describes the synchronizer. On the rising edge of `clk`, `d` is copied to `n1`. At the same time, `n1` is copied to `q`.

HDL Example 4.21 SYNCHRONIZER

Verilog

```
module sync (input      clk,
             input      d,
             output reg q);

  reg n1;

  always @ (posedge clk)
    begin
      n1 <= d;
      q <= n1;
    end
endmodule
```

`n1` must be declared as a `reg` because it is an internal signal used on the left hand side of `<=` in an `always` statement. Also notice that the `begin/end` construct is necessary because multiple statements appear in the `always` statement. This is analogous to { } in C or Java. The `begin/end` was not needed in the `flopr` example because `if/else` counts as a single statement.

VHDL

```
library IEEE; use IEEE.STD_LOGIC_1164.all;

entity sync is
  port (clk: in  STD_LOGIC;
        d:   in  STD_LOGIC;
        q:   out STD_LOGIC);
end;

architecture good of sync is
  signal n1: STD_LOGIC;
begin
  process (clk) begin
    if clk'event and clk = '1' then
      n1 <= d;
      q <= n1;
    end if;
  end process;
end;
```

`n1` must be declared as a `signal` because it is an internal signal used in the module.

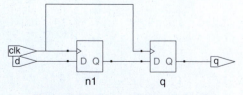

Figure 4.20 `sync` **synthesized circuit**

4.4.5 Latches

Recall from Section 3.2.2 that a D latch is transparent when the clock is HIGH, allowing data to flow from input to output. The latch becomes opaque when the clock is LOW, retaining its old state. HDL Example 4.22 shows the idiom for a D latch.

Not all synthesis tools support latches well. Unless you know that your tool does support latches and you have a good reason to use them, avoid them and use edge-triggered flip-flops instead. Furthermore, take care that your HDL does not imply any unintended latches, something that is easy to do if you aren't attentive. Many synthesis tools warn you when a latch is created; if you didn't expect one, track down the bug in your HDL.

4.5 MORE COMBINATIONAL LOGIC

In Section 4.2, we used assignment statements to describe combinational logic behaviorally. Verilog `always` statements and VHDL `process` statements are used to describe sequential circuits, because they remember the old state when no new state is prescribed. However, `always`/`process`

HDL Example 4.22 D LATCH

Verilog

```
module latch(input          clk,
             input    [3:0] d,
             output reg [3:0] q);

  always @ (clk, d)
    if (clk) q <= d;
endmodule
```

The sensitivity list contains both `clk` and `d`, so the `always` statement evaluates any time `clk` or `d` changes. If `clk` is HIGH, `d` flows through to `q`.

q must be declared to be a `reg` because it appears on the left hand side of `<=` in an `always` statement. This does not always mean that `q` is the output of a register.

VHDL

```
library IEEE; use IEEE.STD_LOGIC_1164.all;

entity latch is
  port(clk: in  STD_LOGIC;
       d:   in  STD_LOGIC_VECTOR (3 downto 0);
       q:   out STD_LOGIC_VECTOR (3 downto 0));
end;

architecture synth of latch is
begin
  process(clk, d) begin
    if clk = '1' then q <= d;
    end if;
  end process;
end;
```

The sensitivity list contains both `clk` and `d`, so the `process` evaluates anytime `clk` or `d` changes. If `clk` is HIGH, `d` flows through to `q`.

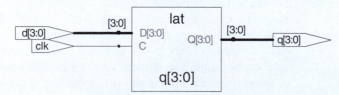

Figure 4.21 `latch` **synthesized circuit**

HDL Example 4.23 INVERTER USING `always/process`

Verilog	**VHDL**
| ```
module inv(input      [3:0] a,
           output reg [3:0] y);

  always @ (*)
    y = ~a;
endmodule
``` | ```
library IEEE; use IEEE.STD_LOGIC_1164.all;

entity inv is
  port(a: in  STD_LOGIC_VECTOR(3 downto 0);
       y: out STD_LOGIC_VECTOR(3 downto 0));
end;

architecture proc of inv is
begin
  process(a) begin
    y <= not a;
  end process;
end;
``` |
| `always @ (*)` reevaluates the statements inside the `always` statement any time any of the signals on the right hand side of <= or = inside the always statement change. Thus, `@ (*)` is a safe way to model combinational logic. In this particular example, `@ (a)` would also have sufficed. | The `begin` and `end process` statements are required in VHDL even though the `process` contains only one assignment. |

The = in the always statement is called a *blocking assignment,* in contrast to the <= nonblocking assignment. In Verilog, it is good practice to use blocking assignments for combinational logic and nonblocking assignments for sequential logic. This will be discussed further in Section 4.5.4.

Note that y must be declared as `reg` because it appears on the left hand side of a <= or = sign in an `always` statement. Nevertheless, y is the output of combinational logic, not a register.

statements can also be used to describe combinational logic behaviorally if the sensitivity list is written to respond to changes in all of the inputs and the body prescribes the output value for every possible input combination. HDL Example 4.23 uses `always/process` statements to describe a bank of four inverters (see Figure 4.3 for the synthesized circuit).

HDLs support *blocking* and *nonblocking assignments* in an `always/process` statement. A group of blocking assignments are evaluated in the order in which they appear in the code, just as one would expect in a standard programming language. A group of nonblocking assignments are evaluated concurrently; all of the statements are evaluated before any of the signals on the left hand sides are updated.

HDL Example 4.24 defines a full adder using intermediate signals p and g to compute s and `cout`. It produces the same circuit from Figure 4.8, but uses `always/process` statements in place of assignment statements.

These two examples are poor applications of `always/process` statements for modeling combinational logic because they require more lines than the equivalent approach with assignment statements from Section 4.2.1. Moreover, they pose the risk of inadvertently implying sequential logic if the inputs are left out of the sensitivity list. However, `case` and `if` statements are convenient for modeling more complicated combinational logic. `case` and `if` statements must appear within `always/process` statements and are examined in the next sections.

Verilog

In a Verilog `always` statement, = indicates a blocking assignment and <= indicates a nonblocking assignment (also called a concurrent assignment).

Do not confuse either type with continuous assignment using the `assign` statement. `assign` statements must be used outside `always` statements and are also evaluated concurrently.

VHDL

In a VHDL `process` statement, : = indicates a blocking assignment and <= indicates a nonblocking assignment (also called a concurrent assignment). This is the first section where : = is introduced.

Nonblocking assignments are made to outputs and to signals. Blocking assignments are made to variables, which are declared in `process` statements (see HDL Example 4.24).

<= can also appear outside `process` statements, where it is also evaluated concurrently.

HDL Example 4.24 FULL ADDER USING `always/process`

Verilog

```
module fulladder(input      a, b, cin,
                 output reg s, cout);
  reg p, g;

  always @ (*)
    begin
      p = a ^ b;            // blocking
      g = a & b;            // blocking

      s = p ^ cin;          // blocking
      cout = g | (p & cin); // blocking
    end
endmodule
```

In this case, an @ (a, b, cin) would have been equivalent to @ (*). However, @ (*) is better because it avoids common mistakes of missing signals in the stimulus list.

For reasons that will be discussed in Section 4.5.4, it is best to use blocking assignments for combinational logic. This example uses blocking assignments, first computing p, then g, then s, and finally cout.

Because p and g appear on the left hand side of an assignment in an `always` statement, they must be declared to be `reg`.

VHDL

```
library IEEE; use IEEE.STD_LOGIC_1164.all;

entity fulladder is
  port(a, b, cin:  in  STD_LOGIC;
       s, cout:    out STD_LOGIC);
end;

architecture synth of fulladder is
begin
  process(a, b, cin)
    variable p, g: STD_LOGIC;
  begin
    p := a xor b; -- blocking
    g := a and b; -- blocking

    s <= p xor cin;
    cout <= g or (p and cin);
  end process;
end;
```

The `process` sensitivity list must include a, b, and cin because combinational logic should respond to changes of any input.

For reasons that will be discussed in Section 4.5.4, it is best to use blocking assignments for intermediate variables in combinational logic. This example uses blocking assignments for p and g so that they get their new values before being used to compute s and cout that depend on them.

Because p and g appear on the left hand side of a blocking assignment (:=) in a `process` statement, they must be declared to be `variable` rather than `signal`. The variable declaration appears before the `begin` in the process where the variable is used.

4.5.1 Case Statements

A better application of using the `always`/`process` statement for combinational logic is a seven-segment display decoder that takes advantage of the `case` statement that must appear inside an `always`/`process` statement.

As you might have noticed in Example 2.10, the design process for large blocks of combinational logic is tedious and prone to error. HDLs offer a great improvement, allowing you to specify the function at a higher level of abstraction, and then automatically synthesize the function into gates. HDL Example 4.25 uses `case` statements to describe a seven-segment display decoder based on its truth table. (See Example 2.10 for a description of the seven-segment display decoder.) The `case`

HDL Example 4.25 SEVEN-SEGMENT DISPLAY DECODER

Verilog

```
module sevenseg(input       [3:0] data,
                output reg [6:0] segments);
  always @ (*)
    case(data)
      //            abc_defg
      0: segments = 7'b111_1110;
      1: segments = 7'b011_0000;
      2: segments = 7'b110_1101;
      3: segments = 7'b111_1001;
      4: segments = 7'b011_0011;
      5: segments = 7'b101_1011;
      6: segments = 7'b101_1111;
      7: segments = 7'b111_0000;
      8: segments = 7'b111_1111;
      9: segments = 7'b111_1011;
      default: segments = 7'b000_0000;
    endcase
endmodule
```

The `case` statement checks the value of `data`. When `data` is 0, the statement performs the action after the colon, setting `segments` to 1111110. The `case` statement similarly checks other `data` values up to 9 (note the use of the default base, base 10).

The `default` clause is a convenient way to define the output for all cases not explicitly listed, guaranteeing combinational logic.

In Verilog, `case` statements must appear inside `always` statements.

VHDL

```
library IEEE; use IEEE.STD_LOGIC_1164.all;

entity seven_seg_decoder is
  port(data:    in  STD_LOGIC_VECTOR (3 downto 0);
       segments: out STD_LOGIC_VECTOR (6 downto 0));
end;

architecture synth of seven_seg_decoder is
begin
  process (data) begin
    case data is
      --                    abcdefg
      when X"0" => segments <= "1111110";
      when X"1" => segments <= "0110000";
      when X"2" => segments <= "1101101";
      when X"3" => segments <= "1111001";
      when X"4" => segments <= "0110011";
      when X"5" => segments <= "1011011";
      when X"6" => segments <= "1011111";
      when X"7" => segments <= "1110000";
      when X"8" => segments <= "1111111";
      when X"9" => segments <= "1111011";
      when others => segments <= "0000000";
    end case;
  end process;
end;
```

The `case` statement checks the value of `data`. When `data` is 0, the statement performs the action after the `=>`, setting `segments` to 1111110. The `case` statement similarly checks other `data` values up to 9 (note the use of X for hexadecimal numbers). The `others` clause is a convenient way to define the output for all cases not explicitly listed, guaranteeing combinational logic.

Unlike Verilog, VHDL supports selected signal assignment statements (see HDL Example 4.6), which are much like `case` statements but can appear outside processes. Thus, there is less reason to use processes to describe combinational logic.

Figure 4.22 sevenseg **synthesized circuit**

statement performs different actions depending on the value of its input. A case statement implies combinational logic if all possible input combinations are defined; otherwise it implies sequential logic, because the output will keep its old value in the undefined cases.

Synplify Pro synthesizes the seven-segment display decoder into a *read-only memory (ROM)* containing the 7 outputs for each of the 16 possible inputs. ROMs are discussed further in Section 5.5.6.

If the default or others clause were left out of the case statement, the decoder would have remembered its previous output anytime data were in the range of 10–15. This is strange behavior for hardware.

Ordinary decoders are also commonly written with case statements. HDL Example 4.26 describes a 3:8 decoder.

4.5.2 If Statements

always/process statements may also contain if statements. The if statement may be followed by an else statement. If all possible input

---

HDL Example 4.26 3:8 DECODER

Verilog

```
module decoder3_8(input      [2:0] a,
                  output reg [7:0] y);
  always @ (*)
    case (a)
      3'b000: y = 8'b00000001;
      3'b001: y = 8'b00000010;
      3'b010: y = 8'b00000100;
      3'b011: y = 8'b00001000;
      3'b100: y = 8'b00010000;
      3'b101: y = 8'b00100000;
      3'b110: y = 8'b01000000;
      3'b111: y = 8'b10000000;
    endcase
endmodule
```

No default statement is needed because all cases are covered.

VHDL

```
library IEEE; use IEEE.STD_LOGIC_1164.all;

entity decoder3_8 is
  port(a: in  STD_LOGIC_VECTOR (2 downto 0);
       y: out STD_LOGIC_VECTOR (7 downto 0));
end;

architecture synth of decoder3_8 is
begin
  process (a) begin
    case a is
      when "000" => y <= "00000001";
      when "001" => y <= "00000010";
      when "010" => y <= "00000100";
      when "011" => y <= "00001000";
      when "100" => y <= "00010000";
      when "101" => y <= "00100000";
      when "110" => y <= "01000000";
      when "111" => y <= "10000000";
    end case;
  end process;
end;
```

No others clause is needed because all cases are covered.

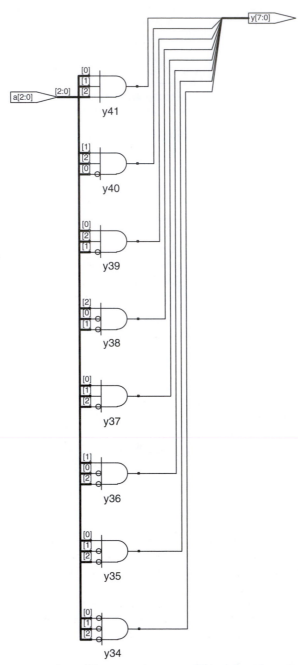

Figure 4.23 decoder3_8 **synthesized circuit**

HDL Example 4.27 PRIORITY CIRCUIT

Verilog

```
module priority(input      [3:0] a,
                output reg [3:0] y);

  always @ (*)
    if      (a[3]) y = 4'b1000;
    else if (a[2]) y = 4'b0100;
    else if (a[1]) y = 4'b0010;
    else if (a[0]) y = 4'b0001;
    else           y = 4'b0000;
endmodule
```

In Verilog, if statements must appear inside of always statements.

VHDL

```
library IEEE; use IEEE.STD_LOGIC_1164.all;

entity priority is
  port (a: in  STD_LOGIC_VECTOR(3 downto 0);
        y: out STD_LOGIC_VECTOR(3 downto 0));
end;

architecture synth of priority is
begin
  process (a) begin
    if    a(3) = '1' then y <= "1000";
    elsif a(2) = '1' then y <= "0100";
    elsif a(1) = '1' then y <= "0010";
    elsif a(0) = '1' then y <= "0001";
    else                  y <= "0000";
    end if;
  end process;
end;
```

Unlike Verilog, VHDL supports conditional signal assignment statements (see HDL Example 4.6), which are much like if statements but can appear outside processes. Thus, there is less reason to use processes to describe combinational logic. (Figure follows on next page.)

---

combinations are handled, the statement implies combinational logic; otherwise, it produces sequential logic (like the latch in Section 4.4.5).

HDL Example 4.27 uses if statements to describe a priority circuit, defined in Section 2.4. Recall that an *N*-input priority circuit sets the output TRUE that corresponds to the most significant input that is TRUE.

4.5.3 Verilog casez*

(This section may be skipped by VHDL users.) Verilog also provides the casez statement to describe truth tables with don't cares (indicated with ? in the casez statement). HDL Example 4.28 shows how to describe a priority circuit with casez.

Synplify Pro synthesizes a slightly different circuit for this module, shown in Figure 4.25, than it did for the priority circuit in Figure 4.24. However, the circuits are logically equivalent.

4.5.4 Blocking and Nonblocking Assignments

The guidelines on page 203 explain when and how to use each type of assignment. If these guidelines are not followed, it is possible to write

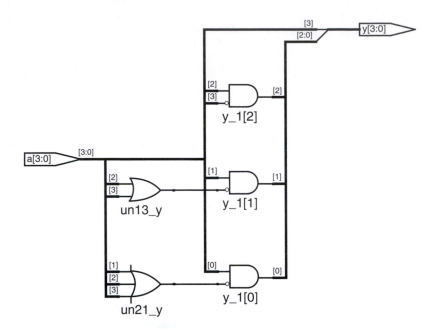

Figure 4.24 priority
synthesized circuit

HDL Example 4.28 PRIORITY CIRCUIT USING casez

```
module priority_casez(input      [3:0] a,
                output reg [3:0] y);

  always @ (*)
    casez (a)
      4'b1???: y = 4'b1000;
      4'b01??: y = 4'b0100;
      4'b001?: y = 4'b0010;
      4'b0001: y = 4'b0001;
      default: y = 4'b0000;
    endcase
endmodule
```
(See figure 4.25.)

code that appears to work in simulation but synthesizes to incorrect hardware. The optional remainder of this section explains the principles behind the guidelines.

Combinational Logic*

The full adder from HDL Example 4.24 is correctly modeled using blocking assignments. This section explores how it operates and how it would differ if nonblocking assignments had been used.

Imagine that a, b, and cin are all initially 0. p, g, s, and cout are thus 0 as well. At some time, a changes to 1, triggering the always/process statement. The four blocking assignments evaluate in

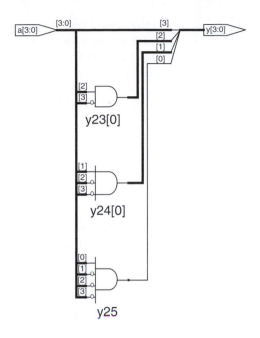

Figure 4.25 `priority_casez`
synthesized circuit

BLOCKING AND NONBLOCKING ASSIGNMENT GUIDELINES

Verilog

1. Use `always @ (posedge clk)` and nonblocking assignments to model synchronous sequential logic.

```
always @ (posedge clk)
  begin
    n1 <= d; // nonblocking
    q <= n1; // nonblocking
  end
```

2. Use continuous assignments to model simple combinational logic.

```
assign y = s ? d1 : d0;
```

3. Use `always @ (*)` and blocking assignments to model more complicated combinational logic where the `always` statement is helpful.

```
always @ (*)
  begin
    p = a ^ b; // blocking
    g = a & b; // blocking
    s = p ^ cin;
    cout = g | (p & cin);
  end
```

4. Do not make assignments to the same signal in more than one `always` statement or continuous assignment statement.

VHDL

1. Use `process(clk)` and nonblocking assignments to model synchronous sequential logic.

```
process (clk) begin
  if clk'event and clk = '1' then
    n1 <= d; -- nonblocking
    q <= n1; -- nonblocking
  end if;
end process;
```

2. Use concurrent assignments outside `process` statements to model simple combinational logic.

```
y <= d0 when s = '0' else d1;
```

3. Use `process(in1, in2, ... )` to model more complicated combinational logic where the `process` is helpful. Use blocking assignments for internal variables.

```
process (a, b, cin)
  variable p, g: STD_LOGIC;
begin
  p := a xor b; -- blocking
  g := a and b; -- blocking
  s <= p xor cin;
  cout <= g or (p and cin);
end process;
```

4. Do not make assignments to the same variable in more than one `process` or concurrent assignment statement.

the order shown here. (In the VHDL code, s and cout are assigned concurrently.) Note that p and g get their new values before s and cout are computed because of the blocking assignments. This is important because we want to compute s and cout using the new values of p and g.

1. $p \leftarrow 1 \oplus 0 = 1$

2. $g \leftarrow 1 \bullet 0 = 0$

3. $s \leftarrow 1 \oplus 0 = 1$

4. $cout \leftarrow 0 + 1 \bullet 0 = 0$

In contrast, HDL Example 4.29 illustrates the use of nonblocking assignments.

Now consider the same case of a rising from 0 to 1 while b and cin are 0. The four nonblocking assignments evaluate concurrently:

$$p \leftarrow 1 \oplus 0 = 1 \quad g \leftarrow 1 \bullet 0 = 0 \quad s \leftarrow 0 \oplus 0 = 0 \quad cout \leftarrow 0 + 0 \bullet 0 = 0$$

Observe that s is computed concurrently with p and hence uses the old value of p, not the new value. Therefore, s remains 0 rather than

---

HDL Example 4.29 FULL ADDER USING NONBLOCKING ASSIGNMENTS

Verilog

```
// nonblocking assignments (not recommended)
module fulladder (input      a, b, cin,
                  output reg s, cout);
  reg p, g;

  always @ (*)
    begin
      p <= a ^ b; // nonblocking
      g <= a & b; // nonblocking

      s <= p ^ cin;
      cout <= g | (p & cin);
    end
endmodule
```

Because p and g appear on the left hand side of an assignment in an always statement, they must be declared to be reg.

VHDL

```
-- nonblocking assignments (not recommended)
library IEEE; use IEEE.STD_LOGIC_1164.all;

entity fulladder is
  port (a, b, cin: in  STD_LOGIC;
        s, cout:   out STD_LOGIC);
end;

architecture nonblocking of fulladder is
  signal p, g: STD_LOGIC;
begin
  process (a, b, cin, p, g) begin
    p <= a xor b; -- nonblocking
    g <= a and b; -- nonblocking

    s <= p xor cin;
    cout <= g or (p and cin);
  end process;
end;
```

Because p and g appear on the left hand side of a nonblocking assignment in a process statement, they must be declared to be signal rather than variable. The signal declaration appears before the begin in the architecture, not the process.

becoming 1. However, p does change from 0 to 1. This change triggers the `always`/`process` statement to evaluate a second time, as follows:

$$p \leftarrow 1 \oplus 0 = 1 \quad g \leftarrow 1 \bullet 0 = 0 \quad s \leftarrow 1 \oplus 0 = 1 \quad cout \leftarrow 0 + 1 \bullet 0 = 0$$

This time, p is already 1, so s correctly changes to 1. The nonblocking assignments eventually reach the right answer, but the `always`/`process` statement had to evaluate twice. This makes simulation slower, though it synthesizes to the same hardware.

Another drawback of nonblocking assignments in modeling combinational logic is that the HDL will produce the wrong result if you forget to include the intermediate variables in the sensitivity list.

Verilog	VHDL
If the sensitivity list of the `always` statement in HDL Example 4.29 were written as `always @ (a, b, cin)` rather than `always @ (*)`, then the statement would not reevaluate when p or g changes. In the previous example, s would be incorrectly left at 0, not 1.	If the sensitivity list of the `process` statement in HDL Example 4.29 were written as `process (a, b, cin)` rather than `process (a, b, cin, p, g)`, then the statement would not reevaluate when p or g changes. In the previous example, s would be incorrectly left at 0, not 1.

Worse yet, some synthesis tools will synthesize the correct hardware even when a faulty sensitivity list causes incorrect simulation. This leads to a mismatch between the simulation results and what the hardware actually does.

Sequential Logic*

The synchronizer from HDL Example 4.21 is correctly modeled using nonblocking assignments. On the rising edge of the clock, d is copied to n1 at the same time that n1 is copied to q, so the code properly describes two registers. For example, suppose initially that $d = 0$, $n1 = 1$, and $q = 0$. On the rising edge of the clock, the following two assignments occur concurrently, so that after the clock edge, $n1 = 0$ and $q = 1$.

$$n1 \leftarrow d = 0 \quad q \leftarrow n1 = 1$$

HDL Example 4.30 tries to describe the same module using blocking assignments. On the rising edge of `clk`, d is copied to n1. Then this new value of n1 is copied to q, resulting in d improperly appearing at both n1 and q. The assignments occur one after the other so that after the clock edge, $q = n1 = 0$.

1. $n1 \leftarrow d = 0$

2. $q \leftarrow n1 = 0$

HDL Example 4.30 BAD SYNCHRONIZER WITH BLOCKING ASSIGNMENTS

Verilog	VHDL
| ```
// Bad implementation using blocking assignments

module syncbad(input    clk,
               input    d,
               output reg q);

  reg n1;

  always @ (posedge clk)
    begin
      n1 = d; // blocking
      q = n1; // blocking
    end
endmodule
``` | ```
-- Bad implementation using blocking assignment

library IEEE; use IEEE.STD_LOGIC_1164.all;

entity syncbad is
  port(clk: in  STD_LOGIC;
       d:   in  STD_LOGIC;
       q:   out STD_LOGIC);
end;

architecture bad of syncbad is
begin
  process (clk)
    variable n1: STD_LOGIC;
  begin
    if clk'event and clk = '1' then
      n1 := d; -- blocking
      q <= n1;
    end if;
  end process;
end;
``` |

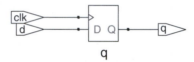

Figure 4.26 syncbad **synthesized circuit**

Because n1 is invisible to the outside world and does not influence the behavior of q, the synthesizer optimizes it away entirely, as shown in Figure 4.26.

The moral of this illustration is to exclusively use nonblocking assignment in always statements when modeling sequential logic. With sufficient cleverness, such as reversing the orders of the assignments, you could make blocking assignments work correctly, but blocking assignments offer no advantages and only introduce the risk of unintended behavior. Certain sequential circuits will not work with blocking assignments no matter what the order.

4.6 FINITE STATE MACHINES

Recall that a finite state machine (FSM) consists of a state register and two blocks of combinational logic to compute the next state and the output given the current state and the input, as was shown in Figure 3.22. HDL descriptions of state machines are correspondingly divided into three parts to model the state register, the next state logic, and the output logic.

HDL Example 4.31 DIVIDE-BY-3 FINITE STATE MACHINE

Verilog

```verilog
module divideby3FSM (input   clk,
                     input   reset,
                     output y);

  reg [1:0] state, nextstate;

  parameter S0 = 2'b00;
  parameter S1 = 2'b01;
  parameter S2 = 2'b10;

  // state register
  always @ (posedge clk, posedge reset)
    if (reset) state <= S0;
    else       state <= nextstate;

  // next state logic
  always @ (*)
    case (state)
      S0: nextstate = S1;
      S1: nextstate = S2;
      S2: nextstate = S0;
      default: nextstate = S0;
    endcase

  // output logic
  assign y = (state == S0);
endmodule
```

The `parameter` statement is used to define constants within a module. Naming the states with parameters is not required, but it makes changing state encodings much easier and makes the code more readable.

Notice how a `case` statement is used to define the state transition table. Because the next state logic should be combinational, a `default` is necessary even though the state $2'b11$ should never arise.

The output, `y`, is 1 when the state is S0. The *equality comparison* a `==` b evaluates to 1 if a equals b and 0 otherwise. The *inequality comparison* a `!=` b does the inverse, evaluating to 1 if a does not equal b.

VHDL

```vhdl
library IEEE; use IEEE.STD_LOGIC_1164.all;
entity divideby3FSM is
  port(clk, reset: in  STD_LOGIC;
       y:              out STD_LOGIC);
end;

architecture synth of divideby3FSM is
  type statetype is (S0, S1, S2);
  signal state, nextstate: statetype;
begin
  -- state register
  process (clk, reset) begin
    if reset = '1' then state <= S0;
    elsif clk'event and clk = '1' then
      state <= nextstate;
    end if;
  end process;

  -- next state logic
  nextstate <= S1 when state = S0 else
               S2 when state = S1 else
               S0;

  -- output logic
  y <= '1' when state = S0 else '0';
end;
```

This example defines a new *enumeration* data type, `statetype`, with three possibilities: S0, S1, and S2. `state` and `nextstate` are `statetype` signals. By using an enumeration instead of choosing the state encoding, VHDL frees the synthesizer to explore various state encodings to choose the best one.

The output, `y`, is 1 when the `state` is S0. The inequality-comparison uses `/=`. To produce an output of 1 when the state is anything but S0, change the comparison to `state /= S0`.

HDL Example 4.31 describes the divide-by-3 FSM from Section 3.4.2. It provides an asynchronous reset to initialize the FSM. The state register uses the ordinary idiom for flip-flops. The next state and output logic blocks are combinational.

The Synplify Pro Synthesis tool just produces a block diagram and state transition diagram for state machines; it does not show the logic gates or the inputs and outputs on the arcs and states. Therefore, be careful that you have specified the FSM correctly in your HDL code. The state transition diagram in Figure 4.27 for the divide-by-3 FSM is analogous to the diagram in Figure 3.28(b). The double circle indicates that

Notice that the synthesis tool uses a 3-bit encoding (Q[2:0]) instead of the 2-bit encoding suggested in the Verilog code.

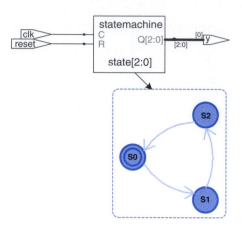

Figure 4.27 dividely3fsm
synthesized circuit

S0 is the reset state. Gate-level implementations of the divide-by-3 FSM were shown in Section 3.4.2.

If, for some reason, we had wanted the output to be HIGH in states S0 and S1, the output logic would be modified as follows.

Verilog	VHDL
``// Output Logic
assign y = (state == S0 | state == S1);```	```-- output logic
y <= '1' when (state = S0 or state = S1) else '0';```

The next two examples describe the snail pattern recognizer FSM from Section 3.4.3. The code shows how to use case and if statements to handle next state and output logic that depend on the inputs as well as the current state. We show both Moore and Mealy modules. In the Moore machine (HDL Example 4.32), the output depends only on the current state, whereas in the Mealy machine (HDL Example 4.33), the output logic depends on both the current state and inputs.

HDL Example 4.32 PATTERN RECOGNIZER MOORE FSM

Verilog

```verilog
module patternMoore(input  clk,
                    input  reset,
                    input  a,
                    output y);

  reg [2:0] state, nextstate;

  parameter S0 = 3'b000;
  parameter S1 = 3'b001;
  parameter S2 = 3'b010;
  parameter S3 = 3'b011;
  parameter S4 = 3'b100;

  // state register
  always @ (posedge clk, posedge reset)
    if (reset) state <= S0;
    else       state <= nextstate;

  // next state logic
  always @ (*)
    case (state)
      S0: if (a) nextstate = S1;
          else   nextstate = S0;
      S1: if (a) nextstate = S2;
          else   nextstate = S0;
      S2: if (a) nextstate = S2;
          else   nextstate = S3;
      S3: if (a) nextstate = S4;
          else   nextstate = S0;
      S4: if (a) nextstate = S2;
          else   nextstate = S0;
      default:   nextstate = S0;
    endcase

  // output logic
  assign y = (state == S4);
endmodule
```

Note how nonblocking assignments (<=) are used in the state register to describe sequential logic, whereas blocking assignments (=) are used in the next state logic to describe combinational logic.

VHDL

```vhdl
library IEEE; use IEEE.STD_LOGIC_1164.all;

entity patternMoore is
  port(clk, reset: in  STD_LOGIC;
       a:          in  STD_LOGIC;
       y:          out STD_LOGIC);
end;

architecture synth of patternMoore is
  type statetype is (S0, S1, S2, S3, S4);
  signal state, nextstate: statetype;
begin
  -- state register
  process(clk, reset) begin
    if reset = '1' then state <= S0;
    elsif clk'event and clk = '1' then
      state <= nextstate;
    end if;
  end process;

  -- next state logic
  process (state, a) begin
    case state is
      when S0 => if a = '1' then
                   nextstate <= S1;
                 else nextstate <= S0;
                 end if;
      when S1 => if a = '1' then
                   nextstate <= S2;
                 else nextstate <= S0;
                 end if;
      when S2 => if a = '1' then
                   nextstate <= S2;
                 else nextstate <= S3;
                 end if;
      when S3 => if a = '1' then
                   nextstate <= S4;
                 else nextstate <= S0;
                 end if;
      when S4 => if a = '1' then
                   nextstate <= S2;
                 else nextstate <= S0;
                 end if;
      when others => nextstate <= S0;
    end case;
  end process;

  -- output logic
  y <= '1' when state = S4 else '0';
end;
```

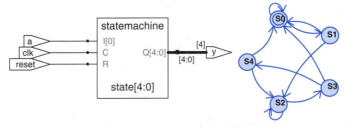

Figure 4.28 patternMoore **synthesized circuit**

HDL Example 4.33 PATTERN RECOGNIZER MEALY FSM

Verilog

```verilog
module patternMealy(input  clk,
                    input  reset,
                    input  a,
                    output y);

  reg [1:0] state, nextstate;

  parameter S0 = 2'b00;
  parameter S1 = 2'b01;
  parameter S2 = 2'b10;
  parameter S3 = 2'b11;

  // state register
  always @ (posedge clk, posedge reset)
    if (reset) state <= S0;
    else       state <= nextstate;

  // next state logic
  always @ (*)
    case (state)
      S0: if (a) nextstate = S1;
          else   nextstate = S0;
      S1: if (a) nextstate = S2;
          else   nextstate = S0;
      S2: if (a) nextstate = S2;
          else   nextstate = S3;
      S3: if (a) nextstate = S1;
          else   nextstate = S0;
      default:   nextstate = S0;
    endcase

  // output logic
  assign y = (a & state == S3);
endmodule
```

VHDL

```vhdl
library IEEE; use IEEE.STD_LOGIC_1164.all;

entity patternMealy is
  port(clk, reset: in  STD_LOGIC;
       a:          in  STD_LOGIC;
       y:          out STD_LOGIC);
end;

architecture synth of patternMealy is
  type statetype is (S0, S1, S2, S3);
  signal state, nextstate: statetype;
begin
  -- state register
  process (clk, reset) begin
    if reset = '1' then state <= S0;
    elsif clk'event and clk = '1' then
      state <= nextstate;
    end if;
  end process;

  -- next state logic
  process(state, a) begin
    case state is
      when S0 => if a = '1' then
                   nextstate <= S1;
                 else nextstate <= S0;
                 end if;
      when S1 => if a = '1' then
                   nextstate <= S2;
                 else nextstate <= S0;
                 end if;
      when S2 => if a = '1' then
                   nextstate <= S2;
                 else nextstate <= S3;
                 end if;
      when S3 => if a = '1' then
                   nextstate <= S1;
                 else nextstate <= S0;
                 end if;
      when others =>  nextstate <= S0;
    end case;
  end process;

  -- output logic
  y <= '1' when (a = '1' and state = S3) else '0';
end;
```

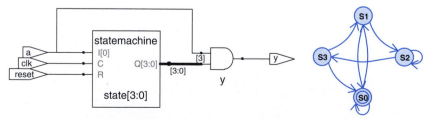

Figure 4.29 patternMealy **synthesized circuit**

4.7 PARAMETERIZED MODULES*

So far all of our modules have had fixed-width inputs and outputs. For example, we had to define separate modules for 4- and 8-bit wide 2:1 multiplexers. HDLs permit variable bit widths using parameterized modules.

HDL Example 4.34 PARAMETERIZED *N*-BIT MULTIPLEXERS

Verilog

```
module mux2
  #(parameter width = 8)
    (input  [width-1:0] d0, d1,
     input             s,
     output [width-1:0] y);

    assign y = s ? d1 : d0;
endmodule
```

Verilog allows a `#(parameter ...)` statement before the inputs and outputs to define parameters. The `parameter` statement includes a default value (8) of the parameter, `width`. The number of bits in the inputs and outputs can depend on this parameter.

```
module mux4_8(input  [7:0] d0, d1, d2, d3,
              input  [1:0] s,
              output [7:0] y);

  wire [7:0] low, hi;

  mux2 lowmux(d0, d1, s[0], low);
  mux2 himux(d2, d3, s[1], hi);
  mux2 outmux(low, hi, s[1], y);
endmodule
```

The 8-bit 4:1 multiplexer instantiates three 2:1 multiplexers using their default widths.

In contrast, a 12-bit 4:1 multiplexer, `mux4_12`, would need to override the default width using `#()` before the instance name, as shown below.

```
module mux4_12(input  [11:0] d0, d1, d2, d3,
               input  [1:0]  s,
               output [11:0] y);

  wire [11:0] low, hi;

  mux2 #(12) lowmux(d0, d1, s[0], low);
  mux2 #(12) himux(d2, d3, s[1], hi);
  mux2 #(12) outmux(low, hi, s[1], y);
endmodule
```

Do not confuse the use of the `#` sign indicating delays with the use of `#( ... )` in defining and overriding parameters.

VHDL

```
library IEEE; use IEEE.STD_LOGIC_1164.all;

entity mux2 is
  generic(width: integer := 8);
  port(d0,
       d1: in  STD_LOGIC_VECTOR(width-1 downto 0);
       s:  in  STD_LOGIC;
       y:  out STD_LOGIC_VECTOR(width-1 downto 0));
end;
architecture synth of mux2 is
begin
  y <= d0 when s = '0' else d1;
end;
```

The `generic` statement includes a default value (8) of `width`. The value is an integer.

```
entity mux4_8 is
  port(d0, d1, d2,
       d3: in  STD_LOGIC_VECTOR(7 downto 0);
       s:  in  STD_LOGIC_VECTOR(1 downto 0);
       y:  out STD_LOGIC_VECTOR(7 downto 0));
end;
architecture struct of mux4_8 is
  component mux2
    generic(width: integer);
    port(d0,
         d1: in  STD_LOGIC_VECTOR(width-1 downto 0);
         s:  in  STD_LOGIC;
         y:  out STD_LOGIC_VECTOR(width-1 downto 0));
  end component;
  signal low, hi: STD_LOGIC_VECTOR(7 downto 0);
begin
  lowmux: mux2 port map(d0, d1, s(0), low);
  himux:  mux2 port map(d2, d3, s(0), hi);
  outmux: mux2 port map(low, hi, s(1), y);
end;
```

The 8-bit 4:1 multiplexer, `mux4_8`, instantiates three 2:1 multiplexers using their default widths.

In contrast, a 12-bit 4:1 multiplexer, `mux4_12`, would need to override the default width using `generic map`, as shown below.

```
lowmux: mux2 generic map(12)
             port map(d0, d1, s(0), low);
himux:  mux2 generic map(12)
             port map(d2, d3, s(0), hi);
outmux: mux2 generic map(12)
             port map(low, hi, s(1), y);
```

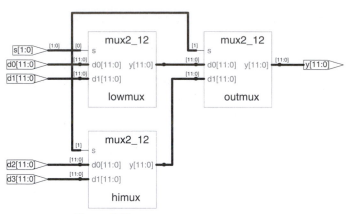

Figure 4.30 mux4_12 **synthesized circuit**

HDL Example 4.35 PARAMETERIZED N:2^N DECODER

Verilog	VHDL

Verilog

```
module decoder #(parameter   N = 3)
                (input     [N−1:0]   a,
                 output reg [2**N−1:0] y);

  always @ (*)
    begin
      y = 0;
      y[a] = 1;
    end
endmodule
```

2**N indicates 2^N.

VHDL

```
library IEEE; use IEEE.STD_LOGIC_1164.all;
use IEEE.STD_LOGIC_UNSIGNED.all;
use IEEE.STD_LOGIC_ARITH.all;

entity decoder is
  generic(N: integer := 3);
  port(a: in  STD_LOGIC_VECTOR(N−1 downto 0);
       y: out STD_LOGIC_VECTOR(2**N−1 downto 0));
end;

architecture synth of decoder is
begin
  process (a)
    variable tmp: STD_LOGIC_VECTOR(2**N−1 downto 0);
    begin
      tmp := CONV_STD_LOGIC_VECTOR(0, 2**N);
      tmp(CONV_INTEGER(a)) := '1';
      y <= tmp;
  end process;
end;
```

2**N indicates 2^N.

    CONV_STD_LOGIC_VECTOR(0, 2**N) produces a STD_LOGIC_VECTOR of length 2^N containing all 0's. It requires the STD_LOGIC_ARITH library. The function is useful in other parameterized functions, such as resettable flip-flops that need to be able to produce constants with a parameterized number of bits. The bit index in VHDL must be an integer, so the CONV_INTEGER function is used to convert a from a STD_LOGIC_VECTOR to an integer.

HDL Example 4.34 declares a parameterized 2:1 multiplexer with a default width of 8, then uses it to create 8- and 12-bit 4:1 multiplexers.

    HDL Example 4.35 shows a decoder, which is an even better application of parameterized modules. A large N:2^N decoder is cumbersome to specify with `case` statements, but easy using parameterized code that simply sets the appropriate output bit to 1. Specifically, the decoder uses blocking assignments to set all the bits to 0, then changes the appropriate bit to 1.

HDLs also provide `generate` statements to produce a variable amount of hardware depending on the value of a parameter. `generate` supports `for` loops and `if` statements to determine how many of what types of hardware to produce. HDL Example 4.36 demonstrates how to use `generate` statements to produce an N-input AND function from a cascade of two-input AND gates.

Use `generate` statements with caution; it is easy to produce a large amount of hardware unintentionally!

HDL Example 4.36 PARAMETERIZED N-INPUT AND GATE

Verilog

```
module andN
  #(parameter width = 8)
   (input [width-1:0] a,
    output           y);

  genvar i;
  wire[width-1:1] x;

  generate
    for (i=1; i<width; i=i+1) begin:forloop
      if (i == 1)
        assign x[1] = a[0] & a[1];
      else
        assign x[i] = a[i] & x[i-1];
    end
  endgenerate
  assign y = x[width-1];
endmodule
```

The `for` statement loops through i = 1, 2, . . . , width−1 to produce many consecutive AND gates. The `begin` in a `generate` `for` loop must be followed by a : and an arbitrary label (`forloop`, in this case).

Of course, writing `assign y = &a` would be much easier!

VHDL

```
library IEEE; use IEEE.STD_LOGIC_1164.all;

entity andN is
  generic (width: integer := 8);
  port (a: in  STD_LOGIC_VECTOR (width-1 downto 0);
        y: out STD_LOGIC);
end;

architecture synth of andN is
  signal i: integer;
  signal x: STD_LOGIC_VECTOR (width-1 downto 1);
begin
  AllBits: for i in 1 to width-1 generate
    LowBit: if i = 1 generate
      A1: x(1) <= a(0) and a(1);
    end generate;
    OtherBits: if i /= 1 generate
      Ai: x(i) <= a(i) and x(i-1);
    end generate;
  end generate;
  y <= x(width-1);
end;
```

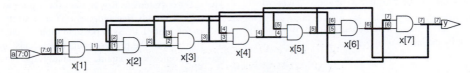

Figure 4.31 andN **synthesized circuit**

4.8 TESTBENCHES

Some tools also call the module to be tested the *unit under test* (UUT).

A *testbench* is an HDL module that is used to test another module, called the *device under test* (DUT). The testbench contains statements to apply inputs to the DUT and, ideally, to check that the correct outputs are produced. The input and desired output patterns are called *test vectors*.

Consider testing the sillyfunction module from Section 4.1.1 that computes $y = \overline{a}\,\overline{b}\,\overline{c} + a\overline{b}\,\overline{c} + a\overline{b}c$. This is a simple module, so we can perform exhaustive testing by applying all eight possible test vectors.

HDL Example 4.37 demonstrates a simple testbench. It instantiates the DUT, then applies the inputs. Blocking assignments and delays are used to apply the inputs in the appropriate order. The user must view the results of the simulation and verify by inspection that the correct outputs are produced. Testbenches are simulated the same as other HDL modules. However, they are not synthesizeable.

HDL Example 4.37 TESTBENCH

Verilog

```
module testbench1 ();
  reg a, b, c;
  wire y;

  // instantiate device under test
  sillyfunction dut (a, b, c, y);

  // apply inputs one at a time
  initial begin
    a = 0; b = 0; c = 0; #10;
    c = 1;              #10;
    b = 1; c = 0;       #10;
    c = 1;              #10;
    a = 1; b = 0; c = 0; #10;
    c = 1;              #10;
    b = 1; c = 0;       #10;
    c = 1;              #10;
  end
endmodule
```

The initial statement executes the statements in its body at the start of simulation. In this case, it first applies the input pattern 000 and waits for 10 time units. It then applies 001 and waits 10 more units, and so forth until all eight possible inputs have been applied. initial statements should be used only in testbenches for simulation, not in modules intended to be synthesized into actual hardware. Hardware has no way of magically executing a sequence of special steps when it is first turned on.

Like signals in always statements, signals in initial statements must be declared to be reg.

VHDL

```
library IEEE; use IEEE.STD_LOGIC_1164.all;

entity testbench1 is -- no inputs or outputs
end;

architecture sim of testbench1 is
  component sillyfunction
    port (a, b, c: in  STD_LOGIC;
          y:       out STD_LOGIC);
  end component;
  signal a, b, c, y: STD_LOGIC;
begin
  -- instantiate device under test
  dut: sillyfunction port map (a, b, c, y);

  -- apply inputs one at a time
  process begin
    a <= '0'; b <= '0'; c <= '0'; wait for 10 ns;
    c <= '1';                     wait for 10 ns;
    b <= '1'; c <= '0';           wait for 10 ns;
    c <= '1';                     wait for 10 ns;
    a <= '1'; b <= '0'; c <= '0'; wait for 10 ns;
    c <= '1';                     wait for 10 ns;
    b <= '1'; c <= '0';           wait for 10 ns;
    c <= '1';                     wait for 10 ns;
    wait; -- wait forever
  end process;
end;
```

The process statement first applies the input pattern 000 and waits for 10 ns. It then applies 001 and waits 10 more ns, and so forth until all eight possible inputs have been applied.

At the end, the process waits indefinitely; otherwise, the process would begin again, repeatedly applying the pattern of test vectors.

Checking for correct outputs is tedious and error-prone. Moreover, determining the correct outputs is much easier when the design is fresh in your mind; if you make minor changes and need to retest weeks later, determining the correct outputs becomes a hassle. A much better approach is to write a self-checking testbench, shown in HDL Example 4.38.

HDL Example 4.38 SELF-CHECKING TESTBENCH

Verilog

```
module testbench2();
  reg a, b, c;
  wire y;

  // instantiate device under test
  sillyfunction dut(a, b, c, y);

  // apply inputs one at a time
  // checking results
  initial begin
    a = 0; b = 0; c = 0; #10;
    if (y !== 1) $display("000 failed.");
    c = 1;             #10;
    if (y !== 0) $display("001 failed.");
    b = 1; c = 0;      #10;
    if (y !== 0) $display("010 failed.");
    c = 1;             #10;
    if (y !== 0) $display("011 failed.");
    a = 1; b = 0; c = 0; #10;
    if (y !== 1) $display("100 failed.");
    c = 1;             #10;
    if (y !== 1) $display("101 failed.");
    b = 1; c = 0;      #10;
    if (y !== 0) $display("110 failed.");
    c = 1;             #10;
    if (y !== 0) $display("111 failed.");
  end
endmodule
```

This module checks y against expectations after each input test vector is applied. In Verilog, comparison using == or != is effective between signals that do not take on the values of x and z. Testbenches use the === and !== operators for comparisons of equality and inequality, respectively, because these operators work correctly with operands that could be x or z. It uses the $display *system task* to print a message on the simulator console if an error occurs. $display is meaningful only in simulation, not synthesis.

VHDL

```
library IEEE; use IEEE.STD_LOGIC_1164.all;

entity testbench2 is -- no inputs or outputs
end;

architecture sim of testbench2 is
  component sillyfunction
    port(a, b, c: in  STD_LOGIC;
         y:       out STD_LOGIC);
  end component;
  signal a, b, c, y: STD_LOGIC;
begin
  -- instantiate device under test
  dut: sillyfunction port map(a, b, c, y);

  -- apply inputs one at a time
  -- checking results
  process begin
    a <= '0'; b <= '0'; c <= '0'; wait for 10 ns;
      assert y = '1' report "000 failed.";
    c <= '1';                     wait for 10 ns;
      assert y = '0' report "001 failed.";
    b <= '1'; c <= '0';           wait for 10 ns;
      assert y = '0' report "010 failed.";
    c <= '1';                     wait for 10 ns;
      assert y = '0' report "011 failed.";
    a <= '1'; b <= '0'; c <= '0'; wait for 10 ns;
      assert y = '1' report "100 failed.";
    c <= '1';                     wait for 10 ns;
      assert y = '1' report "101 failed.";
    b <= '1'; c <= '0';           wait for 10 ns;
      assert y = '0' report "110 failed.";
    c <= '1';                     wait for 10 ns;
      assert y = '0' report "111 failed.";
    wait; -- wait forever
  end process;
end;
```

The assert statement checks a condition and prints the message given in the report clause if the condition is not satisfied. assert is meaningful only in simulation, not in synthesis.

Writing code for each test vector also becomes tedious, especially for modules that require a large number of vectors. An even better approach is to place the test vectors in a separate file. The testbench simply reads the test vectors from the file, applies the input test vector to the DUT, waits, checks that the output values from the DUT match the output vector, and repeats until reaching the end of the test vectors file.

HDL Example 4.39 demonstrates such a testbench. The testbench generates a clock using an `always`/`process` statement with no stimulus list, so that it is continuously reevaluated. At the beginning of the simulation, it reads the test vectors from a text file and pulses `reset` for two cycles. `example.tv` is a text file containing the inputs and expected output written in binary:

```
000_1
001_0
010_0
011_0
100_1
101_1
110_0
111_0
```

HDL Example 4.39 TESTBENCH WITH TEST VECTOR FILE

Verilog

```verilog
module testbench3();
  reg      clk, reset;
  reg      a, b, c, yexpected;
  wire     y;
  reg [31:0] vectornum, errors;
  reg [3:0]  testvectors [10000:0];

  // instantiate device under test
  sillyfunction dut (a, b, c, y);

  // generate clock
  always
    begin
      clk = 1; #5; clk = 0; #5;
    end

  // at start of test, load vectors
  // and pulse reset
  initial
    begin
      $readmemb("example.tv", testvectors);
      vectornum = 0; errors = 0;
      reset = 1; #27; reset = 0;
    end

  // apply test vectors on rising edge of clk
  always @ (posedge clk)
    begin
      #1; {a, b, c, yexpected} =
          testvectors[vectornum];
    end

  // check results on falling edge of clk
  always @ (negedge clk)
    if (~reset) begin // skip during reset
      if (y !== yexpected) begin
```

VHDL

```vhdl
library IEEE; use IEEE.STD_LOGIC_1164.all;
use STD.TEXTIO.all;

entity testbench3 is -- no inputs or outputs
end;

architecture sim of testbench3 is
  component sillyfunction
    port (a, b, c: in  STD_LOGIC;
          y:           out STD_LOGIC);
  end component;
  signal a, b, c, y: STD_LOGIC;
  signal clk, reset: STD_LOGIC;
  signal yexpected:  STD_LOGIC;
  constant MEMSIZE: integer := 10000;
  type tvarray is array (MEMSIZE downto 0) of
    STD_LOGIC_VECTOR (3 downto 0);
  signal testvectors: tvarray;
  shared variable vectornum, errors: integer;
begin
  -- instantiate device under test
  dut: sillyfunction port map (a, b, c, y);

  -- generate clock
  process begin
    clk <= '1'; wait for 5 ns;
    clk <= '0'; wait for 5 ns;
  end process;

  -- at start of test, load vectors
  -- and pulse reset
  process is
    file tv: TEXT;
    variable i, j: integer;
    variable L: line;
    variable ch: character;
```

```
        $display ("Error: inputs = %b", {a, b, c});
        $display (" outputs = %b (%b expected)",
                  y, yexpected);
        errors = errors + 1;
      end
      vectornum = vectornum + 1;
      if (testvectors[vectornum] === 4'bx) begin
        $display ("%d tests completed with %d errors",
                  vectornum, errors);
        $finish;
      end
    end
  end
endmodule
```

$readmemb reads a file of binary numbers into the testvectors array. $readmemh is similar but reads a file of hexadecimal numbers.

The next block of code waits one time unit after the rising edge of the clock (to avoid any confusion if clock and data change simultaneously), then sets the three inputs and the expected output based on the four bits in the current test vector. The next block of code checks the output of the DUT at the negative edge of the clock, after the inputs have had time to propagate through the DUT to produce the output, y. The testbench compares the generated output, y, with the expected output, yexpected, and prints an error if they don't match. %b and %d indicate to print the values in binary and decimal, respectively. For example, $display ("%b %b", y, yexpected); prints the two values, y and yexpected, in binary. %h prints a value in hexadecimal.

This process repeats until there are no more valid test vectors in the testvectors array. $finish terminates the simulation.

Note that even though the Verilog module supports up to 10,001 test vectors, it will terminate the simulation after executing the eight vectors in the file.

```
begin
  -- read file of test vectors
  i := 0;
  FILE_OPEN (tv, "example.tv", READ_MODE);
  while not endfile (tv) loop
    readline (tv, L);
    for j in 0 to 3 loop
      read (L, ch);
      if (ch = '_') then read (L, ch);
      end if;
      if (ch = '0') then
        testvectors (i) (j) <= '0';
      else testvectors (i) (j) <= '1';
      end if;
    end loop;
    i := i + 1;
  end loop;

  vectornum := 0; errors := 0;
  reset <= '1'; wait for 27 ns; reset <= '0';
  wait;
end process;

-- apply test vectors on rising edge of clk
process (clk) begin
  if (clk'event and clk = '1') then

    a <= testvectors (vectornum) (0) after 1 ns;
    b <= testvectors (vectornum) (1) after 1 ns;
    c <= testvectors (vectornum) (2) after 1 ns;
    yexpected <= testvectors (vectornum) (3)
      after 1 ns;
  end if;
end process;

-- check results on falling edge of clk
process (clk) begin
  if (clk'event and clk = '0' and reset = '0') then
    assert y = yexpected
      report "Error: y = " & STD_LOGIC'image(y);
    if (y /= yexpected) then
      errors := errors + 1;
    end if;
    vectornum := vectornum + 1;
    if (is_x (testvectors(vectornum))) then
      if (errors = 0) then
        report "Just kidding --" &
                integer'image (vectornum) &
                "tests completed successfully."
                severity failure;
      else
        report integer'image (vectornum) &
                "tests completed, errors = " &
                integer'image (errors)
                severity failure;
      end if;
    end if;
  end if;
end process;
end;
```

The VHDL code is rather ungainly and uses file reading commands beyond the scope of this chapter, but it gives the sense of what a self-checking testbench looks like.

New inputs are applied on the rising edge of the clock, and the output is checked on the falling edge of the clock. This clock (and `reset`) would also be provided to the DUT if sequential logic were being tested. Errors are reported as they occur. At the end of the simulation, the testbench prints the total number of test vectors applied and the number of errors detected.

The testbench in HDL Example 4.39 is overkill for such a simple circuit. However, it can easily be modified to test more complex circuits by changing the `example.tv` file, instantiating the new DUT, and changing a few lines of code to set the inputs and check the outputs.

4.9 SUMMARY

Hardware description languages (HDLs) are extremely important tools for modern digital designers. Once you have learned Verilog or VHDL, you will be able to specify digital systems much faster than if you had to draw the complete schematics. The debug cycle is also often much faster, because modifications require code changes instead of tedious schematic rewiring. However, the debug cycle can be much *longer* using HDLs if you don't have a good idea of the hardware your code implies.

HDLs are used for both simulation and synthesis. Logic simulation is a powerful way to test a system on a computer before it is turned into hardware. Simulators let you check the values of signals inside your system that might be impossible to measure on a physical piece of hardware. Logic synthesis converts the HDL code into digital logic circuits.

The most important thing to remember when you are writing HDL code is that you are describing real hardware, not writing a computer program. The most common beginner's mistake is to write HDL code without thinking about the hardware you intend to produce. If you don't know what hardware you are implying, you are almost certain not to get what you want. Instead, begin by sketching a block diagram of your system, identifying which portions are combinational logic, which portions are sequential circuits or finite state machines, and so forth. Then write HDL code for each portion, using the correct idioms to imply the kind of hardware you need.

Exercises

The following exercises may be done using your favorite HDL. If you have a simulator available, test your design. Print the waveforms and explain how they prove that it works. If you have a synthesizer available, synthesize your code. Print the generated circuit diagram, and explain why it matches your expectations.

Exercise 4.1 Sketch a schematic of the circuit described by the following HDL code. Simplify the schematic so that it shows a minimum number of gates.

Verilog	VHDL

<pre>module exercise1(input a, b, c,
                 output y, z);
 	
  assign y = a & b & c
	a & b & ~c	a & ~b & c;
		  assign z = a & b
			~a & ~b;
			endmodule</pre>
				<pre>library IEEE; use IEEE.STD_LOGIC_1164.all;
				
				entity exercise1 is
				  port(a, b, c: in STD_LOGIC;
				       y, z: out STD_LOGIC);
				end;
				
				architecture synth of exercise1 is
				begin
				  y <= (a and b and c) or (a and b and (not c)) or
				       (a and (not b) and c);
				  z <= (a and b) or ((not a) and (not b));
				end;</pre>

Exercise 4.2 Sketch a schematic of the circuit described by the following HDL code. Simplify the schematic so that it shows a minimum number of gates.

Verilog	VHDL

<pre>module exercise2(input   [3:0] a,
                 output reg [1:0] y);
 	
  always @(*)
    if   (a[0]) y = 2'b11;
    else if (a[1]) y = 2'b10;
    else if (a[2]) y = 2'b01;
    else if (a[3]) y = 2'b00;
    else   y = a[1:0];
endmodule</pre>
	<pre>library IEEE; use IEEE.STD_LOGIC_1164.all;
	
	entity exercise2 is
	  port(a: in STD_LOGIC_VECTOR(3 downto 0);
	       y: out STD_LOGIC_VECTOR(1 downto 0));
	end;
	
	architecture synth of exercise2 is
	begin
	  process(a) begin
	    if a(0) = '1' then y <= "11";
	    elsif a(1) = '1' then y <= "10";
	    elsif a(2) = '1' then y <= "01";
	    elsif a(3) = '1' then y <= "00";
	    else y <= a(1 downto 0);
	    end if;
	  end process;
	end;</pre>

Exercise 4.3 Write an HDL module that computes a four-input XOR function. The input is $a_{3:0}$, and the output is y.

Exercise 4.4 Write a self-checking testbench for Exercise 4.3. Create a test vector file containing all 16 test cases. Simulate the circuit and show that it works. Introduce an error in the test vector file and show that the testbench reports a mismatch.

Exercise 4.5 Write an HDL module called `minority`. It receives three inputs, a, b, and c. It produces one output, y, that is TRUE if at least two of the inputs are FALSE.

Exercise 4.6 Write an HDL module for a hexadecimal seven-segment display decoder. The decoder should handle the digits A, B, C, D, E, and F as well as 0–9.

Exercise 4.7 Write a self-checking testbench for Exercise 4.6. Create a test vector file containing all 16 test cases. Simulate the circuit and show that it works. Introduce an error in the test vector file and show that the testbench reports a mismatch.

Exercise 4.8 Write an 8:1 multiplexer module called `mux8` with inputs $s_{2:0}$, d0, d1, d2, d3, d4, d5, d6, d7, and output y.

Exercise 4.9 Write a structural module to compute the logic function, $y = a\overline{b} + \overline{b}\,\overline{c} + \overline{a}bc$, using multiplexer logic. Use the 8:1 multiplexer from Exercise 4.8.

Exercise 4.10 Repeat Exercise 4.9 using a 4:1 multiplexer and as many NOT gates as you need.

Exercise 4.11 Section 4.5.4 pointed out that a synchronizer could be correctly described with blocking assignments if the assignments were given in the proper order. Think of a simple sequential circuit that cannot be correctly described with blocking assignments, regardless of order.

Exercise 4.12 Write an HDL module for an eight-input priority circuit.

Exercise 4.13 Write an HDL module for a 2:4 decoder.

Exercise 4.14 Write an HDL module for a 6:64 decoder using three instances of the 2:4 decoders from Exercise 4.13 and a bunch of three-input AND gates.

Exercise 4.15 Write HDL modules that implement the Boolean equations from Exercise 2.7.

Exercise 4.16 Write an HDL module that implements the circuit from Exercise 2.18.

Exercise 4.17 Write an HDL module that implements the logic function from Exercise 2.19. Pay careful attention to how you handle don't cares.

Exercise 4.18 Write an HDL module that implements the functions from Exercise 2.24.

Exercise 4.19 Write an HDL module that implements the priority encoder from Exercise 2.25.

Exercise 4.20 Write an HDL module that implements the binary-to-thermometer code converter from Exercise 2.27.

Exercise 4.21 Write an HDL module implementing the days-in-month function from Question 2.2.

Exercise 4.22 Sketch the state transition diagram for the FSM described by the following HDL code.

Verilog

```verilog
module fsm2 (input  clk, reset,
             input  a, b,
             output y);

  reg [1:0] state, nextstate;

  parameter S0 = 2'b00;
  parameter S1 = 2'b01;
  parameter S2 = 2'b10;
  parameter S3 = 2'b11;

  always @ (posedge clk, posedge reset)
    if (reset) state <= S0;
    else       state <= nextstate;

  always @ (*)
    case (state)
      S0: if (a ^ b) nextstate = S1;
          else       nextstate = S0;
      S1: if (a & b) nextstate = S2;
          else       nextstate = S0;
      S2: if (a | b) nextstate = S3;
          else       nextstate = S0;
      S3: if (a | b) nextstate = S3;
          else       nextstate = S0;
    endcase

  assign y = (state == S1) | (state == S2);
endmodule
```

VHDL

```vhdl
library IEEE; use IEEE.STD_LOGIC_1164.all;

entity fsm2 is
  port (clk, reset: in  STD_LOGIC;
        a, b:       in  STD_LOGIC;
        y:          out STD_LOGIC);
end;

architecture synth of fsm2 is
  type statetype is (S0, S1, S2, S3);
  signal state, nextstate: statetype;
begin
  process (clk, reset) begin
    if reset = '1' then state <= S0;
    elsif clk'event and clk = '1' then
      state <= nextstate;
    end if;
  end process;

  process (state, a, b) begin
    case state is
      when S0 => if (a xor b) = '1' then
                   nextstate <= S1;
                 else nextstate <= S0;
                 end if;
      when S1 => if (a and b) = '1' then
                   nextstate <= S2;
                 else nextstate <= S0;
                 end if;
      when S2 => if (a or b) = '1' then
                   nextstate <= S3;
                 else nextstate <= S0;
                 end if;
      when S3 => if (a or b) = '1' then
                   nextstate <= S3;
                 else nextstate <= S0;
                 end if;
    end case;
  end process;

  y <= '1' when ((state = S1) or (state = S2))
       else '0';
end;
```

Exercise 4.23 Sketch the state transition diagram for the FSM described by the following HDL code. An FSM of this nature is used in a branch predictor on some microprocessors.

Verilog

```
module fsm1(input   clk, reset,
            input   taken, back,
            output  predicttaken);

  reg [4:0] state, nextstate;

  parameter S0 = 5'b00001;
  parameter S1 = 5'b00010;
  parameter S2 = 5'b00100;
  parameter S3 = 5'b01000;
  parameter S4 = 5'b10000;

  always @ (posedge clk, posedge reset)
    if (reset) state <= S2;
    else       state <= nextstate;

  always @ (*)
    case (state)
      S0: if (taken) nextstate = S1;
          else       nextstate = S0;
      S1: if (taken) nextstate = S2;
          else       nextstate = S0;
      S2: if (taken) nextstate = S3;
          else       nextstate = S1;
      S3: if (taken) nextstate = S4;
          else       nextstate = S2;
      S4: if (taken) nextstate = S4;
          else       nextstate = S3;
      default:       nextstate = S2;
    endcase

  assign predicttaken = (state == S4) ||
                        (state == S3) ||
                        (state == S2 && back);
endmodule
```

VHDL

```
library IEEE; use IEEE.STD_LOGIC_1164.all;

entity fsm1 is
  port(clk, reset:  in  STD_LOGIC;
       taken, back: in  STD_LOGIC;
       predicttaken: out STD_LOGIC);
end;

architecture synth of fsm1 is
  type statetype is (S0, S1, S2, S3, S4);
  signal state, nextstate: statetype;
begin
  process (clk, reset) begin
    if reset = '1' then state <= S2;
    elsif clk'event and clk = '1' then
      state <= nextstate;
    end if;
  end process;

  process (state, taken) begin
    case state is
      when S0 => if taken = '1' then
                      nextstate <= S1;
                 else nextstate <= S0;
                 end if;
      when S1 => if taken = '1' then
                      nextstate <= S2;
                 else nextstate <= S0;
                 end if;
      when S2 => if taken = '1' then
                      nextstate <= S3;
                 else nextstate <= S1;
                 end if;
      when S3 => if taken = '1' then
                      nextstate <= S4;
                 else nextstate <= S2;
                 end if;
      when S4 => if taken = '1' then
                      nextstate <= S4;
                 else nextstate <= S3;
                 end if;
      when others => nextstate <= S2;
    end case;
  end process;

  -- output logic
  predicttaken <= '1' when
                   ((state = S4) or (state = S3) or
                    (state = S2 and back = '1'))
                else '0';
end;
```

Exercise 4.24 Write an HDL module for an SR latch.

Exercise 4.25 Write an HDL module for a *JK flip-flop*. The flip-flop has inputs, *clk*, *J*, and *K*, and output *Q*. On the rising edge of the clock, *Q* keeps its old value if $J = K = 0$. It sets *Q* to 1 if $J = 1$, resets *Q* to 0 if $K = 1$, and inverts *Q* if $J = K = 1$.

Exercise 4.26 Write an HDL module for the latch from Figure 3.18. Use one assignment statement for each gate. Specify delays of 1 unit or 1 ns to each gate. Simulate the latch and show that it operates correctly. Then increase the inverter delay. How long does the delay have to be before a race condition causes the latch to malfunction?

Exercise 4.27 Write an HDL module for the traffic light controller from Section 3.4.1.

Exercise 4.28 Write three HDL modules for the factored parade mode traffic light controller from Example 3.8. The modules should be called `controller`, `mode`, and `lights`, and they should have the inputs and outputs shown in Figure 3.33(b).

Exercise 4.29 Write an HDL module describing the circuit in Figure 3.40.

Exercise 4.30 Write an HDL module for the FSM with the state transition diagram given in Figure 3.65 from Exercise 3.19.

Exercise 4.31 Write an HDL module for the FSM with the state transition diagram given in Figure 3.66 from Exercise 3.20.

Exercise 4.32 Write an HDL module for the improved traffic light controller from Exercise 3.21.

Exercise 4.33 Write an HDL module for the daughter snail from Exercise 3.22.

Exercise 4.34 Write an HDL module for the soda machine dispenser from Exercise 3.23.

Exercise 4.35 Write an HDL module for the Gray code counter from Exercise 3.24.

Exercise 4.36 Write an HDL module for the UP/DOWN Gray code counter from Exercise 3.25.

Exercise 4.37 Write an HDL module for the FSM from Exercise 3.26.

Exercise 4.38 Write an HDL module for the FSM from Exercise 3.27.

Exercise 4.39 Write an HDL module for the serial two's complementer from Question 3.2.

Exercise 4.40 Write an HDL module for the circuit in Exercise 3.28.

Exercise 4.41 Write an HDL module for the circuit in Exercise 3.29.

Exercise 4.42 Write an HDL module for the circuit in Exercise 3.30.

Exercise 4.43 Write an HDL module for the circuit in Exercise 3.31. You may use the full adder from Section 4.2.5.

Verilog Exercises

The following exercises are specific to Verilog.

Exercise 4.44 What does it mean for a signal to be declared reg in Verilog?

Exercise 4.45 Rewrite the syncbad module from HDL Example 4.30. Use nonblocking assignments, but change the code to produce a correct synchronizer with two flip-flops.

Exercise 4.46 Consider the following two Verilog modules. Do they have the same function? Sketch the hardware each one implies.

```
module code1(input        clk, a, b, c,
             output reg y);
  reg x;

  always @ (posedge clk) begin
    x <= a & b;
    y <= x | c;
  end
endmodule

module code2(input        a, b, c, clk,
             output reg y);
  reg x;

  always @ (posedge clk) begin
    y <= x | c;
    x <= a & b;
  end
endmodule
```

Exercise 4.47 Repeat Exercise 4.46 if the <= is replaced by = in every assignment.

Exercise 4.48 The following Verilog modules show errors that the authors have seen students make in the laboratory. Explain the error in each module and show how to fix it.

(a)
```verilog
module latch (input              clk,
              input       [3:0] d,
              output reg [3:0] q);

    always @ (clk)
        if (clk) q <= d;
endmodule
```

(b)
```verilog
module gates (input       [3:0] a, b,
              output reg [3:0] y1, y2, y3, y4, y5);

    always @ (a)
        begin
            y1 = a & b;
            y2 = a | b;
            y3 = a ^ b;
            y4 = ~(a & b);
            y5 = ~(a | b);
        end
endmodule
```

(c)
```verilog
module mux2 (input       [3:0] d0, d1,
             input              s,
             output reg [3:0] y);

    always @ (posedge s)
        if (s) y <= d1;
        else   y <= d0;
endmodule
```

(d)
```verilog
module twoflops (input        clk,
                 input        d0, d1,
                 output reg q0, q1);

    always @ (posedge clk)
        q1 = d1;
        q0 = d0;
endmodule
```

(e)
```verilog
module FSM(input        clk,
           input        a,
           output reg out1, out2);

    reg state;

    // next state logic and register (sequential)
    always @ (posedge clk)
       if(state == 0) begin
          if(a)   state <= 1;
       end else begin
          if(~a) state <= 0;
       end

    always @ (*) // output logic (combinational)
       if(state == 0) out1 = 1;
       else            out2 = 1;
endmodule
```

(f)
```verilog
module priority(input        [3:0] a,
                output reg [3:0] y);

    always @ (*)
       if      (a[3]) y = 4'b1000;
       else if(a[2]) y = 4'b0100;
       else if(a[1]) y = 4'b0010;
       else if(a[0]) y = 4'b0001;
endmodule
```

(g)
```verilog
module divideby3FSM(input   clk,
                    input   reset,
                    output out);

    reg [1:0] state, nextstate;

    parameter S0 = 2'b00;
    parameter S1 = 2'b01;
    parameter S2 = 2'b10;

    // State Register
    always @ (posedge clk, posedge reset)
       if(reset) state <= S0;
       else      state <= nextstate;

    // Next State Logic
    always @ (state)
       case(state)
         S0: nextstate = S1;
         S1: nextstate = S2;
          2: nextstate = S0;
       endcase

    // Output Logic
    assign out = (state == S2);
endmodule
```

(h)
```
module mux2tri(input    [3:0] d0, d1,
               input          s,
               output [3:0] y);

   tristate t0 (d0, s, y);
   tristate t1 (d1, s, y);
endmodule
```

(i)
```
module floprsen(input           clk,
                input           reset,
                input           set,
                input     [3:0] d,
                output reg [3:0] q);

   always @ (posedge clk, posedge reset)
      if (reset) q <= 0;
      else       q <= d;

   always @ (set)
      if (set)   q <= 1;
endmodule
```

(j)
```
module and3(input      a, b, c,
            output reg y);

   reg tmp;

   always @ (a, b, c)
   begin
      tmp <= a & b;
      y   <= tmp & c;
   end
endmodule
```

VHDL Exercises

The following exercises are specific to VHDL.

Exercise 4.49 In VHDL, why is it necessary to write

```
q <= '1' when state = S0 else '0';
```

rather than simply

```
q <= (state = S0);
```

Exercise 4.50 Each of the following VHDL modules contains an error. For brevity, only the architecture is shown; assume that the library use clause and entity declaration are correct. Explain the error and show how to fix it.

(a)
```
architecture synth of latch is
begin
  process (clk) begin
    if clk = '1' then q <= d;
    end if;
  end process;
end;
```

(b)
```
architecture proc of gates is
begin
  process (a) begin
    y1 <= a and b;
    y2 <= a or b;
    y3 <= a xor b;
    y4 <= a nand b;
    y5 <= a nor b;
  end process;
end;
```

(c)
```
architecture synth of flop is
begin
  process (clk)
    if clk'event and clk = '1' then
      q <= d;
end;
```

(d)
```
architecture synth of priority is
begin
  process (a) begin
    if    a(3) = '1' then y <= "1000";
    elsif a(2) = '1' then y <= "0100";
    elsif a(1) = '1' then y <= "0010";
    elsif a(0) = '1' then y <= "0001";
    end if;
  end process;
end;
```

(e)
```
architecture synth of divideby3FSM is
  type statetype is (S0, S1, S2);
  signal state, nextstate: statetype;
begin
  process (clk, reset) begin
    if reset = '1' then state <= S0;
    elsif clk'event and clk = '1' then
      state <= nextstate;
    end if;
  end process;
```

```
      process (state) begin
        case state is
          when S0 => nextstate <= S1;
          when S1 => nextstate <= S2;
          when S2 => nextstate <= S0;
        end case;
      end process;

    q <= '1' when state = S0 else '0';
  end;
```

(f)   ```
architecture struct of mux2 is
  component tristate
    port (a: in STD_LOGIC_VECTOR (3 downto 0);
          en: in STD_LOGIC;
          y: out STD_LOGIC_VECTOR (3 downto 0));
  end component;
begin
  t0: tristate port map (d0, s, y);
  t1: tristate port map (d1, s, y);
end;
```

(g)    ```
architecture asynchronous of flopr is
begin
  process (clk, reset) begin
    if reset = '1' then
      q <= '0';
    elsif clk'event and clk = '1' then
      q <= d;
    end if;
  end process;

  process (set) begin
    if set = '1' then
      q <= '1';
    end if;
  end process;
end;
```

(h)   ```
architecture synth of mux3 is
begin
  y <= d2 when s(1) else
       d1 when s(0) else d0;
end;
```
```

Interview Questions

The following exercises present questions that have been asked at interviews for digital design jobs.

Question 4.1 Write a line of HDL code that gates a 32-bit bus called `data` with another signal called `sel` to produce a 32-bit `result`. If `sel` is TRUE, `result` = `data`. Otherwise, `result` should be all 0's.

Question 4.2 Explain the difference between blocking and nonblocking assignments in Verilog. Give examples.

Question 4.3 What does the following Verilog statement do?

```
result = | (data[15:0] & 16'hC820);
```

Digital Building Blocks

5

5.1 INTRODUCTION

Up to this point, we have examined the design of combinational and sequential circuits using Boolean equations, schematics, and HDLs. This chapter introduces more elaborate combinational and sequential building blocks used in digital systems. These blocks include arithmetic circuits, counters, shift registers, memory arrays, and logic arrays. These building blocks are not only useful in their own right, but they also demonstrate the principles of hierarchy, modularity, and regularity. The building blocks are hierarchically assembled from simpler components such as logic gates, multiplexers, and decoders. Each building block has a well-defined interface and can be treated as a black box when the underlying implementation is unimportant. The regular structure of each building block is easily extended to different sizes. In Chapter 7, we use many of these building blocks to build a microprocessor.

5.2 ARITHMETIC CIRCUITS

Arithmetic circuits are the central building blocks of computers. Computers and digital logic perform many arithmetic functions: addition, subtraction, comparisons, shifts, multiplication, and division. This section describes hardware implementations for all of these operations.

5.2.1 Addition

Addition is one of the most common operations in digital systems. We first consider how to add two 1-bit binary numbers. We then extend to N-bit binary numbers. Adders also illustrate trade-offs between speed and complexity.

Half Adder

We begin by building a 1-bit *half adder*. As shown in Figure 5.1, the half adder has two inputs, A and B, and two outputs, S and C_{out}. S is the

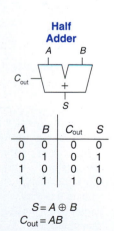

Half Adder

A	B	C_{out}	S
0	0	0	0
0	1	0	1
1	0	0	1
1	1	1	0

$$S = A \oplus B$$
$$C_{out} = AB$$

FIGURE 5.1 **1-bit half adder**

233

sum of A and B. If A and B are both 1, S is 2, which cannot be represented with a single binary digit. Instead, it is indicated with a carry out, C_{out}, in the next column. The half adder can be built from an XOR gate and an AND gate.

In a multi-bit adder, C_{out} is added or *carried in* to the next most significant bit. For example, in Figure 5.2, the carry bit shown in blue is the output, C_{out}, of the first column of 1-bit addition and the input, C_{in}, to the second column of addition. However, the half adder lacks a C_{in} input to accept C_{out} of the previous column. The *full adder*, described in the next section, solves this problem.

Full Adder

A *full adder*, introduced in Section 2.1, accepts the carry in, C_{in}, as shown in Figure 5.3. The figure also shows the output equations for S and C_{out}.

Carry Propagate Adder

An N-bit adder sums two N-bit inputs, A and B, and a carry in, C_{in}, to produce an N-bit result, S, and a carry out, C_{out}. It is commonly called a *carry propagate adder* (CPA) because the carry out of one bit propagates into the next bit. The symbol for a CPA is shown in Figure 5.4; it is drawn just like a full adder except that A, B, and S are busses rather than single bits. Three common CPA implementations are called ripple-carry adders, carry-lookahead adders, and prefix adders.

Ripple-Carry Adder

The simplest way to build an N-bit carry propagate adder is to chain together N full adders. The C_{out} of one stage acts as the C_{in} of the next stage, as shown in Figure 5.5 for 32-bit addition. This is called a *ripple-carry adder*. It is a good application of modularity and regularity: the full adder module is reused many times to form a larger system. The ripple-carry adder has the disadvantage of being slow when N is large. S_{31} depends on C_{30}, which depends on C_{29}, which depends on C_{28}, and so forth all the way back to C_{in}, as shown in blue in Figure 5.5. We say that the carry *ripples* through the carry chain. The delay of the adder, t_{ripple}, grows directly with the number of bits, as given in Equation 5.1, where t_{FA} is the delay of a full adder.

$$t_{ripple} = Nt_{FA} \tag{5.1}$$

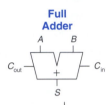

$$
\begin{array}{c}
1 \\
0001 \\
+0101 \\
\hline
0110
\end{array}
$$

Figure 5.2 Carry bit

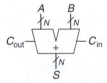

Full Adder

C_{in}	A	B	C_{out}	S
0	0	0	0	0
0	0	1	0	1
0	1	0	0	1
0	1	1	1	0
1	0	0	0	1
1	0	1	1	0
1	1	0	1	0
1	1	1	1	1

$$S = A \oplus B \oplus C_{in}$$
$$C_{out} = AB + AC_{in} + BC_{in}$$

FIGURE 5.3 1-bit full adder

Figure 5.4 Carry propagate adder

Schematics typically show signals flowing from left to right. Arithmetic circuits break this rule because the carries flow from right to left (from the least significant column to the most significant column).

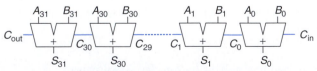

Figure 5.5 32-bit ripple-carry adder

Carry-Lookahead Adder

The fundamental reason that large ripple-carry adders are slow is that the carry signals must propagate through every bit in the adder. A *carry-lookahead* adder is another type of carry propagate adder that solves this problem by dividing the adder into *blocks* and providing circuitry to quickly determine the carry out of a block as soon as the carry in is known. Thus it is said to *look ahead* across the blocks rather than waiting to ripple through all the full adders inside a block. For example, a 32-bit adder may be divided into eight 4-bit blocks.

Carry-lookahead adders use *generate* (G) and *propagate* (P) signals that describe how a column or block determines the carry out. The *i*th column of an adder is said to *generate* a carry if it produces a carry out independent of the carry in. The *i*th column of an adder is guaranteed to generate a carry, C_i, if A_i and B_i are both 1. Hence G_i, the generate signal for column *i*, is calculated as $G_i = A_i B_i$. The column is said to *propagate* a carry if it produces a carry out whenever there is a carry in. The *i*th column will propagate a carry in, C_{i-1}, if either A_i or B_i is 1. Thus, $P_i = A_i + B_i$. Using these definitions, we can rewrite the carry logic for a particular column of the adder. The *i*th column of an adder will generate a carryout, C_i, if it either generates a carry, G_i, or propagates a carry in, $P_i C_{i-1}$. In equation form,

$$C_i = A_i B_i + (A_i + B_i) C_{i-1} = G_i + P_i C_{i-1} \qquad (5.2)$$

The generate and propagate definitions extend to multiple-bit blocks. A block is said to generate a carry if it produces a carry out independent of the carry in to the block. The block is said to propagate a carry if it produces a carry out whenever there is a carry in to the block. We define $G_{i:j}$ and $P_{i:j}$ as generate and propagate signals for blocks spanning columns *i* through *j*.

A block generates a carry if the most significant column generates a carry, or if the most significant column propagates a carry and the previous column generated a carry, and so forth. For example, the generate logic for a block spanning columns 3 through 0 is

$$G_{3:0} = G_3 + P_3 (G_2 + P_2 (G_1 + P_1 G_0)) \qquad (5.3)$$

A block propagates a carry if all the columns in the block propagate the carry. For example, the propagate logic for a block spanning columns 3 through 0 is

$$P_{3:0} = P_3 P_2 P_1 P_0 \qquad (5.4)$$

Using the block generate and propagate signals, we can quickly compute the carry out of the block, C_i, using the carry in to the block, C_j.

$$C_i = G_{i:j} + P_{i:j} C_j \qquad (5.5)$$

Throughout the ages, people have used many devices to perform arithmetic. Toddlers count on their fingers (and some adults stealthily do too). The Chinese and Babylonians invented the abacus as early as 2400 BC. Slide rules, invented in 1630, were in use until the 1970's, when scientific hand calculators became prevalent. Computers and digital calculators are ubiquitous today. What will be next?

Figure 5.6(a) shows a 32-bit carry-lookahead adder composed of eight 4-bit blocks. Each block contains a 4-bit ripple-carry adder and some lookahead logic to compute the carry out of the block given the carry in, as shown in Figure 5.6(b). The AND and OR gates needed to compute the single-bit generate and propagate signals, G_i and P_i, from A_i and B_i are left out for brevity. Again, the carry-lookahead adder demonstrates modularity and regularity.

All of the CLA blocks compute the single-bit and block generate and propagate signals simultaneously. The critical path starts with computing G_0 and $G_{3:0}$ in the first CLA block. C_{in} then advances directly to C_{out} through the AND/OR gate in each block until the last. For a large adder, this is much faster than waiting for the carries to ripple through each consecutive bit of the adder. Finally, the critical path through the last block contains a short ripple-carry adder. Thus, an N-bit adder divided into k-bit blocks has a delay

$$t_{CLA} = t_{pg} + t_{pg\_block} + \left(\frac{N}{k} - 1\right) t_{AND-OR} + k t_{FA} \qquad (5.6)$$

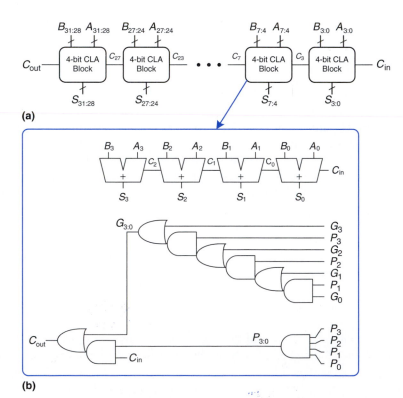

Figure 5.6 (a) 32-bit *carry-lookahead adder (CLA)*, (b) 4-bit CLA block

where t_{pg} is the delay of the individual generate/propagate gates (a single AND or OR gate) to generate P and G, t_{pg_block} is the delay to find the generate/propagate signals $P_{i:j}$ and $G_{i:j}$ for a k-bit block, and t_{AND_OR} is the delay from C_{in} to C_{out} through the AND/OR logic of the k-bit CLA block. For $N > 16$, the carry-lookahead adder is generally much faster than the ripple-carry adder. However, the adder delay still increases linearly with N.

Example 5.1 RIPPLE-CARRY ADDER AND CARRY-LOOKAHEAD
ADDER DELAY

Compare the delays of a 32-bit ripple-carry adder and a 32-bit carry-lookahead adder with 4-bit blocks. Assume that each two-input gate delay is 100 ps and that a full adder delay is 300 ps.

Solution: According to Equation 5.1, the propagation delay of the 32-bit ripple-carry adder is 32×300 ps $= 9.6$ ns.

The CLA has $t_{pg} = 100$ ps, $t_{pg\_block} = 6 \times 100$ ps $= 600$ ps, and $t_{AND\_OR} = 2 \times 100$ ps $= 200$ ps. According to Equation 5.6, the propagation delay of the 32-bit carry-lookahead adder with 4-bit blocks is thus 100 ps $+$ 600 ps $+ (32/4 - 1) \times 200$ ps $+ (4 \times 300$ ps$) = 3.3$ ns, almost three times faster than the ripple-carry adder.

Prefix Adder*

Prefix adders extend the generate and propagate logic of the carry-lookahead adder to perform addition even faster. They first compute G and P for pairs of columns, then for blocks of 4, then for blocks of 8, then 16, and so forth until the generate signal for every column is known. The sums are computed from these generate signals.

In other words, the strategy of a prefix adder is to compute the carry in, C_{i-1}, for each column, i, as quickly as possible, then to compute the sum, using

$$S_i = (A_i \oplus B_i) \oplus C_{i-1} \tag{5.7}$$

Define column $i = -1$ to hold C_{in}, so $G_{-1} = C_{in}$ and $P_{-1} = 0$. Then $C_{i-1} = G_{i-1:-1}$ because there will be a carry out of column $i-1$ if the block spanning columns $i-1$ through -1 generates a carry. The generated carry is either generated in column $i-1$ or generated in a previous column and propagated. Thus, we rewrite Equation 5.7 as

$$S_i = (A_i \oplus B_i) \oplus G_{i-1:-1} \tag{5.8}$$

Hence, the main challenge is to rapidly compute all the block generate signals $G_{-1:-1}$, $G_{0:-1}$, $G_{1:-1}$, $G_{2:-1}$, $\ldots$, $G_{N-2:-1}$. These signals, along with $P_{-1:-1}$, $P_{0:-1}$, $P_{1:-1}$, $P_{2:-1}$, $\ldots$, $P_{N-2:-1}$, are called *prefixes*.

Early computers used ripple carry adders, because components were expensive and ripple carry adders used the least hardware. Virtually all modern PCs use prefix adders on critical paths, because transistors are now cheap and speed is of great importance.

Figure 5.7 shows an $N = 16$-bit prefix adder. The adder begins with a *precomputation* to form P_i and G_i for each column from A_i and B_i using AND and OR gates. It then uses $\log_2 N = 4$ levels of black cells to form the prefixes of $G_{i:j}$ and $P_{i:j}$. A black cell takes inputs from the upper part of a block spanning bits $i:k$ and from the lower part spanning bits $k-1:j$. It combines these parts to form generate and propagate signals for the entire block spanning bits $i:j$, using the equations.

$$G_{i:j} \;=\; G_{i:k} \;+\; P_{i:k}\, G_{k-1:j} \tag{5.9}$$

$$P_{i:j} \;=\; P_{i:k}\, P_{k-1:j} \tag{5.10}$$

In other words, a block spanning bits $i:j$ will generate a carry if the upper part generates a carry or if the upper part propagates a carry generated in the lower part. The block will propagate a carry if both the

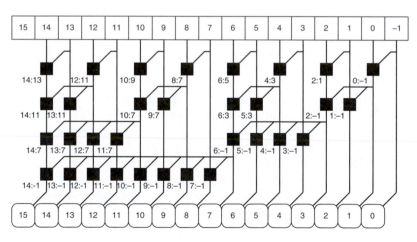

Figure 5.7 **16-bit prefix adder**

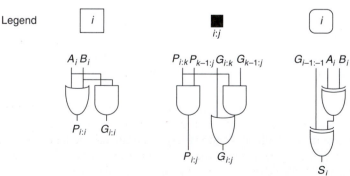

upper and lower parts propagate the carry. Finally, the prefix adder computes the sums using Equation 5.8.

In summary, the prefix adder achieves a delay that grows logarithmically rather than linearly with the number of columns in the adder. This speedup is significant, especially for adders with 32 or more bits, but it comes at the expense of more hardware than a simple carry-lookahead adder. The network of black cells is called a *prefix tree*.

The general principle of using prefix trees to perform computations in time that grows logarithmically with the number of inputs is a powerful technique. With some cleverness, it can be applied to many other types of circuits (see, for example, Exercise 5.7).

The critical path for an N-bit prefix adder involves the precomputation of P_i and G_i followed by $\log_2 N$ stages of black prefix cells to obtain all the prefixes. $G_{i-1:-1}$ then proceeds through the final XOR gate at the bottom to compute S_i. Mathematically, the delay of an N-bit prefix adder is

$$t_{PA} = t_{pg} + \log_2 N(t_{pg\_prefix}) + t_{XOR} \qquad (5.11)$$

where $t_{pg-prefix}$ is the delay of a black prefix cell.

Example 5.2 PREFIX ADDER DELAY

Compute the delay of a 32-bit prefix adder. Assume that each two-input gate delay is 100 ps.

Solution: The propagation delay of each black prefix cell, t_{pg_prefix}, is 200 ps (i.e., two gate delays). Thus, using Equation 5.11, the propagation delay of the 32-bit prefix adder is $100 \text{ ps} + \log_2(32) \times 200 \text{ ps} + 100 \text{ ps} = 1.2 \text{ ns}$, which is about three times faster than the carry-lookahead adder and eight times faster than the ripple-carry adder from Example 5.1. In practice, the benefits are not quite this great, but prefix adders are still substantially faster than the alternatives.

Putting It All Together

This section introduced the half adder, full adder, and three types of carry propagate adders: ripple-carry, carry-lookahead, and prefix adders. Faster adders require more hardware and therefore are more expensive and power-hungry. These trade-offs must be considered when choosing an appropriate adder for a design.

Hardware description languages provide the + operation to specify a CPA. Modern synthesis tools select among many possible implementations, choosing the cheapest (smallest) design that meets the speed requirements. This greatly simplifies the designer's job. HDL Example 5.1 describes a CPA with carries in and out.

HDL Example 5.1 ADDER

Verilog	VHDL

`module adder #(parameter N = 8)`
`          (input  [N−1:0] a, b,`
`           input       cin,`
`           output [N−1:0] s,`
`           output       cout);`
 	
`  assign {cout, s} = a + b + cin;`
`endmodule`
	`library IEEE; use IEEE.STD_LOGIC_1164.ALL;`
	`use IEEE.STD_LOGIC_UNSIGNED.ALL;`
	
	`entity adder is`
	`  generic (N: integer := 8);`
	`  port (a, b:   in  STD_LOGIC_VECTOR(N−1 downto 0);`
	`        cin:    in  STD_LOGIC;`
	`        s:      out STD_LOGIC_VECTOR(N−1 downto 0);`
	`        cout:   out STD_LOGIC);`
	`end;`
	
	`architecture synth of adder is`
	`  signal result: STD_LOGIC_VECTOR(N downto 0);`
	`begin`
	`  result   <= ("0" & a) + ("0" & b) + cin;`
	`  s        <= result (N−1 downto 0);`
	`  cout     <= result (N);`
	`end;`

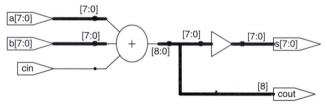

Figure 5.8 Synthesized adder

5.2.2 Subtraction

Recall from Section 1.4.6 that adders can add positive and negative numbers using two's complement number representation. Subtraction is almost as easy: flip the sign of the second number, then add. Flipping the sign of a two's complement number is done by inverting the bits and adding 1.

To compute $Y = A - B$, first create the two's complement of B: Invert the bits of B to obtain $\overline{B}$ and add 1 to get $-B = \overline{B} + 1$. Add this quantity to A to get $Y = A + \overline{B} + 1 = A - B$. This sum can be performed with a single CPA by adding $A + \overline{B}$ with $C_{in} = 1$. Figure 5.9 shows the symbol for a subtractor and the underlying hardware for performing $Y = A - B$. HDL Example 5.2 describes a subtractor.

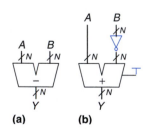

Figure 5.9 Subtractor:
(a) symbol, (b) implementation

5.2.3 Comparators

A *comparator* determines whether two binary numbers are equal or if one is greater or less than the other. A comparator receives two N-bit binary numbers, A and B. There are two common types of comparators.

HDL Example 5.2 SUBTRACTOR

Verilog	VHDL
| ```
module subtractor #(parameter N = 8)
                  (input  [N-1:0] a, b,
                   output [N-1:0] y);

  assign y = a - b;
endmodule
``` | ```
library IEEE; use IEEE.STD_LOGIC_1164.ALL;
use IEEE.STD_LOGIC_UNSIGNED.ALL;

entity subtractor is
  generic (N: integer := 8);
  port (a, b: in  STD_LOGIC_VECTOR(N-1 downto 0);
               y: out STD_LOGIC_VECTOR(N-1 downto 0));
end;

architecture synth of subtractor is
begin
  y <= a - b;
end;
``` |

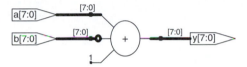

Figure 5.10 Synthesized subtractor

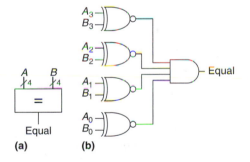

(a)　　(b)

Figure 5.11 4-bit equality comparator: (a) symbol, (b) implementation

An *equality comparator* produces a single output indicating whether A is equal to B ($A == B$). A *magnitude comparator* produces one or more outputs indicating the relative values of A and B.

The equality comparator is the simpler piece of hardware. Figure 5.11 shows the symbol and implementation of a 4-bit equality comparator. It first checks to determine whether the corresponding bits in each column of A and B are equal, using XNOR gates. The numbers are equal if all of the columns are equal.

Magnitude comparison is usually done by computing $A - B$ and looking at the sign (most significant bit) of the result, as shown in Figure 5.12. If the result is negative (i.e., the sign bit is 1), then A is less than B. Otherwise A is greater than or equal to B.

HDL Example 5.3 shows how to use various comparison operations.

Figure 5.12 *N*-bit magnitude comparator

HDL Example 5.3 COMPARATORS

Verilog

```
module comparators # (parameter N = 8)
                (input [N-1:0] a, b,
                 output       eq, neq,
                 output       lt, lte,
                 output       gt, gte);

  assign eq  = (a == b);
  assign neq = (a != b);
  assign lt  = (a < b);
  assign lte = (a <= b);
  assign gt  = (a > b);
  assign gte = (a >= b);
endmodule
```

VHDL

```
library IEEE; use IEEE.STD_LOGIC_1164.ALL;
entity comparators is
  generic (N: integer := 8);
  port (a, b: in STD_LOGIC_VECTOR(N-1 downto 0);
          eq, neq, lt,
          lte, gt, gte: out STD_LOGIC);
end;

architecture synth of comparators is
begin
  eq  <= '1' when (a = b)   else '0';
  neq <= '1' when (a /= b)  else '0';
  lt  <= '1' when (a < b)   else '0';
  lte <= '1' when (a <= b)  else '0';
  gt  <= '1' when (a > b)   else '0';
  gte <= '1' when (a >= b)  else '0';
end;
```

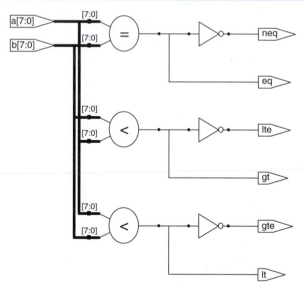

Figure 5.13 Synthesized comparators

5.2.4 ALU

Figure 5.14 ALU symbol

An *Arithmetic/Logical Unit* (*ALU*) combines a variety of mathematical and logical operations into a single unit. For example, a typical ALU might perform addition, subtraction, magnitude comparison, AND, and OR operations. The ALU forms the heart of most computer systems.

Figure 5.14 shows the symbol for an N-bit ALU with N-bit inputs and outputs. The ALU receives a control signal, F, that specifies which

Table 5.1 ALU operations

$F_{2:0}$	Function
000	A AND B
001	A OR B
010	A + B
011	not used
100	A AND $\overline{B}$
101	A OR $\overline{B}$
110	A − B
111	SLT

function to perform. Control signals will generally be shown in blue to
distinguish them from the data. Table 5.1 lists typical functions that the
ALU can perform. The SLT function is used for magnitude comparison
and will be discussed later in this section.

Figure 5.15 shows an implementation of the ALU. The ALU contains an N-bit adder and N two-input AND and OR gates. It also
contains an inverter and a multiplexer to optionally invert input B when
the F_2 control signal is asserted. A 4:1 multiplexer chooses the desired
function based on the $F_{1:0}$ control signals.

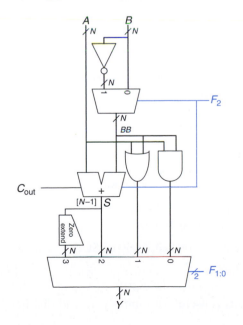

Figure 5.15 *N*-bit ALU

More specifically, the arithmetic and logical blocks in the ALU operate on A and BB. BB is either B or $\overline{B}$, depending on F_2. If $F_{1:0} = 00$, the output multiplexer chooses A AND BB. If $F_{1:0} = 01$, the ALU computes A OR BB. If $F_{1:0} = 10$, the ALU performs addition or subtraction. Note that F_2 is also the carry in to the adder. Also remember that $\overline{B} + 1 = -B$ in two's complement arithmetic. If $F_2 = 0$, the ALU computes $A + B$. If $F_2 = 1$, the ALU computes $A + \overline{B} + 1 = A - B$.

When $F_{2:0} = 111$, the ALU performs the *set if less than* (*SLT*) operation. When $A < B$, $Y = 1$. Otherwise, $Y = 0$. In other words, Y is set to 1 if A is less than B.

SLT is performed by computing $S = A - B$. If S is negative (i.e., the sign bit is set), $A < B$. The *zero extend unit* produces an N-bit output by concatenating its 1-bit input with 0's in the most significant bits. The sign bit (the $N-1^{\text{th}}$ bit) of S is the input to the zero extend unit.

Example 5.3 SET LESS THAN

Configure a 32-bit ALU for the SLT operation. Suppose $A = 25_{10}$ and $B = 32_{10}$. Show the control signals and output, Y.

Solution: Because $A < B$, we expect Y to be 1. For SLT, $F_{2:0} = 111$. With $F_2 = 1$, this configures the adder unit as a subtractor with an output, S, of $25_{10} - 32_{10} = -7_{10} = 1111 \ldots 1001_2$. With $F_{1:0} = 11$, the final multiplexer sets $Y = S_{31} = 1$.

Some ALUs produce extra outputs, called *flags*, that indicate information about the ALU output. For example, an *overflow flag* indicates that the result of the adder overflowed. A *zero flag* indicates that the ALU output is 0.

The HDL for an N-bit ALU is left to Exercise 5.9. There are many variations on this basic ALU that support other functions, such as XOR or equality comparison.

5.2.5 Shifters and Rotators

Shifters and *rotators* move bits and multiply or divide by powers of 2. As the name implies, a shifter shifts a binary number left or right by a specified number of positions. There are several kinds of commonly used shifters:

▶ **Logical shifter**—shifts the number to the left (LSL) or right (LSR) and fills empty spots with 0's.

Ex: 11001 LSR 2 = 00110; 11001 LSL 2 = 00100

▶ **Arithmetic shifter**—is the same as a logical shifter, but on right shifts fills the most significant bits with a copy of the old most significant bit (msb). This is useful for multiplying and dividing signed numbers (see Sections 5.2.6 and 5.2.7). Arithmetic shift left (ASL) is the same as logical shift left (LSL).

Ex: 11001 ASR 2 = 11110; 11001 ASL 2 = 00100

▶ **Rotator**—rotates number in circle such that empty spots are filled with bits shifted off the other end.

Ex: 11001 ROR 2 = 01110; 11001 ROL 2 = 00111

An N-bit shifter can be built from N $N{:}1$ multiplexers. The input is shifted by 0 to $N-1$ bits, depending on the value of the $\log_2 N$-bit select lines. Figure 5.16 shows the symbol and hardware of 4-bit shifters. The operators $<<$, $>>$, and $>>>$ typically indicate shift left, logical shift right, and arithmetic shift right, respectively. Depending on the value of the 2-bit shift amount, $shamt_{1:0}$, the output, Y, receives the input, A, shifted by 0 to 3 bits. For all shifters, when $shamt_{1:0} = 00$, $Y = A$. Exercise 5.14 covers rotator designs.

A left shift is a special case of multiplication. A left shift by N bits multiplies the number by 2^N. For example, $000011_2 << 4 = 110000_2$ is equivalent to $3_{10} \times 2^4 = 48_{10}$.

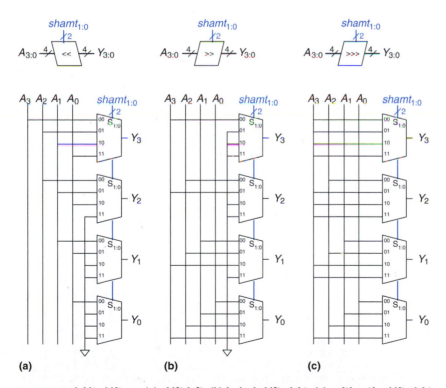

Figure 5.16 4-bit shifters: (a) shift left, (b) logical shift right, (c) arithmetic shift right

An arithmetic right shift is a special case of division. An arithmetic right shift by N bits divides the number by 2^N. For example, $11100_2 >>> 2 = 11111_2$ is equivalent to $-4_{10}/2^2 = -1_{10}$.

5.2.6 Multiplication*

Multiplication of unsigned binary numbers is similar to decimal multiplication but involves only 1's and 0's. Figure 5.17 compares multiplication in decimal and binary. In both cases, *partial products* are formed by multiplying a single digit of the multiplier with the entire multiplicand. The shifted partial products are summed to form the result.

In general, an $N \times N$ multiplier multiplies two N-bit numbers and produces a $2N$-bit result. The partial products in binary multiplication are either the multiplicand or all 0's. Multiplication of 1-bit binary numbers is equivalent to the AND operation, so AND gates are used to form the partial products.

Figure 5.18 shows the symbol, function, and implementation of a 4 $\times$ 4 multiplier. The multiplier receives the multiplicand and multiplier, A and B, and produces the product, P. Figure 5.18(b) shows how partial products are formed. Each partial product is a single multiplier bit (B_3, B_2, B_1, or B_0) AND the multiplicand bits (A_3, A_2, A_1, A_0). With N-bit

Figure 5.17 Multiplication:
(a) decimal, (b) binary

```
        230      multiplicand        0101
      ×  42      multiplier        × 0111
        460      partial             0101
      + 920      products           0101
       9660                         0101
                                  + 0000
                 result           0100011

  2 30×42 = 9660                  5×7 = 35
       (a)                            (b)
```

Figure 5.18 4 × 4 multiplier:
(a) symbol, (b) function,
(c) implementation

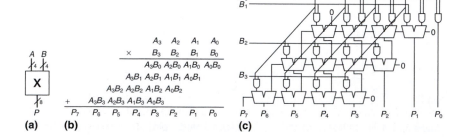

(a)   (b)   (c)

operands, there are N partial products and $N - 1$ stages of 1-bit adders. For example, for a 4×4 multiplier, the partial product of the first row is B_0 AND (A_3, A_2, A_1, A_0). This partial product is added to the shifted second partial product, B_1 AND (A_3, A_2, A_1, A_0). Subsequent rows of AND gates and adders form and add the remaining partial products.

The HDL for a multiplier is in HDL Example 5.4. As with adders, many different multiplier designs with different speed/cost trade-offs exist. Synthesis tools may pick the most appropriate design given the timing constraints.

HDL Example 5.4 MULTIPLIER

Verilog	VHDL
| ```
module multiplier # (parameter N = 8)
                (input  [N-1:0]   a, b,
                 output [2*N-1:0] y);

  assign y = a * b;
endmodule
``` | ```
library IEEE; use IEEE.STD_LOGIC_1164.ALL;
use IEEE.STD_LOGIC_UNSIGNED.ALL;

entity multiplier is
  generic (N: integer := 8);
  port (a, b: in  STD_LOGIC_VECTOR(N-1 downto 0);
            y: out STD_LOGIC_VECTOR(2*N-1 downto 0));
end;

architecture synth of multiplier is
begin
  y <= a * b;
end;
``` |

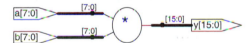

Figure 5.19 Synthesized multiplier

5.2.7 Division*

Binary division can be performed using the following algorithm for normalized unsigned numbers in the range $[2^{N}-1, 2^{N-1}]$:

```
R = A
for i = N-1 to 0
  D = R - B
  if D < 0 then    Q_i = 0, R' = R   // R < B
  else             Q_i = 1, R' = D   // R ≥ B
  if i ≠ 0 then R = 2R'
```

The *partial remainder, R,* is initialized to the dividend, *A*. The divisor, *B*, is repeatedly subtracted from this partial remainder to determine whether it fits. If the difference, *D*, is negative (i.e., the sign bit of *D* is 1), then the quotient bit, Q_i, is 0 and the difference is discarded. Otherwise, Q_i is 1,

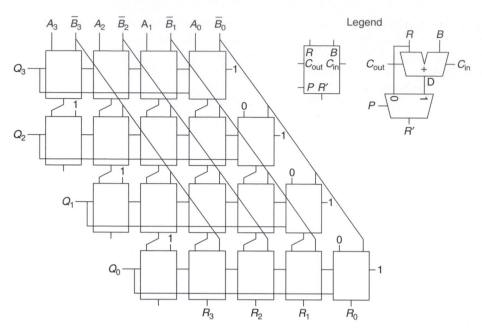

Figure 5.20 Array divider

and the partial remainder is updated to be the difference. In any event, the partial remainder is then doubled (left-shifted by one column), and the process repeats. The result satisfies $\frac{A}{B} = \left(Q + \frac{R}{B}\right)2^{-(N-1)}$.

Figure 5.20 shows a schematic of a 4-bit array divider. The divider computes A/B and produces a quotient, Q, and a remainder, R. The legend shows the symbol and schematic for each block in the array divider. The signal P indicates whether $R - B$ is negative. It is obtained from the C_{out} output of the leftmost block in the row, which is the sign of the difference.

The delay of an N-bit array divider increases proportionally to N^2 because the carry must ripple through all N stages in a row before the sign is determined and the multiplexer selects R or D. This repeats for all N rows. Division is a slow and expensive operation in hardware and therefore should be used as infrequently as possible.

5.2.8 Further Reading

Computer arithmetic could be the subject of an entire text. *Digital Arithmetic*, by Ercegovac and Lang, is an excellent overview of the entire field. *CMOS VLSI Design*, by Weste and Harris, covers high-performance circuit designs for arithmetic operations.

5.3 NUMBER SYSTEMS

Computers operate on both integers and fractions. So far, we have only considered representing signed or unsigned integers, as introduced in Section 1.4. This section introduces fixed- and floating-point number systems that can also represent rational numbers. Fixed-point numbers are analogous to decimals; some of the bits represent the integer part, and the rest represent the fraction. Floating-point numbers are analogous to scientific notation, with a mantissa and an exponent.

5.3.1 Fixed-Point Number Systems

Fixed-point notation has an implied *binary point* between the integer and fraction bits, analogous to the decimal point between the integer and fraction digits of an ordinary decimal number. For example, Figure 5.21(a) shows a fixed-point number with four integer bits and four fraction bits. Figure 5.21(b) shows the implied binary point in blue, and Figure 5.21(c) shows the equivalent decimal value.

(a) 01101100

(b) 0110.1100

(c) $2^2 + 2^1 + 2^{-1} + 2^{-2} = 6.75$

Figure 5.21 Fixed-point notation of 6.75 with four integer bits and four fraction bits

Signed fixed-point numbers can use either two's complement or sign/magnitude notations. Figure 5.22 shows the fixed-point representation of -2.375 using both notations with four integer and four fraction bits. The implicit binary point is shown in blue for clarity. In sign/magnitude form, the most significant bit is used to indicate the sign. The two's complement representation is formed by inverting the bits of the absolute value and adding a 1 to the least significant (rightmost) bit. In this case, the least significant bit position is in the 2^{-4} column.

(a) 0010.0110

(b) 1010.0110

(c) 1101.1010

Figure 5.22 Fixed-point representation of -2.375: (a) absolute value, (b) sign and magnitude, (c) two's complement

Like all binary number representations, fixed-point numbers are just a collection of bits. There is no way of knowing the existence of the binary point except through agreement of those people interpreting the number.

Example 5.4 ARITHMETIC WITH FIXED-POINT NUMBERS

Compute $0.75 + -0.625$ using fixed-point numbers.

Solution: First convert 0.625, the magnitude of the second number, to fixed-point binary notation. $0.625 \geq 2^{-1}$, so there is a 1 in the 2^{-1} column, leaving $0.625 - 0.5 = 0.125$. Because $0.125 < 2^{-2}$, there is a 0 in the 2^{-2} column. Because $0.125 \geq 2^{-3}$, there is a 1 in the 2^{-3} column, leaving $0.125 - 0.125 = 0$. Thus, there must be a 0 in the 2^{-4} column. Putting this all together, $0.625_{10} = 0000.1010_2$

Use two's complement representation for signed numbers so that addition works correctly. Figure 5.23 shows the conversion of -0.625 to fixed-point two's complement notation.

Figure 5.24 shows the fixed-point binary addition and the decimal equivalent for comparison. Note that the leading 1 in the binary fixed-point addition of Figure 5.24(a) is discarded from the 8-bit result.

Fixed-point number systems are commonly used for banking and financial applications that require precision but not a large range.

Figure 5.23 Fixed-point two's complement conversion

```
  0000.1010    Binary Magnitude
  1111.0101    One's Complement
+        1    Add 1
  1111.0110    Two's Complement
```

Figure 5.24 Addition: (a) binary fixed-point (b) decimal equivalent

```
  0000.1100           0.75
+ 1111.0110        + (−0.625)
 10000.0010           0.125
     (a)               (b)
```

Figure 5.25 Floating-point numbers

$$\pm M \times B^E$$

5.3.2 Floating-Point Number Systems*

Floating-point numbers are analogous to scientific notation. They circumvent the limitation of having a constant number of integer and fractional bits, allowing the representation of very large and very small numbers. Like scientific notation, floating-point numbers have a *sign, mantissa* (M), *base* (B), and *exponent* (E), as shown in Figure 5.25. For example, the number 4.1×10^3 is the decimal scientific notation for 4100. It has a mantissa of 4.1, a base of 10, and an exponent of 3. The decimal point *floats* to the position right after the most significant digit. Floating-point numbers are base 2 with a binary mantissa. 32 bits are used to represent 1 sign bit, 8 exponent bits, and 23 mantissa bits.

Example 5.5 32-BIT FLOATING-POINT NUMBERS

Show the floating-point representation of the decimal number 228.

Solution: First convert the decimal number into binary: $228_{10} = 11100100_2 = 1.11001_2 \times 2^7$. Figure 5.26 shows the 32-bit encoding, which will be modified later for efficiency. The sign bit is positive (0), the 8 exponent bits give the value 7, and the remaining 23 bits are the mantissa.

Figure 5.26 32-bit floating-point version 1

```
 1 bit     8 bits                      23 bits
┌──┬──────────────┬───────────────────────────────────────┐
│ 0│  00000111    │ 111 0010 0000 0000 0000 0000           │
└──┴──────────────┴───────────────────────────────────────┘
 Sign  Exponent                      Mantissa
```

In binary floating-point, the first bit of the mantissa (to the left of the binary point) is always 1 and therefore need not be stored. It is called the *implicit leading one*. Figure 5.27 shows the modified floating-point representation of $228_{10} = 11100100_2 \times 2^0 = 1.11001_2 \times 2^7$. The implicit leading one is not included in the 23-bit mantissa for efficiency. Only the fraction bits are stored. This frees up an extra bit for useful data.

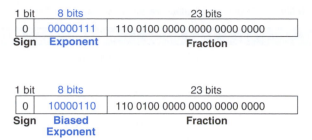

Figure 5.27 Floating-point version 2

Figure 5.28 IEEE 754 floating-point notation

We make one final modification to the exponent field. The exponent needs to represent both positive and negative exponents. To do so, floating-point uses a *biased* exponent, which is the original exponent plus a constant bias. 32-bit floating-point uses a bias of 127. For example, for the exponent 7, the biased exponent is $7 + 127 = 134 = 10000110_2$. For the exponent -4, the biased exponent is: $-4 + 127 = 123 = 01111011_2$. Figure 5.28 shows $1.11001_2 \times 2^7$ represented in floating-point notation with an implicit leading one and a biased exponent of 134 (7 + 127). This notation conforms to the IEEE 754 floating-point standard.

Special Cases: 0, $\pm\infty$, and NaN

The IEEE floating-point standard has special cases to represent numbers such as zero, infinity, and illegal results. For example, representing the number zero is problematic in floating-point notation because of the implicit leading one. Special codes with exponents of all 0's or all 1's are reserved for these special cases. Table 5.2 shows the floating-point representations of 0, $\pm\infty$, and NaN. As with sign/magnitude numbers, floating-point has both positive and negative 0. NaN is used for numbers that don't exist, such as $\sqrt{-1}$ or $\log_2(-5)$.

Single- and Double-Precision Formats

So far, we have examined 32-bit floating-point numbers. This format is also called *single-precision*, *single*, or *float*. The IEEE 754 standard also

As may be apparent, there are many reasonable ways to represent floating-point numbers. For many years, computer manufacturers used incompatible floating-point formats. Results from one computer could not directly be interpreted by another computer.

The Institute of Electrical and Electronics Engineers solved this problem by defining the *IEEE 754 floating-point standard* in 1985 defining floating-point numbers. This floating-point format is now almost universally used and is the one discussed in this section.

Table 5.2 IEEE 754 floating-point notations for 0, $\pm\infty$, and NaN

Number	Sign	Exponent	Fraction
0	X	00000000	0000000000000000000000000
∞	0	11111111	0000000000000000000000000
$-\infty$	1	11111111	0000000000000000000000000
NaN	X	11111111	non-zero

Table 5.3 Single- and double-precision floating-point formats

Format	Total Bits	Sign Bits	Exponent Bits	Fraction Bits
single	32	1	8	23
double	64	1	11	52

Floating-point cannot represent some numbers exactly, like 1.7. However, when you type 1.7 into your calculator, you see exactly 1.7, not 1.69999.... To handle this, some applications, such as calculators and financial software, use *binary coded decimal* (BCD) numbers or formats with a base 10 exponent. BCD numbers encode each decimal digit using four bits with a range of 0 to 9. For example the BCD fixed-point notation of 1.7 with four integer bits and four fraction bits would be 0001.0111. Of course, nothing is free. The cost is increased complexity in arithmetic hardware and wasted encodings (A–F encodings are not used), and thus decreased performance. So for compute-intensive applications, floating-point is much faster.

defines 64-bit *double-precision* (also called *double*) numbers that provide greater precision and greater range. Table 5.3 shows the number of bits used for the fields in each format.

Excluding the special cases mentioned earlier, normal single-precision numbers span a range of $\pm 1.175494 \times 10^{-38}$ to $\pm 3.402824 \times 10^{38}$. They have a precision of about seven significant decimal digits (because $2^{-24} \approx 10^{-7}$). Similarly, normal double-precision numbers span a range of $\pm 2.22507385850720 \times 10^{-308}$ to $\pm 1.79769313486232 \times 10^{308}$ and have a precision of about 15 significant decimal digits.

Rounding

Arithmetic results that fall outside of the available precision must round to a neighboring number. The rounding modes are: (1) round down, (2) round up, (3) round toward zero, and (4) round to nearest. The default rounding mode is round to nearest. In the round to nearest mode, if two numbers are equally near, the one with a 0 in the least significant position of the fraction is chosen.

Recall that a number *overflows* when its magnitude is too large to be represented. Likewise, a number *underflows* when it is too tiny to be represented. In round to nearest mode, overflows are rounded up to $\pm\infty$ and underflows are rounded down to 0.

Floating-Point Addition

Addition with floating-point numbers is not as simple as addition with two's complement numbers. The steps for adding floating-point numbers with the same sign are as follows:

1. Extract exponent and fraction bits.

2. Prepend leading 1 to form the mantissa.

3. Compare exponents.

4. Shift smaller mantissa if necessary.

5. Add mantissas.

6. Normalize mantissa and adjust exponent if necessary.

7. Round result.

8. Assemble exponent and fraction back into floating-point number.

Figure 5.29 shows the floating-point addition of 7.875 (1.11111×2^2) and 0.1875 (1.1×2^{-3}). The result is 8.0625 (1.0000001×2^3). After the fraction and exponent bits are extracted and the implicit leading 1 is prepended in steps 1 and 2, the exponents are compared by subtracting the smaller exponent from the larger exponent. The result is the number of bits by which the smaller number is shifted to the right to align the implied binary point (i.e., to make the exponents equal) in step 4. The aligned numbers are added. Because the sum has a mantissa that is greater than or equal to 2.0, the result is normalized by shifting it to the right one bit and incrementing the exponent. In this example, the result is exact, so no rounding is necessary. The result is stored in floating-point notation by removing the implicit leading one of the mantissa and prepending the sign bit.

> Floating-point arithmetic is usually done in hardware to make it fast. This hardware, called the *floating-point unit* (*FPU*), is typically distinct from the *central processing unit* (*CPU*). The infamous *floating-point division* (*FDIV*) bug in the Pentium FPU cost Intel $475 million to recall and replace defective chips. The bug occurred simply because a lookup table was not loaded correctly.

Floating-point numbers

0	10000001	111 1100 0000 0000 0000 0000
0	01111100	100 0000 0000 0000 0000 0000

Exponent   **Fraction**

Step 1

10000001	111 1100 0000 0000 0000 0000
01111100	100 0000 0000 0000 0000 0000

Step 2

10000001	1.111 1100 0000 0000 0000 0000
01111100	1.100 0000 0000 0000 0000 0000

Step 3

10000001	1.111 1100 0000 0000 0000 0000
− 01111100	1.100 0000 0000 0000 0000 0000

101 (shift amount)

Step 4

10000001	1.111 1100 0000 0000 0000 0000
10000001	0.000 0110 0000 0000 0000 0000	00000

Step 5

10000001	1.111 1100 0000 0000 0000 0000
10000001	+ 0.000 0110 0000 0000 0000 0000

10.000 0010 0000 0000 0000 0000

Step 6

10000001	10.000 0010 0000 0000 0000 0000 >> 1
+ 1	
10000010	1.000 0001 0000 0000 0000 0000

Step 7   (No rounding necessary)

Step 8

0	10000010	000 0001 0000 0000 0000 0000

Figure 5.29 Floating-point addition

CLK

Q N

Reset

Figure 5.30 Counter symbol

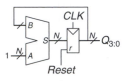

Figure 5.31 N-bit counter

5.4 SEQUENTIAL BUILDING BLOCKS

This section examines sequential building blocks, including counters and shift registers.

5.4.1 Counters

An N-bit *binary counter*, shown in Figure 5.30, is a sequential arithmetic circuit with clock and reset inputs and an N-bit output, Q. *Reset* initializes the output to 0. The counter then advances through all 2^N possible outputs in binary order, incrementing on the rising edge of the clock.

Figure 5.31 shows an N-bit counter composed of an adder and a resettable register. On each cycle, the counter adds 1 to the value stored in the register. HDL Example 5.5 describes a binary counter with asynchronous reset.

Other types of counters, such as Up/Down counters, are explored in Exercises 5.37 through 5.40.

HDL Example 5.5 COUNTER

Verilog

```
module counter #(parameter N = 8)
              (input           clk,
               input           reset,
               output reg [N-1:0] q);

  always @ (posedge clk or posedge reset)
    if (reset) q <= 0;
    else       q <= q + 1;
endmodule
```

VHDL

```
library IEEE; use IEEE.STD_LOGIC_1164.ALL;
use IEEE.STD_LOGIC_UNSIGNED.ALL;
use IEEE.STD_LOGIC_ARITH.ALL;

entity counter is
  generic (N: integer := 8);
  port (clk,
             reset: in STD_LOGIC;
             q: buffer STD_LOGIC_VECTOR(N-1 downto 0));
end;

architecture synth of counter is
begin
  process (clk, reset) begin
    if reset = '1' then
      q <= CONV_STD_LOGIC_VECTOR (0, N);
    elsif clk'event and clk = '1' then
      q <= q + 1;
    end if;
  end process;
end;
```

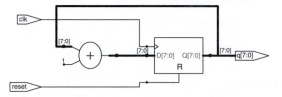

Figure 5.32 Synthesized counter

5.4.2 Shift Registers

A *shift register* has a clock, a serial input, S_{in}, a serial output, S_{out}, and N parallel outputs, $Q_{N-1:0}$, as shown in Figure 5.33. On each rising edge of the clock, a new bit is shifted in from S_{in} and all the subsequent contents are shifted forward. The last bit in the shift register is available at S_{out}. Shift registers can be viewed as *serial-to-parallel converters*. The input is provided serially (one bit at a time) at S_{in}. After N cycles, the past N inputs are available in parallel at Q.

A shift register can be constructed from N flip-flops connected in series, as shown in Figure 5.34. Some shift registers also have a reset signal to initialize all of the flip-flops.

A related circuit is a *parallel-to-serial* converter that loads N bits in parallel, then shifts them out one at a time. A shift register can be modified to perform both serial-to-parallel and parallel-to-serial operations by adding a parallel input, $D_{N-1:0}$, and a control signal, *Load*, as shown in Figure 5.35. When *Load* is asserted, the flip-flops are loaded in parallel from the D inputs. Otherwise, the shift register shifts normally. HDL Example 5.6 describes such a shift register.

Scan Chains*

Shift registers are often used to test sequential circuits using a technique called *scan chains*. Testing combinational circuits is relatively straightforward. Known inputs called *test vectors* are applied, and the outputs are checked against the expected result. Testing sequential circuits is more difficult, because the circuits have state. Starting from a known initial condition, a large number of cycles of test vectors may be needed to put the circuit into a desired state. For example, testing that the most significant bit of a 32-bit counter advances from 0 to 1 requires resetting the counter, then applying 2^{31} (about two billion) clock pulses!

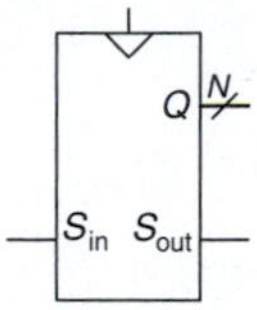

Figure 5.33 Shift register symbol

Don't confuse *shift registers* with the *shifters* from Section 5.2.5. Shift registers are sequential logic blocks that shift in a new bit on each clock edge. Shifters are unclocked combinational logic blocks that shift an input by a specified amount.

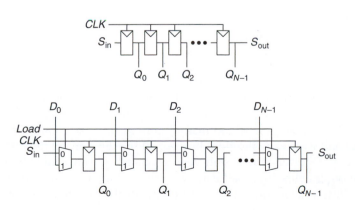

Figure 5.34 Shift register schematic

Figure 5.35 Shift register with parallel load

HDL Example 5.6 SHIFT REGISTER WITH PARALLEL LOAD

Verilog

```
module shiftreg # (parameter N = 8)
              (input              clk,
               input              reset, load,
               input              sin,
               input     [N-1:0]  d,
               output reg [N-1:0] q,
               output             sout);

  always @ (posedge clk or posedge reset)
    if (reset)     q <= 0;
    else if (load) q <= d;
    else           q <= {q[N-2:0], sin};

  assign sout = q[N-1];
endmodule
```

VHDL

```
library IEEE; use IEEE.STD_LOGIC_1164.ALL;
use IEEE.STD_LOGIC_ARITH.ALL;
use IEEE.STD_LOGIC_UNSIGNED.ALL;

entity shiftreg is
  generic (N: integer := 8);
  port(clk, reset,
       load: in    STD_LOGIC;
       sin: in     STD_LOGIC;
       d:   in     STD_LOGIC_VECTOR(N-1 downto 0);
       q: buffer   STD_LOGIC_VECTOR(N-1 downto 0);
       sout: out   STD_LOGIC);
end;

architecture synth of shiftreg is
begin
  process (clk, reset) begin
    if reset = '1' then
      q <= CONV_STD_LOGIC_VECTOR (0, N);
    elsif clk'event and clk = '1' then
      if load = '1' then
        q <= d;
      else
        q <= q(N-2 downto 0) & sin;
      end if;
    end if;
  end process;
  sout <= q(N-1);
end;
```

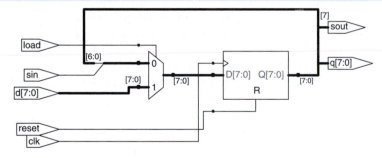

Figure 5.36 Synthesized shiftreg

To solve this problem, designers like to be able to directly observe and control all the state of the machine. This is done by adding a test mode in which the contents of all flip-flops can be read out or loaded with desired values. Most systems have too many flip-flops to dedicate individual pins to read and write each flip-flop. Instead, all the flip-flops in the system are connected together into a shift register called a scan chain. In normal operation, the flip-flops load data from their *D* input and ignore the scan chain. In test mode, the flip-flops serially shift their contents out and shift

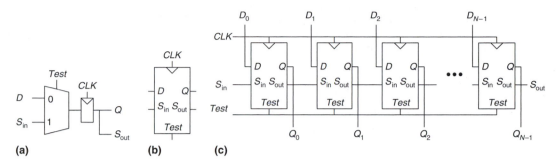

Figure 5.37 Scannable flip-flop: (a) schematic, (b) symbol, and (c) N-bit scannable register

in new contents using S_{in} and S_{out}. The load multiplexer is usually integrated into the flip-flop to produce a *scannable flip-flop*. Figure 5.37 shows the schematic and symbol for a scannable flip-flop and illustrates how the flops are cascaded to build an *N*-bit scannable register.

For example, the 32-bit counter could be tested by shifting in the pattern $011111\ldots111$ in test mode, counting for one cycle in normal mode, then shifting out the result, which should be $100000\ldots000$. This requires only $32 + 1 + 32 = 65$ cycles.

5.5 MEMORY ARRAYS

The previous sections introduced arithmetic and sequential circuits for manipulating data. Digital systems also require *memories* to store the data used and generated by such circuits. Registers built from flip-flops are a kind of memory that stores small amounts of data. This section describes *memory arrays* that can efficiently store large amounts of data.

The section begins with an overview describing characteristics shared by all memory arrays. It then introduces three types of memory arrays: dynamic random access memory (DRAM), static random access memory (SRAM), and read only memory (ROM). Each memory differs in the way it stores data. The section briefly discusses area and delay trade-offs and shows how memory arrays are used, not only to store data but also to perform logic functions. The section finishes with the HDL for a memory array.

5.5.1 Overview

Figure 5.38 shows a generic symbol for a memory array. The memory is organized as a two-dimensional array of memory cells. The memory reads or writes the contents of one of the rows of the array. This row is

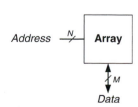

Figure 5.38 Generic memory array symbol

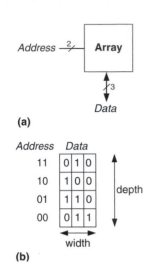

Figure 5.39 4 × 3 memory array: (a) symbol, (b) function

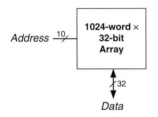

Figure 5.40 32 Kb array: depth = 2^{10} = 1024 words, width = 32 bits

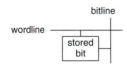

Figure 5.41 Bit cell

specified by an *Address*. The value read or written is called *Data*. An array with *N*-bit addresses and *M*-bit data has 2^N rows and *M* columns. Each row of data is called a *word*. Thus, the array contains 2^N *M*-bit words.

Figure 5.39 shows a memory array with two address bits and three data bits. The two address bits specify one of the four rows (data words) in the array. Each data word is three bits wide. Figure 5.39(b) shows some possible contents of the memory array.

The *depth* of an array is the number of rows, and the *width* is the number of columns, also called the word size. The size of an array is given as *depth* × *width*. Figure 5.39 is a 4-word × 3-bit array, or simply 4 × 3 array. The symbol for a 1024-word × 32-bit array is shown in Figure 5.40. The total size of this array is 32 kilobits (Kb).

Bit Cells

Memory arrays are built as an array of *bit cells*, each of which stores 1 bit of data. Figure 5.41 shows that each bit cell is connected to a *wordline* and a *bitline*. For each combination of address bits, the memory asserts a single wordline that activates the bit cells in that row. When the wordline is HIGH, the stored bit transfers to or from the bitline. Otherwise, the bitline is disconnected from the bit cell. The circuitry to store the bit varies with memory type.

To read a bit cell, the bitline is initially left floating (Z). Then the wordline is turned ON, allowing the stored value to drive the bitline to 0 or 1. To write a bit cell, the bitline is strongly driven to the desired value. Then the wordline is turned ON, connecting the bitline to the stored bit. The strongly driven bitline overpowers the contents of the bit cell, writing the desired value into the stored bit.

Organization

Figure 5.42 shows the internal organization of a 4 × 3 memory array. Of course, practical memories are much larger, but the behavior of larger arrays can be extrapolated from the smaller array. In this example, the array stores the data from Figure 5.39(b).

During a memory read, a wordline is asserted, and the corresponding row of bit cells drives the bitlines HIGH or LOW. During a memory write, the bitlines are driven HIGH or LOW first and then a wordline is asserted, allowing the bitline values to be stored in that row of bit cells. For example, to read *Address* 10, the bitlines are left floating, the decoder asserts $wordline_2$, and the data stored in that row of bit cells, 100, reads out onto the *Data* bitlines. To write the value 001 to *Address* 11, the bitlines are driven to the value 001, then $wordline_3$ is asserted and the new value (001) is stored in the bit cells.

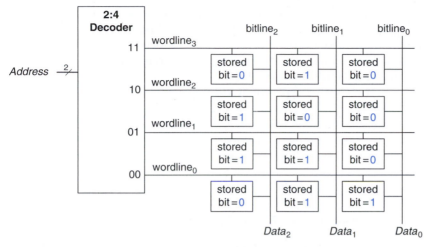

Figure 5.42 **4 $\times$ 3 memory array**

Memory Ports

All memories have one or more *ports*. Each port gives read and/or write access to one memory address. The previous examples were all single-ported memories.

Multiported memories can access several addresses simultaneously. Figure 5.43 shows a three-ported memory with two read ports and one write port. Port 1 reads the data from address *A1* onto the read data output *RD1*. Port 2 reads the data from address *A2* onto *RD2*. Port 3 writes the data from the write data input, *WD3*, into address *A3* on the rising edge of the clock if the write enable, *WE3*, is asserted.

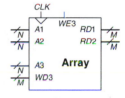

Figure 5.43 **Three-ported memory**

Memory Types

Memory arrays are specified by their size (depth $\times$ width) and the number and type of ports. All memory arrays store data as an array of bit cells, but they differ in how they store bits.

Memories are classified based on how they store bits in the bit cell. The broadest classification is *random access memory (RAM)* versus *read only memory (ROM)*. RAM is *volatile*, meaning that it loses its data when the power is turned off. ROM is *nonvolatile*, meaning that it retains its data indefinitely, even without a power source.

RAM and ROM received their names for historical reasons that are no longer very meaningful. RAM is called *random* access memory because any data word is accessed with the same delay as any other. A sequential access memory, such as a tape recorder, accesses nearby data more quickly than faraway data (e.g., at the other end of the tape).

Robert Dennard, 1932–. Invented DRAM in 1966 at IBM. Although many were skeptical that the idea would work, by the mid-1970s DRAM was in virtually all computers. He claims to have done little creative work until, arriving at IBM, they handed him a patent notebook and said, "put all your ideas in there." Since 1965, he has received 35 patents in semiconductors and micro-electronics. (Photo courtesy of IBM.)

ROM is called *read only* memory because, historically, it could only be read but not written. These names are confusing, because ROMs are randomly accessed too. Worse yet, most modern ROMs can be written as well as read! The important distinction to remember is that RAMs are volatile and ROMs are nonvolatile.

The two major types of RAMs are *dynamic RAM (DRAM)* and *static RAM (SRAM)*. Dynamic RAM stores data as a charge on a capacitor, whereas static RAM stores data using a pair of cross-coupled inverters. There are many flavors of ROMs that vary by how they are written and erased. These various types of memories are discussed in the subsequent sections.

5.5.2 Dynamic Random Access Memory

Dynamic RAM (DRAM, pronounced "dee-ram") stores a bit as the presence or absence of charge on a capacitor. Figure 5.44 shows a DRAM bit cell. The bit value is stored on a capacitor. The nMOS transistor behaves as a switch that either connects or disconnects the capacitor from the bitline. When the wordline is asserted, the nMOS transistor turns ON, and the stored bit value transfers to or from the bitline.

As shown in Figure 5.45(a), when the capacitor is charged to V_{DD}, the stored bit is 1; when it is discharged to GND (Figure 5.45(b)), the stored bit is 0. The capacitor node is *dynamic* because it is not actively driven HIGH or LOW by a transistor tied to V_{DD} or GND.

Upon a read, data values are transferred from the capacitor to the bitline. Upon a write, data values are transferred from the bitline to the capacitor. Reading destroys the bit value stored on the capacitor, so the data word must be restored (rewritten) after each read. Even when DRAM is not read, the contents must be refreshed (read and rewritten) every few milliseconds, because the charge on the capacitor gradually leaks away.

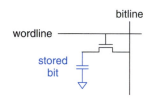

Figure 5.44 DRAM bit cell

5.5.3 Static Random Access Memory (SRAM)

Static RAM (SRAM, pronounced "es-ram") is *static* because stored bits do not need to be refreshed. Figure 5.46 shows an SRAM bit cell. The data bit is stored on cross-coupled inverters like those described in Section 3.2. Each cell has two outputs, bitline and bitline. When the wordline is asserted, both nMOS transistors turn on, and data values are transferred to or from the bitlines. Unlike DRAM, if noise degrades the value of the stored bit, the cross-coupled inverters restore the value.

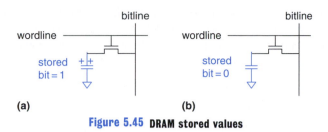

Figure 5.45 DRAM stored values

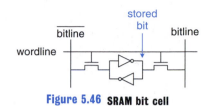

Figure 5.46 SRAM bit cell

Table 5.4 Memory comparison

Memory Type	Transistors per Bit Cell	Latency
flip-flop	~20	fast
SRAM	6	medium
DRAM	1	slow

5.5.4 Area and Delay

Flip-flops, SRAMs, and DRAMs are all volatile memories, but each has different area and delay characteristics. Table 5.4 shows a comparison of these three types of volatile memory. The data bit stored in a flip-flop is available immediately at its output. But flip-flops take at least 20 transistors to build. Generally, the more transistors a device has, the more area, power, and cost it requires. DRAM latency is longer than that of SRAM because its bitline is not actively driven by a transistor. DRAM must wait for charge to move (relatively) slowly from the capacitor to the bitline. DRAM also has lower throughput than SRAM, because it must refresh data periodically and after a read.

Memory latency and throughput also depend on memory size; larger memories tend to be slower than smaller ones if all else is the same. The best memory type for a particular design depends on the speed, cost, and power constraints.

5.5.5 Register Files

Digital systems often use a number of registers to store temporary variables. This group of registers, called a *register file,* is usually built as a small, multiported SRAM array, because it is more compact than an array of flip-flops.

Figure 5.47 shows a 32-register × 32-bit three-ported register file built from a three-ported memory similar to that of Figure 5.43. The

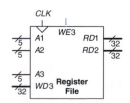

Figure 5.47 32 × 32 register file with two read ports and one write port

register file has two read ports (*A1/RD1* and *A2/RD2*) and one write port (*A3/WD3*). The 5-bit addresses, *A1*, *A2*, and *A3*, can each access all $2^5 = 32$ registers. So, two registers can be read and one register written simultaneously.

5.5.6 Read Only Memory

Read only memory (ROM) stores a bit as the presence or absence of a transistor. Figure 5.48 shows a simple ROM bit cell. To read the cell, the bitline is weakly pulled HIGH. Then the wordline is turned ON. If the transistor is present, it pulls the bitline LOW. If it is absent, the bitline remains HIGH. Note that the ROM bit cell is a combinational circuit and has no state to "forget" if power is turned off.

The contents of a ROM can be indicated using *dot notation*. Figure 5.49 shows the dot notation for a 4-word × 3-bit ROM containing the data from Figure 5.39. A dot at the intersection of a row (wordline) and a column (bitline) indicates that the data bit is 1. For example, the top wordline has a single dot on $Data_1$, so the data word stored at *Address* 11 is 010.

Conceptually, ROMs can be built using two-level logic with a group of AND gates followed by a group of OR gates. The AND gates produce all possible minterms and hence form a decoder. Figure 5.50 shows the ROM of Figure 5.49 built using a decoder and OR gates. Each dotted row in Figure 5.49 is an input to an OR gate in Figure 5.50. For data bits with a single dot, in this case $Data_0$, no OR gate is needed. This representation of a ROM is interesting because it shows how the ROM can perform any two-level logic function. In practice, ROMs are built from transistors instead of logic gates, to reduce their size and cost. Section 5.6.3 explores the transistor-level implementation further.

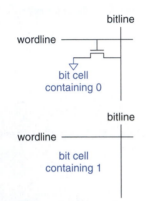

Figure 5.48 ROM bit cells containing 0 and 1

Figure 5.49 4 × 3 ROM: dot notation

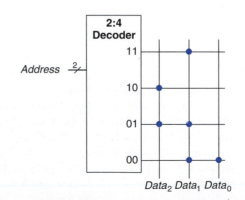

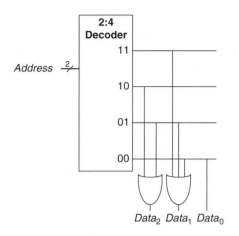

Figure 5.50 4 × 3 ROM implementation using gates

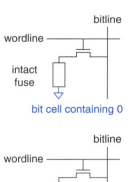

bit cell containing 0

bit cell containing 1

Figure 5.51 Fuse-programmable ROM bit cell

The contents of the ROM bit cell in Figure 5.48 are specified during manufacturing by the presence or absence of a transistor in each bit cell. A *programmable ROM* (*PROM*, pronounced like the dance) places a transistor in every bit cell but provides a way to connect or disconnect the transistor to ground.

Figure 5.51 shows the bit cell for a *fuse-programmable ROM*. The user programs the ROM by applying a high voltage to selectively blow fuses. If the fuse is present, the transistor is connected to GND and the cell holds a 0. If the fuse is destroyed, the transistor is disconnected from ground and the cell holds a 1. This is also called a one-time programmable ROM, because the fuse cannot be repaired once it is blown.

Reprogrammable ROMs provide a reversible mechanism for connecting or disconnecting the transistor to GND. *Erasable PROMs* (*EPROMs*, pronounced "e-proms") replace the nMOS transistor and fuse with a *floating-gate transistor*. The floating gate is not physically attached to any other wires. When suitable high voltages are applied, electrons tunnel through an insulator onto the floating gate, turning on the transistor and connecting the bitline to the wordline (decoder output). When the EPROM is exposed to intense ultraviolet (UV) light for about half an hour, the electrons are knocked off the floating gate, turning the transistor off. These actions are called *programming* and *erasing*, respectively. *Electrically erasable PROMs* (*EEPROMs*, pronounced "e-e-proms" or "double-e proms") and *Flash* memory use similar principles but include circuitry on the chip for erasing as well as programming, so no UV light is necessary. EEPROM bit cells are individually erasable; Flash memory erases larger blocks of bits and is cheaper because fewer erasing circuits are needed. In 2006, Flash

Flash memory drives with Universal Serial Bus (USB) connectors have replaced floppy disks and CDs for sharing files because Flash costs have dropped so dramatically.

Programmable ROMs can be configured with a device programmer like the one shown below. The device programmer is attached to a computer, which specifies the type of ROM and the data values to program. The device programmer blows fuses or injects charge onto a floating gate on the ROM. Thus the programming process is sometimes called *burning* a ROM.

memory costs less than $25 per GB, and the price continues to drop by 30 to 40% per year. Flash has become an extremely popular way to store large amounts of data in portable battery-powered systems such as cameras and music players.

In summary, modern ROMs are not really read only; they can be programmed (written) as well. The difference between RAM and ROM is that ROMs take a longer time to write but are nonvolatile.

5.5.7 Logic Using Memory Arrays

Although they are used primarily for data storage, memory arrays can also perform combinational logic functions. For example, the $Data_2$ output of the ROM in Figure 5.49 is the XOR of the two *Address* inputs. Likewise $Data_0$ is the NAND of the two inputs. A 2^N-word $\times$ M-bit memory can perform any combinational function of N inputs and M outputs. For example, the ROM in Figure 5.49 performs three functions of two inputs.

Memory arrays used to perform logic are called *lookup tables (LUTs)*. Figure 5.52 shows a 4-word $\times$ 1-bit memory array used as a lookup table to perform the function $Y = AB$. Using memory to perform logic, the user can look up the output value for a given input combination (address). Each address corresponds to a row in the truth table, and each data bit corresponds to an output value.

5.5.8 Memory HDL

HDL Example 5.7 describes a 2^N-word $\times$ M-bit RAM. The RAM has a synchronous enabled write. In other words, writes occur on the rising

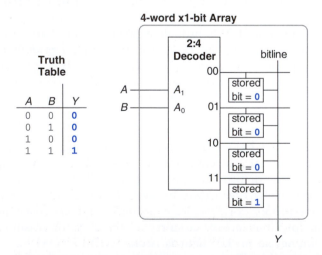

Figure 5.52 4-word $\times$ 1-bit memory array used as a lookup table

---

HDL Example 5.7 RAM

Verilog

```verilog
module ram # (parameter N = 6, M = 32)
               (input          clk,
                input          we,
                input  [N-1:0] adr,
                input  [M-1:0] din,
                output [M-1:0] dout);

  reg [M-1:0] mem [2**N-1:0];

  always @ (posedge clk)
    if (we) mem [adr] <= din;

  assign dout = mem[adr];
endmodule
```

VHDL

```vhdl
library IEEE; use IEEE.STD_LOGIC_1164.ALL;
use IEEE.STD_LOGIC_ARITH.ALL;
use IEEE.STD_LOGIC_UNSIGNED.ALL;

entity ram_array is
  generic (N: integer := 6; M: integer := 32);
  port (clk,
        we:   in  STD_LOGIC;
        adr:  in  STD_LOGIC_VECTOR(N-1 downto 0);
        din:  in  STD_LOGIC_VECTOR(M-1 downto 0);
        dout: out STD_LOGIC_VECTOR(M-1 downto 0));
end;

architecture synth of ram_array is
  type mem_array is array ((2**N-1) downto 0)
      of STD_LOGIC_VECTOR (M-1 downto 0);
  signal mem: mem_array;
begin
  process (clk) begin
    if clk' event and clk = '1' then
      if we = '1' then
        mem (CONV_INTEGER (adr)) <= din;
      end if;
    end if;
  end process;

  dout <= mem (CONV_INTEGER (adr));
end;
```

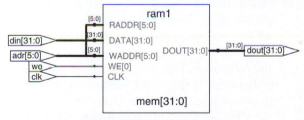

Figure 5.53 Synthesized ram

---

edge of the clock if the write enable, *we,* is asserted. Reads occur immediately. When power is first applied, the contents of the RAM are unpredictable.

HDL Example 5.8 describes a 4-word × 3-bit ROM. The contents of the ROM are specified in the HDL `case` statement. A ROM as small as this one may be synthesized into logic gates rather than an array. Note that the seven-segment decoder from HDL Example 4.25 synthesizes into a ROM in Figure 4.22.

HDL Example 5.8 ROM

Verilog	VHDL
| ```verilog
module rom (input      [1:0] adr,
            output reg [2:0] dout);

  always @ (adr)
    case (adr)
      2'b00: dout <= 3'b011;
      2'b01: dout <= 3'b110;
      2'b10: dout <= 3'b100;
      2'b11: dout <= 3'b010;
    endcase
endmodule
``` | ```vhdl
library IEEE; use IEEE.STD_LOGIC_1164.all;

entity rom is
  port (adr: in  STD_LOGIC_VECTOR(1 downto 0);
        dout: out STD_LOGIC_VECTOR(2 downto 0));
end;

architecture synth of rom is
begin
  process (adr) begin
    case adr is
      when "00" => dout <= "011";
      when "01" => dout <= "110";
      when "10" => dout <= "100";
      when "11" => dout <= "010";
    end case;
  end process;
end;
``` |

5.6 LOGIC ARRAYS

Like memory, gates can be organized into regular arrays. If the connections are made programmable, these *logic arrays* can be configured to perform any function without the user having to connect wires in specific ways. The regular structure simplifies design. Logic arrays are mass produced in large quantities, so they are inexpensive. Software tools allow users to map logic designs onto these arrays. Most logic arrays are also *re*configurable, allowing designs to be modified without replacing the hardware. Reconfigurability is valuable during development and is also useful in the field, because a system can be upgraded by simply downloading the new configuration.

This section introduces two types of logic arrays: *programmable logic arrays* (PLAs), and *field programmable gate arrays* (FPGAs). PLAs, the older technology, perform only combinational logic functions. FPGAs can perform both combinational and sequential logic.

5.6.1 Programmable Logic Array

Programmable logic arrays (PLAs) implement two-level combinational logic in sum-of-products (SOP) form. PLAs are built from an AND array followed by an OR array, as shown in Figure 5.54. The inputs (in true and complementary form) drive an AND array, which produces implicants, which in turn are ORed together to form the outputs. An $M \times N \times P$-bit PLA has M inputs, N implicants, and P outputs.

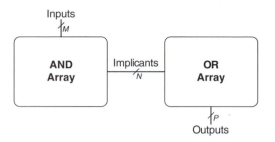

Figure 5.54 $M \times N \times$ **P-bit PLA**

Figure 5.55 shows the dot notation for a $3 \times 3 \times 2$-bit PLA performing the functions $X = \overline{A}\overline{B}C + AB\overline{C}$ and $Y = A\overline{B}$. Each row in the AND array forms an implicant. Dots in each row of the AND array indicate which literals comprise the implicant. The AND array in Figure 5.55 forms three implicants: $\overline{A}\overline{B}C$, $AB\overline{C}$, and $A\overline{B}$. Dots in the OR array indicate which implicants are part of the output function.

Figure 5.56 shows how PLAs can be built using two-level logic. An alternative implementation is given in Section 5.6.3.

ROMs can be viewed as a special case of PLAs. A 2^M-word $\times$ N-bit ROM is simply an $M \times 2^M \times N$-bit PLA. The decoder behaves as an AND plane that produces all 2^M minterms. The ROM array behaves as an OR plane that produces the outputs. If the function does not depend on all 2^M minterms, a PLA is likely to be smaller than a ROM. For example, an 8-word $\times$ 2-bit ROM is required to perform the same functions performed by the $3 \times 3 \times 2$-bit PLA shown in Figures 5.55 and 5.56.

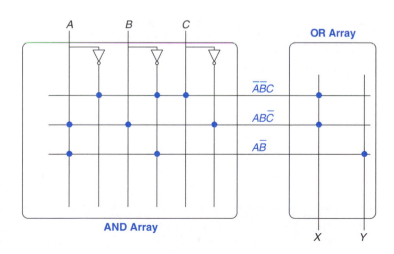

Figure 5.55 $3 \times 3 \times 2$-bit **PLA: dot notation**

Figure 5.56 $3 \times 3 \times$ 2-bit PLA using two-level logic

A   B   C

$\overline{A}\overline{B}C$

$AB\overline{C}$

$A\overline{B}$

OR ARRAY

AND ARRAY

X   Y

Programmable logic devices (PLDs) are souped-up PLAs that add registers and various other features to the basic AND/OR planes. However, PLDs and PLAs have largely been displaced by FPGAs, which are more flexible and efficient for building large systems.

5.6.2 Field Programmable Gate Array

A *field programmable gate array* (FPGA) is an array of reconfigurable gates. Using software programming tools, a user can implement designs on the FPGA using either an HDL or a schematic. FPGAs are more powerful and more flexible than PLAs for several reasons. They can implement both combinational and sequential logic. They can also implement multilevel logic functions, whereas PLAs can only implement two-level logic. Modern FPGAs integrate other useful functions such as built-in multipliers and large RAM arrays.

FPGAs are built as an array of *configurable logic blocks (CLBs)*. Figure 5.57 shows the block diagram of the Spartan FPGA introduced by Xilinx in 1998. Each CLB can be configured to perform combinational or sequential functions. The CLBs are surrounded by *input/output blocks (IOBs)* for interfacing with external devices. The IOBs connect CLB inputs and outputs to pins on the chip package. CLBs can connect to other CLBs and IOBs through programmable routing channels. The remaining blocks shown in the figure aid in programming the device.

Figure 5.58 shows a single CLB for the Spartan FPGA. Other brands of FPGAs are organized somewhat differently, but the same general principles apply. The CLB contains lookup tables (LUTs), configurable multiplexers, and registers. The FPGA is configured by specifying the contents of the lookup tables and the select signals for the multiplexers.

FPGAs are the brains of many consumer products, including automobiles, medical equipment, and media devices like MP3 players. The Mercedes Benz S-Class series, for example, has over a dozen Xilinx FPGAs or PLDs for uses ranging from entertainment to navigation to cruise control systems. FPGAs allow for quick time to market and make debugging or adding features late in the design process easier.

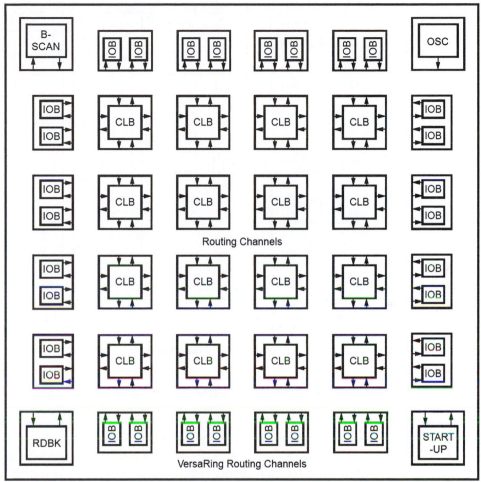

Figure 5.57 **Spartan block diagram**

DS060_01_081100

Each Spartan CLB has three LUTs: the four-input F- and G-LUTs, and the three-input H-LUT. By loading the appropriate values into the lookup tables, the F- and G-LUTs can each be configured to perform any function of up to four variables, and the H-LUT can perform any function of up to three variables.

Configuring the FPGA also involves choosing the select signals that determine how the multiplexers route data through the CLB. For example, depending on the multiplexer configuration, the H-LUT may receive one of its inputs from either DIN or the F-LUT. Similarly, it receives another input from either SR or the G-LUT. The third input always comes from H1.

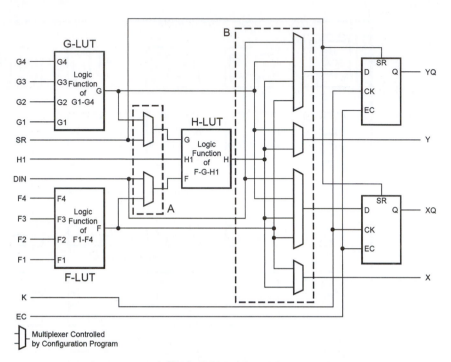

Figure 5.58 Spartan CLB

The FPGA produces two combinational outputs, *X* and *Y*. Depending on the multiplexer configuration, *X* comes from either the F- or H-LUT. *Y* comes from either the G- or H-LUT. These outputs can be connected to other CLBs via the routing channels

The CLB also contains two flip-flops. Depending on the configuration, the flip-flop inputs may come from DIN or from the F-, G-, or H-LUT. The flip-flop outputs, *XQ* and *YQ*, also can be connected to other CLBs via the routing channels.

In summary, the CLB can perform up to two combinational and/or two registered functions. All of the functions can involve at least four variables, and some can involve up to nine.

The designer configures an FPGA by first creating a schematic or HDL description of the design. The design is then synthesized onto the FPGA. The synthesis tool determines how the LUTs, multiplexers, and routing channels should be configured to perform the specified functions. This configuration information is then downloaded to the FPGA.

Because Xilinx FPGAs store their configuration information in SRAM, they can be easily reprogrammed. They may download the SRAM contents from a computer in the laboratory or from an EEPROM chip when the system is turned on. Some manufacturers include EEPROM directly on the FPGA or use one-time programmable fuses to configure the FPGA.

Example 5.6 FUNCTIONS BUILT USING CLBS

Explain how to configure a CLB to perform the following functions: (a) $X = \overline{A}\,\overline{B}C + AB\overline{C}$ and $Y = A\overline{B}$; (b) $Y = JKLMPQR$; (c) a divide-by-3 counter with binary state encoding (see Figure 3.29(a)).

Solution: (a) Configure the F-LUT to compute X and the G-LUT to compute Y, as shown in Figure 5.59. Inputs $F3$, $F2$, and $F1$ are A, B, and C, respectively (these connections are set by the routing channels). Inputs $G2$ and $G1$ are A and B. $F4$, $G4$, and $G3$ are don't cares (and may be connected to 0). Configure the final multiplexers to select X from the F-LUT and Y from the G-LUT. In general, a CLB can compute any two functions, of up to four variables each, in this fashion.

(b) Configure the F-LUT to compute $F = JKLM$ and the G-LUT to compute $G = PQR$. Then configure the H-LUT to compute $H = FG$. Configure the final multiplexer to select Y from the H-LUT. This configuration is shown in Figure 5.60. In general, a CLB can compute certain functions of up to nine variables in this way.

(c) The FSM has two bits of state ($S_{1:0}$) and one output (Y). The next state depends on the two bits of current state. Use the F-LUT and G-LUT to compute the next state from the current state, as shown in Figure 5.61. Use the two flip-flops to hold this state. The flip-flops have a dedicated reset input from the SR signal in the CLB. The registered outputs are fed back to the inputs using the routing channels, as indicated by the dashed blue lines. In general, another CLB might be necessary to compute the output Y. However, in this case, $Y = S_0'$, so Y can come from the same F-LUT used to compute S_0'. Hence, the entire FSM fits in a single CLB. In general, an FSM requires at least one CLB for every two bits of state, and it may require more CLBs for the output or next state logic if they are too complex to fit in a single LUT.

| (A) | (B) | (C) | (X) |
F4	F3	F2	F1	F
X	0	0	0	0
X	0	0	1	1
X	0	1	0	0
X	0	1	1	0
X	1	0	0	0
X	1	0	1	0
X	1	1	0	1
X	1	1	1	0

| (A) | (B) | (Y) |
G4	G3	G2	G1	G
X	X	0	0	0
X	X	0	1	0
X	X	1	0	1
X	X	1	1	0

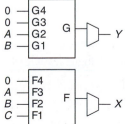

Figure 5.59 CLB configuration for two functions of up to four inputs each

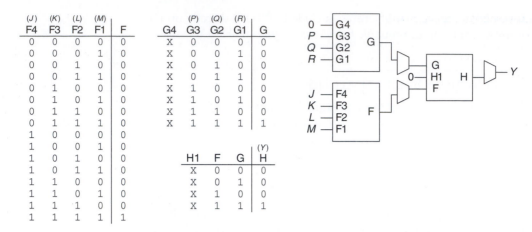

(J) F4	(K) F3	(L) F2	(M) F1	F
0	0	0	0	0
0	0	0	1	0
0	0	1	0	0
0	0	1	1	0
0	1	0	0	0
0	1	0	1	0
0	1	1	0	0
0	1	1	1	0
1	0	0	0	0
1	0	0	1	0
1	0	1	0	0
1	0	1	1	0
1	1	0	0	0
1	1	0	1	0
1	1	1	0	0
1	1	1	1	1

(P) G4	(Q) G3	(R) G2	G1	G
X	0	0	0	0
X	0	0	1	0
X	0	1	0	0
X	0	1	1	0
X	1	0	0	0
X	1	0	1	0
X	1	1	0	0
X	1	1	1	1

H1	F	G	(Y) H
X	0	0	0
X	0	1	0
X	1	0	0
X	1	1	1

Figure 5.60 CLB configuration for one function of more than four inputs

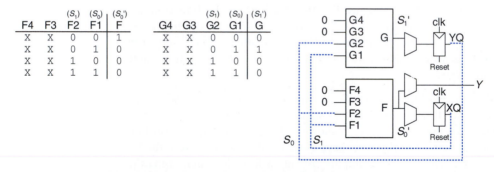

F4	F3	(S₁) F2	(S₀) F1	(S₀') F
X	X	0	0	1
X	X	0	1	0
X	X	1	0	0
X	X	1	1	0

G4	G3	(S₁) G2	(S₀) G1	(S₁') G
X	X	0	0	0
X	X	0	1	1
X	X	1	0	0
X	X	1	1	0

Figure 5.61 CLB configuration for FSM with two bits of state

Example 5.7 CLB DELAY

Alyssa P. Hacker is building a finite state machine that must run at 200 MHz. She uses a Spartan 3 FPGA with the following specifications: $t_{CLB} = 0.61$ ns per CLB; $t_{setup} = 0.53$ ns and $t_{pcq} = 0.72$ ns for all flip-flops. What is the maximum number of CLBs her design can use? You can ignore interconnect delay.

Solution: Alyssa uses Equation 3.13 to solve for the maximum propagation delay of the logic: $t_{pd} \le T_c - (t_{pcq} + t_{setup})$.

Thus, $t_{pd} \le 5$ ns $- (0.72$ ns $+ 0.53$ ns$)$, so $t_{pd} \le 3.75$ ns. The delay of each CLB, t_{CLB}, is 0.61 ns, and the maximum number of CLBs, N, is $Nt_{CLB} \le 3.75$ ns. Thus, $N = 6$.

5.6.3 Array Implementations*

To minimize their size and cost, ROMs and PLAs commonly use pseudo-nMOS or dynamic circuits (see Section 1.7.8) instead of conventional logic gates.

Figure 5.62(a) shows the dot notation for a 4×3-bit ROM that performs the following functions: $X = A \oplus B$, $Y = \overline{A} + B$, and $Z = \overline{AB}$. These are the same functions as those of Figure 5.49, with the address inputs renamed A and B and the data outputs renamed X, Y, and Z. The pseudo-nMOS implementation is given in Figure 5.62(b). Each decoder output is connected to the gates of the nMOS transistors in its row. Remember that in pseudo-nMOS circuits, the weak pMOS transistor pulls the output HIGH *only if* there is no path to GND through the pull-down (nMOS) network.

Pull-down transistors are placed at every junction without a dot. The dots from the dot notation diagram of Figure 5.62(a) are left faintly visible in Figure 5.62(b) for easy comparison. The weak pull-up transistors pull the output HIGH for each wordline without a pull-down transistor. For example, when $AB = 11$, the 11 wordline is HIGH and transistors on X and Z turn on and pull those outputs LOW. The Y output has no transistor connecting to the 11 wordline, so Y is pulled HIGH by the weak pull-up.

PLAs can also be built using pseudo-nMOS circuits, as shown in Figure 5.63 for the PLA from Figure 5.55. Pull-down (nMOS) transistors are placed on the *complement* of dotted literals in the AND array and on dotted rows in the OR array. The columns in the OR array are sent through an inverter before they are fed to the output bits. Again, the blue dots from the dot notation diagram of Figure 5.55 are left faintly visible in Figure 5.63 for easy comparison.

Many ROMs and PLAs use dynamic circuits in place of pseudo-nMOS circuits. Dynamic gates turn the pMOS transistor ON for only part of the time, saving power when the pMOS is OFF and the result is not needed. Aside from this, dynamic and pseudo-nMOS memory arrays are similar in design and behavior.

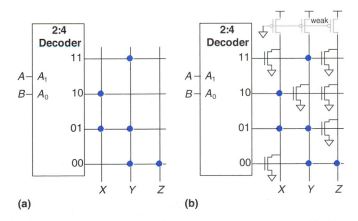

(a)   **(b)**

Figure 5.62 ROM implementation: (a) dot notation, (b) pseudo-nMOS circuit

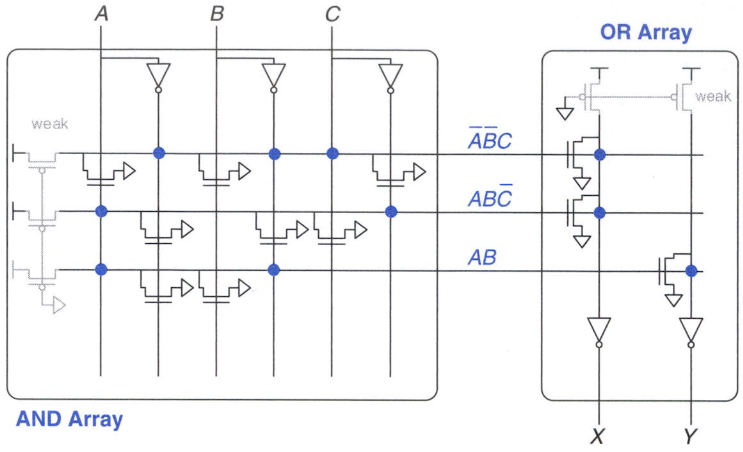

Figure 5.63 $3 \times 3 \times 2$-bit PLA using pseudo-nMOS circuits

5.7 SUMMARY

This chapter introduced digital building blocks used in many digital systems. These blocks include arithmetic circuits such as adders, subtractors, comparators, shifters, multipliers, and dividers; sequential circuits such as counters and shift registers; and arrays for memory and logic. The chapter also explored fixed-point and floating-point representations of fractional numbers. In Chapter 7, we use these building blocks to build a microprocessor.

Adders form the basis of most arithmetic circuits. A half adder adds two 1-bit inputs, A and B, and produces a sum and a carry out. A full adder extends the half adder to also accept a carry in. N full adders can be cascaded to form a carry propagate adder (CPA) that adds two N-bit numbers. This type of CPA is called a ripple-carry adder because the carry ripples through each of the full adders. Faster CPAs can be constructed using lookahead or prefix techniques.

A subtractor negates the second input and adds it to the first. A magnitude comparator subtracts one number from another and determines the relative value based on the sign of the result. A multiplier forms partial products using AND gates, then sums these bits using full adders. A divider repeatedly subtracts the divisor from the partial remainder and checks the sign of the difference to determine the quotient bits. A counter uses an adder and a register to increment a running count.

Fractional numbers are represented using fixed-point or floating-point forms. Fixed-point numbers are analogous to decimals, and floating-point numbers are analogous to scientific notation. Fixed-point numbers use ordinary arithmetic circuits, whereas floating-point numbers require more elaborate hardware to extract and process the sign, exponent, and mantissa.

Large memories are organized into arrays of words. The memories have one or more ports to read and/or write the words. Volatile memories, such as SRAM and DRAM, lose their state when the power is turned off. SRAM is faster than DRAM but requires more transistors. A register file is a small multiported SRAM array. Nonvolatile memories, called ROMs, retain their state indefinitely. Despite their names, most modern ROMs can be written.

Arrays are also a regular way to build logic. Memory arrays can be used as lookup tables to perform combinational functions. PLAs are composed of dedicated connections between configurable AND and OR arrays; they only implement combinational logic. FPGAs are composed of many small lookup tables and registers; they implement combinational and sequential logic. The lookup table contents and their interconnections can be configured to perform any logic function. Modern FPGAs are easy to reprogram and are large and cheap enough to build highly sophisticated digital systems, so they are widely used in low- and medium-volume commercial products as well as in education.

EXERCISES

Exercise 5.1 What is the delay for the following types of 64-bit adders? Assume that each two-input gate delay is 150 ps and that a full adder delay is 450 ps.

(a) a ripple-carry adder

(b) a carry-lookahead adder with 4-bit blocks

(c) a prefix adder

Exercise 5.2 Design two adders: a 64-bit ripple-carry adder and a 64-bit carry-lookahead adder with 4-bit blocks. Use only two-input gates. Each two-input gate is 15 μm^2, has a 50 ps delay, and has 20 pF of total gate capacitance. You may assume that the static power is negligible.

(a) Compare the area, delay, and power of the adders (operating at 100 MHz).

(b) Discuss the trade-offs between power, area, and delay.

Exercise 5.3 Explain why a designer might choose to use a ripple-carry adder instead of a carry-lookahead adder.

Exercise 5.4 Design the 16-bit prefix adder of Figure 5.7 in an HDL. Simulate and test your module to prove that it functions correctly.

Exercise 5.5 The prefix network shown in Figure 5.7 uses black cells to compute all of the prefixes. Some of the block propagate signals are not actually necessary. Design a "gray cell" that receives G and P signals for bits $i{:}k$ and $k - 1{:}j$ but produces only $G_{i:j}$, not $P_{i:j}$. Redraw the prefix network, replacing black cells with gray cells wherever possible.

Exercise 5.6 The prefix network shown in Figure 5.7 is not the only way to calculate all of the prefixes in logarithmic time. The *Kogge-Stone* network is another common prefix network that performs the same function using a different connection of black cells. Research Kogge-Stone adders and draw a schematic similar to Figure 5.7 showing the connection of black cells in a Kogge-Stone adder.

Exercise 5.7 Recall that an N-input priority encoder has $\log_2 N$ outputs that encodes which of the N inputs gets priority (see Exercise 2.25).

(a) Design an N-input priority encoder that has delay that increases logarithmically with N. Sketch your design and give the delay of the circuit in terms of the delay of its circuit elements.

(b) Code your design in HDL. Simulate and test your module to prove that it functions correctly.

Exercise 5.8 Design the following comparators for 32-bit numbers. Sketch the schematics.

(a) not equal

(b) greater than

(c) less than or equal to

Exercise 5.9 Design the 32-bit ALU shown in Figure 5.15 using your favorite HDL. You can make the top-level module either behavioral or structural.

Exercise 5.10 Add an *Overflow* output to the 32-bit ALU from Exercise 5.9. The output is TRUE when the result of the adder overflows. Otherwise, it is FALSE.

(a) Write a Boolean equation for the *Overflow* output.

(b) Sketch the Overflow circuit.

(c) Design the modified ALU in an HDL.

Exercise 5.11 Add a *Zero* output to the 32-bit ALU from Exercise 5.9. The output is TRUE when $Y == 0$.

Exercise 5.12 Write a testbench to test the 32-bit ALU from Exercise 5.9, 5.10, or 5.11. Then use it to test the ALU. Include any test vector files necessary. Be sure to test enough corner cases to convince a reasonable skeptic that the ALU functions correctly.

Exercise 5.13 Design a shifter that always shifts a 32-bit input left by 2 bits. The input and output are both 32 bits. Explain the design in words and sketch a schematic. Implement your design in your favourite HDL.

Exercise 5.14 Design 4-bit left and right rotators. Sketch a schematic of your design. Implement your design in your favourite HDL.

Exercise 5.15 Design an 8-bit left shifter using only 24 2:1 multiplexers. The shifter accepts an 8-bit input, A, and a 3-bit shift amount, $shamt_{2:0}$. It produces an 8-bit output, Y. Sketch the schematic.

Exercise 5.16 Explain how to build any N-bit shifter or rotator using only $N\log_2 N$ 2:1 multiplexers.

Exercise 5.17 The *funnel shifter* in Figure 5.64 can perform any N-bit shift or rotate operation. It shifts a $2N$-bit input right by k bits. The output, Y, is the N least significant bits of the result. The most significant N bits of the input are called B and the least significant N bits are called C. By choosing appropriate values of B, C, and k, the funnel shifter can perform any type of shift or rotate. Explain what these values should be in terms of A, *shamt*, and N for

(a)   logical right shift of A by *shamt*.

(b)   arithmetic right shift of A by *shamt*.

(c)   left shift of A by *shamt*.

(d)   right rotate of A by *shamt*.

(e)   left rotate of A by *shamt*.

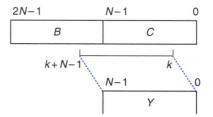

Figure 5.64 Funnel shifter

Exercise 5.18 Find the critical path for the 4×4 multiplier from Figure 5.18 in terms of an AND gate delay (t_{AND}) and a full adder delay (t_{FA}). What is the delay of an $N \times N$ multiplier built in the same way?

Exercise 5.19 Design a multiplier that handles two's complement numbers.

Exercise 5.20 A *sign extension unit* extends a two's complement number from M to N ($N > M$) bits by copying the most significant bit of the input into the upper bits of the output (see Section 1.4.6). It receives an M-bit input, A, and produces an N-bit output, Y. Sketch a circuit for a sign extension unit with a 4-bit input and an 8-bit output. Write the HDL for your design.

Exercise 5.21 A *zero extension unit* extends an unsigned number from M to N bits ($N > M$) by putting zeros in the upper bits of the output. Sketch a circuit for a zero extension unit with a 4-bit input and an 8-bit output. Write the HDL for your design.

Exercise 5.22 Compute $111001.000_2/001100.000_2$ in binary using the standard division algorithm from elementary school. Show your work.

Exercise 5.23 What is the range of numbers that can be represented by the following number systems?

(a) 24-bit unsigned fixed-point numbers with 12 integer bits and 12 fraction bits

(b) 24-bit sign and magnitude fixed-point numbers with 12 integer bits and 12 fraction bits

(c) 24-bit two's complement fixed-point numbers with 12 integer bits and 12 fraction bits

Exercise 5.24 Express the following base 10 numbers in 16-bit fixed-point sign/magnitude format with eight integer bits and eight fraction bits. Express your answer in hexadecimal.

(a) −13.5625

(b)   42.3125

(c) −17.15625

Exercise 5.25 Express the base 10 numbers in Exercise 5.24 in 16-bit fixed-point two's complement format with eight integer bits and eight fraction bits. Express your answer in hexadecimal.

Exercise 5.26 Express the base 10 numbers in Exercise 5.24 in IEEE 754 single-precision floating-point format. Express your answer in hexadecimal.

Exercise 5.27 Convert the following two's complement binary fixed-point numbers to base 10.

(a) 0101.1000

(b) 1111.1111

(c) 1000.0000

Exercise 5.28 When adding two floating-point numbers, the number with the smaller exponent is shifted. Why is this? Explain in words and give an example to justify your explanation.

Exercise 5.29 Add the following IEEE 754 single-precision floating-point numbers.

(a) C0D20004 + 72407020

(b) C0D20004 + 40DC0004

(c) (5FBE4000 + 3FF80000) + DFDE4000
     (Why is the result counterintuitive? Explain.)

Exercise 5.30 Expand the steps in section 5.3.2 for performing floating-point addition to work for negative as well as positive floating-point numbers.

Exercise 5.31 Consider IEEE 754 single-precision floating-point numbers.

(a) How many numbers can be represented by IEEE 754 single-precision floating-point format? You need not count $\pm\infty$ or NaN.

(b) How many additional numbers could be represented if $\pm\infty$ and NaN were not represented?

(c) Explain why $\pm\infty$ and NaN are given special representations.

Exercise 5.32 Consider the following decimal numbers: 245 and 0.0625.

(a) Write the two numbers using single-precision floating-point notation. Give your answers in hexadecimal.

(b) Perform a magnitude comparison of the two 32-bit numbers from part (a). In other words, interpret the two 32-bit numbers as two's complement numbers and compare them. Does the integer comparison give the correct result?

(c) You decide to come up with a new single-precision floating-point notation. Everything is the same as the IEEE 754 single-precision floating-point standard, except that you represent the exponent using two's complement instead of a bias. Write the two numbers using your new standard. Give your answers in hexadecimal.

(e) Does integer comparison work with your new floating-point notation from part (d)?

(f) Why is it convenient for integer comparison to work with floating-point numbers?

Exercise 5.33 Design a single-precision floating-point adder using your favorite HDL. Before coding the design in an HDL, sketch a schematic of your design. Simulate and test your adder to prove to a skeptic that it functions correctly. You may consider positive numbers only and use round toward zero (truncate). You may also ignore the special cases given in Table 5.2.

Exercise 5.34 In this problem, you will explore the design of a 32-bit floating-point multiplier. The multiplier has two 32-bit floating-point inputs and produces a 32-bit floating-point output. You may consider positive numbers only and use round toward zero (truncate). You may also ignore the special cases given in Table 5.2.

(a) Write the steps necessary to perform 32-bit floating-point multiplication.

(b) Sketch the schematic of a 32-bit floating-point multiplier.

(c) Design a 32-bit floating-point multiplier in an HDL. Simulate and test your multiplier to prove to a skeptic that it functions correctly.

Exercise 5.35 In this problem, you will explore the design of a 32-bit prefix adder.

(a) Sketch a schematic of your design.

(b) Design the 32-bit prefix adder in an HDL. Simulate and test your adder to prove that it functions correctly.

(c) What is the delay of your 32-bit prefix adder from part (a)? Assume that each two-input gate delay is 100 ps.

(d) Design a pipelined version of the 32-bit prefix adder. Sketch the schematic of your design. How fast can your pipelined prefix adder run? Make the design run as fast as possible.

(e) Design the pipelined 32-bit prefix adder in an HDL.

Exercise 5.36 An incrementer adds 1 to an N-bit number. Build an 8-bit incrementer using half adders.

Exercise 5.37 Build a 32-bit synchronous *Up/Down counter*. The inputs are *Reset* and *Up*. When *Reset* is 1, the outputs are all 0. Otherwise, when $Up = 1$, the circuit counts up, and when $Up = 0$, the circuit counts down.

Exercise 5.38 Design a 32-bit counter that adds 4 at each clock edge. The counter has reset and clock inputs. Upon reset, the counter output is all 0.

Exercise 5.39 Modify the counter from Exercise 5.38 such that the counter will either increment by 4 or load a new 32-bit value, D, on each clock edge, depending on a control signal, *PCSrc*. When $PCSrc = 1$, the counter loads the new value D.

Exercise 5.40 An N-bit *Johnson counter* consists of an N-bit shift register with a reset signal. The output of the shift register (S_{out}) is inverted and fed back to the input (S_{in}). When the counter is reset, all of the bits are cleared to 0.

(a) Show the sequence of outputs, $Q_{3:0}$, produced by a 4-bit Johnson counter starting immediately after the counter is reset.

(b) How many cycles elapse until an N-bit Johnson counter repeats its sequence? Explain.

(c) Design a decimal counter using a 5-bit Johnson counter, ten AND gates, and inverters. The decimal counter has a clock, a reset, and ten one-hot outputs, $Y_{9:0}$. When the counter is reset, Y_0 is asserted. On each subsequent cycle, the next output should be asserted. After ten cycles, the counter should repeat. Sketch a schematic of the decimal counter.

(d) What advantages might a Johnson counter have over a conventional counter?

Exercise 5.41 Write the HDL for a 4-bit scannable flip-flop like the one shown in Figure 5.37. Simulate and test your HDL module to prove that it functions correctly.

Exercise 5.42 The English language has a good deal of redundancy that allows us to reconstruct garbled transmissions. Binary data can also be transmitted in redundant form to allow error correction. For example, the number 0 could be coded as 00000 and the number 1 could be coded as 11111. The value could then be sent over a noisy channel that might flip up to two of the bits. The receiver could reconstruct the original data because a 0 will have at least three of the five received bits as 0's; similarly a 1 will have at least three 1's.

(a) Propose an encoding to send 00, 01, 10, or 11 encoded using five bits of information such that all errors that corrupt one bit of the encoded data can be corrected. Hint: the encodings 00000 and 11111 for 00 and 11, respectively, will not work.

(b) Design a circuit that receives your five-bit encoded data and decodes it to 00, 01, 10, or 11, even if one bit of the transmitted data has been changed.

(c) Suppose you wanted to change to an alternative 5-bit encoding. How might you implement your design to make it easy to change the encoding without having to use different hardware?

Exercise 5.43 Flash EEPROM, simply called Flash memory, is a fairly recent invention that has revolutionized consumer electronics. Research and explain how Flash memory works. Use a diagram illustrating the floating gate. Describe how a bit in the memory is programmed. Properly cite your sources.

Exercise 5.44 The extraterrestrial life project team has just discovered aliens living on the bottom of Mono Lake. They need to construct a circuit to classify the aliens by potential planet of origin based on measured features available from the NASA probe: greenness, brownness, sliminess, and ugliness. Careful consultation with xenobiologists leads to the following conclusions:

▶ If the alien is green and slimy or ugly, brown, and slimy, it might be from Mars.

▶ If the critter is ugly, brown, and slimy, or green and neither ugly nor slimy, it might be from Venus.

▶ If the beastie is brown and neither ugly nor slimy or is green and slimy, it might be from Jupiter.

Note that this is an inexact science; for example, a life form which is mottled green and brown and is slimy but not ugly might be from either Mars or Jupiter.

(a) Program a $4 \times 4 \times 3$ PLA to identify the alien. You may use dot notation.

(b) Program a 16×3 ROM to identify the alien. You may use dot notation.

(c) Implement your design in an HDL.

Exercise 5.45 Implement the following functions using a single 16×3 ROM. Use dot notation to indicate the ROM contents.

(a) $X = AB + B\overline{C}D + \overline{A}\overline{B}$

(b) $Y = AB + BD$

(c) $Z = A + B + C + D$

Exercise 5.46 Implement the functions from Exercise 5.45 using an $4 \times 8 \times 3$ PLA. You may use dot notation.

Exercise 5.47 Specify the size of a ROM that you could use to program each of the following combinational circuits. Is using a ROM to implement these functions a good design choice? Explain why or why not.

(a) a 16-bit adder/subtractor with C_{in} and C_{out}

(b) an 8×8 multiplier

(c) a 16-bit priority encoder (see Exercise 2.25)

Exercise 5.48 Consider the ROM circuits in Figure 5.65. For each row, can the circuit in column I be replaced by an equivalent circuit in column II by proper programming of the latter's ROM?

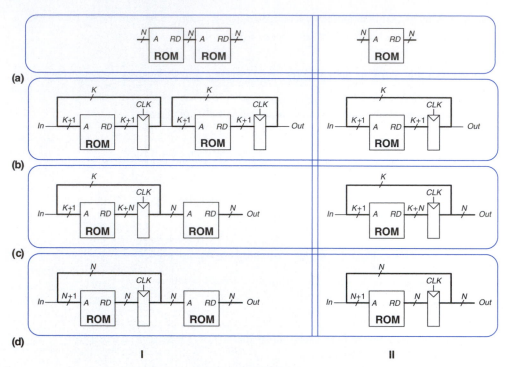

Figure 5.65 ROM circuits

Exercise 5.49 Give an example of a nine-input function that can be performed using only one Spartan FPGA CLB. Give an example of an eight-input function that cannot be performed using only one CLB.

Exercise 5.50 How many Spartan FPGA CLBs are required to perform each of the following functions? Show how to configure one or more CLBs to perform the function. You should be able to do this by inspection, without performing logic synthesis.

(a) The combinational function from Exercise 2.7(c).

(b) The combinational function from Exercise 2.9(c).

(c) The two-output function from Exercise 2.15.

(d) The function from Exercise 2.24.

(e) A four-input priority encoder (see Exercise 2.25).

(f) An eight-input priority encoder (see Exercise 2.25).

(g) A 3:8 decoder.

(h) A 4-bit carry propagate adder (with no carry in or out).

(i) The FSM from Exercise 3.19.

(j) The Gray code counter from Exercise 3.24.

Exercise 5.51 Consider the Spartan CLB shown in Figure 5.58. It has the following specifications: $t_{pd} = t_{cd} = 2.7$ ns per CLB; $t_{setup} = 3.9$ ns, $t_{hold} = 0$ ns, and $t_{pcq} = 2.8$ ns for all flip-flops.

(a) What is the minimum number of Spartan CLBs required to implement the FSM of Figure 3.26?

(b) Without clock skew, what is the fastest clock frequency at which this FSM will run reliably?

(c) With 5 ns of clock skew, what is the fastest frequency at which the FSM will run reliably?

Exercise 5.52 You would like to use an FPGA to implement an M&M sorter with a color sensor and motors to put red candy in one jar and green candy in another. The design is to be implemented as an FSM using a Spartan XC3S200 FPGA, a chip from the Spartan 3 series family. It is considerably faster than the original Spartan FPGA. According to the data sheet, the FPGA has timing characteristics shown in Table 5.5. Assume that the design is small enough that wire delay is negligible.

Table 5.5 Spartan 3 XC3S200 timing

Name	Value (ns)
t_{pcq}	0.72
t_{setup}	0.53
t_{hold}	0
t_{pd} (per CLB)	0.61
t_{skew}	0

You would like your FSM to run at 100 MHz. What is the maximum number of CLBs on the critical path? What is the fastest speed at which the FSM will run?

Interview Questions

The following exercises present questions that have been asked at interviews for digital design jobs.

Question 5.1 What is the largest possible result of multiplying two unsigned N-bit numbers?

Question 5.2 *Binary coded decimal* (BCD) representation uses four bits to encode each decimal digit. For example 42_{10} is represented as 01000010_{BCD}. Explain in words why processors might use BCD representation.

Question 5.3 Design hardware to add two 8-bit unsigned BCD numbers (see Question 5.2). Sketch a schematic for your design, and write an HDL module for the BCD adder. The inputs are A, B, and C_{in}, and the outputs are S and C_{out}. C_{in} and C_{out} are 1-bit carries, and A, B, and S are 8-bit BCD numbers.

JUMP

FETCH

ADD

Architecture

6.1 INTRODUCTION

The previous chapters introduced digital design principles and building blocks. In this chapter, we jump up a few levels of abstraction to define the *architecture* of a computer (see Figure 1.1). The architecture is the programmer's view of a computer. It is defined by the instruction set (language), and operand locations (registers and memory). Many different architectures exist, such as IA-32, MIPS, SPARC, and PowerPC.

The first step in understanding any computer architecture is to learn its language. The words in a computer's language are called *instructions*. The computer's vocabulary is called the instruction set. All programs running on a computer use the same *instruction set*. Even complex software applications, such as word processing and spreadsheet applications, are eventually compiled into a series of simple instructions such as add, subtract, and jump. Computer instructions indicate both the operation to perform and the operands to use. The operands may come from memory, from registers, or from the instruction itself.

Computer hardware understands only 1's and 0's, so instructions are encoded as binary numbers in a format called *machine language*. Just as we use letters to encode human language, computers use binary numbers to encode machine language. Microprocessors are digital systems that read and execute machine language instructions. However, humans consider reading machine language to be tedious, so we prefer to represent the instructions in a symbolic format, called *assembly language*.

The instruction sets of different architectures are more like different dialects than different languages. Almost all architectures define basic instructions, such as add, subtract, and jump, that operate on memory or registers. Once you have learned one instruction set, understanding others is fairly straightforward.

A computer architecture does not define the underlying hardware implementation. Often, many different hardware implementations of a single architecture exist. For example, Intel and Advanced Micro Devices (AMD) sell various microprocessors belonging to the same IA-32 architecture. They all can run the same programs, but they use different underlying hardware and therefore offer trade-offs in performance, price, and power. Some microprocessors are optimized for high-performance servers, whereas others are optimized for long battery life in laptop computers. The specific arrangement of registers, memories, ALUs, and other building blocks to form a microprocessor is called the *microarchitecture* and will be the subject of Chapter 7. Often, many different microarchitectures exist for a single architecture.

In this text, we introduce the MIPS architecture that was first developed by John Hennessy and his colleagues at Stanford in the 1980s. MIPS processors are used by, among others, Silicon Graphics, Nintendo, and Cisco. We start by introducing the basic instructions, operand locations, and machine language formats. We then introduce more instructions used in common programming constructs, such as branches, loops, array manipulations, and procedure calls.

Throughout the chapter, we motivate the design of the MIPS architecture using four principles articulated by Patterson and Hennessy: (1) simplicity favors regularity; (2) make the common case fast; (3) smaller is faster; and (4) good design demands good compromises.

6.2 ASSEMBLY LANGUAGE

Assembly language is the human-readable representation of the computer's native language. Each assembly language instruction specifies both the operation to perform and the operands on which to operate. We introduce simple arithmetic instructions and show how these operations are written in assembly language. We then define the MIPS instruction operands: registers, memory, and constants.

We assume that you already have some familiarity with a *high-level programming language* such as C, C++, or Java. (These languages are practically identical for most of the examples in this chapter, but where they differ, we will use C.)

6.2.1 Instructions

The most common operation computers perform is addition. Code Example 6.1 shows code for adding variables b and c and writing the result to a. The program is shown on the left in a high-level language (using the syntax of C, C++, and Java), and then rewritten on the right in MIPS assembly language. Note that statements in a C program end with a semicolon.

Code Example 6.1 ADDITION

High-Level Code	MIPS Assembly Code
a = b + c;	add a, b, c

Code Example 6.2 SUBTRACTION

High-Level Code	MIPS Assembly Code
a = b − c;	sub a, b, c

The first part of the assembly instruction, add, is called the *mnemonic* and indicates what operation to perform. The operation is performed on b and c, the *source operands*, and the result is written to a, the *destination operand*.

Code Example 6.2 shows that subtraction is similar to addition. The instruction format is the same as the add instruction except for the operation specification, sub. This consistent instruction format is an example of the first design principle:

Design Principle 1: Simplicity favors regularity.

Instructions with a consistent number of operands—in this case, two sources and one destination—are easier to encode and handle in hardware. More complex high-level code translates into multiple MIPS instructions, as shown in Code Example 6.3.

In the high-level language examples, single-line comments begin with // and continue until the end of the line. Multiline comments begin with /* and end with */. In assembly language, only single-line comments are used. They begin with # and continue until the end of the line. The assembly language program in Code Example 6.3 requires a temporary variable, t, to store the intermediate result. Using multiple assembly

mnemonic (pronounced *ni-mon-ik*) comes from the Greek word μιμνΕσκεστηαι, to remember. The assembly language mnemonic is easier to remember than a machine language pattern of 0's and 1's representing the same operation.

Code Example 6.3 MORE COMPLEX CODE

High-Level Code		MIPS Assembly Code	
a = b + c − d;	// single-line comment	sub t, c, d	# t = c − d
	/* multiple-line	add a, b, t	# a = b + t
	comment */		

language instructions to perform more complex operations is an example of the second design principle of computer architecture:

Design Principle 2: Make the common case fast.

The MIPS instruction set makes the common case fast by including only simple, commonly used instructions. The number of instructions is kept small so that the hardware required to decode the instruction and its operands can be simple, small, and fast. More elaborate operations that are less common are performed using sequences of multiple simple instructions. Thus, MIPS is a *reduced instruction set computer (RISC)* architecture. Architectures with many complex instructions, such as Intel's IA-32 architecture, are *complex instruction set computers (CISC)*. For example, IA-32 defines a "string move" instruction that copies a string (a series of characters) from one part of memory to another. Such an operation requires many, possibly even hundreds, of simple instructions in a RISC machine. However, the cost of implementing complex instructions in a CISC architecture is added hardware and overhead that slows down the simple instructions.

A RISC architecture minimizes the hardware complexity and the necessary instruction encoding by keeping the set of distinct instructions small. For example, an instruction set with 64 simple instructions would need $\log_2 64 = 6$ bits to encode the operation. An instruction set with 256 complex instructions would need $\log_2 256 = 8$ bits of encoding per instruction. In a CISC machine, even though the complex instructions may be used only rarely, they add overhead to all instructions, even the simple ones.

6.2.2 Operands: Registers, Memory, and Constants

An instruction operates on *operands*. In Code Example 6.1 the variables a, b, and c are all operands. But computers operate on 1's and 0's, not variable names. The instructions need a physical location from which to retrieve the binary data. Operands can be stored in registers or memory, or they may be *constants* stored in the instruction itself. Computers use various locations to hold operands, to optimize for speed and data capacity. Operands stored as constants or in registers are accessed quickly, but they hold only a small amount of data. Additional data must be accessed from memory, which is large but slow. MIPS is called a 32-bit architecture because it operates on 32-bit data. (The MIPS architecture has been extended to 64 bits in commercial products, but we will consider only the 32-bit form in this book.)

Registers

Instructions need to access operands quickly so that they can run fast. But operands stored in memory take a long time to retrieve. Therefore, most architectures specify a small number of registers that hold commonly used operands. The MIPS architecture uses 32 registers, called the *register set* or *register file*. The fewer the registers, the faster they can be accessed. This leads to the third design principle:

Design Principle 3: Smaller is faster.

Looking up information from a small number of relevant books on your desk is a lot faster than searching for the information in the stacks at a library. Likewise, reading data from a small set of registers (for example, 32) is faster than reading it from 1000 registers or a large memory. A small register file is typically built from a small SRAM array (see Section 5.5.3). The SRAM array uses a small decoder and bitlines connected to relatively few memory cells, so it has a shorter critical path than a large memory does.

Code Example 6.4 shows the add instruction with register operands. MIPS register names are preceded by the $ sign. The variables a, b, and c are arbitrarily placed in $s0, $s1, and $s2. The name $s1 is pronounced "register s1" or "dollar s1". The instruction adds the 32-bit values contained in $s1 (b) and $s2 (c) and writes the 32-bit result to $s0 (a).

MIPS generally stores variables in 18 of the 32 registers: $s0 – $s7, and $t0 – $t9. Register names beginning with $s are called *saved* registers. Following MIPS convention, these registers store variables such as a, b, and c. Saved registers have special connotations when they are used with procedure calls (see Section 6.4.6). Register names beginning with $t are called *temporary* registers. They are used for storing temporary variables. Code Example 6.5 shows MIPS assembly code using a temporary register, $t0, to store the intermediate calculation of c – d.

Code Example 6.4 REGISTER OPERANDS

High-Level Code	MIPS Assembly Code
a = b + c;	# $s0 = a, $s1 = b, $s2 = c add $s0, $s1, $s2 # a = b + c

---

Code Example 6.5 TEMPORARY REGISTERS

High-Level Code	MIPS Assembly Code

a = b + c – d;	# $s0 = a, $s1 = b, $s2 = c, $s3 = d
	
	  sub $t0, $s2, $s3 # t = c – d
	  add $s0, $s1, $t0 # a = b + t

Example 6.1 TRANSLATING HIGH-LEVEL CODE TO ASSEMBLY
LANGUAGE

Translate the following high-level code into assembly language. Assume variables
a-c are held in registers $s0-$s2 and f-j are in $s3-$s7.

```
a = b - c;
f = (g + h) - (i + j);
```

Solution: The program uses four assembly language instructions.

```
# MIPS assembly code
# $s0 = a, $s1 = b, $s2 = c, $s3 = f, $s4 = g, $s5 = h,
# $s6 = i, $s7 = j
  sub $s0, $s1, $s2   # a = b - c
  add $t0, $s4, $s5   # $t0 = g + h
  add $t1, $s6, $s7   # $t1 = i + j
  sub $s3, $t0, $t1   # f = (g + h) - (i + j)
```

The Register Set

The MIPS architecture defines 32 registers. Each register has a name and a
number ranging from 0 to 31. Table 6.1 lists the name, number, and use for
each register. $0 always contains the value 0 because this constant is so fre-
quently used in computer programs. We have also discussed the $s and $t
registers. The remaining registers will be described throughout this chapter.

Table 6.1 MIPS register set

Name	Number	Use
$0	0	the constant value 0
$at	1	assembler temporary
$v0-$v1	2–3	procedure return values
$a0-$a3	4–7	procedure arguments
$t0-$t7	8–15	temporary variables
$s0-$s7	16–23	saved variables
$t8-$t9	24–25	temporary variables
$k0-$k1	26–27	operating system (OS) temporaries
$gp	28	global pointer
$sp	29	stack pointer
$fp	30	frame pointer
$ra	31	procedure return address

Register Numbers

```
Word
Address          Data
   •              •            •
   •              •            •
   •              •            •
00000003    4 0 F 3 0 7 8 8   Word 3
00000002    0 1 E E 2 8 4 2   Word 2
00000001    F 2 F 1 A C 0 7   Word 1
00000000    A B C D E F 7 8   Word 0
```

Figure 6.1 Word-addressable memory

Memory

If registers were the only storage space for operands, we would be confined to simple programs with no more than 32 variables. However, data can also be stored in memory. When compared to the register file, memory has many data locations, but accessing it takes a longer amount of time. Whereas the register file is small and fast, memory is large and slow. For this reason, commonly used variables are kept in registers. By using a combination of memory and registers, a program can access a large amount of data fairly quickly. As described in Section 5.5, memories are organized as an array of data words. The MIPS architecture uses 32-bit memory addresses and 32-bit data words.

MIPS uses a byte-addressable memory. That is, each byte in memory has a unique address. However, for explanation purposes only, we first introduce a word-addressable memory, and afterward describe the MIPS byte-addressable memory.

Figure 6.1 shows a memory array that is *word-addressable*. That is, each 32-bit data word has a unique 32-bit address. Both the 32-bit word address and the 32-bit data value are written in hexadecimal in Figure 6.1. For example, data 0xF2F1AC07 is stored at memory address 1. Hexadecimal constants are written with the prefix 0x. By convention, memory is drawn with low memory addresses toward the bottom and high memory addresses toward the top.

MIPS uses the *load word* instruction, lw, to read a data word from memory into a register. Code Example 6.6 loads memory word 1 into $s3.

The lw instruction specifies the *effective address* in memory as the sum of a *base address* and an *offset*. The base address (written in parentheses in the instruction) is a register. The offset is a constant (written before the parentheses). In Code Example 6.6, the base address

Code Example 6.6 READING WORD-ADDRESSABLE MEMORY

Assembly Code

```
# This assembly code (unlike MIPS) assumes word-addressable memory
  lw $s3, 1($0)    # read memory word 1 into $s3
```

Code Example 6.7 WRITING WORD-ADDRESSABLE MEMORY

Assembly Code

```
# This assembly code (unlike MIPS) assumes word-addressable memory
  sw  $s7, 5($0)      # write $s7 to memory word 5
```

Figure 6.2 Byte-addressable memory

Word Address	Data	
0000000C	4 0 F 3 0 7 8 8	Word 3
00000008	0 1 E E 2 8 4 2	Word 2
00000004	F 2 F 1 A C 0 7	Word 1
00000000	A B C D E F 7 8	Word 0

width = 4 bytes

is $0, which holds the value 0, and the offset is 1, so the lw instruction reads from memory address ($0 + 1) = 1. After the load word instruction (lw) is executed, $s3 holds the value 0xF2F1AC07, which is the data value stored at memory address 1 in Figure 6.1.

Similarly, MIPS uses the *store word* instruction, sw, to write a data word from a register into memory. Code Example 6.7 writes the contents of register $s7 into memory word 5. These examples have used $0 as the base address for simplicity, but remember that any register can be used to supply the base address.

The previous two code examples have shown a computer architecture with a word-addressable memory. The MIPS memory model, however, is byte-addressable, *not* word-addressable. Each data byte has a unique address. A 32-bit word consists of four 8-bit bytes. So each word address is a multiple of 4, as shown in Figure 6.2. Again, both the 32-bit word address and the data value are given in hexadecimal.

Code Example 6.8 shows how to read and write words in the MIPS byte-addressable memory. The word address is four times the word number. The MIPS assembly code reads words 0, 2, and 3 and writes words 1, 8, and 100. The offset can be written in decimal or hexadecimal.

The MIPS architecture also provides the lb and sb instructions that load and store single bytes in memory rather than words. They are similar to lw and sw and will be discussed further in Section 6.4.5.

Byte-addressable memories are organized in a *big-endian* or *little-endian* fashion, as shown in Figure 6.3. In both formats, the *most significant byte* (MSB) is on the left and the *least significant byte* (LSB) is on the right. In big-endian machines, bytes are numbered starting with 0

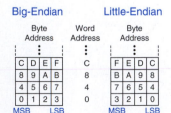

Figure 6.3 Big- and little-endian memory addressing

Code Example 6.8 ACCESSING BYTE-ADDRESSABLE MEMORY

MIPS Assembly Code

```
lw  $s0, 0($0)       # read data word 0 (0xABCDEF78) into $s0
lw  $s1, 8($0)       # read data word 2 (0x01EE2842) into $s1
lw  $s2, 0xC($0)     # read data word 3 (0x40F30788) into $s2
sw  $s3, 4($0)       # write $s3 to data word 1
sw  $s4, 0x20($0)    # write $s4 to data word 8
sw  $s5, 400($0)     # write $s5 to data word 100
```

at the big (most significant) end. In little-endian machines, bytes are numbered starting with 0 at the little (least significant) end. Word addresses are the same in both formats and refer to the same four bytes. Only the addresses of bytes within a word differ.

Example 6.2 BIG- AND LITTLE-ENDIAN MEMORY

Suppose that $s0 initially contains 0x23456789. After the following program is run on a big-endian system, what value does $s0 contain? In a little-endian system? `lb $s0, 1($0)` loads the data at byte address $(1 + \$0) = 1$ into the least significant byte of $s0. `lb` is discussed in detail in Section 6.4.5.

```
sw  $s0, 0($0)
lb  $s0, 1($0)
```

Solution: Figure 6.4 shows how big- and little-endian machines store the value 0x23456789 in memory word 0. After the load byte instruction, `lb $s0, 1($0)`, $s0 would contain 0x00000045 on a big-endian system and 0x00000067 on a little-endian system.

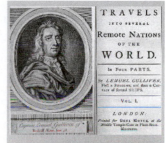

The terms big-endian and little-endian come from Jonathan Swift's *Gulliver's Travels*, first published in 1726 under the pseudonym of Isaac Bickerstaff. In his stories the Lilliputian king required his citizens (the Little-Endians) to break their eggs on the little end. The Big-Endians were rebels who broke their eggs on the big end.

The terms were first applied to computer architectures by Danny Cohen in his paper "On Holy Wars and a Plea for Peace" published on April Fools Day, 1980 (*USC/ISI IEN 137*). (Photo courtesy The Brotherton Collection, IEEDS University Library.)

```
            Big-Endian       Little-Endian
                           Word
Byte Address  0  1  2  3  Address  3  2  1  0  Byte Address
Data Value   23 45 67 89     0    23 45 67 89  Data Value
             MSB    LSB             MSB    LSB
```

Figure 6.4 Big-endian and little-endian data storage

IBM's PowerPC (formerly found in Macintosh computers) uses big-endian addressing. Intel's IA-32 architecture (found in PCs) uses little-endian addressing. Some MIPS processors are little-endian, and some are big-endian.[1] The choice of endianness is completely arbitrary but leads to hassles when sharing data between big-endian and little-endian computers. In examples in this text, we will use little-endian format whenever byte ordering matters.

---

[1] SPIM, the MIPS simulator that comes with this text, uses the endianness of the machine it is run on. For example, when using SPIM on an Intel IA-32 machine, the memory is little-endian. With an older Macintosh or Sun SPARC machine, memory is big-endian.

In the MIPS architecture, word addresses for lw and sw must be *word aligned*. That is, the address must be divisible by 4. Thus, the instruction lw $s0, 7($0) is an illegal instruction. Some architectures, such as IA-32, allow non-word-aligned data reads and writes, but MIPS requires strict alignment for simplicity. Of course, byte addresses for load byte and store byte, lb and sb, need not be word aligned.

Constants/Immediates

Load word and store word, lw and sw, also illustrate the use of *constants* in MIPS instructions. These constants are called *immediates*, because their values are immediately available from the instruction and do not require a register or memory access. Add immediate, addi, is another common MIPS instruction that uses an immediate operand. addi adds the immediate specified in the instruction to a value in a register, as shown in Code Example 6.9.

The immediate specified in an instruction is a 16-bit two's complement number in the range [−32768, 32767]. Subtraction is equivalent to adding a negative number, so, in the interest of simplicity, there is no subi instruction in the MIPS architecture.

Recall that the add and sub instructions use three register operands. But the lw, sw, and addi instructions use two register operands and a constant. Because the instruction formats differ, lw and sw instructions violate design principle 1: simplicity favors regularity. However, this issue allows us to introduce the last design principle:

Code Example 6.9 IMMEDIATE OPERANDS

High-Level Code	MIPS Assembly Code

a = a + 4;
b = a − 12;
	# $s0 = a, $s1 = b
	  addi $s0, $s0, 4 # a = a + 4
	  addi $s1, $s0, −12 # b = a − 12

Design Principle 4: Good design demands good compromises.

A single instruction format would be simple but not flexible. The MIPS instruction set makes the compromise of supporting three instruction formats. One format, used for instructions such as add and sub, has three register operands. Another, used for instructions such as lw and addi, has two register operands and a 16-bit immediate. A third, to be discussed later, has a 26-bit immediate and no registers. The next section discusses the three MIPS instruction formats and shows how they are encoded into binary.

6.3 MACHINE LANGUAGE

Assembly language is convenient for humans to read. However, digital circuits understand only 1's and 0's. Therefore, a program written in assembly language is translated from mnemonics to a representation using only 1's and 0's, called *machine language*.

MIPS uses 32-bit instructions. Again, simplicity favors regularity, and the most regular choice is to encode all instructions as words that can be stored in memory. Even though some instructions may not require all 32 bits of encoding, variable-length instructions would add too much complexity. Simplicity would also encourage a single instruction format, but, as already mentioned, that is too restrictive. MIPS makes the compromise of defining three instruction formats: R-type, I-type, and J-type. This small number of formats allows for some regularity among all the types, and thus simpler hardware, while also accommodating different instruction needs, such as the need to encode large constants in the instruction. *R-type* instructions operate on three registers. *I-type* instructions operate on two registers and a 16-bit immediate. *J-type* (jump) instructions operate on one 26-bit immediate. We introduce all three formats in this section but leave the discussion of J-type instructions for Section 6.4.2.

6.3.1 R-type Instructions

The name R-type is short for *register-type*. R-type instructions use three registers as operands: two as sources, and one as a destination. Figure 6.5 shows the R-type machine instruction format. The 32-bit instruction has six fields: op, rs, rt, rd, shamt, and funct. Each field is five or six bits, as indicated.

The operation the instruction performs is encoded in the two fields highlighted in blue: op (also called opcode or operation code) and funct (also called the function). All R-type instructions have an opcode of 0. The specific R-type operation is determined by the funct field. For example, the opcode and funct fields for the add instruction are 0 (000000_2) and 32 (100000_2), respectively. Similarly, the sub instruction has an opcode and funct field of 0 and 34.

The operands are encoded in the three fields: rs, rt, and rd. The first two registers, rs and rt, are the source registers; rd is the destination

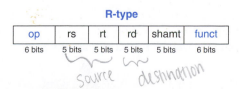

R-type

op	rs	rt	rd	shamt	funct
6 bits	5 bits	5 bits	5 bits	5 bits	6 bits

source   destination

Figure 6.5 R-type machine instruction format

rs is short for "register source." rt comes after rs alphabetically and usually indicates the second register source.

register. The fields contain the register numbers that were given in Table 6.1. For example, $s0 is register 16.

The fifth field, shamt, is used only in shift operations. In those instructions, the binary value stored in the 5-bit shamt field indicates the amount to shift. For all other R-type instructions, shamt is 0.

Figure 6.6 shows the machine code for the R-type instructions add and sub. Notice that the destination is the first register in an assembly language instruction, but it is the third register field (rd) in the machine language instruction. For example, the assembly instruction add $s0, $s1, $s2 has rs = $s1 (17), rt = $s2 (18), and rd = $s0 (16).

Tables B.1 and B.2 in Appendix B define the opcode values for all MIPS instructions and the funct field values for R-type instructions.

Assembly Code		Field Values						Machine Code						
	op	rs	rt	rd	shamt	funct		op	rs	rt	rd	shamt	funct	
add $s0, $s1, $s2	0	17	18	16	0	32		000000	10001	10010	10000	00000	100000	(0x02328020)
sub $t0, $t3, $t5	0	11	13	8	0	34		000000	01011	01101	01000	00000	100010	(0x016D4022)
	6 bits	5 bits	5 bits	5 bits	5 bits	6 bits		6 bits	5 bits	5 bits	5 bits	5 bits	6 bits	

Figure 6.6 Machine code for R-type instructions

Example 6.3 TRANSLATING ASSEMBLY LANGUAGE TO MACHINE LANGUAGE

Translate the following assembly language statement into machine language.

add $t0, $s4, $s5

Solution: According to Table 6.1, $t0, $s4, and $s5 are registers 8, 20, and 21. According to Tables B.1 and B.2, add has an opcode of 0 and a funct code of 32. Thus, the fields and machine code are given in Figure 6.7. The easiest way to write the machine language in hexadecimal is to first write it in binary, then look at consecutive groups of four bits, which correspond to hexadecimal digits (indicated in blue). Hence, the machine language instruction is 0x02954020.

Assembly Code		Field Values						Machine Code						
	op	rs	rt	rd	shamt	funct		op	rs	rt	rd	shamt	funct	
add $t0, $s4, $s5	0	20	21	8	0	32		000000	10100	10101	01000	00000	100000	(0x02954020)
	6 bits	5 bits	5 bits	5 bits	5 bits	6 bits		0	2	9	5	4	0	2	0

Figure 6.7 Machine code for the R-type instruction of Example 6.3

6.3.2 I-Type Instructions

The name I-type is short for *immediate-type*. I-type instructions use two register operands and one immediate operand. Figure 6.8 shows the I-type machine instruction format. The 32-bit instruction has four fields: op, rs, rt, and imm. The first three fields, op, rs, and rt, are like those of R-type instructions. The imm field holds the 16-bit immediate.

The operation is determined solely by the opcode, highlighted in blue. The operands are specified in the three fields, rs, rt, and imm. rs and imm are always used as source operands. rt is used as a destination for some instructions (such as addi and lw) but as another source for others (such as sw).

Figure 6.9 shows several examples of encoding I-type instructions. Recall that negative immediate values are represented using 16-bit two's complement notation. rt is listed first in the assembly language instruction when it is used as a destination, but it is the second register field in the machine language instruction.

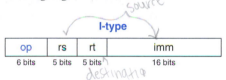

Figure 6.8 I-type instruction format

Assembly Code														

Field Values

	op	rs	rt	imm
addi $s0, $s1, 5	8	17	16	5
addi $t0, $s3, −12	8	19	8	−12
lw $t2, 32($0)	35	0	10	32
sw $s1, 4($t1)	43	9	17	4
	6 bits	5 bits	5 bits	16 bits

Machine Code

op	rs	rt	imm	
001000	10001	10000	0000 0000 0000 0101	(0x22300005)
001000	10011	01000	1111 1111 1111 0100	(0x2268FFF4)
100011	00000	01010	0000 0000 0010 0000	(0x8C0A0020)
101011	01001	10001	0000 0000 0000 0100	(0xAD310004)
6 bits	5 bits	5 bits	16 bits	

Figure 6.9 Machine code for I-type instructions

Example 6.4 TRANSLATING I-TYPE ASSEMBLY INSTRUCTIONS INTO MACHINE CODE

Translate the following I-type instruction into machine code.

```
lw $s3, −24($s4)
```

Solution: According to Table 6.1, $s3 and $s4 are registers 19 and 20, respectively. Table B.1 indicates that lw has an opcode of 35. rs specifies the base address, $s4, and rt specifies the destination register, $s3. The immediate, imm, encodes the 16-bit offset, −24. Thus, the fields and machine code are given in Figure 6.10.

Figure 6.10 **Machine code for the I-type instruction**

I-type instructions have a 16-bit immediate field, but the immediates are used in 32-bit operations. For example, lw adds a 16-bit offset to a 32-bit base register. What should go in the upper half of the 32 bits? For positive immediates, the upper half should be all 0's, but for negative immediates, the upper half should be all 1's. Recall from Section 1.4.6 that this is called *sign extension*. An N-bit two's complement number is sign-extended to an M-bit number ($M > N$) by copying the sign bit (most significant bit) of the N-bit number into all of the upper bits of the M-bit number. Sign-extending a two's complement number does not change its value.

Most MIPS instructions sign-extend the immediate. For example, addi, lw, and sw do sign extension to support both positive and negative immediates. An exception to this rule is that logical operations (andi, ori, xori) place 0's in the upper half; this is called *zero extension* rather than sign extension. Logical operations are discussed further in Section 6.4.1.

6.3.3 J-type Instructions

The name J-type is short for *jump-type*. This format is used only with jump instructions (see Section 6.4.2). This instruction format uses a single 26-bit address operand, addr, as shown in Figure 6.11. Like other formats, J-type instructions begin with a 6-bit opcode. The remaining bits are used to specify an address, addr. Further discussion and machine code examples of J-type instructions are given in Sections 6.4.2 and 6.5.

6.3.4 Interpreting Machine Language Code

To interpret machine language, one must decipher the fields of each 32-bit instruction word. Different instructions use different formats, but all formats start with a 6-bit opcode field. Thus, the best place to begin is to look at the opcode. If it is 0, the instruction is R-type; otherwise it is I-type or J-type.

Figure 6.11 **J-type instruction format**

Example 6.5 TRANSLATING MACHINE LANGUAGE TO ASSEMBLY
LANGUAGE

Translate the following machine language code into assembly language.

```
0x2237FFF1
0x02F34022
```

Solution: First, we represent each instruction in binary and look at the six most significant bits to find the opcode for each instruction, as shown in Figure 6.12. The opcode determines how to interpret the rest of the bits. The opcodes are 001000_2 (8_{10}) and 000000_2 (0_{10}), indicating an addi and R-type instruction, respectively. The funct field of the R-type instruction is 100010_2 (34_{10}), indicating that it is a sub instruction. Figure 6.12 shows the assembly code equivalent of the two machine instructions.

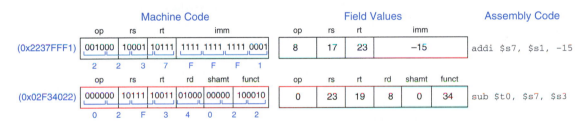

Figure 6.12 Machine code to assembly code translation

6.3.5 The Power of the Stored Program

A program written in machine language is a series of 32-bit numbers representing the instructions. Like other binary numbers, these instructions can be stored in memory. This is called the *stored program* concept, and it is a key reason why computers are so powerful. Running a different program does not require large amounts of time and effort to reconfigure or rewire hardware; it only requires writing the new program to memory. Instead of dedicated hardware, the stored program offers *general purpose* computing. In this way, a computer can execute applications ranging from a calculator to a word processor to a video player simply by changing the stored program.

Instructions in a stored program are retrieved, or *fetched*, from memory and executed by the processor. Even large, complex programs are simplified to a series of memory reads and instruction executions.

Figure 6.13 shows how machine instructions are stored in memory. In MIPS programs, the instructions are normally stored starting at address 0x00400000. Remember that MIPS memory is byte addressable, so 32-bit (4-byte) instruction addresses advance by 4 bytes, not 1.

Assembly Code	Machine Code
lw $t2, 32($0)	0x8C0A0020
add $s0, $s1, $s2	0x02328020
addi $t0, $s3, -12	0x2268FFF4
sub $t0, $t3, $t5	0x016D4022

Stored Program

Address	Instructions
⋮	⋮
0040000C	0 1 6 D 4 0 2 2
00400008	2 2 6 8 F F F 4
00400004	0 2 3 2 8 0 2 0
00400000	8 C 0 A 0 0 2 0 ← PC
⋮	⋮

Main Memory

Figure 6.13 Stored program

To run or *execute* the stored program, the processor fetches the instructions from memory sequentially. The fetched instructions are then decoded and executed by the digital hardware. The address of the current instruction is kept in a 32-bit register called the *program counter* (PC). The PC is separate from the 32 registers shown previously in Table 6.1.

To execute the code in Figure 6.13, the operating system sets the PC to address 0x00400000. The processor reads the instruction at that memory address and executes the instruction, 0x8C0A0020. The processor then increments the PC by 4, to 0x00400004, fetches and executes that instruction, and repeats.

The *architectural state* of a microprocessor holds the state of a program. For MIPS, the architectural state consists of the register file and PC. If the operating system saves the architectural state at some point in the program, it can interrupt the program, do something else, then restore the state such that the program continues properly, unaware that it was ever interrupted. The architectural state is also of great importance when we build a microprocessor in Chapter 7.

6.4 PROGRAMMING

Software languages such as C or Java are called high-level programming languages, because they are written at a more abstract level than assembly language. Many high-level languages use common software constructs such as arithmetic and logical operations, if/else statements, for and while loops, array indexing, and procedure calls. In this section, we explore how to translate these high-level constructs into MIPS assembly code.

6.4.1 Arithmetic/Logical Instructions

The MIPS architecture defines a variety of arithmetic and logical instructions. We introduce these instructions briefly here, because they are necessary to implement higher-level constructs.

Ada Lovelace, 1815–1852. Wrote the first computer program. It calculated the Bernoulli numbers using Charles Babbage's Analytical Engine. She was the only legitimate child of the poet Lord Byron.

Source Registers

$s1	1111	1111	1111	1111	0000	0000	0000	0000
$s2	0100	0110	1010	0001	1111	0000	1011	0111

Assembly Code		Result								
and $s3, $s1, $s2	$s3	0100	0110	1010	0001	0000	0000	0000	0000
or $s4, $s1, $s2	$s4	1111	1111	1111	1111	1111	0000	1011	0111
xor $s5, $s1, $s2	$s5	1011	1001	0101	1110	1111	0000	1011	0111
nor $s6, $s1, $s2	$s6	0000	0000	0000	0000	0000	1111	0100	1000

Figure 6.14 Logical operations

Logical Instructions

MIPS logical operations include `and`, `or`, `xor`, and `nor`. These R-type instructions operate bit-by-bit on two source registers and write the result to the destination register. Figure 6.14 shows examples of these operations on the two source values 0xFFFF0000 and 0x46A1F0B7. The figure shows the values stored in the destination register, `rd`, after the instruction executes.

The `and` instruction is useful for *masking* bits (i.e., forcing unwanted bits to 0). For example, in Figure 6.14, 0xFFFF0000 AND 0x46A1F0B7 = 0x46A10000. The `and` instruction masks off the bottom two bytes and places the unmasked top two bytes of $s2, 0x46A1, in $s3. Any subset of register bits can be masked.

The `or` instruction is useful for combining bits from two registers. For example, 0x347A0000 OR 0x000072FC = 0x347A72FC, a combination of the two values.

MIPS does not provide a NOT instruction, but A NOR $0 = NOT A, so the NOR instruction can substitute.

Logical operations can also operate on immediates. These I-type instructions are `andi`, `ori`, and `xori`. `nori` is not provided, because the same functionality can be easily implemented using the other instructions, as will be explored in Exercise 6.11. Figure 6.15 shows examples of the `andi`, `ori`, and `xori` instructions. The figure gives the values of

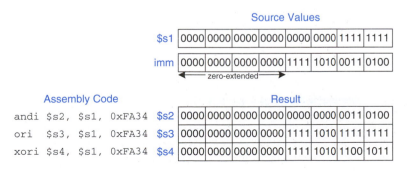

Source Values

$s1	0000	0000	0000	0000	0000	0000	1111	1111
imm	0000	0000	0000	0000	1111	1010	0011	0100

zero-extended

Assembly Code		Result								
andi $s2, $s1, 0xFA34	$s2	0000	0000	0000	0000	0000	0000	0011	0100
ori $s3, $s1, 0xFA34	$s3	0000	0000	0000	0000	1111	1010	1111	1111
xori $s4, $s1, 0xFA34	$s4	0000	0000	0000	0000	1111	1010	1100	1011

Figure 6.15 Logical operations with immediates

the source register and immediate, and the value of the destination register, rt, after the instruction executes. Because these instructions operate on a 32-bit value from a register and a 16-bit immediate, they first zero-extend the immediate to 32 bits.

Shift Instructions

Shift instructions shift the value in a register left or right by up to 31 bits. Shift operations multiply or divide by powers of two. MIPS shift operations are sll (shift left logical), srl (shift right logical), and sra (shift right arithmetic).

As discussed in Section 5.2.5, left shifts always fill the least significant bits with 0's. However, right shifts can be either logical (0's shift into the most significant bits) or arithmetic (the sign bit shifts into the most significant bits). Figure 6.16 shows the machine code for the R-type instructions sll, srl, and sra. rt (i.e., $s1) holds the 32-bit value to be shifted, and shamt gives the amount by which to shift (4). The shifted result is placed in rd.

Figure 6.17 shows the register values for the shift instructions sll, srl, and sra. Shifting a value left by N is equivalent to multiplying it by 2^N. Likewise, arithmetically shifting a value right by N is equivalent to dividing it by 2^N, as discussed in Section 5.2.5.

MIPS also has variable-shift instructions: sllv (shift left logical variable), srlv (shift right logical variable), and srav (shift right arithmetic variable). Figure 6.18 shows the machine code for these instructions.

Assembly Code		op	rs	rt	rd	shamt	funct		op	rs	rt	rd	shamt	funct	
sll $t0, $s1,	4	0	0	17	8	4	0		000000	00000	10001	01000	00100	000000	(0x00114100)
srl $s2, $s1,	4	0	0	17	18	4	2		000000	00000	10001	10010	00100	000010	(0x00119102)
sra $s3, $s1,	4	0	0	17	19	4	3		000000	00000	10001	10011	00100	000011	(0x00119903)
		6 bits	5 bits	5 bits	5 bits	5 bits	6 bits		6 bits	5 bits	5 bits	5 bits	5 bits	6 bits	

Field Values | Machine Code

Figure 6.16 Shift instruction machine code

Source Values

$s1   1111 0011 0000 0000 0000 0010 1010 1000

shamt   00100

Figure 6.17 Shift operations

Assembly Code	Result								
sll $t0, $s1, 4	$t0	0011	0000	0000	0000	0010	1010	1000	0000
srl $s2, $s1, 4	$s2	0000	1111	0011	0000	0000	0000	0010	1010
sra $s3, $s1, 4	$s3	1111	1111	0011	0000	0000	0000	0010	1010

Assembly Code	op	rs	rt	rd	shamt	funct	op	rs	rt	rd	shamt	funct	
			Field Values						**Machine Code**				
sllv $s3, $s1, $s2	0	18	17	19	0	4	000000	10010	10001	10011	00000	000100	(0x02519804)
srlv $s4, $s1, $s2	0	18	17	20	0	6	000000	10010	10001	10100	00000	000110	(0x0251A006)
srav $s5, $s1, $s2	0	18	17	21	0	7	000000	10010	10001	10101	00000	000111	(0x0251A807)
	6 bits	5 bits	5 bits	5 bits	5 bits	6 bits	6 bits	5 bits	5 bits	5 bits	5 bits	6 bits	

Figure 6.18 Variable-shift instruction machine code

Source Values

$s1	1111	0011	0000	0100	0000	0010	1010	1000

$s2	0000	0000	0000	0000	0000	0000	0000	**1000**

Assembly Code		**Result**							
sllv $s3, $s1, $s2	$s3	0000	0100	0000	0010	1010	1000	0000	0000
srlv $s4, $s1, $s2	$s4	0000	0000	1111	0011	0000	0100	0000	0010
srav $s5, $s1, $s2	$s5	1111	1111	1111	0011	0000	0100	0000	0010

Figure 6.19 Variable-shift operations

rt (i.e., $s1) holds the value to be shifted, and the five least significant bits of rs (i.e., $s2) give the amount to shift. The shifted result is placed in rd, as before. The shamt field is ignored and should be all 0's. Figure 6.19 shows register values for each type of variable-shift instruction.

Generating Constants

The addi instruction is helpful for assigning 16-bit constants, as shown in Code Example 6.10.

Code Example 6.10 16-BIT CONSTANT

High-Level Code	MIPS Assembly code
int a = 0x4f3c;	```# $s0 = a``` ``` addi $s0, $0, 0x4f3c # a = 0x4f3c```

Code Example 6.11 32-BIT CONSTANT

High-Level Code	MIPS Assembly Code

int a = 0x6d5e4f3c;	```# $s0 = a```
	``` lui $s0, 0x6d5e # a = 0x6d5e0000```
	``` ori $s0, $s0, 0x4f3c # a = 0x6d5e4f3c```

The int data type in C refers to a word of data representing a two's complement integer. MIPS uses 32-bit words, so an int represents a number in the range $[-2^{31}, 2^{31}-1]$.

To assign 32-bit constants, use a load upper immediate instruction (lui) followed by an or immediate (ori) instruction, as shown in Code Example 6.11. lui loads a 16-bit immediate into the upper half of a register and sets the lower half to 0. As mentioned earlier, ori merges a 16-bit immediate into the lower half.

Multiplication and Division Instructions*

Multiplication and division are somewhat different from other arithmetic operations. Multiplying two 32-bit numbers produces a 64-bit product. Dividing two 32-bit numbers produces a 32-bit quotient and a 32-bit remainder.

hi and lo are not among the usual 32 MIPS registers, so special instructions are needed to access them. mfhi $s2 (move from hi) copies the value in hi to $s2. mflo $s3 (move from lo) copies the value in lo to $s3. hi and lo are technically part of the architectural state; however, we generally ignore these registers in this book.

The MIPS architecture has two special-purpose registers, hi and lo, which are used to hold the results of multiplication and division. mult $s0, $s1 multiplies the values in $s0 and $s1. The 32 most significant bits are placed in hi and the 32 least significant bits are placed in lo. Similarly, div $s0, $s1 computes $s0/$s1. The quotient is placed in lo and the remainder is placed in hi.

6.4.2 Branching

An advantage of a computer over a calculator is its ability to make decisions. A computer performs different tasks depending on the input. For example, if/else statements, case statements, while loops, and for loops all conditionally execute code depending on some test.

To sequentially execute instructions, the program counter increments by 4 after each instruction. *Branch* instructions modify the program counter to skip over sections of code or to go back to repeat previous code. *Conditional branch* instructions perform a test and branch only if the test is TRUE. *Unconditional branch* instructions, called *jumps*, always branch.

Conditional Branches

The MIPS instruction set has two conditional branch instructions: branch if equal (beq) and branch if not equal (bne). beq branches when the values in two registers are equal, and bne branches when they are not equal. Code Example 6.12 illustrates the use of beq. Note that branches are written as beq $rs, $rt, imm, where $rs is the first source register. This order is reversed from most I-type instructions.

When the program in Code Example 6.12 reaches the branch if equal instruction (beq), the value in $s0 is equal to the value in $s1, so the branch is *taken*. That is, the next instruction executed is the add instruction just after the *label* called target. The two instructions directly after the branch and before the label are not executed.

Assembly code uses labels to indicate instruction locations in the program. When the assembly code is translated into machine code, these

---

Code Example 6.12 CONDITIONAL BRANCHING USING beq

MIPS Assembly Code

```
addi  $s0, $0, 4        # $s0 = 0 + 4 = 4
addi  $s1, $0, 1        # $s1 = 0 + 1 = 1
sll   $s1, $s1, 2       # $s1 = 1 << 2 = 4
beq   $s0, $s1, target  # $s0 == $s1, so branch is taken
addi  $s1, $s1, 1       # not executed
sub   $s1, $s1, $s0     # not executed

target:
add   $s1, $s1, $s0     # $s1 = 4 + 4 = 8
```

---

labels are translated into instruction addresses (see Section 6.5). MIPS assembly labels are followed by a (:) and cannot use reserved words, such as instruction mnemonics. Most programmers indent their instructions but not the labels, to help make labels stand out.

Code Example 6.13 shows an example using the branch if not equal instruction (bne). In this case, the branch is *not taken* because $s0 is equal to $s1, and the code continues to execute directly after the bne instruction. All instructions in this code snippet are executed.

Code Example 6.13 CONDITIONAL BRANCHING USING bne

MIPS Assembly Code

```
addi  $s0, $0, 4        # $s0 = 0 + 4 = 4
addi  $s1, $0, 1        # $s1 = 0 + 1 = 1
sll   $s1, $s1, 2       # $s1 = 1 << 2 = 4
bne   $s0, $s1, target  # $s0 == $s1, so branch is not taken
addi  $s1, $s1, 1       # $s1 = 4 + 1 = 5
sub   $s1, $s1, $s0     # $s1 = 5 - 4 = 1

target:
add   $s1, $s1, $s0     # $s1 = 1 + 4 = 5
```

Jump

A program can unconditionally branch, or *jump*, using the three types of jump instructions: jump (j), jump and link (jal), and jump register (jr). Jump (j) jumps directly to the instruction at the specified label. Jump and link (jal) is similar to j but is used by procedures to save a return address, as will be discussed in Section 6.4.6. Jump register (jr) jumps to the address held in a register. Code Example 6.14 shows the use of the jump instruction (j).

After the j target instruction, the program in Code Example 6.14 unconditionally continues executing the add instruction at the label target. All of the instructions between the jump and the label are skipped.

j and jal are J-type instructions. jr is an R-type instruction that uses only the rs operand.

Code Example 6.14 UNCONDITIONAL BRANCHING USING j

MIPS Assembly Code

```
    addi   $s0, $0, 4      # $s0 = 4
    addi   $s1, $0, 1      # $s1 = 1
    j      target          # jump to target
    addi   $s1, $s1, 1     # not executed
    sub    $s1, $s1, $s0   # not executed
target:
    add    $s1, $s1, $s0   # $s1 = 1 + 4 = 5
```

Code Example 6.15 UNCONDITIONAL BRANCHING USING jr

MIPS Assembly Code

```
0x00002000   addi   $s0, $0, 0x2010   # $s0 = 0x2010
0x00002004   jr     $s0               # jump to 0x00002010
0x00002008   addi   $s1, $0, 1        # not executed
0x0000200c   sra    $s1, $s1, 2       # not executed
0x00002010   lw     $s3, 44 ($s1)     # executed after jr instruction
```

Code Example 6.15 shows the use of the jump register instruction (jr). Instruction addresses are given to the left of each instruction. jr $s0 jumps to the address held in $s0, 0x00002010.

6.4.3 Conditional Statements

if statements, if/else statements, and case statements are conditional statements commonly used by high-level languages. They each conditionally execute a *block* of code consisting of one or more instructions. This section shows how to translate these high-level constructs into MIPS assembly language.

If Statements

An if statement executes a block of code, the *if block*, only when a condition is met. Code Example 6.16 shows how to translate an if statement into MIPS assembly code.

Code Example 6.16 if STATEMENT

High-Level Code	MIPS Assembly Code

`if (i == j)`
  `f = g + h;`
 	
`f = f - i;`
	`# $s0 = f, $s1 = g, $s2 = h, $s3 = i, $s4 = j`
	`    bne $s3, $s4, L1    # if i ! = j, skip if block`
	`    add $s0, $s1, $s2   # if block: f = g + h`
	`L1:`
	`    sub $s0, $s0, $s3   # f = f - i`

The assembly code for the `if` statement tests the opposite condition of the one in the high-level code. In Code Example 6.16, the high-level code tests for `i == j`, and the assembly code tests for `i != j`. The `bne` instruction branches (skips the `if` block) when `i != j`. Otherwise, `i == j`, the branch is not taken, and the `if` block is executed as desired.

If/Else Statements

`if/else` statements execute one of two blocks of code depending on a condition. When the condition in the `if` statement is met, the *if block* is executed. Otherwise, the *else block* is executed. Code Example 6.17 shows an example `if/else` statement.

Like `if` statements, `if/else` assembly code tests the opposite condition of the one in the high-level code. For example, in Code Example 6.17, the high-level code tests for `i == j`. The assembly code tests for the opposite condition (`i != j`). If that opposite condition is TRUE, `bne` skips the `if` block and executes the `else` block. Otherwise, the `if` block executes and finishes with a jump instruction (`j`) to jump past the `else` block.

Code Example 6.17 `if/else` **STATEMENT**

High-Level Code	MIPS Assembly Code

`if (i == j)`
`  f = g + h;`
 	
`else`
`  f = f - i;`
	`# $s0 = f, $s1 = g,  $s2 = h, $s3 = i, $s4 = j`
	`  bne $s3, $s4, else  # if i ! = j, branch to else`
	`  add $s0, $s1, $s2  # if block: f = g + h`
	`  j  L2        # skip past the else block`
	`else:`
	`  sub $s0, $s0, $s3  # else block: f = f - i`
	`L2:`

Switch/Case Statements*

`switch/case` statements execute one of several blocks of code depending on the conditions. If no conditions are met, the `default` block is executed. A `case` statement is equivalent to a series of *nested* `if/else` statements. Code Example 6.18 shows two high-level code snippets with the same functionality: they calculate the fee for an *ATM* (*automatic teller machine*) withdrawal of $20, $50, or $100, as defined by `amount`. The MIPS assembly implementation is the same for both high-level code snippets.

6.4.4 Getting Loopy

Loops repeatedly execute a block of code depending on a condition. `for` loops and `while` loops are common loop constructs used by high-level languages. This section shows how to translate them into MIPS assembly language.

Code Example 6.18 switch/case STATEMENT

High-Level Code	MIPS Assembly Code

```
switch (amount) {
  case 20: fee = 2; break;




  case 50: fee = 3; break;




  case 100: fee = 5; break;




  default: fee = 0;

}

// equivalent function using if/else statements
  if      (amount == 20)  fee = 2;
  else if (amount == 50)  fee = 3;
  else if (amount == 100) fee = 5;
  else                    fee = 0;
```

```
# $s0 = amount, $s1 = fee

case20:
  addi $t0, $0,  20     # $t0 = 20
  bne  $s0, $t0, case50 # i == 20? if not,
                        #   skip to case50
  addi $s1, $0,  2      # if so, fee = 2
  j    done             # and break out of case
case50:
  addi $t0, $0,  50     # $t0 = 50
  bne  $s0, $t0, case100 # i == 50? if not,
                        #   skip to case100
  addi $s1, $0,  3      # if so, fee = 3
  j    done             # and break out of case
case100:
  addi $t0, $0,  100    # $t0 = 100
  bne  $s0, $t0, default # i == 100? if not,
                        #   skip to default
  addi $s1, $0,  5      # if so, fee = 5
  j    done             # and break out of case
default:
  add  $s1, $0, $0      # charge = 0

done:
```

While Loops

while loops repeatedly execute a block of code until a condition is *not* met. The while loop in Code Example 6.19 determines the value of x such that $2^x = 128$. It executes seven times, until pow = 128.

Like if/else statements, the assembly code for while loops tests the opposite condition of the one given in the high-level code. If that opposite condition is TRUE, the while loop is finished.

Code Example 6.19 while LOOP

High-Level Code	MIPS Assembly Code

```
int pow = 1;
int x   = 0;




while (pow != 128)
{
  pow = pow * 2;
  x = x + 1;
}
```

```
# $s0 = pow, $s1 = x
  addi $s0, $0, 1      # pow = 1
  addi $s1, $0, 0      # x = 0

  addi $t0, $0, 128    # t0 = 128 for comparison
while:
  beq  $s0, $t0, done  # if pow == 128, exit while
  sll  $s0, $s0, 1     # pow = pow * 2
  addi $s1, $s1, 1     # x = x + 1
  j    while
done:
```

In Code Example 6.19, the while loop compares pow to 128 and exits the loop if it is equal. Otherwise it doubles pow (using a left shift), increments x, and jumps back to the start of the while loop.

For Loops

for loops, like while loops, repeatedly execute a block of code until a condition is *not* met. However, for loops add support for a *loop variable*, which typically keeps track of the number of loop executions. A general format of the for loop is

```
for (initialization; condition; loop operation)
```

The *initialization* code executes before the for loop begins. The *condition* is tested at the beginning of each loop. If the condition is not met, the loop exits. The *loop operation* executes at the end of each loop.

Code Example 6.20 adds the numbers from 0 to 9. The loop variable, i, is initialized to 0 and is incremented at the end of each loop iteration. At the beginning of each iteration, the for loop executes only when i is not equal to 10. Otherwise, the loop is finished. In this case, the for loop executes 10 times. for loops can be implemented using a while loop, but the for loop is often convenient.

Magnitude Comparison

So far, the examples have used beq and bne to perform equality or inequality comparisons and branches. MIPS provides the *set less than* instruction, slt, for magnitude comparison. slt sets rd to 1 when rs < rt. Otherwise, rd is 0.

Code Example 6.20 for LOOP

High-Level Code

```
int sum = 0;




for (i = 0; i != 10; i = i + 1) {
  sum = sum + i;



}

// equivalent to the following while loop
int sum = 0;
int i = 0;
while (i != 10) {
  sum = sum + i;
  i = i + 1;
}
```

MIPS Assembly Code

```
# $s0 = i, $s1 = sum
    add   $s1, $0, $0    # sum = 0
    addi  $s0, $0, 0     # i   = 0
    addi  $t0, $0, 10    # $t0 = 10
for:
    beq   $s0, $t0, done # if i == 10, branch to done
    add   $s1, $s1, $s0  # sum = sum + i
    addi  $s0, $s0, 1    # increment i
    j     for
done:
```

Example 6.6 LOOPS USING slt

The following high-level code adds the powers of 2 from 1 to 100. Translate it into assembly language.

```
// high-level code

int sum = 0;
for (i = 1; i < 101; i = i * 2)
  sum = sum + i;
```

Solution: The assembly language code uses the set less than (slt) instruction to perform the less than comparison in the for loop.

```
# MIPS assembly code

# $s0 = i, $s1 = sum
  addi $s1, $0, 0    # sum = 0
  addi $s0, $0, 1    # i = 1
  addi $t0, $0, 101  # $t0 = 101

loop:
  slt $t1, $s0, $t0    # if (i < 101) $t1 = 1, else $t1 = 0
  beq $t1, $0, done    # if $t1 == 0 (i >= 101), branch to done
  add $s1, $s1, $s0    # sum = sum + i
  sll $s0, $s0, 1      # i = i * 2
  j   loop

done:
```

Exercise 6.12 explores how to use slt for other magnitude comparisons including greater than, greater than or equal, and less than or equal.

6.4.5 Arrays

Arrays are useful for accessing large amounts of similar data. An array is organized as sequential data addresses in memory. Each array element is identified by a number called its *index*. The number of elements in the array is called the *size* of the array. This section shows how to access array elements in memory.

Array Indexing

Figure 6.20 shows an array of five integers stored in memory. The *index* ranges from 0 to 4. In this case, the array is stored in a processor's main memory starting at *base address* 0x10007000. The base address gives the address of the first array element, array[0].

Code Example 6.21 multiplies the first two elements in array by 8 and stores them back in the array.

The first step in accessing an array element is to load the base address of the array into a register. Code Example 6.21 loads the base address

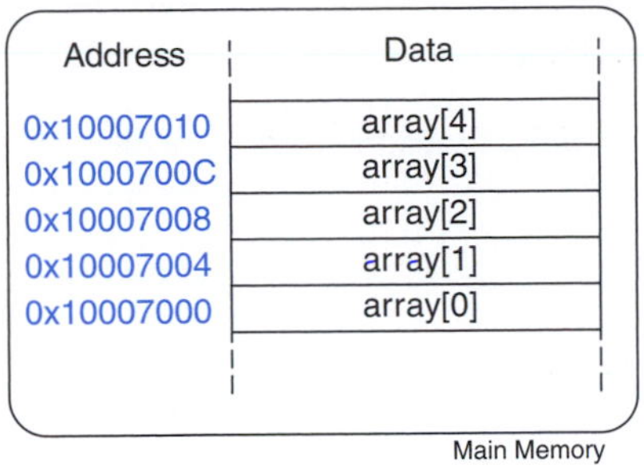

Figure 6.20 Five-entry array with base address of 0x10007000

Code Example 6.21 ACCESSING ARRAYS

High-Level Code	MIPS Assembly Code
`int array [5];`	``` # $s0 = base address of array lui $s0, 0x1000 # $s0 = 0x10000000 ori $s0, $s0, 0x7000 # $s0 = 0x10007000 ```
`array[0] = array[0] * 8;`	``` lw $t1, 0($s0) # $t1 = array[0] sll $t1, $t1, 3 # $t1 = $t1 << 3 = $t1 * 8 sw $t1, 0($s0) # array[0] = $t1 ```
`array[1] = array[1] * 8;`	``` lw $t1, 4($s0) # $t1 = array[1] sll $t1, $t1, 3 # $t1 = $t1 << 3 = $t1 * 8 sw $t1, 4($s0) # array[1] = $t1 ```

---

into $s0. Recall that the load upper immediate (lui) and or immediate (ori) instructions can be used to load a 32-bit constant into a register.

Code Example 6.21 also illustrates why lw takes a base address and an offset. The base address points to the start of the array. The offset can be used to access subsequent elements of the array. For example, array[1] is stored at memory address 0x10007004 (one word or four bytes after array[0]), so it is accessed at an offset of 4 past the base address.

You might have noticed that the code for manipulating each of the two array elements in Code Example 6.21 is essentially the same except for the index. Duplicating the code is not a problem when accessing two array elements, but it would become terribly inefficient for accessing all of the elements in a large array. Code Example 6.22 uses a for loop to multiply by 8 all of the elements of a 1000-element array stored at a base address of 0x23B8F000.

Figure 6.21 shows the 1000-element array in memory. The index into the array is now a variable (i) rather than a constant, so we cannot take advantage of the immediate offset in lw. Instead, we compute the address of the ith element and store it in $t0. Remember that each array element is a word but that memory is byte addressed, so the offset from

Code Example 6.22 ACCESSING ARRAYS USING A `for` LOOP

High-Level Code	MIPS Assembly Code
<pre>int i;
int array[1000];

for (i=0; i < 1000; i = i + 1) {

  array[i] = array[i] * 8;

}</pre> | <pre># $s0 = array base address, $s1 = i
initialization code
  lui $s0, 0x23B8   # $s0 = 0x23B80000
  ori $s0, $s0, 0xF000 # $s0 = 0x23B8F000
  addi $s1, $0   # i = 0
  addi $t2, $0, 1000   # $t2 = 1000

loop:
  slt $t0, $s1, $t2   # i < 1000?
  beq $t0, $0, done   # if not then done
  sll $t0, $s1, 2   # $t0 = i * 4 (byte offset)
  add $t0, $t0, $s0   # address of array[i]
  lw $t1, 0($t0)   # $t1 = array[i]
  sll $t1, $t1, 3   # $t1 = array[i] * 8
  sw $t1, 0($t0)   # array[i] = array[i] * 8
  addi $s1, $s1, 1   # i = i + 1
  j   loop   # repeat
done:</pre> |

Figure 6.21 Memory holding array[1000] starting at base address 0x23B8F000

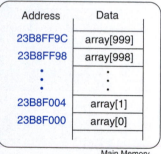

Address	Data
23B8FF9C	array[999]
23B8FF98	array[998]
⋮	⋮
23B8F004	array[1]
23B8F000	array[0]

Main Memory

the base address is $i * 4$. Shifting left by 2 is a convenient way to multiply by 4 in MIPS assembly language. This example readily extends to an array of any size.

Bytes and Characters

Numbers in the range $[-128, 127]$ can be stored in a single byte rather than an entire word. Because there are much fewer than 256 characters on an English language keyboard, English characters are often represented by bytes. The C language uses the type `char` to represent a byte or character.

Early computers `lacked a standard mapping between bytes and English characters, so exchanging text between computers was difficult. In 1963, the American Standards Association published the *American Standard Code for Information Interchange (ASCII)*, which assigns each text character a unique byte value. Table 6.2 shows these character encodings for printable characters. The ASCII values are given in hexadecimal. Lower-case and upper-case letters differ by 0x20 (32).

Other program languages, such as Java, use different character encodings, most notably *Unicode*. Unicode uses 16 bits to represent each character, so it supports accents, umlauts, and Asian languages. For more information, see www.unicode.org.

MIPS provides load byte and store byte instructions to manipulate bytes or characters of data: load byte unsigned (lbu), load byte (lb), and store byte (sb). All three are illustrated in Figure 6.22.

Table 6.2 ASCII encodings

#	Char	#	Char	#	Char	#	Char	#	Char	#	Char
20	space	30	0	40	@	50	P	60	`	70	p
21	!	31	1	41	A	51	Q	61	a	71	q
22	"	32	2	42	B	52	R	62	b	72	r
23	#	33	3	43	C	53	S	63	c	73	s
24	$	34	4	44	D	54	T	64	d	74	t
25	%	35	5	45	E	55	U	65	e	75	u
26	&	36	6	46	F	56	V	66	f	76	v
27	'	37	7	47	G	57	W	67	g	77	w
28	(	38	8	48	H	58	X	68	h	78	x
29	)	39	9	49	I	59	Y	69	i	79	y
2A	*	3A	:	4A	J	5A	Z	6A	j	7A	z
2B	+	3B	;	4B	K	5B	[	6B	k	7B	{
2C	,	3C	<	4C	L	5C	\	6C	l	7C	|
2D	-	3D	=	4D	M	5D	]	6D	m	7D	}
2E	.	3E	>	4E	N	5E	^	6E	n	7E	~
2F	/	3F	?	4F	O	5F	_	6F	o		

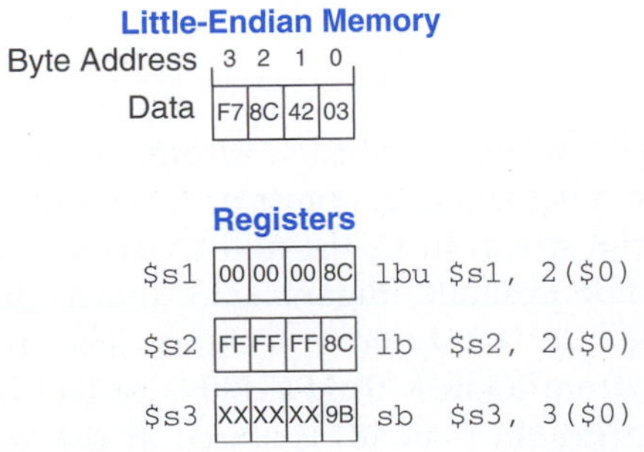

ASCII codes developed from earlier forms of character encoding. Beginning in 1838, telegraph machines used Morse code, a series of dots (.) and dashes (−), to represent characters. For example, the letters A, B, C, and D were represented as .−, − . . ., −.−., and −.., respectively. The number of dots and dashes varied with each letter. For efficiency, common letters used shorter codes.

In 1874, Jean-Maurice-Emile Baudot invented a 5-bit code called the Baudot code. For example, A, B, C, and D were represented as 00011, 11001, 01110, and 01001. However, the 32 possible encodings of this 5-bit code were not sufficient for all the English characters. But 8-bit encoding was. Thus, as electronic communication became prevalent, 8-bit ASCII encoding emerged as the standard.

Little-Endian Memory

Byte Address 3 2 1 0
Data F7 8C 42 03

Registers

$s1 00 00 00 8C   lbu $s1, 2($0)

$s2 FF FF FF 8C   lb $s2, 2($0)

$s3 XX XX XX 9B   sb $s3, 3($0)

Figure 6.22 Instructions for loading and storing bytes

Load byte unsigned (1bu) zero-extends the byte, and load byte (1b) sign-extends the byte to fill the entire 32-bit register. Store byte (sb) stores the least significant byte of the 32-bit register into the specified byte address in memory. In Figure 6.22, 1bu loads the byte at memory address 2 into the least significant byte of $s1 and fills the remaining register bits with 0. 1b loads the sign-extended byte at memory address 2 into $s2. sb stores the least significant byte of $s3 into memory byte 3; it replaces 0xF7 with 0x9B. The more significant bytes of $s3 are ignored.

Example 6.7 USING 1b AND sb TO ACCESS A CHARACTER ARRAY

The following high-level code converts a ten-entry array of characters from lower-case to upper-case by subtracting 32 from each array entry. Translate it into MIPS assembly language. Remember that the address difference between array elements is now 1 byte, not 4 bytes. Assume that $s0 already holds the base address of chararray.

```
// high-level code

char chararray[10];
int i;
for (i = 0; i != 10; i = i + 1)
  chararray[i] = chararray[i] - 32;
```

Solution:

```
# MIPS assembly code
# $s0 = base address of chararray, $s1 = i

        addi $s1, $0, 0      # i = 0
        addi $t0, $0, 10     # $t0 = 10
loop:   beq  $t0, $s1, done  # if i == 10, exit loop
        add  $t1, $s1, $s0    # $t1 = address of chararray[i]
        lb   $t2, 0($t1)      # $t2 = array[i]
        addi $t2, $t2, -32    # convert to upper case: $t1 = $t1 - 32
        sb   $t2, 0($t1)      # store new value in array:
                             # chararray[i] = $t1
        addi $s1, $s1, 1      # i = i + 1
        j    loop             # repeat
done:
```

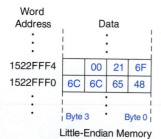

Figure 6.23 shows data table:

Word Address	Data
1522FFF4	00 21 6F
1522FFF0	6C 6C 65 48

Byte 3 ⋯ Byte 0

Little-Endian Memory

Figure 6.23 The string "Hello!" stored in memory

A series of characters is called a *string*. Strings have a variable length, so programming languages must provide a way to determine the length or end of the string. In C, the null character (0x00) signifies the end of a string. For example, Figure 6.23 shows the string "Hello!" (0x48 65 6C 6C 6F 21 00) stored in memory. The string is seven bytes long and extends from address 0x1522FFF0 to 0x1522FFF6. The first character of the string (H = 0x48) is stored at the lowest byte address (0x1522FFF0).

6.4.6 Procedure Calls

High-level languages often use *procedures* (also called *functions*) to reuse frequently accessed code and to make a program more readable. Procedures have inputs, called *arguments*, and an output, called the *return value*. Procedures should calculate the return value and cause no other unintended side effects.

When one procedure calls another, the calling procedure, the *caller*, and the called procedure, the *callee*, must agree on where to put the arguments and the return value. In MIPS, the caller conventionally places up to four arguments in registers $a0-$a3 before making the procedure call, and the callee places the return value in registers $v0-$v1 before finishing. By following this convention, both procedures know where to find the arguments and return value, even if the caller and callee were written by different people.

The callee must not interfere with the function of the caller. Briefly, this means that the callee must know where to return to after it completes and it must not trample on any registers or memory needed by the caller. The caller stores the *return address* in $ra at the same time it jumps to the callee using the jump and link instruction (jal). The callee must not overwrite any architectural state or memory that the caller is depending on. Specifically, the callee must leave the saved registers, $s0-$s7, $ra, and the *stack*, a portion of memory used for temporary variables, unmodified.

This section shows how to call and return from a procedure. It shows how procedures access input arguments and the return value and how they use the stack to store temporary variables.

Procedure Calls and Returns

MIPS uses the *jump and link* instruction (jal) to call a procedure and the *jump register* instruction (jr) to return from a procedure. Code Example 6.23 shows the main procedure calling the simple procedure. main is the caller, and simple is the callee. The simple procedure is called with no input arguments and generates no return value; it simply returns to the caller. In Code Example 6.23, instruction addresses are given to the left of each MIPS instruction in hexadecimal.

Code Example 6.23 simple PROCEDURE CALL

High-Level Code	MIPS Assembly Code
```int main() { simple(); . . . } // void means the function returns no value void simple() { return; }```	```0x00400200 main: jal simple # call procedure 0x00400204 . . . 0x00401020 simple: jr $ra # return```

Jump and link (jal) and jump register (jr $ra) are the two essential instructions needed for a procedure call. jal performs two functions: it stores the address of the *next* instruction (the instruction after jal) in the return address register ($ra), and it jumps to the target instruction.

In Code Example 6.23, the main procedure calls the simple procedure by executing the jump and link (jal) instruction. jal jumps to the simple label and stores 0x00400204 in $ra. The simple procedure returns immediately by executing the instruction jr $ra, jumping to the instruction address held in $ra. The main procedure then continues executing at this address, 0x00400204.

Input Arguments and Return Values

The simple procedure in Code Example 6.23 is not very useful, because it receives no input from the calling procedure (main) and returns no output. By MIPS convention, procedures use $a0-$a3 for input arguments and $v0-$v1 for the return value. In Code Example 6.24, the procedure diffofsums is called with four arguments and returns one result.

According to MIPS convention, the calling procedure, main, places the procedure arguments, from left to right, into the input registers, $a0-$a3. The called procedure, diffofsums, stores the return value in the return register, $v0.

A procedure that returns a 64-bit value, such as a double-precision floating point number, uses both return registers, $v0 and $v1. When a procedure with more than four arguments is called, the additional input arguments are placed on the stack, which we discuss next.

Code Example 6.24 has some subtle errors. Code Examples 6.25 and 6.26 on page 323 show improved versions of the program.

Code Example 6.24 PROCEDURE CALL WITH ARGUMENTS AND RETURN VALUES

High-Level Code

```
int main ()
{
  int y;

    . . .

  y = diffofsums (2, 3, 4, 5);

    . . .
}

int diffofsums (int f, int g, int h, int i)
{
  int result;

  result = (f + g) - (h + i);
  return result;
}
```

MIPS Assembly Code

```
# $s0 = y

main:
    . . .
    addi $a0, $0, 2    # argument 0 = 2
    addi $a1, $0, 3    # argument 1 = 3
    addi $a2, $0, 4    # argument 2 = 4
    addi $a3, $0, 5    # argument 3 = 5
    jal diffofsums     # call procedure
    add $s0, $v0, $0   # y = returned value
    . . .

# $s0 = result
diffofsums:
    add $t0, $a0, $a1  # $t0 = f + g
    add $t1, $a2, $a3  # $t1 = h + i
    sub $s0, $t0, $t1  # result = (f + g) - (h + i)
    add $v0, $s0, $0   # put return value in $v0
    jr $ra             # return to caller
```

The Stack

The *stack* is memory that is used to save local variables within a procedure. The stack expands (uses more memory) as the processor needs more scratch space and contracts (uses less memory) when the processor no longer needs the variables stored there. Before explaining how procedures use the stack to store temporary variables, we explain how the stack works.

The stack is a *last-in-first-out (LIFO) queue*. Like a stack of dishes, the last item *pushed* onto the stack (the top dish) is the first one that can be pulled (*popped*) off. Each procedure may allocate stack space to store local variables but must deallocate it before returning. The *top of the stack*, is the most recently allocated space. Whereas a stack of dishes grows up in space, the MIPS stack grows *down* in memory. The stack expands to lower memory addresses when a program needs more scratch space.

Figure 6.24 shows a picture of the stack. The *stack pointer*, $sp, is a special MIPS register that points to the top of the stack. A *pointer* is a fancy name for a memory address. It points to (gives the address of) data. For example, in Figure 6.24(a) the stack pointer, $sp, holds the address value 0x7FFFFFFC and points to the data value 0x12345678. $sp points to the top of the stack, the lowest accessible memory address on the stack. Thus, in Figure 6.24(a), the stack cannot access memory below memory word 0x7FFFFFFC.

The stack pointer ($sp) starts at a high memory address and decrements to expand as needed. Figure 6.24(b) shows the stack expanding to allow two more data words of temporary storage. To do so, $sp decrements by 8 to become 0x7FFFFFF4. Two additional data words, 0xAABBCCDD and 0x11223344, are temporarily stored on the stack.

One of the important uses of the stack is to save and restore registers that are used by a procedure. Recall that a procedure should calculate a return value but have no other unintended side effects. In particular, it should not modify any registers besides the one containing the return value, $v0. The diffofsums procedure in Code Example 6.24 violates this rule because it modifies $t0, $t1, and $s0. If main had been using $t0, $t1, or $s0 before the call to diffofsums, the contents of these registers would have been corrupted by the procedure call.

To solve this problem, a procedure saves registers on the stack before it modifies them, then restores them from the stack before it returns. Specifically, it performs the following steps.

1. Makes space on the stack to store the values of one or more registers.

2. Stores the values of the registers on the stack.

3. Executes the procedure using the registers.

4. Restores the original values of the registers from the stack.

5. Deallocates space on the stack.

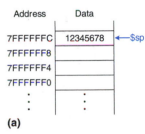

Address	Data	
7FFFFFFC	12345678	←$sp
7FFFFFF8		
7FFFFFF4		
7FFFFFF0		

(a)

Address	Data	
7FFFFFFC	12345678	
7FFFFFF8	AABBCCDD	
7FFFFFF4	11223344	←$sp
7FFFFFF0		

(b)

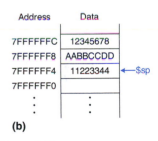

Figure 6.24 The stack

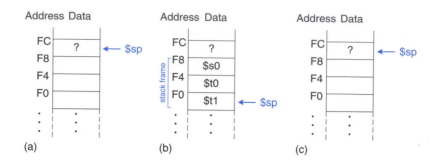

Figure 6.25 The stack (a) before, (b) during, and (c) after diffofsums **procedure call**

Code Example 6.25 shows an improved version of diffofsums that saves and restores $t0, $t1, and $s0. The new lines are indicated in blue. Figure 6.25 shows the stack before, during, and after a call to the diffofsums procedure from Code Example 6.25. diffofsums makes room for three words on the stack by decrementing the stack pointer ($sp) by 12. It then stores the current values of $s0, $t0, and $t1 in the newly allocated space. It executes the rest of the procedure, changing the values in these three registers. At the end of the procedure, diffofsums restores the values of $s0, $t0, and $t1 from the stack, deallocates its stack space, and returns. When the procedure returns, $v0 holds the result, but there are no other side effects: $s0, $t0, $t1, and $sp have the same values as they did before the procedure call.

The stack space that a procedure allocates for itself is called its *stack frame*. diffofsums's stack frame is three words deep. The principle of modularity tells us that each procedure should access only its own stack frame, not the frames belonging to other procedures.

Preserved Registers

Code Example 6.25 assumes that temporary registers $t0 and $t1 must be saved and restored. If the calling procedure does not use those registers, the effort to save and restore them is wasted. To avoid this waste, MIPS divides registers into *preserved* and *nonpreserved* categories. The preserved registers include $s0-$s7 (hence their name, *saved*). The nonpreserved registers include $t0-$t9 (hence their name, *temporary*). A procedure must save and restore any of the preserved registers that it wishes to use, but it can change the nonpreserved registers freely.

Code Example 6.26 shows a further improved version of diffofsums that saves only $s0 on the stack. $t0 and $t1 are nonpreserved registers, so they need not be saved.

Remember that when one procedure calls another, the former is the *caller* and the latter is the *callee*. The callee must save and restore any preserved registers that it wishes to use. The callee may change any of the nonpreserved registers. Hence, if the caller is holding active data in a

Code Example 6.25 PROCEDURE SAVING REGISTERS ON THE STACK

MIPS Assembly Code

```
# $s0 = result
diffofsums:
  addi $sp, $sp, -12  # make space on stack to store three registers
  sw   $s0, 8($sp)    # save $s0 on stack
  sw   $t0, 4($sp)    # save $t0 on stack
  sw   $t1, 0($sp)    # save $t1 on stack
  add  $t0, $a0, $a1  # $t0 = f + g
  add  $t1, $a2, $a3  # $t1 = h + i
  sub  $s0, $t0, $t1  # result = (f + g) - (h + i)
  add  $v0, $s0, $0   # put return value in $v0
  lw   $t1, 0($sp)    # restore $t1 from stack
  lw   $t0, 4($sp)    # restore $t0 from stack
  lw   $s0, 8($sp)    # restore $s0 from stack
  addi $sp, $sp, 12   # deallocate stack space
  jr   $ra            # return to caller
```

Code Example 6.26 PROCEDURE SAVING PRESERVED REGISTERS ON THE STACK

MIPS Assembly Code

```
# $s0 = result
diffofsums:
  addi $sp, $sp, -4   # make space on stack to store one register
  sw   $s0, 0($sp)    # save $s0 on stack
  add  $t0, $a0, $a1  # $t0 = f + g
  add  $t1, $a2, $a3  # $t1 = h + i
  sub  $s0, $t0, $t1  # result = (f + g) - (h + i)
  add  $v0, $s0, $0   # put return value in $v0
  lw   $s0, 0($sp)    # restore $s0 from stack
  addi $sp, $sp, 4    # deallocate stack space
  jr   $ra            # return to caller
```

nonpreserved register, the caller needs to save that nonpreserved register before making the procedure call and then needs to restore it afterward. For these reasons, preserved registers are also called *callee-save*, and nonpreserved registers are called *caller-save*.

Table 6.3 summarizes which registers are preserved. $s0-$s7 are generally used to hold local variables within a procedure, so they must be saved. $ra must also be saved, so that the procedure knows where to return. $t0-$t9 are used to hold temporary results before they are assigned to local variables. These calculations typically complete before a procedure call is made, so they are not preserved, and it is rare that the caller needs to save them. $a0-$a3 are often overwritten in the process of calling a procedure. Hence, they must be saved by the caller if the caller depends on any of its own arguments after a called procedure returns. $v0-$v1 certainly should not be preserved, because the callee returns its result in these registers.

Table 6.3 Preserved and nonpreserved registers

Preserved	Nonpreserved
Saved registers: $s0-$s7	Temporary registers: $t0-$t9
Return address: $ra	Argument registers: $a0-$a3
Stack pointer: $sp	Return value registers: $v0-$v1
Stack above the stack pointer	Stack below the stack pointer

The stack above the stack pointer is automatically preserved as long as the callee does not write to memory addresses above $sp. In this way, it does not modify the stack frame of any other procedures. The stack pointer itself is preserved, because the callee deallocates its stack frame before returning by adding back the same amount that it subtracted from $sp at the beginning of the procedure.

Recursive Procedure Calls

A procedure that does not call others is called a *leaf* procedure; an example is diffofsums. A procedure that does call others is called a *nonleaf* procedure. As mentioned earlier, nonleaf procedures are somewhat more complicated because they may need to save nonpreserved registers on the stack before they call another procedure, and then restore those registers afterward. Specifically, the caller saves any nonpreserved registers ($t0-$t9 and $a0-$a3) that are needed after the call. The callee saves any of the preserved registers ($s0-$s7 and $ra) that it intends to modify.

A *recursive* procedure is a nonleaf procedure that calls itself. The factorial function can be written as a recursive procedure call. Recall that $factorial(n) = n \times (n - 1) \times (n - 2) \times \ldots \times 2 \times 1$. The factorial function can be rewritten recursively as $factorial(n) = n \times factorial(n - 1)$. The factorial of 1 is simply 1. Code Example 6.27 shows the factorial function written as a recursive procedure. To conveniently refer to program addresses, we assume that the program starts at address 0x90.

The factorial procedure might modify $a0 and $ra, so it saves them on the stack. It then checks whether n < 2. If so, it puts the return value of 1 in $v0, restores the stack pointer, and returns to the caller. It does not have to reload $ra and $a0 in this case, because they were never modified. If n > 1, the procedure recursively calls factorial(n−1). It then restores the value of n ($a0) and the return address ($ra) from the stack, performs the multiplication, and returns this result. The multiply instruction (mul $v0, $a0, $v0) multiplies $a0 and $v0 and places the result in $v0. It is discussed further in Section 6.7.1.

Code Example 6.27 factorial RECURSIVE PROCEDURE CALL

High-Level Code	MIPS Assembly Code

```
int factorial (int n) {




  if (n <= 1)
      return 1;



  else
      return (n * factorial (n-1));
}
```

```
0x90   factorial:   addi   $sp, $sp, -8    # make room on stack
0x94                sw     $a0, 4($sp)     # store $a0
0x98                sw     $ra, 0($sp)     # store $ra
0x9C                addi   $t0, $0, 2      # $t0 = 2
0xA0                slt    $t0, $a0, $t0   # a <= 1 ?
0xA4                beq    $t0, $0, else   # no: goto else
0xA8                addi   $v0, $0, 1      # yes: return 1
0xAC                addi   $sp, $sp, 8     # restore $sp
0xB0                jr     $ra             # return
0xB4   else:        addi   $a0, $a0, -1    # n = n - 1
0xB8                jal    factorial       # recursive call
0xBC                lw     $ra, 0($sp)     # restore $ra
0xC0                lw     $a0, 4($sp)     # restore $a0
0xC4                addi   $sp, $sp, 8     # restore $sp
0xC8                mul    $v0, $a0, $v0   # n * factorial (n-1)
0xCC                jr     $ra             # return
```

Figure 6.26 shows the stack when executing factorial(3). We assume that $sp initially points to 0xFC, as shown in Figure 6.26(a). The procedure creates a two-word stack frame to hold $a0 and $ra. On the first invocation, factorial saves $a0 (holding n = 3) at 0xF8 and $ra at 0xF4, as shown in Figure 6.26(b). The procedure then changes $a0 to n = 2 and recursively calls factorial(2), making $ra hold 0xBC. On the second invocation, it saves $a0 (holding n = 2) at 0xF0 and $ra at 0xEC. This time, we know that $ra contains 0xBC. The procedure then changes $a0 to n = 1 and recursively calls factorial(1). On the third invocation, it saves $a0 (holding n = 1) at 0xE8 and $ra at 0xE4. This time, $ra again contains 0xBC. The third invocation of

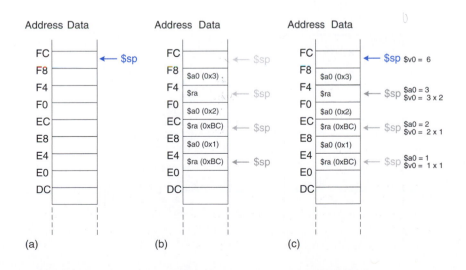

Figure 6.26 Stack during factorial **procedure call when** n = **3: (a) before call, (b) after last recursive call, (c) after return**

factorial returns the value 1 in $v0 and deallocates the stack frame before returning to the second invocation. The second invocation restores n to 2, restores $ra to 0xBC (it happened to already have this value), deallocates the stack frame, and returns $v0 = 2 × 1 = 2 to the first invocation. The first invocation restores n to 3, restores $ra to the return address of the caller, deallocates the stack frame, and returns $v0 = 3 × 2 = 6. Figure 6.26(c) shows the stack as the recursively called procedures return. When factorial returns to the caller, the stack pointer is in its original position (0xFC), none of the contents of the stack above the pointer have changed, and all of the preserved registers hold their original values. $v0 holds the return value, 6.

Additional Arguments and Local Variables*

Procedures may have more than four input arguments and local variables. The stack is used to store these temporary values. By MIPS convention, if a procedure has more than four arguments, the first four are passed in the argument registers as usual. Additional arguments are passed on the stack, just above $sp. The *caller* must expand its stack to make room for the additional arguments. Figure 6.27(a) shows the caller's stack for calling a procedure with more than four arguments.

A procedure can also declare local variables or arrays. *Local* variables are declared within a procedure and can be accessed only within that procedure. Local variables are stored in $s0-$s7; if there are too many local variables, they can also be stored in the procedure's stack frame. In particular, local arrays are stored on the stack.

Figure 6.27(b) shows the organization of a callee's stack frame. The frame holds the procedure's own arguments (if it calls other procedures), the return address, and any of the saved registers that the procedure will

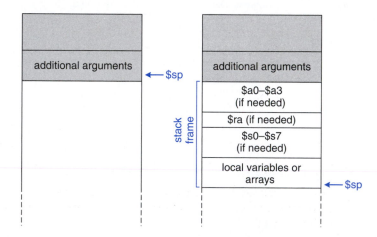

Figure 6.27 Stack usage: (left) before call, (right) after call

modify. It also holds local arrays and any excess local variables. If the callee has more than four arguments, it finds them in the caller's stack frame. Accessing additional input arguments is the one exception in which a procedure can access stack data not in its own stack frame.

6.5 ADDRESSING MODES

MIPS uses five *addressing modes*: register-only, immediate, base, PC-relative, and pseudo-direct. The first three modes (register-only, immediate, and base addressing) define modes of reading and writing operands. The last two (PC-relative and pseudo-direct addressing) define modes of writing the program counter, PC.

Register-Only Addressing

Register-only addressing uses registers for all source and destination operands. All R-type instructions use register-only addressing.

Immediate Addressing

Immediate addressing uses the 16-bit immediate along with registers as operands. Some I-type instructions, such as add immediate (addi) and load upper immediate (lui), use immediate addressing.

Base Addressing

Memory access instructions, such as load word (lw) and store word (sw), use *base addressing*. The effective address of the memory operand is found by adding the base address in register rs to the sign-extended 16-bit offset found in the immediate field.

PC-relative Addressing

Conditional branch instructions use *PC-relative addressing* to specify the new value of the PC if the branch is taken. The signed offset in the immediate field is added to the PC to obtain the new PC; hence, the branch destination address is said to be *relative* to the current PC.

Code Example 6.28 shows part of the factorial procedure from Code Example 6.27. Figure 6.28 shows the machine code for the beq instruction. The *branch target address (BTA)* is the address of the next instruction to execute if the branch is taken. The beq instruction in Figure 6.28 has a BTA of 0xB4, the instruction address of the else label.

The 16-bit immediate field gives the number of instructions between the BTA and the instruction *after* the branch instruction (the instruction at PC+4). In this case, the value in the immediate field of beq is 3 because the BTA (0xB4) is 3 instructions past PC+4 (0xA8).

The processor calculates the BTA from the instruction by sign-extending the 16-bit immediate, multiplying it by 4 (to convert words to bytes), and adding it to PC+4.

Code Example 6.28 CALCULATING THE BRANCH TARGET ADDRESS

MIPS Assembly Code

```
0xA4            beq  $t0, $0, else
0xA8            addi $v0, $0, 1
0xAC            addi $sp, $sp, 8
0xB0            jr   $ra
0xB4    else:   addi $a0, $a0, −1
0xB8            jal  factorial
```

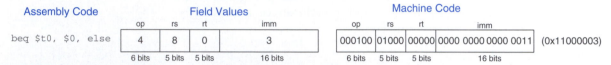

Figure 6.28 **Machine code for** beq

Example 6.8 CALCULATING THE IMMEDIATE FIELD
FOR PC-RELATIVE ADDRESSING

Calculate the immediate field and show the machine code for the branch not equal (bne) instruction in the following program.

```
# MIPS assembly code
0x40 loop:  add  $t1, $a0, $s0
0x44        lb   $t1, 0($t1)
0x48        add  $t2, $a1, $s0
0x4C        sb   $t1, 0($t2)
0x50        addi $s0, $s0, 1
0x54        bne  $t1, $0, loop
0x58        lw   $s0, 0($sp)
```

Solution: Figure 6.29 shows the machine code for the bne instruction. Its branch target address, 0x40, is 6 instructions behind PC+4 (0x58), so the immediate field is −6.

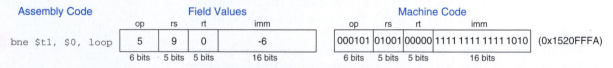

Figure 6.29 bne **machine code**

Pseudo-Direct Addressing

In *direct addressing*, an address is specified in the instruction. The jump instructions, j and jal, ideally would use direct addressing to specify a

Code Example 6.29 CALCULATING THE JUMP TARGET ADDRESS

MIPS Assembly Code
```
0x0040005C          jal     sum
...
0x004000A0  sum:    add     $v0, $a0, $a1
```

32-bit *jump target address* (*JTA*) to indicate the instruction address to execute next.

Unfortunately, the J-type instruction encoding does not have enough bits to specify a full 32-bit JTA. Six bits of the instruction are used for the opcode, so only 26 bits are left to encode the JTA. Fortunately, the two least significant bits, $JTA_{1:0}$, should always be 0, because instructions are word aligned. The next 26 bits, $JTA_{27:2}$, are taken from the addr field of the instruction. The four most significant bits, $JTA_{31:28}$, are obtained from the four most significant bits of PC+4. This addressing mode is called *pseudo-direct*.

Code Example 6.29 illustrates a jal instruction using pseudo-direct addressing. The JTA of the jal instruction is 0x004000A0. Figure 6.30 shows the machine code for this jal instruction. The top four bits and bottom two bits of the JTA are discarded. The remaining bits are stored in the 26-bit address field (addr).

The processor calculates the JTA from the J-type instruction by appending two 0's and prepending the four most significant bits of PC+4 to the 26-bit address field (addr).

Because the four most significant bits of the JTA are taken from PC+4, the jump range is limited. The range limits of branch and jump instructions are explored in Exercises 6.23 to 6.26. All J-type instructions, j and jal, use pseudo-direct addressing.

Note that the jump register instruction, jr, is *not* a J-type instruction. It is an R-type instruction that jumps to the 32-bit value held in register rs.

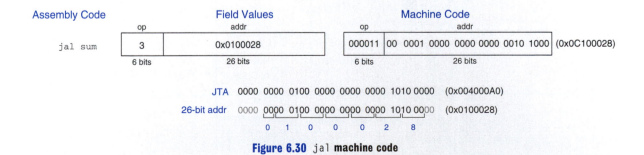

Figure 6.30 jal **machine code**

6.6 LIGHTS, CAMERA, ACTION: COMPILING, ASSEMBLING, AND LOADING

Up until now, we have shown how to translate short high-level code snippets into assembly and machine code. This section describes how to compile and assemble a complete high-level program and how to load the program into memory for execution.

We begin by introducing the MIPS *memory map*, which defines where code, data, and stack memory are located. We then show the steps of code execution for a sample program.

6.6.1 The Memory Map

With 32-bit addresses, the MIPS *address space* spans 2^{32} bytes = 4 gigabytes (GB). Word addresses are divisible by 4 and range from 0 to 0xFFFFFFFC. Figure 6.31 shows the MIPS memory map. The MIPS architecture divides the address space into four parts or *segments*: the text segment, global data segment, dynamic data segment, and reserved segments. The following sections describes each segment.

The Text Segment

The *text segment* stores the machine language program. It is large enough to accommodate almost 256 MB of code. Note that the four most significant bits of the address in the text space are all 0, so the j instruction can directly jump to any address in the program.

The Global Data Segment

The *global data segment* stores global variables that, in contrast to local variables, can be seen by all procedures in a program. Global variables

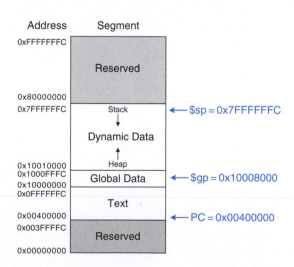

Figure 6.31 MIPS memory map

are defined at *start-up*, before the program begins executing. These variables are declared outside the main procedure in a C program and can be accessed by any procedure. The global data segment is large enough to store 64 KB of global variables.

Global variables are accessed using the global pointer ($gp), which is initialized to 0x100080000. Unlike the stack pointer ($sp), $gp does not change during program execution. Any global variable can be accessed with a 16-bit positive or negative offset from $gp. The offset is known at assembly time, so the variables can be efficiently accessed using base addressing mode with constant offsets.

The Dynamic Data Segment

The *dynamic data segment* holds the stack and the *heap*. The data in this segment are not known at start-up but are dynamically allocated and deallocated throughout the execution of the program. This is the largest segment of memory used by a program, spanning almost 2 GB of the address space.

As discussed in Section 6.4.6, the stack is used to save and restore registers used by procedures and to hold local variables such as arrays. The stack grows downward from the top of the dynamic data segment (0x7FFFFFFC) and is accessed in last-in-first-out (LIFO) order.

The heap stores data that is allocated by the program during runtime. In C, memory allocations are made by the malloc function; in C++ and Java, new is used to allocate memory. Like a heap of clothes on a dorm room floor, heap data can be used and discarded in any order. The heap grows upward from the bottom of the dynamic data segment.

If the stack and heap ever grow into each other, the program's data can become corrupted. The memory allocator tries to ensure that this never happens by returning an out-of-memory error if there is insufficient space to allocate more dynamic data.

The Reserved Segments

The *reserved segments* are used by the operating system and cannot directly be used by the program. Part of the reserved memory is used for interrupts (see Section 7.7) and for memory-mapped I/O (see Section 8.5).

Grace Hopper, 1906–1992. Graduated from Yale University with a Ph.D. in mathematics. Developed the first compiler while working for the Remington Rand Corporation and was instrumental in developing the COBOL programming language. As a naval officer, she received many awards, including a World War II Victory Medal and the National Defence Service Medal.

6.6.2 Translating and Starting a Program

Figure 6.32 shows the steps required to translate a program from a high-level language into machine language and to start executing that program. First, the high-level code is compiled into assembly code. The assembly code is assembled into machine code in an *object file*. The linker combines the machine code with object code from libraries and other files to produce an entire executable program. In practice, most compilers perform all three steps of compiling, assembling, and linking. Finally, the loader loads

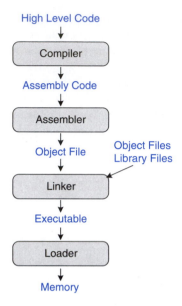

Figure 6.32 Steps for translating and starting a program

the program into memory and starts execution. The remainder of this section walks through these steps for a simple program.

Step 1: Compilation

A compiler translates high-level code into assembly language. Code Example 6.30 shows a simple high-level program with three global

---

Code Example 6.30 COMPILING A HIGH-LEVEL PROGRAM

High-Level Code	MIPS Assembly Code

`int f, g, y; // global variables`	`.data`
	`f:`
	`g:`
	`y:`

`int main (void)`
`{`
`  f = 2;`
`  g = 3;`
`  y = sum (f, g);`
`  return y;`
`}`
	`.text`
	`main:`
	`  addi  $sp, $sp, -4  # make stack frame`
	`  sw    $ra, 0($sp)   # store $ra on stack`
	`  addi  $a0, $0, 2    # $a0 = 2`
	`  sw    $a0, f        # f = 2`
	`  addi  $a1, $0, 3    # $a1 = 3`
	`  sw    $a1, g        # g = 3`
	`  jal   sum           # call sum procedure`
	`  sw    $v0, y        # y = sum (f, g)`
	`  lw    $ra, 0($sp)   # restore $ra from stack`
	`  addi  $sp, $sp, 4   # restore stack pointer`
	`  jr    $ra           # return to operating system`

`int sum (int a, int b) {`
`  return (a + b);`
`}`
	`sum:`
	`  add   $v0, $a0, $a1 # $v0 = a + b`
	`  jr    $ra           # return to caller`

variables and two procedures, along with the assembly code produced by a typical compiler. The .data and .text keywords are *assembler directives* that indicate where the text and data segments begin. Labels are used for global variables f, g, and y. Their storage location will be determined by the assembler; for now, they are left as symbols in the code.

Step 2: Assembling

The assembler turns the assembly language code into an *object file* containing machine language code. The assembler makes two passes through the assembly code. On the first pass, the assembler assigns instruction addresses and finds all the *symbols*, such as labels and global variable names. The code after the first assembler pass is shown here.

```
0x00400000   main:   addi $sp, $sp, −4
0x00400004           sw   $ra, 0($sp)
0x00400008           addi $a0, $0, 2
0x0040000C           sw   $a0, f
0x00400010           addi $a1, $0, 3
0x00400014           sw   $a1, g
0x00400018           jal  sum
0x0040001C           sw   $v0, y
0x00400020           lw   $ra, 0($sp)
0x00400024           addi $sp, $sp, 4
0x00400028           jr   $ra
0x0040002C   sum:    add  $v0, $a0, $a1
0x00400030           jr   $ra
```

The names and addresses of the symbols are kept in a *symbol table*, as shown in Table 6.4 for this code. The symbol addresses are filled in after the first pass, when the addresses of labels are known. Global variables are assigned storage locations in the global data segment of memory, starting at memory address 0x10000000.

On the second pass through the code, the assembler produces the machine language code. Addresses for the global variables and labels are taken from the symbol table. The machine language code and symbol table are stored in the object file.

Table 6.4 Symbol table

Symbol	Address
f	0x10000000
g	0x10000004
y	0x10000008
main	0x00400000
sum	0x0040002C

Step 3: Linking

Most large programs contain more than one file. If the programmer changes only one of the files, it would be wasteful to recompile and reassemble the other files. In particular, programs often call procedures in library files; these library files almost never change. If a file of high-level code is not changed, the associated object file need not be updated.

The job of the linker is to combine all of the object files into one machine language file called the *executable*. The linker relocates the data and instructions in the object files so that they are not all on top of each other. It uses the information in the symbol tables to adjust the addresses of global variables and of labels that are relocated.

In our example, there is only one object file, so no relocation is necessary. Figure 6.33 shows the executable file. It has three sections: the executable file header, the text segment, and the data segment. The executable file header reports the text size (code size) and data size (amount of globally declared data). Both are given in units of bytes. The text segment gives the instructions and the addresses where they are to be stored.

The figure shows the instructions in human-readable format next to the machine code for ease of interpretation, but the executable file includes only machine instructions. The data segment gives the address of each global variable. The global variables are addressed with respect to the base address given by the global pointer, $gp. For example, the

Figure 6.33 Executable

Executable file header	Text Size	Data Size	
	0x34 (52 bytes)	0xC (12 bytes)	
Text segment	Address	Instruction	
	0x00400000	0x23BDFFFC	addi $sp, $sp, −4
	0x00400004	0xAFBF0000	sw $ra, 0 ($sp)
	0x00400008	0x20040002	addi $a0, $0, 2
	0x0040000C	0xAF848000	sw $a0, 0x8000 ($gp)
	0x00400010	0x20050003	addi $a1, $0, 3
	0x00400014	0xAF858004	sw $a1, 0x8004 ($gp)
	0x00400018	0x0C10000B	jal 0x0040002C
	0x0040001C	0xAF828008	sw $v0, 0x8008 ($gp)
	0x00400020	0x8FBF0000	lw $ra, 0 ($sp)
	0x00400024	0x23BD0004	addi $sp, $sp, −4
	0x00400028	0x03E00008	jr $ra
	0x0040002C	0x00851020	add $v0, $a0, $a1
	0x00400030	0x03E0008	jr $ra
Data segment	Address	Data	
	0x10000000	f	
	0x10000004	g	
	0x10000008	y	

first store instruction, sw $a0, 0x8000($gp), stores the value 2 to the global variable f, which is located at memory address 0x10000000. Remember that the offset, 0x8000, is a 16-bit signed number that is sign-extended and added to the base address, $gp. So, $gp + 0x8000 = 0x10008000 + 0xFFFF8000 = 0x10000000, the memory address of variable f.

Step 4: Loading

The operating system loads a program by reading the text segment of the executable file from a storage device (usually the hard disk) into the text segment of memory. The operating system sets $gp to 0x10008000 (the middle of the global data segment) and $sp to 0x7FFFFFFC (the top of the dynamic data segment), then performs a jal 0x00400000 to jump to the beginning of the program. Figure 6.34 shows the memory map at the beginning of program execution.

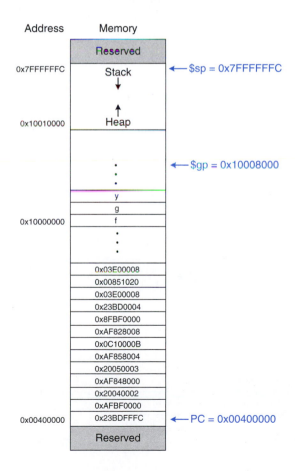

Figure 6.34 Executable loaded in memory

6.7 ODDS AND ENDS*

This section covers a few optional topics that do not fit naturally elsewhere in the chapter. These topics include pseudoinstructions, exceptions, signed and unsigned arithmetic instructions, and floating-point instructions.

6.7.1 Pseudoinstructions

If an instruction is not available in the MIPS instruction set, it is probably because the same operation can be performed using one or more existing MIPS instructions. Remember that MIPS is a reduced instruction set computer (RISC), so the instruction size and hardware complexity are minimized by keeping the number of instructions small.

However, MIPS defines *pseudoinstructions* that are not actually part of the instruction set but are commonly used by programmers and compilers. When converted to machine code, pseudoinstructions are translated into one or more MIPS instructions.

Table 6.5 gives examples of pseudoinstructions and the MIPS instructions used to implement them. For example, the load immediate pseudoinstruction (li) loads a 32-bit constant using a combination of lui and ori instructions. The multiply pseudoinstruction (mul) provides a three-operand multiply, multiplying two registers and putting the 32 least significant bits of the result into a third register. The no operation pseudoinstruction (nop, pronounced "no op") performs no operation. The PC is incremented by 4 upon its execution. No other registers or memory values are altered. The machine code for the nop instruction is 0x00000000.

Some pseudoinstructions require a temporary register for intermediate calculations. For example, the pseudoinstruction beq $t2, $imm_{15:0}$, Loop compares $t2 to a 16-bit immediate, $imm_{15:0}$. This pseudoinstruction

Table 6.5 Pseudoinstructions

Pseudoinstruction	Corresponding MIPS Instructions
li $s0, 0x1234AA77	lui $s0, 0x1234 ori $s0, 0xAA77
mul $s0, $s1, $s2	mult $s1, $s2 mflo $s0
clear $t0	add $t0, $0, $0
move $s1, $s2	add $s2, $s1, $0
nop	sll $0, $0, 0

Table 6.6 Pseudoinstruction using $at

Pseudoinstruction	Corresponding MIPS Instructions
beq $t2, imm$_{15:0}$, Loop	addi $at, $0, imm$_{15:0}$ beq $t2, $at, Loop

requires a temporary register in which to store the 16-bit immediate. Assemblers use the assembler register, $at, for such purposes. Table 6.6 shows how the assembler uses $at in converting a pseudoinstruction to real MIPS instructions. We leave it as Exercise 6.31 to implement other pseudoinstructions such as rotate left (rol) and rotate right (ror).

6.7.2 Exceptions

An *exception* is like an unscheduled procedure call that jumps to a new address. Exceptions may be caused by hardware or software. For example, the processor may receive notification that the user pressed a key on a keyboard. The processor may stop what it is doing, determine which key was pressed, save it for future reference, then resume the program that was running. Such a hardware exception triggered by an input/output (I/O) device such as a keyboard is often called an *interrupt*. Alternatively, the program may encounter an error condition such as an undefined instruction. The program then jumps to code in the *operating system* (*OS*), which may choose to terminate the offending program. Software exceptions are sometimes called *traps*. Other causes of exceptions include division by zero, attempts to read nonexistent memory, hardware malfunctions, debugger breakpoints, and arithmetic overflow (see Section 6.7.3).

The processor records the cause of an exception and the value of the PC at the time the exception occurs. It then jumps to the *exception handler* procedure. The exception handler is code (usually in the OS) that examines the cause of the exception and responds appropriately (by reading the keyboard on a hardware interrupt, for example). It then returns to the program that was executing before the exception took place. In MIPS, the exception handler is always located at 0x80000180. When an exception occurs, the processor always jumps to this instruction address, regardless of the cause.

The MIPS architecture uses a special-purpose register, called the Cause register, to record the cause of the exception. Different codes are used to record different exception causes, as given in Table 6.7. The exception handler code reads the Cause register to determine how to handle the exception. Some other architectures jump to a different exception handler for each different cause instead of using a Cause register.

MIPS uses another special-purpose register called the Exception Program Counter (EPC) to store the value of the PC at the time an exception

Table 6.7 Exception cause codes

Exception	Cause
hardware interrupt	0x00000000
system call	0x00000020
breakpoint/divide by 0	0x00000024
undefined instruction	0x00000028
arithmetic overflow	0x00000030

takes place. The processor returns to the address in EPC after handling the exception. This is analogous to using $ra to store the old value of the PC during a jal instruction.

The EPC and Cause registers are not part of the MIPS register file. The mfc0 (move from coprocessor 0) instruction copies these and other special-purpose registers into one of the general purpose registers. Coprocessor 0 is called the *MIPS processor control*; it handles interrupts and processor diagnostics. For example, mfc0 $t0, Cause copies the Cause register into $t0.

The syscall and break instructions cause traps to perform system calls or debugger breakpoints. The exception handler uses the EPC to look up the instruction and determine the nature of the system call or breakpoint by looking at the fields of the instruction.

In summary, an exception causes the processor to jump to the exception handler. The exception handler saves registers on the stack, then uses mfc0 to look at the cause and respond accordingly. When the handler is finished, it restores the registers from the stack, copies the return address from EPC to $k0 using mfc0, and returns using jr $k0.

$k0 and $k1 are included in the MIPS register set. They are reserved by the OS for exception handling. They do not need to be saved and restored during exceptions.

6.7.3 Signed and Unsigned Instructions

Recall that a binary number may be signed or unsigned. The MIPS architecture uses two's complement representation of signed numbers. MIPS has certain instructions that come in signed and unsigned flavors, including addition and subtraction, multiplication and division, set less than, and partial word loads.

Addition and Subtraction

Addition and subtraction are performed identically whether the number is signed or unsigned. However, the interpretation of the results is different.

As mentioned in Section 1.4.6, if two large signed numbers are added together, the result may incorrectly produce the opposite sign. For example, adding the following two huge positive numbers gives a negative result: 0x7FFFFFFF + 0x7FFFFFFF = 0xFFFFFFFE = −2. Similarly, adding two huge negative numbers gives a positive result, 0x80000001 + 0x80000001 = 0x00000002. This is called arithmetic *overflow*.

The C language ignores arithmetic overflows, but other languages, such as Fortran, require that the program be notified. As mentioned in Section 6.7.2, the MIPS processor takes an exception on arithmetic overflow. The program can decide what to do about the overflow (for example, it might repeat the calculation with greater precision to avoid the overflow), then return to where it left off.

MIPS provides signed and unsigned versions of addition and subtraction. The signed versions are add, addi, and sub. The unsigned versions are addu, addiu, and subu. The two versions are identical except that signed versions trigger an exception on overflow, whereas unsigned versions do not. Because C ignores exceptions, C programs technically use the unsigned versions of these instructions.

Multiplication and Division

Multiplication and division behave differently for signed and unsigned numbers. For example, as an unsigned number, 0xFFFFFFFF represents a large number, but as a signed number it represents −1. Hence, 0xFFFFFFFF × 0xFFFFFFFF would equal 0xFFFFFFFE00000001 if the numbers were unsigned but 0x0000000000000001 if the numbers were signed.

Therefore, multiplication and division come in both signed and unsigned flavors. mult and div treat the operands as signed numbers. multu and divu treat the operands as unsigned numbers.

Set Less Than

Set less than instructions can compare either two registers (slt) or a register and an immediate (slti). Set less than also comes in signed (slt and slti) and unsigned (sltu and sltiu) versions. In a signed comparison, 0x80000000 is less than any other number, because it is the most negative two's complement number. In an unsigned comparison, 0x80000000 is greater than 0x7FFFFFFF but less than 0x80000001, because all numbers are positive.

Beware that sltiu sign-extends the immediate before treating it as an unsigned number. For example, sltiu $s0, $s1, 0x8042 compares $s1 to 0xFFFF8042, treating the immediate as a large positive number.

Loads

As described in Section 6.4.5, byte loads come in signed (lb) and unsigned (lbu) versions. lb sign-extends the byte, and lbu zero-extends the byte to fill the entire 32-bit register. Similarly, MIPS provides signed and unsigned half-word loads (lh and lhu), which load two bytes into the lower half and sign- or zero-extend the upper half of the word.

6.7.4 Floating-Point Instructions

The MIPS architecture defines an optional floating-point coprocessor, known as coprocessor 1. In early MIPS implementations, the floating-point coprocessor was a separate chip that users could purchase if they needed fast floating-point math. In most recent MIPS implementations, the floating-point coprocessor is built in alongside the main processor.

MIPS defines 32 32-bit floating-point registers, $f0-$f31. These are separate from the ordinary registers used so far. MIPS supports both single- and double-precision IEEE floating point arithmetic. Double-precision (64-bit) numbers are stored in pairs of 32-bit registers, so only the 16 even-numbered registers ($f0, $f2, $f4, . . . , $f30) are used to specify double-precision operations. By convention, certain registers are reserved for certain purposes, as given in Table 6.8.

Floating-point instructions all have an opcode of 17 (10001_2). They require both a funct field and a cop (coprocessor) field to indicate the type of instruction. Hence, MIPS defines the *F-type* instruction format for floating-point instructions, shown in Figure 6.35. Floating-point instructions come in both single- and double-precision flavors. cop = 16 (10000_2) for single-precision instructions or 17 (10001_2) for double-precision instructions. Like R-type instructions, F-type instructions have two source operands, fs and ft, and one destination, fd.

Instruction precision is indicated by .s and .d in the mnemonic. Floating-point arithmetic instructions include addition (add.s, add.d), subtraction (sub.sz, sub.d), multiplication (mul.s, mul.d), and division (div.s, div.d) as well as negation (neg.s, neg.d) and absolute value (abs.s, abs.d).

Table 6.8 MIPS floating-point register set

Name	Number	Use
$fv0-$fv1	0, 2	procedure return values
$ft0-$ft3	4, 6, 8, 10	temporary variables
$fa0-$fa1	12, 14	procedure arguments
$ft4-$ft5	16, 18	temporary variables
$fs0-$fs5	20, 22, 24, 26, 28, 30	saved variables

Figure 6.35 F-type machine instruction format

F-type

op	cop	ft	fs	fd	funct
6 bits	5 bits	5 bits	5 bits	5 bits	6 bits

Floating-point branches have two parts. First, a compare instruction is used to set or clear the *floating-point condition flag* (fpcond). Then, a conditional branch checks the value of the flag. The compare instructions include equality (c.seq.s/c.seq.d), less than (c.lt.s/c.lt.d), and less than or equal to (c.le.s/c.le.d). The conditional branch instructions are bc1f and bc1t that branch if fpcond is FALSE or TRUE, respectively. Inequality, greater than or equal to, and greater than comparisons are performed with seq, lt, and le, followed by bc1f.

Floating-point registers are loaded and stored from memory using lwc1 and swc1. These instructions move 32 bits, so two are necessary to handle a double-precision number.

6.8 REAL-WORLD PERSPECTIVE: IA-32 ARCHITECTURE*   ← STOP! End of Midterm 2

Almost all personal computers today use IA-32 architecture microprocessors. IA-32 is a 32-bit architecture originally developed by Intel. AMD also sells IA-32 compatible microprocessors.

The IA-32 architecture has a long and convoluted history dating back to 1978, when Intel announced the 16-bit 8086 microprocessor. IBM selected the 8086 and its cousin, the 8088, for IBM's first personal computers. In 1985, Intel introduced the 32-bit 80386 microprocessor, which was backward compatible with the 8086, so it could run software developed for earlier PCs. Processor architectures compatible with the 80386 are called IA-32 or x86 processors. The Pentium, Core, and Athlon processors are well known IA-32 processors. Section 7.9 describes the evolution of IA-32 microprocessors in more detail.

Various groups at Intel and AMD over many years have shoehorned more instructions and capabilities into the antiquated architecture. The result is far less elegant than MIPS. As Patterson and Hennessy explain, "this checkered ancestry has led to an architecture that is difficult to explain and impossible to love." However, software compatibility is far more important than technical elegance, so IA-32 has been the *de facto* PC standard for more than two decades. More than 100 million IA-32 processors are sold every year. This huge market justifies more than $5 billion of research and development annually to continue improving the processors.

IA-32 is an example of a *Complex Instruction Set Computer* (CISC) architecture. In contrast to RISC architectures such as MIPS, each CISC instruction can do more work. Programs for CISC architectures usually require fewer instructions. The instruction encodings were selected to be more compact, so as to save memory, when RAM was far more expensive than it is today; instructions are of variable length and are often less than 32 bits. The trade-off is that complicated instructions are more difficult to decode and tend to execute more slowly.

Table 6.9 Major differences between MIPS and IA-32

Feature	MIPS	IA-32
# of registers	32 general purpose	8, some restrictions on purpose
# of operands	3 (2 source, 1 destination)	2 (1 source, 1 source/destination)
operand location	registers or immediates	registers, immediates, or memory
operand size	32 bits	8, 16, or 32 bits
condition codes	no	yes
instruction types	simple	simple and complicated
instruction encoding	fixed, 4 bytes	variable, 1–15 bytes

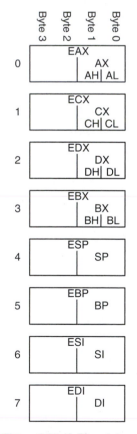

Figure 6.36 IA-32 registers

This section introduces the IA-32 architecture. The goal is not to make you into an IA-32 assembly language programmer, but rather to illustrate some of the similarities and differences between IA-32 and MIPS. We think it is interesting to see how IA-32 works. However, none of the material in this section is needed to understand the rest of the book. Major differences between IA-32 and MIPS are summarized in Table 6.9.

6.8.1 IA-32 Registers

The 8086 microprocessor provided eight 16-bit registers. It could separately access the upper and lower eight bits of some of these registers. When the 32-bit 80386 was introduced, the registers were extended to 32 bits. These registers are called EAX, ECX, EDX, EBX, ESP, EBP, ESI, and EDI. For backward compatibility, the bottom 16 bits and some of the bottom 8-bit portions are also usable, as shown in Figure 6.36.

The eight registers are almost, but not quite, general purpose. Certain instructions cannot use certain registers. Other instructions always put their results in certain registers. Like $sp in MIPS, ESP is normally reserved for the stack pointer.

The IA-32 program counter is called EIP (the *extended instruction pointer*). Like the MIPS PC, it advances from one instruction to the next or can be changed with branch, jump, and subroutine call instructions.

6.8.2 IA-32 Operands

MIPS instructions always act on registers or immediates. Explicit load and store instructions are needed to move data between memory and the registers. In contrast, IA-32 instructions may operate on registers, immediates, or memory. This partially compensates for the small set of registers.

MIPS instructions generally specify three operands: two sources and one destination. IA-32 instructions specify only two operands. The first is a source. The second is both a source and the destination. Hence, IA-32 instructions always overwrite one of their sources with the result. Table 6.10 lists the combinations of operand locations in IA-32. All of the combinations are possible except memory to memory.

Like MIPS, IA-32 has a 32-bit memory space that is byte-addressable. However, IA-32 also supports a much wider variety of memory *addressing modes*. The memory location is specified with any combination of a *base register, displacement*, and a *scaled index register*. Table 6.11 illustrates these combinations. The displacement can be an 8-, 16-, or 32-bit value. The scale multiplying the index register can be 1, 2, 4, or 8. The base + displacement mode is equivalent to the MIPS base addressing mode for loads and stores. The scaled index provides an easy way to access arrays or structures of 2-, 4-, or 8-byte elements without having to issue a sequence of instructions to generate the address.

Table 6.10 Operand locations

Source/Destination	Source	Example	Meaning
register	register	add EAX, EBX	EAX <- EAX + EBX
register	immediate	add EAX, 42	EAX <- EAX + 42
register	memory	add EAX, [20]	EAX <- EAX + Mem[20]
memory	register	add [20], EAX	Mem[20] <- Mem[20] + EAX
memory	immediate	add [20], 42	Mem[20] <- Mem[20] + 42

Table 6.11 Memory addressing modes

Example	Meaning	Comment
add EAX, [20]	EAX <- EAX + Mem[20]	displacement
add EAX, [ESP]	EAX <- EAX + Mem[ESP]	base addressing
add EAX, [EDX+40]	EAX <- EAX + Mem[EDX+40]	base + displacement
add EAX, [60+EDI*4]	EAX <- EAX + Mem[60+EDI*4]	displacement + scaled index
add EAX, [EDX+80+EDI*2]	EAX <- EAX + Mem[EDX+80+EDI*2]	base + displacement + scaled index

Table 6.12 Instructions acting on 8-, 16-, or 32-bit data

Example	Meaning	Data Size
add AH, BL	AH <- AH + BL	8-bit
add AX, −1	AX <- AX + 0xFFFF	16-bit
add EAX, EDX	EAX <- EAX + EDX	32-bit

While MIPS always acts on 32-bit words, IA-32 instructions can operate on 8-, 16-, or 32-bit data. Table 6.12 illustrates these variations.

6.8.3 Status Flags

IA-32, like many CISC architectures, uses *status flags* (also called *condition codes*) to make decisions about branches and to keep track of carries and arithmetic overflow. IA-32 uses a 32-bit register, called EFLAGS, that stores the status flags. Some of the bits of the EFLAGS register are given in Table 6.13. Other bits are used by the operating system.

The architectural state of an IA-32 processor includes EFLAGS as well as the eight registers and the EIP.

6.8.4 IA-32 Instructions

IA-32 has a larger set of instructions than MIPS. Table 6.14 describes some of the general purpose instructions. IA-32 also has instructions for floating-point arithmetic and for arithmetic on multiple short data elements packed into a longer word. D indicates the destination (a register or memory location), and S indicates the source (a register, memory location, or immediate).

Note that some instructions always act on specific registers. For example, 32 × 32-bit multiplication always takes one of the sources from EAX and always puts the 64-bit result in EDX and EAX. LOOP always

Table 6.13 Selected EFLAGS

Name	Meaning
CF (Carry Flag)	Carry out generated by last arithmetic operation. Indicates overflow in unsigned arithmetic. Also used for propagating the carry between words in multiple-precision arithmetic.
ZF (Zero Flag)	Result of last operation was zero.
SF (Sign Flag)	Result of last operation was negative (msb = 1).
OF (Overflow Flag)	Overflow of two's complement arithmetic.

Table 6.14 Selected IA-32 instructions

Instruction	Meaning	Function
ADD/SUB	add/subtract	D = D + S / D = D − S
ADDC	add with carry	D = D + S + CF
INC/DEC	increment/decrement	D = D + 1 / D = D − 1
CMP	compare	Set flags based on D − S
NEG	negate	D = −D
AND/OR/XOR	logical AND/OR/XOR	D = D op S
NOT	logical NOT	D = $\overline{D}$
IMUL/MUL	signed/unsigned multiply	EDX:EAX = EAX × D
IDIV/DIV	signed/unsigned divide	EDX:EAX/D EAX = Quotient; EDX = Remainder
SAR/SHR	arithmetic/logical shift right	D = D >>> S / D = D >> S
SAL/SHL	left shift	D = D << S
ROR/ROL	rotate right/left	Rotate D by S
RCR/RCL	rotate right/left with carry	Rotate CF and D by S
BT	bit test	CF = D[S] (the S*th* bit of D)
BTR/BTS	bit test and reset/set	CF = D[S]; D[S] = 0 / 1
TEST	set flags based on masked bits	Set flags based on D AND S
MOV	move	D = S
PUSH	push onto stack	ESP = ESP − 4; Mem[ESP] = S
POP	pop off stack	D = MEM[ESP]; ESP = ESP + 4
CLC, STC	clear/set carry flag	CF = 0 / 1
JMP	unconditional jump	relative jump: EIP = EIP + S absolute jump: EIP = S
Jcc	conditional jump	if (flag) EIP = EIP + S
LOOP	loop	ECX = ECX − 1 if ECX ≠ 0 EIP = EIP + imm
CALL	procedure call	ESP = ESP − 4; MEM[ESP] = EIP; EIP = S
RET	procedure return	EIP = MEM[ESP]; ESP = ESP + 4

Table 6.15 Selected branch conditions

Instruction	Meaning	Function After cmp d, s
JZ/JE	jump if ZF = 1	jump if D = S
JNZ/JNE	jump if ZF = 0	jump if D ≠ S
JGE	jump if SF = OF	jump if D ≥ S
JG	jump if SF = OF and ZF = 0	jump if D > S
JLE	jump if SF ≠ OF or ZF = 1	jump if D ≤ S
JL	jump if SF ≠ OF	jump if D < S
JC/JB	jump if CF = 1	
JNC	jump if CF = 0	
JO	jump if OF = 1	
JNO	jump if OF = 0	
JS	jump if SF = 1	
JNS	jump if SF = 0	

stores the loop counter in ECX. PUSH, POP, CALL, and RET use the stack pointer, ESP.

Conditional jumps check the flags and branch if the appropriate condition is met. They come in many flavors. For example, JZ jumps if the zero flag (ZF) is 1. JNZ jumps if the zero flag is 0. The jumps usually follow an instruction, such as the compare instruction (CMP), that sets the flags. Table 6.15 lists some of the conditional jumps and how they depend on the flags set by a prior compare operation.

6.8.5 IA-32 Instruction Encoding

The IA-32 instruction encodings are truly messy, a legacy of decades of piecemeal changes. Unlike MIPS, whose instructions are uniformly 32 bits, IA-32 instructions vary from 1 to 15 bytes, as shown in Figure 6.37.[2] The opcode may be 1, 2, or 3 bytes. It is followed by four optional fields: ModR/M, SIB, Displacement, and Immediate. ModR/M specifies an addressing mode. SIB specifies the scale, index, and base

---

[2] It is possible to construct 17-byte instructions if all the optional fields are used. However, IA-32 places a 15-byte limit on the length of legal instructions.

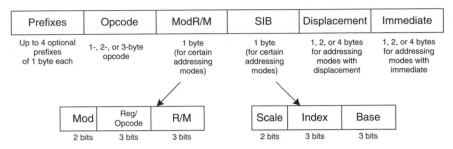

Figure 6.37 **IA-32 instruction encodings**

registers in certain addressing modes. `Displacement` indicates a 1-, 2-, or 4-byte displacement in certain addressing modes. And `Immediate` is a 1-, 2-, or 4-byte constant for instructions using an immediate as the source operand. Moreover, an instruction can be preceded by up to four optional byte-long prefixes that modify its behavior.

The `ModR/M` byte uses the 2-bit `Mod` and 3-bit `R/M` field to specify the addressing mode for one of the operands. The operand can come from one of the eight registers, or from one of 24 memory addressing modes. Due to artifacts in the encodings, the `ESP` and `EBP` registers are not available for use as the base or index register in certain addressing modes. The `Reg` field specifies the register used as the other operand. For certain instructions that do not require a second operand, the `Reg` field is used to specify three more bits of the `opcode`.

In addressing modes using a scaled index register, the `SIB` byte specifies the index register and the scale (1, 2, 4, or 8). If both a base and index are used, the `SIB` byte also specifies the base register.

MIPS fully specifies the instruction in the `opcode` and `funct` fields of the instruction. IA-32 uses a variable number of bits to specify different instructions. It uses fewer bits to specify more common instructions, decreasing the average length of the instructions. Some instructions even have multiple opcodes. For example, `add AL, imm8` performs an 8-bit add of an immediate to `AL`. It is represented with the 1-byte `opcode`, 0x04, followed by a 1-byte immediate. The `A` register (`AL`, `AX`, or `EAX`) is called the *accumulator*. On the other hand, `add D, imm8` performs an 8-bit add of an immediate to an arbitrary destination, `D` (memory or a register). It is represented with the 1-byte `opcode`, 0x80, followed by one or more bytes specifying `D`, followed by a 1-byte immediate. Many instructions have shortened encodings when the destination is the accumulator.

In the original 8086, the `opcode` specified whether the instruction acted on 8- or 16-bit operands. When the 80386 introduced 32-bit operands, no new opcodes were available to specify the 32-bit form.

Instead, the same opcode was used for both 16- and 32-bit forms. An additional bit in the *code segment descriptor* used by the OS specifies which form the processor should choose. The bit is set to 0 for backward compatibility with 8086 programs, defaulting the opcode to 16-bit operands. It is set to 1 for programs to default to 32-bit operands. Moreover, the programmer can specify prefixes to change the form for a particular instruction. If the prefix 0x66 appears before the opcode, the alternative size operand is used (16 bits in 32-bit mode, or 32 bits in 16-bit mode).

6.8.6 Other IA-32 Peculiarities

The 80286 introduced *segmentation* to divide memory into segments of up to 64 KB in length. When the OS enables segmentation, addresses are computed relative to the beginning of the segment. The processor checks for addresses that go beyond the end of the segment and indicates an error, thus preventing programs from accessing memory outside their own segment. Segmentation proved to be a hassle for programmers and is not used in modern versions of the Windows operating system.

IA-32 contains string instructions that act on entire strings of bytes or words. The operations include moving, comparing, or scanning for a specific value. In modern processors, these instructions are usually slower than performing the equivalent operation with a series of simpler instructions, so they are best avoided.

As mentioned earlier, the 0x66 prefix is used to choose between 16- and 32-bit operand sizes. Other prefixes include ones used to lock the bus (to control access to shared variables in a multiprocessor system), to predict whether a branch will be taken or not, and to repeat the instruction during a string move.

The bane of any architecture is to run out of memory capacity. With 32-bit addresses, IA-32 can access 4 GB of memory. This was far more than the largest computers had in 1985, but by the early 2000s it had become limiting. In 2003, AMD extended the address space and register sizes to 64 bits, calling the enhanced architecture AMD64. AMD64 has a compatibility mode that allows it to run 32-bit programs unmodified while the OS takes advantage of the bigger address space. In 2004, Intel gave in and adopted the 64-bit extensions, renaming them Extended Memory 64 Technology (EM64T). With 64-bit addresses, computers can access 16 exabytes (16 billion GB) of memory.

For those curious about more details of the IA-32 architecture, the *IA-32 Intel Architecture Software Developer's Manual*, is freely available on Intel's Web site.

Intel and Hewlett-Packard jointly developed a new 64-bit architecture called IA-64 in the mid 1990's. It was designed from a clean slate, bypassing the convoluted history of IA-32, taking advantage of 20 years of new research in computer architecture, and providing a 64-bit address space. However, IA-64 has yet to become a market success. Most computers needing the large address space now use the 64-bit extensions of IA-32.

6.8.7 The Big Picture

This section has given a taste of some of the differences between the MIPS RISC architecture and the IA-32 CISC architecture. IA-32 tends to have shorter programs, because a complex instruction is equivalent to a series of simple MIPS instructions and because the instructions are encoded to minimize memory use. However, the IA-32 architecture is a hodgepodge of features accumulated over the years, some of which are no longer useful but must be kept for compatibility with old programs. It has too few registers, and the instructions are difficult to decode. Merely explaining the instruction set is difficult. Despite all these failings, IA-32 is firmly entrenched as the dominant computer architecture for PCs, because the value of software compatibility is so great and because the huge market justifies the effort required to build fast IA-32 microprocessors.

6.9 SUMMARY

To command a computer, you must speak its language. A computer architecture defines how to command a processor. Many different computer architectures are in widespread commercial use today, but once you understand one, learning others is much easier. The key questions to ask when approaching a new architecture are

▶ What is the data word length?

▶ What are the registers?

▶ How is memory organized?

▶ What are the instructions?

MIPS is a 32-bit architecture because it operates on 32-bit data. The MIPS architecture has 32 general-purpose registers. In principle, almost any register can be used for any purpose. However, by convention, certain registers are reserved for certain purposes, for ease of programming and so that procedures written by different programmers can communicate easily. For example, register 0, $0, always holds the constant 0, $ra holds the return address after a jal instruction, and $a0-$a3 and $v0 - $v1 hold the arguments and return value of a procedure. MIPS has a byte-addressable memory system with 32-bit addresses. The memory map was described in Section 6.6.1. Instructions are 32 bits long and must be word aligned. This chapter discussed the most commonly used MIPS instructions.

The power of defining a computer architecture is that a program written for any given architecture can run on many different implementations of that architecture. For example, programs written for the Intel

Pentium processor in 1993 will generally still run (and run much faster) on the Intel Core 2 Duo or AMD Athlon processors in 2006.

In the first part of this book, we learned about the circuit and logic levels of abstraction. In this chapter, we jumped up to the architecture level. In the next chapter, we study microarchitecture, the arrangement of digital building blocks that implement a processor architecture. Microarchitecture is the link between hardware and software engineering. And, we believe it is one of the most exciting topics in all of engineering: you will learn to build your own microprocessor!

Exercises

Exercise 6.1 Give three examples from the MIPS architecture of each of the architecture design principles: (1) simplicity favors regularity; (2) make the common case fast; (3) smaller is faster; and (4) good design demands good compromises. Explain how each of your examples exhibits the design principle.

Exercise 6.2 The MIPS architecture has a register set that consists of 32 32-bit registers. Is it possible to design a computer architecture without a register set? If so, briefly describe the architecture, including the instruction set. What are advantages and disadvantages of this architecture over the MIPS architecture?

Exercise 6.3 Consider memory storage of a 32-bit word stored at memory word 42 in a byte addressable memory.

(a) What is the byte address of memory word 42?

(b) What are the byte addresses that memory word 42 spans?

(c) Draw the number 0xFF223344 stored at word 42 in both big-endian and little-endian machines. Your drawing should be similar to Figure 6.4. Clearly label the byte address corresponding to each data byte value.

Exercise 6.4 Explain how the following program can be used to determine whether a computer is big-endian or little-endian:

```
li $t0, 0xABCD9876
sw $t0, 100($0)
lb $s5, 101($0)
```

Exercise 6.5 Write the following strings using ASCII encoding. Write your final answers in hexadecimal.

(a) SOS

(b) Cool!

(c) (your own name)

Exercise 6.6 Show how the strings in Exercise 6.5 are stored in a byte-addressable memory on (a) a big-endian machine and (b) a little-endian machine starting at memory address 0x1000100C. Use a memory diagram similar to Figure 6.4. Clearly indicate the memory address of each byte on each machine.

Exercise 6.7 Convert the following MIPS assembly code into machine language. Write the instructions in hexadecimal.

```
add  $t0, $s0, $s1
lw   $t0, 0x20($t7)
addi $s0, $0, -10
```

Exercise 6.8 Repeat Exercise 6.7 for the following MIPS assembly code:

```
addi $s0, $0, 73
sw   $t1, -7($t2)
sub  $t1, $s7, $s2
```

Exercise 6.9 Consider I-type instructions.

(a) Which instructions from Exercise 6.8 are I-type instructions?

(b) Sign-extend the 16-bit immediate of each instruction from part (a) so that it becomes a 32-bit number.

Exercise 6.10 Convert the following program from machine language into MIPS assembly language. The numbers on the left are the instruction address in memory, and the numbers on the right give the instruction at that address. Then reverse engineer a high-level program that would compile into this assembly language routine and write it. Explain in words what the program does. $a0 is the input, and it initially contains a positive number, n. $v0 is the output.

```
0x00400000    0x20080000       addi  $t0 $0   0
0x00400004    0x20090001       addi  $t1 $0   1
0x00400008    0x0089502a       slt   $t2 $t0 $t1
0x0040000c    0x15400003       bne   $t0,$0, 3
0x00400010    0x01094020
0x00400014    0x21290002
0x00400018    0x08100002
0x0040001c    0x01001020
```

funct

Exercise 6.11 The nori instruction is not part of the MIPS instruction set, because the same functionality can be implemented using existing instructions. Write a short assembly code snippet that has the following functionality: $t0 = $t1 NOR 0xF234. Use as few instructions as possible.

Exercise 6.12 Implement the following high-level code segments using the slt instruction. Assume the integer variables g and h are in registers $s0 and $s1, respectively.

(a) `if (g > h)`
```
        g = g + h;
    else
        g = g - h;
```

(b) `if (g >= h)`
```
        g = g + 1;
    else
        h = h - 1;
```

(c) `if (g <= h)`
```
        g = 0;
    else
        h = 0;
```

Exercise 6.13 Write a procedure in a high-level language for `int find42(int array[], int size)`. `size` specifies the number of elements in the array. `array` specifies the base address of the array. The procedure should return the index number of the first array entry that holds the value 42. If no array entry is 42, it should return the value −1.

Exercise 6.14 The high-level procedure strcpy copies the character string x to the character string y.

```
// high-level code
void strcpy(char x[], char y[]) {
  int i = 0;

  while (x[i] != 0) {
    y[i] = x[i];
    i = i + 1;
  }
}
```

(a) Implement the strcpy procedure in MIPS assembly code. Use $s0 for i.

(b) Draw a picture of the stack before, during, and after the strcpy procedure call. Assume $sp = 0x7FFFFF00 just before strcpy is called.

Exercise 6.15 Convert the high-level procedure from Exercise 6.13 into MIPS assembly code.

This simple string copy program has a serious flaw: it has no way of knowing that y has enough space to receive x. If a malicious programmer were able to execute strcpy with a long string x, the programmer might be able to write bytes all over memory, possibly even modifying code stored in subsequent memory locations. With some cleverness, the modified code might take over the machine. This is called a buffer overflow attack; it is employed by several nasty programs, including the infamous Blaster worm, which caused an estimated $525 million in damages in 2003.

Exercise 6.16 Each number in the *Fibonacci series* is the sum of the previous two numbers. Table 6.16 lists the first few numbers in the series, *fib(n)*.

Table 6.16 Fibonacci series

n	1	2	3	4	5	6	7	8	9	10	11	. . .
fib(n)	1	1	2	3	5	8	13	21	34	55	89	. . .

(a) What is *fib(n)* for $n = 0$ and $n = -1$?

(b) Write a procedure called fib in a high-level language that returns the Fibonacci number for any nonnegative value of *n*. Hint: You probably will want to use a loop. Clearly comment your code.

(c) Convert the high-level procedure of part (b) into MIPS assembly code. Add comments after every line of code that explain clearly what it does. Use the SPIM simulator to test your code on fib(9).

Exercise 6.17 Consider the MIPS assembly code below. proc1, proc2, and proc3 are non-leaf procedures. proc4 is a leaf procedure. The code is not shown for each procedure, but the comments indicate which registers are used within each procedure.

```
0x00401000    proc1:    . . .         # proc1 uses $s0 and $s1
0x00401020              jal proc2
. . .
0x00401100    proc2:    . . .         # proc2 uses $s2 - $s7
0x0040117C              jal proc3
. . .
0x00401400    proc3:    . . .         # proc3 uses $s1 - $s3
0x00401704              jal proc4
. . .
0x00403008    proc4:    . . .         # proc4 uses no preserved
                                      # registers
0x00403118              jr $ra
```

(a) How many words are the stack frames of each procedure?

(b) Sketch the stack after proc4 is called. Clearly indicate which registers are stored where on the stack. Give values where possible.

Exercise 6.18 Ben Bitdiddle is trying to compute the function $f(a, b) = 2a + 3b$ for nonnegative b. He goes overboard in the use of procedure calls and recursion and produces the following high-level code for procedures f and f2.

```
// high-level code for procedures f and f2
int f(int a, int b) {
  int j;
  j = a;
  return j + a + f2(b);
}

int f2(int x)
{
  int k;
  k = 3;
  if (x == 0) return 0;
  else return k + f2(x-1);
}
```

Ben then translates the two procedures into assembly language as follows. He also writes a procedure, test, that calls the procedure f(5, 3).

```
# MIPS assembly code
# f: $a0 = a, $a1 = b, $s0 = j  f2: $a0 = x, $s0 = k

0x00400000  test: addi $a0, $0, 5     # $a0 = 5 (a = 5)
0x00400004        addi $a1, $0, 3     # $a1 = 3 (b = 3)
0x00400008        jal  f              # call f(5,3)
0x0040000c  loop: j    loop           # and loop forever

0x00400010  f:    addi $sp, $sp, -16  # make room on the stack
                                      # for $s0, $a0, $a1, and $ra
0x00400014        sw   $a1, 12($sp)   # save $a1 (b)
0x00400018        sw   $a0, 8($sp)    # save $a0 (a)
0x0040001c        sw   $ra, 4($sp)    # save $ra
0x00400020        sw   $s0, 0($sp)    # save $s0
0x00400024        add  $s0, $a0, $0   # $s0 = $a0 (j = a)
0x00400028        add  $a0, $a1, $0   # place b as argument for f2
0x0040002c        jal  f2             # call f2(b)
0x00400030        lw   $a0, 8($sp)    # restore $a0 (a) after call
0x00400034        lw   $a1, 12($sp)   # restore $a1 (b) after call
0x00400038        add  $v0, $v0, $s0  # $v0 = f2(b) + j
0x0040003c        add  $v0, $v0, $a0  # $v0 = (f2(b) + j) + a
0x00400040        lw   $s0, 0($sp)    # restore $s0
0x00400044        lw   $ra, 4($sp)    # restore $ra
0x00400048        addi $sp, $sp, 16   # restore $sp (stack pointer)
0x0040004c        jr   $ra            # return to point of call

0x00400050  f2:   addi $sp, $sp, -12  # make room on the stack for
                                      # $s0, $a0, and $ra
0x00400054        sw   $a0, 8($sp)    # save $a0 (x)
0x00400058        sw   $ra, 4($sp)    # save return address
0x0040005c        sw   $s0, 0($sp)    # save $s0
0x00400060        addi $s0, $0, 3     # k = 3
```

```
0x00400064              bne    $a0, $0, else   # x = 0?
0x00400068              addi   $v0, $0, 0      # yes: return value should be 0
0x0040006c              j      done            # and clean up
0x00400070   else: addi   $a0, $a0, -1      # no: $a0 = $a0 - 1 (x = x - 1)
0x00400074              jal    f2              # call f2(x - 1)
0x00400078              lw     $a0, 8($sp)     # restore $a0 (x)
0x0040007c              add    $v0, $v0, $s0   # $v0 = f2(x - 1) + k
0x00400080   done: lw    $s0, 0($sp)     # restore $s0
0x00400084              lw     $ra, 4($sp)     # restore $ra
0x00400088              addi   $sp, $sp, 12    # restore $sp
0x0040008c              jr     $ra             # return to point of call
```

You will probably find it useful to make drawings of the stack similar to the one in Figure 6.26 to help you answer the following questions.

(a) If the code runs starting at test, what value is in $v0 when the program gets to loop? Does his program correctly compute $2a + 3b$?

(b) Suppose Ben deletes the instructions at addresses 0x0040001C and 0x00400040 that save and restore $ra. Will the program (1) enter an infinite loop but not crash; (2) crash (cause the stack to grow beyond the dynamic data segment or the PC to jump to a location outside the program); (3) produce an incorrect value in $v0 when the program returns to loop (if so, what value?), or (4) run correctly despite the deleted lines?

(c) Repeat part (b) when the instructions at the following instruction addresses are deleted:

   (i)   0x00400018 and 0x00400030 (instructions that save and restore $a0)

   (ii) 0x00400014 and 0x00400034 (instructions that save and restore $a1)

   (iii) 0x00400020 and 0x00400040 (instructions that save and restore $s0)

   (iv) 0x00400050 and 0x00400088 (instructions that save and restore $sp)

   (v)   0x0040005C and 0x00400080 (instructions that save and restore $s0)

   (vi) 0x00400058 and 0x00400084 (instructions that save and restore $ra)

   (vii) 0x00400054 and 0x00400078 (instructions that save and restore $a0)

Exercise 6.19 Convert the following beq, j, and jal assembly instructions into machine code. Instruction addresses are given to the left of each instruction.

(a)
```
0x00401000              beq $t0, $s1, Loop
0x00401004                  . . .
0x00401008                  . . .
0x0040100C      Loop:      . . .
```

(b)

```
0x00401000                    beq $t7, $s4, done
   . . .                         . . .
0x00402040      done:  . . .
```

(c)

```
0x0040310C      back:  . . .
   . . .                         . . .
0x00405000                    beq $t9, $s7, back
```

(d)

```
0x00403000                    jal proc
   . . .                         . . .
0x0041147C      proc:  . . .
```

(e)

```
0x00403004      back:  . . .
   . . .                         . . .
0x0040400C      j      back
```

Exercise 6.20 Consider the following MIPS assembly language snippet. The numbers to the left of each instruction indicate the instruction address.

```
                      rd   rs    rt
0x00400028            add  $a0, $a1, $0
0x0040002c            jal  f2
0x00400030 f1:   jr   $ra
0x00400034 f2:   sw   $s0, 0($s2)
0x00400038            bne  $a0, $0, else
0x0040003c            j    f1
0x00400040 else: addi $a0, $a0, -1
0x00400044            j    f2
```

(a) Translate the instruction sequence into machine code. Write the machine code instructions in hexadecimal.

(b) List the addressing mode used at each line of code.

Exercise 6.21 Consider the following C code snippet.

```
// C code
  void set_array(int num) {
  int i;
  int array[10];

  for (i = 0; i < 10; i = i + 1) {
    array[i] = compare(num, i);
  }
 }
 int compare(int a, int b) {
  if (sub(a, b) >= 0)
    return 1;
  else
```

```
    return 0;
  }
  int sub (int a, int b) {
    return a - b;
  }
```

(a) Implement the C code snippet in MIPS assembly language. Use $s0 to hold the variable i. Be sure to handle the stack pointer appropriately. The array is stored on the stack of the set_array procedure (see Section 6.4.6).

(b) Assume set_array is the first procedure called. Draw the status of the stack before calling set_array and during each procedure call. Indicate the names of registers and variables stored on the stack and mark the location of $sp.

(c) How would your code function if you failed to store $ra on the stack?

Exercise 6.22 Consider the following high-level procedure.

```
// high-level code
  int f(int n, int k) {
    int b;

    b = k + 2;
    if (n == 0) b = 10;
    else b = b + (n * n) + f(n - 1, k + 1);
    return b * k;
  }
```

(a) Translate the high-level procedure f into MIPS assembly language. Pay particular attention to properly saving and restoring registers across procedure calls and using the MIPS preserved register conventions. Clearly comment your code. You can use the MIPS mult, mfhi, and mflo instructions. The procedure starts at instruction address 0x00400100. Keep local variable b in $s0.

(b) Step through your program from part (a) by hand for the case of f(2, 4). Draw a picture of the stack similar to the one in Figure 6.26(c). Write the register name and data value stored at each location in the stack and keep track of the stack pointer value ($sp). You might also find it useful to keep track of the values in $a0, $a1, $v0, and $s0 throughout execution. Assume that when f is called, $s0 = 0xABCD and $ra = 0x400004. What is the final value of $v0?

Exercise 6.23 What is the range of instruction addresses to which conditional branches, such as beq and bne, can branch in MIPS? Give your answer in number of instructions relative to the conditional branch instruction.

Exercise 6.24 The following questions examine the limitations of the jump instruction, j. Give your answer in number of instructions relative to the jump instruction.

(a) In the worst case, how far can the jump instruction (j) jump forward (i.e., to higher addresses)? (The worst case is when the jump instruction cannot jump far.) Explain using words and examples, as needed.

(b) In the best case, how far can the jump instruction (j) jump forward? (The best case is when the jump instruction can jump the farthest.) Explain.

(c) In the worst case, how far can the jump instruction (j) jump backward (to lower addresses)? Explain.

(d) In the best case, how far can the jump instruction (j) jump backward? Explain.

Exercise 6.25 Explain why it is advantageous to have a large address field, addr, in the machine format for the jump instructions, j and jal.

Exercise 6.26 Write assembly code that jumps to the instruction 64 Minstructions from the first instruction. Recall that 1 Minstruction = 2^{20} instructions = 1,048,576 instructions. Assume that your code begins at address 0x00400000. Use a minimum number of instructions.

Exercise 6.27 Write a procedure in high-level code that takes a ten-entry array of 32-bit integers stored in little-endian format and converts it to big-endian format. After writing the high-level code, convert it to MIPS assembly code. Comment all your code and use a minimum number of instructions.

Exercise 6.28 Consider two strings: string1 and string2.

(a) Write high-level code for a procedure called concat that concatenates (joins together) the two strings: void concat(char[] string1, char[] string2, char[] stringconcat). The procedure does not return a value. It concatenates string1 and string2 and places the resulting string in stringconcat. You may assume that the character array stringconcat is large enough to accommodate the concatenated string.

(b) Convert the procedure from part (a) into MIPS assembly language.

Exercise 6.29 Write a MIPS assembly program that adds two positive single-precision floating point numbers held in $s0 and $s1. Do not use any of the MIPS floating-point instructions. You need not worry about any of the encodings that are reserved for special purposes (e.g., 0, NANs, INF) or numbers that overflow or underflow. Use the SPIM simulator to test your code. You will need to manually set the values of $s0 and $s1 to test your code. Demonstrate that your code functions reliably.

Exercise 6.30 Show how the following MIPS program would be loaded into memory and executed.

```
# MIPS assembly code
main:
  lw $a0, x
  lw $a1, y
  jal diff
  jr $ra
diff:
  sub $v0, $a0, $a1
  jr $ra
```

(a) First show the instruction address next to each assembly instruction.

(b) Draw the symbol table showing the labels and their addresses.

(c) Convert all instructions into machine code.

(d) How big (how many bytes) are the data and text segments?

(e) Sketch a memory map showing where data and instructions are stored.

Exercise 6.31 Show the MIPS instructions that implement the following pseudoinstructions. You may use the assembler register, $at, but you may not corrupt (overwrite) any other registers.

(a) beq $t1, imm$_{31:0}$, L

(b) ble $t3, $t5, L

(c) bgt $t3, $t5, L

(d) bge $t3, $t5, L

(e) addi $t0, $2, imm$_{31:0}$

(f) lw $t5, imm$_{31:0}$($s0)

(g) rol $t0, $t1, 5 (rotate $t1 left by 5 and put the result in $t0)

(h) ror $s4, $t6, 31 (rotate $t6 right by 31 and put the result in $s4)

Interview Questions

The following exercises present questions that have been asked at interviews for digital design jobs (but are usually open to any assembly language).

Question 6.1 Write MIPS assembly code for swapping the contents of two registers, $t0 and $t1. You may not use any other registers.

Question 6.2 Suppose you are given an array of both positive and negative integers. Write MIPS assembly code that finds the subset of the array with the largest sum. Assume that the array's base address and the number of array elements are in $a0 and $a1, respectively. Your code should place the resulting subset of the array starting at base address $a2. Write code that runs as fast as possible.

Question 6.3 You are given an array that holds a C string. The string forms a sentence. Design an algorithm for reversing the words in the sentence and storing the new sentence back in the array. Implement your algorithm using MIPS assembly code.

Question 6.4 Design an algorithm for counting the number of 1's in a 32-bit number. Implement your algorithm using MIPS assembly code.

Question 6.5 Write MIPS assembly code to reverse the bits in a register. Use as few instructions as possible. Assume the register of interest is $t3.

Question 6.6 Write MIPS assembly code to test whether overflow occurs when $t2 and $t3 are added. Use a minimum number of instructions.

Question 6.7 Design an algorithm for testing whether a given string is a palindrome. (Recall, that a palindrome is a word that is the same forward and backward. For example, the words "wow" and "racecar" are palindromes.) Implement your algorithm using MIPS assembly code.

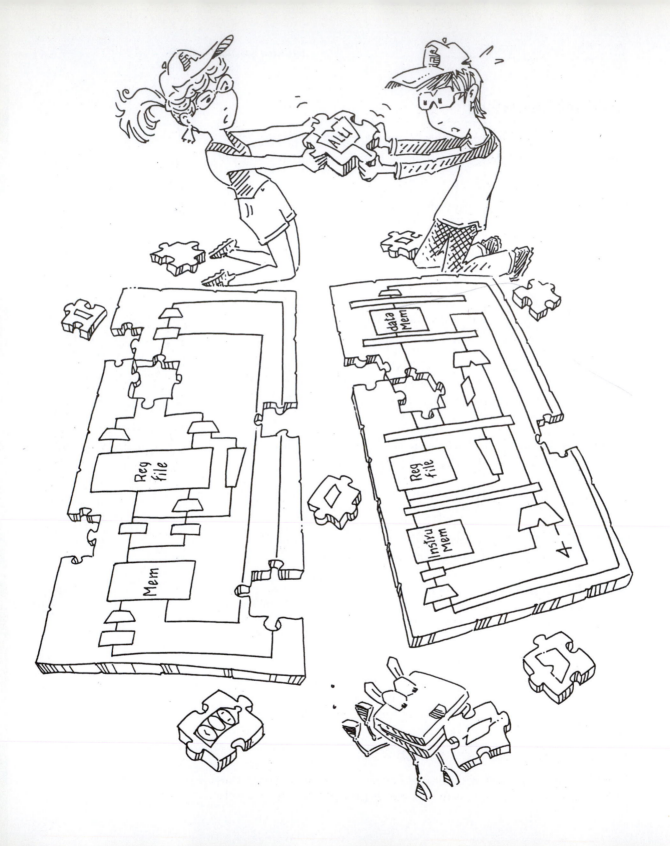

Microarchitecture

7.1 INTRODUCTION

In this chapter, you will learn how to piece together a MIPS microprocessor. Indeed, you will puzzle out three different versions, each with different trade-offs between performance, cost, and complexity.

To the uninitiated, building a microprocessor may seem like black magic. But it is actually relatively straightforward, and by this point you have learned everything you need to know. Specifically, you have learned to design combinational and sequential logic given functional and timing specifications. You are familiar with circuits for arithmetic and memory. And you have learned about the MIPS architecture, which specifies the programmer's view of the MIPS processor in terms of registers, instructions, and memory.

This chapter covers *microarchitecture*, which is the connection between logic and architecture. Microarchitecture is the specific arrangement of registers, ALUs, finite state machines (FSMs), memories, and other logic building blocks needed to implement an architecture. A particular architecture, such as MIPS, may have many different microarchitectures, each with different trade-offs of performance, cost, and complexity. They all run the same programs, but their internal designs vary widely. We will design three different microarchitectures in this chapter to illustrate the trade-offs.

This chapter draws heavily on David Patterson and John Hennessy's classic MIPS designs in their text *Computer Organization and Design*. They have generously shared their elegant designs, which have the virtue of illustrating a real commercial architecture while being relatively simple and easy to understand.

7.1.1 Architectural State and Instruction Set

Recall that a computer architecture is defined by its instruction set and *architectural state*. The architectural state for the MIPS processor consists

David Patterson was the first in his family to graduate from college (UCLA, 1969). He has been a professor of computer science at UC Berkeley since 1977, where he coinvented RISC, the Reduced Instruction Set Computer. In 1984, he developed the SPARC architecture used by Sun Microsystems. He is also the father of *RAID* (*Redundant Array of Inexpensive Disks*) and *NOW* (*Network of Workstations*).

John Hennessy is president of Stanford University and has been a professor of electrical engineering and computer science there since 1977. He coinvented RISC. He developed the MIPS architecture at Stanford in 1984 and cofounded MIPS Computer Systems. As of 2004, more than 300 million MIPS microprocessors have been sold.

In their copious free time, these two modern paragons write textbooks for recreation and relaxation.

of the program counter and the 32 registers. Any MIPS microarchitecture must contain all of this state. Based on the current architectural state, the processor executes a particular instruction with a particular set of data to produce a new architectural state. Some microarchitectures contain additional *nonarchitectural state* to either simplify the logic or improve performance; we will point this out as it arises.

To keep the microarchitectures easy to understand, we consider only a subset of the MIPS instruction set. Specifically, we handle the following instructions:

▶ R-type arithmetic/logic instructions: `add`, `sub`, `and`, `or`, `slt`

▶ Memory instructions: `lw`, `sw`

▶ Branches: `beq`

After building the microarchitectures with these instructions, we extend them to handle `addi` and `j`. These particular instructions were chosen because they are sufficient to write many interesting programs. Once you understand how to implement these instructions, you can expand the hardware to handle others.

7.1.2 Design Process

We will divide our microarchitectures into two interacting parts: the *datapath* and the *control*. The datapath operates on words of data. It contains structures such as memories, registers, ALUs, and multiplexers. MIPS is a 32-bit architecture, so we will use a 32-bit datapath. The control unit receives the current instruction from the datapath and tells the datapath how to execute that instruction. Specifically, the control unit produces multiplexer select, register enable, and memory write signals to control the operation of the datapath.

A good way to design a complex system is to start with hardware containing the state elements. These elements include the memories and the architectural state (the program counter and registers). Then, add blocks of combinational logic between the state elements to compute the new state based on the current state. The instruction is read from part of memory; load and store instructions then read or write data from another part of memory. Hence, it is often convenient to partition the overall memory into two smaller memories, one containing instructions and the other containing data. Figure 7.1 shows a block diagram with the four state elements: the program counter, register file, and instruction and data memories.

In Figure 7.1, heavy lines are used to indicate 32-bit data busses. Medium lines are used to indicate narrower busses, such as the 5-bit address busses on the register file. Narrow blue lines are used to indicate

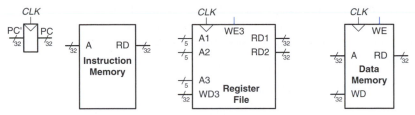

Figure 7.1 State elements of MIPS processor

control signals, such as the register file write enable. We will use this convention throughout the chapter to avoid cluttering diagrams with bus widths. Also, state elements usually have a reset input to put them into a known state at start-up. Again, to save clutter, this reset is not shown.

The *program counter* is an ordinary 32-bit register. Its output, *PC*, points to the current instruction. Its input, *PC'*, indicates the address of the next instruction.

The *instruction memory* has a single read port.[1] It takes a 32-bit instruction address input, *A*, and reads the 32-bit data (i.e., instruction) from that address onto the read data output, *RD*.

The 32-element × 32-bit *register file* has two read ports and one write port. The read ports take 5-bit address inputs, *A1* and *A2*, each specifying one of $2^5 = 32$ registers as source operands. They read the 32-bit register values onto read data outputs *RD1* and *RD2*, respectively. The write port takes a 5-bit address input, *A3*; a 32-bit write data input, *WD*; a write enable input, *WE3*; and a clock. If the write enable is 1, the register file writes the data into the specified register on the rising edge of the clock.

The *data memory* has a single read/write port. If the write enable, *WE*, is 1, it writes data *WD* into address *A* on the rising edge of the clock. If the write enable is 0, it reads address *A* onto *RD*.

The instruction memory, register file, and data memory are all read *combinationally*. In other words, if the address changes, the new data appears at *RD* after some propagation delay; no clock is involved. They are written only on the rising edge of the clock. In this fashion, the state of the system is changed only at the clock edge. The address, data, and write enable must setup sometime before the clock edge and must remain stable until a hold time after the clock edge.

Because the state elements change their state only on the rising edge of the clock, they are synchronous sequential circuits. The microprocessor is

Resetting the PC

At the very least, the program counter must have a reset signal to initialize its value when the processor turns on. MIPS processors initialize the PC to 0xBFC00000 on reset and begin executing code to start up the operating system (OS). The OS then loads an application program at 0x00400000 and begins executing it. For simplicity in this chapter, we will reset the PC to 0x00000000 and place our programs there instead.

---

[1] This is an oversimplification used to treat the instruction memory as a ROM; in most real processors, the instruction memory must be writable so that the OS can load a new program into memory. The multicycle microarchitecture described in Section 7.4 is more realistic in that it uses a combined memory for instructions and data that can be both read and written.

built of clocked state elements and combinational logic, so it too is a synchronous sequential circuit. Indeed, the processor can be viewed as a giant finite state machine, or as a collection of simpler interacting state machines.

7.1.3 MIPS Microarchitectures

In this chapter, we develop three microarchitectures for the MIPS processor architecture: single-cycle, multicycle, and pipelined. They differ in the way that the state elements are connected together and in the amount of nonarchitectural state.

The *single-cycle microarchitecture* executes an entire instruction in one cycle. It is easy to explain and has a simple control unit. Because it completes the operation in one cycle, it does not require any nonarchitectural state. However, the cycle time is limited by the slowest instruction.

The *multicycle microarchitecture* executes instructions in a series of shorter cycles. Simpler instructions execute in fewer cycles than complicated ones. Moreover, the multicycle microarchitecture reduces the hardware cost by reusing expensive hardware blocks such as adders and memories. For example, the adder may be used on several different cycles for several purposes while carrying out a single instruction. The multicycle microprocessor accomplishes this by adding several nonarchitectural registers to hold intermediate results. The multicycle processor executes only one instruction at a time, but each instruction takes multiple clock cycles.

The *pipelined microarchitecture* applies pipelining to the single-cycle microarchitecture. It therefore can execute several instructions simultaneously, improving the throughput significantly. Pipelining must add logic to handle dependencies between simultaneously executing instructions. It also requires nonarchitectural pipeline registers. The added logic and registers are worthwhile; all commercial high-performance processors use pipelining today.

We explore the details and trade-offs of these three microarchitectures in the subsequent sections. At the end of the chapter, we briefly mention additional techniques that are used to get even more speed in modern high-performance microprocessors.

7.2 PERFORMANCE ANALYSIS

As we mentioned, a particular processor architecture can have many microarchitectures with different cost and performance trade-offs. The cost depends on the amount of hardware required and the implementation technology. Each year, CMOS processes can pack more transistors on a chip for the same amount of money, and processors take advantage of these additional transistors to deliver more performance. Precise cost calculations require detailed knowledge of the implementation technology, but in general, more gates and more memory mean more dollars. This section lays the foundation for analyzing performance.

There are many ways to measure the performance of a computer system, and marketing departments are infamous for choosing the method that makes their computer look fastest, regardless of whether the measurement has any correlation to real world performance. For example, Intel and Advanced Micro Devices (AMD) both sell compatible microprocessors conforming to the IA-32 architecture. Intel Pentium III and Pentium 4 microprocessors were largely advertised according to clock frequency in the late 1990s and early 2000s, because Intel offered higher clock frequencies than its competitors. However, Intel's main competitor, AMD, sold Athlon microprocessors that executed programs faster than Intel's chips at the same clock frequency. What is a consumer to do?

The only gimmick-free way to measure performance is by measuring the execution time of a program of interest to you. The computer that executes your program fastest has the highest performance. The next best choice is to measure the total execution time of a collection of programs that are similar to those you plan to run; this may be necessary if you haven't written your program yet or if somebody else who doesn't have your program is making the measurements. Such collections of programs are called *benchmarks*, and the execution times of these programs are commonly published to give some indication of how a processor performs.

The execution time of a program, measured in seconds, is given by Equation 7.1.

$$Execution\ Time = \left(\#\ instructions \right)\left(\frac{cycles}{instruction} \right)\left(\frac{seconds}{cycle} \right) \quad (7.1)$$

The number of instructions in a program depends on the processor architecture. Some architectures have complicated instructions that do more work per instruction, thus reducing the number of instructions in a program. However, these complicated instructions are often slower to execute in hardware. The number of instructions also depends enormously on the cleverness of the programmer. For the purposes of this chapter, we will assume that we are executing known programs on a MIPS processor, so the number of instructions for each program is constant, independent of the microarchitecture.

The number of cycles per instruction, often called *CPI*, is the number of clock cycles required to execute an average instruction. It is the reciprocal of the throughput (instructions per cycle, or *IPC*). Different microarchitectures have different CPIs. In this chapter, we will assume we have an ideal memory system that does not affect the CPI. In Chapter 8, we examine how the processor sometimes has to wait for the memory, which increases the CPI.

The number of seconds per cycle is the clock period, T_c. The clock period is determined by the critical path through the logic on the processor. Different microarchitectures have different clock periods. Logic and circuit designs also significantly affect the clock period. For example, a carry-lookahead adder is faster than a ripple-carry adder. Manufacturing advances have historically doubled transistor speeds every 4–6 years, so a microprocessor built today will be much faster than one from last decade, even if the microarchitecture and logic are unchanged.

The challenge of the microarchitect is to choose the design that minimizes the execution time while satisfying constraints on cost and/or power consumption. Because microarchitectural decisions affect both CPI and T_c and are influenced by logic and circuit designs, determining the best choice requires careful analysis.

There are many other factors that affect overall computer performance. For example, the hard disk, the memory, the graphics system, and the network connection may be limiting factors that make processor performance irrelevant. The fastest microprocessor in the world doesn't help surfing the Internet on a dial-up connection. But these other factors are beyond the scope of this book.

7.3 SINGLE-CYCLE PROCESSOR

We first design a MIPS microarchitecture that executes instructions in a single cycle. We begin constructing the datapath by connecting the state elements from Figure 7.1 with combinational logic that can execute the various instructions. Control signals determine which specific instruction is carried out by the datapath at any given time. The controller contains combinational logic that generates the appropriate control signals based on the current instruction. We conclude by analyzing the performance of the single-cycle processor.

7.3.1 Single-Cycle Datapath

This section gradually develops the single-cycle datapath, adding one piece at a time to the state elements from Figure 7.1. The new connections are emphasized in black (or blue, for new control signals), while the hardware that has already been studied is shown in gray.

The program counter (PC) register contains the address of the instruction to execute. The first step is to read this instruction from instruction memory. Figure 7.2 shows that the PC is simply connected to the address input of the instruction memory. The instruction memory reads out, or *fetches*, the 32-bit instruction, labeled *Instr*.

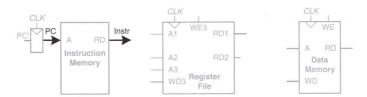

Figure 7.2 Fetch instruction from memory

The processor's actions depend on the specific instruction that was fetched. First we will work out the datapath connections for the lw instruction. Then we will consider how to generalize the datapath to handle the other instructions.

For a lw instruction, the next step is to read the source register containing the base address. This register is specified in the rs field of the instruction, $Instr_{25:21}$. These bits of the instruction are connected to the address input of one of the register file read ports, $A1$, as shown in Figure 7.3. The register file reads the register value onto $RD1$.

The lw instruction also requires an offset. The offset is stored in the immediate field of the instruction, $Instr_{15:0}$. Because the 16-bit immediate might be either positive or negative, it must be sign-extended to 32 bits, as shown in Figure 7.4. The 32-bit sign-extended value is called $SignImm$. Recall from Section 1.4.6 that sign extension simply copies the sign bit (most significant bit) of a short input into all of the upper bits of the longer output. Specifically, $SignImm_{15:0} = Instr_{15:0}$ and $SignImm_{31:16} = Instr_{15}$.

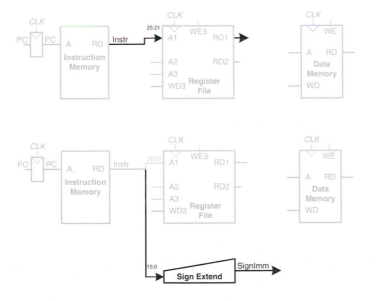

Figure 7.3 Read source operand from register file

Figure 7.4 Sign-extend the immediate

The processor must add the base address to the offset to find the address to read from memory. Figure 7.5 introduces an ALU to perform this addition. The ALU receives two operands, *SrcA* and *SrcB*. *SrcA* comes from the register file, and *SrcB* comes from the sign-extended immediate. The ALU can perform many operations, as was described in Section 5.2.4. The 3-bit *ALUControl* signal specifies the operation. The ALU generates a 32-bit *ALUResult* and a *Zero* flag, that indicates whether *ALUResult* == 0. For a lw instruction, the *ALUControl* signal should be set to 010 to add the base address and offset. *ALUResult* is sent to the data memory as the address for the load instruction, as shown in Figure 7.5.

The data is read from the data memory onto the *ReadData* bus, then written back to the destination register in the register file at the end of the cycle, as shown in Figure 7.6. Port 3 of the register file is the

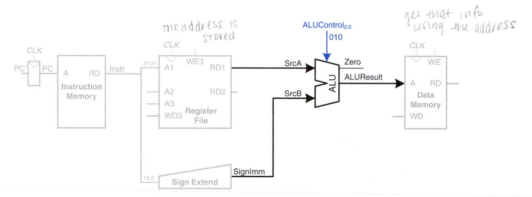

Figure 7.5 Compute memory address

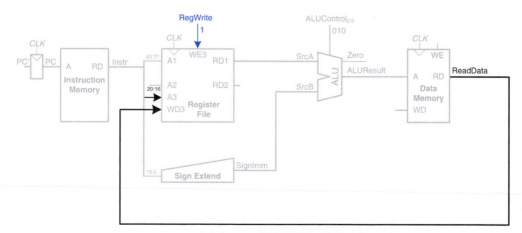

Figure 7.6 Write data back to register file

write port. The destination register for the lw instruction is specified in the rt field, $Instr_{20:16}$, which is connected to the port 3 address input, A3, of the register file. The *ReadData* bus is connected to the port 3 write data input, *WD3*, of the register file. A control signal called *RegWrite* is connected to the port 3 write enable input, *WE3*, and is asserted during a lw instruction so that the data value is written into the register file. The write takes place on the rising edge of the clock at the end of the cycle.

While the instruction is being executed, the processor must compute the address of the next instruction, *PC'*. Because instructions are 32 bits = 4 bytes, the next instruction is at *PC* + 4. Figure 7.7 uses another adder to increment the *PC* by 4. The new address is written into the program counter on the next rising edge of the clock. This completes the datapath for the lw instruction.

Next, let us extend the datapath to also handle the sw instruction. Like the lw instruction, the sw instruction reads a base address from port 1 of the register and sign-extends an immediate. The ALU adds the base address to the immediate to find the memory address. All of these functions are already supported by the datapath.

The sw instruction also reads a second register from the register file and writes it to the data memory. Figure 7.8 shows the new connections for this function. The register is specified in the rt field, $Instr_{20:16}$. These bits of the instruction are connected to the second register file read port, *A2*. The register value is read onto the *RD2* port. It is connected to the write data port of the data memory. The write enable port of the data memory, *WE*, is controlled by *MemWrite*. For a sw instruction, *MemWrite* = 1, to write the data to memory; *ALUControl* = 010, to add the base address

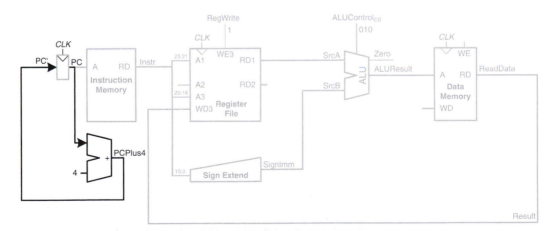

Figure 7.7 Determine address of next instruction for PC

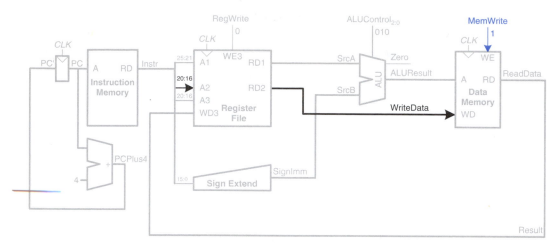

Figure 7.8 Write data to memory for sw **instruction**

and offset; and *RegWrite* = 0, because nothing should be written to the register file. Note that data is still read from the address given to the data memory, but that this *ReadData* is ignored because *RegWrite* = 0.

Next, consider extending the datapath to handle the R-type instructions add, sub, and, or, and slt. All of these instructions read two registers from the register file, perform some ALU operation on them, and write the result back to a third register file. They differ only in the specific ALU operation. Hence, they can all be handled with the same hardware, using different *ALUControl* signals.

Figure 7.9 shows the enhanced datapath handling R-type instructions. The register file reads two registers. The ALU performs an operation on these two registers. In Figure 7.8, the ALU always received its *SrcB* operand from the sign-extended immediate (*SignImm*). Now, we add a multiplexer to choose *SrcB* from either the register file *RD2* port or *SignImm*.

The multiplexer is controlled by a new signal, *ALUSrc*. *ALUSrc* is 0 for R-type instructions to choose *SrcB* from the register file; it is 1 for lw and sw to choose *SignImm*. This principle of enhancing the datapath's capabilities by adding a multiplexer to choose inputs from several possibilities is extremely useful. Indeed, we will apply it twice more to complete the handling of R-type instructions.

In Figure 7.8, the register file always got its write data from the data memory. However, R-type instructions write the *ALUResult* to the register file. Therefore, we add another multiplexer to choose between *ReadData* and *ALUResult*. We call its output *Result*. This multiplexer is controlled by another new signal, *MemtoReg*. *MemtoReg* is 0

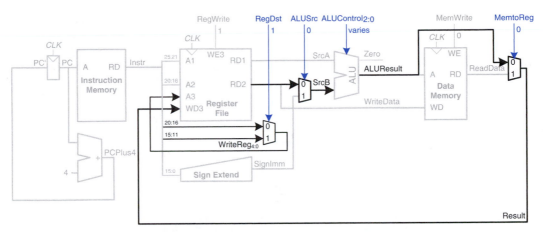

Figure 7.9 Datapath enhancements for R-type instruction

for R-type instructions to choose *Result* from the *ALUResult*; it is 1 for
lw to choose *ReadData*. We don't care about the value of *MemtoReg* for
sw, because sw does not write to the register file.

Similarly, in Figure 7.8, the register to write was specified by the rt
field of the instruction, $Instr_{20:16}$. However, for R-type instructions, the
register is specified by the rd field, $Instr_{15:11}$. Thus, we add a third multiplexer to choose *WriteReg* from the appropriate field of the instruction. The multiplexer is controlled by *RegDst*. *RegDst* is 1 for R-type
instructions to choose *WriteReg* from the rd field, $Instr_{15:11}$; it is 0 for
lw to choose the rt field, $Instr_{20:16}$. We don't care about the value of
RegDst for sw, because sw does not write to the register file.

Finally, let us extend the datapath to handle beq. beq compares
two registers. If they are equal, it takes the branch by adding the branch
offset to the program counter. Recall that the offset is a positive or negative number, stored in the imm field of the instruction, $Instr_{31:26}$. The offset indicates the number of instructions to branch past. Hence, the
immediate must be sign-extended and multiplied by 4 to get the new
program counter value: $PC' = PC + 4 + SignImm \times 4$.

Figure 7.10 shows the datapath modifications. The next *PC* value
for a taken branch, *PCBranch*, is computed by shifting *SignImm* left by
2 bits, then adding it to *PCPlus4*. The left shift by 2 is an easy way to
multiply by 4, because a shift by a constant amount involves just wires.
The two registers are compared by computing *SrcA* − *SrcB* using the
ALU. If *ALUResult* is 0, as indicated by the *Zero* flag from the ALU, the
registers are equal. We add a multiplexer to choose *PC'* from either
PCPlus4 or *PCBranch*. *PCBranch* is selected if the instruction is

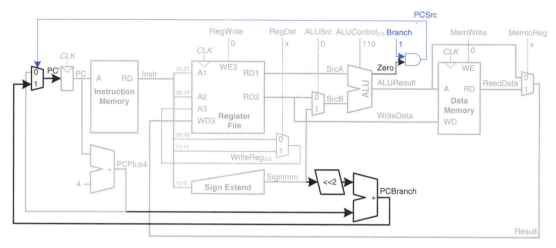

Figure 7.10 Datapath enhancements for beq **instruction**

a branch and the *Zero* flag is asserted. Hence, *Branch* is 1 for beq and 0 for other instructions. For beq, *ALUControl* = 110, so the ALU performs a subtraction. *ALUSrc* = 0 to choose *SrcB* from the register file. *RegWrite* and *MemWrite* are 0, because a branch does not write to the register file or memory. We don't care about the values of *RegDst* and *MemtoReg*, because the register file is not written.

This completes the design of the single-cycle MIPS processor datapath. We have illustrated not only the design itself, but also the design process in which the state elements are identified and the combinational logic connecting the state elements is systematically added. In the next section, we consider how to compute the control signals that direct the operation of our datapath.

7.3.2 Single-Cycle Control

The control unit computes the control signals based on the opcode and funct fields of the instruction, $Instr_{31:26}$ and $Instr_{5:0}$. Figure 7.11 shows the entire single-cycle MIPS processor with the control unit attached to the datapath.

Most of the control information comes from the opcode, but R-type instructions also use the funct field to determine the ALU operation. Thus, we will simplify our design by factoring the control unit into two blocks of combinational logic, as shown in Figure 7.12. The *main decoder* computes most of the outputs from the opcode. It also determines a 2-bit *ALUOp* signal. The ALU decoder uses this *ALUOp* signal in conjunction with the funct field to compute *ALUControl*. The meaning of the *ALUOp* signal is given in Table 7.1.

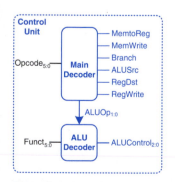

Figure 7.12 Control unit internal structure

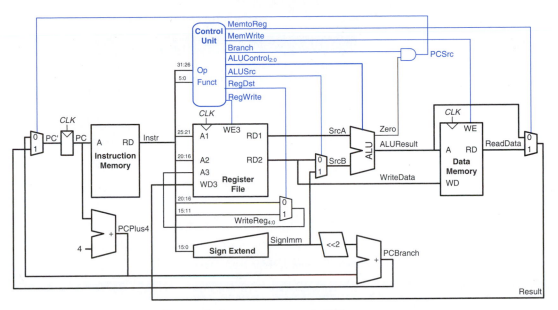

Figure 7.11 Complete single-cycle MIPS processor

Table 7.1 *ALUOp* encoding

ALUOp	Meaning
00	add
01	subtract
10	look at funct field
11	n/a

Table 7.2 is a truth table for the ALU decoder. Recall that the meanings of the three *ALUControl* signals were given in Table 5.1. Because *ALUOp* is never 11, the truth table can use don't care's X1 and 1X instead of 01 and 10 to simplify the logic. When *ALUOp* is 00 or 01, the ALU should add or subtract, respectively. When *ALUOp* is 10, the decoder examines the funct field to determine the *ALUControl*. Note that, for the R-type instructions we implement, the first two bits of the funct field are always 10, so we may ignore them to simplify the decoder.

The control signals for each instruction were described as we built the datapath. Table 7.3 is a truth table for the main decoder that summarizes the control signals as a function of the opcode. All R-type instructions use the same main decoder values; they differ only in the

Table 7.2 **ALU decoder truth table**

ALUOp	Funct	ALUControl
00	X	010 (add)
X1	X	110 (subtract)
1X	100000 (add)	010 (add)
1X	100010 (sub)	110 (subtract)
1X	100100 (and)	000 (and)
1X	100101 (or)	001 (or)
1X	101010 (slt)	111 (set less than)

Table 7.3 **Main decoder truth table**

Instruction	Opcode	RegWrite	RegDst	ALUSrc	Branch	MemWrite	MemtoReg	ALUOp
R-type	000000	1	1	0	0	0	0	10
lw	100011	1	0	1	0	0	1	00
sw	101011	0	X	1	0	1	X	00
beq	000100	0	X	0	1	0	X	01

ALU decoder output. Recall that, for instructions that do not write to the register file (e.g., sw and beq), the *RegDst* and *MemtoReg* control signals are don't cares (X); the address and data to the register write port do not matter because *RegWrite* is not asserted. The logic for the decoder can be designed using your favorite techniques for combinational logic design.

Example 7.1 SINGLE-CYCLE PROCESSOR OPERATION

Determine the values of the control signals and the portions of the datapath that are used when executing an or instruction.

Solution: Figure 7.13 illustrates the control signals and flow of data during execution of the or instruction. The PC points to the memory location holding the instruction, and the instruction memory fetches this instruction.

The main flow of data through the register file and ALU is represented with a dashed blue line. The register file reads the two source operands specified by $Instr_{25:21}$ and $Instr_{20:16}$. SrcB should come from the second port of the register

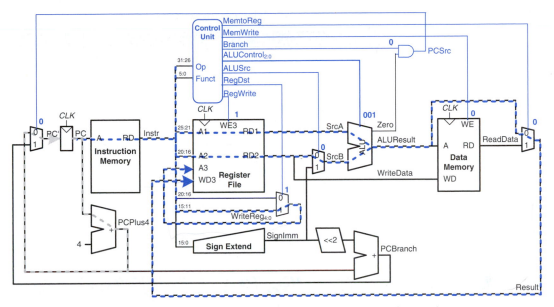

Figure 7.13 Control signals and data flow while executing or instruction

file (not *SignImm*), so *ALUSrc* must be 0. or is an R-type instruction, so *ALUOp* is 10, indicating that *ALUControl* should be determined from the funct field to be 001. *Result* is taken from the ALU, so *MemtoReg* is 0. The result is written to the register file, so *RegWrite* is 1. The instruction does not write memory, so *MemWrite* = 0.

The selection of the destination register is also shown with a dashed blue line. The destination register is specified in the rd field, $Instr_{15:11}$, so *RegDst* = 1.

The updating of the PC is shown with the dashed gray line. The instruction is not a branch, so *Branch* = 0 and, hence, *PCSrc* is also 0. The PC gets its next value from *PCPlus4*.

Note that data certainly does flow through the nonhighlighted paths, but that the value of that data is unimportant for this instruction. For example, the immediate is sign-extended and data is read from memory, but these values do not influence the next state of the system.

7.3.3 More Instructions

We have considered a limited subset of the full MIPS instruction set. Adding support for the addi and j instructions illustrates the principle of how to handle new instructions and also gives us a sufficiently rich instruction set to write many interesting programs. We will see that supporting some instructions simply requires enhancing the main decoder, whereas supporting others also requires more hardware in the datapath.

Example 7.2 `addi` INSTRUCTION

The add immediate instruction, `addi`, adds the value in a register to the immediate and writes the result to another register. The datapath already is capable of this task. Determine the necessary changes to the controller to support `addi`.

Solution: All we need to do is add a new row to the main decoder truth table showing the control signal values for `addi`, as given in Table 7.4. The result should be written to the register file, so *RegWrite* = 1. The destination register is specified in the `rt` field of the instruction, so *RegDst* = 0. *SrcB* comes from the immediate, so *ALUSrc* = 1. The instruction is not a branch, nor does it write memory, so *Branch* = *MemWrite* = 0. The result comes from the ALU, not memory, so *MemtoReg* = 0. Finally, the ALU should add, so *ALUOp* = 00.

Table 7.4 Main decoder truth table enhanced to support `addi`

Instruction	Opcode	RegWrite	RegDst	ALUSrc	Branch	MemWrite	MemtoReg	ALUOp
R-type	000000	1	1	0	0	0	0	10
lw	100011	1	0	1	0	0	1	00
sw	101011	0	X	1	0	1	X	00
beq	000100	0	X	0	1	0	X	01
addi	001000	1	0	1	0	0	0	00

Example 7.3 `j` INSTRUCTION

The jump instruction, `j`, writes a new value into the PC. The two least significant bits of the PC are always 0, because the PC is word aligned (i.e., always a multiple of 4). The next 26 bits are taken from the jump address field in $Instr_{25:0}$. The upper four bits are taken from the old value of the PC.

The existing datapath lacks hardware to compute *PC'* in this fashion. Determine the necessary changes to both the datapath and controller to handle `j`.

Solution: First, we must add hardware to compute the next PC value, *PC'*, in the case of a `j` instruction and a multiplexer to select this next PC, as shown in Figure 7.14. The new multiplexer uses the new *Jump* control signal.

Now we must add a row to the main decoder truth table for the j instruction and a column for the *Jump* signal, as shown in Table 7.5. The *Jump* control signal is 1 for the j instruction and 0 for all others. j does not write the register file or memory, so *RegWrite* = *MemWrite* = 0. Hence, we don't care about the computation done in the datapath, and *RegDst* = *ALUSrc* = *Branch* = *MemtoReg* = *ALUOp* = X.

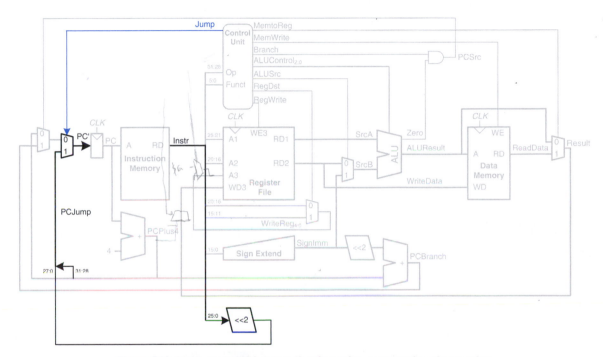

Figure 7.14 Single-cycle MIPS datapath enhanced to support the j instruction

Table 7.5 Main decoder truth table enhanced to support j

Instruction	Opcode	RegWrite	RegDst	ALUSrc	Branch	MemWrite	MemtoReg	ALUOp	Jump
R-type	000000	1	1	0	0	0	0	10	0
lw	100011	1	0	1	0	0	1	00	0
sw	101011	0	X	1	0	1	X	00	0
beq	000100	0	X	0	1	0	X	01	0
addi	001000	1	0	1	0	0	0	00	0
j	000010	0	X	X	X	0	X	XX	1

7.3.4 Performance Analysis

Each instruction in the single-cycle processor takes one clock cycle, so the CPI is 1. The critical path for the lw instruction is shown in Figure 7.15 with a heavy dashed blue line. It starts with the PC loading a new address on the rising edge of the clock. The instruction memory reads the next instruction. The register file reads *SrcA*. While the register file is reading, the immediate field is sign-extended and selected at the *ALUSrc* multiplexer to determine *SrcB*. The ALU adds *SrcA* and *SrcB* to find the effective address. The data memory reads from this address. The *MemtoReg* multiplexer selects *ReadData*. Finally, *Result* must setup at the register file before the next rising clock edge, so that it can be properly written. Hence, the cycle time is

$$T_c = t_{pcq\_PC} + t_{mem} + \max[t_{RFread}, t_{sext}] + t_{mux}$$

$$+ t_{ALU} + t_{mem} + t_{mux} + t_{RFsetup} \tag{7.2}$$

In most implementation technologies, the ALU, memory, and register file accesses are substantially slower than other operations. Therefore, the cycle time simplifies to

$$T_c = t_{pcq\_PC} + 2t_{mem} + t_{RFread} + 2t_{mux} + t_{ALU} + t_{RFsetup} \tag{7.3}$$

The numerical values of these times will depend on the specific implementation technology.

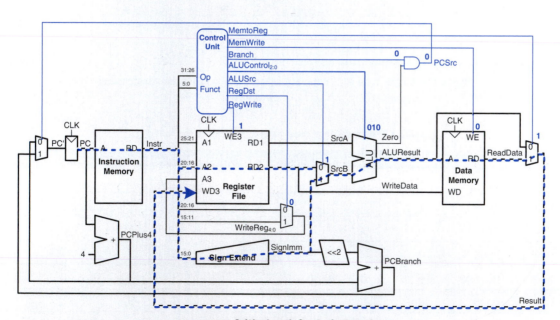

Figure 7.15 Critical path for lw instruction

Other instructions have shorter critical paths. For example, R-type instructions do not need to access data memory. However, we are disciplining ourselves to synchronous sequential design, so the clock period is constant and must be long enough to accommodate the slowest instruction.

Example 7.4 SINGLE-CYCLE PROCESSOR PERFORMANCE

Ben Bitdiddle is contemplating building the single-cycle MIPS processor in a 65 nm CMOS manufacturing process. He has determined that the logic elements have the delays given in Table 7.6. Help him compare the execution time for a program with 100 billion instructions.

Solution: According to Equation 7.3, the cycle time of the single-cycle processor is $T_{c1} = 30 + 2(250) + 150 + 2(25) + 200 + 20 = 950$ ps. We use the subscript "1" to distinguish it from subsequent processor designs. According to Equation 7.1, the total execution time is $T_1 = (100 \times 10^9$ instructions$)(1$ cycle/instruction$)$ $(950 \times 10^{-12}$ s/cycle$) = 95$ seconds.

Table 7.6 Delays of circuit elements

Element	Parameter	Delay (ps)
register clk-to-Q	t_{pcq}	30
register setup	t_{setup}	20
multiplexer	t_{mux}	25
ALU	t_{ALU}	200
memory read	t_{mem}	250
register file read	t_{RFread}	150
register file setup	$t_{RFsetup}$	20

7.4 MULTICYCLE PROCESSOR

The single-cycle processor has three primary weaknesses. First, it requires a clock cycle long enough to support the slowest instruction (lw), even though most instructions are faster. Second, it requires three adders (one in the ALU and two for the PC logic); adders are relatively expensive circuits, especially if they must be fast. And third, it has separate instruction and data memories, which may not be realistic. Most computers have a single large memory that holds both instructions and data and that can be read and written.

The multicycle processor addresses these weaknesses by breaking an instruction into multiple shorter steps. In each short step, the processor can read or write the memory or register file or use the ALU. Different instructions use different numbers of steps, so simpler instructions can complete faster than more complex ones. The processor needs only one adder; this adder is reused for different purposes on various steps. And the processor uses a combined memory for instructions and data. The instruction is fetched from memory on the first step, and data may be read or written on later steps.

We design a multicycle processor following the same procedure we used for the single-cycle processor. First, we construct a datapath by connecting the architectural state elements and memories with combinational logic. But, this time, we also add nonarchitectural state elements to hold intermediate results between the steps. Then we design the controller. The controller produces different signals on different steps during execution of a single instruction, so it is now a finite state machine rather than combinational logic. We again examine how to add new instructions to the processor. Finally, we analyze the performance of the multicycle processor and compare it to the single-cycle processor.

7.4.1 Multicycle Datapath

Again, we begin our design with the memory and architectural state of the MIPS processor, shown in Figure 7.16. In the single-cycle design, we used separate instruction and data memories because we needed to read the instruction memory and read or write the data memory all in one cycle. Now, we choose to use a combined memory for both instructions and data. This is more realistic, and it is feasible because we can read the instruction in one cycle, then read or write the data in a separate cycle. The PC and register file remain unchanged. We gradually build the datapath by adding components to handle each step of each instruction. The new connections are emphasized in black (or blue, for new control signals), whereas the hardware that has already been studied is shown in gray.

The PC contains the address of the instruction to execute. The first step is to read this instruction from instruction memory. Figure 7.17 shows that the PC is simply connected to the address input of the instruction memory. The instruction is read and stored in a new nonarchitectural

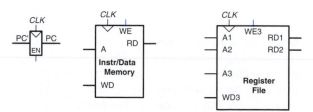

Figure 7.16 State elements with unified instruction/data memory

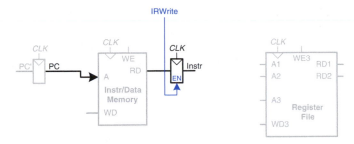

Figure 7.17 Fetch instruction from memory

Instruction Register so that it is available for future cycles. The Instruction Register receives an enable signal, called *IRWrite*, that is asserted when it should be updated with a new instruction.

As we did with the single-cycle processor, we will work out the datapath connections for the lw instruction. Then we will enhance the datapath to handle the other instructions. For a lw instruction, the next step is to read the source register containing the base address. This register is specified in the rs field of the instruction, $Instr_{25:21}$. These bits of the instruction are connected to one of the address inputs, *A1*, of the register file, as shown in Figure 7.18. The register file reads the register onto *RD1*. This value is stored in another nonarchitectural register, *A*.

The lw instruction also requires an offset. The offset is stored in the immediate field of the instruction, $Instr_{15:0}$ and must be sign-extended to 32 bits, as shown in Figure 7.19. The 32-bit sign-extended value is called *SignImm*. To be consistent, we might store *SignImm* in another nonarchitectural register. However, *SignImm* is a combinational function of *Instr* and will not change while the current instruction is being processed, so there is no need to dedicate a register to hold the constant value.

The address of the load is the sum of the base address and offset. We use an ALU to compute this sum, as shown in Figure 7.20. *ALUControl* should be set to 010 to perform an addition. *ALUResult* is stored in a nonarchitectural register called *ALUOut*.

The next step is to load the data from the calculated address in the memory. We add a multiplexer in front of the memory to choose the

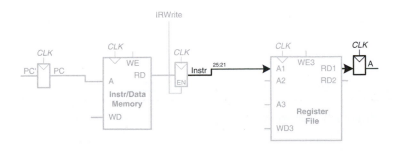

Figure 7.18 Read source operand from register file

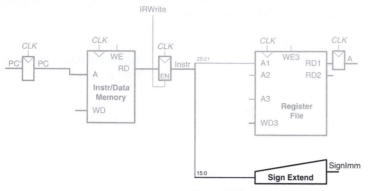

Figure 7.19 Sign-extend the immediate

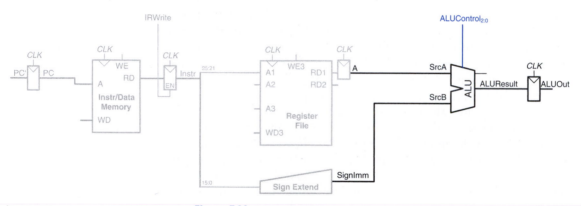

Figure 7.20 Add base address to offset

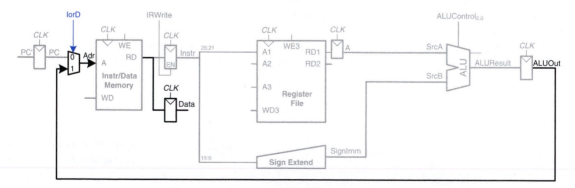

Figure 7.21 Load data from memory

memory address, *Adr*, from either the PC or *ALUOut*, as shown in Figure 7.21. The multiplexer select signal is called *IorD*, to indicate either an instruction or data address. The data read from the memory is stored in another nonarchitectural register, called *Data*. Notice that the address multiplexer permits us to reuse the memory during the lw instruction. On the first step, the address is taken from the PC to fetch the instruction. On a later step, the address is taken from *ALUOut* to load the data. Hence, *IorD* must have different values on different steps. In Section 7.4.2, we develop the FSM controller that generates these sequences of control signals.

Finally, the data is written back to the register file, as shown in Figure 7.22. The destination register is specified by the rt field of the instruction, $Instr_{20:16}$.

While all this is happening, the processor must update the program counter by adding 4 to the old PC. In the single-cycle processor, a separate adder was needed. In the multicycle processor, we can use the existing ALU on one of the steps when it is not busy. To do so, we must insert source multiplexers to choose the PC and the constant 4 as ALU inputs, as shown in Figure 7.23. A two-input multiplexer controlled by *ALUSrcA* chooses either the PC or register *A* as *SrcA*. A four-input multiplexer controlled by *ALUSrcB* chooses either 4 or *SignImm* as *SrcB*. We use the other two multiplexer inputs later when we extend the datapath to handle other instructions. (The numbering of inputs to the multiplexer is arbitrary.) To update the PC, the ALU adds *SrcA* (PC) to *SrcB* (4), and the result is written into the program counter register. The *PCWrite* control signal enables the PC register to be written only on certain cycles.

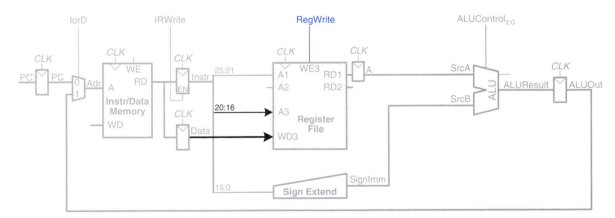

Figure 7.22 Write data back to register file

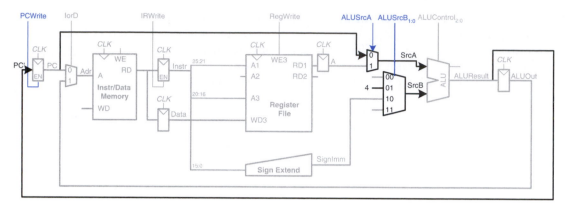

Figure 7.23 Increment PC by 4

This completes the datapath for the lw instruction. Next, let us extend the datapath to also handle the sw instruction. Like the lw instruction, the sw instruction reads a base address from port 1 of the register file and sign-extends the immediate. The ALU adds the base address to the immediate to find the memory address. All of these functions are already supported by existing hardware in the datapath.

The only new feature of sw is that we must read a second register from the register file and write it into the memory, as shown in Figure 7.24. The register is specified in the rt field of the instruction, $Instr_{20:16}$, which is connected to the second port of the register file. When the register is read, it is stored in a nonarchitectural register, B. On the next step, it is sent to the write data port (WD) of the data memory to be written. The memory receives an additional *MemWrite* control signal to indicate that the write should occur.

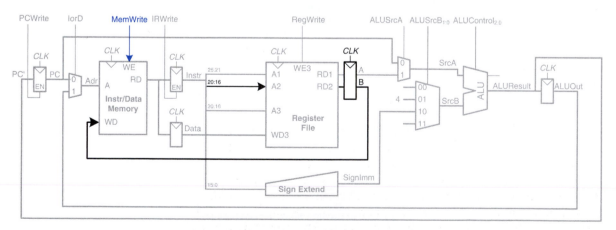

Figure 7.24 Enhanced datapath for sw instruction

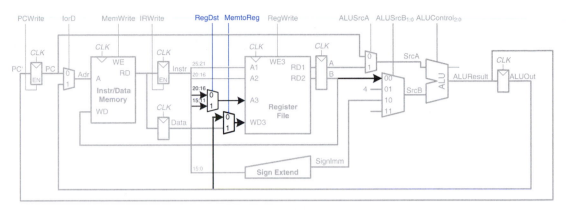

Figure 7.25 Enhanced datapath for R-type instructions

For R-type instructions, the instruction is again fetched, and the two source registers are read from the register file. Another input of the *SrcB* multiplexer is used to choose register *B* as the second source register for the ALU, as shown in Figure 7.25. The ALU performs the appropriate operation and stores the result in *ALUOut*. On the next step, *ALUOut* is written back to the register specified by the rd field of the instruction, $Instr_{15:11}$. This requires two new multiplexers. The *MemtoReg* multiplexer selects whether *WD3* comes from *ALUOut* (for R-type instructions) or from *Data* (for lw). The *RegDst* instruction selects whether the destination register is specified in the rt or rd field of the instruction.

For the beq instruction, the instruction is again fetched, and the two source registers are read from the register file. To determine whether the registers are equal, the ALU subtracts the registers and examines the *Zero* flag. Meanwhile, the datapath must compute the next value of the PC if the branch is taken: $PC' = PC + 4 + SignImm \times 4$. In the single-cycle processor, yet another adder was needed to compute the branch address. In the multicycle processor, the ALU can be reused again to save hardware. On one step, the ALU computes $PC + 4$ and writes it back to the program counter, as was done for other instructions. On another step, the ALU uses this updated PC value to compute $PC + SignImm \times 4$. *SignImm* is left-shifted by 2 to multiply it by 4, as shown in Figure 7.26. The *SrcB* multiplexer chooses this value and adds it to the PC. This sum represents the destination of the branch and is stored in *ALUOut*. A new multiplexer, controlled by *PCSrc*, chooses what signal should be sent to *PC'*. The program counter should be written either when *PCWrite* is asserted or when a branch is taken. A new control signal, *Branch*, indicates that the beq instruction is being executed. The branch is taken if *Zero* is also asserted. Hence, the datapath computes a new PC write

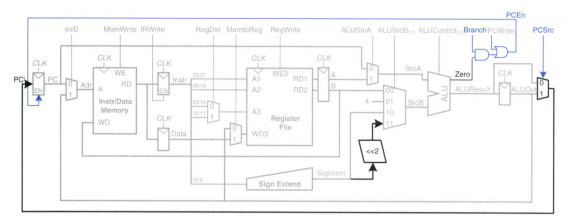

Figure 7.26 Enhanced datapath for beq **instruction**

enable, called *PCEn*, which is TRUE either when *PCWrite* is asserted or when both *Branch* and *Zero* are asserted.

This completes the design of the multicycle MIPS processor datapath. The design process is much like that of the single-cycle processor in that hardware is systematically connected between the state elements to handle each instruction. The main difference is that the instruction is executed in several steps. Nonarchitectural registers are inserted to hold the results of each step. In this way, the ALU can be reused several times, saving the cost of extra adders. Similarly, the instructions and data can be stored in one shared memory. In the next section, we develop an FSM controller to deliver the appropriate sequence of control signals to the datapath on each step of each instruction.

7.4.2 Multicycle Control

As in the single-cycle processor, the control unit computes the control signals based on the opcode and funct fields of the instruction, $Instr_{31:26}$ and $Instr_{5:0}$. Figure 7.27 shows the entire multicycle MIPS processor with the control unit attached to the datapath. The datapath is shown in black, and the control unit is shown in blue.

As in the single-cycle processor, the control unit is partitioned into a main controller and an ALU decoder, as shown in Figure 7.28. The ALU decoder is unchanged and follows the truth table of Table 7.2. Now, however, the main controller is an FSM that applies the proper control signals on the proper cycles or steps. The sequence of control signals depends on the instruction being executed. In the remainder of this section, we will develop the FSM state transition diagram for the main controller.

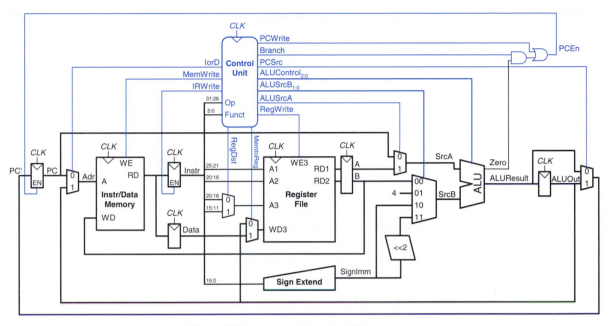

Figure 7.27 Complete multicycle MIPS processor

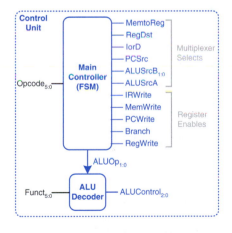

Figure 7.28 Control unit internal structure

The main controller produces multiplexer select and register enable signals for the datapath. The select signals are *MemtoReg*, *RegDst*, *IorD*, *PCSrc*, *ALUSrcB*, and *ALUSrcA*. The enable signals are *IRWrite*, *MemWrite*, *PCWrite*, *Branch*, and *RegWrite*.

To keep the following state transition diagrams readable, only the relevant control signals are listed. Select signals are listed only when their value matters; otherwise, they are don't cares. Enable signals are listed only when they are asserted; otherwise, they are 0.

The first step for any instruction is to fetch the instruction from memory at the address held in the PC. The FSM enters this state on reset. To read memory, $IorD = 0$, so the address is taken from the PC. *IRWrite* is asserted to write the instruction into the instruction register, IR. Meanwhile, the PC should be incremented by 4 to point to the next instruction. Because the ALU is not being used for anything else, the processor can use it to compute $PC + 4$ at the same time that it fetches the instruction. $ALUSrcA = 0$, so *SrcA* comes from the PC. $ALUSrcB = 01$, so *SrcB* is the constant 4. $ALUOp = 00$, so the ALU decoder produces $ALUControl = 010$ to make the ALU add. To update the PC with this new value, $PCSrc = 0$, and *PCWrite* is asserted. These control signals are shown in Figure 7.29. The data flow on this step is shown in Figure 7.30, with the instruction fetch shown using the dashed blue line and the PC increment shown using the dashed gray line.

The next step is to read the register file and decode the instruction. The register file always reads the two sources specified by the rs and rt fields of the instruction. Meanwhile, the immediate is sign-extended. Decoding involves examining the opcode of the instruction to determine what to do next. No control signals are necessary to decode the instruction, but the FSM must wait 1 cycle for the reading and decoding to complete, as shown in Figure 7.31. The new state is highlighted in blue. The data flow is shown in Figure 7.32.

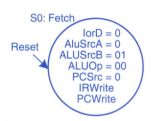

Figure 7.29 Fetch

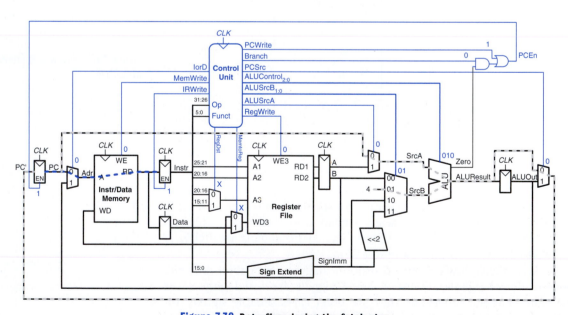

Figure 7.30 Data flow during the fetch step

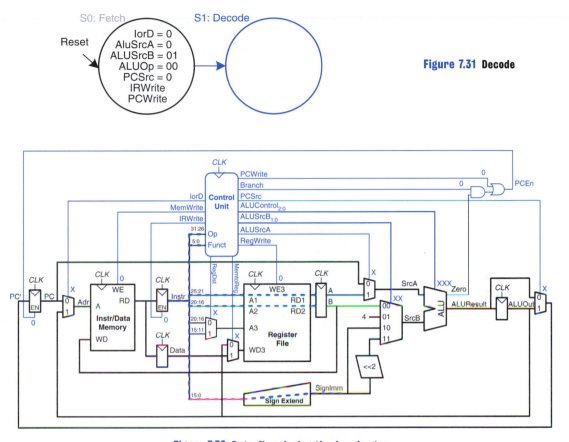

Figure 7.31 Decode

Figure 7.32 Data flow during the decode step

Now the FSM proceeds to one of several possible states, depending on the opcode. If the instruction is a memory load or store (lw or sw), the multicycle processor computes the address by adding the base address to the sign-extended immediate. This requires $ALUSrcA = 1$ to select register A and $ALUSrcB = 10$ to select $SignImm$. $ALUOp = 00$, so the ALU adds. The effective address is stored in the $ALUOut$ register for use on the next step. This FSM step is shown in Figure 7.33, and the data flow is shown in Figure 7.34.

If the instruction is lw, the multicycle processor must next read data from memory and write it to the register file. These two steps are shown in Figure 7.35. To read from memory, $IorD = 1$ to select the memory address that was just computed and saved in $ALUOut$. This address in memory is read and saved in the Data register during step S3. On the next step, S4, $Data$ is written to the register file. $MemtoReg = 1$ to select

Figure 7.33 Memory address
computation

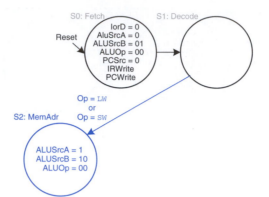

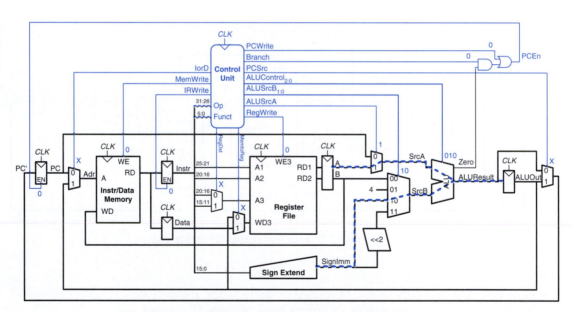

Figure 7.34 Data flow during memory address computation

Data, and *RegDst* = 0 to pull the destination register from the rt field
of the instruction. *RegWrite* is asserted to perform the write, completing
the lw instruction. Finally, the FSM returns to the initial state, S0, to
fetch the next instruction. For these and subsequent steps, try to visualize the data flow on your own.

From state S2, if the instruction is sw, the data read from the second
port of the register file is simply written to memory. *IorD* = 1 to select
the address computed in S2 and saved in *ALUOut*. *MemWrite* is
asserted to write the memory. Again, the FSM returns to S0 to fetch the
next instruction. The added step is shown in Figure 7.36.

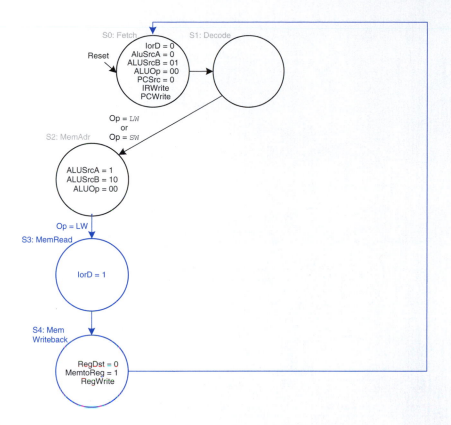

S0: Fetch
S1: Decode

Reset

IorD = 0
AluSrcA = 0
ALUSrcB = 01
ALUOp = 00
PCSrc = 0
IRWrite
PCWrite

Op = LW
or
Op = SW

S2: MemAdr

ALUSrcA = 1
ALUSrcB = 10
ALUOp = 00

Op = LW

S3: MemRead

IorD = 1

S4: Mem
Writeback

RegDst = 0
MemtoReg = 1
RegWrite

Figure 7.35 Memory read

If the opcode indicates an R-type instruction, the multicycle processor must calculate the result using the ALU and write that result to the register file. Figure 7.37 shows these two steps. In S6, the instruction is executed by selecting the *A* and *B* registers (*ALUSrcA* = 1, *ALUSrcB* = 00) and performing the ALU operation indicated by the funct field of the instruction. *ALUOp* = 10 for all R-type instructions. The *ALUResult* is stored in *ALUOut*. In S7, *ALUOut* is written to the register file, *RegDst* = 1, because the destination register is specified in the rd field of the instruction. *MemtoReg* = 0 because the write data, *WD3*, comes from *ALUOut*. *RegWrite* is asserted to write the register file.

For a beq instruction, the processor must calculate the destination address and compare the two source registers to determine whether the branch should be taken. This requires two uses of the ALU and hence might seem to demand two new states. Notice, however, that the ALU was not used during S1 when the registers were being read. The processor might as well use the ALU at that time to compute the destination address by adding the incremented PC, *PC* + 4, to *SignImm* × 4, as shown in

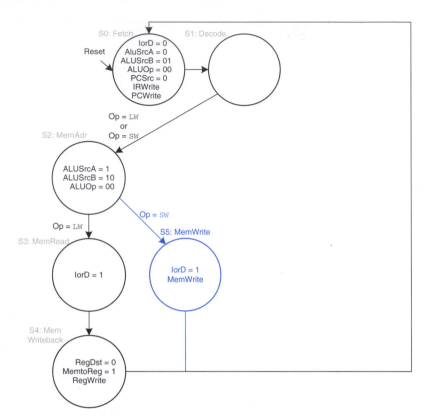

Figure 7.36 Memory write

Figure 7.38 (see page 396). *ALUSrcA* = 0 to select the incremented PC, *ALUSrcB* = 11 to select *SignImm* × 4, and *ALUOp* = 00 to add. The destination address is stored in *ALUOut*. If the instruction is not beq, the computed address will not be used in subsequent cycles, but its computation was harmless. In S8, the processor compares the two registers by subtracting them and checking to determine whether the result is 0. If it is, the processor branches to the address that was just computed. *ALUSrcA* = 1 to select register *A*; *ALUSrcB* = 00 to select register *B*; *ALUOp* = 01 to subtract; *PCSrc* = 1 to take the destination address from *ALUOut*, and *Branch* = 1 to update the PC with this address if the ALU result is 0.[2]

Putting these steps together, Figure 7.39 shows the complete main controller state transition diagram for the multicycle processor (see page 397). Converting it to hardware is a straightforward but tedious task using the techniques of Chapter 3. Better yet, the FSM can be coded in an HDL and synthesized using the techniques of Chapter 4.

---

[2] Now we see why the *PCSrc* multiplexer is necessary to choose *PC′* from either *ALUResult* (in S0) or *ALUOut* (in S8).

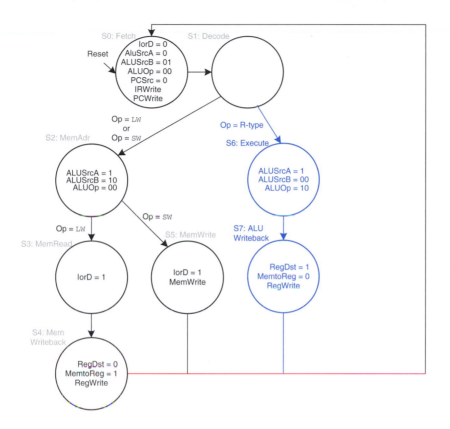

Figure 7.37 Execute R-type operation

7.4.3 More Instructions

As we did in Section 7.3.3 for the single-cycle processor, let us now extend the multicycle processor to support the `addi` and `j` instructions. The next two examples illustrate the general design process to support new instructions.

Example 7.5 `addi` **INSTRUCTION**

Modify the multicycle processor to support `addi`.

Solution: The datapath is already capable of adding registers to immediates, so all we need to do is add new states to the main controller FSM for `addi`, as shown in Figure 7.40 (see page 398). The states are similar to those for R-type instructions. In S9, register A is added to *SignImm* ($ALUSrcA = 1$, $ALUSrcB = 10$, $ALUOp = 00$) and the result, *ALUResult*, is stored in *ALUOut*. In S10, *ALUOut* is written

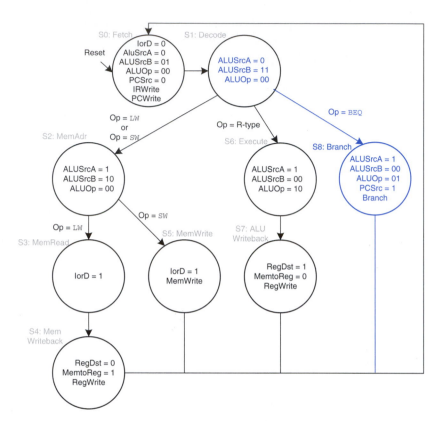

Figure 7.38 Branch

to the register specified by the rt field of the instruction (*RegDst* = 0, *MemtoReg* = 0, *RegWrite* asserted). The astute reader may notice that S2 and S9 are identical and could be merged into a single state.

Example 7.6 j INSTRUCTION

Modify the multicycle processor to support j.

Solution: First, we must modify the datapath to compute the next PC value in the case of a j instruction. Then we add a state to the main controller to handle the instruction.

Figure 7.41 shows the enhanced datapath (see page 399). The jump destination address is formed by left-shifting the 26-bit addr field of the instruction by two bits, then prepending the four most significant bits of the already incremented PC. The *PCSrc* multiplexer is extended to take this address as a third input.

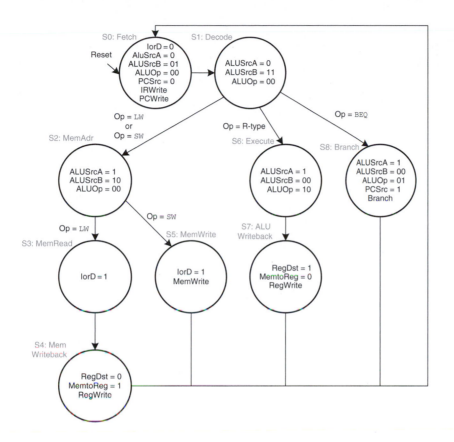

Figure 7.39 Complete multicycle control FSM

Figure 7.42 shows the enhanced main controller (see page 400). The new state, S11, simply selects *PC'* as the *PCJump* value (*PCSrc* = 10) and writes the PC. Note that the *PCSrc* select signal is extended to two bits in S0 and S8 as well.

7.4.4 Performance Analysis

The execution time of an instruction depends on both the number of cycles it uses and the cycle time. Whereas the single-cycle processor performed all instructions in one cycle, the multicycle processor uses varying numbers of cycles for the various instructions. However, the multicycle processor does less work in a single cycle and, thus, has a shorter cycle time.

The multicycle processor requires three cycles for beq and j instructions, four cycles for sw, addi, and R-type instructions, and five cycles for lw instructions. The CPI depends on the relative likelihood that each instruction is used.

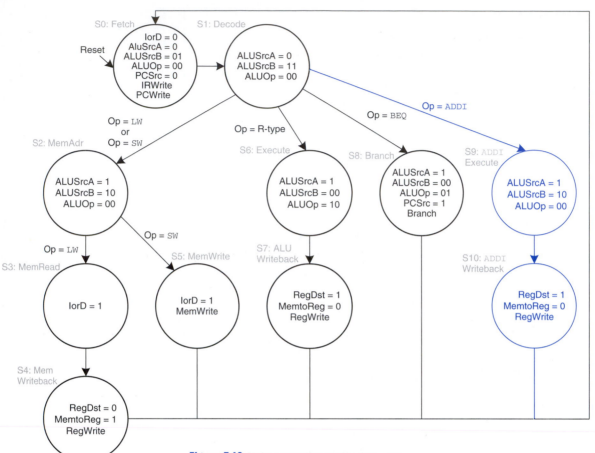

Figure 7.40 Main controller states for `addi`

Example 7.7 MULTICYCLE PROCESSOR CPI

The SPECINT2000 benchmark consists of approximately 25% loads, 10% stores, 11% branches, 2% jumps, and 52% R-type instructions.[3] Determine the average CPI for this benchmark.

Solution: The average CPI is the sum over each instruction of the CPI for that instruction multiplied by the fraction of the time that instruction is used. For this benchmark, Average CPI = $(0.11 + 0.02)(3) + (0.52 + 0.10)(4) + (0.25)(5) = 4.12$. This is better than the worst-case CPI of 5, which would be required if all instructions took the same time.

[3] Data from Patterson and Hennessy, *Computer Organization and Design*, 3rd Edition, Morgan Kaufmann, 2005.

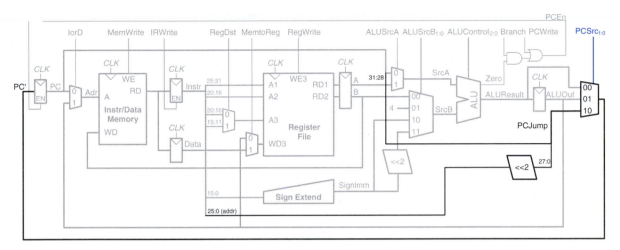

Figure 7.41 Multicycle MIPS datapath enhanced to support the j instruction

Recall that we designed the multicycle processor so that each cycle involved one ALU operation, memory access, or register file access. Let us assume that the register file is faster than the memory and that writing memory is faster than reading memory. Examining the datapath reveals two possible critical paths that would limit the cycle time:

$$T_c = t_{pcq} + t_{mux} + \max(t_{ALU} + t_{mux}, t_{mem}) + t_{setup} \qquad (7.4)$$

The numerical values of these times will depend on the specific implementation technology.

Example 7.8 PROCESSOR PERFORMANCE COMPARISON

Ben Bitdiddle is wondering whether he would be better off building the multicycle processor instead of the single-cycle processor. For both designs, he plans on using a 65 nm CMOS manufacturing process with the delays given in Table 7.6. Help him compare each processor's execution time for 100 billion instructions from the SPECINT2000 benchmark (see Example 7.7).

Solution: According to Equation 7.4, the cycle time of the multicycle processor is $T_{c2} = 30 + 25 + 250 + 20 = 325$ ps. Using the CPI of 4.12 from Example 7.7, the total execution time is $T_2 = (100 \times 10^9$ instructions$)(4.12$ cycles/instruction$)(325 \times 10^{-12}$ s/cycle$) = 133.9$ seconds. According to Example 7.4, the single-cycle processor had a cycle time of $T_{c1} = 950$ ps, a CPI of 1, and a total execution time of 95 seconds.

One of the original motivations for building a multicycle processor was to avoid making all instructions take as long as the slowest one. Unfortunately, this example shows that the multicycle processor is slower than the single-cycle

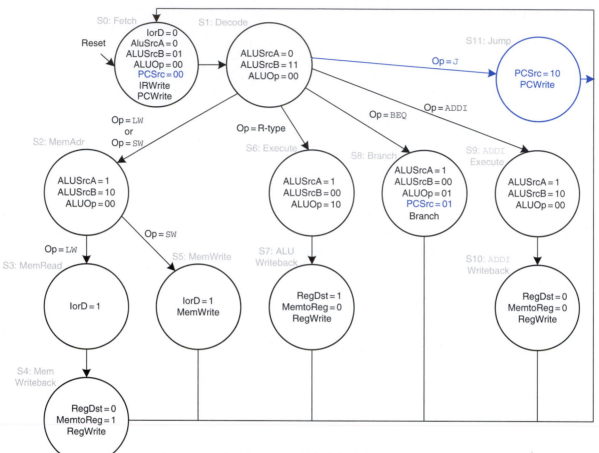

Figure 7.42 Main controller state for j

processor given the assumptions of CPI and circuit element delays. The fundamental problem is that even though the slowest instruction, lw, was broken into five steps, the multicycle processor cycle time was not nearly improved five-fold. This is partly because not all of the steps are exactly the same length, and partly because the 50-ps sequencing overhead of the register clk-to-Q and setup time must now be paid on every step, not just once for the entire instruction. In general, engineers have learned that it is difficult to exploit the fact that some computations are faster than others unless the differences are large.

Compared with the single-cycle processor, the multicycle processor is likely to be less expensive because it eliminates two adders and combines the instruction and data memories into a single unit. It does, however, require five nonarchitectural registers and additional multiplexers.

7.5 PIPELINED PROCESSOR

Pipelining, introduced in Section 3.6, is a powerful way to improve the throughput of a digital system. We design a pipelined processor by subdividing the single-cycle processor into five pipeline stages. Thus, five instructions can execute simultaneously, one in each stage. Because each stage has only one-fifth of the entire logic, the clock frequency is almost five times faster. Hence, the latency of each instruction is ideally unchanged, but the throughput is ideally five times better. Microprocessors execute millions or billions of instructions per second, so throughput is more important than latency. Pipelining introduces some overhead, so the throughput will not be quite as high as we might ideally desire, but pipelining nevertheless gives such great advantage for so little cost that all modern high-performance microprocessors are pipelined.

Reading and writing the memory and register file and using the ALU typically constitute the biggest delays in the processor. We choose five pipeline stages so that each stage involves exactly one of these slow steps. Specifically, we call the five stages *Fetch*, *Decode*, *Execute*, *Memory*, and *Writeback*. They are similar to the five steps that the multicycle processor used to perform lw. In the *Fetch* stage, the processor reads the instruction from instruction memory. In the *Decode* stage, the processor reads the source operands from the register file and decodes the instruction to produce the control signals. In the *Execute* stage, the processor performs a computation with the ALU. In the *Memory* stage, the processor reads or writes data memory. Finally, in the *Writeback* stage, the processor writes the result to the register file, when applicable.

Figure 7.43 shows a timing diagram comparing the single-cycle and pipelined processors. Time is on the horizontal axis, and instructions are on the vertical axis. The diagram assumes the logic element delays from Table 7.6 but ignores the delays of multiplexers and registers. In the single-cycle processor, Figure 7.43(a), the first instruction is read from memory at time 0; next the operands are read from the register file; and then the ALU executes the necessary computation. Finally, the data memory may be accessed, and the result is written back to the register file by 950 ps. The second instruction begins when the first completes. Hence, in this diagram, the single-cycle processor has an instruction latency of $250 + 150 + 200 + 250 + 100 = 950$ ps and a throughput of 1 instruction per 950 ps (1.05 billion instructions per second).

In the pipelined processor, Figure 7.43(b), the length of a pipeline stage is set at 250 ps by the slowest stage, the memory access (in the Fetch or Memory stage). At time 0, the first instruction is fetched from memory. At 250 ps, the first instruction enters the Decode stage, and

402

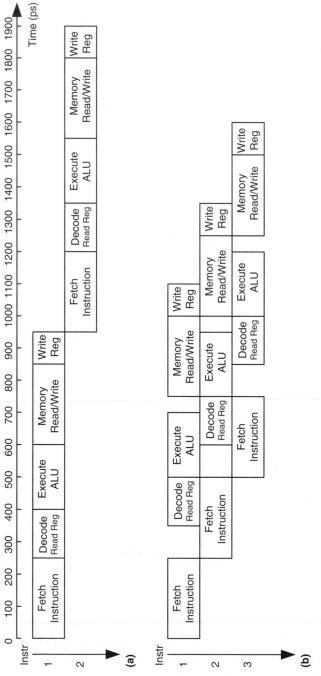

Figure 7.43 Timing diagrams: (a) single-cycle processor, (b) pipelined processor

a second instruction is fetched. At 500 ps, the first instruction executes, the second instruction enters the Decode stage, and a third instruction is fetched. And so forth, until all the instructions complete. The instruction latency is $5 \times 250 = 1250$ ps. The throughput is 1 instruction per 250 ps (4 billion instructions per second). Because the stages are not perfectly balanced with equal amounts of logic, the latency is slightly longer for the pipelined than for the single-cycle processor. Similarly, the throughput is not quite five times as great for a five-stage pipeline as for the single-cycle processor. Nevertheless, the throughput advantage is substantial.

Figure 7.44 shows an abstracted view of the pipeline in operation in which each stage is represented pictorially. Each pipeline stage is represented with its major component—instruction memory (IM), register file (RF) read, ALU execution, data memory (DM), and register file write-back—to illustrate the flow of instructions through the pipeline. Reading across a row shows the clock cycles in which a particular instruction is in each stage. For example, the sub instruction is fetched in cycle 3 and executed in cycle 5. Reading down a column shows what the various pipeline stages are doing on a particular cycle. For example, in cycle 6, the or instruction is being fetched from instruction memory, while $s1 is being read from the register file, the ALU is computing $t5 AND $t6, the data memory is idle, and the register file is writing a sum to $s3. Stages are shaded to indicate when they are used. For example, the data memory is used by lw in cycle 4 and by sw in cycle 8. The instruction memory and ALU are used in every cycle. The register file is written by

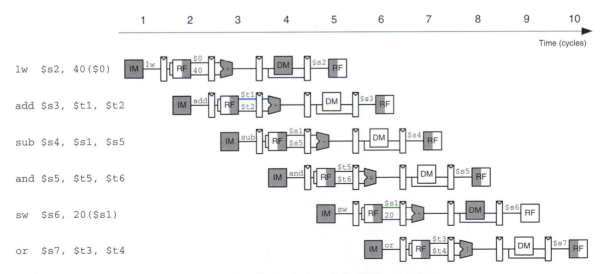

Figure 7.44 Abstract view of pipeline in operation

every instruction except sw. We assume that in the pipelined processor, the register file is written in the first part of a cycle and read in the second part, as suggested by the shading. This way, data can be written and read back within a single cycle.

A central challenge in pipelined systems is handling *hazards* that occur when the results of one instruction are needed by a subsequent instruction before the former instruction has completed. For example, if the add in Figure 7.44 used $s2 rather than $t2, a hazard would occur because the $s2 register has not been written by the lw by the time it is read by the add. This section explores *forwarding, stalls*, and *flushes* as methods to resolve hazards. Finally, this section revisits performance analysis considering sequencing overhead and the impact of hazards.

7.5.1 Pipelined Datapath

The pipelined datapath is formed by chopping the single-cycle datapath into five stages separated by pipeline registers. Figure 7.45(a) shows the single-cycle datapath stretched out to leave room for the pipeline registers. Figure 7.45(b) shows the pipelined datapath formed by inserting four pipeline registers to separate the datapath into five stages. The stages and their boundaries are indicated in blue. Signals are given a suffix (F, D, E, M, or W) to indicate the stage in which they reside.

The register file is peculiar because it is read in the Decode stage and written in the Writeback stage. It is drawn in the Decode stage, but the write address and data come from the Writeback stage. This feedback will lead to pipeline hazards, which are discussed in Section 7.5.3.

One of the subtle but critical issues in pipelining is that all signals associated with a particular instruction must advance through the pipeline in unison. Figure 7.45(b) has an error related to this issue. Can you find it?

The error is in the register file write logic, which should operate in the Writeback stage. The data value comes from *ResultW*, a Writeback stage signal. But the address comes from *WriteRegE*, an Execute stage signal. In the pipeline diagram of Figure 7.44, during cycle 5, the result of the lw instruction would be incorrectly written to register $s4 rather than $s2.

Figure 7.46 shows a corrected datapath. The *WriteReg* signal is now pipelined along through the Memory and Writeback stages, so it remains in sync with the rest of the instruction. *WriteRegW* and *ResultW* are fed back together to the register file in the Writeback stage.

The astute reader may notice that the *PC'* logic is also problematic, because it might be updated with a Fetch or a Memory stage signal (*PCPlus4F* or *PCBranchM*). This control hazard will be fixed in Section 7.5.3.

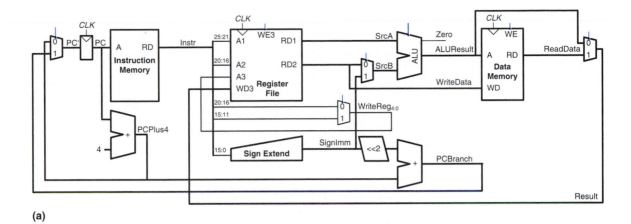

(a)

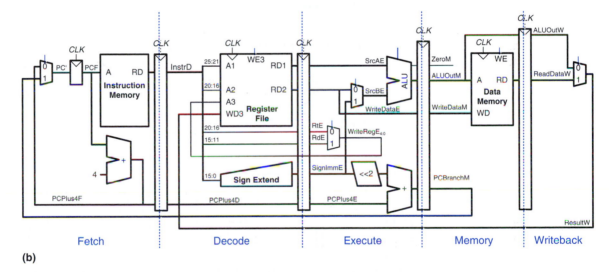

(b)

Figure 7.45 Single-cycle and pipelined datapaths

7.5.2 Pipelined Control

The pipelined processor takes the same control signals as the single-cycle processor and therefore uses the same control unit. The control unit examines the opcode and funct fields of the instruction in the Decode stage to produce the control signals, as was described in Section 7.3.2. These control signals must be pipelined along with the data so that they remain synchronized with the instruction.

The entire pipelined processor with control is shown in Figure 7.47. *RegWrite* must be pipelined into the Writeback stage before it feeds back to the register file, just as *WriteReg* was pipelined in Figure 7.46.

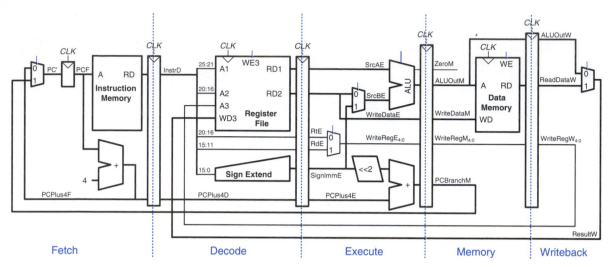

Figure 7.46 Corrected pipelined datapath

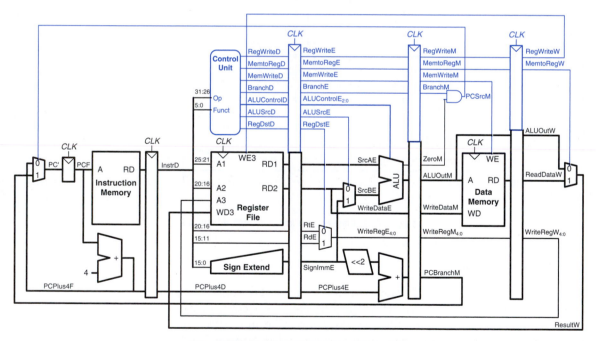

Figure 7.47 Pipelined processor with control

7.5.3 Hazards

In a pipelined system, multiple instructions are handled concurrently. When one instruction is *dependent* on the results of another that has not yet completed, a *hazard* occurs.

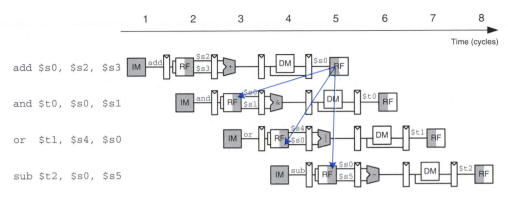

Figure 7.48 Abstract pipeline diagram illustrating hazards

The register file can be read and written in the same cycle. Let us assume that the write takes place during the first half of the cycle and the read takes place during the second half of the cycle, so that a register can be written and read back in the same cycle without introducing a hazard.

Figure 7.48 illustrates hazards that occur when one instruction writes a register ($s0) and subsequent instructions read this register. This is called a *read after write* (*RAW*) hazard. The add instruction writes a result into $s0 in the first half of cycle 5. However, the and instruction reads $s0 on cycle 3, obtaining the wrong value. The or instruction reads $s0 on cycle 4, again obtaining the wrong value. The sub instruction reads $s0 in the second half of cycle 5, obtaining the correct value, which was written in the first half of cycle 5. Subsequent instructions also read the correct value of $s0. The diagram shows that hazards may occur in this pipeline when an instruction writes a register and either of the two subsequent instructions read that register. Without special treatment, the pipeline will compute the wrong result.

On closer inspection, however, observe that the sum from the add instruction is computed by the ALU in cycle 3 and is not strictly needed by the and instruction until the ALU uses it in cycle 4. In principle, we should be able to forward the result from one instruction to the next to resolve the RAW hazard without slowing down the pipeline. In other situations explored later in this section, we may have to stall the pipeline to give time for a result to be computed before the subsequent instruction uses the result. In any event, something must be done to solve hazards so that the program executes correctly despite the pipelining.

Hazards are classified as data hazards or control hazards. A *data hazard* occurs when an instruction tries to read a register that has not yet been written back by a previous instruction. A *control hazard* occurs when the decision of what instruction to fetch next has not been made by the time the fetch takes place. In the remainder of this section, we will enhance the pipelined processor with a hazard unit that detects hazards and handles them appropriately, so that the processor executes the program correctly.

Solving Data Hazards with Forwarding

Some data hazards can be solved by *forwarding* (also called *bypassing*) a result from the Memory or Writeback stage to a dependent instruction in the Execute stage. This requires adding multiplexers in front of the ALU to select the operand from either the register file or the Memory or Writeback stage. Figure 7.49 illustrates this principle. In cycle 4, $s0 is forwarded from the Memory stage of the add instruction to the Execute stage of the dependent and instruction. In cycle 5, $s0 is forwarded from the Writeback stage of the add instruction to the Execute stage of the dependent or instruction.

Forwarding is necessary when an instruction in the Execute stage has a source register matching the destination register of an instruction in the Memory or Writeback stage. Figure 7.50 modifies the pipelined processor to support forwarding. It adds a *hazard detection unit* and two forwarding multiplexers. The hazard detection unit receives the two source registers from the instruction in the Execute stage and the destination registers from the instructions in the Memory and Writeback stages. It also receives the *RegWrite* signals from the Memory and Writeback stages to know whether the destination register will actually be written (for example, the sw and beq instructions do not write results to the register file and hence do not need to have their results forwarded). Note that the *RegWrite* signals are *connected by name*. In other words, rather than cluttering up the diagram with long wires running from the control signals at the top to the hazard unit at the bottom, the connections are indicated by a short stub of wire labeled with the control signal name to which it is connected.

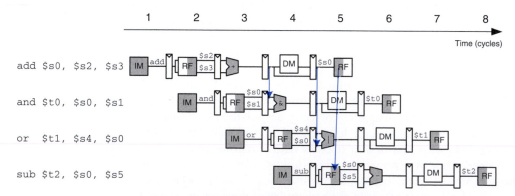

Figure 7.49 Abstract pipeline diagram illustrating forwarding

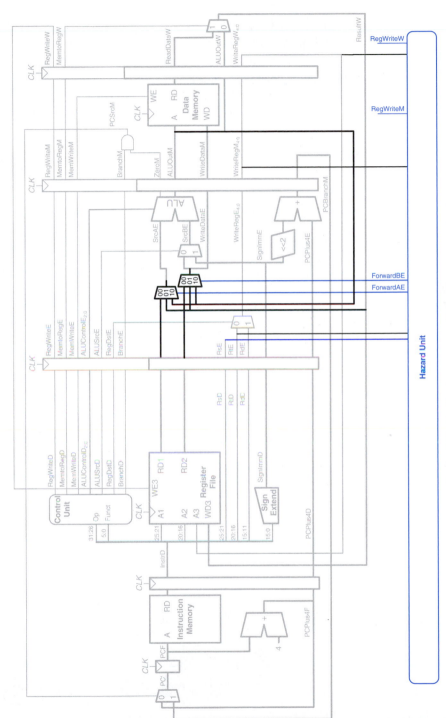

Figure 7.50 Pipelined processor with forwarding to solve hazards

The hazard detection unit computes control signals for the forwarding multiplexers to choose operands from the register file or from the results in the Memory or Writeback stage. It should forward from a stage if that stage will write a destination register and the destination register matches the source register. However, $0 is hardwired to 0 and should never be forwarded. If both the Memory and Writeback stages contain matching destination registers, the Memory stage should have priority, because it contains the more recently executed instruction. In summary, the function of the forwarding logic for *SrcA* is given below. The forwarding logic for *SrcB* (*ForwardBE*) is identical except that it checks rt rather than rs.

```
if        ((rsE != 0) AND (rsE == WriteRegM) AND RegWriteM) then
                                    ForwardAE = 10
else if   ((rsE != 0) AND (rsE == WriteRegW) AND RegWriteW) then
                                    ForwardAE = 01
else                                ForwardAE = 00
```

Solving Data Hazards with Stalls

Forwarding is sufficient to solve RAW data hazards when the result is computed in the Execute stage of an instruction, because its result can then be forwarded to the Execute stage of the next instruction. Unfortunately, the lw instruction does not finish reading data until the end of the Memory stage, so its result cannot be forwarded to the Execute stage of the next instruction. We say that the lw instruction has a *two-cycle latency*, because a dependent instruction cannot use its result until two cycles later. Figure 7.51 shows this problem. The lw instruction receives data from memory at the end of cycle 4. But the and instruction needs that data as a source operand at the beginning of cycle 4. There is no way to solve this hazard with forwarding.

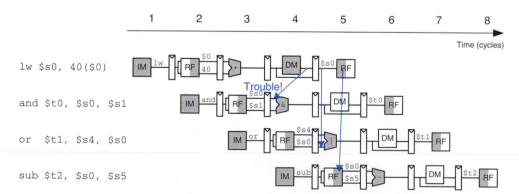

Figure 7.51 Abstract pipeline diagram illustrating trouble forwarding from lw

The alternative solution is to *stall* the pipeline, holding up operation until the data is available. Figure 7.52 shows stalling the dependent instruction (and) in the Decode stage. and enters the Decode stage in cycle 3 and stalls there through cycle 4. The subsequent instruction (or) must remain in the Fetch stage during both cycles as well, because the Decode stage is full.

In cycle 5, the result can be forwarded from the Writeback stage of lw to the Execute stage of and. In cycle 6, source $s0 of the or instruction is read directly from the register file, with no need for forwarding.

Notice that the Execute stage is unused in cycle 4. Likewise, Memory is unused in Cycle 5 and Writeback is unused in cycle 6. This unused stage propagating through the pipeline is called a *bubble*, and it behaves like a nop instruction. The bubble is introduced by zeroing out the Execute stage control signals during a Decode stall so that the bubble performs no action and changes no architectural state.

In summary, stalling a stage is performed by disabling the pipeline register, so that the contents do not change. When a stage is stalled, all previous stages must also be stalled, so that no subsequent instructions are lost. The pipeline register directly after the stalled stage must be cleared to prevent bogus information from propagating forward. Stalls degrade performance, so they should only be used when necessary.

Figure 7.53 modifies the pipelined processor to add stalls for lw data dependencies. The hazard unit examines the instruction in the Execute stage. If it is lw and its destination register (rtE) matches either source operand of the instruction in the Decode stage (rsD or rtD), that instruction must be stalled in the Decode stage until the source operand is ready.

Stalls are supported by adding enable inputs (*EN*) to the Fetch and Decode pipeline registers and a synchronous reset/clear (*CLR*) input to the Execute pipeline register. When a lw stall occurs, *StallD* and *StallF*

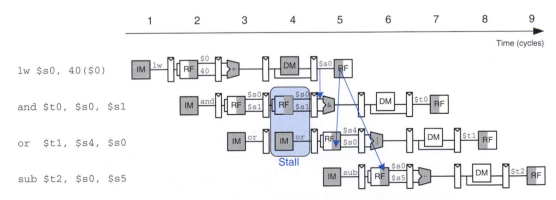

Figure 7.52 Abstract pipeline diagram illustrating stall to solve hazards

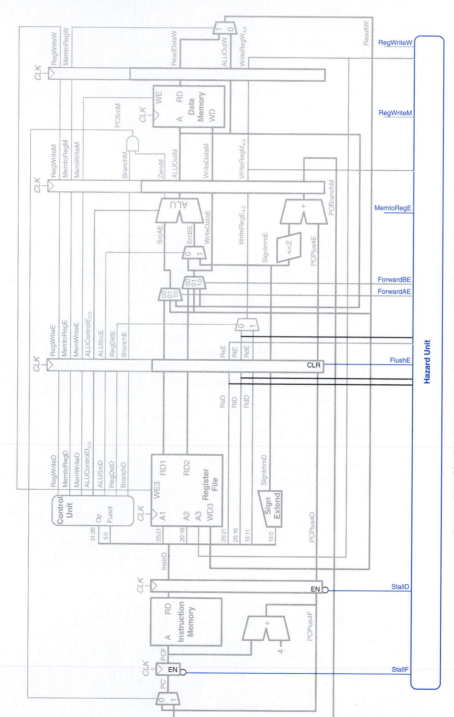

Figure 7.53 Pipelined processor with stalls to solve lw data hazard

are asserted to force the Decode and Fetch stage pipeline registers to hold their old values. *FlushE* is also asserted to clear the contents of the Execute stage pipeline register, introducing a bubble.[4]

The *MemtoReg* signal is asserted for the `lw` instruction. Hence, the logic to compute the stalls and flushes is

```
lwstall = ((rsD  == rtE) OR (rtD == rtE)) AND MemtoRegE
StallF  = StallD = FlushE = lwstall
```

Solving Control Hazards

The `beq` instruction presents a control hazard: the pipelined processor does not know what instruction to fetch next, because the branch decision has not been made by the time the next instruction is fetched.

One mechanism for dealing with the control hazard is to stall the pipeline until the branch decision is made (i.e., *PCSrc* is computed). Because the decision is made in the Memory stage, the pipeline would have to be stalled for three cycles at every branch. This would severely degrade the system performance.

An alternative is to predict whether the branch will be taken and begin executing instructions based on the prediction. Once the branch decision is available, the processor can throw out the instructions if the prediction was wrong. In particular, suppose that we predict that branches are not taken and simply continue executing the program in order. If the branch should have been taken, the three instructions following the branch must be *flushed* (discarded) by clearing the pipeline registers for those instructions. These wasted instruction cycles are called the *branch misprediction penalty*.

Figure 7.54 shows such a scheme, in which a branch from address 20 to address 64 is taken. The branch decision is not made until cycle 4, by which point the and, or, and sub instructions at addresses 24, 28, and 2C have already been fetched. These instructions must be flushed, and the slt instruction is fetched from address 64 in cycle 5. This is somewhat of an improvement, but flushing so many instructions when the branch is taken still degrades performance.

We could reduce the branch misprediction penalty if the branch decision could be made earlier. Making the decision simply requires comparing the values of two registers. Using a dedicated equality comparator is much faster than performing a subtraction and zero detection. If the comparator is fast enough, it could be moved back into the Decode stage, so that the operands are read from the register file and compared to determine the next PC by the end of the Decode stage.

---

[4] Strictly speaking, only the register designations (*RsE*, *RtE*, and *RdE*) and the control signals that might update memory or architectural state (*RegWrite*, *MemWrite*, and *Branch*) need to be cleared; as long as these signals are cleared, the bubble can contain random data that has no effect.

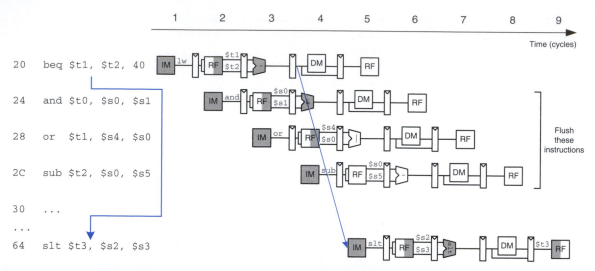

Figure 7.54 Abstract pipeline diagram illustrating flushing when a branch is taken

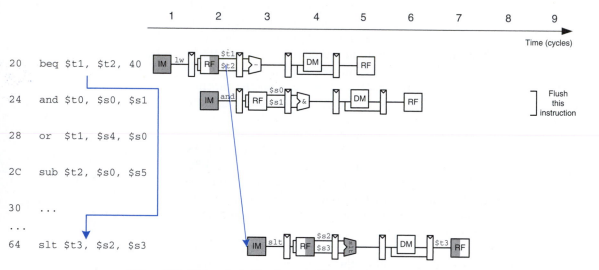

Figure 7.55 Abstract pipeline diagram illustrating earlier branch decision

Figure 7.55 shows the pipeline operation with the early branch decision being made in cycle 2. In cycle 3, the and instruction is flushed and the slt instruction is fetched. Now the branch misprediction penalty is reduced to only one instruction rather than three.

Figure 7.56 modifies the pipelined processor to move the branch decision earlier and handle control hazards. An equality comparator is added to the Decode stage and the *PCSrc* AND gate is moved earlier, so

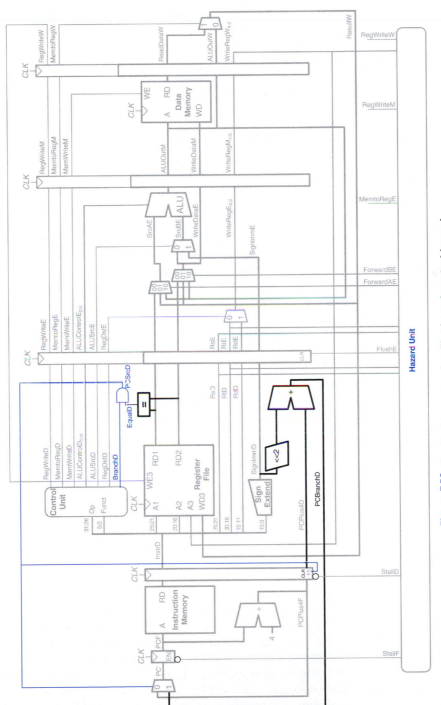

Figure 7.56 Pipelined processor handling branch control hazard

that *PCSrc* can be determined in the Decoder stage rather than the Memory stage. The *PCBranch* adder must also be moved into the Decode stage so that the destination address can be computed in time. The synchronous clear input (*CLR*) connected to *PCSrcD* is added to the Decode stage pipeline register so that the incorrectly fetched instruction can be flushed when a branch is taken.

Unfortunately, the early branch decision hardware introduces a new RAW data hazard. Specifically, if one of the source operands for the branch was computed by a previous instruction and has not yet been written into the register file, the branch will read the wrong operand value from the register file. As before, we can solve the data hazard by forwarding the correct value if it is available or by stalling the pipeline until the data is ready.

Figure 7.57 shows the modifications to the pipelined processor needed to handle the Decode stage data dependency. If a result is in the Writeback stage, it will be written in the first half of the cycle and read during the second half, so no hazard exists. If the result of an ALU instruction is in the Memory stage, it can be forwarded to the equality comparator through two new multiplexers. If the result of an ALU instruction is in the Execute stage or the result of a `lw` instruction is in the Memory stage, the pipeline must be stalled at the Decode stage until the result is ready.

The function of the Decode stage forwarding logic is given below.

```
ForwardAD = (rsD != 0) AND (rsD == WriteRegM) AND RegWriteM
ForwardBD = (rtD != 0) AND (rtD == WriteRegM) AND RegWriteM
```

The function of the stall detection logic for a branch is given below. The processor must make a branch decision in the Decode stage. If either of the sources of the branch depends on an ALU instruction in the Execute stage or on a `lw` instruction in the Memory stage, the processor must stall until the sources are ready.

```
branchstall =
  BranchD AND RegWriteE AND (WriteRegE == rsD OR WriteRegE == rtD)
                          OR
  BranchD AND MemtoRegM AND (WriteRegM == rsD OR WriteRegM == rtD)
```

Now the processor might stall due to either a load or a branch hazard:

```
StallF = StallD = FlushE = lwstall OR branchstall
```

Hazard Summary

In summary, RAW data hazards occur when an instruction depends on the result of another instruction that has not yet been written into the register file. The data hazards can be resolved by forwarding if the result is computed soon enough; otherwise, they require stalling the pipeline until the result is available. Control hazards occur when the decision of what instruction to fetch has not been made by the time the next instruction must be fetched. Control hazards are solved by predicting which

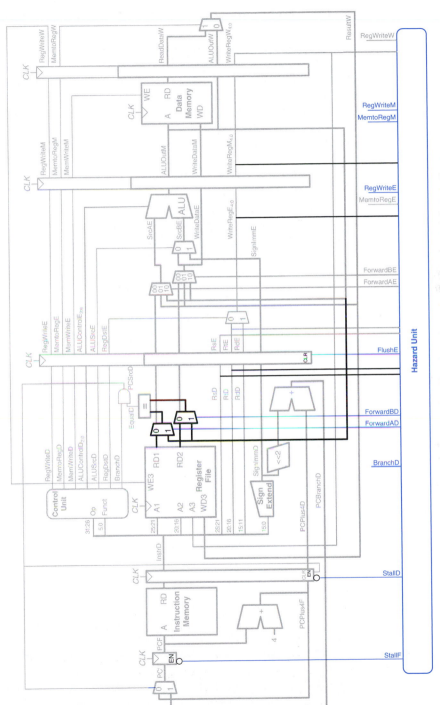

Figure 7.57 Pipelined processor handling data dependencies for branch instructions

instruction should be fetched and flushing the pipeline if the prediction is later determined to be wrong. Moving the decision as early as possible minimizes the number of instructions that are flushed on a misprediction. You may have observed by now that one of the challenges of designing a pipelined processor is to understand all the possible interactions between instructions and to discover all the hazards that may exist. Figure 7.58 shows the complete pipelined processor handling all of the hazards.

7.5.4 More Instructions

Supporting new instructions in the pipelined processor is much like supporting them in the single-cycle processor. However, new instructions may introduce hazards that must be detected and solved.

In particular, supporting addi and j instructions on the pipelined processor requires enhancing the controller, exactly as was described in Section 7.3.3, and adding a jump multiplexer to the datapath after the branch multiplexer. Like a branch, the jump takes place in the Decode stage, so the subsequent instruction in the Fetch stage must be flushed. Designing this flush logic is left as Exercise 7.29.

7.5.5 Performance Analysis

The pipelined processor ideally would have a CPI of 1, because a new instruction is issued every cycle. However, a stall or a flush wastes a cycle, so the CPI is slightly higher and depends on the specific program being executed.

Example 7.9 PIPELINED PROCESSOR CPI

The SPECINT2000 benchmark considered in Example 7.7 consists of approximately 25% loads, 10% stores, 11% branches, 2% jumps, and 52% R-type instructions. Assume that 40% of the loads are immediately followed by an instruction that uses the result, requiring a stall, and that one quarter of the branches are mispredicted, requiring a flush. Assume that jumps always flush the subsequent instruction. Ignore other hazards. Compute the average CPI of the pipelined processor.

Solution: The average CPI is the sum over each instruction of the CPI for that instruction multiplied by the fraction of time that instruction is used. Loads take one clock cycle when there is no dependency and two cycles when the processor must stall for a dependency, so they have a CPI of $(0.6)(1) + (0.4)(2) = 1.4$. Branches take one clock cycle when they are predicted properly and two when they are not, so they have a CPI of $(0.75)(1) + (0.25)(2) = 1.25$. Jumps always have a CPI of 2. All other instructions have a CPI of 1. Hence, for this benchmark, Average CPI = $(0.25)(1.4) + (0.1)(1) + (0.11)(1.25) + (0.02)(2) + (0.52)(1) = 1.15$.

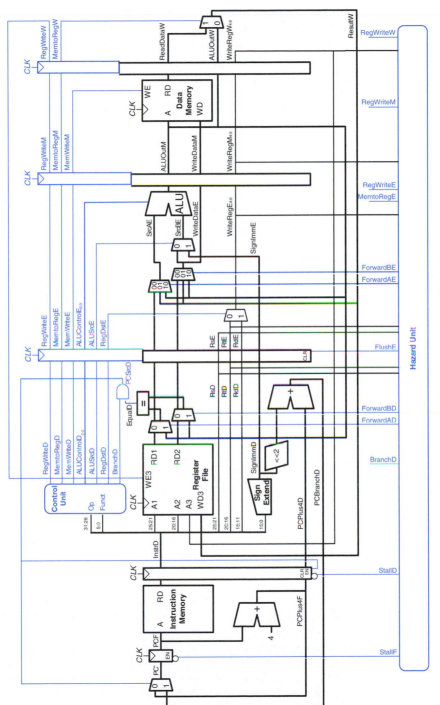

Figure 7.58 Pipelined processor with full hazard handling

419

We can determine the cycle time by considering the critical path in each of the five pipeline stages shown in Figure 7.58. Recall that the register file is written in the first half of the Writeback cycle and read in the second half of the Decode cycle. Therefore, the cycle time of the Decode and Writeback stages is twice the time necessary to do the half-cycle of work.

$$T_c = max \begin{pmatrix} t_{pcq} + t_{mem} + t_{setup} & \text{Fetch} \\ 2(t_{RFread} + t_{mux} + t_{eq} + t_{AND} + t_{mux} + t_{setup}) & \text{Decode} \\ t_{pcq} + t_{mux} + t_{mux} + t_{ALU} + t_{setup} & \text{Execute} \\ t_{pcq} + t_{memwrite} + t_{setup} & \text{Memory} \\ 2(t_{pcq} + t_{mux} + t_{RFwrite}) & \text{Writeback} \end{pmatrix} \qquad (7.5)$$

Example 7.10 PROCESSOR PERFORMANCE COMPARISON

Ben Bitdiddle needs to compare the pipelined processor performance to that of the single-cycle and multicycle processors considered in Example 7.8. Most of the logic delays were given in Table 7.6. The other element delays are 40 ps for an equality comparator, 15 ps for an AND gate, 100 ps for a register file write, and 220 ps for a memory write. Help Ben compare the execution time of 100 billion instructions from the SPECINT2000 benchmark for each processor.

Solution: According to Equation 7.5, the cycle time of the pipelined processor is T_{c3} = max[30 + 250 + 20, 2(150 + 25 + 40 + 15 + 25 + 20), 30 + 25 + 25 + 200 + 20, 30 + 220 + 20, 2(30 + 25 + 100)] = 550 ps. According to Equation 7.1, the total execution time is T_3 = (100 × 10^9 instructions)(1.15 cycles/ instruction)(550 × 10^{-12} s/cycle) = 63.3 seconds. This compares to 95 seconds for the single-cycle processor and 133.9 seconds for the multicycle processor.

The pipelined processor is substantially faster than the others. However, its advantage over the single-cycle processor is nowhere near the five-fold speedup one might hope to get from a five-stage pipeline. The pipeline hazards introduce a small CPI penalty. More significantly, the sequencing overhead (clk-to-Q and setup times) of the registers applies to every pipeline stage, not just once to the overall datapath. Sequencing overhead limits the benefits one can hope to achieve from pipelining.

The careful reader might observe that the Decode stage is substantially slower than the others, because the register file write, read, and branch comparison must all happen in half a cycle. Perhaps moving the branch comparison to the Decode stage was not such a good idea. If branches were resolved in the Execute stage instead, the CPI would increase slightly, because a mispredict would flush two instructions, but the cycle time would decrease substantially, giving an overall speedup.

The pipelined processor is similar in hardware requirements to the single-cycle processor, but it adds a substantial number of pipeline registers, along with multiplexers and control logic to resolve hazards.

7.6 HDL REPRESENTATION*

This section presents HDL code for the single-cycle MIPS processor supporting all of the instructions discussed in this chapter, including addi and j. The code illustrates good coding practices for a moderately complex system. HDL code for the multicycle processor and pipelined processor are left to Exercises 7.22 and 7.33.

In this section, the instruction and data memories are separated from the main processor and connected by address and data busses. This is more realistic, because most real processors have external memory. It also illustrates how the processor can communicate with the outside world.

The processor is composed of a datapath and a controller. The controller, in turn, is composed of the main decoder and the ALU decoder. Figure 7.59 shows a block diagram of the single-cycle MIPS processor interfaced to external memories.

The HDL code is partitioned into several sections. Section 7.6.1 provides HDL for the single-cycle processor datapath and controller. Section 7.6.2 presents the generic building blocks, such as registers and multiplexers, that are used by any microarchitecture. Section 7.6.3

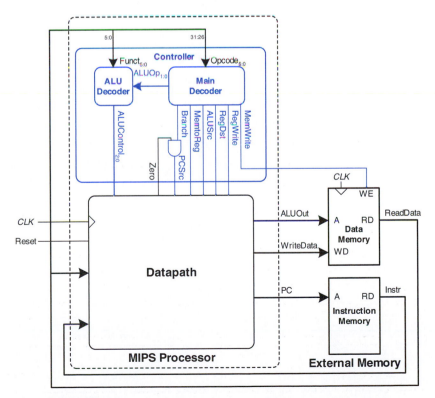

Figure 7.59 MIPS single-cycle processor interfaced to external memory

introduces the testbench and external memories. The HDL is available in electronic form on the this book's Web site (see the preface).

7.6.1 Single-Cycle Processor

The main modules of the single-cycle MIPS processor module are given in the following HDL examples.

HDL Example 7.1 SINGLE-CYCLE MIPS PROCESSOR

Verilog

```verilog
module mips (input          clk, reset,
            output [31:0]  pc,
            input  [31:0]  instr,
            output         memwrite,
            output [31:0]  aluout, writedata,
            input  [31:0]  readdata);

 wire       memtoreg, branch,
            alusrc, regdst, regwrite, jump;
 wire [2:0] alucontrol;

 controller c(instr[31:26], instr[5:0], zero,
             memtoreg, memwrite, pcsrc,
             alusrc, regdst, regwrite, jump,
             alucontrol);
 datapath dp(clk, reset, memtoreg, pcsrc,
             alusrc, regdst, regwrite, jump,
             alucontrol,
             zero, pc, instr,
             aluout, writedata, readdata);
endmodule
```

VHDL

```vhdl
library IEEE; use IEEE.STD_LOGIC_1164.all;
entity mips is -- single cycle MIPS processor
  port(clk, reset:        in  STD_LOGIC;
       pc:                out STD_LOGIC_VECTOR(31 downto 0);
       instr:             in  STD_LOGIC_VECTOR(31 downto 0);
       memwrite:          out STD_LOGIC;
       aluout, writedata: out STD_LOGIC_VECTOR(31 downto 0);
       readdata:          in  STD_LOGIC_VECTOR(31 downto 0));
end;
architecture struct of mips is
  component controller
    port(op, funct:          in  STD_LOGIC_VECTOR(5 downto 0);
         zero:               in  STD_LOGIC;
         memtoreg,memwrite:  out STD_LOGIC;
         pcsrc, alusrc:      out STD_LOGIC;
         regdst, regwrite:   out STD_LOGIC;
         jump:               out STD_LOGIC;
         alucontrol:         out STD_LOGIC_VECTOR(2 downto 0));
  end component;
  component datapath
    port(clk, reset:         in  STD_LOGIC;
         memtoreg, pcsrc:    in  STD_LOGIC;
         alusrc, regdst:     in  STD_LOGIC;
         regwrite, jump:     in  STD_LOGIC;
         alucontrol:         in  STD_LOGIC_VECTOR(2 downto 0);
         zero:               out STD_LOGIC;
         pc:                 buffer STD_LOGIC_VECTOR(31 downto 0);
         instr:              in  STD_LOGIC_VECTOR(31 downto 0);
         aluout, writedata:  buffer STD_LOGIC_VECTOR(31 downto 0);
         readdata:           in  STD_LOGIC_VECTOR(31 downto 0));
  end component;
  signal memtoreg, alusrc, regdst, regwrite, jump, pcsrc:
    STD_LOGIC;
  signal zero: STD_LOGIC;
  signal alucontrol: STD_LOGIC_VECTOR(2 downto 0);
begin
  cont: controller port map(instr(31 downto 26), instr
                           (5 downto 0), zero, memtoreg,
                            memwrite, pcsrc, alusrc, regdst,
                            regwrite, jump, alucontrol);
  dp: datapath port map(clk, reset, memtoreg, pcsrc, alusrc,
                        regdst, regwrite, jump, alucontrol,
                        zero, pc, instr, aluout, writedata,
                        readdata);
end;
```

HDL Example 7.2 CONTROLLER

Verilog

```verilog
module controller(input   [5:0] op, funct,
                  input         zero,
                  output        memtoreg, memwrite,
                  output        pcsrc, alusrc,
                  output        regdst, regwrite,
                  output        jump,
                  output [2:0]  alucontrol);

  wire [1:0] aluop;
  wire       branch;

  maindec md(op, memtoreg, memwrite, branch,
             alusrc, regdst, regwrite, jump,
             aluop);
  aludec ad(funct, aluop, alucontrol);

  assign pcsrc = branch & zero;
endmodule
```

VHDL

```vhdl
library IEEE; use IEEE.STD_LOGIC_1164.all;
entity controller is -- single cycle control decoder
  port(op, funct:          in  STD_LOGIC_VECTOR(5 downto 0);
       zero:               in  STD_LOGIC;
       memtoreg, memwrite: out STD_LOGIC;
       pcsrc, alusrc:      out STD_LOGIC;
       regdst, regwrite:   out STD_LOGIC;
       jump:               out STD_LOGIC;
       alucontrol:         out STD_LOGIC_VECTOR(2 downto 0));
end;

architecture struct of controller is
  component maindec
    port(op:                 in  STD_LOGIC_VECTOR(5 downto 0);
         memtoreg, memwrite: out STD_LOGIC;
         branch, alusrc:     out STD_LOGIC;
         regdst, regwrite:   out STD_LOGIC;
         jump:               out STD_LOGIC;
         aluop:              out STD_LOGIC_VECTOR(1 downto 0));
  end component;
  component aludec
    port(funct:      in  STD_LOGIC_VECTOR(5 downto 0);
         aluop:      in  STD_LOGIC_VECTOR(1 downto 0);
         alucontrol: out STD_LOGIC_VECTOR(2 downto 0));
  end component;
  signal aluop:  STD_LOGIC_VECTOR(1 downto 0);
  signal branch: STD_LOGIC;
begin
  md: maindec port map(op, memtoreg, memwrite, branch,
                       alusrc, regdst, regwrite, jump, aluop);
  ad: aludec port map(funct, aluop, alucontrol);

  pcsrc <= branch and zero;
end;
```

HDL Example 7.3 MAIN DECODER

Verilog

```verilog
module maindec(input  [5:0] op,
               output       memtoreg, memwrite,
               output       branch, alusrc,
               output       regdst, regwrite,
               output       jump,
               output [1:0] aluop);

  reg [8:0] controls;

  assign {regwrite, regdst, alusrc,
          branch, memwrite,
          memtoreg, jump, aluop} = controls;

  always @(*)
    case(op)
      6'b000000: controls <= 9'b110000010; //Rtyp
      6'b100011: controls <= 9'b101001000; //LW
      6'b101011: controls <= 9'b001010000; //SW
      6'b000100: controls <= 9'b000100001; //BEQ
      6'b001000: controls <= 9'b101000000; //ADDI
      6'b000010: controls <= 9'b000000100; //J
      default:   controls <= 9'bxxxxxxxxx; //???
    endcase
endmodule
```

VHDL

```vhdl
library IEEE; use IEEE.STD_LOGIC_1164.all;
entity maindec is -- main control decoder
  port (op:                    in  STD_LOGIC_VECTOR (5 downto 0);
        memtoreg, memwrite:    out STD_LOGIC;
        branch, alusrc:        out STD_LOGIC;
        regdst, regwrite:      out STD_LOGIC;
        jump:                  out STD_LOGIC;
        aluop:                 out STD_LOGIC_VECTOR (1 downto 0));
end;

architecture behave of maindec is
  signal controls: STD_LOGIC_VECTOR(8 downto 0);
begin
  process(op) begin
    case op is
      when "000000" => controls <= "110000010"; -- Rtyp
      when "100011" => controls <= "101001000"; -- LW
      when "101011" => controls <= "001010000"; -- SW
      when "000100" => controls <= "000100001"; -- BEQ
      when "001000" => controls <= "101000000"; -- ADDI
      when "000010" => controls <= "000000100"; -- J
      when others   => controls <= "---------"; -- illegal op
    end case;
  end process;

  regwrite <= controls(8);
  regdst   <= controls(7);
  alusrc   <= controls(6);
  branch   <= controls(5);
  memwrite <= controls(4);
  memtoreg <= controls(3);
  jump     <= controls(2);
  aluop    <= controls(1 downto 0);
end;
```

HDL Example 7.4 ALU DECODER

Verilog

```verilog
module aludec (input      [5:0] funct,
               input      [1:0] aluop,
               output reg [2:0] alucontrol);

  always @(*)
    case (aluop)
      2'b00: alucontrol <= 3'b010; // add
      2'b01: alucontrol <= 3'b110; // sub
      default: case(funct)         // RTYPE
          6'b100000: alucontrol <= 3'b010; // ADD
          6'b100010: alucontrol <= 3'b110; // SUB
          6'b100100: alucontrol <= 3'b000; // AND
          6'b100101: alucontrol <= 3'b001; // OR
          6'b101010: alucontrol <= 3'b111; // SLT
          default:   alucontrol <= 3'bxxx; // ???
        endcase
    endcase
endmodule
```

VHDL

```vhdl
library IEEE; use IEEE.STD_LOGIC_1164.all;
entity aludec is -- ALU control decoder
  port (funct:      in  STD_LOGIC_VECTOR (5 downto 0);
        aluop:      in  STD_LOGIC_VECTOR (1 downto 0);
        alucontrol: out STD_LOGIC_VECTOR (2 downto 0));
end;

architecture behave of aludec is
begin
  process (aluop, funct) begin
    case aluop is
      when "00" => alucontrol <= "010"; -- add (for lb/sb/addi)
      when "01" => alucontrol <= "110"; -- sub (for beq)
      when others => case funct is      -- R-type instructions
                       when "100000" => alucontrol <=
                         "010"; -- add
                       when "100010" => alucontrol <=
                         "110"; -- sub
                       when "100100" => alucontrol <=
                         "000"; -- and
                       when "100101" => alucontrol <=
                         "001"; -- or
                       when "101010" => alucontrol <=
                         "111"; -- slt
                       when others   => alucontrol <=
                         "---"; -- ???
                     end case;
    end case;
  end process;
end;
```

Verilog

```verilog
module datapath(input              clk, reset,
                input              memtoreg, pcsrc,
                input              alusrc, regdst,
                input              regwrite, jump,
                input       [2:0]  alucontrol,
                output             zero,
                output      [31:0] pc,
                input       [31:0] instr,
                output      [31:0] aluout, writedata,
                input       [31:0] readdata);

  wire [4:0]  writereg;
  wire [31:0] pcnext, pcnextbr, pcplus4, pcbranch;
  wire [31:0] signimm, signimmsh;
  wire [31:0] srca, srcb;
  wire [31:0] result;

  // next PC logic
  flopr #(32) pcreg(clk, reset, pcnext, pc);
  adder       pcadd1(pc, 32'b100, pcplus4);
  sl2         immsh(signimm, signimmsh);
  adder       pcadd2(pcplus4, signimmsh, pcbranch);
  mux2 #(32)  pcbrmux(pcplus4, pcbranch, pcsrc,
                      pcnextbr);
  mux2 #(32)  pcmux(pcnextbr, {pcplus4[31:28],
                    instr[25:0], 2'b00},
                    jump, pcnext);

  // register file logic
  regfile     rf(clk, regwrite, instr[25:21],
                 instr[20:16], writereg,
                 result, srca, writedata);
  mux2 #(5)   wrmux(instr[20:16], instr[15:11],
                    regdst, writereg);
  mux2 #(32)  resmux(aluout, readdata,
                     memtoreg, result);
  signext     se(instr[15:0], signimm);

  // ALU logic
  mux2 #(32)  srcbmux(writedata, signimm, alusrc,
                      srcb);
  alu         alu(srca, srcb, alucontrol,
                  aluout, zero);
endmodule
```

VHDL

```vhdl
library IEEE; use IEEE.STD_LOGIC_1164.all; use
IEEE.STD_LOGIC_ARITH.all;
entity datapath is -- MIPS datapath
  port(clk, reset:          in    STD_LOGIC;
       memtoreg, pcsrc:     in    STD_LOGIC;
       alusrc, regdst:      in    STD_LOGIC;
       regwrite, jump:      in    STD_LOGIC;
       alucontrol:          in    STD_LOGIC_VECTOR(2 downto 0);
       zero:                out   STD_LOGIC;
       pc:                  buffer STD_LOGIC_VECTOR(31 downto 0);
       instr:               in    STD_LOGIC_VECTOR(31 downto 0);
       aluout, writedata:   buffer STD_LOGIC_VECTOR(31 downto 0);
       readdata:            in    STD_LOGIC_VECTOR(31 downto 0));
end;

architecture struct of datapath is
  component alu
    port(a, b:       in  STD_LOGIC_VECTOR(31 downto 0);
         alucontrol: in  STD_LOGIC_VECTOR(2 downto 0);
         result:     buffer STD_LOGIC_VECTOR(31 downto 0);
         zero:       out STD_LOGIC);
  end component;
  component regfile
    port(clk:          in  STD_LOGIC;
         we3:          in  STD_LOGIC;
         ra1, ra2, wa3: in  STD_LOGIC_VECTOR(4 downto 0);
         wd3:          in  STD_LOGIC_VECTOR(31 downto 0);
         rd1, rd2:     out STD_LOGIC_VECTOR(31 downto 0));
  end component;
  component adder
    port(a, b: in  STD_LOGIC_VECTOR(31 downto 0);
         y:    out STD_LOGIC_VECTOR(31 downto 0));
  end component;
  component sl2
    port(a: in  STD_LOGIC_VECTOR(31 downto 0);
         y: out STD_LOGIC_VECTOR(31 downto 0));
  end component;
  component signext
    port(a: in  STD_LOGIC_VECTOR(15 downto 0);
         y: out STD_LOGIC_VECTOR(31 downto 0));
  end component;
  component flopr generic(width: integer);
    port(clk, reset: in  STD_LOGIC;
         d:          in  STD_LOGIC_VECTOR(width-1 downto 0);
         q:          out STD_LOGIC_VECTOR(width-1 downto 0));
  end component;
  component mux2 generic(width: integer);
    port(d0, d1: in  STD_LOGIC_VECTOR(width-1 downto 0);
         s:      in  STD_LOGIC;
         y:      out STD_LOGIC_VECTOR(width-1 downto 0));
  end component;
  signal writereg: STD_LOGIC_VECTOR(4 downto 0);
  signal pcjump, pcnext, pcnextbr,
         pcplus4, pcbranch: STD_LOGIC_VECTOR(31 downto 0);
  signal signimm, signimmsh: STD_LOGIC_VECTOR(31 downto 0);
  signal srca, srcb, result: STD_LOGIC_VECTOR(31 downto 0);
begin
  -- next PC logic
  pcjump <= pcplus4(31 downto 28) & instr(25 downto 0) & "00";
  pcreg: flopr generic map(32) port map(clk, reset, pcnext, pc);
  pcadd1: adder port map(pc, X"00000004", pcplus4);
  immsh: sl2 port map(signimm, signimmsh);
  pcadd2: adder port map(pcplus4, signimmsh, pcbranch);
  pcbrmux: mux2 generic map(32) port map(pcplus4, pcbranch,
                                         pcsrc, pcnextbr);
  pcmux: mux2 generic map(32) port map(pcnextbr, pcjump, jump,
                                       pcnext);

  -- register file logic
  rf: regfile port map(clk, regwrite, instr(25 downto 21),
                       instr(20 downto 16), writereg, result, srca,
                       writedata);
  wrmux: mux2 generic map(5) port map(instr(20 downto 16),
         instr(15 downto 11), regdst, writereg);
  resmux: mux2 generic map(32) port map(aluout, readdata,
                                         memtoreg, result);
  se: signext port map(instr(15 downto 0), signimm);

  -- ALU logic
  srcbmux: mux2 generic map (32) port map(writedata, signimm,
                                          alusrc, srcb);
  mainalu: alu port map(srca, srcb, alucontrol, aluout, zero);
end;
```

425

7.6.2 Generic Building Blocks

This section contains generic building blocks that may be useful in any MIPS microarchitecture, including a register file, adder, left shift unit, sign-extension unit, resettable flip-flop, and multiplexer. The HDL for the ALU is left to Exercise 5.9.

HDL Example 7.6 REGISTER FILE

Verilog

```
module regfile (input         clk,
                input         we3,
                input  [4:0]  ra1, ra2, wa3,
                input  [31:0] wd3,
                output [31:0] rd1, rd2);

  reg [31:0] rf[31:0];

  // three ported register file
  // read two ports combinationally
  // write third port on rising edge of clock
  // register 0 hardwired to 0

  always @(posedge clk)
    if (we3) rf[wa3] <= wd3;

  assign rd1 = (ra1 != 0) ? rf[ra1] : 0;
  assign rd2 = (ra2 != 0) ? rf[ra2] : 0;
endmodule
```

VHDL

```
library IEEE; use IEEE.STD_LOGIC_1164.all;
use IEEE.STD_LOGIC_UNSIGNED.all;
entity regfile is -- three-port register file
  port(clk:          in  STD_LOGIC;
       we3:          in  STD_LOGIC;
       ra1, ra2, wa3:in  STD_LOGIC_VECTOR(4 downto 0);
       wd3:          in  STD_LOGIC_VECTOR(31 downto 0);
       rd1, rd2:     out STD_LOGIC_VECTOR(31 downto 0));
end;

architecture behave of regfile is
  type ramtype is array (31 downto 0) of STD_LOGIC_VECTOR (31
                        downto 0);
  signal mem: ramtype;
begin
  -- three-ported register file
  -- read two ports combinationally
  -- write third port on rising edge of clock
  process(clk) begin
   if clk'event and clk = '1' then
    if we3 = '1' then mem(CONV_INTEGER(wa3)) <= wd3;
    end if;
   end if;
  end process;
  process (ra1, ra2) begin
    if(conv_integer(ra1) = 0) then rd1 <= X"00000000";
        -- register 0 holds 0
    else rd1 <= mem(CONV_INTEGER(ra1));
    end if;
    if(conv_integer(ra2) = 0) then rd2 <= X"00000000";
    else rd2 <= mem(CONV_INTEGER(ra2));
    end if;
  end process;
end;
```

HDL Example 7.7 ADDER

Verilog

```
module adder (input  [31:0] a, b,
              output [31:0] y);

  assign y = a + b;
endmodule
```

VHDL

```
library IEEE; use IEEE.STD_LOGIC_1164.all;
use IEEE.STD_LOGIC_UNSIGNED.all;
entity adder is - adder
  port (a, b: in  STD_LOGIC_VECTOR(31 downto 0);
        y:    out STD_LOGIC_VECTOR(31 downto 0));
end;

architecture behave of adder is
begin
  y <= a + b;
end;
```

HDL Example 7.8 LEFT SHIFT (MULTIPLY BY 4)

Verilog

```
module sl2(input  [31:0] a,
          output [31:0] y);

  // shift left by 2
  assign y = {a[29:01], 2'b00};
endmodule
```

VHDL

```
library IEEE; use IEEE.STD_LOGIC_1164.all;
entity sl2 is -- shift left by 2
  port(a: in  STD_LOGIC_VECTOR(31 downto 0);
       y: out STD_LOGIC_VECTOR(31 downto 0));
end;

architecture behave of sl2 is
begin
  y <= a(29 downto 0) & "00";
end;
```

HDL Example 7.9 SIGN EXTENSION

Verilog

```
module signext(input  [15:0] a,
               output [31:0] y);

  assign y = {{16{a[15]}}, a};
endmodule
```

VHDL

```
library IEEE; use IEEE.STD_LOGIC_1164.all;
entity signext is -- sign extender
port(a: in  STD_LOGIC_VECTOR (15 downto 0);
     y: out STD_LOGIC_VECTOR (31 downto 0));
end;

architecture behave of signext is
begin
  y <= X"0000" & a when a(15) = '0' else X"ffff" & a;
end;
```

HDL Example 7.10 RESETTABLE FLIP-FLOP

Verilog

```
module flopr #(parameter WIDTH = 8)
             (input              clk, reset,
              input      [WIDTH-1:0] d,
              output reg [WIDTH-1:0] q);

  always @(posedge clk, posedge reset)
    if (reset) q <= 0;
    else       q <= d;
endmodule
```

VHDL

```
library IEEE; use IEEE.STD_LOGIC_1164.all; use
IEEE.STD_LOGIC_ARITH.all;
entity flopr is -- flip-flop with synchronous reset
  generic(width: integer);
  port(clk, reset: in  STD_LOGIC;
       d:          in  STD_LOGIC_VECTOR(width-1 downto 0);
       q:          out STD_LOGIC_VECTOR(width-1 downto 0));
end;

architecture asynchronous of flopr is
begin
  process(clk, reset) begin
    if reset = '1' then q <= CONV_STD_LOGIC_VECTOR(0, width);
    elsif clk'event and clk = '1' then
      q <= d;
    end if;
  end process;
end;
```

HDL Example 7.11 2:1 MULTIPLEXER

Verilog	VHDL
| ```verilog
module mux2 #(parameter WIDTH = 8)
             (input  [WIDTH-1:0] d0, d1,
              input              s,
              output [WIDTH-1:0] y);

  assign y = s ? d1 : d0;
endmodule
``` | ```vhdl
library IEEE; use IEEE.STD_LOGIC_1164.all;
entity mux2 is -- two-input multiplexer
  generic (width: integer);
  port (d0, d1: in  STD_LOGIC_VECTOR(width-1 downto 0);
        s:      in  STD_LOGIC;
        y:      out STD_LOGIC_VECTOR(width-1 downto 0));
end;

architecture behave of mux2 is
begin
  y <= d0 when s = '0' else d1;
end;
``` |

7.6.3 Testbench

The MIPS testbench loads a program into the memories. The program in Figure 7.60 exercises all of the instructions by performing a computation that should produce the correct answer only if all of the instructions are functioning properly. Specifically, the program will write the value 7 to address 84 if it runs correctly, and is unlikely to do so if the hardware is buggy. This is an example of *ad hoc* testing.

```
# mipstest.asm
# David_Harris@hmc.edu 9 November 2005
#
# Test the MIPS processor.
# add, sub, and, or, slt, addi, lw, sw, beq, j
# If successful, it should write the value 7 to address 84
```

#	Assembly	Description	Address	Machine	
main:	addi $2, $0, 5	# initialize $2 = 5	0	20020005	20020005
	addi $3, $0, 12	# initialize $3 = 12	4	2003000c	2003000c
	addi $7, $3, -9	# initialize $7 = 3	8	2067fff7	2067fff7
	or $4, $7, $2	# $4 <= 3 or 5 = 7	c	00e22025	00e22025
	and $5, $3, $4	# $5 <= 12 and 7 = 4	10	00642824	00642824
	add $5, $5, $4	# $5 = 4 + 7 = 11	14	00a42820	00a42820
	beq $5, $7, end	# shouldn't be taken	18	10a7000a	10a7000a
	slt $4, $3, $4	# $4 = 12 < 7 = 0	1c	0064202a	0064202a
	beq $4, $0, around	# should be taken	20	10800001	10800001
	addi $5, $0, 0	# shouldn't happen	24	20050000	20050000
around:	slt $4, $7, $2	# $4 = 3 < 5 = 1	28	00e2202a	00e2202a
	add $7, $4, $5	# $7 = 1 + 11 = 12	2c	00853820	00853820
	sub $7, $7, $2	# $7 = 12 - 5 = 7	30	00e23822	00e23822
	sw $7, 68($3)	# [80] = 7	34	ac670044	ac670044
	lw $2, 80($0)	# $2 = [80] = 7	38	8c020050	8c020050
	j end	# should be taken	3c	08000011	08000011
	addi $2, $0, 1	# shouldn't happen	40	20020001	20020001
end:	sw $2, 84($0)	# write adr 84 = 7	44	ac020054	ac020054

Figure 7.60 Assembly and machine code for MIPS test program

Figure 7.61 Contents of
memfile.dat

The machine code is stored in a hexadecimal file called `memfile.dat` (see Figure 7.61), which is loaded by the testbench during simulation. The file consists of the machine code for the instructions, one instruction per line.

The testbench, top-level MIPS module, and external memory HDL code are given in the following examples. The memories in this example hold 64 words each.

HDL Example 7.12 MIPS TESTBENCH

Verilog

```verilog
module testbench();

  reg    clk;
  reg    reset;

  wire [31:0] writedata, dataadr;
  wire        memwrite;

  // instantiate device to be tested
  top dut(clk, reset, writedata, dataadr, memwrite);

  // initialize test
  initial
    begin
      reset <= 1; # 22; reset <= 0;
    end

  // generate clock to sequence tests
  always
    begin
      clk <= 1; # 5; clk <= 0; # 5;
    end

  // check results
  always @ (negedge clk)
    begin
      if (memwrite) begin
        if (dataadr === 84 & writedata === 7) begin
          $display ("Simulation succeeded");
          $stop;
        end else if (dataadr !== 80) begin
          $display ("Simulation failed");
          $stop;
        end
      end
    end
endmodule
```

VHDL

```vhdl
library IEEE;
use IEEE.STD_LOGIC_1164.all; use IEEE.STD_LOGIC_UNSIGNED.all;
entity testbench is
end;

architecture test of testbench is
  component top
    port(clk, reset:        in  STD_LOGIC;
         writedata, dataadr: out STD_LOGIC_VECTOR(31 downto 0);
         memwrite:           out STD_LOGIC);
  end component;
  signal writedata, dataadr:  STD_LOGIC_VECTOR(31 downto 0);
  signal clk, reset, memwrite: STD_LOGIC;

begin
  -- instantiate device to be tested
  dut: top port map (clk, reset, writedata, dataadr, memwrite);

  -- Generate clock with 10 ns period
  process begin
    clk <= '1';
    wait for 5 ns;
    clk <= '0';
    wait for 5 ns;
  end process;

  -- Generate reset for first two clock cycles
  process begin
    reset <= '1';
    wait for 22 ns;
    reset <= '0';
    wait;
  end process;

  -- check that 7 gets written to address 84
  -- at end of program
  process (clk) begin
    if (clk'event and clk = '0' and memwrite = '1') then
      if (conv_integer(dataadr) = 84 and conv_integer
          (writedata) = 7) then
        report "Simulation succeeded";
      elsif (dataadr /= 80) then
        report "Simulation failed";
      end if;
    end if;
  end process;
end;
```

HDL Example 7.13 MIPS TOP-LEVEL MODULE

Verilog

```
module top (input          clk, reset,
            output [31:0] writedata, dataadr,
            output         memwrite);

  wire [31:0] pc, instr, readdata;

  // instantiate processor and memories
  mips mips (clk, reset, pc, instr, memwrite, dataadr,
             writedata, readdata);
  imem imem (pc[7:2], instr);
  dmem dmem (clk, memwrite, dataadr, writedata,
             readdata);
endmodule
```

VHDL

```
library IEEE;
use IEEE.STD_LOGIC_1164.all; use IEEE.STD_LOGIC_UNSIGNED.all;
entity top is -- top-level design for testing
  port (clk, reset:         in      STD_LOGIC;
        writedata, dataadr: buffer STD_LOGIC_VECTOR (31 downto
                                                        0);
        memwrite:           buffer STD_LOGIC);
end;

architecture test of top is
  component mips
    port (clk, reset:     in  STD_LOGIC;
          pc:                out STD_LOGIC_VECTOR (31 downto 0);
          instr:             in  STD_LOGIC_VECTOR (31 downto 0);
          memwrite:          out STD_LOGIC;
          aluout, writedata: out STD_LOGIC_VECTOR (31 downto 0);
          readdata:          in  STD_LOGIC_VECTOR (31 downto 0));
  end component;
  component imem
    port (a:  in  STD_LOGIC_VECTOR (5 downto 0)
          rd: out STD_LOGIC_VECTOR (31 downto 0));
  end component;
  component dmem
    port (clk, we: in  STD_LOGIC;
          a, wd:   in  STD_LOGIC_VECTOR (31 downto 0);
          rd:      out STD_LOGIC_VECTOR (31 downto 0));
  end component;
  signal pc, instr,
         readdata: STD_LOGIC_VECTOR (31 downto 0);
begin
  -- instantiate processor and memories
  mips1: mips port map (clk, reset, pc, instr, memwrite,
                        dataadr, writedata, readdata);
  imem1: imem port map (pc (7 downto 2), instr);
  dmem1: dmem port map (clk, memwrite, dataadr, writedata,
                        readdata);
end;
```

HDL Example 7.14 MIPS DATA MEMORY

```
module dmem (input          clk, we,
             input  [31:0] a, wd,
             output [31:0] rd);

  reg [31:0] RAM[63:0];

  assign rd = RAM[a[31:2]]; // word aligned

  always @(posedge clk)
    if (we)
      RAM[a[31:2]] <= wd;
endmodule
```

```
library IEEE;
use IEEE.STD_LOGIC_1164.all; use STD.TEXTIO.all;
use IEEE.STD_LOGIC_UNSIGNED.all; use IEEE.STD_LOGIC_ARITH.all;
entity dmem is -- data memory
  port (clk, we: in  STD_LOGIC;
        a, wd:   in  STD_LOGIC_VECTOR (31 downto 0);
        rd:      out STD_LOGIC_VECTOR (31 downto 0));
end;

architecture behave of dmem is
begin
  process is
    type ramtype is array (63 downto 0) of STD_LOGIC_VECTOR
                                         (31 downto 0);
    variable mem: ramtype;
  begin
    -- read or write memory
    loop
      if clk'event and clk = '1' then
        if (we = '1') then mem (CONV_INTEGER (a(7 downto
                                            2))): = wd;
        end if;
      end if;
      rd <= mem (CONV_INTEGER (a (7 downto 2)));
      wait on clk, a;
    end loop;
  end process;
end;
```

HDL Example 7.15 MIPS INSTRUCTION MEMORY

Verilog

```verilog
module imem(input  [5:0]  a,
            output [31:0] rd);

  reg [31:0] RAM[63:0];

  initial
    begin
      $readmemh ("memfile.dat",RAM);
    end

  assign rd = RAM[a]; // word aligned
endmodule
```

VHDL

```vhdl
library IEEE;
use IEEE.STD_LOGIC_1164.all; use STD.TEXTIO.all;
use IEEE.STD_LOGIC_UNSIGNED.all; use IEEE.STD_LOGIC_ARITH.all;

entity imem is -- instruction memory
  port(a:  in  STD_LOGIC_VECTOR (5 downto 0);
       rd: out STD_LOGIC_VECTOR (31 downto 0));
end;

architecture behave of imem is
begin
  process is
    file mem_file: TEXT;
    variable L: line;
    variable ch: character;
    variable index, result: integer;
    type ramtype is array (63 downto 0) of STD_LOGIC_VECTOR
                        (31 downto 0);
    variable mem: ramtype;
  begin
    -- initialize memory from file
    for i in 0 to 63 loop -- set all contents low
      mem(conv_integer(i)) := CONV_STD_LOGIC_VECTOR (0, 32);
    end loop;
    index := 0;
    FILE_OPEN(mem_file, "C:/mips/memfile.dat", READ_MODE);
    while not endfile(mem_file) loop
      readline(mem_file, L);
      result := 0;
      for i in 1 to 8 loop
        read(L, ch);
        if '0' <= ch and ch <= '9' then
          result := result*16 + character'pos(ch) -
                    character'pos('0');
        elsif 'a' <= ch and ch <= 'f' then
          result := result*16 + character'pos(ch) -
                    character'pos('a') + 10;
        else report "Format error on line" & integer'image
          (index) severity error;
        end if;
      end loop;
      mem(index) := CONV_STD_LOGIC_VECTOR (result, 32);
      index := index + 1;
    end loop;

    -- read memory
    loop
      rd <= mem(CONV_INTEGER(a));
      wait on a;
    end loop;
  end process;
end;
```

7.7 EXCEPTIONS*

Section 6.7.2 introduced exceptions, which cause unplanned changes in the flow of a program. In this section, we enhance the multicycle processor to support two types of exceptions: undefined instructions and arithmetic overflow. Supporting exceptions in other microarchitectures follows similar principles.

As described in Section 6.7.2, when an exception takes place, the processor copies the PC to the EPC register and stores a code in the Cause register indicating the source of the exception. Exception causes include 0x28 for undefined instructions and 0x30 for overflow (see Table 6.7). The processor then jumps to the exception handler at memory address 0x80000180. The exception handler is code that responds to the exception. It is part of the operating system.

Also as discussed in Section 6.7.2, the exception registers are part of *Coprocessor 0*, a portion of the MIPS processor that is used for system functions. Coprocessor 0 defines up to 32 special-purpose registers, including Cause and EPC. The exception handler may use the `mfc0` (move from coprocessor 0) instruction to copy these special-purpose registers into a general-purpose register in the register file; the Cause register is Coprocessor 0 register 13, and EPC is register 14.

To handle exceptions, we must add EPC and Cause registers to the datapath and extend the *PCSrc* multiplexer to accept the exception handler address, as shown in Figure 7.62. The two new registers have write enables, *EPCWrite* and *CauseWrite*, to store the PC and exception cause when an exception takes place. The cause is generated by a multiplexer

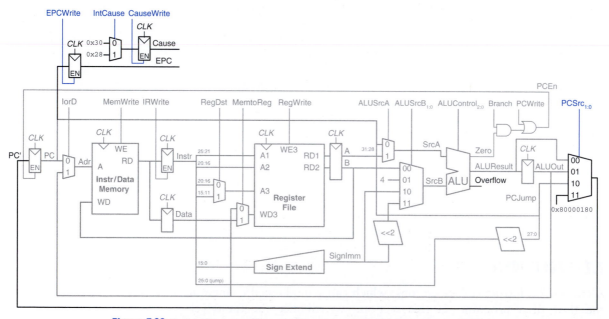

Figure 7.62 Datapath supporting overflow and undefined instruction exceptions

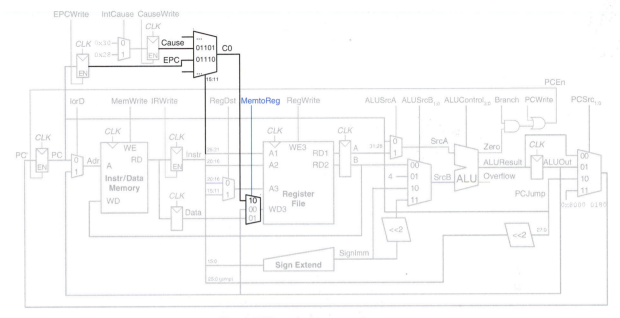

Figure 7.63 Datapath supporting mfc0

that selects the appropriate code for the exception. The ALU must also generate an overflow signal, as was discussed in Section 5.2.4.[5]

To support the mfc0 instruction, we also add a way to select the Coprocessor 0 registers and write them to the register file, as shown in Figure 7.63. The mfc0 instruction specifies the Coprocessor 0 register by $Instr_{15:11}$; in this diagram, only the Cause and EPC registers are supported. We add another input to the *MemtoReg* multiplexer to select the value from Coprocessor 0.

The modified controller is shown in Figure 7.64. The controller receives the overflow flag from the ALU. It generates three new control signals: one to write the EPC, a second to write the Cause register, and a third to select the Cause. It also includes two new states to support the two exceptions and another state to handle mfc0.

If the controller receives an undefined instruction (one that it does not know how to handle), it proceeds to S12, saves the PC in EPC, writes 0x28 to the Cause register, and jumps to the exception handler. Similarly, if the controller detects arithmetic overflow on an add or sub instruction, it proceeds to S13, saves the PC in EPC, writes 0x30

---

[5] Strictly speaking, the ALU should assert overflow only for add and sub, not for other ALU instructions.

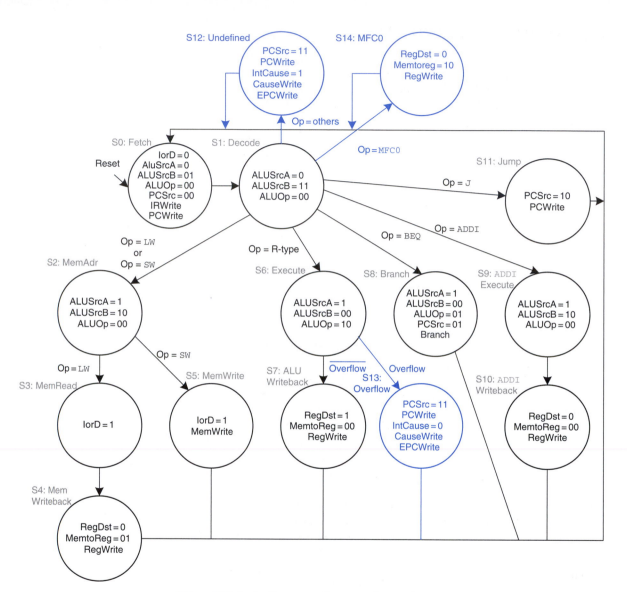

Figure 7.64 Controller supporting exceptions and mfc0

in the Cause register, and jumps to the exception handler. Note that, when an exception occurs, the instruction is discarded and the register file is not written. When a mfc0 instruction is decoded, the processor goes to S14 and writes the appropriate Coprocessor 0 register to the main register file.

7.8 ADVANCED MICROARCHITECTURE*

High-performance microprocessors use a wide variety of techniques to run programs faster. Recall that the time required to run a program is proportional to the period of the clock and to the number of clock cycles per instruction (CPI). Thus, to increase performance we would like to speed up the clock and/or reduce the CPI. This section surveys some existing speedup techniques. The implementation details become quite complex, so we will focus on the concepts. Hennessy & Patterson's *Computer Architecture* text is a definitive reference if you want to fully understand the details.

Every 2 to 3 years, advances in CMOS manufacturing reduce transistor dimensions by 30% in each direction, doubling the number of transistors that can fit on a chip. A manufacturing process is characterized by its *feature size*, which indicates the smallest transistor that can be reliably built. Smaller transistors are faster and generally consume less power. Thus, even if the microarchitecture does not change, the clock frequency can increase because all the gates are faster. Moreover, smaller transistors enable placing more transistors on a chip. Microarchitects use the additional transistors to build more complicated processors or to put more processors on a chip. Unfortunately, power consumption increases with the number of transistors and the speed at which they operate (see Section 1.8). Power consumption is now an essential concern. Microprocessor designers have a challenging task juggling the trade-offs among speed, power, and cost for chips with billions of transistors in some of the most complex systems that humans have ever built.

7.8.1 Deep Pipelines

Aside from advances in manufacturing, the easiest way to speed up the clock is to chop the pipeline into more stages. Each stage contains less logic, so it can run faster. This chapter has considered a classic five-stage pipeline, but 10 to 20 stages are now commonly used.

The maximum number of pipeline stages is limited by pipeline hazards, sequencing overhead, and cost. Longer pipelines introduce more dependencies. Some of the dependencies can be solved by forwarding, but others require stalls, which increase the CPI. The pipeline registers between each stage have sequencing overhead from their setup time and clk-to-Q delay (as well as clock skew). This sequencing overhead makes adding more pipeline stages give diminishing returns. Finally, adding more stages increases the cost because of the extra pipeline registers and hardware required to handle hazards.

Example 7.11 DEEP PIPELINES

Consider building a pipelined processor by chopping up the single-cycle processor into N stages ($N \geq 5$). The single-cycle processor has a propagation delay of 900 ps through the combinational logic. The sequencing overhead of a register is 50 ps. Assume that the combinational delay can be arbitrarily divided into any number of stages and that pipeline hazard logic does not increase the delay. The five-stage pipeline in Example 7.9 has a CPI of 1.15. Assume that each additional stage increases the CPI by 0.1 because of branch mispredictions and other pipeline hazards. How many pipeline stages should be used to make the processor execute programs as fast as possible?

Solution: If the 900-ps combinational logic delay is divided into N stages and each stage also pays 50 ps of sequencing overhead for its pipeline register, the cycle time is $T_c = 900/N + 50$. The CPI is $1.15 + 0.1(N - 5)$. The time per instruction, or instruction time, is the product of the cycle time and the CPI. Figure 7.65 plots the cycle time and instruction time versus the number of stages. The instruction time has a minimum of 231 ps at $N = 11$ stages. This minimum is only slightly better than the 250 ps per instruction achieved with a six-stage pipeline.

In the late 1990s and early 2000s, microprocessors were marketed largely based on clock frequency ($1/T_c$). This pushed microprocessors to use very deep pipelines (20 to 31 stages on the Pentium 4) to maximize the clock frequency, even if the benefits for overall performance were questionable. Power is proportional to clock frequency and also increases with the number of pipeline registers, so now that power consumption is so important, pipeline depths are decreasing.

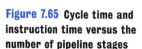

Figure 7.65 Cycle time and instruction time versus the number of pipeline stages

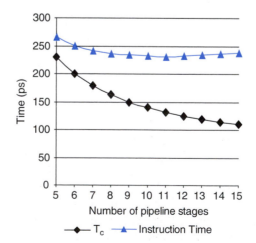

7.8.2 Branch Prediction

An ideal pipelined processor would have a CPI of 1. The branch mispre-diction penalty is a major reason for increased CPI. As pipelines get deeper, branches are resolved later in the pipeline. Thus, the branch mis-prediction penalty gets larger, because all the instructions issued after the mispredicted branch must be flushed. To address this problem, most pipelined processors use a *branch predictor* to guess whether the branch should be taken. Recall that our pipeline from Section 7.5.3 simply pre-dicted that branches are never taken.

Some branches occur when a program reaches the end of a loop (e.g., a `for` or `while` statement) and branches back to repeat the loop. Loops tend to be executed many times, so these backward branches are usually taken. The simplest form of branch prediction checks the direc-tion of the branch and predicts that backward branches should be taken. This is called *static branch prediction*, because it does not depend on the history of the program.

Forward branches are difficult to predict without knowing more about the specific program. Therefore, most processors use *dynamic branch predictors*, which use the history of program execution to guess whether a branch should be taken. Dynamic branch predictors maintain a table of the last several hundred (or thousand) branch instructions that the processor has executed. The table, sometimes called a *branch target buffer*, includes the destination of the branch and a history of whether the branch was taken.

To see the operation of dynamic branch predictors, consider the fol-lowing loop code from Code Example 6.20. The loop repeats 10 times, and the `beq` out of the loop is taken only on the last time.

```
add  $s1, $0, $0      # sum = 0
add  $s0, $0, $0      # i   = 0
addi $t0, $0, 10      # $t0 = 10

for:
  beq  $s0, $t0, done # if i == 10, branch to done
  add  $s1, $s1, $s0  # sum = sum + i
  addi $s0, $s0, 1    # increment i
  j    for
done:
```

A *one-bit dynamic branch predictor* remembers whether the branch was taken the last time and predicts that it will do the same thing the next time. While the loop is repeating, it remembers that the `beq` was not taken last time and predicts that it should not be taken next time. This is a correct prediction until the last branch of the loop, when the branch does get taken. Unfortunately, if the loop is run again, the branch predictor remembers that the last branch was taken. Therefore,

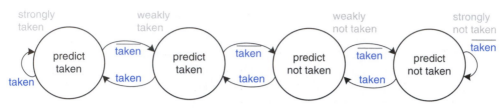

Figure 7.66 2-bit branch predictor state transition diagram

it incorrectly predicts that the branch should be taken when the loop is first run again. In summary, a 1-bit branch predictor mispredicts the first and last branches of a loop.

A 2-bit dynamic branch predictor solves this problem by having four states: *strongly taken, weakly taken, weakly not taken*, and *strongly not taken*, as shown in Figure 7.66. When the loop is repeating, it enters the "strongly not taken" state and predicts that the branch should not be taken next time. This is correct until the last branch of the loop, which is taken and moves the predictor to the "weakly not taken" state. When the loop is first run again, the branch predictor correctly predicts that the branch should not be taken and reenters the "strongly not taken" state. In summary, a 2-bit branch predictor mispredicts only the last branch of a loop.

As one can imagine, branch predictors may be used to track even more history of the program to increase the accuracy of predictions. Good branch predictors achieve better than 90% accuracy on typical programs.

The branch predictor operates in the Fetch stage of the pipeline so that it can determine which instruction to execute on the next cycle. When it predicts that the branch should be taken, the processor fetches the next instruction from the branch destination stored in the branch target buffer. By keeping track of both branch and jump destinations in the branch target buffer, the processor can also avoid flushing the pipeline during jump instructions.

7.8.3 Superscalar Processor

A *superscalar processor* contains multiple copies of the datapath hardware to execute multiple instructions simultaneously. Figure 7.67 shows a block diagram of a two-way superscalar processor that fetches and executes two instructions per cycle. The datapath fetches two instructions at a time from the instruction memory. It has a six-ported register file to read four source operands and write two results back in each cycle. It also contains two ALUs and a two-ported data memory to execute the two instructions at the same time.

A *scalar* processor acts on one piece of data at a time. A *vector* processor acts on several pieces of data with a single instruction. A *superscalar* processor issues several instructions at a time, each of which operates on one piece of data.

Our MIPS pipelined processor is a scalar processor. Vector processors were popular for supercomputers in the 1980s and 1990s because they efficiently handled the long vectors of data common in scientific computations. Modern high-performance microprocessors are superscalar, because issuing several independent instructions is more flexible than processing vectors.

However, modern processors also include hardware to handle short vectors of data that are common in multimedia and graphics applications. These are called *single instruction multiple data* (*SIMD*) units.

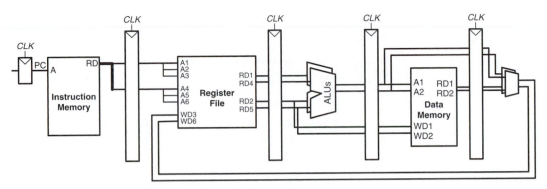

Figure 7.67 Superscalar datapath

Figure 7.68 shows a pipeline diagram illustrating the two-way superscalar processor executing two instructions on each cycle. For this program, the processor has a CPI of 0.5. Designers commonly refer to the reciprocal of the CPI as the *instructions per cycle*, or *IPC*. This processor has an IPC of 2 on this program.

Executing many instructions simultaneously is difficult because of dependencies. For example, Figure 7.69 shows a pipeline diagram running a program with data dependencies. The dependencies in the code are shown in blue. The add instruction is dependent on $t0, which is produced by the lw instruction, so it cannot be issued at the same time as lw. Indeed, the add instruction stalls for yet another cycle so that lw can forward $t0 to add in cycle 5. The other dependencies (between

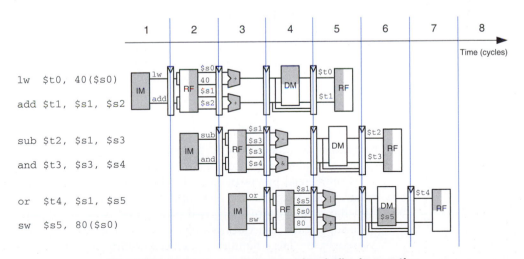

Figure 7.68 Abstract view of a superscalar pipeline in operation

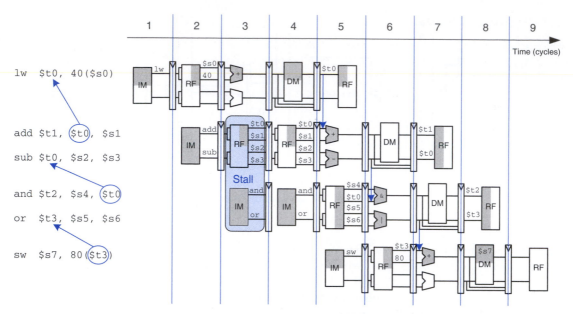

Figure 7.69 Program with data dependencies

sub and and based on $t0, and between or and sw based on $t3) are handled by forwarding results produced in one cycle to be consumed in the next. This program, also given below, requires five cycles to issue six instructions, for an IPC of 1.17.

```
lw  $t0, 40($s0)
add $t1, $t0, $s1
sub $t0, $s2, $s3
and $t2, $s4, $t0
or  $t3, $s5, $s6
sw  $s7, 80($t3)
```

Recall that parallelism comes in temporal and spatial forms. Pipelining is a case of temporal parallelism. Multiple execution units is a case of spatial parallelism. Superscalar processors exploit both forms of parallelism to squeeze out performance far exceeding that of our single-cycle and multicycle processors.

Commercial processors may be three-, four-, or even six-way super-scalar. They must handle control hazards such as branches as well as data hazards. Unfortunately, real programs have many dependencies, so wide superscalar processors rarely fully utilize all of the execution units. Moreover, the large number of execution units and complex forwarding networks consume vast amounts of circuitry and power.

7.8.4 Out-of-Order Processor

To cope with the problem of dependencies, an *out-of-order processor* looks ahead across many instructions to *issue*, or begin executing, independent instructions as rapidly as possible. The instructions can be issued in a different order than that written by the programmer, as long as dependencies are honored so that the program produces the intended result.

Consider running the same program from Figure 7.69 on a two-way superscalar out-of-order processor. The processor can issue up to two instructions per cycle from anywhere in the program, as long as dependencies are observed. Figure 7.70 shows the data dependencies and the operation of the processor. The classifications of dependencies as RAW and WAR will be discussed shortly. The constraints on issuing instructions are described below.

- **Cycle 1**

  – The `lw` instruction issues.

  – The `add`, `sub`, and `and` instructions are dependent on `lw` by way of `$t0`, so they cannot issue yet. However, the `or` instruction is independent, so it also issues.

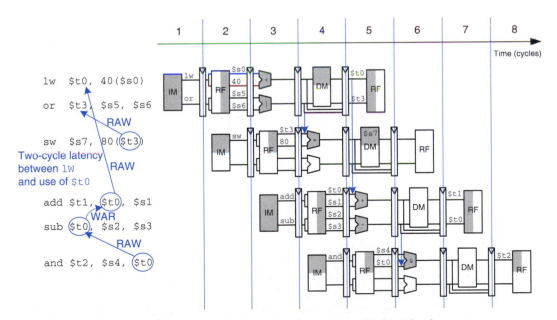

Figure 7.70 Out-of-order execution of a program with dependencies

▶ **Cycle 2**

– Remember that there is a two-cycle latency between when a `lw` instruction issues and when a dependent instruction can use its result, so `add` cannot issue yet because of the $t0 dependence. `sub` writes $t0, so it cannot issue before `add`, lest `add` receive the wrong value of $t0. `and` is dependent on `sub`.

– Only the `sw` instruction issues.

▶ **Cycle 3**

– On cycle 3, $t0 is available, so `add` issues. `sub` issues simultaneously, because it will not write $t0 until after `add` consumes $t0.

▶ **Cycle 4**

– The `and` instruction issues. $t0 is forwarded from `sub` to `and`.

The out-of-order processor issues the six instructions in four cycles, for an IPC of 1.5.

The dependence of `add` on `lw` by way of $t0 is a read after write (RAW) hazard. `add` must not read $t0 until after `lw` has written it. This is the type of dependency we are accustomed to handling in the pipelined processor. It inherently limits the speed at which the program can run, even if infinitely many execution units are available. Similarly, the dependence of `sw` on `or` by way of $t3 and of `and` on `sub` by way of $t0 are RAW dependencies.

The dependence between `sub` and `add` by way of $t0 is called a *write after read* (*WAR*) hazard or an *antidependence*. `sub` must not write $t0 before `add` reads $t0, so that `add` receives the correct value according to the original order of the program. WAR hazards could not occur in the simple MIPS pipeline, but they may happen in an out-of-order processor if the dependent instruction (in this case, `sub`) is moved too early.

A WAR hazard is not essential to the operation of the program. It is merely an artifact of the programmer's choice to use the same register for two unrelated instructions. If the `sub` instruction had written $t4 instead of $t0, the dependency would disappear and `sub` could be issued before `add`. The MIPS architecture only has 32 registers, so sometimes the programmer is forced to reuse a register and introduce a hazard just because all the other registers are in use.

A third type of hazard, not shown in the program, is called *write after write* (*WAW*) or an *output dependence*. A WAW hazard occurs if an instruction attempts to write a register after a subsequent instruction has already written it. The hazard would result in the wrong value being written to the register. For example, in the following program, add and sub both write $t0. The final value in $t0 should come from sub according to the order of the program. If an out-of-order processor attempted to execute sub first, the WAW hazard would occur.

```
add $t0, $s1, $s2
sub $t0, $s3, $s4
```

WAW hazards are not essential either; again, they are artifacts caused by the programmer's using the same register for two unrelated instructions. If the sub instruction were issued first, the program could eliminate the WAW hazard by discarding the result of the add instead of writing it to $t0. This is called *squashing* the add.[6]

Out-of-order processors use a table to keep track of instructions waiting to issue. The table, sometimes called a *scoreboard*, contains information about the dependencies. The size of the table determines how many instructions can be considered for issue. On each cycle, the processor examines the table and issues as many instructions as it can, limited by the dependencies and by the number of execution units (e.g., ALUs, memory ports) that are available.

The *instruction level parallelism* (*ILP*) is the number of instructions that can be executed simultaneously for a particular program and microarchitecture. Theoretical studies have shown that the ILP can be quite large for out-of-order microarchitectures with perfect branch predictors and enormous numbers of execution units. However, practical processors seldom achieve an ILP greater than 2 or 3, even with six-way superscalar datapaths with out-of-order execution.

7.8.5 Register Renaming

Out-of-order processors use a technique called *register renaming* to eliminate WAR hazards. Register renaming adds some nonarchitectural *renaming registers* to the processor. For example, a MIPS processor might add 20 renaming registers, called $r0-$r19. The programmer cannot use these registers directly, because they are not part of the architecture. However, the processor is free to use them to eliminate hazards.

For example, in the previous section, a WAR hazard occurred between the sub and add instructions based on reusing $t0. The out-of-order processor could *rename* $t0 to $r0 for the sub instruction. Then

---

[6] You might wonder why the add needs to be issued at all. The reason is that out-of-order processors must guarantee that all of the same exceptions occur that would have occurred if the program had been executed in its original order. The add potentially may produce an overflow exception, so it must be issued to check for the exception, even though the result can be discarded.

sub could be executed sooner, because $r0 has no dependency on the add instruction. The processor keeps a table of which registers were renamed so that it can consistently rename registers in subsequent dependent instructions. In this example, $t0 must also be renamed to $r0 in the and instruction, because it refers to the result of sub.

Figure 7.71 shows the same program from Figure 7.70 executing on an out-of-order processor with register renaming. $t0 is renamed to $r0 in sub and and to eliminate the WAR hazard. The constraints on issuing instructions are described below.

▶ **Cycle 1**

–   The lw instruction issues.

–   The add instruction is dependent on lw by way of $t0, so it cannot issue yet. However, the sub instruction is independent now that its destination has been renamed to $r0, so sub also issues.

▶ **Cycle 2**

–   Remember that there is a two-cycle latency between when a lw issues and when a dependent instruction can use its result, so add cannot issue yet because of the $t0 dependence.

–   The and instruction is dependent on sub, so it can issue. $r0 is forwarded from sub to and.

–   The or instruction is independent, so it also issues.

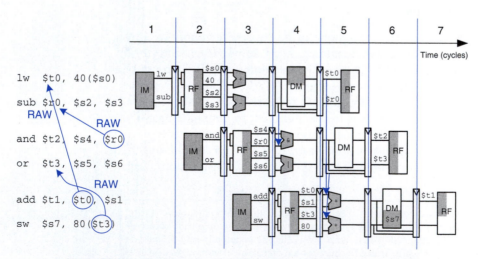

Figure 7.71 Out-of-order execution of a program using register renaming

▶ **Cycle 3**

   – On cycle 3, `$t0` is available, so `add` issues. `$t3` is also available, so `sw` issues.

The out-of-order processor with register renaming issues the six instructions in three cycles, for an IPC of 2.

7.8.6 Single Instruction Multiple Data

The term *SIMD* (pronounced "sim-dee") stands for *single instruction multiple data*, in which a single instruction acts on multiple pieces of data in parallel. A common application of SIMD is to perform many short arithmetic operations at once, especially for graphics processing. This is also called *packed* arithmetic.

For example, a 32-bit microprocessor might pack four 8-bit data elements into one 32-bit word. Packed add and subtract instructions operate on all four data elements within the word in parallel. Figure 7.72 shows a packed 8-bit addition summing four pairs of 8-bit numbers to produce four results. The word could also be divided into two 16-bit elements. Performing packed arithmetic requires modifying the ALU to eliminate carries between the smaller data elements. For example, a carry out of $a_0 + b_0$ should not affect the result of $a_1 + b_1$.

Short data elements often appear in graphics processing. For example, a pixel in a digital photo may use 8 bits to store each of the red, green, and blue color components. Using an entire 32-bit word to process one of these components wastes the upper 24 bits. When the components from four adjacent pixels are packed into a 32-bit word, the processing can be performed four times faster.

SIMD instructions are even more helpful for 64-bit architectures, which can pack eight 8-bit elements, four 16-bit elements, or two 32-bit elements into a single 64-bit word. SIMD instructions are also used for floating-point computations; for example, four 32-bit single-precision floating-point values can be packed into a single 128-bit word.

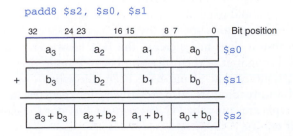

Figure 7.72 **Packed arithmetic: four simultaneous 8-bit additions**

7.8.7 Multithreading

Because the ILP of real programs tends to be fairly low, adding more execution units to a superscalar or out-of-order processor gives diminishing returns. Another problem, discussed in Chapter 8, is that memory is much slower than the processor. Most loads and stores access a smaller and faster memory, called a *cache*. However, when the instructions or data are not available in the cache, the processor may stall for 100 or more cycles while retrieving the information from the main memory. Multithreading is a technique that helps keep a processor with many execution units busy even if the ILP of a program is low or the program is stalled waiting for memory.

To explain multithreading, we need to define a few new terms. A program running on a computer is called a *process*. Computers can run multiple processes simultaneously; for example, you can play music on a PC while surfing the web and running a virus checker. Each process consists of one or more *threads* that also run simultaneously. For example, a word processor may have one thread handling the user typing, a second thread spell-checking the document while the user works, and a third thread printing the document. In this way, the user does not have to wait, for example, for a document to finish printing before being able to type again.

In a conventional processor, the threads only give the illusion of running simultaneously. The threads actually take turns being executed on the processor under control of the OS. When one thread's turn ends, the OS saves its architectural state, loads the architectural state of the next thread, and starts executing that next thread. This procedure is called *context switching*. As long as the processor switches through all the threads fast enough, the user perceives all of the threads as running at the same time.

A multithreaded processor contains more than one copy of its architectural state, so that more than one thread can be active at a time. For example, if we extended a MIPS processor to have four program counters and 128 registers, four threads could be available at one time. If one thread stalls while waiting for data from main memory, the processor could context switch to another thread without any delay, because the program counter and registers are already available. Moreover, if one thread lacks sufficient parallelism to keep all the execution units busy, another thread could issue instructions to the idle units.

Multithreading does not improve the performance of an individual thread, because it does not increase the ILP. However, it does improve the overall throughput of the processor, because multiple threads can use processor resources that would have been idle when executing a single thread. Multithreading is also relatively inexpensive to implement, because it replicates only the PC and register file, not the execution units and memories.

7.8.8 Multiprocessors

A *multiprocessor* system consists of multiple processors and a method for communication between the processors. A common form of multiprocessing in computer systems is *symmetric multiprocessing* (*SMP*), in which two or more identical processors share a single main memory.

The multiple processors may be separate chips or multiple *cores* on the same chip. Modern processors have enormous numbers of transistors available. Using them to increase the pipeline depth or to add more execution units to a superscalar processor gives little performance benefit and is wasteful of power. Around the year 2005, computer architects made a major shift to build multiple copies of the processor on the same chip; these copies are called cores.

Multiprocessors can be used to run more threads simultaneously or to run a particular thread faster. Running more threads simultaneously is easy; the threads are simply divided up among the processors. Unfortunately typical PC users need to run only a small number of threads at any given time. Running a particular thread faster is much more challenging. The programmer must divide the thread into pieces to perform on each processor. This becomes tricky when the processors need to communicate with each other. One of the major challenges for computer designers and programmers is to effectively use large numbers of processor cores.

Other forms of multiprocessing include asymmetric multiprocessing and clusters. *Asymmetric multiprocessors* use separate specialized microprocessors for separate tasks. For example, a cell phone contains a *digital signal processor* (*DSP*) with specialized instructions to decipher the wireless data in real time and a separate conventional processor to interact with the user, manage the phone book, and play games. In *clustered multiprocessing*, each processor has its own local memory system. Clustering can also refer to a group of PCs connected together on the network running software to jointly solve a large problem.

7.9 REAL-WORLD PERSPECTIVE: IA-32 MICROARCHITECTURE*

Section 6.8 introduced the IA-32 architecture used in almost all PCs. This section tracks the evolution of IA-32 processors through progressively faster and more complicated microarchitectures. The same principles we have applied to the MIPS microarchitectures are used in IA-32.

Intel invented the first single-chip microprocessor, the 4-bit 4004, in 1971 as a flexible controller for a line of calculators. It contained 2300 transistors manufactured on a 12-mm^2 sliver of silicon in a process with a 10-μm feature size and operated at 750 KHz. A photograph of the chip taken under a microscope is shown in Figure 7.73.

Scientists searching for signs of extraterrestrial intelligence use the world's largest clustered multiprocessors to analyze radio telescope data for patterns that might be signs of life in other solar systems. The cluster consists of personal computers owned by more than 3.8 million volunteers around the world.

When a computer in the cluster is idle, it fetches a piece of the data from a centralized server, analyzes the data, and sends the results back to the server. You can volunteer your computer's idle time for the cluster by visiting setiathome.berkeley.edu.

Figure 7.73 **4004 microprocessor chip**

In places, columns of four similar-looking structures are visible, as one would expect in a 4-bit microprocessor. Around the periphery are *bond wires*, which are used to connect the chip to its package and the circuit board.

The 4004 inspired the 8-bit 8008, then the 8080, which eventually evolved into the 16-bit 8086 in 1978 and the 80286 in 1982. In 1985, Intel introduced the 80386, which extended the 8086 architecture to 32 bits and defined the IA-32 architecture. Table 7.7 summarizes major Intel IA-32 microprocessors. In the 35 years since the 4004, transistor feature size has shrunk 160-fold, the number of transistors

Table 7.7 **Evolution of Intel IA-32 microprocessors**

Processor	Year	Feature Size (μm)	Transistors	Frequency (MHz)	Microarchitecture
80386	1985	1.5–1.0	275k	16–25	multicycle
80486	1989	1.0–0.6	1.2M	25–100	pipelined
Pentium	1993	0.8–0.35	3.2–4.5M	60–300	superscalar
Pentium II	1997	0.35–0.25	7.5M	233–450	out of order
Pentium III	1999	0.25–0.18	9.5M–28M	450–1400	out of order
Pentium 4	2001	0.18–0.09	42–178M	1400–3730	out of order
Pentium M	2003	0.13–0.09	77–140M	900–2130	out of order
Core Duo	2005	0.065	152M	1500–2160	dual core

on a chip has increased by five orders of magnitude, and the operating frequency has increased by almost four orders of magnitude. No other field of engineering has made such astonishing progress in such a short time.

The 80386 is a multicycle processor. The major components are labeled on the chip photograph in Figure 7.74. The 32-bit datapath is clearly visible on the left. Each of the columns processes one bit of data. Some of the control signals are generated using a *microcode* PLA that steps through the various states of the control FSM. The memory management unit in the upper right controls access to the external memory.

The 80486, shown in Figure 7.75, dramatically improved performance using pipelining. The datapath is again clearly visible, along with the control logic and microcode PLA. The 80486 added an on-chip floating-point unit; previous Intel processors either sent floating-point instructions to a separate coprocessor or emulated them in software. The 80486 was too fast for external memory to keep up, so it incorporated an 8-KB cache onto the chip to hold the most commonly used instructions and data. Chapter 8 describes caches in more detail and revisits the cache systems on Intel IA-32 processors.

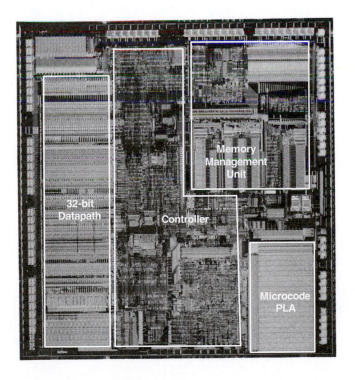

Figure 7.74 **80386 microprocessor chip**

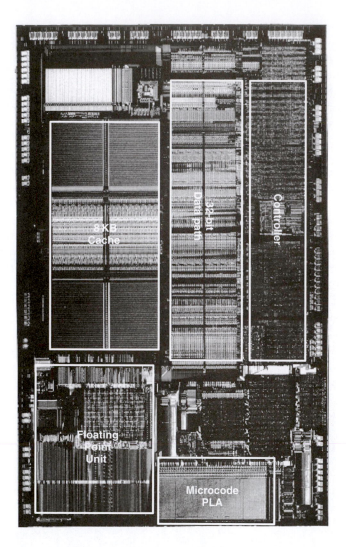

Figure 7.75 80486
microprocessor chip

The Pentium processor, shown in Figure 7.76, is a superscalar processor capable of executing two instructions simultaneously. Intel switched to the name Pentium instead of 80586 because AMD was becoming a serious competitor selling interchangeable 80486 chips, and part numbers cannot be trademarked. The Pentium uses separate instruction and data caches. It also uses a branch predictor to reduce the performance penalty for branches.

The Pentium Pro, Pentium II, and Pentium III processors all share a common out-of-order microarchitecture, code named P6. The complex IA-32 instructions are broken down into one or more micro-ops similar to MIPS instructions. The micro-ops are then executed on a fast out-of-order execution core with an 11-stage pipeline. Figure 7.77 shows the Pentium III. The 32-bit datapath is called the Integer Execution Unit (IEU). The floating-point datapath is called the Floating Point Unit

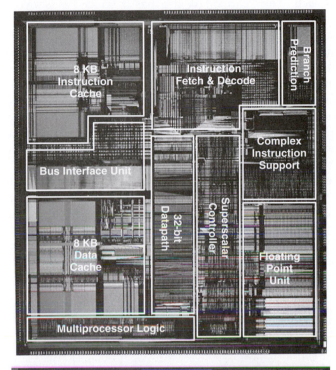

Figure 7.76 Pentium microprocessor chip

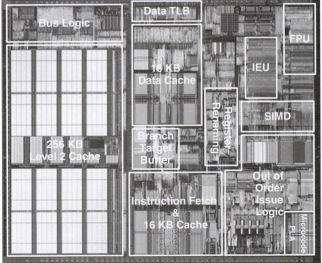

Figure 7.77 Pentium III microprocessor chip

(FPU). The processor also has a SIMD unit to perform packed operations on short integer and floating-point data. A larger portion of the chip is dedicated to issuing instructions out-of-order than to actually executing the instructions. The instruction and data caches have grown to 16 KB each. The Pentium III also has a larger but slower 256-KB second-level cache on the same chip.

By the late 1990s, processors were marketed largely on clock speed. The Pentium 4 is another out-of-order processor with a very deep pipeline to achieve extremely high clock frequencies. It started with 20 stages, and later versions adopted 31 stages to achieve frequencies greater than 3 GHz. The chip, shown in Figure 7.78, packs in 42 to 178 million transistors (depending on the cache size), so even the major execution units are difficult to see on the photograph. Decoding three IA-32 instructions per cycle is impossible at such high clock frequencies because the instruction encodings are so complex and irregular. Instead, the processor predecodes the instructions into simpler micro-ops, then stores the micro-ops in a memory called a *trace cache*. Later versions of the Pentium 4 also perform multithreading to increase the throughput of multiple threads.

The Pentium 4's reliance on deep pipelines and high clock speed led to extremely high power consumption, sometimes more than 100 W. This is unacceptable in laptops and makes cooling of desktops expensive.

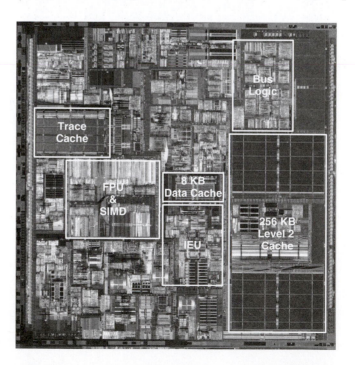

Figure 7.78 Pentium 4 microprocessor chip

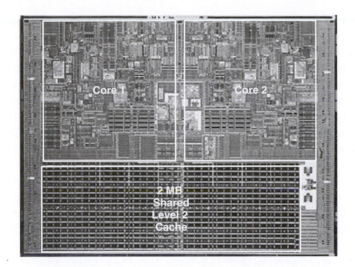

Figure 7.79 Core Duo microprocessor chip

Intel discovered that the older P6 architecture could achieve comparable performance at much lower clock speed and power. The Pentium M uses an enhanced version of the P6 out-of-order microarchitecture with 32-KB instruction and data caches and a 1- to 2-MB second-level cache. The Core Duo is a multicore processor based on two Pentium M cores connected to a shared 2-MB second-level cache. The individual functional units in Figure 7.79 are difficult to see, but the two cores and the large cache are clearly visible.

7.10 SUMMARY

This chapter has described three ways to build MIPS processors, each with different performance and cost trade-offs. We find this topic almost magical: how can such a seemingly complicated device as a microprocessor actually be simple enough to fit in a half-page schematic? Moreover, the inner workings, so mysterious to the uninitiated, are actually reasonably straightforward.

The MIPS microarchitectures have drawn together almost every topic covered in the text so far. Piecing together the microarchitecture puzzle illustrates the principles introduced in previous chapters, including the design of combinational and sequential circuits, covered in Chapters 2 and 3; the application of many of the building blocks described in Chapter 5; and the implementation of the MIPS architecture, introduced in Chapter 6. The MIPS microarchitectures can be described in a few pages of HDL, using the techniques from Chapter 4.

Building the microarchitectures has also heavily used our techniques for managing complexity. The microarchitectural abstraction forms the link between the logic and architecture abstractions, forming the crux of this book on digital design and computer architecture. We also use the abstractions of block diagrams and HDL to succinctly describe the arrangement of components. The microarchitectures exploit regularity and modularity, reusing a library of common building blocks such as ALUs, memories, multiplexers, and registers. Hierarchy is used in numerous ways. The microarchitectures are partitioned into the datapath and control units. Each of these units is built from logic blocks, which can be built from gates, which in turn can be built from transistors using the techniques developed in the first five chapters.

This chapter has compared single-cycle, multicycle, and pipelined microarchitectures for the MIPS processor. All three microarchitectures implement the same subset of the MIPS instruction set and have the same architectural state. The single-cycle processor is the most straight-forward and has a CPI of 1.

The multicycle processor uses a variable number of shorter steps to execute instructions. It thus can reuse the ALU, rather than requiring several adders. However, it does require several nonarchitectural registers to store results between steps. The multicycle design in principle could be faster, because not all instructions must be equally long. In practice, it is generally slower, because it is limited by the slowest steps and by the sequencing overhead in each step.

The pipelined processor divides the single-cycle processor into five relatively fast pipeline stages. It adds pipeline registers between the stages to separate the five instructions that are simultaneously executing. It nominally has a CPI of 1, but hazards force stalls or flushes that increase the CPI slightly. Hazard resolution also costs some extra hardware and design complexity. The clock period ideally could be five times shorter than that of the single-cycle processor. In practice, it is not that short, because it is limited by the slowest stage and by the sequencing overhead in each stage. Nevertheless, pipelining provides substantial performance benefits. All modern high-performance microprocessors use pipelining today.

Although the microarchitectures in this chapter implement only a subset of the MIPS architecture, we have seen that supporting more instructions involves straightforward enhancements of the datapath and controller. Supporting exceptions also requires simple modifications.

A major limitation of this chapter is that we have assumed an ideal memory system that is fast and large enough to store the entire program and data. In reality, large fast memories are prohibitively expensive. The next chapter shows how to get most of the benefits of a large fast memory with a small fast memory that holds the most commonly used information and one or more larger but slower memories that hold the rest of the information.

Exercises

Exercise 7.1 Suppose that one of the following control signals in the single-cycle MIPS processor has a *stuck-at-0 fault*, meaning that the signal is always 0, regardless of its intended value. What instructions would malfunction? Why?

(a) *RegWrite*

(b) $ALUOp_1$

(c) *MemWrite*

Exercise 7.2 Repeat Exercise 7.1, assuming that the signal has a stuck-at-1 fault.

Exercise 7.3 Modify the single-cycle MIPS processor to implement one of the following instructions. See Appendix B for a definition of the instructions. Mark up a copy of Figure 7.11 to indicate the changes to the datapath. Name any new control signals. Mark up a copy of Table 7.8 to show the changes to the main decoder. Describe any other changes that are required.

(a) sll   R[rd] = R[rs] << shamt   R-type

(b) lui   R[rt] = {imm, 16'b0}

(c) slti   R[rt] = (R[rs] < sign txt Im] ? 1 : 0

(d) blez   if(rs ≤ 0) PC = BTA

(e) jal   jump & link $ra = PC+4   PC = JTA   R[31] = PC+4

(f) lh

Table 7.8 Main decoder truth table to mark up with changes

Instruction	Opcode	RegWrite	RegDst	ALUSrc	Branch	MemWrite	MemtoReg	ALUOp
R-type	000000	1	1	0	0	0	0	10
lw	100011	1	0	1	0	0	1	00
sw	101011	0	X	1	0	1	X	00
beq	000100	0	X	0	1	0	X	01

Exercise 7.4 Many processor architectures have a *load with postincrement* instruction, which updates the index register to point to the next memory word after completing the load. lwinc $rt, imm($rs) is equivalent to the following two instructions:

```
lw   $rt, imm($rs)
addi $rs, $rs, 4
```

lw = R[rt] = M[R[rs] + signExt

addi = R[rs] = R[rs] + signExt

Repeat Exercise 7.3 for the `lwinc` instruction. Is it possible to add the instruction without modifying the register file?

Exercise 7.5 Add a single-precision floating-point unit to the single-cycle MIPS processor to handle `add.s`, `sub.s`, and `mul.s`. Assume that you have single-precision floating-point adder and multiplier units available. Explain what changes must be made to the datapath and the controller.

Exercise 7.6 Your friend is a crack circuit designer. She has offered to redesign one of the units in the single-cycle MIPS processor to have half the delay. Using the delays from Table 7.6, which unit should she work on to obtain the greatest speedup of the overall processor, and what would the cycle time of the improved machine be?

Exercise 7.7 Consider the delays given in Table 7.6. Ben Bitdiddle builds a prefix adder that reduces the ALU delay by 20 ps. If the other element delays stay the same, find the new cycle time of the single-cycle MIPS processor and determine how long it takes to execute a benchmark with 100 billion instructions.

Exercise 7.8 Suppose one of the following control signals in the multicycle MIPS processor has a stuck-at-0 fault, meaning that the signal is always 0, regardless of its intended value. What instructions would malfunction? Why?

(a) *MemtoReg*
(b) *ALUOp$_0$*
(c) *PCSrc*

Exercise 7.9 Repeat Exercise 7.8, assuming that the signal has a stuck-at-1 fault.

Exercise 7.10 Modify the HDL code for the single-cycle MIPS processor, given in Section 7.6.1, to handle one of the new instructions from Exercise 7.3. Enhance the testbench, given in Section 7.6.3 to test the new instruction.

Exercise 7.11 Modify the multicycle MIPS processor to implement one of the following instructions. See Appendix B for a definition of the instructions. Mark up a copy of Figure 7.27 to indicate the changes to the datapath. Name any new control signals. Mark up a copy of Figure 7.39 to show the changes to the controller FSM. Describe any other changes that are required.

(a) `srlv`
(b) `ori`
(c) `xori`
(d) `jr`
(e) `bne`
(f) `lbu`

Exercise 7.12 Repeat Exercise 7.4 for the multicycle MIPS processor. Show the changes to the multicycle datapath and control FSM. Is it possible to add the instruction without modifying the register file?

Exercise 7.13 Repeat Exercise 7.5 for the multicycle MIPS processor.

Exercise 7.14 Suppose that the floating-point adder and multiplier from Exercise 7.13 each take two cycles to operate. In other words, the inputs are applied at the beginning of one cycle, and the output is available in the second cycle. How does your answer to Exercise 7.13 change?

Exercise 7.15 Your friend, the crack circuit designer, has offered to redesign one of the units in the multicycle MIPS processor to be much faster. Using the delays from Table 7.6, which unit should she work on to obtain the greatest speedup of the overall processor? How fast should it be? (Making it faster than necessary is a waste of your friend's effort.) What is the cycle time of the improved processor?

Exercise 7.16 Repeat Exercise 7.7 for the multicycle processor.

Exercise 7.17 Suppose the multicycle MIPS processor has the component delays given in Table 7.6. Alyssa P. Hacker designs a new register file that has 40% less power but twice as much delay. Should she switch to the slower but lower power register file for her multicycle processor design?

Exercise 7.18 Goliath Corp claims to have a patent on a three-ported register file. Rather than fighting Goliath in court, Ben Bitdiddle designs a new register file that has only a single read/write port (like the combined instruction and data memory). Redesign the MIPS multicycle datapath and controller to use his new register file.

Exercise 7.19 What is the CPI of the redesigned multicycle MIPS processor from Exercise 7.18? Use the instruction mix from Example 7.7.

Exercise 7.20 How many cycles are required to run the following program on the multicycle MIPS processor? What is the CPI of this program?

```
    addi $s0, $0, 5    # sum = 5

while:
    beq  $s0, $0, done# if result > 0, execute the while block
    addi $s0, $s0, -1 # while block: result = result - 1  .
    j    while

done:
```

Exercise 7.21 Repeat Exercise 7.20 for the following program.

```
        add   $s0, $0, $0    # i = 0
        add   $s1, $0, $0    # sum = 0
        addi  $t0, $0, 10    # $t0 = 10

    loop:
        slt   $t1, $s0, $t0 # if (i < 10), $t1 = 1, else $t1 = 0
        beq   $t1, $0, done # if $t1 == 0 (i >= 10), branch to done
        add   $s1, $s1, $s0 # sum = sum + i
        addi  $s0, $s0, 1   # increment i
        j loop
    done:
```

Exercise 7.22 Write HDL code for the multicycle MIPS processor. The processor should be compatible with the following top-level module. The mem module is used to hold both instructions and data. Test your processor using the testbench from Section 7.6.3.

```
module top(input         clk, reset,
           output [31:0] writedata, adr,
           output        memwrite);

  wire [31:0] readdata;

  // instantiate processor and memories
  mips mips(clk, reset, adr, writedata, memwrite, readdata);
  mem mem(clk, memwrite, adr, writedata, readdata);

  endmodule

module mem(input         clk, we,
           input  [31:0] a, wd,
           output [31:0] rd);

  reg [31:0] RAM[63:0];

  initial
   begin
    $readmemh("memfile.dat",RAM);
   end

assign rd = RAM[a[31:2]]; // word aligned
   always @ (posedge clk)
     if (we)
      RAM[a[31:2]] <= wd;
endmodule
```

Exercise 7.23 Extend your HDL code for the multicycle MIPS processor from Exercise 7.22 to handle one of the new instructions from Exercise 7.11. Enhance the testbench to test the new instruction.

Exercise 7.24 The pipelined MIPS processor is running the following program. Which registers are being written, and which are being read on the fifth cycle?

```
add $s0, $t0, $t1
sub $s1, $t2, $t3
and $s2, $s0, $s1
or  $s3, $t4, $t5
slt $s4, $s2, $s3
```

Exercise 7.25 Using a diagram similar to Figure 7.52, show the forwarding and stalls needed to execute the following instructions on the pipelined MIPS processor.

```
add $t0, $s0, $s1
sub $t0, $t0, $s2
lw  $t1, 60($t0)
and $t2, $t1, $t0
```

Exercise 7.26 Repeat Exercise 7.25 for the following instructions.

```
add $t0, $s0, $s1
lw  $t1, 60($s2)
sub $t2, $t0, $s3
and $t3, $t1, $t0
```

Exercise 7.27 How many cycles are required for the pipelined MIPS processor to issue all of the instructions for the program in Exercise 7.21? What is the CPI of the processor on this program?

Exercise 7.28 Explain how to extend the pipelined MIPS processor to handle the addi instruction.

Exercise 7.29 Explain how to extend the pipelined processor to handle the j instruction. Give particular attention to how the pipeline is flushed when a jump takes place.

Exercise 7.30 Examples 7.9 and 7.10 point out that the pipelined MIPS processor performance might be better if branches take place during the Execute stage rather than the Decode stage. Show how to modify the pipelined processor from Figure 7.58 to branch in the Execute stage. How do the stall and flush signals change? Redo Examples 7.9 and 7.10 to find the new CPI, cycle time, and overall time to execute the program.

Exercise 7.31 Your friend, the crack circuit designer, has offered to redesign one of the units in the pipelined MIPS processor to be much faster. Using the delays from Table 7.6 and Example 7.10, which unit should she work on to obtain the greatest speedup of the overall processor? How fast should it be? (Making it faster than necessary is a waste of your friend's effort.) What is the cycle time of the improved processor?

Exercise 7.32 Consider the delays from Table 7.6 and Example 7.10. Now suppose that the ALU were 20% faster. Would the cycle time of the pipelined MIPS processor change? What if the ALU were 20% slower?

Exercise 7.33 Write HDL code for the pipelined MIPS processor. The processor should be compatible with the top-level module from HDL Example 7.13. It should support all of the instructions described in this chapter, including addi and j (see Exercises 7.28 and 7.29). Test your design using the testbench from HDL Example 7.12.

Exercise 7.34 Design the hazard unit shown in Figure 7.58 for the pipelined MIPS processor. Use an HDL to implement your design. Sketch the hardware that a synthesis tool might generate from your HDL.

Exercise 7.35 A *nonmaskable interrupt* (NMI) is triggered by an input pin to the processor. When the pin is asserted, the current instruction should finish, then the processor should set the Cause register to 0 and take an exception. Show how to modify the multicycle processor in Figures 7.63 and 7.64 to handle nonmaskable interrupts.

Interview Questions

The following exercises present questions that have been asked at interviews for digital design jobs.

Question 7.1 Explain the advantages of pipelined microprocessors.

Question 7.2 If additional pipeline stages allow a processor to go faster, why don't processors have 100 pipeline stages?

Question 7.3 Describe what a hazard is in a microprocessor and explain ways in which it can be resolved. What are the pros and cons of each way?

Question 7.4 Describe the concept of a superscalar processor and its pros and cons.

Memory Systems

8.1 INTRODUCTION

Computer system performance depends on the memory system as well as the processor microarchitecture. Chapter 7 assumed an ideal memory system that could be accessed in a single clock cycle. However, this would be true only for a very small memory—or a very slow processor! Early processors were relatively slow, so memory was able to keep up. But processor speed has increased at a faster rate than memory speeds. DRAM memories are currently 10 to 100 times slower than processors. The increasing gap between processor and DRAM memory speeds demands increasingly ingenious memory systems to try to approximate a memory that is as fast as the processor. This chapter investigates practical memory systems and considers trade-offs of speed, capacity, and cost.

The processor communicates with the memory system over a *memory interface*. Figure 8.1 shows the simple memory interface used in our multicycle MIPS processor. The processor sends an address over the *Address* bus to the memory system. For a read, *MemWrite* is 0 and the memory returns the data on the *ReadData* bus. For a write, *MemWrite* is 1 and the processor sends data to memory on the *WriteData* bus.

The major issues in memory system design can be broadly explained using a metaphor of books in a library. A library contains many books on the shelves. If you were writing a term paper on the meaning of dreams, you might go to the library[1] and pull Freud's *The Interpretation of Dreams* off the shelf and bring it to your cubicle. After skimming it, you might put it back and pull out Jung's *The Psychology of the*

---

[1] We realize that library usage is plummeting among college students because of the Internet. But we also believe that libraries contain vast troves of hard-won human knowledge that are not electronically available. We hope that Web searching does not completely displace the art of library research.

Figure 8.1 The memory interface

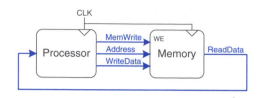

Unconscious. You might then go back for another quote from *Interpretation of Dreams*, followed by yet another trip to the stacks for Freud's *The Ego and the Id*. Pretty soon you would get tired of walking from your cubicle to the stacks. If you are clever, you would save time by keeping the books in your cubicle rather than schlepping them back and forth. Furthermore, when you pull a book by Freud, you could also pull several of his other books from the same shelf.

This metaphor emphasizes the principle, introduced in Section 6.2.1, of making the common case fast. By keeping books that you have recently used or might likely use in the future at your cubicle, you reduce the number of time-consuming trips to the stacks. In particular, you use the principles of *temporal* and *spatial locality*. Temporal locality means that if you have used a book recently, you are likely to use it again soon. Spatial locality means that when you use one particular book, you are likely to be interested in other books on the same shelf.

The library itself makes the common case fast by using these principles of locality. The library has neither the shelf space nor the budget to accommodate all of the books in the world. Instead, it keeps some of the lesser-used books in deep storage in the basement. Also, it may have an interlibrary loan agreement with nearby libraries so that it can offer more books than it physically carries.

In summary, you obtain the benefits of both a large collection and quick access to the most commonly used books through a hierarchy of storage. The most commonly used books are in your cubicle. A larger collection is on the shelves. And an even larger collection is available, with advanced notice, from the basement and other libraries. Similarly, memory systems use a hierarchy of storage to quickly access the most commonly used data while still having the capacity to store large amounts of data.

Memory subsystems used to build this hierarchy were introduced in Section 5.5. Computer memories are primarily built from dynamic RAM (DRAM) and static RAM (SRAM). Ideally, the computer memory system is fast, large, and cheap. In practice, a single memory only has two of these three attributes; it is either slow, small, or expensive. But computer systems can approximate the ideal by combining a fast small cheap memory and a slow large cheap memory. The fast memory stores the most commonly used data and instructions, so on average the memory system appears fast. The large memory stores the remainder of the data and instructions, so the overall capacity is large. The combination of two cheap memories is much less expensive than a single large fast memory. These principles extend to using an entire hierarchy of memories of increasing capacity and decreasing speed.

Computer memory is generally built from DRAM chips. In 2006, a typical PC had a *main memory* consisting of 256 MB to 1 GB of DRAM, and DRAM cost about $100 per gigabyte (GB). DRAM prices have declined at about 30% per year for the last three decades, and memory capacity has grown at the same rate, so the total cost of the memory in a PC has remained roughly constant. Unfortunately, DRAM speed has improved by only about 7% per year, whereas processor performance has improved at a rate of 30 to 50% per year, as shown in Figure 8.2. The plot shows memory and processor speeds with the 1980 speeds as a baseline. In about 1980, processor and memory speeds were the same. But performance has diverged since then, with memories badly lagging.

DRAM could keep up with processors in the 1970s and early 1980's, but it is now woefully too slow. The DRAM access time is one to two orders of magnitude longer than the processor cycle time (tens of nanoseconds, compared to less than one nanosecond).

To counteract this trend, computers store the most commonly used instructions and data in a faster but smaller memory, called a *cache*. The cache is usually built out of SRAM on the same chip as the processor. The cache speed is comparable to the processor speed, because SRAM is inherently faster than DRAM, and because the on-chip memory eliminates lengthy delays caused by traveling to and from a separate chip. In 2006, on-chip SRAM costs were on the order of $10,000/GB, but the cache is relatively small (kilobytes to a few megabytes), so the overall

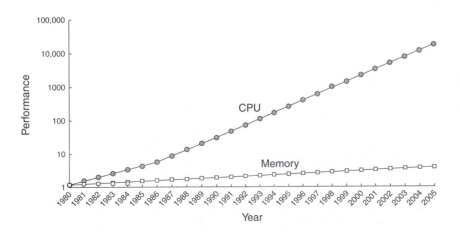

Figure 8.2 Diverging processor and memory performance Adapted with permission from Hennessy and Patterson, *Computer Architecture: A Quantitative Approach*, 3rd ed., Morgan Kaufmann, 2003.

cost is low. Caches can store both instructions and data, but we will refer to their contents generically as "data."

If the processor requests data that is available in the cache, it is returned quickly. This is called a cache *hit*. Otherwise, the processor retrieves the data from main memory (DRAM). This is called a cache *miss*. If the cache hits most of the time, then the processor seldom has to wait for the slow main memory, and the average access time is low.

The third level in the memory hierarchy is the *hard disk*, or *hard drive*. In the same way that a library uses the basement to store books that do not fit in the stacks, computer systems use the hard disk to store data that does not fit in main memory. In 2006, a hard disk cost less than $1/GB and had an access time of about 10 ms. Hard disk costs have decreased at 60%/year but access times scarcely improved. The hard disk provides an illusion of more capacity than actually exists in the main memory. It is thus called *virtual memory*. Like books in the basement, data in virtual memory takes a long time to access. Main memory, also called *physical memory*, holds a subset of the virtual memory. Hence, the main memory can be viewed as a cache for the most commonly used data from the hard disk.

Figure 8.3 summarizes the memory hierarchy of the computer system discussed in the rest of this chapter. The processor first seeks data in a small but fast cache that is usually located on the same chip. If the data is not available in the cache, the processor then looks in main memory. If the data is not there either, the processor fetches the data from virtual memory on the large but slow hard disk. Figure 8.4 illustrates this capacity and speed trade-off in the memory hierarchy and lists typical costs and access times in 2006 technology. As access time decreases, speed increases.

Section 8.2 introduces memory system performance analysis. Section 8.3 explores several cache organizations, and Section 8.4 delves into virtual memory systems. To conclude, this chapter explores how processors can access input and output devices, such as keyboards and monitors, in much the same way as they access memory. Section 8.5 investigates such memory-mapped I/O.

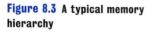

Figure 8.3 A typical memory hierarchy

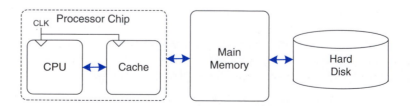

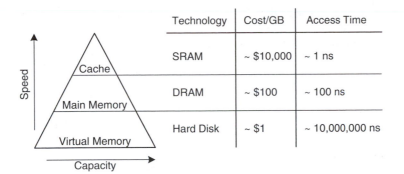

Figure 8.4 Memory hierarchy components, with typical characteristics in 2006

8.2 MEMORY SYSTEM PERFORMANCE ANALYSIS

Designers (and computer buyers) need quantitative ways to measure the performance of memory systems to evaluate the cost-benefit trade-offs of various alternatives. Memory system performance metrics are *miss rate* or *hit rate* and *average memory access time*. Miss and hit rates are calculated as:

$$Miss\ Rate = \frac{Number\ of\ misses}{Number\ of\ total\ memory\ accesses} = 1 - Hit\ Rate$$

$$\hspace{10cm} (8.1)$$

$$Hit\ Rate = \frac{Number\ of\ hits}{Number\ of\ total\ memory\ accesses} = 1 - Miss\ Rate$$

Example 8.1 CALCULATING CACHE PERFORMANCE

Suppose a program has 2000 data access instructions (loads or stores), and 1250 of these requested data values are found in the cache. The other 750 data values are supplied to the processor by main memory or disk memory. What are the miss and hit rates for the cache?

Solution: The miss rate is $750/2000 = 0.375 = 37.5\%$. The hit rate is $1250/2000 = 0.625 = 1 - 0.375 = 62.5\%$.

Average memory access time (AMAT) is the average time a processor must wait for memory per load or store instruction. In the typical computer system from Figure 8.3, the processor first looks for the data in the cache. If the cache misses, the processor then looks in main memory. If the main memory misses, the processor accesses virtual memory on the hard disk. Thus, *AMAT* is calculated as:

$$AMAT = t_{cache} + MR_{cache}(t_{MM} + MR_{MM}t_{VM}) \hspace{2cm} (8.2)$$

where t_{cache}, t_{MM}, and t_{VM} are the access times of the cache, main memory, and virtual memory, and MR_{cache} and MR_{MM} are the cache and main memory miss rates, respectively.

Example 8.2 CALCULATING AVERAGE MEMORY ACCESS TIME

Suppose a computer system has a memory organization with only two levels of hierarchy, a cache and main memory. What is the average memory access time given the access times and miss rates given in Table 8.1?

Solution: The average memory access time is $1 + 0.1(100) = 11$ cycles.

Table 8.1 Access times and miss rates

Memory Level	Access Time (Cycles)	Miss Rate
Cache	1	10%
Main Memory	100	0%

Example 8.3 IMPROVING ACCESS TIME

An 11-cycle average memory access time means that the processor spends ten cycles waiting for data for every one cycle actually using that data. What cache miss rate is needed to reduce the average memory access time to 1.5 cycles given the access times in Table 8.1?

Solution: If the miss rate is m, the average access time is $1 + 100m$. Setting this time to 1.5 and solving for m requires a cache miss rate of 0.5%.

Gene Amdahl, 1922–. Most famous for Amdahl's Law, an observation he made in 1965. While in graduate school, he began designing computers in his free time. This side work earned him his Ph.D. in theoretical physics in 1952. He joined IBM immediately after graduation, and later went on to found three companies, including one called Amdahl Corporation in 1970.

As a word of caution, performance improvements might not always be as good as they sound. For example, making the memory system ten times faster will not necessarily make a computer program run ten times as fast. If 50% of a program's instructions are loads and stores, a tenfold memory system improvement only means a 1.82-fold improvement in program performance. This general principle is called *Amdahl's Law*, which says that the effort spent on increasing the performance of a subsystem is worthwhile only if the subsystem affects a large percentage of the overall performance.

8.3 CACHES

A cache holds commonly used memory data. The number of data words that it can hold is called the *capacity*, *C*. Because the capacity of the cache is smaller than that of main memory, the computer system designer must choose what subset of the main memory is kept in the cache.

When the processor attempts to access data, it first checks the cache for the data. If the cache hits, the data is available immediately. If the cache misses, the processor fetches the data from main memory and places it in the cache for future use. To accommodate the new data, the cache must *replace* old data. This section investigates these issues in cache design by answering the following questions: (1) What data is held in the cache? (2) How is the data found? and (3) What data is replaced to make room for new data when the cache is full?

When reading the next sections, keep in mind that the driving force in answering these questions is the inherent spatial and temporal locality of data accesses in most applications. Caches use spatial and temporal locality to predict what data will be needed next. If a program accesses data in a random order, it would not benefit from a cache.

As we explain in the following sections, caches are specified by their capacity (C), number of sets (S), block size (b), number of blocks (B), and degree of associativity (N).

Although we focus on data cache loads, the same principles apply for fetches from an instruction cache. Data cache store operations are similar and are discussed further in Section 8.3.4.

> *Cache*: a hiding place especially for concealing and preserving provisions or implements.
>
> – Merriam Webster Online Dictionary. 2006. http://www.merriam-webster.com

8.3.1 What Data Is Held in the Cache?

An ideal cache would anticipate all of the data needed by the processor and fetch it from main memory ahead of time so that the cache has a zero miss rate. Because it is impossible to predict the future with perfect accuracy, the cache must guess what data will be needed based on the past pattern of memory accesses. In particular, the cache exploits temporal and spatial locality to achieve a low miss rate.

Recall that temporal locality means that the processor is likely to access a piece of data again soon if it has accessed that data recently. Therefore, when the processor loads or stores data that is not in the cache, the data is copied from main memory into the cache. Subsequent requests for that data hit in the cache.

Recall that spatial locality means that, when the processor accesses a piece of data, it is also likely to access data in nearby memory locations. Therefore, when the cache fetches one word from memory, it may also fetch several adjacent words. This group of words is called a *cache block*. The number of words in the cache block, b, is called the *block size*. A cache of capacity C contains $B = C/b$ blocks.

The principles of temporal and spatial locality have been experimentally verified in real programs. If a variable is used in a program, the same variable is likely to be used again, creating temporal locality. If an element in an array is used, other elements in the same array are also likely to be used, creating spatial locality.

8.3.2 How Is the Data Found?

A cache is organized into S *sets*, each of which holds one or more blocks of data. The relationship between the address of data in main memory and the location of that data in the cache is called the *mapping*. Each memory address maps to exactly one set in the cache. Some of the address bits are used to determine which cache set contains the data. If the set contains more than one block, the data may be kept in any of the blocks in the set.

Caches are categorized based on the number of blocks in a set. In a *direct mapped* cache, each set contains exactly one block, so the cache has $S = B$ sets. Thus, a particular main memory address maps to a unique block in the cache. In an *N-way set associative* cache, each set contains N blocks. The address still maps to a unique set, with $S = B/N$ sets. But the data from that address can go in any of the N blocks in that set. A *fully associative* cache has only $S = 1$ set. Data can go in any of the B blocks in the set. Hence, a fully associative cache is another name for a B-way set associative cache.

To illustrate these cache organizations, we will consider a MIPS memory system with 32-bit addresses and 32-bit words. The memory is byte-addressable, and each word is four bytes, so the memory consists of 2^{30} words aligned on word boundaries. We analyze caches with an eight-word capacity (C) for the sake of simplicity. We begin with a one-word block size (b), then generalize later to larger blocks.

Direct Mapped Cache

A *direct mapped* cache has one block in each set, so it is organized into $S = B$ sets. To understand the mapping of memory addresses onto cache blocks, imagine main memory as being mapped into b-word blocks, just as the cache is. An address in block 0 of main memory maps to set 0 of the cache. An address in block 1 of main memory maps to set 1 of the cache, and so forth until an address in block $B - 1$ of main memory maps to block $B - 1$ of the cache. There are no more blocks of the cache, so the mapping wraps around, such that block B of main memory maps to block 0 of the cache.

This mapping is illustrated in Figure 8.5 for a direct mapped cache with a capacity of eight words and a block size of one word. The cache has eight sets, each of which contains a one-word block. The bottom two bits of the address are always 00, because they are word aligned. The next $\log_2 8 = 3$ bits indicate the set onto which the memory address maps. Thus, the data at addresses 0x00000004, 0x00000024, . . . ,

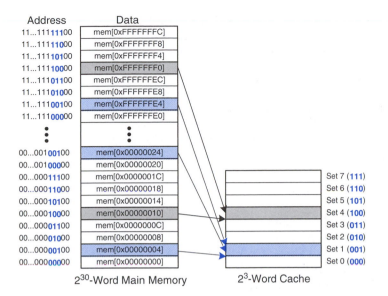

Address   Data
11...11**11**1100   mem[0xFFFFFFFC]
11...11**11**1000   mem[0xFFFFFFF8]
11...11**10**1100   mem[0xFFFFFFF4]
11...11**10**1000   mem[0xFFFFFFF0]
11...11**01**1100   mem[0xFFFFFFEC]
11...11**01**1000   mem[0xFFFFFFE8]
11...11**00**1100   mem[0xFFFFFFE4]
11...11**00**1000   mem[0xFFFFFFE0]

⋮   ⋮

00...001**00**100   mem[0x00000024]
00...001**00**000   mem[0x00000020]
00...000**11**100   mem[0x0000001C]
00...000**11**000   mem[0x00000018]
00...000**10**100   mem[0x00000014]
00...000**10**000   mem[0x00000010]
00...000**01**100   mem[0x0000000C]
00...000**01**000   mem[0x00000008]
00...000**00**100   mem[0x00000004]
00...000**00**000   mem[0x00000000]

2^{30}-Word Main Memory

Set 7 (**111**)
Set 6 (**110**)
Set 5 (**101**)
Set 4 (**100**)
Set 3 (**011**)
Set 2 (**010**)
Set 1 (**001**)
Set 0 (**000**)

2^3-Word Cache

Figure 8.5 Mapping of main memory to a direct mapped cache

0xFFFFFFE4 all map to set 1, as shown in blue. Likewise, data at addresses 0x00000010, . . . , 0xFFFFFFF0 all map to set 4, and so forth. Each main memory address maps to exactly one set in the cache.

Example 8.4 CACHE FIELDS

To what cache set in Figure 8.5 does the word at address 0x00000014 map? Name another address that maps to the same set.

Solution: The two least significant bits of the address are 00, because the address is word aligned. The next three bits are 101, so the word maps to set 5. Words at addresses 0x34, 0x54, 0x74, . . . , 0xFFFFFFF4 all map to this same set.

Because many addresses map to a single set, the cache must also keep track of the address of the data actually contained in each set. The least significant bits of the address specify which set holds the data. The remaining most significant bits are called the *tag* and indicate which of the many possible addresses is held in that set.

In our previous example, the two least significant bits of the 32-bit address are called the *byte offset*, because they indicate the byte within the word. The next three bits are called the *set bits*, because they indicate the set to which the address maps. (In general, the number of set bits is $\log_2 S$.) The remaining 27 tag bits indicate the memory address of the data stored in a given cache set. Figure 8.6 shows the cache fields for address 0xFFFFFFE4. It maps to set 1 and its tag is all 1's.

Figure 8.6 Cache fields for address 0xFFFFFFE4 when mapping to the cache in Figure 8.5

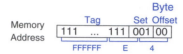

Example 8.5 CACHE FIELDS

Find the number of set and tag bits for a direct mapped cache with 1024 (2^{10}) sets and a one-word block size. The address size is 32 bits.

Solution: A cache with 2^{10} sets requires $\log_2(2^{10}) = 10$ set bits. The two least significant bits of the address are the byte offset, and the remaining $32 - 10 - 2 = 20$ bits form the tag.

Sometimes, such as when the computer first starts up, the cache sets contain no data at all. The cache uses a *valid bit* for each set to indicate whether the set holds meaningful data. If the valid bit is 0, the contents are meaningless.

Figure 8.7 shows the hardware for the direct mapped cache of Figure 8.5. The cache is constructed as an eight-entry SRAM. Each entry, or set, contains one line consisting of 32 bits of data, 27 bits of tag, and 1 valid bit. The cache is accessed using the 32-bit address. The two least significant bits, the byte offset bits, are ignored for word accesses. The next three bits, the set bits, specify the entry or set in the cache. A load instruction reads the specified entry from the cache and checks the tag and valid bits. If the tag matches the most significant

Figure 8.7 Direct mapped cache with 8 sets

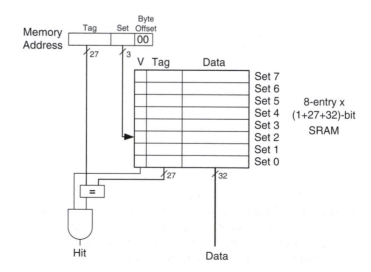

27 bits of the address and the valid bit is 1, the cache hits and the data is returned to the processor. Otherwise, the cache misses and the memory system must fetch the data from main memory.

Example 8.6 TEMPORAL LOCALITY WITH A DIRECT MAPPED CACHE

Loops are a common source of temporal and spatial locality in applications. Using the eight-entry cache of Figure 8.7, show the contents of the cache after executing the following silly loop in MIPS assembly code. Assume that the cache is initially empty. What is the miss rate?

```
        addi  $t0, $0, 5
loop:   beq   $t0, $0, done
        lw    $t1, 0x4($0)
        lw    $t2, 0xC($0)
        lw    $t3, 0x8($0)
        addi  $t0, $t0, −1
        j     loop
done:
```

Solution: The program contains a loop that repeats for five iterations. Each iteration involves three memory accesses (loads), resulting in 15 total memory accesses. The first time the loop executes, the cache is empty and the data must be fetched from main memory locations 0x4, 0xC, and 0x8 into cache sets 1, 3, and 2, respectively. However, the next four times the loop executes, the data is found in the cache. Figure 8.8 shows the contents of the cache during the last request to memory address 0x4. The tags are all 0 because the upper 27 bits of the addresses are 0. The miss rate is 3/15 = 20%.

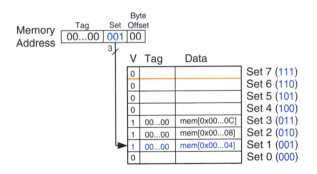

Figure 8.8 Direct mapped cache contents

When two recently accessed addresses map to the same cache block, a *conflict* occurs, and the most recently accessed address *evicts* the previous one from the block. Direct mapped caches have only one block in each set, so two addresses that map to the same set always cause a conflict. The example on the next page illustrates conflicts.

Example 8.7 CACHE BLOCK CONFLICT

What is the miss rate when the following loop is executed on the eight-word direct mapped cache from Figure 8.7? Assume that the cache is initially empty.

```
      addi $t0, $0, 5
loop: beq  $t0, $0, done
      lw   $t1, 0x4($0)
      lw   $t2, 0x24($0)
      addi $t0, $t0, −1
      j    loop
done:
```

Solution: Memory addresses 0x4 and 0x24 both map to set 1. During the initial execution of the loop, data at address 0x4 is loaded into set 1 of the cache. Then data at address 0x24 is loaded into set 1, evicting the data from address 0x4. Upon the second execution of the loop, the pattern repeats and the cache must refetch data at address 0x4, evicting data from address 0x24. The two addresses conflict, and the miss rate is 100%.

Multi-way Set Associative Cache

An *N-way set associative* cache reduces conflicts by providing N blocks in each set where data mapping to that set might be found. Each memory address still maps to a specific set, but it can map to any one of the N blocks in the set. Hence, a direct mapped cache is another name for a one-way set associative cache. N is also called the *degree of associativity* of the cache.

Figure 8.9 shows the hardware for a $C = 8$-word, $N = 2$-way set associative cache. The cache now has only $S = 4$ sets rather than 8.

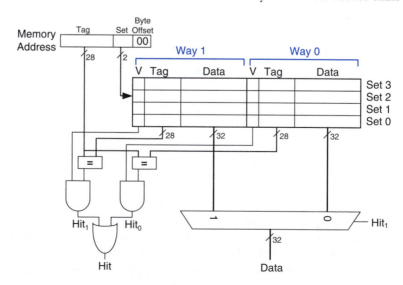

Figure 8.9 Two-way set associative cache

Thus, only $\log_2 4 = 2$ set bits rather than 3 are used to select the set. The tag increases from 27 to 28 bits. Each set contains two *ways* or degrees of associativity. Each way consists of a data block and the valid and tag bits. The cache reads blocks from both ways in the selected set and checks the tags and valid bits for a hit. If a hit occurs in one of the ways, a multiplexer selects data from that way.

Set associative caches generally have lower miss rates than direct mapped caches of the same capacity, because they have fewer conflicts. However, set associative caches are usually slower and somewhat more expensive to build because of the output multiplexer and additional comparators. They also raise the question of which way to replace when both ways are full; this is addressed further in Section 8.3.3. Most commercial systems use set associative caches.

Example 8.8 SET ASSOCIATIVE CACHE MISS RATE

Repeat Example 8.7 using the eight-word two-way set associative cache from Figure 8.9.

Solution: Both memory accesses, to addresses 0x4 and 0x24, map to set 1. However, the cache has two ways, so it can accommodate data from both addresses. During the first loop iteration, the empty cache misses both addresses and loads both words of data into the two ways of set 1, as shown in Figure 8.10. On the next four iterations, the cache hits. Hence, the miss rate is $2/10 = 20\%$. Recall that the direct mapped cache of the same size from Example 8.7 had a miss rate of 100%.

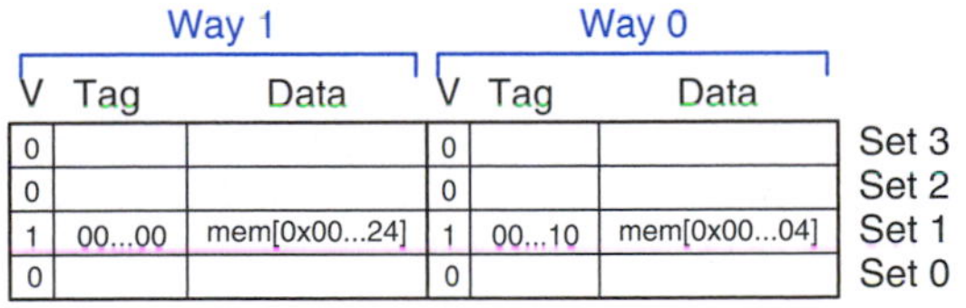

	Way 1			Way 0		
V	Tag	Data	V	Tag	Data	
0			0			Set 3
0			0			Set 2
1	00...00	mem[0x00...24]	1	00...10	mem[0x00...04]	Set 1
0			0			Set 0

Figure 8.10 Two-way set associative cache contents

Fully Associative Cache

A *fully associative* cache contains a single set with B ways, where B is the number of blocks. A memory address can map to a block in any of these ways. A fully associative cache is another name for a B-way set associative cache with one set.

Figure 8.11 shows the SRAM array of a fully associative cache with eight blocks. Upon a data request, eight tag comparisons (not shown) must be made, because the data could be in any block. Similarly, an 8:1 multiplexer chooses the proper data if a hit occurs. Fully associative caches tend

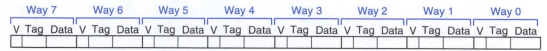

Figure 8.11 Eight-block fully associative cache

to have the fewest conflict misses for a given cache capacity, but they require more hardware for additional tag comparisons. They are best suited to relatively small caches because of the large number of comparators.

Block Size

The previous examples were able to take advantage only of temporal locality, because the block size was one word. To exploit spatial locality, a cache uses larger blocks to hold several consecutive words.

The advantage of a block size greater than one is that when a miss occurs and the word is fetched into the cache, the adjacent words in the block are also fetched. Therefore, subsequent accesses are more likely to hit because of spatial locality. However, a large block size means that a fixed-size cache will have fewer blocks. This may lead to more conflicts, increasing the miss rate. Moreover, it takes more time to fetch the missing cache block after a miss, because more than one data word is fetched from main memory. The time required to load the missing block into the cache is called the *miss penalty*. If the adjacent words in the block are not accessed later, the effort of fetching them is wasted. Nevertheless, most real programs benefit from larger block sizes.

Figure 8.12 shows the hardware for a $C = 8$-word direct mapped cache with a $b = 4$-word block size. The cache now has only $B = C/b = 2$ blocks. A direct mapped cache has one block in each set, so this cache is

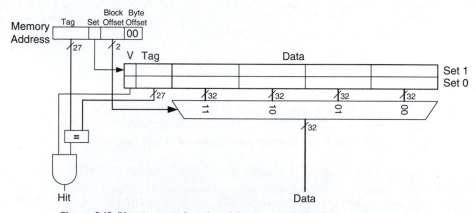

Figure 8.12 Direct mapped cache with two sets and a four-word block size

Tag Set Block Offset Byte Offset

Memory Address | 100...100 | 1 | 11 | 00 |

800000   9   C

organized as two sets. Thus, only $\log_2 2 = 1$ bit is used to select the set. A multiplexer is now needed to select the word within the block. The multiplexer is controlled by the $\log_2 4 = 2$ *block offset bits* of the address. The most significant 27 address bits form the tag. Only one tag is needed for the entire block, because the words in the block are at consecutive addresses.

Figure 8.13 shows the cache fields for address 0x8000009C when it maps to the direct mapped cache of Figure 8.12. The byte offset bits are always 0 for word accesses. The next $\log_2 b = 2$ block offset bits indicate the word within the block. And the next bit indicates the set. The remaining 27 bits are the tag. Therefore, word 0x8000009C maps to set 1, word 3 in the cache. The principle of using larger block sizes to exploit spatial locality also applies to associative caches.

Example 8.9 SPATIAL LOCALITY WITH A DIRECT MAPPED CACHE

Repeat Example 8.6 for the eight-word direct mapped cache with a four-word block size.

Solution: Figure 8.14 shows the contents of the cache after the first memory access. On the first loop iteration, the cache misses on the access to memory address 0x4. This access loads data at addresses 0x0 through 0xC into the cache block. All subsequent accesses (as shown for address 0xC) hit in the cache. Hence, the miss rate is $1/15 = 6.67\%$.

Block Byte
Tag   Set Offset Offset

Memory Address | 00...00 | 0 | 11 | 00 |

V Tag   Data

| 0 | | | | | | Set 1 |
| 1 | 00...00 | mem[0x00...0C] | mem[0x00...08] | mem[0x00...04] | mem[0x00...00] | Set 0 |

Figure 8.14 Cache contents with a block size (*b*) of four words

Putting It All Together

Caches are organized as two-dimensional arrays. The rows are called sets, and the columns are called ways. Each entry in the array consists of

Table 8.2 Cache organizations

Organization	Number of Ways (N)	Number of Sets (S)
direct mapped	1	B
set associative	1 < N < B	B/N
fully associative	B	1

a data block and its associated valid and tag bits. Caches are characterized by

▸ capacity C

▸ block size b (and number of blocks, $B = C/b$)

▸ number of blocks in a set (N)

Table 8.2 summarizes the various cache organizations. Each address in memory maps to only one set but can be stored in any of the ways.

Cache capacity, associativity, set size, and block size are typically powers of 2. This makes the cache fields (tag, set, and block offset bits) subsets of the address bits.

Increasing the associativity, N, usually reduces the miss rate caused by conflicts. But higher associativity requires more tag comparators. Increasing the block size, b, takes advantage of spatial locality to reduce the miss rate. However, it decreases the number of sets in a fixed sized cache and therefore could lead to more conflicts. It also increases the miss penalty.

8.3.3 What Data Is Replaced?

In a direct mapped cache, each address maps to a unique block and set. If a set is full when new data must be loaded, the block in that set is replaced with the new data. In set associative and fully associative caches, the cache must choose which block to evict when a cache set is full. The principle of temporal locality suggests that the best choice is to evict the least recently used block, because it is least likely to be used again soon. Hence, most associative caches have a *least recently used* (*LRU*) replacement policy.

In a two-way set associative cache, a *use bit*, U, indicates which way within a set was least recently used. Each time one of the ways is used, U is adjusted to indicate the other way. For set associative caches with more than two ways, tracking the least recently used way becomes complicated. To simplify the problem, the ways are often divided into two groups and U indicates which *group* of ways was least recently used.

Upon replacement, the new block replaces a random block within the least recently used group. Such a policy is called *pseudo-LRU* and is good enough in practice.

Example 8.10 **LRU REPLACEMENT**

Show the contents of an eight-word two-way set associative cache after executing the following code. Assume LRU replacement, a block size of one word, and an initially empty cache.

```
lw $t0, 0x04($0)
lw $t1, 0x24($0)
lw $t2, 0x54($0)
```

Solution: The first two instructions load data from memory addresses 0x4 and 0x24 into set 1 of the cache, shown in Figure 8.15(a). $U = 0$ indicates that data in way 0 was the least recently used. The next memory access, to address 0x54, also maps to set 1 and replaces the least recently used data in way 0, as shown in Figure 8.15(b), The use bit, U, is set to 1 to indicate that data in way 1 was the least recently used.

		Way 1			Way 0		
V	U	Tag	Data	V	Tag	Data	
0	0			0			Set 3 (11)
0	0			0			Set 2 (10)
1	0	00...010	mem[0x00...24]	1	00...000	mem[0x00...04]	Set 1 (01)
0	0			0			Set 0 (00)

(a)

		Way 1			Way 0		
V	U	Tag	Data	V	Tag	Data	
0	0			0			Set 3 (11)
0	0			0			Set 2 (10)
1	1	00...010	mem[0x00...24]	1	00...101	mem[0x00...54]	Set 1 (01)
0	0			0			Set 0 (00)

(b)

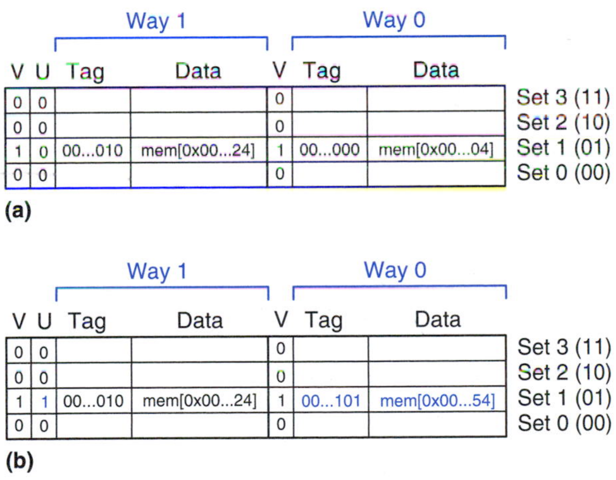

Figure 8.15 **Two-way associative cache with LRU replacement**

8.3.4 Advanced Cache Design*

Modern systems use multiple levels of caches to decrease memory access time. This section explores the performance of a two-level caching system and examines how block size, associativity, and cache capacity affect miss rate. The section also describes how caches handle stores, or writes, by using a write-through or write-back policy.

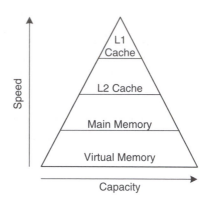

Figure 8.16 Memory hierarchy with two levels of cache

Multiple-Level Caches

Large caches are beneficial because they are more likely to hold data of interest and therefore have lower miss rates. However, large caches tend to be slower than small ones. Modern systems often use two levels of caches, as shown in Figure 8.16. The first-level (L1) cache is small enough to provide a one- or two-cycle access time. The second-level (L2) cache is also built from SRAM but is larger, and therefore slower, than the L1 cache. The processor first looks for the data in the L1 cache. If the L1 cache misses, the processor looks in the L2 cache. If the L2 cache misses, the processor fetches the data from main memory. Some modern systems add even more levels of cache to the memory hierarchy, because accessing main memory is so slow.

Example 8.11 SYSTEM WITH AN L2 CACHE

Use the system of Figure 8.16 with access times of 1, 10, and 100 cycles for the L1 cache, L2 cache, and main memory, respectively. Assume that the L1 and L2 caches have miss rates of 5% and 20%, respectively. Specifically, of the 5% of accesses that miss the L1 cache, 20% of those also miss the L2 cache. What is the average memory access time ($AMAT$)?

Solution: Each memory access checks the L1 cache. When the L1 cache misses (5% of the time), the processor checks the L2 cache. When the L2 cache misses (20% of the time), the processor fetches the data from main memory. Using Equation 8.2, we calculate the average memory access time as follows: 1 cycle + 0.05[10 cycles + 0.2(100 cycles)] = 2.5 cycles

The L2 miss rate is high because it receives only the "hard" memory accesses, those that miss in the L1 cache. If all accesses went directly to the L2 cache, the L2 miss rate would be about 1%.

Reducing Miss Rate

Cache misses can be reduced by changing capacity, block size, and/or associativity. The first step to reducing the miss rate is to understand the causes of the misses. The misses can be classified as compulsory, capacity, and conflict. The first request to a cache block is called a *compulsory miss*, because the block must be read from memory regardless of the cache design. *Capacity misses* occur when the cache is too small to hold all concurrently used data. *Conflict misses* are caused when several addresses map to the same set and evict blocks that are still needed.

Changing cache parameters can affect one or more type of cache miss. For example, increasing cache capacity can reduce conflict and capacity misses, but it does not affect compulsory misses. On the other hand, increasing block size could reduce compulsory misses (due to spatial locality) but might actually *increase* conflict misses (because more addresses would map to the same set and could conflict).

Memory systems are complicated enough that the best way to evaluate their performance is by running benchmarks while varying cache parameters. Figure 8.17 plots miss rate versus cache size and degree of associativity for the SPEC2000 benchmark. This benchmark has a small number of compulsory misses, shown by the dark region near the x-axis. As expected, when cache size increases, capacity misses decrease. Increased associativity, especially for small caches, decreases the number of conflict misses shown along the top of the curve.

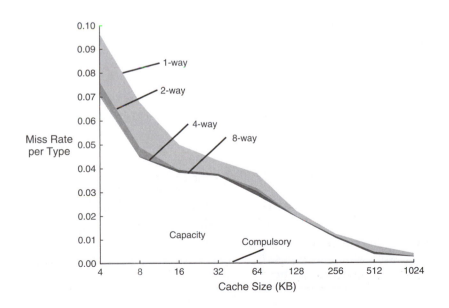

Figure 8.17 Miss rate versus cache size and associativity on SPEC2000 benchmark
Adapted with permission from Hennessy and Patterson, *Computer Architecture: A Quantitative Approach*, 3rd ed., Morgan Kaufmann, 2003.

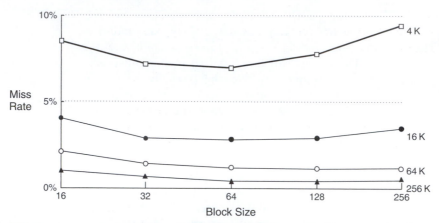

Figure 8.18 Miss rate versus block size and cache size on SPEC92 benchmark Adapted with permission from Hennessy and Patterson, *Computer Architecture: A Quantitative Approach*, 3rd ed., Morgan Kaufmann, 2003.

Increasing associativity beyond four or eight ways provides only small decreases in miss rate.

As mentioned, miss rate can also be decreased by using larger block sizes that take advantage of spatial locality. But as block size increases, the number of sets in a fixed size cache decreases, increasing the probability of conflicts. Figure 8.18 plots miss rate versus block size (in number of bytes) for caches of varying capacity. For small caches, such as the 4-KB cache, increasing the block size beyond 64 bytes *increases* the miss rate because of conflicts. For larger caches, increasing the block size does not change the miss rate. However, large block sizes might still increase execution time because of the larger miss penalty, the time required to fetch the missing cache block from main memory on a miss.

Write Policy

The previous sections focused on memory loads. Memory stores, or writes, follow a similar procedure as loads. Upon a memory store, the processor checks the cache. If the cache misses, the cache block is fetched from main memory into the cache, and then the appropriate word in the cache block is written. If the cache hits, the word is simply written to the cache block.

Caches are classified as either write-through or write-back. In a *write-through* cache, the data written to a cache block is simultaneously written to main memory. In a *write-back* cache, a *dirty bit* (D) is associated with each cache block. D is 1 when the cache block has been written and 0 otherwise. Dirty cache blocks are written back to main memory only when they are evicted from the cache. A write-through cache requires no dirty bit but usually requires more main memory writes than a write-back cache. Modern caches are usually write-back, because main memory access time is so large.

Example 8.12 WRITE-THROUGH VERSUS WRITE-BACK

Suppose a cache has a block size of four words. How many main memory accesses are required by the following code when using each write policy: write-through or write-back?

```
sw $t0, 0x0($0)
sw $t0, 0xC($0)
sw $t0, 0x8($0)
sw $t0, 0x4($0)
```

Solution: All four store instructions write to the same cache block. With a write-through cache, each store instruction writes a word to main memory, requiring four main memory writes. A write-back policy requires only one main memory access, when the dirty cache block is evicted.

8.3.5 The Evolution of MIPS Caches*

Table 8.3 traces the evolution of cache organizations used by the MIPS processor from 1985 to 2004. The major trends are the introduction of multiple levels of cache, larger cache capacity, and increased associativity. These trends are driven by the growing disparity between CPU frequency and main memory speed and the decreasing cost of transistors. The growing difference between CPU and memory speeds necessitates a lower miss rate to avoid the main memory bottleneck, and the decreasing cost of transistors allows larger cache sizes.

Table 8.3 MIPS cache evolution*

Year	CPU	MHz	L1 Cache	L2 Cache
1985	R2000	16.7	none	none
1990	R3000	33	32 KB direct mapped	none
1991	R4000	100	8 KB direct mapped	1 MB direct mapped
1995	R10000	250	32 KB two-way	4 MB two-way
2001	R14000	600	32 KB two-way	16 MB two-way
2004	R16000A	800	64 KB two-way	16 MB two-way

* Adapted from D. Sweetman, *See MIPS Run*, Morgan Kaufmann, 1999.

8.4 VIRTUAL MEMORY

Most modern computer systems use a *hard disk* (also called a *hard drive*) as the lowest level in the memory hierarchy (see Figure 8.4). Compared with the ideal large, fast, cheap memory, a hard disk is large and cheap but terribly slow. The disk provides a much larger capacity than is possible with a cost-effective main memory (DRAM). However, if a significant fraction of memory accesses involve the disk, performance is dismal. You may have encountered this on a PC when running too many programs at once.

Figure 8.19 shows a hard disk with the lid of its case removed. As the name implies, the hard disk contains one or more rigid disks or *platters*, each of which has a *read/write head* on the end of a long triangular arm. The head moves to the correct location on the disk and reads or writes data magnetically as the disk rotates beneath it. The head takes several milliseconds to *seek* the correct location on the disk, which is fast from a human perspective but millions of times slower than the processor.

Figure 8.19 Hard disk

The objective of adding a hard disk to the memory hierarchy is to inexpensively give the illusion of a very large memory while still providing the speed of faster memory for most accesses. A computer with only 128 MB of DRAM, for example, could effectively provide 2 GB of memory using the hard disk. This larger 2-GB memory is called *virtual memory*, and the smaller 128-MB main memory is called *physical memory*. We will use the term physical memory to refer to main memory throughout this section.

Programs can access data anywhere in virtual memory, so they must use *virtual addresses* that specify the location in virtual memory. The physical memory holds a subset of most recently accessed virtual memory. In this way, physical memory acts as a cache for virtual memory. Thus, most accesses hit in physical memory at the speed of DRAM, yet the program enjoys the capacity of the larger virtual memory.

Virtual memory systems use different terminologies for the same caching principles discussed in Section 8.3. Table 8.4 summarizes the analogous terms. Virtual memory is divided into *virtual pages*, typically 4 KB in size. Physical memory is likewise divided into *physical pages* of the same size. A virtual page may be located in physical memory (DRAM) or on the disk. For example, Figure 8.20 shows a virtual memory that is larger than physical memory. The rectangles indicate pages. Some virtual pages are present in physical memory, and some are located on the disk. The process of determining the physical address from the virtual address is called *address translation*. If the processor attempts to access a virtual address that is not in physical memory, a *page fault* occurs, and the operating system loads the page from the hard disk into physical memory.

To avoid page faults caused by conflicts, any virtual page can map to any physical page. In other words, physical memory behaves as a fully associative cache for virtual memory. In a conventional fully associative cache, every cache block has a comparator that checks the most significant address bits against a tag to determine whether the request hits in

> A computer with 32-bit addresses can access a maximum of 2^{32} bytes = 4 GB of memory. This is one of the motivations for moving to 64-bit computers, which can access far more memory.

Table 8.4 Analogous cache and virtual memory terms

Cache	Virtual Memory
Block	Page
Block size	Page size
Block offset	Page offset
Miss	Page fault
Tag	Virtual page number

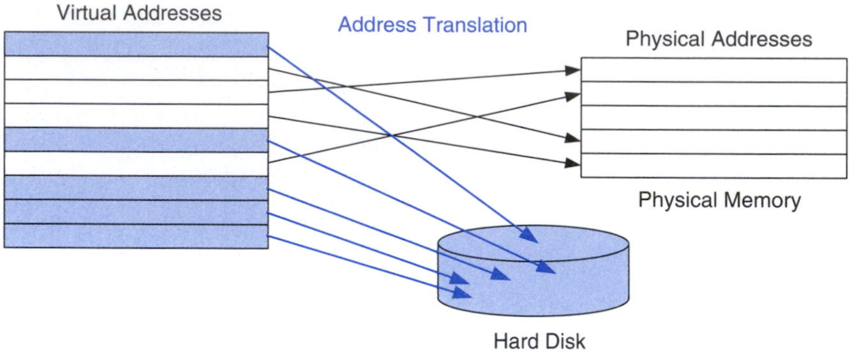

Virtual Addresses   Address Translation   Physical Addresses

Figure 8.20 Virtual and physical pages

the block. In an analogous virtual memory system, each physical page would need a comparator to check the most significant virtual address bits against a tag to determine whether the virtual page maps to that physical page.

A realistic virtual memory system has so many physical pages that providing a comparator for each page would be excessively expensive. Instead, the virtual memory system uses a page table to perform address translation. A page table contains an entry for each virtual page, indicating its location in physical memory or that it is on the disk. Each load or store instruction requires a page table access followed by a physical memory access. The page table access translates the virtual address used by the program to a physical address. The physical address is then used to actually read or write the data.

The page table is usually so large that it is located in physical memory. Hence, each load or store involves two physical memory accesses: a page table access, and a data access. To speed up address translation, a translation lookaside buffer (TLB) caches the most commonly used page table entries.

The remainder of this section elaborates on address translation, page tables, and TLBs.

8.4.1 Address Translation

In a system with virtual memory, programs use virtual addresses so that they can access a large memory. The computer must translate these virtual addresses to either find the address in physical memory or take a page fault and fetch the data from the hard disk.

Recall that virtual memory and physical memory are divided into pages. The most significant bits of the virtual or physical address specify the virtual or physical *page number*. The least significant bits specify the word within the page and are called the *page offset*.

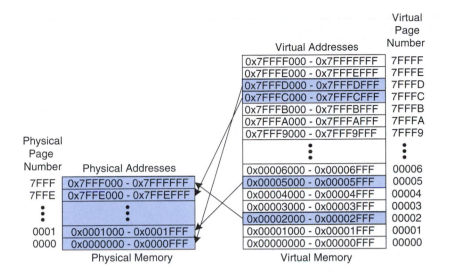

Figure 8.21 Physical and virtual pages

Figure 8.21 illustrates the page organization of a virtual memory system with 2 GB of virtual memory and 128 MB of physical memory divided into 4-KB pages. MIPS accommodates 32-bit addresses. With a 2-GB = 2^{31}-byte virtual memory, only the least significant 31 virtual address bits are used; the 32nd bit is always 0. Similarly, with a 128-MB = 2^{27}-byte physical memory, only the least significant 27 physical address bits are used; the upper 5 bits are always 0.

Because the page size is 4 KB = 2^{12} bytes, there are $2^{31}/2^{12} = 2^{19}$ virtual pages and $2^{27}/2^{12} = 2^{15}$ physical pages. Thus, the virtual and physical page numbers are 19 and 15 bits, respectively. Physical memory can only hold up to 1/16th of the virtual pages at any given time. The rest of the virtual pages are kept on disk.

Figure 8.21 shows virtual page 5 mapping to physical page 1, virtual page 0x7FFFC mapping to physical page 0x7FFE, and so forth. For example, virtual address 0x53F8 (an offset of 0x3F8 within virtual page 5) maps to physical address 0x13F8 (an offset of 0x3F8 within physical page 1). The least significant 12 bits of the virtual and physical addresses are the same (0x3F8) and specify the page offset within the virtual and physical pages. Only the page number needs to be translated to obtain the physical address from the virtual address.

Figure 8.22 illustrates the translation of a virtual address to a physical address. The least significant 12 bits indicate the page offset and require no translation. The upper 19 bits of the virtual address specify the *virtual page number* (VPN) and are translated to a 15-bit *physical page number* (PPN). The next two sections describe how page tables and TLBs are used to perform this address translation.

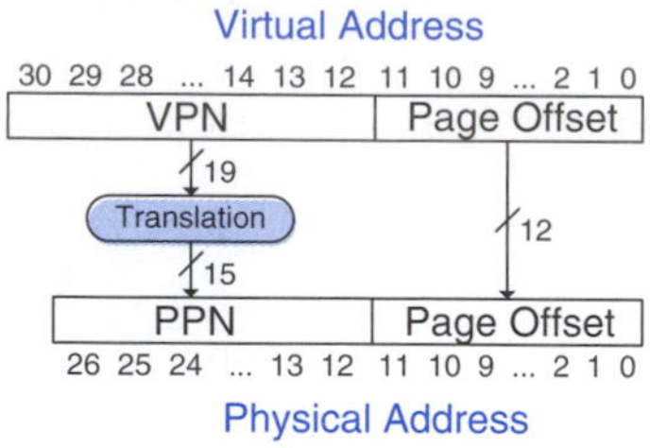

Figure 8.22 Translation from virtual address to physical address

---

Example 8.13 VIRTUAL ADDRESS TO PHYSICAL ADDRESS
                TRANSLATION

Find the physical address of virtual address 0x247C using the virtual memory system shown in Figure 8.21.

Solution: The 12-bit page offset (0x47C) requires no translation. The remaining 19 bits of the virtual address give the virtual page number, so virtual address 0x247C is found in virtual page 0x2. In Figure 8.21, virtual page 0x2 maps to physical page 0x7FFF. Thus, virtual address 0x247C maps to physical address 0x7FFF47C.

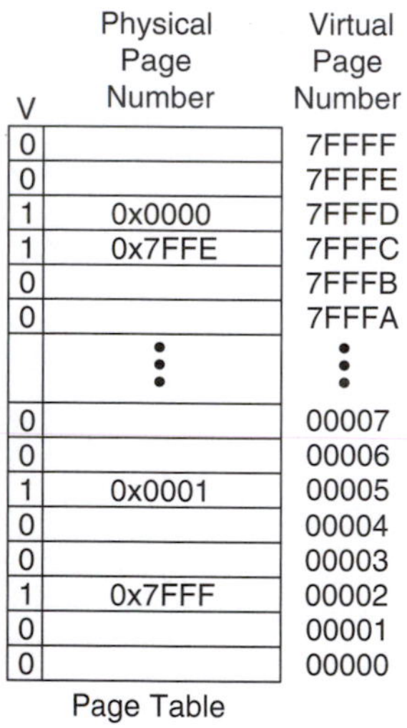

8.4.2 The Page Table

The processor uses a *page table* to translate virtual addresses to physical addresses. Recall that the page table contains an entry for each virtual page. This entry contains a physical page number and a valid bit. If the valid bit is 1, the virtual page maps to the physical page specified in the entry. Otherwise, the virtual page is found on disk.

Because the page table is so large, it is stored in physical memory. Let us assume for now that it is stored as a contiguous array, as shown in Figure 8.23. This page table contains the mapping of the memory system of Figure 8.21. The page table is indexed with the virtual page number (VPN). For example, entry 5 specifies that virtual page 5 maps to physical page 1. Entry 6 is invalid ($V = 0$), so virtual page 6 is located on disk.

Figure 8.23 The page table for Figure 8.21

Example 8.14 USING THE PAGE TABLE TO PERFORM ADDRESS
                TRANSLATION

Find the physical address of virtual address 0x247C using the page table shown in Figure 8.23.

Solution: Figure 8.24 shows the virtual address to physical address translation for virtual address 0x247C. The 12-bit page offset requires no translation. The remaining 19 bits of the virtual address are the virtual page number, 0x2, and give the index into the page table. The page table maps virtual page 0x2 to physical page 0x7FFF. So, virtual address 0x247C maps to physical address 0x7FFF47C. The least significant 12 bits are the same in both the physical and the virtual address.

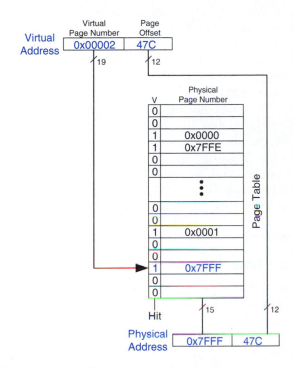

Figure 8.24 Address translation using the page table

   The page table can be stored anywhere in physical memory, at the discretion of the OS. The processor typically uses a dedicated register, called the *page table register*, to store the base address of the page table in physical memory.

   To perform a load or store, the processor must first translate the virtual address to a physical address and then access the data at that physical address. The processor extracts the virtual page number from the virtual address and adds it to the page table register to find the physical address of the page table entry. The processor then reads this page table entry from physical memory to obtain the physical page number. If the entry is valid, it merges this physical page number with the page offset to create the physical address. Finally, it reads or writes data at this physical address. Because the page table is stored in physical memory, each load or store involves two physical memory accesses.

8.4.3 The Translation Lookaside Buffer

Virtual memory would have a severe performance impact if it required a page table read on every load or store, doubling the delay of loads and stores. Fortunately, page table accesses have great temporal locality. The temporal and spatial locality of data accesses and the large page size mean that many consecutive loads or stores are likely to reference the same page. Therefore, if the processor remembers the last page table entry that it read, it can probably reuse this translation without rereading the page table. In general, the processor can keep the last several page table entries in a small cache called a *translation lookaside buffer* (TLB). The processor "looks aside" to find the translation in the TLB before having to access the page table in physical memory. In real programs, the vast majority of accesses hit in the TLB, avoiding the time-consuming page table reads from physical memory.

A TLB is organized as a fully associative cache and typically holds 16 to 512 entries. Each TLB entry holds a virtual page number and its corresponding physical page number. The TLB is accessed using the virtual page number. If the TLB hits, it returns the corresponding physical page number. Otherwise, the processor must read the page table in physical memory. The TLB is designed to be small enough that it can be accessed in less than one cycle. Even so, TLBs typically have a hit rate of greater than 99%. The TLB decreases the number of memory accesses required for most load or store instructions from two to one.

Example 8.15 USING THE TLB TO PERFORM ADDRESS TRANSLATION

Consider the virtual memory system of Figure 8.21. Use a two-entry TLB or explain why a page table access is necessary to translate virtual addresses 0x247C and 0x5FB0 to physical addresses. Suppose the TLB currently holds valid translations of virtual pages 0x2 and 0x7FFFD.

Solution: Figure 8.25 shows the two-entry TLB with the request for virtual address 0x247C. The TLB receives the virtual page number of the incoming address, 0x2, and compares it to the virtual page number of each entry. Entry 0 matches and is valid, so the request hits. The translated physical address is the physical page number of the matching entry, 0x7FFF, concatenated with the page offset of the virtual address. As always, the page offset requires no translation.

The request for virtual address 0x5FB0 misses in the TLB. So, the request is forwarded to the page table for translation.

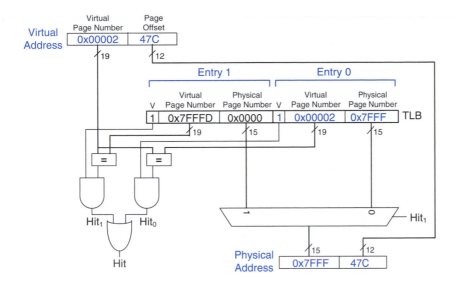

Figure 8.25 Address translation using a two-entry TLB

8.4.4 Memory Protection

So far this section has focused on using virtual memory to provide a fast, inexpensive, large memory. An equally important reason to use virtual memory is to provide protection between concurrently running programs.

As you probably know, modern computers typically run several programs or *processes* at the same time. All of the programs are simultaneously present in physical memory. In a well-designed computer system, the programs should be protected from each other so that no program can crash or hijack another program. Specifically, no program should be able to access another program's memory without permission. This is called *memory protection*.

Virtual memory systems provide memory protection by giving each program its own *virtual address space*. Each program can use as much memory as it wants in that virtual address space, but only a portion of the virtual address space is in physical memory at any given time. Each program can use its entire virtual address space without having to worry about where other programs are physically located. However, a program can access only those physical pages that are mapped in its page table. In this way, a program cannot accidentally or maliciously access another program's physical pages, because they are not mapped in its page table. In some cases, multiple programs access common instructions or data. The operating system adds control bits to each page table entry to determine which programs, if any, can write to the shared physical pages.

8.4.5 Replacement Policies*

Virtual memory systems use write-back and an approximate least recently used (LRU) replacement policy. A write-through policy, where each write to physical memory initiates a write to disk, would be impractical. Store instructions would operate at the speed of the disk instead of the speed of the processor (milliseconds instead of nanoseconds). Under the write-back policy, the physical page is written back to disk only when it is evicted from physical memory. Writing the physical page back to disk and reloading it with a different virtual page is called *swapping*, so the disk in a virtual memory system is sometimes called *swap space*. The processor swaps out one of the least recently used physical pages when a page fault occurs, then replaces that page with the missing virtual page. To support these replacement policies, each page table entry contains two additional status bits: a dirty bit, D, and a use bit, U.

The dirty bit is 1 if any store instructions have changed the physical page since it was read from disk. When a physical page is swapped out, it needs to be written back to disk only if its dirty bit is 1; otherwise, the disk already holds an exact copy of the page.

The use bit is 1 if the physical page has been accessed recently. As in a cache system, exact LRU replacement would be impractically complicated. Instead, the OS approximates LRU replacement by periodically resetting all the use bits in the page table. When a page is accessed, its use bit is set to 1. Upon a page fault, the OS finds a page with $U = 0$ to swap out of physical memory. Thus, it does not necessarily replace the least recently used page, just one of the least recently used pages.

8.4.6 Multilevel Page Tables*

Page tables can occupy a large amount of physical memory. For example, the page table from the previous sections for a 2 GB virtual memory with 4 KB pages would need 2^{19} entries. If each entry is 4 bytes, the page table is $2^{19} \times 2^2$ bytes $= 2^{21}$ bytes $= 2$ MB.

To conserve physical memory, page tables can be broken up into multiple (usually two) levels. The first-level page table is always kept in physical memory. It indicates where small second-level page tables are stored in virtual memory. The second-level page tables each contain the actual translations for a range of virtual pages. If a particular range of translations is not actively used, the corresponding second-level page table can be swapped out to the hard disk so it does not waste physical memory.

In a two-level page table, the virtual page number is split into two parts: the *page table number* and the *page table offset*, as shown in Figure 8.26. The page table number indexes the first-level page table, which must reside in physical memory. The first-level page table entry gives the base address of the second-level page table or indicates that

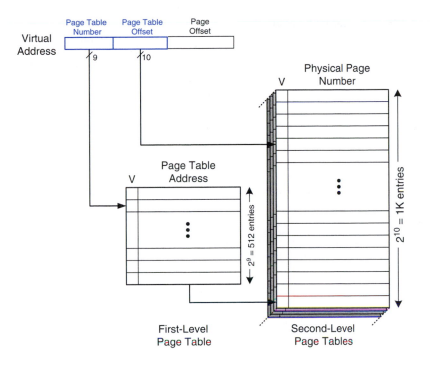

Figure 8.26 Hierarchical page tables

it must be fetched from disk when V is 0. The page table offset indexes the second-level page table. The remaining 12 bits of the virtual address are the page offset, as before, for a page size of $2^{12} = 4$ KB.

In Figure 8.26 the 19-bit virtual page number is broken into 9 and 10 bits, to indicate the page table number and the page table offset, respectively. Thus, the first-level page table has $2^9 = 512$ entries. Each of these 512 second-level page tables has $2^{10} = 1$ K entries. If each of the first- and second-level page table entries is 32 bits (4 bytes) and only two second-level page tables are present in physical memory at once, the hierarchical page table uses only $(512 \times 4$ bytes$) + 2 \times (1$ K $\times 4$ bytes$) = 10$ KB of physical memory. The two-level page table requires a fraction of the physical memory needed to store the entire page table (2 MB). The drawback of a two-level page table is that it adds yet another memory access for translation when the TLB misses.

Example 8.16 USING A MULTILEVEL PAGE TABLE FOR ADDRESS
              TRANSLATION

Figure 8.27 shows the possible contents of the two-level page table from Figure 8.26. The contents of only one second-level page table are shown. Using this two-level page table, describe what happens on an access to virtual address 0x003FEFB0.

Solution: As always, only the virtual page number requires translation. The most significant nine bits of the virtual address, 0x0, give the page table number, the index into the first-level page table. The first-level page table at entry 0x0 indicates that the second-level page table is resident in memory ($V = 1$) and its physical address is 0x2375000.

The next ten bits of the virtual address, 0x3FE, are the page table offset, which gives the index into the second-level page table. Entry 0 is at the bottom of the second-level page table, and entry 0x3FF is at the top. Entry 0x3FE in the second-level page table indicates that the virtual page is resident in physical memory ($V = 1$) and that the physical page number is 0x23F1. The physical page number is concatenated with the page offset to form the physical address, 0x23F1FB0.

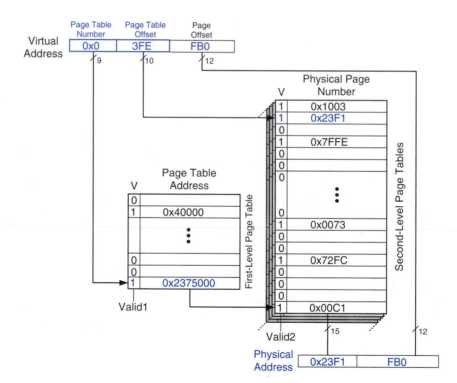

Figure 8.27 Address translation using a two-level page table

8.5 MEMORY-MAPPED I/O*

Processors also use the memory interface to communicate with *input/output (I/O) devices* such as keyboards, monitors, and printers. A processor accesses an I/O device using the address and data busses in the same way that it accesses memory.

A portion of the address space is dedicated to I/O devices rather than memory. For example, suppose that addresses in the range

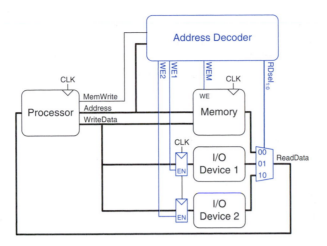

Figure 8.28 Support hardware for memory-mapped I/O

0xFFFF0000 to 0xFFFFFFFF are used for I/O. Recall from Section 6.6.1 that these addresses are in a reserved portion of the memory map. Each I/O device is assigned one or more memory addresses in this range. A store to the specified address sends data to the device. A load receives data from the device. This method of communicating with I/O devices is called *memory-mapped I/O*.

In a system with memory-mapped I/O, a load or store may access either memory or an I/O device. Figure 8.28 shows the hardware needed to support two memory-mapped I/O devices. An *address decoder* determines which device communicates with the processor. It uses the *Address* and *MemWrite* signals to generate control signals for the rest of the hardware. The *ReadData* multiplexer selects between memory and the various I/O devices. Write-enabled registers hold the values written to the I/O devices.

Some architectures, notably IA-32, use specialized instructions instead of memory-mapped I/O to communicate with I/O devices. These instructions are of the following form, where device1 and device2 are the unique ID of the peripheral device:

```
lwio $t0, device1
swio $t0, device2
```

This type of communication with I/O devices is called *programmed I/O*.

Example 8.17 COMMUNICATING WITH I/O DEVICES

Suppose I/O Device 1 in Figure 8.28 is assigned the memory address 0xFFFFFFF4. Show the MIPS assembly code for writing the value 7 to I/O Device 1 and for reading the output value from I/O Device 1.

Solution: The following MIPS assembly code writes the value 7 to I/O Device 1.[2]

```
addi $t0, $0, 7
sw   $t0, 0xFFF4($0)
```

The address decoder asserts *WE1* because the address is 0xFFFFFFF4 and *MemWrite* is TRUE. The value on the *WriteData* bus, 7, is written into the register connected to the input pins of I/O Device 1.

---

[2] Recall that the 16-bit immediate 0xFFF4 is sign-extended to the 32-bit value 0xFFFFFFF4.

To read from I/O Device 1, the processor performs the following MIPS assembly code.

```
lw $t1, 0xFFF4($0)
```

The address decoder sets $RDsel_{1:0}$ to 01, because it detects the address 0xFFFFFFF4 and *MemWrite* is FALSE. The output of I/O Device 1 passes through the multiplexer onto the *ReadData* bus and is loaded into `$t1` in the processor.

Software that communicates with an I/O device is called a *device driver*. You have probably downloaded or installed device drivers for your printer or other I/O device. Writing a device driver requires detailed knowledge about the I/O device hardware. Other programs call functions in the device driver to access the device without having to understand the low-level device hardware.

To illustrate memory-mapped I/O hardware and software, the rest of this section describes interfacing a commercial speech synthesizer chip to a MIPS processor.

Speech Synthesizer Hardware

See www.speechchips.com for more information about the SP0256 and the allophone encodings.

The Radio Shack SP0256 speech synthesizer chip generates robot-like speech. Words are composed of one or more *allophones*, the fundamental units of sound. For example, the word "hello" uses five allophones represented by the following symbols in the SP0256 speech chip: HH1 EH LL AX OW. The speech synthesizer uses 6-bit codes to represent 64 different allophones that appear in the English language. For example, the five allophones for the word "hello" correspond to the hexadecimal values 0x1B, 0x07, 0x2D, 0x0F, 0x20, respectively. The processor sends a series of allophones to the speech synthesizer, which drives a speaker to blabber the sounds.

Figure 8.29 shows the pinout of the SP0256 speech chip. The I/O pins highlighted in blue are used to interface with the MIPS processor to produce speech. Pins $A_{6:1}$ receive the 6-bit allophone encoding from the processor. The allophone sound is produced on the *Digital Out* pin. The *Digital Out* signal is first amplified and then sent to a speaker. The other two highlighted pins, *SBY* and $\overline{ALD}$, are status and control pins. When the *SBY* output is 1, the speech chip is standing by and is ready to receive a new allophone. On the falling edge of the address load input $\overline{ALD}$, the speech chip reads the allophone specified by $A_{6:1}$. Other pins, such as power and ground (V_{DD} and V_{SS}) and the clock (*OSC1*), must be connected as shown but are not driven by the processor.

Figure 8.30 shows the speech synthesizer interfaced to the MIPS processor. The processor uses three memory-mapped I/O addresses to communicate with the speech synthesizer. We arbitrarily have chosen

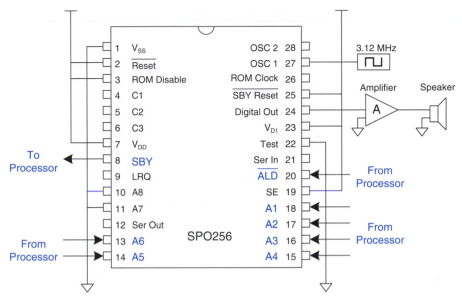

Figure 8.29 SP0256 speech synthesizer chip pinout

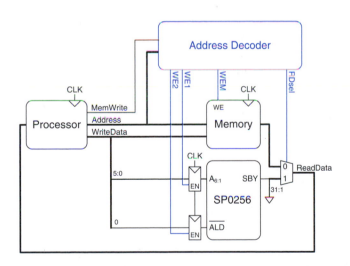

Figure 8.30 Hardware for driving the SP0256 speech synthesizer

that the $A_{6:1}$ port is mapped to address 0xFFFFFF00, $\overline{ALD}$ to 0xFFFFFF04, and *SBY* to 0xFFFFFF08. Although the *WriteData* bus is 32 bits, only the least significant 6 bits are used for $A_{6:1}$, and the least significant bit is used for $\overline{ALD}$; the other bits are ignored. Similarly, *SBY* is read on the least significant bit of the *ReadData* bus; the other bits are 0.

Speech Synthesizer Device Driver

The device driver controls the speech synthesizer by sending an appropriate series of allophones over the memory-mapped I/O interface. It follows the protocol expected by the SPO256 chip, given below:

- Set $\overline{ALD}$ to 1

- Wait until the chip asserts SBY to indicate that it is finished speaking the previous allophone and is ready for the next

- Write a 6-bit allophone to $A_{6:1}$

- Reset $\overline{ALD}$ to 0 to initiate speech

This sequence can be repeated for any number of allophones. The MIPS assembly in Code Example 8.1 writes five allophones to the speech chip. The allophone encodings are stored as 32-bit values in a five-entry array starting at memory address 0x10000000.

Code Example 8.1 SPEECH CHIP DEVICE DRIVER

```
init:
      addi $t1, $0, 1      # $t1 = 1 (value to write to ALD)
      addi $t2, $0, 20     # $t2 = array size * 4
      lui  $t3, 0x1000     # $t3 = array base address
      addi $t4, $0, 0      # $t4 = 0 (array index)

start:
      sw   $t1, 0xFF04($0) # ALD =1
loop:
      lw   $t5, 0xFF08($0) # $t5 = SBY
      beq  $0,  $t5, loop  # loop until SBY == 1

      add  $t5, $t3, $t4   # $t5 = address of allophone
      lw   $t5, 0($t5)     # $t5 = allophone
      sw   $t5, 0xFF00($0) # A6:1 = allophone
      sw   $0,  0xFF04($0) # ALD = 0 to initiate speech
      addi $t4, $t4, 4     # increment array index
      beq  $t4, $t2, done  # last allophone in array?
      j    start           # repeat

done:
```

The assembly code in Code Example 8.1 *polls*, or repeatedly checks, the *SBY* signal to determine when the speech chip is ready to receive a new allophone. The code functions correctly but wastes valuable processor cycles that could be used to perform useful work. Instead of polling, the processor could use an *interrupt* connected to *SBY*. When *SBY* rises, the processor stops what it is doing and jumps to code that handles the interrupt. In the case of the speech synthesizer, the interrupt handler would send the next allophone, then let the processor resume what it was doing before the interrupt. As described in Section 6.7.2, the processor handles interrupts like any other exception.

8.6 REAL-WORLD PERSPECTIVE: IA-32 MEMORY AND I/O SYSTEMS*

As processors get faster, they need ever more elaborate memory hierarchies to keep a steady supply of data and instructions flowing. This section describes the memory systems of IA-32 processors to illustrate the progression. Section 7.9 contained photographs of the processors, highlighting the on-chip caches. IA-32 also has an unusual programmed I/O system that differs from the more common memory-mapped I/O.

8.6.1 IA-32 Cache Systems

The 80386, initially produced in 1985, operated at 16 MHz. It lacked a cache, so it directly accessed main memory for all instructions and data. Depending on the speed of the memory, the processor might get an immediate response, or it might have to pause for one or more cycles for the memory to react. These cycles are called *wait states*, and they increase the CPI of the processor. Microprocessor clock frequencies have increased by at least 25% per year since then, whereas memory latency has scarcely diminished. The delay from when the processor sends an address to main memory until the memory returns the data can now exceed 100 processor clock cycles. Therefore, caches with a low miss rate are essential to good performance. Table 8.5 summarizes the evolution of cache systems on Intel IA-32 processors.

The 80486 introduced a unified write-through cache to hold both instructions and data. Most high-performance computer systems also provided a larger second-level cache on the motherboard using commercially available SRAM chips that were substantially faster than main memory.

The Pentium processor introduced separate instruction and data caches to avoid contention during simultaneous requests for data and instructions. The caches used a write-back policy, reducing the communication with main memory. Again, a larger second-level cache (typically 256–512 KB) was usually offered on the motherboard.

The P6 series of processors (Pentium Pro, Pentium II, and Pentium III) were designed for much higher clock frequencies. The second-level cache on the motherboard could not keep up, so it was moved closer to the processor to improve its latency and throughput. The Pentium Pro was packaged in a *multichip module* (MCM) containing both the processor chip and a second-level cache chip, as shown in Figure 8.31. Like the Pentium, the processor had separate 8-KB level 1 instruction and data

Table 8.5 Evolution of Intel IA-32 microprocessor memory systems

Processor	Year	Frequency (MHz)	Level 1 Data Cache	Level 1 Instruction Cache	Level 2 Cache
80386	1985	16–25	none	none	none
80486	1989	25–100	8 KB unified		none on chip
Pentium	1993	60–300	8 KB	8 KB	none on chip
Pentium Pro	1995	150–200	8 KB	8 KB	256 KB–1 MB on MCM
Pentium II	1997	233–450	16 KB	16 KB	256–512 KB on cartridge
Pentium III	1999	450–1400	16 KB	16 KB	256–512 KB on chip
Pentium 4	2001	1400–3730	8–16 KB	12 K op trace cache	256 KB–2 MB on chip
Pentium M	2003	900–2130	32 KB	32 KB	1–2 MB on chip
Core Duo	2005	1500–2160	32 KB/core	32 KB/core	2 MB shared on chip

caches. However, these caches were *nonblocking*, so that the out-of-order processor could continue executing subsequent cache accesses even if the cache missed a particular access and had to fetch data from main memory. The second-level cache was 256 KB, 512 KB, or 1 MB in size and could operate at the same speed as the processor. Unfortunately, the MCM packaging proved too expensive for high-volume manufacturing. Therefore, the Pentium II was sold in a lower-cost cartridge containing the processor and the second-level cache. The level 1 caches were doubled in size to compensate for the fact that the second-level cache operated at half the processor's speed. The Pentium III integrated a full-speed second-level cache directly onto the same chip as the processor. A cache on the same chip can operate at better latency and throughput, so it is substantially more effective than an off-chip cache of the same size.

The Pentium 4 offered a nonblocking level 1 data cache. It switched to a *trace cache* to store instructions after they had been decoded into micro-ops, avoiding the delay of redecoding each time instructions were fetched from the cache.

The Pentium M design was adapted from the Pentium III. It further increased the level 1 caches to 32 KB each and featured a 1- to 2-MB level 2 cache. The Core Duo contains two modified Pentium M processors and

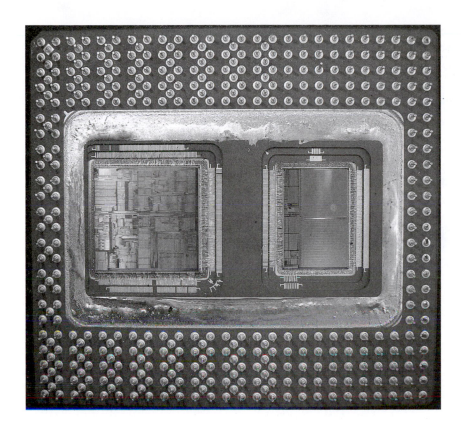

Figure 8.31 Pentium Pro multichip module with processor (left) and 256-KB cache (right) in a pin grid array (PGA) package (Courtesy Intel.)

a shared 2-MB cache on one chip. The shared cache is used for communication between the processors: one can write data to the cache, and the other can read it.

8.6.2 IA-32 Virtual Memory

IA-32 processors operate in either real mode or protected mode. *Real mode* is backward compatible with the original 8086. It only uses 20 bits of addresses, limiting memory to 1 MB, and it does not allow virtual memory.

Protected mode was introduced with the 80286 and extended to 32-bit addresses with the 80386. It supports virtual memory with 4-KB pages. It also provides memory protection so that one program cannot access the pages belonging to other programs. Hence, a buggy or malicious program cannot crash or corrupt other programs. All modern operating systems now use protected mode.

A 32-bit address permits up to 4 GB of memory. Processors since the Pentium Pro have bumped the memory capacity to 64 GB using a

Although memory protection became available in the hardware in the early 1980s, Microsoft Windows took almost 15 years to take advantage of the feature and prevent bad programs from crashing the entire computer. Until the release of Windows 2000, consumer versions of Windows were notoriously unstable. The lag between hardware features and software support can be extremely long.

technique called *physical address extension*. Each process uses 32-bit addresses. The virtual memory system maps these addresses onto a larger 36-bit virtual memory space. It uses different page tables for each process, so that each process can have its own address space of up to 4 GB.

8.6.3 IA-32 Programmed I/O

Most architectures use memory-mapped I/O, described in Section 8.5, in which programs access I/O devices by reading and writing memory locations. IA-32 uses *programmed I/O*, in which special IN and OUT instructions are used to read and write I/O devices. IA-32 defines 2^{16} I/O ports. The IN instruction reads one, two, or four bytes from the port specified by DX into AL, AX, or EAX. OUT is similar, but writes the port.

Connecting a peripheral device to a programmed I/O system is similar to connecting it to a memory-mapped system. When accessing an I/O port, the processor sends the port number rather than the memory address on the 16 least significant bits of the address bus. The device reads or writes data from the data bus. The major difference is that the processor also produces an $M/\overline{IO}$ signal. When $M/\overline{IO} = 1$, the processor is accessing memory. When it is 0, the process is accessing one of the I/O devices. The address decoder must also look at $M/\overline{IO}$ to generate the appropriate enables for main memory and for the I/O devices. I/O devices can also send interrupts to the processor to indicate that they are ready to communicate.

8.7 SUMMARY

Memory system organization is a major factor in determining computer performance. Different memory technologies, such as DRAM, SRAM, and hard disks, offer trade-offs in capacity, speed, and cost. This chapter introduced cache and virtual memory organizations that use a hierarchy of memories to approximate an ideal large, fast, inexpensive memory. Main memory is typically built from DRAM, which is significantly slower than the processor. A cache reduces access time by keeping commonly used data in fast SRAM. Virtual memory increases the memory capacity by using a hard disk to store data that does not fit in the main memory. Caches and virtual memory add complexity and hardware to a computer system, but the benefits usually outweigh the costs. All modern personal computers use caches and virtual memory. Most processors also use the memory interface to communicate with I/O devices. This is called memory-mapped I/O. Programs use load and store operations to access the I/O devices.

EPILOGUE

This chapter brings us to the end of our journey together into the realm of digital systems. We hope this book has conveyed the beauty and thrill of the art as well as the engineering knowledge. You have learned to design combinational and sequential logic using schematics and hardware description languages. You are familiar with larger building blocks such as multiplexers, ALUs, and memories. Computers are one of the most fascinating applications of digital systems. You have learned how to program a MIPS processor in its native assembly language and how to build the processor and memory system using digital building blocks. Throughout, you have seen the application of abstraction, discipline, hierarchy, modularity, and regularity. With these techniques, we have pieced together the puzzle of a microprocessor's inner workings. From cell phones to digital television to Mars rovers to medical imaging systems, our world is an increasingly digital place.

Imagine what Faustian bargain Charles Babbage would have made to take a similar journey a century and a half ago. He merely aspired to calculate mathematical tables with mechanical precision. Today's digital systems are yesterday's science fiction. Might Dick Tracy have listened to iTunes on his cell phone? Would Jules Verne have launched a constellation of global positioning satellites into space? Could Hippocrates have cured illness using high-resolution digital images of the brain? But at the same time, George Orwell's nightmare of ubiquitous government surveillance becomes closer to reality each day. And rogue states develop nuclear weapons using laptop computers more powerful than the room-sized supercomputers that simulated Cold War bombs. The microprocessor revolution continues to accelerate. The changes in the coming decades will surpass those of the past. You now have the tools to design and build these new systems that will shape our future. With your newfound power comes profound responsibility. We hope that you will use it, not just for fun and riches, but also for the benefit of humanity.

Exercises

Exercise 8.1 In less than one page, describe four everyday activities that exhibit temporal or spatial locality. List two activities for each type of locality, and be specific.

Exercise 8.2 In one paragraph, describe two short computer applications that exhibit temporal and/or spatial locality. Describe how. Be specific.

Exercise 8.3 Come up with a sequence of addresses for which a direct mapped cache with a size (capacity) of 16 words and block size of 4 words outperforms a fully associative cache with least recently used (LRU) replacement that has the same capacity and block size.

Exercise 8.4 Repeat Exercise 8.3 for the case when the fully associative cache outperforms the direct mapped cache.

Exercise 8.5 Describe the trade-offs of increasing each of the following cache parameters while keeping the others the same:

(a) block size

(b) associativity

(c) cache size

Exercise 8.6 Is the miss rate of a two-way set associative cache always, usually, occasionally, or never better than that of a direct mapped cache of the same capacity and block size? Explain.

Exercise 8.7 Each of the following statements pertains to the miss rate of caches. Mark each statement as true or false. Briefly explain your reasoning; present a counterexample if the statement is false.

(a) A two-way set associative cache always has a lower miss rate than a direct mapped cache with the same block size and total capacity.

(b) A 16-KB direct mapped cache always has a lower miss rate than an 8-KB direct mapped cache with the same block size.

(c) An instruction cache with a 32-byte block size usually has a lower miss rate than an instruction cache with an 8-byte block size, given the same degree of associativity and total capacity.

Exercise 8.8 A cache has the following parameters: b, block size given in numbers of words; S, number of sets; N, number of ways; and A, number of address bits.

(a) In terms of the parameters described, what is the cache capacity, C?

(b) In terms of the parameters described, what is the total number of bits required to store the tags?

(c) What are S and N for a fully associative cache of capacity C words with block size b?

(d) What is S for a direct mapped cache of size C words and block size b?

Exercise 8.9 A 16-word cache has the parameters given in Exercise 8.8. Consider the following repeating sequence of lw addresses (given in hexadecimal):

40 44 48 4C 70 74 78 7C 80 84 88 8C 90 94 98 9C 0 4 8 C 10 14 18 1C 20

Assuming least recently used (LRU) replacement for associative caches, determine the effective miss rate if the sequence is input to the following caches, ignoring startup effects (i.e., compulsory misses).

(a) direct mapped cache, $S = 16$, $b = 1$ word

(b) fully associative cache, $N = 16$, $b = 1$ word

(c) two-way set associative cache, $S = 8$, $b = 1$ word

(d) direct mapped cache, $S = 8$, $b = 2$ words

Exercise 8.10 Suppose you are running a program with the following data access pattern. The pattern is executed only once.

0x0, 0x8, 0x10, 0x18, 0x20, 0x28

(a) If you use a direct mapped cache with a cache size of 1 KB and a block size of 8 bytes (2 words), how many sets are in the cache?

(b) With the same cache and block size as in part (a), what is the miss rate of the direct mapped cache for the given memory access pattern?

(c) For the given memory access pattern, which of the following would decrease the miss rate the most? (Cache capacity is kept constant.) Circle one.

(i) Increasing the degree of associativity to 2.

(ii) Increasing the block size to 16 bytes.

(iii) Either (i) or (ii).

(iv) Neither (i) nor (ii).

Exercise 8.11 You are building an instruction cache for a MIPS processor. It has a total capacity of $4C = 2^{c+2}$ bytes. It is $N = 2^n$-way set associative ($N \geq 8$), with a block size of $b = 2^{b'}$ bytes ($b \geq 8$). Give your answers to the following questions in terms of these parameters.

(a) Which bits of the address are used to select a word within a block?

(b) Which bits of the address are used to select the set within the cache?

(c) How many bits are in each tag?

(d) How many tag bits are in the entire cache?

Exercise 8.12 Consider a cache with the following parameters: N (associativity) = 2, b (block size) = 2 words, W (word size) = 32 bits, C (cache size) = 32 K words, A (address size) = 32 bits. You need consider only word addresses.

(a) Show the tag, set, block offset, and byte offset bits of the address. State how many bits are needed for each field.

(b) What is the size of *all* the cache tags in bits?

(c) Suppose each cache block also has a valid bit (V) and a dirty bit (D). What is the size of each cache set, including data, tag, and status bits?

(d) Design the cache using the building blocks in Figure 8.32 and a small number of two-input logic gates. The cache design must include tag storage, data storage, address comparison, data output selection, and any other parts you feel are relevant. Note that the multiplexer and comparator blocks may be any size (n or p bits wide, respectively), but the SRAM blocks must be 16 K × 4 bits. Be sure to include a neatly labeled block diagram.

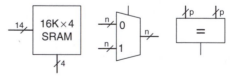

Figure 8.32 Building blocks

Exercise 8.13 You've joined a hot new Internet startup to build wrist watches with a built-in pager and Web browser. It uses an embedded processor with a multilevel cache scheme depicted in Figure 8.33. The processor includes a small on-chip cache in addition to a large off-chip second-level cache. (Yes, the watch weighs 3 pounds, but you should see it surf!)

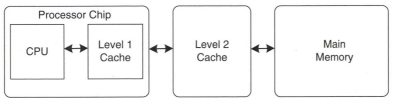

Figure 8.33 Computer system

Assume that the processor uses 32-bit physical addresses but accesses data only on word boundaries. The caches have the characteristics given in Table 8.6. The DRAM has an access time of t_m and a size of 512 MB.

Table 8.6 Memory characteristics

Characteristic	On-chip Cache	Off-chip Cache
organization	four-way set associative	direct mapped
hit rate	A	B
access time	t_a	t_b
block size	16 bytes	16 bytes
number of blocks	512	256K

(a) For a given word in memory, what is the total number of locations in which it might be found in the on-chip cache and in the second-level cache?

(b) What is the size, in bits, of each tag for the on-chip cache and the second-level cache?

(c) Give an expression for the average memory read access time. The caches are accessed in sequence.

(d) Measurements show that, for a particular problem of interest, the on-chip cache hit rate is 85% and the second-level cache hit rate is 90%. However, when the on-chip cache is disabled, the second-level cache hit rate shoots up to 98.5%. Give a brief explanation of this behavior.

Exercise 8.14 This chapter described the least recently used (LRU) replacement policy for multiway associative caches. Other, less common, replacement policies include first-in-first-out (FIFO) and random policies. FIFO replacement evicts the block that has been there the longest, regardless of how recently it was accessed. Random replacement randomly picks a block to evict.

(a) Discuss the advantages and disadvantages of each of these replacement policies.

(b) Describe a data access pattern for which FIFO would perform better than LRU.

Exercise 8.15 You are building a computer with a hierarchical memory system that consists of separate instruction and data caches followed by main memory. You are using the MIPS multicycle processor from Figure 7.41 running at 1 GHz.

(a) Suppose the instruction cache is perfect (i.e., always hits) but the data cache has a 5% miss rate. On a cache miss, the processor stalls for 60 ns to access main memory, then resumes normal operation. Taking cache misses into account, what is the average memory access time?

(b) How many clock cycles per instruction (CPI) on average are required for load and store word instructions considering the non-ideal memory system?

(c) Consider the benchmark application of Example 7.7 that has 25% loads, 10% stores, 11% branches, 2% jumps, and 52% R-type instructions.[3] Taking the non-ideal memory system into account, what is the average CPI for this benchmark?

(d) Now suppose that the instruction cache is also non-ideal and has a 7% miss rate. What is the average CPI for the benchmark in part (c)? Take into account both instruction and data cache misses.

Exercise 8.16 If a computer uses 64-bit virtual addresses, how much virtual memory can it access? Note that 2^{40} bytes = 1 *terabyte*, 2^{50} bytes = 1 *petabyte*, and 2^{60} bytes = 1 *exabyte*.

Exercise 8.17 A supercomputer designer chooses to spend $1 million on DRAM and the same amount on hard disks for virtual memory. Using the prices from Figure 8.4, how much physical and virtual memory will the computer have? How many bits of physical and virtual addresses are necessary to access this memory?

---

[3] Data from Patterson and Hennessy, *Computer Organization and Design*, 3rd Edition, Morgan Kaufmann, 2005. Used with permission.

Exercise 8.18 Consider a virtual memory system that can address a total of 2^{32} bytes. You have unlimited hard disk space, but are limited to only 8 MB of semiconductor (physical) memory. Assume that virtual and physical pages are each 4 KB in size.

(a) How many bits is the physical address?

(b) What is the maximum number of virtual pages in the system?

(c) How many physical pages are in the system?

(d) How many bits are the virtual and physical page numbers?

(e) Suppose that you come up with a direct mapped scheme that maps virtual pages to physical pages. The mapping uses the least significant bits of the virtual page number to determine the physical page number. How many virtual pages are mapped to each physical page? Why is this "direct mapping" a bad plan?

(f) Clearly, a more flexible and dynamic scheme for translating virtual addresses into physical addresses is required than the one described in part (d). Suppose you use a page table to store mappings (translations from virtual page number to physical page number). How many page table entries will the page table contain?

(g) Assume that, in addition to the physical page number, each page table entry also contains some status information in the form of a valid bit (V) and a dirty bit (D). How many bytes long is each page table entry? (Round up to an integer number of bytes.)

(h) Sketch the layout of the page table. What is the total size of the page table in bytes?

Exercise 8.19 You decide to speed up the virtual memory system of Exercise 8.18 by using a translation lookaside buffer (TLB). Suppose your memory system has the characteristics shown in Table 8.7. The TLB and cache miss rates indicate how often the requested entry is not found. The main memory miss rate indicates how often page faults occur.

Table 8.7 Memory characteristics

Memory Unit	Access Time (Cycles)	Miss Rate
TLB	1	0.05%
cache	1	2%
main memory	100	0.0003%
disk	1,000,000	0%

(a)   What is the average memory access time of the virtual memory system before and after adding the TLB? Assume that the page table is always resident in physical memory and is never held in the data cache.

(b)   If the TLB has 64 entries, how big (in bits) is the TLB? Give numbers for data (physical page number), tag (virtual page number), and valid bits of each entry. Show your work clearly.

(c)   Sketch the TLB. Clearly label all fields and dimensions.

(d)   What size SRAM would you need to build the TLB described in part (c)? Give your answer in terms of depth $\times$ width.

Exercise 8.20 Suppose the MIPS multicycle processor described in Section 7.4 uses a virtual memory system.

(a)   Sketch the location of the TLB in the multicycle processor schematic.

(b)   Describe how adding a TLB affects processor performance.

Exercise 8.21 The virtual memory system you are designing uses a single-level page table built from dedicated hardware (SRAM and associated logic). It supports 25-bit virtual addresses, 22-bit physical addresses, and 2^{16}-byte (64 KB) pages. Each page table entry contains a physical page number, a valid bit (V) and a dirty bit (D).

(a)   What is the total size of the page table, in bits?

(b)   The operating system team proposes reducing the page size from 64 to 16 KB, but the hardware engineers on your team object on the grounds of added hardware cost. Explain their objection.

(c)   The page table is to be integrated on the processor chip, along with the on-chip cache. The on-chip cache deals only with physical (not virtual) addresses. Is it possible to access the appropriate set of the on-chip cache concurrently with the page table access for a given memory access? Explain briefly the relationship that is necessary for concurrent access to the cache set and page table entry.

(d)   Is it possible to perform the tag comparison in the on-chip cache concurrently with the page table access for a given memory access? Explain briefly.

Exercise 8.22 Describe a scenario in which the virtual memory system might affect how an application is written. Be sure to include a discussion of how the page size and physical memory size affect the performance of the application.

Exercise 8.23 Suppose you own a personal computer (PC) that uses 32-bit virtual addresses.

(a) What is the maximum amount of virtual memory space each program can use?

(b) How does the size of your PC's hard disk affect performance?

(c) How does the size of your PC's physical memory affect performance?

Exercise 8.24 Use MIPS memory-mapped I/O to interact with a user. Each time the user presses a button, a pattern of your choice displays on five light-emitting diodes (LEDs). Suppose the input button is mapped to address 0xFFFFFF10 and the LEDs are mapped to address 0xFFFFFF14. When the button is pushed, its output is 1; otherwise it is 0.

(a) Write MIPS code to implement this functionality.

(b) Draw a schematic similar to Figure 8.30 for this memory-mapped I/O system.

(c) Write HDL code to implement the address decoder for your memory-mapped I/O system.

Exercise 8.25 Finite state machines (FSMs), like the ones you built in Chapter 3, can also be implemented in software.

(a) Implement the traffic light FSM from Figure 3.25 using MIPS assembly code. The inputs (T_A and T_B) are memory-mapped to bit 1 and bit 0, respectively, of address 0xFFFFF000. The two 3-bit outputs (L_A and L_B) are mapped to bits 0–2 and bits 3–5, respectively, of address 0xFFFFF004. Assume one-hot output encodings for each light, L_A and L_B; red is 100, yellow is 010, and green is 001.

(b) Draw a schematic similar to Figure 8.30 for this memory-mapped I/O system.

(c) Write HDL code to implement the address decoder for your memory-mapped I/O system.

Interview Questions

The following exercises present questions that have been asked on interviews.

Question 8.1 Explain the difference between direct mapped, set associative, and fully associative caches. For each cache type, describe an application for which that cache type will perform better than the other two.

Question 8.2 Explain how virtual memory systems work.

Question 8.3 Explain the advantages and disadvantages of using a virtual memory system.

Question 8.4 Explain how cache performance might be affected by the virtual page size of a memory system.

Question 8.5 Can addresses used for memory-mapped I/O be cached? Explain why or why not.

Digital System Implementation

A.1 INTRODUCTION

This appendix introduces practical issues in the design of digital systems. The material in this appendix is not necessary for understanding the rest of the book. However, it seeks to demystify the process of building real digital systems. Moreover, we believe that the best way to understand digital systems is to build and debug them yourself in the laboratory.

Digital systems are usually built using one or more chips. One strategy is to connect together chips containing individual logic gates or larger elements such as arithmetic/logical units (ALUs) or memories. Another is to use programmable logic, which contains generic arrays of circuitry that can be programmed to perform specific logic functions. Yet a third is to design a custom integrated circuit containing the specific logic necessary for the system. These three strategies offer trade-offs in cost, speed, power consumption, and design time that are explored in the following sections. This appendix also examines the physical packaging and assembly of circuits, the transmission lines that connect the chips, and the economics of digital systems.

A.2 74XX LOGIC

In the 1970s and 1980s, many digital systems were built from simple chips, each containing a handful of logic gates. For example, the 7404 chip contains six NOT gates, the 7408 contains four AND gates, and the 7474 contains two flip-flops. These chips are collectively referred to as *74xx-series* logic. They were sold by many manufacturers, typically for 10 to 25 cents per chip. These chips are now largely obsolete, but they are still handy for simple digital systems or class projects, because they are so inexpensive and easy to use. 74xx-series chips are commonly sold in 14-pin *dual inline packages* (DIPs).

74LS04 inverter chip in a 14-pin dual inline package. The part number is on the first line. LS indicates the logic family (see Section A.6). The N suffix indicates a DIP package. The large S is the logo of the manufacturer, Signetics. The bottom two lines of gibberish are codes indicating the batch in which the chip was manufactured.

A.2.1 Logic Gates

Figure A.1 shows the pinout diagrams for a variety of popular 74xx-series chips containing basic logic gates. These are sometimes called *small-scale integration (SSI)* chips, because they are built from a few transistors. The 14-pin packages typically have a notch at the top or a dot on the top left to indicate orientation. Pins are numbered starting with 1 in the upper left and going counterclockwise around the package. The chips need to receive power (V_{DD} = 5 V) and ground (GND = 0 V) at pins 14 and 7, respectively. The number of logic gates on the chip is determined by the number of pins. Note that pins 3 and 11 of the 7421 chip are not connected (NC) to anything. The 7474 flip-flop has the usual *D, CLK,* and *Q* terminals. It also has a complementary output, $\overline{Q}$. Moreover, it receives asynchronous set (also called preset, or *PRE*) and reset (also called clear, or *CLR*) signals. These are active low; in other words, the flop sets when $\overline{PRE}$ = 0, resets when $\overline{CLR}$ = 0, and operates normally when $\overline{PRE} = \overline{CLR}$ = 1.

A.2.2 Other Functions

The 74xx series also includes somewhat more complex logic functions, including those shown in Figures A.2 and A.3. These are called *medium-scale integration (MSI)* chips. Most use larger packages to accommodate more inputs and outputs. Power and ground are still provided at the upper right and lower left, respectively, of each chip. A general functional description is provided for each chip. See the manufacturer's data sheets for complete descriptions.

A.3 PROGRAMMABLE LOGIC

Programmable logic consists of arrays of circuitry that can be configured to perform specific logic functions. We have already introduced three forms of programmable logic: programmable read only memories (PROMs), programmable logic arrays (PLAs), and field programmable gate arrays (FPGAs). This section shows chip implementations for each of these. Configuration of these chips may be performed by blowing on-chip fuses to connect or disconnect circuit elements. This is called *one-time programmable (OTP)* logic because, once a fuse is blown, it cannot be restored. Alternatively, the configuration may be stored in a memory that can be reprogrammed at will. Reprogrammable logic is convenient in the laboratory, because the same chip can be reused during development.

A.3.1 PROMs

As discussed in Section 5.5.7, PROMs can be used as lookup tables. A 2^N-word $\times$ *M*-bit PROM can be programmed to perform any combinational function of *N* inputs and *M* outputs. Design changes simply

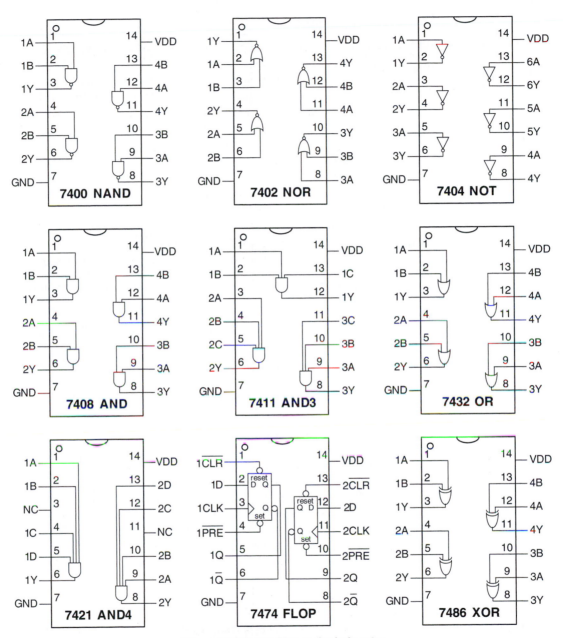

Figure A.1 Common 74xx-series logic gates

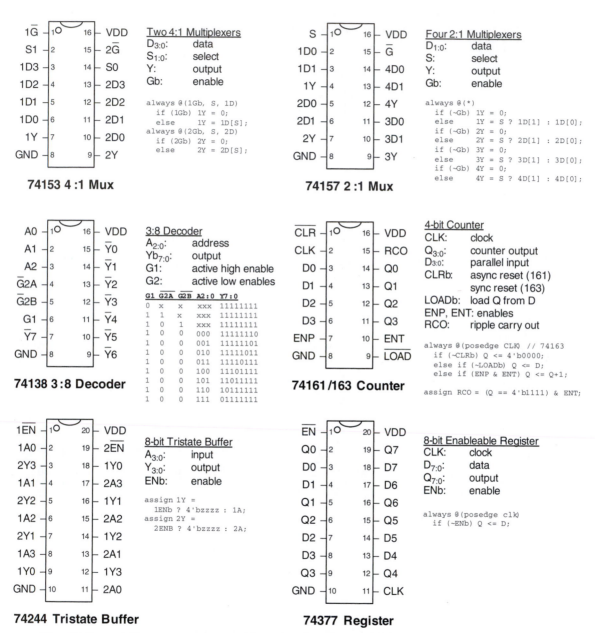

Note: Verilog variable names cannot start with numbers, but the names in the example code in Figure A.2 are chosen to match the manufacturer's data sheet.

Figure A.2 Medium-scale integration chips

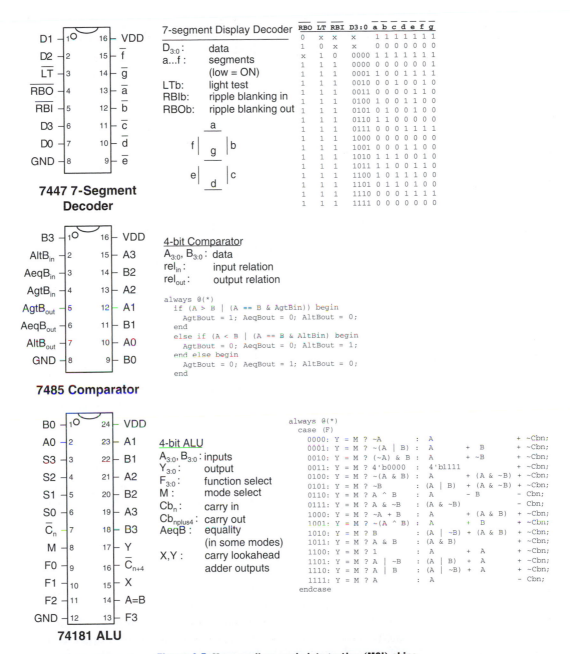

Figure A.3 More medium-scale integration (MSI) chips

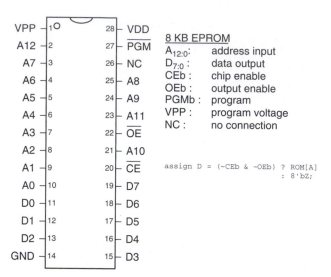

Figure A.4 2764 8KB EPROM

8 KB EPROM

$A_{12:0}$:	address input
$D_{7:0}$:	data output
CEb:	chip enable
OEb:	output enable
PGMb:	program
VPP:	program voltage
NC:	no connection

```
assign D = (~CEb & ~OEb) ? ROM[A]
                         : 8'bZ;
```

involve replacing the contents of the PROM rather than rewiring connections between chips. Lookup tables are useful for small functions but become prohibitively expensive as the number of inputs grows.

For example, the classic 2764 8-KB (64-Kb) erasable PROM (EPROM) is shown in Figure A.4. The EPROM has 13 address lines to specify one of the 8K words and 8 data lines to read the byte of data at that word. The chip enable and output enable must both be asserted for data to be read. The maximum propagation delay is 200 ps. In normal operation, $\overline{PGM} = 1$ and *VPP* is not used. The EPROM is usually programmed on a special programmer that sets $\overline{PGM} = 0$, applies 13 V to *VPP*, and uses a special sequence of inputs to configure the memory.

Modern PROMs are similar in concept but have much larger capacities and more pins. Flash memory is the cheapest type of PROM, selling for about $30 per gigabyte in 2006. Prices have historically declined by 30 to 40% per year.

A.3.2 PLAs

As discussed in Section 5.6.1, PLAs contain AND and OR planes to compute any combinational function written in sum-of-products form. The AND and OR planes can be programmed using the same techniques for PROMs. A PLA has two columns for each input and one column for each output. It has one row for each minterm. This organization is more efficient than a PROM for many functions, but the array still grows excessively large for functions with numerous I/Os and minterms.

Many different manufacturers have extended the basic PLA concept to build *programmable logic devices* (*PLDs*) that include registers.

The 22V10 is one of the most popular classic PLDs. It has 12 dedicated input pins and 10 outputs. The outputs can come directly from the PLA or from clocked registers on the chip. The outputs can also be fed back into the PLA. Thus, the 22V10 can directly implement FSMs with up to 12 inputs, 10 outputs, and 10 bits of state. The 22V10 costs about $2 in quantities of 100. PLDs have been rendered mostly obsolete by the rapid improvements in capacity and cost of FPGAs.

A.3.3 FPGAs

As discussed in Section 5.6.2, FPGAs consist of arrays of *configurable logic blocks* (*CLBs*) connected together with programmable wires. The CLBs contain small lookup tables and flip-flops. FPGAs scale gracefully to extremely large capacities, with thousands of lookup tables. Xilinx and Altera are two of the leading FPGA manufacturers.

Lookup tables and programmable wires are flexible enough to implement any logic function. However, they are an order of magnitude less efficient in speed and cost (chip area) than hard-wired versions of the same functions. Thus, FPGAs often include specialized blocks, such as memories, multipliers, and even entire microprocessors.

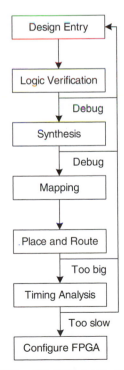

Figure A.5 FPGA design flow

Figure A.5 shows the design process for a digital system on an FPGA. The design is usually specified with a hardware description language (HDL), although some FPGA tools also support schematics. The design is then simulated. Inputs are applied and compared against expected outputs to *verify* that the logic is correct. Usually some debugging is required. Next, logic *synthesis* converts the HDL into Boolean functions. Good synthesis tools produce a schematic of the functions, and the prudent designer examines these schematics, as well as any warnings produced during synthesis, to ensure that the desired logic was produced. Sometimes sloppy coding leads to circuits that are much larger than intended or to circuits with asynchronous logic. When the synthesis results are good, the FPGA tool *maps* the functions onto the CLBs of a specific chip. The *place and route* tool determines which functions go in which lookup tables and how they are wired together. Wire delay increases with length, so critical circuits should be placed close together. If the design is too big to fit on the chip, it must be reengineered. *Timing analysis* compares the timing constraints (e.g., an intended clock speed of 100 MHz) against the actual circuit delays and reports any errors. If the logic is too slow, it may have to be redesigned or pipelined differently. When the design is correct, a file is generated specifying the contents of all the CLBs and the programming of all the wires on the FPGA. Many FPGAs store this *configuration* information in static RAM that must be reloaded each time the FPGA is turned on. The FPGA can download this information from a computer in the laboratory, or can read it from a nonvolatile ROM when power is first applied.

Example A.1 FPGA TIMING ANALYSIS

Alyssa P. Hacker is using an FPGA to implement an M&M sorter with a color sensor and motors to put red candy in one jar and green candy in another. Her design is implemented as an FSM, and she is using a Spartan XC3S200 FPGA, a chip from the Spartan 3 series family. According to the data sheet, the FPGA has the timing characteristics shown in Table A.1. Assume that the design is small enough that wire delay is negligible.

Alyssa would like her FSM to run at 100 MHz. What is the maximum number of CLBs on the critical path? What is the fastest speed at which her FSM could possibly run?

SOLUTION: At 100 MHz, the cycle time, T_c, is 10 ns. Alyssa uses Equation 3.13 figure to out the minimum combinational propagation delay, t_{pd}, at this cycle time:

$$t_{pd} \leq 10 \text{ ns} - (0.72 \text{ ns} + 0.53 \text{ ns}) = 8.75 \text{ ns} \qquad (A.1)$$

Alyssa's FSM can use at most 14 consecutive CLBs (8.75/0.61) to implement the next-state logic.

The fastest speed at which an FSM will run on a Spartan 3 FPGA is when it is using a single CLB for the next state logic. The minimum cycle time is

$$T_c \geq 0.61 \text{ ns} + 0.72 \text{ ns} + 0.53 \text{ ns} = 1.86 \text{ ns} \qquad (A.2)$$

Therefore, the maximum frequency is 538 MHz.

Table A.1 Spartan 3 XC3S200 timing

name	value (ns)
t_{pcq}	0.72
t_{setup}	0.53
t_{hold}	0
t_{pd} (per CLB)	0.61
t_{skew}	0

Xilinx advertises the XC3S100E FPGA with 1728 lookup tables and flip-flops for $2 in quantities of 500,000 in 2006. In more modest quantities, medium-sized FPGAs typically cost about $10, and the largest

FPGAs cost hundreds or even thousands of dollars. The cost has declined at approximately 30% per year, so FPGAs are becoming extremely popular.

A.4 APPLICATION-SPECIFIC INTEGRATED CIRCUITS

Application-specific integrated circuits (ASICs) are chips designed for a particular purpose. Graphics accelerators, network interface chips, and cell phone chips are common examples of ASICS. The ASIC designer places transistors to form logic gates and wires the gates together. Because the ASIC is hardwired for a specific function, it is typically several times faster than an FPGA and occupies an order of magnitude less chip area (and hence cost) than an FPGA with the same function. However, the *masks* specifying where transistors and wires are located on the chip cost hundreds of thousands of dollars to produce. The fabrication process usually requires 6 to 12 weeks to manufacture, package, and test the ASICs. If errors are discovered after the ASIC is manufactured, the designer must correct the problem, generate new masks, and wait for another batch of chips to be fabricated. Hence, ASICs are suitable only for products that will be produced in large quantities and whose function is well defined in advance.

Figure A.6 shows the ASIC design process, which is similar to the FPGA design process of Figure A.5. Logic verification is especially important because correction of errors after the masks are produced is expensive. Synthesis produces a *netlist* consisting of logic gates and connections between the gates; the gates in this netlist are placed, and the wires are routed between gates. When the design is satisfactory, masks are generated and used to fabricate the ASIC. A single speck of dust can ruin an ASIC, so the chips must be tested after fabrication. The fraction of manufactured chips that work is called the *yield*; it is typically 50 to 90%, depending on the size of the chip and the maturity of the manufacturing process. Finally, the working chips are placed in packages, as will be discussed in Section A.7.

A.5 DATA SHEETS

Integrated circuit manufacturers publish *data sheets* that describe the functions and performance of their chips. It is essential to read and understand the data sheets. One of the leading sources of errors in digital systems comes from misunderstanding the operation of a chip.

Data sheets are usually available from the manufacturer's Web site. If you cannot locate the data sheet for a part and do not have clear documentation from another source, don't use the part. Some of the entries in the data sheet may be cryptic. Often the manufacturer publishes data books containing data sheets for many related parts. The

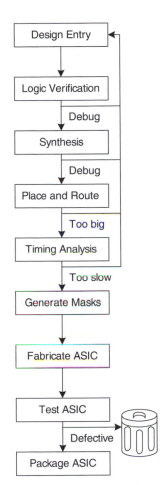

Figure A.6 ASIC design flow

beginning of the data book has additional explanatory information. This information can usually be found on the Web with a careful search.

This section dissects the Texas Instruments (TI) data sheet for a 74HC04 inverter chip. The data sheet is relatively simple but illustrates many of the major elements. TI still manufacturers a wide variety of 74xx-series chips. In the past, many other companies built these chips too, but the market is consolidating as the sales decline.

Figure A.7 shows the first page of the data sheet. Some of the key sections are highlighted in blue. The title is SN54HC04, SN74HC04 HEX INVERTERS. HEX INVERTERS means that the chip contains six inverters. SN indicates that TI is the manufacturer. Other manufacture codes include MC for Motorola and DM for National Semiconductor. You can generally ignore these codes, because all of the manufacturers build compatible 74xx-series logic. HC is the logic family (high speed CMOS). The logic family determines the speed and power consumption of the chip, but not the function. For example, the 7404, 74HC04, and 74LS04 chips all contain six inverters, but they differ in performance and cost. Other logic families are discussed in Section A.6. The 74xx chips operate across the commercial or industrial temperature range (0 to 70 °C or −40 to 85 °C, respectively), whereas the 54xx chips operate across the military temperature range (−55 to 125 °C) and sell for a higher price but are otherwise compatible.

The 7404 is available in many different packages, and it is important to order the one you intended when you make a purchase. The packages are distinguished by a suffix on the part number. N indicates a *plastic dual inline package* (PDIP), which fits in a breadboard or can be soldered in through-holes in a printed circuit board. Other packages are discussed in Section A.7.

The function table shows that each gate inverts its input. If A is HIGH (H), Y is LOW (L) and vice versa. The table is trivial in this case but is more interesting for more complex chips.

Figure A.8 shows the second page of the data sheet. The logic diagram indicates that the chip contains inverters. The *absolute maximum* section indicates conditions beyond which the chip could be destroyed. In particular, the power supply voltage (V_{CC}, also called V_{DD} in this book) should not exceed 7 V. The continuous output current should not exceed 25 mA. The *thermal resistance* or impedance, θ_{JA}, is used to calculate the temperature rise caused by the chip's dissipating power. If the *ambient* temperature in the vicinity of the chip is T_A and the chip dissipates P_{chip}, then the temperature on the chip itself at its *junction* with the package is

$$T_J = T_A + P_{\text{chip}}\,\theta_{JA} \qquad\qquad (A.3)$$

For example, if a 7404 chip in a plastic DIP package is operating in a hot box at 50 °C and consumes 20 mW, the junction temperature will

SN54HC04, SN74HC04
HEX INVERTERS

SCLS078D – DECEMBER 1982 – REVISED JULY 2003

- Wide Operating Voltage Range of 2 V to 6 V
- Outputs Can Drive Up To 10 LSTTL Loads
- Low Power Consumption, 20-μA Max I_{CC}

- Typical tpd = 8 ns
- $\pm$4-mA Output Drive at 5 V
- Low Input Current of 1 μA Max

SN54HC04 . . . J OR W PACKAGE
SN74HC04 . . . D, N, NS, OR PW PACKAGE
(TOPVIEW)

```
1A  [ 1    14 ] V_CC
1Y  [ 2    13 ] 6A
2A  [ 3    12 ] 6Y
2Y  [ 4    11 ] 5A
3A  [ 5    10 ] 5Y
3Y  [ 6     9 ] 4A
GND [ 7     8 ] 4Y
```

SN54HC04 . . . FK PACKAGE
(TOPVIEW)

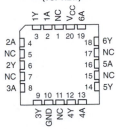

NC – No internal connection

description/ordering information

The 'HC04 devices contain six independent inverters. They perform the Boolean function $Y = \overline{A}$ in positive logic.

ORDERING INFORMATION

T_A	PACKAGE†		ORDERABLE PARTNUMBER	TOP-SIDE MARKING
–40°C to 85°C	PDIP – N	Tube of 25	SN74HC04N	SN74HC04N
	SOIC – D	Tube of 50	SN74HC04D	HC04
		Reel of 2500	SN74HC04DR	
		Reel of 250	SN74HC04DT	
	SOP – NS	Reel of 2000	SN74HC04NSR	HC04
	TSSOP – PW	Tube of 90	SN74HC04PW	HC04
		Reel of 2000	SN74HC04PWR	
		Reel of 250	SN74HC04PWT	
–55°C to 125°C	CDIP – J	Tube of 25	SNJ54HC04J	SNJ54HC04J
	CFP – W	Tube of 150	SNJ54HC04W	SNJ54HC04W
	LCCC – FK	Tube of 55	SNJ54HC04FK	SNJ54HC04FK

† Package drawings, standard packing quantities, thermal data, symbolization, and PCB design guidelines are available at www.ti.com/sc/package.

FUNCTION TABLE
(each inverter)

INPUT A	OUTPUT Y
H	L
L	H

 Please be aware that an important notice concerning availability, standard warranty, and use in critical applications of Texas Instruments semiconductor products and disclaimers there to appears at the end of this data sheet.

TEXAS INSTRUMENTS
POST OFFICE BOX 655303 ● DALLAS, TEXAS 75265

Figure A.7 7404 data sheet page 1

SN54HC04, SN74HC04
HEX INVERTERS

SCLS078D – DECEMBER 1982 – REVISED JULY 2003

logic diagram (positive logic)

absolute maximum ratings over operating free-air temperature range (unless otherwise noted)†

Supply voltage range, V_{CC} .... –0.5 V to 7 V
Input clamp current, I_{IK} ($V_I < 0$ or $V_I > V_{CC}$) (see Note 1) .... ±20 mA
Output clamp current, I_{OK} ($V_O < 0$ or $V_O > V_{CC}$) (see Note 1) .... ±20 mA
Continuous output current, I_O ($V_O = 0$ to V_{CC}) .... ±25 mA
Continuous current through V_{CC} or GND .... ±50 mA
Package thermal impedance, θ_{JA} (see Note 2): D package .... 86° C/W
                                                                     N package .... 80° C/W
                                                                     NS package .... 76° C/W
                                                                     PW package .... 131° C/W
Storage temperature range, T_{stg} .... –65° C to 150° C

† Stresses beyond those listed under "absolute maximum ratings" may cause permanent damage to the device. These are stress ratings only, and functional operation of the device at these or any other conditions beyond those indicated under "recommended operating conditions" is not implied. Exposure to absolute-maximum-rated conditions for extended periods may affect device reliability.

NOTES: 1. The input and output voltage ratings may be exceeded if the input and output current ratings are observed.
            2. The package thermal impedance is calculated in accordance with JESD 51-7.

recommended operating conditions (see Note 3)

			SN54HC04			SN74HC04			UNIT
			MIN	NOM	MAX	MIN	NOM	MAX	
V_{CC}	Supply voltage		2	5	6	2	5	6	V
V_{IH}	High-level input voltage	V_{CC} = 2 V	1.5			1.5			V
		V_{CC} = 4.5 V	3.15			3.15			
		V_{CC} = 6 V	4.2			4.2			
V_{IL}	Low-level input voltage	V_{CC} = 2 V			0.5			0.5	V
		V_{CC} = 4.5 V			1.35			1.35	
		V_{CC} = 6 V			1.8			1.8	
V_I	Input voltage		0		V_{CC}	0		V_{CC}	V
V_O	Output voltage		0		V_{CC}	0		V_{CC}	V
$\Delta t/\Delta v$	Input transition rise/fall time	V_{CC} = 2 V			1000			1000	ns
		V_{CC} = 4.5 V			500			500	
		V_{CC} = 6 V			400			400	
T_A	Operating free-air temperature		–55		125	–40		85	°C

NOTE 3: All unused inputs of the device must be held at V_{CC} or GND to ensure proper device operation. Refer to the TI application report, *Implications of Slow or Floating CMOS Inputs*, literature number SCBA004.

**TEXAS
INSTRUMENTS**
POST OFFICE BOX 655303 ● DALLAS, TEXAS 75265

Figure A.8 7404 datasheet page 2

climb to $50°C + 0.02$ W $\times$ $80°C/W = 51.6°C$. Internal power dissipation is seldom important for 74xx-series chips, but it becomes important for modern chips that dissipate tens of watts or more.

The *recommended operating conditions* define the environment in which the chip should be used. Within these conditions, the chip should meet specifications. These conditions are more stringent than the absolute maximums. For example, the power supply voltage should be between 2 and 6 V. The input logic levels for the HC logic family depend on V_{DD}. Use the 4.5 V entries when $V_{DD} = 5$ V, to allow for a 10% droop in the power supply caused by noise in the system.

Figure A.9 shows the third page of the data sheet. The *electrical characteristics* describe how the device performs when used within the recommended operating conditions if the inputs are held constant. For example, if $V_{CC} = 5$ V (and droops to 4.5 V) and the output current, I_{OH}/I_{OL} does not exceed 20 μA, $V_{OH} = 4.4$ V and $V_{OL} = 0.1$ V in the worst case. If the output current increases, the output voltages become less ideal, because the transistors on the chip struggle to provide the current. The HC logic family uses CMOS transistors that draw very little current. The current into each input is guaranteed to be less than 1000 nA and is typically only 0.1 nA at room temperature. The *quiescent* power supply current (I_{DD}) drawn while the chip is idle is less than 20 μA. Each input has less than 10 pF of capacitance.

The *switching characteristics* define how the device performs when used within the recommended operating conditions if the inputs change. The *propagation delay, t_{pd},* is measured from when the input passes through 0.5 V_{CC} to when the output passes through 0.5 V_{CC}. If V_{CC} is nominally 5 V and the chip drives a capacitance of less than 50 pF, the propagation delay will not exceed 24 ns (and typically will be much faster). Recall that each input may present 10 pF, so the chip cannot drive more than five identical chips at full speed. Indeed, stray capacitance from the wires connecting chips cuts further into the useful load. The *transition time*, also called the rise/fall time, is measured as the output transitions between 0.1 V_{CC} and 0.9 V_{CC}.

Recall from Section 1.8 that chips consume both *static* and *dynamic* power. Static power is low for HC circuits. At 85 °C, the maximum quiescent supply current is 20 μA. At 5 V, this gives a static power consumption of 0.1 mW. The dynamic power depends on the capacitance being driven and the switching frequency. The 7404 has an internal power dissipation capacitance of 20 pF per inverter. If all six inverters on the 7404 switch at 10 MHz and drive external loads of 25 pF, then the dynamic power given by Equation 1.4 is $\frac{1}{2}(6)(20$ pF $+$ 25 pF)$(5^2)(10$ MHz$) = 33.75$ mW and the maximum total power is 33.85 mW.

SN54HC04, SN74HC04
HEX INVERTERS

SCLS078D – DECEMBER 1982 – REVISED JULY 2003

electrical characteristics over recommended operating free-air temperature range (unless otherwise noted)

PARAMETER	TEST CONDITIONS		V_{CC}	$T_A = 25°C$			SN54HC04		SN74HC04		UNIT
				MIN	TYP	MAX	MIN	MAX	MIN	MAX	
V_{OH}	$V_I = V_{IH}$ or V_{IL}	$I_{OH} = -20\,\mu A$	2 V	1.9	1.998		1.9		1.9		V
			4.5 V	4.4	4.499		4.4		4.4		
			6 V	5.9	5.999		5.9		5.9		
		$I_{OH} = -4\,mA$	4.5 V	3.98	4.3		3.7		3.84		
		$I_{OH} = -5.2\,mA$	6 V	5.48	5.8		5.2		5.34		
V_{OL}	$V_I = V_{IH}$ or V_{IL}	$I_{OL} = 20\,\mu A$	2 V		0.002	0.1		0.1		0.1	V
			4.5 V		0.001	0.1		0.1		0.1	
			6 V		0.001	0.1		0.1		0.1	
		$I_{OL} = 4\,mA$	4.5 V		0.17	0.26		0.4		0.33	
		$I_{OL} = 5.2\,mA$	6 V		0.15	0.26		0.4		0.33	
I_I	$V_I = V_{CC}$ or 0		6 V		±0.1	±100		±1000		±1000	nA
I_{CC}	$V_I = V_{CC}$ or 0, $I_O = 0$		6 V			2		40		20	μA
C_I			2 V to 6 V		3	10		10		10	pF

switching characteristics over recommended operating free-air temperature range, CL = 50 pF (unless otherwise noted) (see Figure 1)

PARAMETER	FROM (INPUT)	TO (OUTPUT)	V_{CC}	$T_A = 25°C$			SN54HC04		SN74HC04		UNIT
				MIN	TYP	MAX	MIN	MAX	MIN	MAX	
t_{pd}	A	Y	2 V		45	95		145		120	ns
			4.5 V		9	19		29		24	
			6 V		8	16		25		20	
t_t		Y	2 V		38	75		110		95	ns
			4.5 V		8	15		22		19	
			6 V		6	13		19		16	

operating characteristics, $T_A = 25°C$

PARAMETER		TEST CONDITIONS	TYP	UNIT
C_{pd}	Power dissipation capacitance per inverter	No load	20	pF

TEXAS
INSTRUMENTS
POST OFFICE BOX 655303 ● DALLAS, TEXAS 75265

Figure A.9 7404 datasheet page 3

A.6 LOGIC FAMILIES

The 74xx-series logic chips have been manufactured using many different technologies, called *logic families*, that offer different speed, power, and logic level trade-offs. Other chips are usually designed to be compatible with some of these logic families. The original chips, such as the 7404, were built using bipolar transistors in a technology called *Transistor-Transistor Logic* (TTL). Newer technologies add one or more letters after the 74 to indicate the logic family, such as 74LS04, 74HC04, or 74AHCT04. Table A.2 summarizes the most common 5-V logic families.

Advances in bipolar circuits and process technology led to the *Schottky* (S) and *Low-Power Schottky* (LS) families. Both are faster than TTL. Schottky draws more power, whereas Low-power Schottky draws less. *Advanced Schottky* (AS) and *Advanced Low-Power Schottky* (ALS) have improved speed and power compared to S and LS. *Fast* (F) logic is faster and draws less power than AS. All of these families provide more current for LOW outputs than for HIGH outputs and hence have asymmetric logic levels. They conform to the "TTL" logic levels: $V_{IH} = 2$ V, $V_{IL} = 0.8$ V, $V_{OH} > 2.4$ V, and $V_{OL} < 0.5$ V.

Table A.2 Typical specifications for 5-V logic families

Characteristic	Bipolar / TTL						CMOS		CMOS / TTL Compatible	
	TTL	S	LS	AS	ALS	F	HC	AHC	HCT	AHCT
t_{pd} (ns)	22	9	12	7.5	10	6	21	7.5	30	7.7
V_{IH} (V)	2	2	2	2	2	2	3.15	3.15	2	2
V_{IL} (V)	0.8	0.8	0.8	0.8	0.8	0.8	1.35	1.35	0.8	0.8
V_{OH} (V)	2.4	2.7	2.7	2.5	2.5	2.5	3.84	3.8	3.84	3.8
V_{OL} (V)	0.4	0.5	0.5	0.5	0.5	0.5	0.33	0.44	0.33	0.44
I_{OH} (mA)	0.4	1	0.4	2	0.4	1	4	8	4	8
I_{OL} (mA)	16	20	8	20	8	20	4	8	4	8
I_{IL} (mA)	1.6	2	0.4	0.5	0.1	0.6	0.001	0.001	0.001	0.001
I_{IH} (mA)	0.04	0.05	0.02	0.02	0.02	0.02	0.001	0.001	0.001	0.001
I_{DD} (mA)	33	54	6.6	26	4.2	15	0.02	0.02	0.02	0.02
C_{pd} (pF)	n/a						20	12	20	14
cost[*] (US $)	obsolete	0.57	0.29	0.53	0.33	0.20	0.15	0.15	0.15	0.15

[*] Per unit in quantities of 1000 for the 7408 from Texas Instruments in 2006

As CMOS circuits matured in the 1980s and 1990s, they became popular because they draw very little power supply or input current. The *High Speed CMOS (HC)* and *Advanced High Speed CMOS (AHC)* families draw almost no static power. They also deliver the same current for HIGH and LOW outputs. They conform to the "CMOS" logic levels: V_{IH} = 3.15 V, V_{IL} = 1.35 V, V_{OH} > 3.8 V, and V_{OL} < 0.44 V. Unfortunately, these levels are incompatible with TTL circuits, because a TTL HIGH output of 2.4 V may not be recognized as a legal CMOS HIGH input. This motivates the use of *High Speed TTL-compatible CMOS (HCT)* and *Advanced High Speed TTL-compatible CMOS (AHCT)*, which accept TTL input logic levels and generate valid CMOS output logic levels. These families are slightly slower than their pure CMOS counterparts. All CMOS chips are sensitive to *electrostatic discharge (ESD)* caused by static electricity. Ground yourself by touching a large metal object before handling CMOS chips, lest you zap them.

The 74xx-series logic is inexpensive. The newer logic families are often cheaper than the obsolete ones. The LS family is widely available and robust and is a popular choice for laboratory or hobby projects that have no special performance requirements.

The 5-V standard collapsed in the mid-1990s, when transistors became too small to withstand the voltage. Moreover, lower voltage offers lower power consumption. Now 3.3, 2.5, 1.8, 1.2, and even lower voltages are commonly used. The plethora of voltages raises challenges in communicating between chips with different power supplies. Table A.3 lists some of the low-voltage logic families. Not all 74xx parts are available in all of these logic families.

All of the low-voltage logic families use CMOS transistors, the workhorse of modern integrated circuits. They operate over a wide range of V_{DD}, but the speed degrades at lower voltage. *Low-Voltage CMOS (LVC)* logic and *Advanced Low-Voltage CMOS (ALVC)* logic are commonly used at 3.3, 2.5, or 1.8 V. LVC withstands inputs up to 5.5 V, so it can receive inputs from 5-V CMOS or TTL circuits. *Advanced Ultra-Low-Voltage CMOS (AUC)* is commonly used at 2.5, 1.8, or 1.2 V and is exceptionally fast. Both ALVC and AUC withstand inputs up to 3.6 V, so they can receive inputs from 3.3-V circuits.

FPGAs often offer separate voltage supplies for the internal logic, called the *core*, and for the input/output (I/O) pins. As FPGAs have advanced, the core voltage has dropped from 5 to 3.3, 2.5, 1.8, and 1.2 V to save power and avoid damaging the very small transistors. FPGAs have configurable I/Os that can operate at many different voltages, so as to be compatible with the rest of the system.

Table A.3 Typical specifications for low-voltage logic families

V_{dd} (V)	LVC			ALVC			AUC		
	3.3	2.5	1.8	3.3	2.5	1.8	2.5	1.8	1.2
t_{pd} (ns)	4.1	6.9	9.8	2.8	3	?[1]	1.8	2.3	3.4
V_{IH} (V)	2	1.7	1.17	2	1.7	1.17	1.7	1.17	0.78
V_{IL} (V)	0.8	0.7	0.63	0.8	0.7	0.63	0.7	0.63	0.42
V_{OH} (V)	2.2	1.7	1.2	2	1.7	1.2	1.8	1.2	0.8
V_{OL} (V)	0.55	0.7	0.45	0.55	0.7	0.45	0.6	0.45	0.3
I_O (mA)	24	8	4	24	12	12	9	8	3
I_I (mA)		0.02			0.005			0.005	
I_{DD} (mA)		0.01			0.01			0.01	
C_{pd} (pF)	10	9.8	7	27.5	23	?*	17	14	14
cost (US $)		0.17			0.20			not available	

* Delay and capacitance not available at the time of writing

A.7 PACKAGING AND ASSEMBLY

Integrated circuits are typically placed in *packages* made of plastic or ceramic. The packages serve a number of functions, including connecting the tiny metal I/O pads of the chip to larger pins in the package for ease of connection, protecting the chip from physical damage, and spreading the heat generated by the chip over a larger area to help with cooling. The packages are placed on a breadboard or printed circuit board and wired together to assemble the system.

Packages

Figure A.10 shows a variety of integrated circuit packages. Packages can be generally categorized as *through-hole* or *surface mount* (SMT). Through-hole packages, as their name implies, have pins that can be inserted through holes in a printed circuit board or into a socket. *Dual inline packages* (DIPs) have two rows of pins with 0.1-inch spacing between pins. *Pin grid arrays* (PGAs) support more pins in a smaller package by placing the pins under the package. SMT packages are soldered directly to the surface of a printed circuit board without using holes. Pins on SMT parts are called *leads*. The *thin small outline package* (TSOP) has two rows of closely spaced leads (typically 0.02-inch spacing). *Plastic leaded chip carriers* (PLCCs) have J-shaped leads on all four

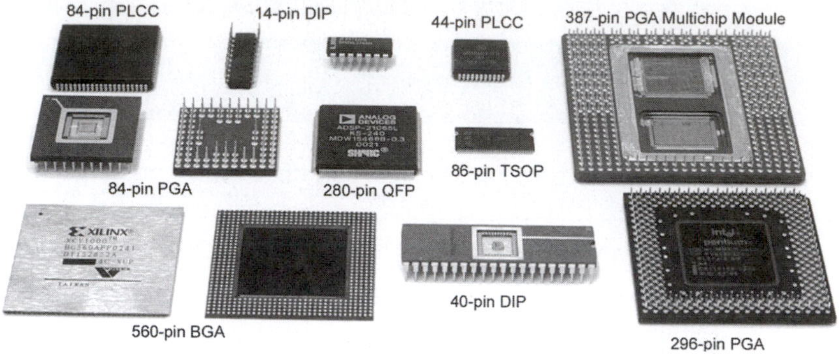

Figure A.10 Integrated circuit packages

sides, with 0.05-inch spacing. They can be soldered directly to a board or placed in special sockets. *Quad flat packs (QFPs)* accommodate a large number of pins using closely spaced legs on all four sides. *Ball grid arrays (BGAs)* eliminate the legs altogether. Instead, they have hundreds of tiny solder balls on the underside of the package. They are carefully placed over matching pads on a printed circuit board, then heated so that the solder melts and joins the package to the underlying board.

Breadboards

DIPs are easy to use for prototyping, because they can be placed in a *breadboard*. A breadboard is a plastic board containing rows of sockets, as shown in Figure A.11. All five holes in a row are connected together. Each pin of the package is placed in a hole in a separate row. Wires can be placed in adjacent holes in the same row to make connections to the pin. Breadboards often provide separate columns of connected holes running the height of the board to distribute power and ground.

Figure A.11 shows a breadboard containing a majority gate built with a 74LS08 AND chip and a 74LS32 OR chip. The schematic of the circuit is shown in Figure A.12. Each gate in the schematic is labeled with the chip (08 or 32) and the pin numbers of the inputs and outputs (see Figure A.1). Observe that the same connections are made on the breadboard. The inputs are connected to pins 1, 2, and 5 of the 08 chip, and the output is measured at pin 6 of the 32 chip. Power and ground are connected to pins 14 and 7, respectively, of each chip, from the vertical power and ground columns that are attached to the banana plug receptacles, Vb and Va. Labeling the schematic in this way and checking off connections as they are made is a good way to reduce the number of mistakes made during breadboarding.

Unfortunately, it is easy to accidentally plug a wire in the wrong hole or have a wire fall out, so breadboarding requires a great deal of care (and usually some debugging in the laboratory). Breadboards are suited only to prototyping, not production.

Figure A.11 Majority circuit on breadboard

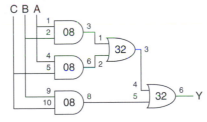

Figure A.12 Majority gate schematic with chips and pins identified

Printed Circuit Boards

Instead of breadboarding, chip packages may be soldered to a *printed circuit board* (PCB). The PCB is formed of alternating layers of conducting copper and insulating epoxy. The copper is etched to form wires called *traces*. Holes called *vias* are drilled through the board and plated with metal to connect between layers. PCBs are usually designed with *computer-aided design* (CAD) tools. You can etch and drill your own simple boards in the laboratory, or you can send the board design to a specialized factory for inexpensive mass production. Factories have turnaround times of days (or weeks, for cheap mass production runs) and typically charge a few hundred dollars in setup fees and a few dollars per board for moderately complex boards built in large quantities.

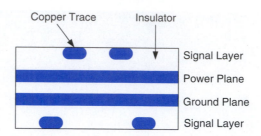

PCB traces are normally made of copper because of its low resistance. The traces are embedded in an insulating material, usually a green, fire-resistant plastic called FR4. A PCB also typically has copper power and ground layers, called *planes*, between signal layers. Figure A.13 shows a cross-section of a PCB. The signal layers are on the top and bottom, and the power and ground planes are embedded in the center of the board. The power and ground planes have low resistance, so they distribute stable power to components on the board. They also make the capacitance and inductance of the traces uniform and predictable.

Figure A.14 shows a PCB for a 1970s vintage Apple II+ computer. At the top is a Motorola 6502 microprocessor. Beneath are six 16-Kb ROM chips forming 12 KB of ROM containing the operating system. Three rows of eight 16-Kb DRAM chips provide 48 KB of RAM. On the right are several rows of 74xx-series logic for memory address decoding and other functions. The lines between chips are traces that wire the chips together. The dots at the ends of some of the traces are vias filled with metal.

Putting It All Together

Most modern chips with large numbers of inputs and outputs use SMT packages, especially QFPs and BGAs. These packages require a printed circuit board rather than a breadboard. Working with BGAs is especially challenging because they require specialized assembly equipment. Moreover, the balls cannot be probed with a voltmeter or oscilloscope during debugging in the laboratory, because they are hidden under the package.

In summary, the designer needs to consider packaging early on to determine whether a breadboard can be used during prototyping and whether BGA parts will be required. Professional engineers rarely use breadboards when they are confident of connecting chips together correctly without experimentation.

A.8 TRANSMISSION LINES

We have assumed so far that wires are *equipotential* connections that have a single voltage along their entire length. Signals actually propagate along wires at the speed of light in the form of electromagnetic waves. If the wires are short enough or the signals change slowly, the equipotential assumption

Figure A.14 Apple II+ circuit board

is good enough. When the wire is long or the signal is very fast, the *transmission time* along the wire becomes important to accurately determine the circuit delay. We must model such wires as *transmission lines,* in which a wave of voltage and current propagates at the speed of light. When the wave reaches the end of the line, it may reflect back along the line. The reflection may cause noise and odd behaviors unless steps are taken to limit it. Hence, the digital designer must consider transmission line behavior to accurately account for the delay and noise effects in long wires.

Electromagnetic waves travel at the speed of light in a given medium, which is fast but not instantaneous. The speed of light depends on the *permittivity*, ε, and *permeability*, μ, of the medium[2]: $v = \dfrac{1}{\sqrt{\mu\varepsilon}} = \dfrac{1}{\sqrt{LC}}$.

---

[2] The capacitance, C, and inductance, L, of a wire are related to the permittivity and permeability of the physical medium in which the wire is located.

The speed of light in free space is $v = c = 3 \times 10^8$ m/s. Signals in a PCB travel at about half this speed, because the FR4 insulator has four times the permittivity of air. Thus, PCB signals travel at about 1.5×10^8 m/s, or 15 cm/ns. The time delay for a signal to travel along a transmission line of length l is

$$t_d = l/v \qquad (A.4)$$

The *characteristic impedance* of a transmission line, Z_0 (pronounced "Z-naught"), is the ratio of voltage to current in a wave traveling along the line: $Z_0 = V/I$. It is *not* the resistance of the wire (a good transmission line in a digital system typically has negligible resistance). Z_0 depends on the inductance and capacitance of the line (see the derivation in Section A.8.7) and typically has a value of 50 to 75 Ω.

$$Z_0 = \sqrt{\frac{L}{C}} \qquad (A.5)$$

Figure A.15 shows the symbol for a transmission line. The symbol resembles a *coaxial cable* with an inner signal conductor and an outer grounded conductor like that used in television cable wiring.

The key to understanding the behavior of transmission lines is to visualize the wave of voltage propagating along the line at the speed of light. When the wave reaches the end of the line, it may be absorbed or reflected, depending on the termination or load at the end. Reflections travel back along the line, adding to the voltage already on the line. Terminations are classified as matched, open, short, or mismatched. The following subsections explore how a wave propagates along the line and what happens to the wave when it reaches the termination.

A.8.1 Matched Termination

Figure A.16 shows a transmission line of length l with a *matched termination*, which means that the load impedance, Z_L, is equal to the characteristic impedance, Z_0. The transmission line has a characteristic impedance of 50 Ω. One end of the line is connected to a voltage

Figure A.15 Transmission line symbol

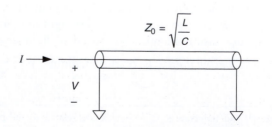

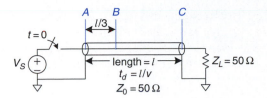

**Figure A.16 Transmission line
with matched termination**

source through a switch that closes at time $t = 0$. The other end is connected to the 50 Ω matched load. This section analyzes the voltages and currents at points A, B, and C—at the beginning of the line, one-third of the length along the line, and at the end of the line, respectively.

Figure A.17 shows the voltages at points A, B, and C over time. Initially, there is no voltage or current flowing in the transmission line, because the switch is open. At time $t = 0$, the switch closes, and the voltage source launches a wave with voltage $V = V_S$ along the line. Because the characteristic impedance is Z_0, the wave has current $I = V_S/Z_0$. The voltage reaches the beginning of the line (point A) immediately, as shown in Figure A.17(a). The wave propagates along the line at the speed of light. At time $t_d/3$, the wave reaches point B. The voltage at this point abruptly rises from 0 to V_S, as shown in Figure A.17(b). At time t_d, the *incident wave* reaches point C at the end of the line, and the voltage rises there too. All of the current, I, flows into the resistor, Z_L, producing a voltage across the resistor of $Z_L I = Z_L(V_S/Z_0) = V_S$ because $Z_L = Z_0$. This voltage is consistent with the wave flowing along the transmission line. Thus, the wave is *absorbed* by the load impedance, and the transmission line reaches its *steady state*.

In steady state, the transmission line behaves like an ideal equipotential wire because it is, after all, just a wire. The voltage at all points along the line must be identical. Figure A.18 shows the steady-state equivalent model of the circuit in Figure A.16. The voltage is V_S everywhere along the wire.

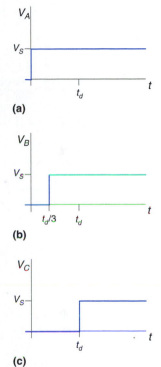

**Figure A.17 Voltage waveforms
for Figure A.16 at points A, B,
and C**

Example A.2 TRANSMISSION LINE WITH MATCHED SOURCE AND
LOAD TERMINATIONS

Figure A.19 shows a transmission line with matched source and load impedances Z_S and Z_L. Plot the voltage at nodes A, B, and C versus time. When does the system reach steady-state, and what is the equivalent circuit at steady-state?

SOLUTION: When the voltage source has a source impedance, Z_S, in series with the transmission line, part of the voltage drops across Z_S, and the remainder

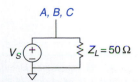

**Figure A.18 Equivalent circuit of
Figure A.16 at steady state**

Figure A.19 Transmission line with matched source and load impedances

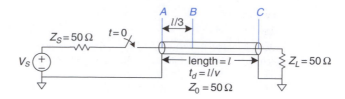

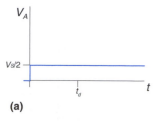

(a)

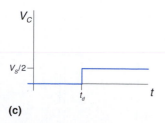

(b)

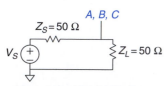

(c)

Figure A.20 Voltage waveforms for Figure A.19 at points A, B, and C

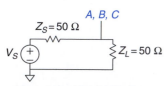

Figure A.21 Equivalent circuit of Figure A.19 at steady state

propagates down the transmission line. At first, the transmission line behaves as an impedance Z_0, because the load at the end of the line cannot possibly influence the behavior of the line until a speed of light delay has elapsed. Hence, by the *voltage divider equation*, the incident voltage flowing down the line is

$$V = V_S \left(\frac{Z_0}{Z_0 + Z_S} \right) = \frac{V_S}{2} \qquad (A.6)$$

Thus, at $t = 0$, a wave of voltage, $V = \frac{V_S}{2}$, is sent down the line from point A. Again, the signal reaches point B at time $t_d/3$ and point C at t_d, as shown in Figure A.20. All of the current is absorbed by the load impedance Z_L, so the circuit enters steady-state at $t = t_d$. In steady-state, the entire line is at $V_S/2$, just as the steady-state equivalent circuit in Figure A.21 would predict.

A.8.2 Open Termination

When the load impedance is not equal to Z_0, the termination cannot absorb all of the current, and some of the wave must be reflected. Figure A.22 shows a transmission line with an open load termination. No current can flow through an open termination, so the current at point C must always be 0.

The voltage on the line is initially zero. At $t = 0$, the switch closes and a wave of voltage, $V = V_S \frac{Z_0}{Z_0 + Z_S} = \frac{V_S}{2}$, begins propagating down the line. Notice that this initial wave is the same as that of Example A.2 and is independent of the termination, because the load at the end of the line cannot influence the behavior at the beginning until at least t_d has elapsed. This wave reaches point B at $t_d/3$ and point C at t_d as shown in Figure A.23.

When the incident wave reaches point C, it cannot continue forward because the wire is open. It must instead reflect back toward the source. The reflected wave also has voltage $V = \frac{V_S}{2}$, because the open termination reflects the entire wave.

The voltage at any point is the sum of the incident and reflected waves. At time $t = t_d$, the voltage at point C is $V = \frac{V_S}{2} + \frac{V_S}{2} = V_S$. The reflected wave reaches point B at $5t_d/3$ and point A at $2t_d$. When it reaches point A, the wave is absorbed by the source termination

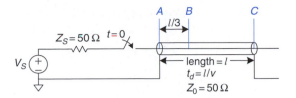

Figure A.22 Transmission line with open load termination

impedance that matches the characteristic impedance of the line. Thus, the system reaches steady state at time $t = 2t_d$, and the transmission line becomes equivalent to an equipotential wire with voltage V_S and current $I = 0$.

A.8.3 Short Termination

Figure A.24 shows a transmission line terminated with a short circuit to ground. Thus, the voltage at point C must always be 0.

As in the previous examples, the voltages on the line are initially 0. When the switch closes, a wave of voltage, $V = \frac{V_S}{2}$, begins propagating down the line (Figure A.25). When it reaches the end of the line, it must reflect with opposite polarity. The reflected wave, with voltage $V = \frac{-V_S}{2}$, adds to the incident wave, ensuring that the voltage at point C remains 0. The reflected wave reaches the source at time $t = 2t_d$ and is absorbed by the source impedance. At this point, the system reaches steady state, and the transmission line is equivalent to an equipotential wire with voltage $V = 0$.

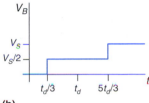

(a)

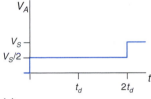

(b)

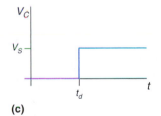

(c)

Figure A.23 Voltage waveforms for Figure A.22 at points A, B, and C

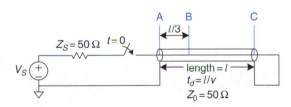

Figure A.24 Transmission line with short termination

A.8.4 Mismatched Termination

The termination impedance is said to be *mismatched* when it does not equal the characteristic impedance of the line. In general, when an incident wave reaches a mismatched termination, part of the wave is absorbed and part is reflected. The reflection coefficient, k_r, indicates the fraction of the incident wave (V_i) that is reflected: $V_r = k_r V_i$.

Section A.8.8 derives the reflection coefficient using conservation of current arguments. It shows that, when an incident wave flowing along a

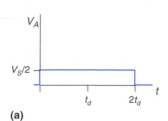

(a)

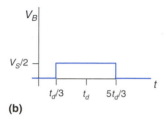

(b)

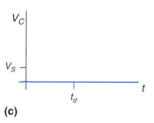

(c)

Figure A.25 **Voltage waveforms for Figure A.24 at points A, B, and C**

transmission line of characteristic impedance Z_0 reaches a termination impedance, Z_T, at the end of the line, the reflection coefficient is

$$k_r = \frac{Z_T - Z_0}{Z_T + Z_0} \tag{A.7}$$

Note a few special cases. If the termination is an open circuit ($Z_T = \infty$), $k_r = 1$, because the incident wave is entirely reflected (so the current out the end of the line remains zero). If the termination is a short circuit ($Z_T = 0$), $k_r = -1$, because the incident wave is reflected with negative polarity (so the voltage at the end of the line remains zero). If the termination is a matched load ($Z_T = Z_0$), $k_r = 0$, because the incident wave is absorbed.

Figure A.26 illustrates reflections in a transmission line with a *mismatched load termination* of 75 Ω. $Z_T = Z_L = 75$ Ω, and $Z_0 = 50$ Ω, so $k_r = 1/5$. As in previous examples, the voltage on the line is initially 0. When the switch closes, a wave of voltage, $V = \frac{V_S}{2}$, propagates down the line, reaching the end at $t = t_d$. When the incident wave reaches the termination at the end of the line, one fifth of the wave is reflected, and the remaining four fifths flows into the load impedance. Thus, the reflected wave has a voltage $V = \frac{V_S}{2} \times \frac{1}{5} = \frac{V_S}{10}$. The total voltage at point C is the sum of the incoming and reflected voltages, $V_C = \frac{V_S}{2} + \frac{V_S}{10} = \frac{3V_S}{5}$. At $t = 2t_d$, the reflected wave reaches point A, where it is absorbed by the matched 50 Ω termination, Z_S. Figure A.27 plots the voltages and currents along the line. Again, note that, in steady state (in this case at time $t > 2t_d$), the transmission line is equivalent to an equipotential wire, as shown in Figure A.28. At steady-state, the system acts like a voltage divider, so

$$V_A = V_B = V_C = V_S \left(\frac{Z_L}{Z_L + Z_S} \right) = V_S \left(\frac{75\,\Omega}{75\,\Omega + 50\,\Omega} \right) = \frac{3V_S}{5}$$

Reflections can occur at both ends of the transmission line. Figure A.29 shows a transmission line with a source impedance, Z_S, of 450 Ω and an open termination at the load. The reflection coefficients at the load and source, k_{rL} and k_{rS}, are 4/5 and 1, respectively. In this case, waves reflect off both ends of the transmission line until a steady state is reached.

The *bounce diagram*, shown in Figure A.30, helps visualize reflections off both ends of the transmission line. The horizontal axis represents

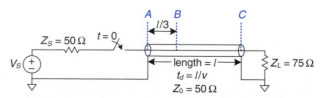

Figure A.26 **Transmission line with mismatched termination**

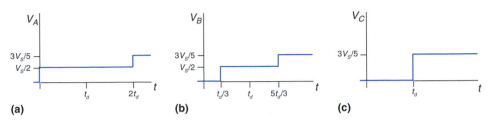

Figure A.27 Voltage waveforms for Figure A.26 at points *A*, *B*, and *C*

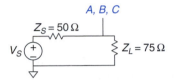

Figure A.28 Equivalent circuit of Figure A.26 at steady-state

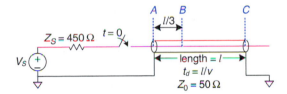

Figure A.29 Transmission line with mismatched source and load terminations

distance along the transmission line, and the vertical axis represents time, increasing downward. The two sides of the bounce diagram represent the source and load ends of the transmission line, points *A* and *C*. The incoming and reflected signal waves are drawn as diagonal lines between points *A* and *C*. At time $t = 0$, the source impedance and transmission line behave as a voltage divider, launching a voltage wave of $\frac{V_S}{10}$ from point *A* toward point *C*. At time $t = t_d$, the signal reaches point *C* and is completely reflected ($k_{rL} = 1$). At time $t = 2t_d$, the reflected wave of $\frac{V_S}{10}$ reaches point *A* and is reflected with a reflection coefficient, $k_{rS} = 4/5$, to produce a wave of $\frac{2V_S}{25}$ traveling toward point *C*, and so forth.

The voltage at a given time at any point on the transmission line is the sum of all the incident and reflected waves. Thus, at time $t = 1.1t_d$, the voltage at point *C* is $\frac{V_S}{10} + \frac{V_S}{10} = \frac{V_S}{5}$. At time $t = 3.1t_d$, the voltage at point *C* is $\frac{V_S}{10} + \frac{V_S}{10} + \frac{2V_S}{25} + \frac{2V_S}{25} = \frac{9V_S}{25}$, and so forth. Figure A.31 plots the voltages against time. As *t* approaches infinity, the voltages approach steady-state with $V_A = V_B = V_C = V_S$.

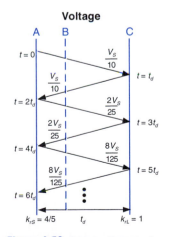

Figure A.30 Bounce diagram for Figure A.29

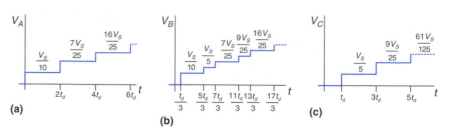

Figure A.31 Voltage and current waveforms for Figure A.29

A.8.5 When to Use Transmission Line Models

Transmission line models for wires are needed whenever the wire delay, t_d, is longer than a fraction (e.g., 20%) of the edge rates (rise or fall times) of a signal. If the wire delay is shorter, it has an insignificant effect on the propagation delay of the signal, and the reflections dissipate while the signal is transitioning. If the wire delay is longer, it must be considered in order to accurately predict the propagation delay and waveform of the signal. In particular, reflections may distort the digital characteristic of a waveform, resulting in incorrect logic operations.

Recall that signals travel on a PCB at about 15 cm/ns. For TTL logic, with edge rates of 10 ns, wires must be modeled as transmission lines only if they are longer than 30 cm (10 ns × 15 cm/ns × 20%). PCB traces are usually less than 30 cm, so most traces can be modeled as ideal equipotential wires. In contrast, many modern chips have edge rates of 2 ns or less, so traces longer than about 6 cm (about 2.5 inches) must be modeled as transmission lines. Clearly, use of edge rates that are crisper than necessary just causes difficulties for the designer.

Breadboards lack a ground plane, so the electromagnetic fields of each signal are nonuniform and difficult to model. Moreover, the fields interact with other signals. This can cause strange reflections and crosstalk between signals. Thus, breadboards are unreliable above a few megahertz.

In contrast, PCBs have good transmission lines with consistent characteristic impedance and velocity along the entire line. As long as they are terminated with a source or load impedance that is matched to the impedance of the line, PCB traces do not suffer from reflections.

A.8.6 Proper Transmission Line Terminations

There are two common ways to properly terminate a transmission line, shown in Figure A.32. In *parallel termination* (Figure A.32(a)), the driver has a low impedance ($Z_S \approx 0$). A load resistor (Z_L) with impedance Z_0 is placed in parallel with the load (between the input of the receiver gate and

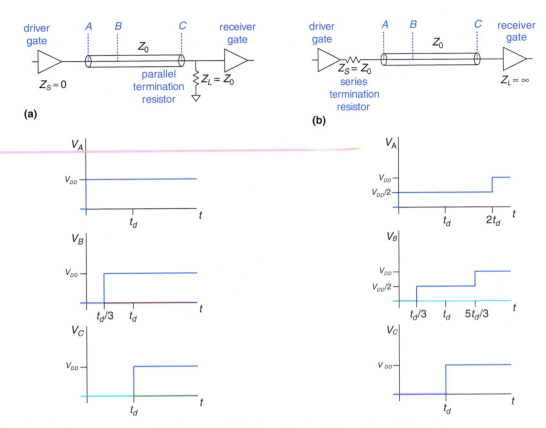

Figure A.32 Termination schemes: (a) parallel, (b) series

ground). When the driver switches from 0 to V_{DD}, it sends a wave with voltage V_{DD} down the line. The wave is absorbed by the matched load termination, and no reflections take place. In *series termination* (Figure A.32(b)), a source resistor (Z_S) is placed in series with the driver to raise the source impedance to Z_0. The load has a high impedance $(Z_L \approx \infty)$. When the driver switches, it sends a wave with voltage $V_{DD}/2$ down the line. The wave reflects at the open circuit load and returns, bringing the voltage on the line up to V_{DD}. The wave is absorbed at the source termination. Both schemes are similar in that the voltage at the receiver transitions from 0 to V_{DD} at $t = t_d$, just as one would desire. They differ in power consumption and in the waveforms that appear elsewhere along the line. Parallel termination dissipates power continuously through the load resistor when the line is at a high voltage. Series termination dissipates no DC power, because the load is an open circuit. However, in series terminated lines, points near the middle of the transmission line initially see a voltage of $V_{DD}/2$, until the reflection returns. If other gates are attached to the middle of the line, they will momentarily see an illegal logic level. Therefore, series termination works best for *point-to-point* communication with a single driver and a single receiver. Parallel termination is better for a *bus* with multiple receivers, because receivers at the middle of the line never see an illegal logic level.

A.8.7 Derivation of Z_0*

Z_0 is the ratio of voltage to current in a wave propagating along a transmission line. This section derives Z_0; it assumes some previous knowledge of resistor-inductor-capacitor (RLC) circuit analysis.

Imagine applying a step voltage to the input of a semi-infinite transmission line (so that there are no reflections). Figure A.33 shows the semi-infinite line and a model of a segment of the line of length dx. R, L, and C, are the values of resistance, inductance, and capacitance per unit length. Figure A.33(b) shows the transmission line model with a resistive component, R. This is called a *lossy* transmission line model, because energy is dissipated, or lost, in the resistance of the wire. However, this loss is often negligible, and we can simplify analysis by ignoring the resistive component and treating the transmission line as an *ideal* transmission line, as shown in Figure A.33(c).

Voltage and current are functions of time and space throughout the transmission line, as given by Equations A.8 and A.9.

$$\frac{\partial}{\partial x}V(x,\,t) = L\frac{\partial}{\partial t}\,I(x,\,t) \tag{A.8}$$

$$\frac{\partial}{\partial x}I(x,\,t) = C\frac{\partial}{\partial t}\,V(x,\,t) \tag{A.9}$$

Taking the space derivative of Equation A.8 and the time derivative of Equation A.9 and substituting gives Equation A.10, the *wave equation*.

$$\frac{\partial^2}{\partial x^2}V(x,\,t) = LC\frac{\partial^2}{\partial t^2}\,I(x,\,t) \tag{A.10}$$

Z_0 is the ratio of voltage to current in the transmission line, as illustrated in Figure A.34(a). Z_0 must be independent of the length of the line, because the behavior of the wave cannot depend on things at a distance. Because it is independent of length, the impedance must still equal Z_0 after the addition of a small amount of transmission line, dx, as shown in Figure A.34(b).

Figure A.33 Transmission line models: (a) semi-infinite cable, (b) lossy, (c) ideal

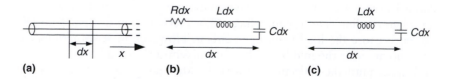

(a)   (b)   (c)

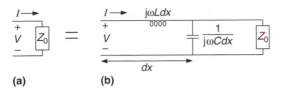

Figure A.34 Transmission line model: (a) for entire line and (b) with additional length, *dx*

Using the impedances of an inductor and a capacitor, we rewrite the relationship of Figure A.34 in equation form:

$$Z_0 = j\omega L dx + [Z_0 \| (1/(j\omega C dx))] \tag{A.11}$$

Rearranging, we get

$$Z_0^2(j\omega C) - j\omega L + \omega^2 Z_0 L C dx = 0 \tag{A.12}$$

Taking the limit as *dx* approaches 0, the last term vanishes and we find that

$$Z_0 = \sqrt{\frac{L}{C}} \tag{A.13}$$

A.8.8 Derivation of the Reflection Coefficient*

The reflection coefficient, k_r, is derived using conservation of current. Figure A.35 shows a transmission line with characteristic impedance, Z_0, and load impedance, Z_L. Imagine an incident wave of voltage V_i and current I_i. When the wave reaches the termination, some current, I_L, flows through the load impedance, causing a voltage drop, V_L. The remainder of the current reflects back down the line in a wave of voltage, V_r, and current, I_r. Z_0 is the ratio of voltage to current in waves propagating along the line, so $\frac{V_i}{I_i} = \frac{V_r}{I_r} = Z_0$.

The voltage on the line is the sum of the voltages of the incident and reflected waves. The current flowing in the positive direction on the line is the difference between the currents of the incident and reflected waves.

$$V_L = V_i + V_r \tag{A.14}$$

$$I_L = I_i - I_r \tag{A.15}$$

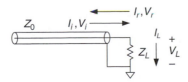

Figure A.35 Transmission line showing incoming, reflected, and load voltages and currents

Using Ohm's law and substituting for I_L, I_i, and I_r in Equation A.15, we get

$$\frac{V_i + V_r}{Z_L} = \frac{V_i}{Z_0} - \frac{V_r}{Z_0} \tag{A.16}$$

Rearranging, we solve for the reflection coefficient, k_r:

$$\frac{V_r}{V_i} = \frac{Z_L - Z_0}{Z_L + Z_0} = k_r \tag{A.17}$$

A.8.9 Putting It All Together

Transmission lines model the fact that signals take time to propagate down long wires because the speed of light is finite. An ideal transmission line has uniform inductance, L, and capacitance, C, per unit length and zero resistance. The transmission line is characterized by its characteristic impedance, Z_0, and delay, t_d, which can be derived from the inductance, capacitance, and wire length. The transmission line has significant delay and noise effects on signals whose rise/fall times are less than about $5t_d$. This means that, for systems with 2 ns rise/fall times, PCB traces longer than about 6 cm must be analyzed as transmission lines to accurately understand their behavior.

A digital system consisting of a gate driving a long wire attached to the input of a second gate can be modeled with a transmission line as shown in Figure A.36. The voltage source, source impedance (Z_S), and switch model the first gate switching from 0 to 1 at time 0. The driver gate cannot supply infinite current; this is modeled by Z_S. Z_S is usually small for a logic gate, but a designer may choose to add a resistor in series with the gate to raise Z_S and match the impedance of the line. The input to the second gate is modeled as Z_L. CMOS circuits usually have little input current, so Z_L may be close to infinity. The designer may also choose to add a resistor in parallel with the second gate, between the gate input and ground, so that Z_L matches the impedance of the line.

Figure A.36 Digital system modeled with transmission line

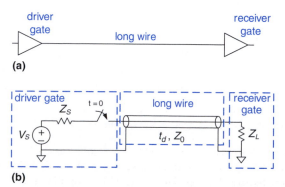

When the first gate switches, a wave of voltage is driven onto the transmission line. The source impedance and transmission line form a voltage divider, so the voltage of the incident wave is

$$V_i = V_S \frac{Z_0}{Z_0 + Z_S} \tag{A.18}$$

At time t_d, the wave reaches the end of the line. Part is absorbed by the load impedance, and part is reflected. The reflection coefficient, k_r, indicates the portion that is reflected: $k_r = V_r/V_i$, where V_r is the voltage of the reflected wave and V_i is the voltage of the incident wave.

$$k_r = \frac{Z_L - Z_0}{Z_L + Z_0} \tag{A.19}$$

The reflected wave adds to the voltage already on the line. It reaches the source at time $2t_d$, where part is absorbed and part is again reflected. The reflections continue back and forth, and the voltage on the line eventually approaches the value that would be expected if the line were a simple equipotential wire.

A.9 ECONOMICS

Although digital design is so much fun that some of us would do it for free, most designers and companies intend to make money. Therefore, economic considerations are a major factor in design decisions.

The cost of a digital system can be divided into *nonrecurring engineering costs* (NRE), and *recurring costs*. NRE accounts for the cost of designing the system. It includes the salaries of the design team, computer and software costs, and the costs of producing the first working unit. The fully loaded cost of a designer in the United States in 2006 (including salary, health insurance, retirement plan, and a computer with design tools) is roughly $200,000 per year, so design costs can be significant. Recurring costs are the cost of each additional unit; this includes components, manufacturing, marketing, technical support, and shipping.

The sales price must cover not only the cost of the system but also other costs such as office rental, taxes, and salaries of staff who do not directly contribute to the design (such as the janitor and the CEO). After all of these expenses, the company should still make a profit.

Example A.3 BEN TRIES TO MAKE SOME MONEY

Ben Bitdiddle has designed a crafty circuit for counting raindrops. He decides to sell the device and try to make some money, but he needs help deciding what implementation to use. He decides to use either an FPGA or an ASIC. The development kit to design and test the FPGA costs $1500. Each FPGA costs $17. The ASIC costs $600,000 for a mask set and $4 per chip.

Regardless of what chip implementation he chooses, Ben needs to mount the packaged chip on a printed circuit board (PCB), which will cost him $1.50 per board. He thinks he can sell 1000 devices per month. Ben has coerced a team of bright undergraduates into designing the chip for their senior project, so it doesn't cost him anything to design.

If the sales price has to be twice the cost (100% profit margin), and the product life is 2 years, which implementation is the better choice?

SOLUTION: Ben figures out the total cost for each implementation over 2 years, as shown in Table A.4. Over 2 years, Ben plans on selling 24,000 devices, and the total cost is given in Table A.4 for each option. If the product life is only two years, the FPGA option is clearly superior. The per-unit cost is $445,500/24,000 = $18.56, and the sales price is $37.13 per unit to give a 100% profit margin. The ASIC option would have cost $732,000/24,000 = $30.50 and would have sold for $61 per unit.

Table A.4 ASIC vs FPGA costs

Cost	ASIC	FPGA
NRE	$600,000	$1500
chip	$4	$17
PCB	$1.50	$1.50
TOTAL	$600,000 + (24,000 × $5.50) = $732,000	$1500 + (24,000 × $18.50) = $445,500
per unit	$30.50	$18.56

Example A.4 BEN GETS GREEDY

After seeing the marketing ads for his product, Ben thinks he can sell even more chips per month than originally expected. If he were to choose the ASIC option, how many devices per month would he have to sell to make the ASIC option more profitable than the FPGA option?

SOLUTION: Ben solves for the minimum number of units, N, that he would need to sell in 2 years:

$$\$600,000 + (N \times \$5.50) = \$1500 + (N \times \$18.50)$$

Solving the equation gives $N = 46,039$ units, or 1919 units per month. He would need to almost double his monthly sales to benefit from the ASIC solution.

Example A.5 BEN GETS LESS GREEDY

Ben realizes that his eyes have gotten too big for his stomach, and he doesn't think he can sell more than 1000 devices per month. But he does think the product life can be longer than 2 years. At a sales volume of 1000 devices per month, how long would the product life have to be to make the ASIC option worthwhile?

SOLUTION: If Ben sells more than 46,039 units in total, the ASIC option is the best choice. So, Ben would need to sell at a volume of 1000 per month for at least 47 months (rounding up), which is almost 4 years. By then, his product is likely to be obsolete.

Chips are usually purchased from a distributor rather than directly from the manufacturer (unless you are ordering tens of thousands of units). Digikey (www.digikey.com) is a leading distributor that sells a wide variety of electronics. Jameco (www.jameco.com) and All Electronics (www.allelectronics.com) have eclectic catalogs that are competitively priced and well suited to hobbyists.

MIPS Instructions

This appendix summarizes MIPS instructions used in this book. Tables B.1–B.3 define the `opcode` and `funct` fields for each instruction, along with a short description of what the instruction does. The following notations are used:

- ▶ `[reg]:`   contents of the register
- ▶ `imm:`   16-bit immediate field of the I-type instruction
- ▶ `addr:`   26-bit address field of the J-type instruction
- ▶ `SignImm:`   sign-extended immediate

  = `{{16{imm[15]}}, imm}`

- ▶ `ZeroImm:`   zero-extended immediate

  = `{16'b0, imm}`

- ▶ `Address:`   `[rs] + SignImm`
- ▶ `[Address]:`   contents of memory location `Address`
- ▶ `BTA:`   branch target address[1]

  = `PC + 4 + (SignImm << 2)`

- ▶ `JTA:`   jump target address

  = `{(PC + 4)[31:28], addr, 2'b0}`

---

[1] The SPIM simulator has no branch delay slot, so BTA is PC + (SignImm << 2). Thus, if you use the SPIM assembler to create machine code for a real MIPS processor, you must decrement the immediate field by 1 to compensate.

Table B.1 Instructions, sorted by opcode

Opcode	Name	Description	Operation
000000 (0)	R-type	all R-type instructions	see Table B.2
000001 (1) (rt = 0/1)	bltz/bgez	branch less than zero/ branch greater than or equal to zero	if ([rs] < 0) PC = BTA/ if ([rs] ≥ 0) PC = BTA
000010 (2)	j	jump	PC = JTA
000011 (3)	jal	jump and link	$ra = PC+4, PC = JTA
000100 (4)	beq	branch if equal	if ([rs]==[rt]) PC = BTA
000101 (5)	bne	branch if not equal	if ([rs]!=[rt]) PC = BTA
000110 (6)	blez	branch if less than or equal to zero	if ([rs] ≤ 0) PC = BTA
000111 (7)	bgtz	branch if greater than zero	if ([rs] > 0) PC = BTA
001000 (8)	addi	add immediate	[rt] = [rs] + SignImm
001001 (9)	addiu	add immediate unsigned	[rt] = [rs] + SignImm
001010 (10)	slti	set less than immediate	[rs] < SignImm ? [rt]=1 : [rt]=0
001011 (11)	sltiu	set less than immediate unsigned	[rs] < SignImm ? [rt]=1 : [rt]=0
001100 (12)	andi	and immediate	[rt] = [rs] & ZeroImm
001101 (13)	ori	or immediate	[rt] = [rs] | ZeroImm
001110 (14)	xori	xor immediate	[rt] = [rs] ^ ZeroImm
001111 (15)	lui	load upper immediate	[rt] = {Imm, 16'b0}
010000 (16) (rs = 0/4)	mfc0, mtc0	move from/to coprocessor 0	[rt] = [rd]/[rd] = [rt] (rd is in coprocessor 0)
010001 (17)	F-type	fop = 16/17: F-type instructions	see Table B.3
010001 (17) (rt = 0/1)	bc1f/bc1t	fop = 8: branch if fpcond is FALSE/TRUE	if (fpcond == 0) PC = BTA/ if (fpcond == 1) PC = BTA
100000 (32)	lb	load byte	[rt] = SignExt ([Address]$_{7:0}$)
100001 (33)	lh	load halfword	[rt] = SignExt ([Address]$_{15:0}$)
100011 (35)	lw	load word	[rt] = [Address]
100100 (36)	lbu	load byte unsigned	[rt] = ZeroExt ([Address]$_{7:0}$)
100101 (37)	lhu	load halfword unsigned	[rt] = ZeroExt ([Address]$_{15:0}$)
101000 (40)	sb	store byte	[Address]$_{7:0}$ = [rt]$_{7:0}$

(continued)

Table B.1 Instructions, sorted by opcode—Cont'd

Opcode	Name	Description	Operation
101001 (41)	sh	store halfword	$[Address]_{15:0} = [rt]_{15:0}$
101011 (43)	sw	store word	[Address] = [rt]
110001 (49)	lwc1	load word to FP coprocessor 1	[ft] = [Address]
111001 (56)	swc1	store word to FP coprocessor 1	[Address] = [ft]

Table B.2 R-type instructions, sorted by funct field

Funct	Name	Description	Operation
000000 (0)	sll	shift left logical	[rd] = [rt] << shamt
000010 (2)	srl	shift right logical	[rd] = [rt] >> shamt
000011 (3)	sra	shift right arithmetic	[rd] = [rt] >>> shamt
000100 (4)	sllv	shift left logical variable	$[rd] = [rt] << [rs]_{4:0}$ assembly: sllv rd, rt, rs
000110 (6)	srlv	shift right logical variable	$[rd] = [rt] >> [rs]_{4:0}$ assembly: srlv rd, rt, rs
000111 (7)	srav	shift right arithmetic variable	$[rd] = [rt] >>> [rs]_{4:0}$ assembly: srav rd, rt, rs
001000 (8)	jr	jump register	PC = [rs]
001001 (9)	jalr	jump and link register	$ra = PC + 4, PC = [rs]
001100 (12)	syscall	system call	system call exception
001101 (13)	break	break	break exception
010000 (16)	mfhi	move from hi	[rd] = [hi]
010001 (17)	mthi	move to hi	[hi] = [rs]
010010 (18)	mflo	move from lo	[rd] = [lo]
010011 (19)	mtlo	move to lo	[lo] = [rs]
011000 (24)	mult	multiply	{[hi], [lo]} = [rs] × [rt]
011001 (25)	multu	multiply unsigned	{[hi], [lo]} = [rs] × [rt]
011010 (26)	div	divide	[lo] = [rs]/[rt], [hi] = [rs]%[rt]

(continued)

Table B.2 R-type instructions, sorted by funct field—Cont'd

Funct	Name	Description	Operation
011011 (27)	divu	divide unsigned	`[lo] = [rs]/[rt]`, `[hi] = [rs]%[rt]`
100000 (32)	add	add	`[rd] = [rs] + [rt]`
100001 (33)	addu	add unsigned	`[rd] = [rs] + [rt]`
100010 (34)	sub	subtract	`[rd] = [rs] − [rt]`
100011 (35)	subu	subtract unsigned	`[rd] = [rs] − [rt]`
100100 (36)	and	and	`[rd] = [rs] & [rt]`
100101 (37)	or	or	`[rd] = [rs]	[rt]`
100110 (38)	xor	xor	`[rd] = [rs] ∧ [rt]`
100111 (39)	nor	nor	`[rd] = ~([rs] | [rt])`
101010 (42)	slt	set less than	`[rs] < [rt] ? [rd] = 1 : [rd] = 0`
101011 (43)	sltu	set less than unsigned	`[rs] < [rt] ? [rd] = 1 : [rd] = 0`

Table B.3 F-type instructions (`fop = 16/17`)

Funct	Name	Description	Operation
000000 (0)	add.s/add.d	FP add	`[fd] = [fs] + [ft]`
000001 (1)	sub.s/sub.d	FP subtract	`[fd] = [fs] − [ft]`
000010 (2)	mul.s/mul.d	FP multiply	`[fd] = [fs] * [ft]`
000011 (3)	div.s/div.d	FP divide	`[fd] = [fs]/[ft]`
000101 (5)	abs.s/abs.d	FP absolute value	`[fd] = ([fs] < 0) ? [−fs] : [fs]`
000111 (7)	neg.s/neg.d	FP negation	`[fd] = [−fs]`
111010 (58)	c.seq.s/c.seq.d	FP equality comparison	`fpcond = ([fs] == [ft])`
111100 (60)	c.lt.s/c.lt.d	FP less than comparison	`fpcond = ([fs] < [ft])`
111110 (62)	c.le.s/c.le.d	FP less than or equal comparison	`fpcond = ([fs] ≤ [ft])`

Further Reading

Berlin L., *The Man Behind the Microchip: Robert Noyce and the Invention of Silicon Valley*, Oxford University Press, 2005.
> The fascinating biography of Robert Noyce, an inventor of the microchip and founder of Fairchild and Intel. For anyone thinking of working in Silicon Valley, this book gives insights into the culture of the region, a culture influenced more heavily by Noyce than any other individual.

Colwell R., *The Pentium Chronicles: The People, Passion, and Politics Behind Intel's Landmark Chips*, Wiley, 2005.
> An insider's tale of the development of several generations of Intel's Pentium chips, told by one of the leaders of the project. For those considering a career in the field, this book offers views into the managment of huge design projects and a behind-the-scenes look at one of the most significant commercial microprocessor lines.

Ercegovac M., and Lang T., *Digital Arithmetic*, Morgan Kaufmann, 2003.
> The most complete text on computer arithmetic systems. An excellent resource for building high-quality arithmetic units for computers.

Hennessy J., and Patterson D., *Computer Architecture: A Quantitative Approach, 4th ed.*, Morgan Kaufmann, 2006.
> The authoritative text on advanced computer architecture. If you are intrigued about the inner workings of cutting-edge microprocessors, this is the book for you.

Kidder T., *The Soul of a New Machine*, Back Bay Books, 1981.
> A classic story of the design of a computer system. Three decades later, the story is still a page-turner and the insights on project managment and technology still ring true.

Pedroni V., *Circuit Design with VHDL*, MIT Press, 2004.
> A reference showing how to design circuits with VHDL.

Thomas D., and Moorby P., *The Verilog Hardware Description Language, 5th ed.*, Kluwer Academic Publishers, 2002.

Ciletti M., *Advanced Digital Design with the Verilog HDL*, Prentice Hall, 2003.
> Both excellent references covering Verilog in more detail.

Verilog IEEE Standard (IEEE STD 1364).

> The IEEE standard for the Verilog Hardware Description Language; last updated in 2001. Available at *ieeexplore.ieee.org*.

VHDL IEEE Standard (IEEE STD 1076).

> The IEEE standard for VHDL; last updated in 2004. Available from IEEE. Available at *ieeexplore.ieee.org*.

Wakerly J., *Digital Design: Principles and Practices, 4th ed.*, Prentice Hall, 2006.

> A comprehensive and readable text on digital design, and an excellent reference book.

Weste N., and Harris D., *CMOS VLSI Design, 3rd ed.*, Addison-Wesley, 2005.

> Very Large Scale Integration (VLSI) Design is the art and science of building chips containing oodles of transistors. This book, coauthored by one of our favorite writers, spans the field from the beginning through the most advanced techniques used in commercial products.

Index